African American Folklore

African American Folklore

An Encyclopedia for Students

ANAND PRAHLAD, EDITOR

BLOOMSBURY ACADEMIC
NEW YORK • LONDON • OXFORD • NEW DELHI • SYDNEY

BLOOMSBURY ACADEMIC
Bloomsbury Publishing Inc
1385 Broadway, New York, NY 10018, USA
50 Bedford Square, London, WC1B 3DP, UK
29 Earlsfort Terrace, Dublin 2, Ireland

BLOOMSBURY, BLOOMSBURY ACADEMIC and the Diana logo
are trademarks of Bloomsbury Publishing Plc

First published in the United States of America by ABC-CLIO 2016
Paperback edition published by Bloomsbury Academic 2024

Cover design by Silverander Communications
Cover photos: Voodoo Priestess Ava Kay Jones poses in the Louisiana Superdome in New Orleans,
December 30, 2000. (Andrew J. Cohoon/AP Photo); Carved totem pole, Montgomery, Louisiana,
March 26, 2007. (Alex Brandon/AP Photo); Breakdancing young man in graffi ti area.
(Izabela Habur/iStockphoto); Graffi ti wall. (kiyoko/iStockphoto); Playing trumpet. (Lise Gagne/iStockphoto)

Bloomsbury Publishing Inc does not have any control over, or responsibility for,
any third-party websites referred to or in this book. All internet addresses given
in this book were correct at the time of going to press. The author and publisher
regret any inconvenience caused if addresses have changed or sites have
ceased to exist, but can accept no responsibility for any such changes.

Library of Congress Cataloging-in-Publication Data
Names: Prahlad, Anand, author.
Title: African American folklore : an encyclopedia for students / Anand
Prahlad, editor.
Description: Santa Barbara, California : Greenwood, an Imprint of ABC-CLIO,
LLC, [2016] | Includes bibliographical references and index.
Identifiers: LCCN 2016005233 | ISBN 9781610699297 |
ISBN 9781610699303 (ebook)
Subjects: LCSH: African Americans—Folklore—Encyclopedias. | African
Americans—Social life and customs—Encyclopedias. | Folklore—United
States—Encyclopedias. | Tales—United States—Encyclopedias.
Classification: LCC GR111.A47 A35 2016 | DDC 398.2089/96073—dc23
LC record available at https://lccn.loc.gov/2016005233

ISBN: HB: 978-1-6106-9929-7
PB: 979-8-7651-1620-3
ePDF: 978-1-6106-9930-3
eBook: 979-8-2160-4294-5

To find out more about our authors and books visit www.bloomsbury.com
and sign up for our newsletters.

Contents

Introduction

What Is African American Folklore and Why Study It?

Folklore is the art of everyday life, the artistic expressions that people learn informally, often just by being members of a community. It includes, among other things, the stories and jokes that people tell, proverbs that are offered as words of wisdom, gestures, dances, games that people play, superstitions, and beliefs that guide people's thinking, religion, rituals, and festivals. Folklore also includes material expressions, such as quilting, instrument making, costumes, basket making, graffiti, architectural designs, food making, and tattoos. Because it is learned informally, without institutional mandates and formal structures, it is often unrecognized and undervalued as art.

Folklore is often thought of as being old, and often it is. Folklore has conventionally been defined as traditional (passed down from generation to generation), anonymously created (as opposed to literature, in which the author is known), orally transmitted, and existing in multiple versions. These traits still hold true for most forms of folklore, but not for all of them. With the emergence of technology, such as the Internet, many kinds of folklore are circulated in visual and written forms rather than being orally transmitted, and are shared electronically rather than being shared in face-to-face communication.

In contemporary folklore studies, folklore has been most succinctly defined as "artistic communication in small groups." As such, contemporary folklore is as concerned with the communication as it is with the actual texts. The text would be the written example of the folklore item, such as a folktale in a book. The study of the performance would include concerns that could not be answered by simply reading the text. How does a person perform the actual telling of the story? What aesthetics influence the way the tale is told? How do others respond and interact with the taleteller? What are some of the meanings of the story at that particular moment, among that particular group of people? So, the study of folklore is rooted in ethnographic methodology and experience. Folklorists go out and collect folklore from ordinary people, and listen to expressions as they are being performed. We are concerned with not just the texts of tales, sermons, or proverbs, etc., but also with the mindsets and attitudes that give rise to expressions, and the dynamics of how they are communicated.

Although most Westerners have been socialized to equate "folk" with ancient or backward people and imagine that "others" have mythology, superstitions, tales, etc., in fact, folklore continues to play a significant role in the lives of people in the modern, technological world. Everyone is the folk. People of all social backgrounds, classes, educational levels, and ethnicities tell stories, jokes, and proverbs; have folk beliefs, religions (mythologies), and rituals; participate in festivals and dances; and prepare and consume foods. Just as they have for thousands of years, most people live in families and/or communities held together by networks of folk traditions.

Folklore is usually divided into genres, or categories for study and archiving. Narrative genres (those that involve stories) include myths, legends, folktales, fables, jokes, prayers, testimonies, sermons, and toasts, among others; and minor oral genres include such forms as proverbs, superstitions, riddles, and folk speech. There are many folklore dictionaries, collections, and encyclopedias that contain either a combination of genres or focus just on one.

The scope of this encyclopedia includes African American folklore of the United States. These are the folk expressions and traditions of everyday life found among people of African descent. Although this folklore has African, European, and even Native American influences, it is characterized by its uniqueness. It is born out of the historical circumstances of enslavement and oppression and reflects the spirits of determination and resistance that have been necessary for survival in America. Further, it embodies resilience and celebration, and a distinctive creativity and will to forge new identities and to create and maintain systems of cultural knowledge, belief, and practice. This is the folklore of diverse African American communities and groups from across the country, distinguished by such factors as regional influences, linguistic varieties, educational and socioeconomic levels, and religious persuasions. The entries in the encyclopedia represent those that have been the most pervasive, enduring, and, in some ways, core to what can be called a "pan" African American identity. For example, not all African Americans are Baptists, or even Christian; however, the influence of the black Baptist church has been pervasive. The many forms of expression that grew out of the black Baptist church have been foundational to the development of most black music and oral genres, from spirituals to hip-hop. Similarly, forms such as "signifying," "hush harbors," or "hoodoo," which were found in slave societies, continue to have tremendous influence on diverse areas of African American culture. They often resonate in cultural and political realms beyond folk performances—in literature, film, visual art, television, and political speeches, for example.

The study of this material is important for many reasons. First, African American folklore furthers our understanding of black history and of American history in general. In the 1960s and 1970s, American historians became aware that one way to gain a more comprehensive picture of American and African American history was to seriously study oral narratives. Because white Americans had written most of the history books, and because those books relied on written documents and pre-existing assumptions that were biased against African Americans, they did not offer accurate or comprehensive accounts of many events and issues. Historians such as Lawrence Levine (*Black Culture, Black Consciousness*) and Edward Genovese (*Roll Jordan Roll*) offered radical revisions of American history by researching folklore and transcriptions of oral narratives. Theirs are generally considered more accurate accounts of the slavery and postslavery periods than those by previous historians. More importantly, they humanized black people. Reading the oral narratives of African Americans can provide more personal, emotional, and descriptive information that deepens our insights in ways that history books cannot.

Another reason to study African American folklore is to gain a greater understanding of black cultural perspectives; for example, aesthetics. A major contribution of scholars such as Melville Herskovits and Robert Farris Thompson is their argument that African Americans retained many basic aesthetic components of the African cultures from which they came. Before Herskovits, it was believed that all aspects of African cultures had been lost during the slave trade. Thanks to the work of such scholars as these, it is now commonly accepted that black folklore is rooted in African cultural aesthetics mixed with other influences, such as European and Native American. These aesthetics apply to dance, music, religion, speech, religious practices, crafts, etc., and are among the fundamental threads that connect many different forms of folklore, from varying groups, regions, and time periods.

Cultural perspectives also include ideology, identity, ways of perceiving outside groups, and ways of perceiving one's social, political, and historical circumstances. Articulating social problems and offering strategies for dealing with those problems are basic functions of folklore. So folklore reflects cultural anxieties, fears, hopes, and dreams of the group in which it is found. For example, Brer Rabbit tales reflect problems that confronted enslaved and oppressed people, such as the scarcity of food, or the fear of being killed. But they also pose strategies for coping with these issues. Similarly, hip-hop music and lyrics reflect contemporary issues confronting African Americans and strategies for coping with and overcoming these problems. So folklore can provide an index of cultural issues, feelings about these issues, and possible cultural solutions and strategies for coping with them.

Finally, the study of African American folklore is important in understanding the fabric of American culture. As many scholars have noted, African American folklore has played a major role in shaping the spirit and soul of the Americas. It permeates American culture in more ways than are commonly recognized. American popular music, for example, emerged out of black folk musical traditions such as blues and jazz. American popular dance, from the Charleston to the twist to the boogaloo to break dancing to hip-hop dance, are rooted in the aesthetics of black dance. The same can be said of popular speech, and especially the speech of white youth subcultures since the 1950s. This is equally true of black religion, foodways, and healing traditions, among others, but most importantly, the aesthetics underlying these forms have had a profound impact on American cultural expression and identity. If one wants to understand rock and roll, one has to understand the blues; however, one first has to understand the black religious forms out of which the blues grew.

African American folklore is a priceless resource for students and educators interested in contemporary Western culture. These materials have profoundly influenced the concept of "Americanness," which includes modes of self-expression and self-presentation as well as spirituality and religion, music, fashion, speech, and general ways of being in the world.

Challenges in the Study of African American Folklore

The field of folklore studies has struggled to gain respectability in American schools since becoming an academic field in the late 19th century. One of the reasons for this is that many people associate the term "folk" with the lower class and the uneducated, and with those considered ignorant or backward. This association has made it difficult for educators to appreciate the value of studying folk culture or to know how to approach its study even when its value has been acknowledged. Therefore, fields such as history, literature, sociology, and psychology have overshadowed folklore.

This problem is complicated by the nature of folklore materials. Folklore is often blatantly outside of mainstream social values and aesthetics. When judged by mainstream, polite, and educated values, folklore is frequently perceived as obscene, vulgar, and politically incorrect. It reflects what people really think, do, and say in the privacy of their own folk groups, and it is not written or created with a middle-class audience in mind. Adding race makes the introduction of folklore into classrooms an even more complex proposition. Educators often wrestle with texts containing overtly racial materials, in fear of offending people or otherwise violating social etiquette regarding conversations about race.

One issue that arises when considering the study of African American folklore is that many important books in the field were written in time periods when the language and attitudes about race were different than they are today. The earliest writings are from late 19th-century observations about slave cultures. These early writings reflected the prevailing colonial attitudes of the day, which assumed white superiority and considered Africans and other people of color to be savages and less than human. On one hand, these writings helped to preserve knowledge about some of the folklore elements in slave cultures. On the other hand, however, they are infused with racist attitudes. For this reason, they can be disturbing for modern readers. Joel Chandler Harris's *Uncle Remus* is a case in point. The Brer Rabbit stories recorded by Harris have proven to be accurate renderings of traditional tales that existed during the slavery period within the Southern United States and other parts of the black diaspora. However, Harris's creation of the taleteller, Uncle Remus, and his choice for Remus to narrate tales to the young son of a slaveholder affect the readers' experience of the tales.

Harris's creation of Uncle Remus was not unusual for the time in which it was written. It was a part of a literary tradition in which white Southern authors sought to reinforce the idea that slaves had been happy and content with their lives and that they enjoyed entertaining and taking care of white children and white families. Like similar writings of that time, the book promotes negative stereotypes of African Americans. Although Harris's book, *Uncle Remus,* was not unique, it became *the* collection that captured the hearts of mainstream America. Uncle Remus became even more popular with the release of the Walt Disney movie *Song of the South,* based on the Uncle Remus stories. Originally shown in U.S. theaters in 1946, the movie was rereleased by Disney in 1956, 1972, 1980, and 1986. Unfortunately, *Uncle Remus* became, and continues to be, for many Americans, the defining example of black folklore.

A part of the stereotype that continues to resonate for readers is the use of dialect that made it seem as if the black characters were of lesser intelligence than the white characters. Harris was writing in the tradition of black dialect fiction shared by authors such as Thomas Nelson Page, who was famous for his novel, *In Ole Virginia* (1887). In this tradition, slaves or newly freed blacks were depicted as "contented plantation darkies" or helpless and nostalgic freedmen. The tradition was so firmly entrenched that even black authors were influenced by it and, to some extent, forced to write in this genre to get their work published. It was in this context that Charles Chesnutt, the first major African American novelist, had his collection of stories, *The Conjure Woman,* published.

Dialect was also a part of scholarly collections and studies of African American folklore preceding the publication of *Uncle Remus.* For example, one of the major collections of slave spirituals was Allen, Ware, and Garrison's *Slave Songs of the United States*, published in 1867. In 1888, the second issue of the *Journal of American Folklore* issued a call for the serious study of black folklore of the Southern United States. But even serious studies of black folklore often contained dialect, although for different reasons.

The exaggerated uses of dialect gave way to more accurate renderings into the second half of the 20th century. However, even works by black folklorists such as Zora Neale Hurston employ dialect. But this is in effort to maintain a certain cultural integrity that would be compromised if authors simply translated everything they collected into standard, grammatical English. A core aspect of anthropological and folkloric ethnography is the emphasis on representing the speech of those from which one collects as accurately as possible. Because so much of a culture is embedded in the language, it would be a misrepresentation, when dialect is spoken, to change it to "standard English." There can be worlds of difference between the use of "ain't" and "are not," and this difference might reflect important aspects of the historical, cultural, and even political identities of the speaker.

In the latter half of the 20th century, writings on black folklore, at least among academic authors, moved gradually away from stereotypical and racist depictions of African Americans and toward more racially sensitive and humanistic presentations. Scholars and collectors became better able to validate the worldviews and aesthetics of black folklore and to view these materials on their own terms rather than through the lenses of white, middle-class norms. The late 20th century also saw the expansion of scholarly interest beyond Southern and rural traditions. Studies began to concentrate on urban traditions and on expressive arts that had previously received little or no attention, such as urban legends and rumors, toasts, urban blues, and jazz. But some of this material also offers its own challenges. For example, the language of forms such as toasts, jokes, the dozens, rap, and hip-hop is often culturally sensitive for a different reason. In these cases, the issue is not so much the racism reflected in dialect, but obscene and misogynistic language. As is the case with many early collections of folklore, these contemporary urban genres are important to our understanding of black culture and folk traditions. The study of folklore is of what people really think and feel, and how they really express those thoughts and feelings.

In studying African American folklore, one engages material that is often racially sensitive, such as images or allusions to offensive stereotypes, disturbing historical references, and obscenity. Whenever possible, the discussions and examples of folklore in the encyclopedia avoid potentially disturbing language, although, there are cases in which this is not possible (the language of quoted passages, for example, cannot be altered). There are texts that may be difficult for modern readers, but that represent the only recorded examples of important forms of folklore. Hence, whatever appears in the encyclopedia is in the interest of providing important information, explaining necessary issues, and offering a deeper understanding of African American culture and folklore. Overall, however, what permeates the entries in the encyclopedia is the enduring legacy of extraordinary creativity and expressive genius, emotional substance, uncompromising engagement with social reality, and the universal spirit of determination that is reflected in black folklore.

Using the Encyclopedia

Features of This Encyclopedia

Much of the information in *African American Folklore: An Encyclopedia for Students* is highly condensed. The encyclopedia begins with an alphabetical list of 134 entries. This initial list may not be very helpful to students or teachers when thinking about projects, however, and so it is followed by "Suggested Research Clusters." The clusters are topics that are related to each other, and might help to facilitate individual or group projects. For example, different groups of students in a classroom might be assigned different clusters, and individual students in the group might take specific topics in that cluster. Or, individual students might be better able to decide on a project by perusing the entries in a cluster that interests them. In some cases, the entries are detailed enough to serve as the major source of information for a project or paper, but in other cases, they are considerably shorter, and additional research would be required. Readers are encouraged to consult the references in the "Further Reading" sections at the end of each entry and in the encyclopedia's bibliography at the back of the volume for additional sources. Some of these sources will probably not be available in a high school library; however, they may be available in a public library. Other sources are available online.

One can find film and video performances of many African American folklore topics in online sites, such as YouTube. There are also films available at such sites as http://www.folkstreams.net and http://www.pbs.org, and from cultural centers such as the Smithsonian Institution and the Center for Southern Folklore.

Teachers might also consider having students do projects in which they collect folklore from family and friends. Most students now have the equipment to record audio and video with their cell phones. It should be stressed, however, that the standard rules of collecting are to respect those from whom we gather folklore at all times, and to never use their images or audio unless they give us written permission.

To further facilitate readers' understanding of the connections between topics, related entries are boldfaced in the text of essays. An index follows the bibliography and provides access to the encyclopedia's contents. The "About the Editor, Advisors, and Contributors" section follows the index, and contains short biographies of the scholars and researchers who wrote the essays in this encyclopedia.

African American folklore offers a rich and diverse body of materials that will surely engage students interested in black traditional culture and expressive forms. This volume provides a significant overview of African American folklore that will be useful for the student, the teacher, and the interested reader. I hope that it encourages the use of these materials in a diverse range of classrooms and provides substantial information for readers wishing to explore some of these topics.

Alphabetical List of Entries

Suggested Research Cluster

Arts/Crafts
Aerosol Art
Basket Weaving
Blacksmithing
Bottle Trees
Film
Instruments, Folk
Pottery
Quilting
Visionary Artists
Wood Carving
Yard Art

Characters
Bad Man, The
Biblical Characters
Devil, The
Dicy, Aunt
Field Negro/House Negro
Fox, Brer
Henry, John
Jemima, Aunt
Jim Crow
Lawman, The
Monkey, The Signifying
Preacher Tales
Rabbit, Brer
Remus, Uncle
Stagolee
Tom, Uncle
Tortoise
Trickster

Dance and Play
Break Dancing
Cheerleading
Dance
Double Dutch
Dozens, The
Games, Folk

Jump Rope Rhymes/Games
Sports
Stepping

Foodways
Barbecue
Chitterlings
Folk Foods
Gumbo
Soul Food

Festivals
Christmas
Congo Square
Election Day
Family Reunions
Festivals
Juneteenth
Kwanzaa
Mardi Gras
Pinkster Celebrations

Folk Groups
Africa
Fraternity Folkore
Gay and Lesbian Folklore
Gullah
Jook/Juke
Native American and African American
     Folklore
Paper Bag Test
Porch Sitters
Sorority Folklore
South, The
Sports

Healing and Magic
Bottle Trees
Black Cat Bone
Caul

Charms
Conjure
Crossroads, The
Herbalism
Hoodoo
John the Conqueror, High
Magic Shops
Mojo

Hip-Hop
Aerosol Art
Bitch
Break Dancing
Hip-hop
Ho
Rap
Toasts

Music
Banjo
Blues
Field Hollers
Gospel Music
Hip-hop
Instruments, Folk
Jazz
Sacred Steel Guitar
Singing and Praying Bands
Slide Guitar
Soul
Spirituals
Work Songs
Zydeco

Religion and Ritual
Baptism
Biblical Characters
Church, The Black
Conversion Narratives
Devil, The
Funerals
Gospel Music
Grave Decorations
Hush/Bush Harbors
Jordan (River, Land)
Jumping the Broom
Laying on Hands
Mythology
Praise Houses
Prayer

Preacher, The
Ring Shout
Sermons
Shout
Spirituals
Testifying
Wakes

Speech and Language
Baad
Cool
CP Time
Dozens, The
Drylongso
"Forty Acres and a Mule"
Grapevine, The
Jivin'
Mother Wit
Nonverbal Communication
Proverbs
Rap
Sass/Sassy
Signifying
Soul
Speech, Folk

Storytelling and Narrative
Barbershop, The
Briar Patch
Fables
Flying Africans
Folktales
Fox, Brer
Jokes
Legends
Night Riders
Pimp, The
Preacher Tales
Rabbit, Brer
Remus, Uncle
Rumors
Signifying
Slave Narratives
Storytelling
Titanic, The
Toasts
Tortoise
Trains
Trickster

A

AEROSOL ART

This public painting tradition is associated with graffiti. Graffiti includes various inscriptions, illicit marks, or figure drawings upon walls or other surfaces. Graffiti is usually placed anonymously and is usually visible to the public. For example, graffiti artists use the walls of garages, public restrooms, buildings, and jail cells as well as highway overpasses and medians for their clandestine messages. To the larger society this constitutes vandalism, but there is a movement in the modern art world and among socially conscious individuals that deems the expression, social message, and creativity of graffiti as true art or "art of the streets." Because of the illicit nature of graffiti and to accommodate the need for size, visibility, speed, and convenience, the most common medium used is spray paint (although pen, pencil, paintbrush, and colored marking pens are also used).

Some of the earliest known African American graffiti emerged in response to political events. For example, in the late 1960s the Black Panther Party in the San Francisco Bay Area of California used graffiti to express its dissatisfaction with the then-current racial, social, and economic plight of African Americans of the region and in the United States in general. Political graffiti has also arisen at times from sudden emergency situations (e.g., riots) in response to political legislation, in party politics, or upon the death of a prominent political or social leader. For instance, after the assassinations of Rev. Dr. Martin Luther King and Malcolm X, graffiti was seen during riots in the Watts area of Los Angeles, in Newark, New Jersey, and in Memphis, Tennessee. More recently, graffiti was used in response to the Rodney King trial verdict in South Central Los Angeles. Graffiti has also been associated in some cases with urban gangs. The content and form of gang graffiti consists of cryptic codes and initials styled with specialized messages. Gang members have sometimes used graffiti to indicate group membership, to distinguish enemies and allies, and especially to mark boundaries that are territorial and ideological.

Aerosol art began as a kind of graffiti art, which had its origins in New York City. Commonly referred to as "**hip-hop**" or "New York style," it is derived from a tradition of subway painting that originated in New York during the 1960s, an era marked by social unrest. For example, such forces as the civil rights struggle, the black power and women's liberation movements, and protests against the Vietnam War, set the tone for the times. The emergence of aerosol art was one among many forms of social protest. This is reflected in the "bombing" (painting) of subway trains in direct response to the bombing of Cambodia and Vietnam by the United States. As such, aerosol art is best understood in the context of African American resistance movements, which have historically used coded languages and subversive tactics to break out of confined spaces. Aerosol art should further be considered in the context of the visual culture of New York City, which has, as one of its most prominent features, large-scale advertising. So aerosol artists—who traditionally refer to themselves as "writers" and are often offended by the term "graffiti artists"—were speaking to multiple audiences. These included the corporate world, represented by the proliferation of visible advertisements; political authorities; the masses of poor, upper- and middle-class New York residents; tourists; and each other. Ivor Miller compares aerosol art to celebrations of Caribbean Carnival in New York City, in that they both represent instances of New World Africans taking over public spaces that had historically been denied to them. Miller writes:

> Through their activities, the subway painters remapped the city. By visually communicating via the trains, they drew attention to the city's marginal neighborhoods and the nature of life on the streets. The subways were designed to carry workers in from the margins to downtown offices. Many writers therefore targeted specific trains they knew would circulate their paintings throughout the city, a concept they accurately call "goin' all city." (Miller, 4)

Some have compared the artwork on trains to Trojan horses, while others view it as assaults on the very nerve centers of the city.

Like participants in other resistance movements, New York aerosol writers had strong communities that were characterized by the construction of new identities and language and by a belief in the importance of maintaining links to ancestral spiritual traditions (Miller, 13). In true guerrilla fashion, early artists stole their aerosol paint from stores, then stole into train layups dressed in the uniforms of the Metropolitan Transit Authority and spent the night painting. Like other artists within a community, they were consistently inspired and challenged by each other's creations. Artists renamed themselves, many being guided by the belief that a name conveys someone's spiritual essence. Some of the most prominent figures in the movement were PHASE 2, DAZE, VULCAN, RIFF, BLADE, COCO 144, MICO, STAY HIGH, and CASE 2. Names were a central feature of aerosol culture, functioning in part to camouflage the identities of artists but always with some deeper significance. Many artists use several names, and signatures are an important element of the paintings; in fact, at times the art has revolved around the signature. Like many other forms of New World African expression, aerosol art is marked by syncretism, or fusion. Artists had a diversity of cultural backgrounds, although the most pervasive influences came from African American, Caribbean, and Latin American sources. Artists also drew from a wide range of influences in developing their individual styles, including calligraphy, Egyptian hieroglyphics, underground comics by authors such as R. Crumb and Vaughn Bodé, the Hebrew and Arabic alphabets, science fiction art and literature, and advertising.

The kinetic element of aerosol art is one of its distinguishing features. As Miller describes the artists, "When painting surfaces that could be reached while standing, they moved in fluid, dance-like gestures to achieve the flowing lines important to their elegant styles" (Miller, 4). This does not consider the many paintings done in seemingly impossible places, while artists hung in the air. However, the motion inherent in the painting process is only a part of what is involved with the tradition. The style of aerosol art seeks to breathe rhythm into the Roman alphabet. Miller suggests parallels between patterns in African visual art, African American **quilting**, funk music, and hip-hop rhythms. There is a close association between hip-hop and aerosol cultures, including overlaps in dialect, speech, and dance forms. PHASE 2, for example, was the artist responsible for rap pioneer Kool DJ Herc's posters, and he is also himself a **rap** artist. Aerosol painting is stylized in such a way as to suggest dynamism, motion, and rhythm, whether one imagines **jazz** or hip-hop. The effects of the paintings were intensified when they were viewed on moving trains.

In part because of efforts made by the Metropolitan Transit Authority to stop what it saw simply as acts of vandalism, the tradition of aerosol art has moved away from the trains as a canvas of first choice. Murals painted on landscapes such as handball courts and other public, community sites represent one of the many contemporary directions in which the tradition has grown. Many of the most famous aerosol artists have by now become successful in the mainstream art world, following a trend of galleries showcasing their art—much of which is now on canvas. For example, PHASE 2, WAYNE, and MARE represent artists who have taken the reins in developing careers and businesses in publishing, videos, graphic design, fashion, and other forms of art. (Although art critics have often suggested that artists such as Keith Haring and Jean-Michel Basquiat were graffiti or aerosol artists, many in the aerosol communities do not claim them. For many aerosol artists, membership in the community rests in part on commitment to ideals consistent with black and Latin power movements.)

The tradition of aerosol art and graffiti has by no means perished. To the contrary, like hip-hop, the music it is most associated with, aerosol art has taken the globe by storm and is popular among marginalized and counterculture groups around the world. It has even become appropriated by mainstream commercial culture and is used in advertising to appeal primarily to youth cultures. It is even being offered as an option for home decor (boardecoration.com). The tradition has also entered the electronic realm and is featured on thousands of Web sites, some of which are devoted specifically to this art form. Although art in this form is inherently temporary, photographers and fans have ensured its legacy by devoting Web sites and other publications to photographs that were taken of paintings going back to the 1970s. The global impact of aerosol art on the art world has been recognized by exhibitions in museums such as the Brooklyn Museum, the Smithsonian Institution, the Museum of the City of New York, the Institute of Contemporary Art in Boston, and in contemporary magazines and art books. New York remains, however, "the Mecca of graffiti culture" (Felisbret). Many aerosol artists have continued to be successful in the art world and in related professions. James Prigoff writes:

> Many of the artists have graduated from the streets to run their own businesses. They are involved in digital imaging services, clothing manufacturing, art galleries, magazines, advertising and consulting, all jobs complimented by the knowledge they acquired in the streets. (Forward, in Felisbret)

Aerosol art by Daze, one of the most famous early graffiti artists. (Patrick Aventurier/Getty Images)

Aerosol art is an American art form, an innovative style and language rooted in African-derived aesthetics, now with multiethnic, multinational communities.

Anand Prahlad and Jack T. Cooper

See also: Visionary Artists

Further Reading

Blumberg, Jess, 2008, "Aerosol Art," *Smithsonian Magazine*; Felisbret, Eric, 2009, *Graffiti and Street Art,* (New York: Harry N. Abrams); Chalfant, Henry, and James Prigoff, 1987, *Spraycan Art* (London: Thames and Hudson, Ltd.); Ensminger, David A., 2011, *Visual Vitriol: The Street Art and Subcultures of the Punk and Hardcore Generation* (Jackson: University Press of Mississippi); Miller, Ivor L., 2012 [2002], *Aerosol Kingdom: Subway Painters of New York City* (Jackson: University Press of Mississippi); Rabine, Leslie W., 2014, "These Walls Belong to Everybody: The Graffiti Art Movement in Dakar," *African Studies Quarterly: The Online Journal of African Studies* 14 (3): 89–112.

AFRICA

Elements of contemporary African American folklore can be traced to African cultural origins. Those elements of African cultures that were retained by Africans transported to the New World during the trans-Atlantic slave trade are known as *Africanisms* and also referred to as *syncretisms*, *retentions*, or *survivals*. The concept of Africanisms was developed by the late Melville Herskovits, a pioneer in the development of the field of African American studies, and can be defined as including those elements, cultural motifs, and patterns of behavior he and later scholars observed in African societies and, subsequently, in North and South America and the Caribbean. In attempting to discover the answers to the questions "What is innate?" and "What is cultural or learned?" Herskovits and other scholars asserted that the trauma of the Middle Passage had not destroyed the culturally derived understandings, worldviews, values, and patterns of social interaction of those who were enslaved. Rather, those basic modes of organizing their social worlds and shared cultural knowledge had been retained and incorporated into the New World environments in which the transported and transplanted Africans found themselves.

With regard to these retentions, or Africanisms, as they have influenced African American folklore, it is important to understand the elements that constitute folklore. While folklore includes **folktales** and folk literature, it is not limited to those elements of nonelite, traditional cultural expressions. Folklore also contains the nonelite customs of any group of people who share the knowledge of those customs and can act upon that shared knowledge in a culturally acceptable, recognized, and appropriate way. "Folk" can be broadly defined as two or more individuals who have at least one shared cultural attribute in common that brings them together, fosters their interaction on an ongoing basis, serves to shape their behavior, and serves to construct a shared understanding of appropriate responses to patterns of behavior among them. "Lore" can be broadly defined as a people's time-tested body of knowledge and beliefs about how the world works and why it works the way it does. This knowledge is reflected in a diverse array of African-derived folk practices among African Americans and people of the African diaspora. Thus, for African Americans, folklore has served to forge a cultural cohesion and maintenance of an African-derived worldview in the face of the historic cultural rupture created by the trade of enslaved African people in the 17th, 18th, and 19th centuries.

The specific sites of the origins of Africans enslaved in the New World are not definitively known because of the inconsistencies of record keeping during the trade in slaves. However, the western and central regions of Africa are generally accepted by scholars as the points of origin and source of generalized cultural retentions among people of the African diaspora. These include the present-day nations of Senegal, Gambia, Guinea-Bissau, Guinea, Sierra Leone, Liberia, the Ivory Coast, Ghana, Benin, Nigeria, Cameroon, Gabon, the Congo, and Angola. The regions encompassed by these nations are generally accepted as those from which the largest percentage of African peoples captured or sold into slavery originated.

While some scholars have questioned the validity of claims of African cultural retentions in the United States, others have argued for the persistence of cultural continuities, or survivals, of African culture among African-descended populations in both North and South America. Herskovits, in defiance of the scholarly and popular belief of his time and in an effort to discover the interrelationships of the processes of cultural and biological forms of behavior, argued that patterns of expressive forms and social structures found among African-descended peoples had survived rather than been erased from consciousness by the trauma of enslavement. While it would be erroneous to unequivocally assert that cultural traits from African cultures from which people were bought and sold as slaves were transferred intact among black people in the New World, scholarship suggests that cultural survivals occurred within the folk culture and folklore of African Americans in the forms of language and verbal arts, family structure, music, bodily adornment, art (such as **basket weaving**, **wood carving**, and metal working), communalism and economic reciprocity, **dance**, superstitions and folk beliefs, spirituality, food preferences and food preparation styles, and folkways (such as naming practices and **storytelling**). The influence of Africa on African American folklore in the areas of language and language arts, family structure, communalism and economic reciprocity, music, bodily adornment, and spirituality is covered below.

Language and Language Arts

A form of oral expression derived from a West African context is exemplified in the *griot* tradition of males serving as the bearers, retainers, and conveyers of their given peoples' history. The *griot* tradition of deeply held values and beliefs related to respect for elders, the existing social order, nature, ancestors, and the value of mothers and children continued in the folktales, **proverbs**, and riddles shared among Africans in an evolving African American folk culture. The use of double entendre in the tales and lore found in West African cultures is also a characteristic of the tales and stories found in slave communities. It is also represented in the practices of **signifying** or, more contemporarily, "snapping," or "snaps," as well as in the lyrics of **blues** songs of the 1920s through the 1950s heard in both northern and southern urban and rural black communities. Another example of indirection in the use of language among African Americans in the urban North is the practice of "playin' **the dozens**," also known as "talking about somebody's mama."

Family Structure

Respect for mothers and elders, the practice of maintaining extended family ties, and the establishment of fictive kinship relationships characterizes African family structures, and these patterns of familial relations remain in practice among African American families in the United States. Women, viewed as mothers within the family (whether monogamous or polygamous), the community, and the community's spiritual and religious organizations, have historically and traditionally been respected and revered in the African context. These traditions were maintained in the New World setting. The central role of women in family structure is a pattern that served to ensure the survival of African-descended people during enslavement and following the emancipation of 1863. While slave masters often sold fathers of children (and the children themselves) away from the children's mothers, the women of reproductive age were more often kept by their owners. Thus, the women, following tradition, served as anchors for both their biological and social families within the community of enslaved people. This continued after emancipation as well as during the great wave of migration from the **South** to the North that began in the 1920s.

Respect for the elders of the family and the community is a tradition that remains in place throughout all African societies. Deference is given to the wisdom of the elders based on their life experience and the knowledge of their families and people that reside within them. This deference and respect continues to be in evidence among African American families, particularly in (but not limited to) families and communities in the southern United States. African American families are noted for the adaptive pattern of claiming, or "taking in," non-blood-related children and, often, adults who are incorporated into the family and recognized in kinship relationships as being aunts, uncles, "big momma," "little momma," and generically as cousins. Despite the rupture of enslavement, this pattern of family formation and fictive kinship can be traced to African origins and remains in practice among African Americans.

Communalism and Economic Reciprocity

Extended family practices, as noted above, also include economic cooperation through a pooling of resources (financial, social, emotional) that, in effect, serves to create and extend a network of reciprocal relationships. This practice of pooling resources can be found in Africa and throughout the diaspora; *esusu* among the Yoruba of Nigeria, *susu* among Trinidadians, and Haitian *combite* are examples of established mechanisms of a tradition of such economic reciprocity and communalism. In the United States, this practice of mutual aid has been demonstrated formally within churches, mutual aid societies and associations, sisterhoods, brotherhoods, sororities, and fraternities. This pattern has been demonstrated informally among black Americans through a variety of exchanges of goods and services within families and among community members in both urban and rural settings.

Music

An extension of the oral tradition among Africans and African Americans can be found in African American–based musical expression, which is noted for antiphony, the call-and-response patterning in vocal and instrumental versions of both sacred and secular music. Call-and-response patterning is a continuation of a generalized West African oral folk tradition that is reflected in numerous contexts among enslaved Africans in the North American New World setting, from the "cries," which were songs used to pace the rhythm of work in cotton and tobacco fields during enslavement, to the Mississippi and Alabama chain-gang songs recorded by Alan Lomax in the 1950s, and from the rhythms of the songs of the Virginia gandy dancers (railroad workers) to the instrumental call-and-response heard in African American **jazz**. Herskovits noted the significance of West African musical forms in terms of complexity with regard to scale, rhythm, and the generally polyrhythmic structure of such forms. Derivations of these forms were to be found during the enslavement period in the work and play (social) songs, **field hollers**, and **spirituals.** During later eras, these forms were evident in both rural and urban blues, ragtime, and jazz music as well as in the sacred domain through folk and urban **gospel music**. In musical expression, call-and-response and polyrhythmic patterning (both vocal and instrumental) were, and remain, at the core of African-derived forms of folklore and folk knowledge as they are conveyed in the context of contemporary African American folk cultures.

Material Culture

Many forms of African American material culture bear direct or indirect influences of African cultures and aesthetics. For example, most dance styles and even some of the names of dances are rooted in African cultures. So, too, are the aesthetics and functions of dances, including dance as a means of communicating with the divine. Traditions of food preparation, instrument making, boat building and fishing, husbandry, gestures, herbalism, wood carving, ironwork, pottery, architecture, and painting among different groups and in diverse regions of the United States have roots in African traditions and ideology.

African culture has also played a major role in the aesthetics of bodily adornment among African Americans. The elaborate braid designs worn by women in many West African societies serve as a prototype for similar designs worn by both female and male African Americans. The practice of elaborate braid designs continues to the present time throughout Africa and the African diaspora, as can be seen in the braiding worn currently by African Americans—young and elderly, female and male, urban and rural. Braided hair also serves a functional purpose in tropical regions of Africa—the braiding exposes the scalp and allows for cooling of the body through evaporation of perspiration. The same purpose, in addition to adornment and grooming, could very well have served to sustain the practice initially in the United States, particularly in those regions noted for extremely high summer temperatures. The retention of this mode of hairdressing currently serves as a statement of cultural identity among African Americans.

The practice of bodily adornment through the wearing of jewelry is another African American practice that can be traced to African origins. The great leaders of West African societies, most notably rulers of the present-day nations of Ghana and Nigeria, are noted for their lavish displays of bodily adornments of gold jewelry—rings, earrings, necklaces, all of which signify the regal status of the wearer. The elaborately woven kente cloth robes worn by paramount chiefs and noted for their brilliant coloring and patterning (designs that symbolize and embody narratives extolling the virtues and characteristics of the wearers) also serve as prototypes for contemporary cultural survivals among African Americans, who demonstrate a similar approach to making a statement about identity and status through the incorporation of modified and adapted versions of kente cloth itself and vivid colors in clothing as a statement of status and an awareness of style.

Spirituality

Cultures throughout the African diaspora manifest the influence of Africa on spirituality and the religious expression of that spirituality. Vivid examples of the almost universal influence of Africa on African American religious practices appear in music and language and verbal arts in the form of spirituals and in an intensity of emotional expression in the traditional **black church** in America. While secular songs of enslaved Africans reflected an African belief in the ability to triumph over adversity, the spirituals drew on an African-derived "trust in God as the primary source of their empowerment. In those songs they sang about their faith in a God who they unquestionably believed was concerned about their well-being" (Paris, 563). Likewise, the cadences and rhythms of the spirituals, the call-and-response patterning of the words, and the notes of music served to convey the mixed emotions of sorrow and joy in longing for divine justice to prevail in the face of adversity and the steadfast belief in a higher power that could, and would, deliver that justice. This belief is conveyed in the lyrics of the spirituals. Traditional African religion celebrates and affirms life, "with God serving as the apex of being and humankind as the center" (Creel, 74). African American spirituality and religious practices likewise serve as celebrations and affirmations of life, despite its challenges and adversities, through musical expression and the power of the spoken word in the sermons offered in the churches of black America.

In addition to the manifestation of African cultural survivals in religious expression as demonstrated by the theology of spirituals, the syncretic religions of Santería, Vodou, and Candomblé also developed. These religions are African-based, with origins in the devotional system of the Yoruba pantheon of orishas (deities). Originating in Cuba and Puerto Rico (Santería), Haiti (Vodou) and Brazil (Candomblé), the practice of these religions enabled Africans enslaved in these nations to adapt their familiar orisha-based African religion to the religion of the slave owners, which, in these instances, was Catholicism. The saints of the Catholic Church thus share characteristics and qualities with the orishas of Yoruba. Because of the trade in slaves between the Caribbean islands and southern gulf states such as Louisiana, Mississippi, Alabama, and Texas, as well as the presence of African priests (male and female) already among the captive population in the southern United States, the Yoruba religion survived and was continuously practiced by Africans throughout the diaspora, with adaptations and accommodations within the New World settings. A resurgence and revitalization of these Yoruba-based religions among African Americans began in the 1960s, primarily in urban areas of the Northeast, Midwest, and West Coast, and continues to the present time.

Besides the more obvious connections between continental Africa and New World African spiritualities, links can be found at the level of performance styles, aesthetics, and philosophy. Thus many beliefs and practices in Christian denominations are related to those in the religions mentioned above; for example, the prevalence of direct interaction with deities, spirits, or other supernatural forces (e.g., being "ridden" by loas in Vodou, or being taken by the Holy Ghost in evangelistic Christian worship). Other commonalities include the belief in music as a channel through which people can communicate with the divine, and a dynamic, body-centered approach to worship. Recent studies suggest that many of these continuities are as integral to many African American communities in contemporary society as they were in earlier periods of history.

Adrianne R. Andrews

Further Reading

Araujo, Ana Lucia, 2014, *Shadows of the Slave Past: Memory, Heritage, and Slavery* (New York, NY: Routledge); Archer, Jermaine O., 2009, *Antebellum Slave Narratives: Cultural and Political Expressions of Africa* (Routledge); Cartwright, Keith, 2013, *Sacral Grooves, Limbo Gateways: Travels in Deep Southern Time, Circum-Caribbean Space, Afro-creole Authority* (University of Georgia Press); Creel, Margaret W., 1990, "Gullah Attitudes toward Life and Death," in *Africanisms in American Culture,* ed. J. E. Holloway (Bloomington and Indianapolis: Indiana University Press), pp. 69–97; Epega, Afolabi, 1993, "Preface," in *The Way of the Orisa: Empowering Your Life through the Ancient African Religion of Ifa*, Philip J. Neimark (San Francisco: Harper San Francisco), pp. xv–xvi; Ferris, William, ed., 1983, *Afro-American Folk Art and Crafts* (Jackson: University Press of Mississippi); Herskovits, Frances S., ed., 1966, *The New World Negro: Selected Papers in Afroamerican Studies* (Bloomington and Indianapolis: Indiana University Press); Herskovits, Melville J., 1941, *The Myth of the Negro Past* (Boston: Beacon Press); Holloway, Joseph E., ed., 1990, *Africanisms in American Culture* (Bloomington and Indianapolis: Indiana University Press); Paris, Peter J., 1998, "Basic African American Values: Gifts to the World," in *Soundings* 81 (3–4): 553–570; Pinn, Anthony B., 2009, *Black Religion and Aesthetics: Religious Thought and Life in Africa and the African Diaspora* (New York, NY: Palgrave Macmillan); Thompson, Robert Farris, 1984 [1983], *Flash of the Spirit: African and Afro-American Art and Philosophy* (New York: Vintage Books); Valdes, Vanessa, ed., 2012, *The Future is Now: A New Look at African Diaspora Studies* (Newcastle upon Tyne, United Kingdom: Cambridge Scholars Publishing).

AFRICANS, FLYING
See Flying Africans

B

BAAD

Meaning stylishly and irreverently good, this adjective is related to the "**Bad Man**" in African American folklore and often is used in the phrase "baad ass" to describe a person or thing. While the term encapsulates an African-derived emphasis on ornamentation, style, and self presentation, it has a distinctly New World African, urban flavor. As much as anything, baad refers to an attitude, a toughness, and indifference to mainstream white values and authority. While it refers to behavior and mental disposition, it also translates into aesthetics and is a criterion by which not only people, but also performances are judged. Culturally, baad is a defiant stance against mainstream institutional values that confine and oppress black people and black expression. For example, in the mainstream, elaborate adornment, bright colors, and militant attitudes are considered transgressions. Hence, bold and elaborate decoration of one's car or of one's body is a protest of mainstream values and a declaration of pride in a different cultural aesthetic. Baad is often associated with the "Bad Man" figures, such as those in **toasts,** songs, and other genres (e.g., Stagolee, Dolemite, John Henry, Railroad Bill, Sweetback, and Shaft). It is also applicable to historical figures, such as Harriet Tubman, Huey Newton, or Malcolm X, and to cultural expressions, such as performances by artists like Miles Davis, Nina Simone, or Prince.

Anand Prahlad

Further Reading

Dunn, Stephane, 2008, *"Baad Bitches" and Sassy Supermamas: Black Power Action Films,* (Urbana: University of Illinois Press); Roberts, John W., 1989, *From Trickster to Bad-man: The Black Folk Hero in Slavery and Freedom* (Philadelphia: University of Pennsylvania Press); Semley, John, 2010, "Who's Bleeding Whom? Analyzing the Cultural Flows of Blaxploitation Cinema, Then and Now," *Cineaction* 80: 22.

BAD MAN, THE

The Bad Man is a recurring figure in African American folklore, representing the rebellious character of those black men who refuse to submit to authority and who may use violence to achieve their ends. Just as the Uncle Tom figure epitomizes the passive "Good Negro" who meekly accepts his inferior position, the Bad Man epitomizes the belligerent and unpredictable "Bad N*gger" who neither respects nor expects justice.

In its broadest sense, the figure of the Bad Man in the United States may encompass two main types: (1) those whose rebellion is directed against the predominant culture controlled by whites, and (2) those who turn upon everyone in their way, whether black or white, usually with amoral violence. In the first category can be found both historical and contemporary figures: gangster rappers, political activists, and successful athletes such as Jack Johnson and Dennis Rodman. In the second category can be found folkloric figures such as Railroad Bill, **Stagolee**, and John Hardy, whose exploits are celebrated in ballads and legends, and also fictional characters created by novelists, such as Bigger Thomas in Richard Wright's *Native Son* and Cholly Breedlove in Toni Morrison's *The Bluest Eye*.

In many cases, the folklore of the Bad Man is derived from actual historical figures. Perhaps the best known is Railroad Bill ("so mean and so bad," as the ballad goes), based on the life of Morris Slater from the piney woods of southern Alabama. After refusing to register his rifle in accordance with state law and firing at sheriff's deputies, Slater escaped and remained a fugitive for three years. He survived primarily by robbing freight trains and threatening the life of anyone who crossed his path. Finally, on March 7, 1896, Slater was shot and killed by a lawman, but legends of his meanness and supernatural prowess persist in many regions. A similar figure is John Hardy ("a mean and desperate man," as the ballad goes), who killed a fellow worker in a West Virginia crap game over a twenty-five-cent bet and was hanged for the crime in January 1894.

The decade of the 1890s is also when the ballads and legends of Stagolee (also known as Staggerlee, Stackolee, etc.) first emerged, apparently based on the murder of Billy Lyons by Lee Shelton, a **pimp** known as Stack Lee, in St. Louis on December 25, 1895. However, the stories and songs quickly overtook any historical facts, and it was not long before Stagolee had become a notorious Bad Man, a boastful bully, and a cruel, remorseless killer.

Several scholars have noted that the typical black Bad Man is rarely sentimentalized or romanticized like many white outlaw heroes and social bandits such as Jesse James, Billy the Kid, or John Dillinger, who follow in the folkloric traditions of Robin Hood and thus are good men driven to bad behavior. However, other scholars have observed that the black Bad Man is often endowed with **trickster**-like qualities, enabling him to break the rules of white society with wit and humor, much like some of the earlier trickster heroes who defied the conventions of slavery. The rise of the folkloric Bad Man in the late 19th century may therefore be seen as a means for expressing in a vicarious way attitudes of defiance and rebellion against the white authorities, who were reacting to the African American gains of Reconstruction with the Jim Crow laws of segregation.

James I. Deutsch

Further Reading

Brown, Cecil, 2003, *Stagolee Shot Billy* (Cambridge, MA: Harvard University Press); Bryant, Jerry H., 2003, *"Born in a Mighty Bad Land": The Violent Man in African American Folklore and Fiction* (Bloomington: Indiana University Press); Levine, Lawrence W., 1977, *Black Culture and Black Consciousness: Afro-American Folk Thought from Slavery to*

Freedom (New York: Oxford University Press); Munby, Jonathan, 2011, *Under a Bad Sign: Criminal Self-Representation in African American Popular Culture* (Chicago: University of Chicago Press); Nyawalo, Mich Yonah, 2012, "From Trickster to Badman to 'Gangsta': Globalizing the Badman Mythoform in Hip-Hop Music," ProQuest Dissertations Publishing; Nyawalo, Mich, 2013, "From Badman to Gangsta: Double Consciousness and Authenticity, from African-American Folklore to Hip Hop," *Popular Music and Society* 36 (4): 460–75; Roberts, John W., 1989, *From Trickster to Badman: The Black Folk Hero in Slavery and Freedom* (Philadelphia: University of Pennsylvania Press); Rolston, Simon, 2013, "Prison Life Writing, African American Narrative Strategies, and Bad: The Autobiography of James Carr." *Multi-Ethnic Literature of the United States* 38 (4): 191–215; Williams, Shawn, 2007, *I'm a Bad Man: African American Vernacular Culture and the Making of Muhammad Ali* (Lulu).

BANJO

The banjo is a plucked lute with a hide- or plastic-covered sound chamber, four to five strings, and a bridge. This symbol of Appalachia is heard around the world, but Africans brought the *banjar* with them to America, and the banjo that developed from it eventually helped create the sounds used in American minstrel, ragtime, **blues**, **jazz**, old-time, country, bluegrass, and other musical styles. The banjo retained the short drone African thumb string of the *banjar* but replaced the gourd body with a cheese-box (or sometimes inset-rim) wooden sound chamber.

In previous times, African praise singers and memory keepers played the Mali *molo* and *ngoni*, the Jolas *akonting*, the Wolof *halam*, and other West African lutes for singing and dancing in local rituals. Enslaved Africans brought or made gourd *banjars* in the colony of Maryland by 1740 and in Virginia by 1744. In 1789 on the Wilderness Road near Knoxville in Appalachia, frontiersmen and women "danced around" to the music of black *banjies*, and the instrument was played on the banks of the Ohio River in Wheeling, West Virginia, in 1806. Rex Ellis writes that banjo music "provided a temporary escape from the realities of broken families, violence, death, dismemberment, disease, and the loss of freedom that was part of the system of chattel slavery (42)." For almost a century, only blacks seem to have played the *banjar* (built with a pole or sometimes a flat neck); it echoed their homeland traditions, inspired their improvised lyric songs, and paced their frolic dances. Field hands and river roustabouts from different African regions exchanged **field hollers**; shanties; rowing, corn shucking, and *banjar* songs; **spirituals**; and **dance** music. Later they worked on the railroads and in the mines. In a call-and-response structure with repeating riffs, *banjar* music is more rhythmically complex and less melodically intricate than Scots and Irish music. With special tunings, the Upland South *banjar* repertoire of lyric songs is conversational and often includes animal songs that celebrate a **trickster** (often a fox instead of **Brer Rabbit**) that are symbolic of survival during slavery and later.

Most of the black mentors of mountain and minstrel apprentices remain unidentified, but Picayune Butler influenced whites in New Orleans and remained famous for 25 years on the rivers to Cincinnati and even in New York City. Butler sang on the street and in competitions, and his banjo songs and journeys prefigure the traveling country bluesman. No later than the 1830s, whites (especially the Irish and Scots) took up the gourd *banjar* and its African American thumping playing style. By 1842, the Virginian Joel Sweeney, of Irish heritage, either popularized or invented the five-string, open-back, wooden-rim banjo that resulted from the black and white musical exchange. The African short thumb string already existed; his fifth string was added in today's fourth-string position to expand the banjo's possibilities for Celtic melodies.

The standardized fiddle, easy to carry and echoing the outlawed bagpipes, had arrived with the Scotch-Irish, Germans, and others during the 18th century. Soon the banjo moved from local frolics and dances to court days and the circus and on to the minstrel stage. Early minstrels respected African American musicianship and soon put the Scotch-Irish fiddle and African banjo together; their musical exchange, like the cocreation of the banjo from the *banjar*, symbolizes American egalitarianism at work. The minstrels traveled widely, and their routines continued to explore black and white musical and social relations in the new country, but soon the routines became increasingly commercial and cruelly satiric.

After steamboat travel took off in 1850, enslaved African Americans (leased by their southern masters) often worked side by side with Irish and German laborers. In the evenings, cabin boys played music, buck danced, and did the cakewalk. Blacks and whites played jigs and reels (e.g., "Natchez under the Hill"), "jump up" songs, and old lonesome "breakdowns." During the Civil War regional exchange expanded. In waterfront dancehalls in Cincinnati, no later than 1876, black roustabouts and white longshoremen paired the banjo and fiddle. Twelve such songs played by African Americans are documented. Black and white exchange resulted in minstrelsy, at least three types of banjo songs, and the merging of the fiddle and banjo.

The downstroking ("thumping" or "clawhammer") style of old-time banjo peaked in the early 20th century among blacks (e.g., Virginians Josh Thomas, Rufus Kasey, and Leonard Bowles) and white mountain songsters. African American makers of old-time banjos included the fathers of Kasey and fellow Virginian John Jackson. However, early in the 20th century, many blacks put down their banjos to set their songs with increasingly assertive commentary to the now readily available guitar to create the blues.

Two-finger, up-picking styles, acquired from African Americans before 1865, influenced minstrel styles in parlors and orchestral concert halls as the banjo was introduced to genteel society. After World War II, fingerpicking banjo and gospel singing laid the groundwork for the hard-driving bluegrass style and its industrial context. In the 1950s and 1960s, old-time banjo influenced the folk revival. The first Black Banjo Gathering took place in spring 2005 in an attempt to help reclaim the banjo for African Americans and perpetuate its diverse traditions. From the arrival of the *banjar* in the United States to the present, the banjo has made an intense contribution to the country's indigenous music and its interaction with song and dance.

Cecelia Conway

Further Reading

Andersen, Leslie, 2015, "African American Roots and Branches of the 5-String Banjo: A Selective Videography." *Notes* 72 (1): 203; Burrison, John A., 2007, *Roots of a Region: Southern Folk Culture* (University of Mississippi Press); Charry, Eric, 2000, *Mande Music: Traditional and Modern Music of the Maninka and Mandinka of Western Africa* (Chicago: The University of Chicago Press); Cole, Thomas B., 2014, "The Banjo Lesson: Henry Ossawa Tanner," *Jama* 311 (17): 1714–5; Conway, Cecelia, 1995, *African Banjo Echoes in Appalachia* (Knoxville: University of Tennessee Press); Conway, Cecelia, 2005, "Black Banjo Songsters" in *Black Music Research Journal*; Conway, Cecelia, and Scott Odell, 1998, *Black Banjo Songsters of North Carolina and Virginia*, CD liner notes (Smithsonian Folkways); Coolen, Michael Theodore, 1984, "Senegambia Archetypes for the American Folk Banjo," *Western Folklore* 43: 146–161; Ellis, Rex, 2011, "Banjos," in *World of a Slave: Encyclopedia of the Material Life of Slaves in the United States,* editors Martha B. Katz-Hyman, and Kym S. Rice (ABC-CLIO), pp. 40–44; Epstein, Dena J., 1977, *Sinful Tunes and Spirituals: Black Folk Music in the Civil War* (Urbana: University of Illinois Press); Gura, Philip F., and James F. Bollman, 1999, *America's Instrument: The Banjo in the Nineteenth Century* (Chapel Hill: The University of North Carolina Press); Kubik, Gerhard, "South Africa: The Southern African Periphery: Banjo Traditions in Zambia and Malawi," *The World of Music* 31 (1): 3–39; Levine, Lawrence W., 1977, *Black Culture and Consciousness: Afro-American Folk Thought from Slavery to Freedom* (New York: Oxford University Press); Nathan, Hans, 1977 [1962], *Dan Emmett and the Rise of Early Negro Minstrelsy* (Norman: University of Oklahoma Press); Oliver, Paul, ed., 1970, *Savannah Syncopators: African Retentions in the Blues*, the Blues Series (New York: Stein and Day); Pecknold, Diane, 2013, *Hidden in the Mix: The African American Presence in Country Music* (Durham, NC: Duke University Press); Sacks, Howard L., and Judith Rose, 1993, *Way up North in Dixie: A Black Family's Claim to the Confederate Anthem* (Washington, DC: Smithsonian Institution Press); Webb, Robert Lloyd, 1984, *Ring the Banjar: The Banjo in America from Folklore to Factory* (Cambridge: The MIT Museum).

BAPTISM

This ritual is crucial to one's admission into the Christian church or conversion to Christianity. Among the Baptists, baptism takes the form of water immersion in a local lake or river. John Bivens, a resident of the Sea Islands, described the baptisms that he witnessed. First, he observed, the church members gathered at the church, from which point they would march in pairs to the river, led by the pastor and the deacons. "Dis is a solemn time," Bivens remarked, "an duh candidates an deah friens an relatives all rejoice."The participants prepared themselves by singing **spirituals** along the way. "Wen we git tuh duh ribbuh some uh duh folks is so happy an dey scream an jump round so much dat some uh duh udduhs hab tuh hole em," Bivens continued. Then, one by one, each candidate was led into the water for his or her submersion (Georgia Writers' Project, 92). Elizabeth Roberts provided one explanation for the insistence upon a river baptism when she explained that baptisms were always performed when the tide was on its way out "so duh watuh will wash duh sins away" (Georgia Writers' Project, 113).

Most African American Christians looked upon baptism as the death and rebirth of the spirit. That this process would take place in the water is quite significant. Especially for Africans and African Americans of Kongolese heritage, "water was perceived as a barrier separating this world from the next," wrote historian Jason Young (p. 84). The close connection between submersion and rebirth is explained in part by art historian Robert Farris Thompson. He described the Bakongo cross, an ideogram found among the Kongolese, as an object with four points, sometimes joined by a circle. These four points are the "four moments of the sun." Envision these four points as marking north, west, east, and south. The easternmost point marks dawn, the beginning of life. As the sun ascends, so does life, until the individual finds himself or herself at noon, where life flourishes. The western point, sunset, marks the end of life, while the southern point, midnight, represents life just before the new dawn—the world where the spirit waits to be reborn. The points marking west and east are joined by a horizontal line referred to as the Kalunga line, which is envisioned as a body of water. Beneath the Kalunga line, under the water, is the southern, fourth point, which marks the moment of death and rebirth. The world of the dead, the world of the spirits, thus resides below the Kalunga line, below the water.

When converts were submerged under the water by a minister, then, they came into contact with God. Immediately following her conversion, one resident of the Sea Islands emerged exclaiming, "Oh Jedus . . . uh see Gawd onduhneet' de water! Uh fin' me Gawd. 'E look 'puntopme!" (Young, 83). Crossing between worlds—between the human earth above the water and the spiritual world beneath it—meant that, for a short time, the converts entered into the land of the dead. "I knew at that time that I was in another world, and I knew that I had left my earthly body behind," wrote a new convert (Young, 84). Elizabeth Roberts described the process by saying that the candidates were "buried in baptism" (Georgia Writers' Project, 113).

Anthropologist Melville Herskovits has also suggested that water baptism, which is "indispensable for affiliation with the Baptist Church," and the African meanings associated with water baptism help to explain the preponderance of African American converts to that faith. "River spirits are among the most powerful of those inhabiting the supernatural world," Herskovits found. He further asserted that priests of river cults, known for their "intransigence," were frequently sold out of **Africa** as slaves; thus a significant number would have found their way to the New World. The Baptist church, with its emphasis on emotionalism, its basis in the folk realm, and its "autonomous organization that was in line with the tradition of local self-direction congenial to African practice" made it appealing. To these priests and their followers, however, the most attractive feature of the Baptist faith would have been the submersion ritual. Worshippers of the water spirits would rush into the water to be tangibly connected to those spirits, so a religion that marked its conversion with a ritual that encouraged its followers to connect to God while submerged in the river had obvious attractions (Herskovits, 232–233).

Certainly there were differences between the two religious practices, but the similarities are also significant. Among African tribes that worshipped water spirits, Herskovits observed, it was spirit possession that drove the devotee "threshing into the stream" to attain that physical proximity to the spirits. In the United States, "Negro Baptists do not run into the water under possession by African gods." However, when the convert is submerged, "the spirit descends on him at that moment, if at all, and a possession hysteria develops that in its outward appearance, at least, is almost indistinguishable from the possession brought on by the African water deities" (Herskovits, 233–234).

A final parallel between African cultural practices and water baptism appears in the clothing worn by the candidates; the color white was closely associated with the baptismal process. Numerous sources describe candidates for baptism wearing white robes. For example, Bivens remarked that "duh candidates comes all dressed ready fuh baptism in long wite robes" (Georgia Writers' Project, 92). Young explains that this emphasis on the color white marks a connection between the Sea Islands and the Kongo. "For the Kongolese the color white evoked the underworld whose inhabitants were commonly figured as white-skinned" (Young, 83). As part of many spiritual rituals, Kongolese men and women would whiten their skin by rubbing kaolin, a white, clay-like substance, on themselves. Africans in the United States continued the association of whiteness with spirituality by adorning themselves in white for this most sacred ritual of symbolic death and rebirth; they then put their white robes away "to serve as their shrouds one day" (Young, 85).

Jennifer Hildebrand

Further Reading

Battle, Michael, 2006, *The Black Church in America: African American Christian Spirituality* (Malden; MA: Blackwell Publishers); Georgia Writers' Project, 1986 [1940], *Drums and Shadows* (Athens: University of Georgia Press); Haldeman, Scott, 2007, *Towards Liturgies that Reconcile: Race and Ritual Among African-American and European-American Protestants* Burlington, VT: Ashgate); Harvey, Paul, 2011, *Through the Storm, through the Night: A History of African American Christianity* (Lanham, MD: Rowman & Littlefield Publishers); Herskovits, Melville, 1958 [1941], *Myth of the Negro Past* (Boston: Beacon Press); Thomas, Kenneth, and Hugh Tulloch, 2008, *The Religious Dancing of American Slaves, 1820–1865: Spiritual Ecstasy at Baptisms, Funerals, and Sunday Meetings* (NY: Edward Mellen Press); Thompson, Robert Farris, and Joseph Cornet, 1981, *Four Moments of the Sun* (Washington, DC: National Gallery of Art); Young, Jason, 2002, "Rituals of Resistance: The Making of an African-Atlantic Religious Complex in Kongo and along the Sea Islands of the Slave South," PhD diss., University of California, Riverside.

BARBECUE

Barbecue is a cuisine produced by cooking meat slowly over a fire and basting it with a highly seasoned sauce. There are several possible origins for the word itself and for the cooking method. The most widely accepted is that the word is a modification of the word *barbacoa* and that enslaved African Americans learned the technique of barbecue while in the West Indies en route to North America. Evidence of this lies in reports by Spanish explorers that Taino-Arawak and Carib peoples used a wooden framework they called a *babracot*, which was placed over a small bed of coals to roast, dry, and smoke meat. The Spanish modified the word to *barbacoa*, and the English to "barbecue." The word appeared in print in English for the first time in 1661, and the poet Alexander Pope used it in 1732.

As early as 1705, Virginia passed a law forbidding the shooting of firearms at barbecuing parties, indicating that these events had become common. George Washington refers in his diaries to barbecuing parties he attended and gave. On plantations before emancipation, barbecue was usually prepared by African American cooks, whether it was to be eaten by enslaved workers or by the slaveholder and his family and friends. To a large degree, that practice continued after the Civil War. Even in white restaurants during the **Jim Crow** period, the cooking of barbecue was often done by African Americans. Nonetheless, white Southerners have been reluctant to view barbecue as an element of black cuisine, and there is considerable controversy surrounding this point.

There is reason to believe that the enslaved people who were taken to Texas by the Austin colony took barbecue with them. The cooking methods that were used primarily on pork in the deep **South** were applied to beef, which was more plentiful in the west. The result was Texas barbecue. During the great wave of migration in the early 20th century, African Americans took barbecue with them to the North, along with **blues** music and sanctified churches, and cities such as Chicago, Detroit, and Kansas City also gained reputations as producers of good barbecue—the ultimate accolade.

Barbecue is culturally significant in the American South and to African Americans across the country because of its central role in celebrations, community organizing, and political gatherings in both black and white communities, beginning during the antebellum period and continuing to the present. The first **Juneteenth** celebration, in Galveston, Texas, on June 19, 1865, was a barbecue, and the first integrated political event in South Carolina after Reconstruction was a barbecue celebrating the election of Governor Donald Russell in 1963. In the black community, barbecues were held to raise funds for churches, orphanages, and the civil rights movement.

In the works of African American writers, barbecues are often symbolic of community feeling itself. Ralph Ellison, Alice Walker, and Zora Neale Hurston are only a few of those who have brought their characters together at barbecues or spoken of the barbecue as a place of unity and reconciliation. In *Dust Tracks on a Road*, Hurston wrote, "Maybe all of us who do not have the good fortune to meet or meet again, in this world, will meet at a barbecue."

In recent years, writers have drawn attention to the black tradition of barbecue being overlooked. While barbecue has taken a more prominent place in American cuisine, having television programs devoted to it and the elevation of white restaurant owners to a position beside chefs of other kinds of food, African Americans have been largely left out. There is even a National Barbecue Month (May), in which pitmasters are profiled in media such as magazines and television. Miller writes, "What's regularly missing in these features are shout-outs to African Americans" (eatcroacy.cnn.com).

Kathleen Thompson

See also: Festivals; Folk Foods; Soul Food

Further Reading

Douglas, Mary, ed., 1984, *Food in the Social Order* (New York: Russell Sage Foundation); Lovegren, Sylvia, "Barbecue," *American Heritage* 3: 36; Lussenhop, Jessica, 2015, "Black pitmasters left out of US barbecue boom," *BBC News Magazine,* August 24; Miller, Adrian, 2012, "Barbecue Digest: Don't Whitewash BBQ," (eatocracy.cnn.com) June 21; Miller, Adrian, 2014, *Soul Food: The Surprising Story of an American Cuisine One Plate at a Time* (Chapel Hill: The University of North Carolina Press); Opie, Frederick Douglass, 2010, *Hog and Hominy: Soul Food from Africa to America* (New York: Columbia University Press); Twitty, Michael W., 2015, "Barbecue is an American Tradition—of Enslaved Africans and Native Americans," (theguardian.com), July 4; Walsh, Robb, 2003, "Barbecue in Black and White: Carving Racism out of Texas Barbecue Mythology," Houston Press, May 1; Warnes, Andrew, 2006, "Guantánamo, Eatonville, Accompong: Barbecue and the Diaspora in the Writings of Zora Neale Hurston," *Journal of American Studies* 40 (2): 367–89; Warnes, Andrew, 2010, *Savage Barbecue: Race, Culture, and the Invention of America's First Food.* (Athens: University of Georgia Press).

BARBERSHOP, THE

African American barbershops are more than functional environs where African American men go to obtain a haircut. They also serve as cultural refuges and psychic sanctuaries. Barbershops are safe havens where African American men shed the masks displayed for psychic and bodily survival in an often racialized and masculinized public sphere. Like the beauty shop, the **jook** joint, the church, and sites of **hip-hop** freestyle competitions, barbershops are marketplaces of talk and discourse, quasi/counter public sites of ritual, rhetorical education, and knowledge production where communal and cultural affirmation and exchange occur. There, African American men deploy straight-no-chaser black male opinions and truths. As eloquently articulated by Ralph Ellison in *Shadow and Act*, "There is no place like a Negro barbershop for hearing what Negroes really believe" (Ellison, 9).

Barbershops reflect the historical and rhetorical antecedents of what enslaved Africans and African Americans referred to as **hush harbors** or **bush harbors**. These were places such as thickets, woods, and slave cabins where African Americans would go to avoid having their discourse policed and monitored, where they could develop counternarratives and frames reflecting their own experiences. Peter Randolph, an escaped slave who was emancipated in 1847, gave a paradigmatic description of a hush harbor in Virginia: "Not being allowed to hold meetings on the plantation, the slaves assemble in the swamps, out of the reach of patrols. They have an understanding among themselves as to the time and place of getting together" (Randolph, 67). Given that certain kinds of black talk are still monitored and trivialized as being angry, militant, radical, or slang, barbershops still serve an important function in the circulation of African American males' hidden transcripts and understandings of the world. From Paul Laurence Dunbar's *An Ante-Bellum Sermon* through Toni Morrison's *Song of Solomon* to the *Barbershop* movies, the

African American barbershop on U Street in Washington, D.C., ca. 1942. (Corbis)

pervasiveness of both the hush harbor and the barbershop in African American folk, popular, and expressive culture is apparent.

In antebellum America, many European immigrants avoided working in service industries such as hair service, as the jobs were deemed beneath their station. As a result of this and the gender oppression of black women, one of the more lucrative occupations for black males was that of the African American barber, typically with an exclusive, pampered, white clientele. With their access to whites and to the economic advantages that accompanied such access, barbers and barbering possessed social prestige in African American communities. One of the reasons that black folks held barbers in such high esteem is that barbers were known for their commitment to African American communities. For example, William Watson was a Cincinnati barber and former slave who purchased freedom for his mother and siblings and invested in building **black churches**. Another, Pierre Toussant, was one of the first black philanthropists. Two barbers, John Vashon and Lewis Woodson, cofounded the first all-black university, Wilberforce University. However, postbellum and post-Reconstruction America changed the economic and spatial lot of African American barbers. In the late 19th century, German and Italian immigrants competed with black barbers, siphoning away white customers, driving black customers out of downtown areas, and creating separate black economies. Because of this racial segregation of hair care, black barbershop customers eventually became more racially homogeneous and more class heterogeneous, as African

Americans of all economic levels sought cultural refuge and affirmation outside the hostility of the public sphere. Barbershops became repositories of African American folk culture, stock markets of cultural exchange, and schools of knowledge production.

In *Ella Baker & the Black Freedom Movement: A Radical Democratic Vision*, Barbara Ransby discusses how "from her own point of view, her [Ella Baker's] political education was derived not only from her formal training at Shaw University but also from what she learned on the streets and in meeting places and union halls of New York City, as well as at rural and urban churches, barbershops, and kitchen tables throughout the South" (Ransby, 363). Richard Wright, Toni Morrison, John Oliver Killens, Keith Gilyard, Lonnie Elder III, Henry Louis Gates Jr., Amiri Baraka, Jay-Z, and a wide variety of African American scholars, artists, writers, theorists, and everyday people have either written or talked about the African American barbershop. **Blues**, **rap**, ghetto/street literature, and other forms of African American folk and vernacular refer to the barbershop. Melvin Murphy's *Barber Shop Talk: The Other Side of Black Men*, and Melissa Victoria Harris-Lacwell's *Barbershops, Bibles, and Bet: Everyday, Talk and Black Political Thought* provide evidence of the continuing importance of the barbershop to African American life. Studies by Brunson and Wood, Davis, and Marowa-Wilkerson offer additional insights into the many ways in which barbershops play significant roles in African American communities. For example, some barbershops have begun offering information about health and diet, focusing on problems such as hypertension and diabetes, and including free blood pressure readings (Davis, 140). As the spatial and discursive segregation of working-class and poor African Americans continues in the face of deindustrialization and globalization, barbershops appear as if they will remain important in the future as black public spheres.

Vorris Nunley

Further Reading

Bristol, Douglas Walter, 2009, *Knights of the Razor: Black Barbers in Slavery and Freedom* (Baltimore: Johns Hopkins University Press); Brunson, Rod, and Patricia Wood, 2011, "Geographics of Resilient Social Networks: The Role of African American Barbershops," in *Urban Geography*, Vol. 32, Issue 2, pp. 228–243; Davis, Olga, 2013, "Barbershop Cuisine: African American Foodways and Narratives of Health in the Black Barbershop," in *International Journal of Men's Health*, Vol. 12, No. 2, pp. 138–149; Ellison, Ralph, 1964, *Shadow and Act* (New York: Random House); Harris-Lacwell, Melissa Victoria, 2004, *Barbershops, Bibles, and Bet: Everyday Talk and Black Political Thought* (Princeton, NJ: Princeton University Press); Marowa-Wilkerson, Tendai M., "The Use of Mobile Phones in an African American Barbershop," Dissertation, University of Illinois, Urbana-Champaign; Mills, Quincy T., 2013, *Cutting Along the Color Line: Black Barbers and Barber Shops in America* (Philadelphia: University of Pennsylvania Press); Murphy, Melvin, 1998, *Barber Shop Talk: The Other Side of Black Men* (Merrifield, VA: Melvin Murphy); Nunley, Vorris, 2011, *Keepin' It Hushed: The Barbershop and African American Hush Harbor Rhetoric* (Detroit: Wayne State University Press); Randolph, Peter, 1893, *From Slave Cabin to Pulpit. The Autobiography of Rev. Peter Randolph: The Southern Question Illustrated and Sketches of Slave Life* (Boston: J. H. Earle); Ransby, Barbara,

2003, *Ella Baker & the Black Freedom Movement: A Radical Democratic Vision* (Chapel Hill: The University of North Carolina Press).

BASKET WEAVING

Basket weaving was one of many skills carried by Africans across the Atlantic that proved essential to the success of rice as an export crop. African American folk arts provide an important area of study for scholars interested in tracing the transmission of African cultural patterns across the Atlantic and the ways in which those patterns persisted and changed in the United States. **Pottery**, **wood carving**, work implements, jewelry, and woven baskets all communicated important information regarding this process. "The coiled baskets of the Sea Islands," observed John Michael Vlach, "are perhaps the most noteworthy examples of distinctly Afro-American craft" (Vlach, 1990, 7). Judith Wragg Chase contends, "On the American plantations, basketry was preserved in purer form than most other crafts. Shapes, uses, and technique of manufacture are similar to those of Africa" (Chase, 59).

Alfred Graham, the first teacher of basketry at Penn Center on Saint Helena island (initially a center of learning for blacks during Reconstruction) said that he learned the skill in **Africa** and brought it with him to the United States while young (Davis, 160). Anthropologist Melville Herskovits observed that "pottery of a high grade, basketry, and iron work are found everywhere" throughout West Africa (Georgia Writers' Project, 247). Gerald L. Davis added Central and even South Africa to the list of areas on that continent where basketry skills appeared (Davis, 153). Vlach indicated that the "coiled grass basket is known all across the continent of Africa, and although a similar technology is also found among Euro- and Native Americans, the relationship between African and Afro-American examples is particularly striking." He added that "Senegambian baskets" could be "interchanged for Sea Island baskets" (Vlach, 1990, 7). The similarities that he noted appeared in "form, materials, techniques of sewing, and use" (Vlach, 1999 [1991], 21). Another collector explained that the similarity was in "weave pattern, design, and final product"; these characteristics linked the flat and "fanner" baskets of the Carolinas to Nigeria, Togo, Benin, and Ghana (Jones-Jackson, 18).

The baskets made on the Sea Islands off the coast of Georgia and South Carolina can be divided into two basic groups. The first group, work baskets, allowed slaves in the United States to use familiar objects while performing forced labor. Work baskets served many purposes, including "winnowing rice, carrying clothing, cradling infants, fanning, [and] sorting foods" (Jones-Jackson, 18). Work baskets produced by African descendants in the United States took on many forms. Perhaps the most common was the fanner, a wide but shallow basket used as a companion to the mortar and pestle to separate the husk from the rice kernel. The average fanner measured two feet in diameter. First, freshly harvested rice would be placed within a mortar. A pair of workers, sometimes boys, sometimes women, would pound the rice using pestles. "The beaters seized the pestles in the middle, raising

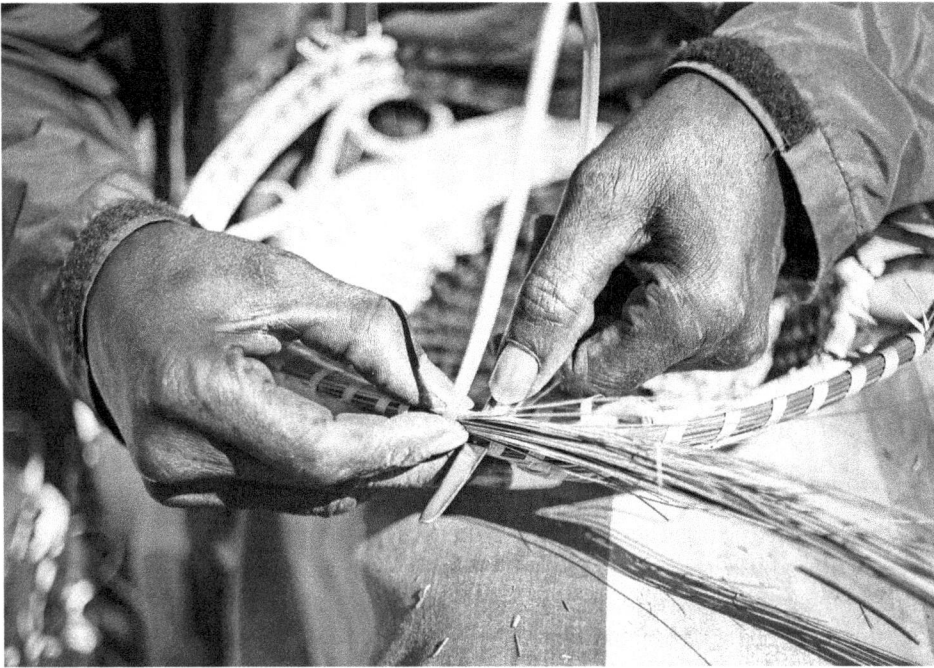

Sixty-year-old Eugene Gilliard weaves a traditional Gullah sweetgrass basket. (Pete Marovich/Corbis)

them and letting them fall so quickly and evenly that the beating of the rice was not considered a difficult task, although often the pestle would be tied to the limb of a tree so the tension would pull the pestle up to aid in the task." Rice pounding was a skill that needed to be learned, requiring both an awareness of technique and a sensitivity to rhythm. "The pounding of the pestles in the mortars of American plantations," observed Chase, "was as regular and rhythmical as the sound of the African drum." The versions of the fanner, the pestle, and the mortar (usually a hollowed-out log) used in the United States, Chase observed, were "identical to those used in Africa for hundreds of years" (Chase, 59–60).

With the husk still on but loosened, the rice would be transferred to fanners—wide, circular-shaped baskets with a flat bottom and very shallow sides. Two methods were then available. The fanner could be held up so that the wind might scatter its contents. The heavier rice would fall into waiting baskets on the ground, while the chaff would be carried away by the wind. If any of the chaff remained, the process would be repeated. Another option required the worker to toss the rice using the fanner. While the contents were airborne, the wind would carry away the husk, and then the worker would catch the grains of rice as they fell. Once the husk was separated, the rice would be stored in yet another basket, also crafted by slaves using the coiling technique, though of course with much deeper sides and a lid.

The fanner, like the knowledge requisite for the success of rice as an export crop in the United States and the coiling technique employed in making it, came from Africa. Historian Peter Wood observed:

Those Africans who are accustomed to growing rice on one side of the Atlantic, and who found themselves raising the same crop on the other side, did not markedly alter their annual routine. When New World slaves planted in the Spring by pressing a hole with the heel and covering the seeds with the foot, the motion used was demonstrably similar to that employed in West Africa. In Summer, when Carolina Blacks moved through the rice fields in a row, hoeing in unison to work songs, the pattern of cultivation was not one imposed by European owners but rather one learned from West African forebears. And in October when the threshed grain was "fanned" in the wind, the wide winnowing baskets were made by Black hands after an African design. (Vlach, 1999 [1991], 20–21)

Indeed, it has been suggested that the strain of rice grown in South Carolina was imported from Madagascar (Heywood). Chase suggests, moreover, that the African style of growing and gathering rice was observed in South Carolina "as recently as 1926" (Chase, 59).

Other tasks to which slaves were assigned in the United States mirrored tasks performed in Africa: gathering eggs, fruits, and vegetables, for example. In each case, a strong basket was required, so it should be no surprise that Africans in the United States would turn to the same methods as were used in Africa to construct such tools. Other instruments made of fibers—brooms, fly whisks, and mats, for example—also show signs of cultural persistence (Chase, 59).

Africans and their descendents in the United States also made what are commonly referred to as "show baskets," the second type of basketry. These baskets tend to be lighter and made to serve an aesthetic purpose rather than a work-related one. Weavers might use color, pattern, or texture to vary the baskets and make them more attractive to customers. The function of the basket also changed when it was made for a commercial audience: show baskets might be purses or vases, or they might hold a candle (Jones-Jackson, 18).

Baskets found in the United States were made of several different materials, and the weaver's choice was often determined by the purpose the basket was expected to serve. Bulrush, rushel, or rush (Juncus roemericanus), "a long tough brown grass found along the 'salt-water coast' and alongside the brook-like inland salt-water ways that meander about in the South Carolina Low Country," was used to make baskets that came to be known as "rushel baskets." The advantage to this material was twofold—it was both durable and lightweight. Robert Shaw observed that baskets made with rush were more frequently made by men during the time of slavery, as their hands, calloused by work in the field, could more easily manipulate the material (Davis, 159, 162–163; Shaw, 191).

The bark of the white oak might also be employed in basket making, especially in baskets that would be used to carry heavy loads. The basket maker would have to soak strips of the white oak until they became pliable, and then he or she could manipulate them. Heavier baskets, like those made from rush or white oak, were usually sewn together using oak splints (Davis, 159, 162–163; Shaw, 191).

Another common material, sweet grass (*Sporobulus gracilis* and similar species as well as *Muhlenbergia capillaries* or *M. filipe*) appeared predominantly in coil baskets.

Basket makers found sweet grass in wooded areas rather than marsh areas and generally worked with strips 18 to 24 inches in length. Some basket makers preferred harvesting sweet grass only after it had dried, while others wove it while green, allowing it to dry after being incorporated into a basket. Sweet grass was much softer, finer, and more pliable than rush, allowing for the winding of thinner coils (Davis, 159, 162–163; Shaw, 191).

Long-leafed pine needles (*Pinus palustris* Mill.) provided another option for coil baskets. Though shorter than the strands of sweet grass (usually four to eight inches), they were more solid. Pine needles and sweet grass, being softer materials, could be sewn together using palmetto leaves. Such baskets were more likely to have been sewn by women and used within the house, often as sewing or yarn baskets (Davis, 159, 162–163; Shaw, 191).

The technique for weaving baskets has been described at length in other books. The following description allows the reader to get a basic sense of the process as well as to note the way in which regional variety appeared in a weaver's work:

> Most of the baskets follow a simple coiling technique with a knot used as a base. The free ends of the sweet grass bundle are folded and then wound around the knot to begin a coil. Then an opening is pierced in the center knot and a strip of palm leaf is pulled through the opening, wrapped around the grass coil, and pulled back through a second opening made in the knot to anchor or station the coil. As this process is repeated, the coil begins to circle out from the center knot to create a basket base that is circular or oval. From this base, the basket is constructed by changing the angle at which one circular row is fastened to another. The palm stitch in the Mt. Pleasant baskets does not interlock with the stitches in previous rows of the coil. Consequently, the stitches appear to radiate out from the center knot in a linear way, much like the spokes of a wheel. (Jones-Jackson, 21)

Not surprisingly, given its prevalence among African descendants in America, the coiling technique had its roots in West Africa: "The woven trays used in the Sea Islands are made with the sewing technique called coiling, which is paramount in West Africa; more interesting is the fact that, as in Africa, the coils, in all instances examined, are laid on in a clockwise direction" (Herskovits, 147).

Indeed, whether during slavery or presently, basketry allows the perseverance of African and African American customs in several ways. On a basic level, the technique of basket making was reproduced; novices were taught how to collect and prepare the right materials, how to sew them together, how to produce different styles of baskets, and (especially in the later, commercial era of basket making) how to augment the basic design. The latter might be accomplished, for example, by using pine needles in a coil basket made predominantly of sweet grass; the former are darker and create a color contrast. On a second level, during the process of basket making a history of the family and its basketry skills might have been shared. Children might have learned about their extended family or their ancestors by learning about them as basket sewers. On a third level, coming together to work on baskets provided an opportunity for social exchange unrelated to basket-making skills. Stories and tales could be exchanged, or **work songs** might be sung to hurry along the process. In these ways, African and African American heritage was recorded and transmitted orally, much as it had been in Africa.

When interviewed in the late 1930s by Georgia Writers' Project workers (part of the Works Progress Administration [WPA] created during the Great Depression), John Haynes claimed that, as a basket maker, he was continuing a family tradition. In his family, father passed on to son the skills requisite for excellence in basketry, **wood carving**, and weaving. A wood carver known as "Stick Daddy" because of his skillfully carved walking sticks likewise observed that such talents were handed down in families through the male line. "Muh granfathuh, Pharo Cooper, he used tuh make things frum wood an straw, sech as baskets an cheahs [chairs] an tables an othuh things fuh the home. I guess I sawt of inherited it frum him" (Georgia Writers' Project, 8, 26). Such had been the tradition for many generations, connecting artists like Haynes in the United States to their ancestors in Africa.

Basketry in the 20th and 21st centuries continues to reflect African traditions, especially among skilled craftsmen and craftswomen in the Sea Islands. "Fanners are still used in West Africa," observed Shaw, "and modern examples are virtually identical to those from antebellum rice plantations." The use of the baskets, rather than the process of making them, is more likely to have changed. African American baskets are now more commonly made to fuel the tourist trade. The paving of Route 17, the highway between Mount Pleasant and Charleston, South Carolina, opened up the area to tourists in the early 1930s, and many African American craftsmen and craftswomen seized upon this commercial opportunity. They built stands on the side of the highway and shifted their technique somewhat. White middle-class women, their primary market, had little need for work baskets but were eager to purchase the unique bread baskets, wastebaskets, handbags, and other items geared more toward decoration that they saw along the highway (Shaw, 194).

Basket weavers priced their wares according to the amount of labor and skill they felt that they put into the product. The size of the basket and the intricacy of the design were factored in as well. The prices were known within the community of weavers, and if one consented to sell a basket for a price lower than the experienced community agreed that it was worth, the sales skills of the weaver were questioned (Jones-Jackson, 22).

As basketry sales allowed adults to support their families, they also provided an opportunity to continue an important cultural and familial tradition. "Adults taught this art to children," observed Chase, "exactly as it had been taught to them, so that the method continued without interruption." She described the African system of handing down this knowledge as an apprenticeship and maintained that the same system of education continued in the 20th century in the United States. The young students experimented on flat mats first, slowly graduating into the more skilled craft of basketry. Boys and girls both learned how to make baskets, though in the United States the boys usually left the task to the women when they reached puberty and their skills were demanded in the field. Women, therefore, became the primary basket makers. Nonetheless, the process remains a familial or communal concern.

Younger children took part by gathering the material to be used and sometimes by starting the first coils. These "starters" were considered helpers and apprentices to the "master" basket sewer. This master was usually a matriarch of the family, and she passed her skill along to her daughters and granddaughters. When boys took part in the basket-making process, it was usually only until age 18, and they were primarily gatherers of materials. After age 45, some men returned to basket making as a way to augment their income (Chase, 59; Davis, 177–178).

As they continue the tradition begun by their ancestors, these artists maintain a connection to their historical roots in Africa and in American slavery. "My ancestors were far away from their homeland against their will," said Mary Jackson. "They were fortunate to have a skill that allowed them to be kept together. The intent of the plantation owners was to separate families so they would lose their identities. Because of the valuable skill [my forebears] had, they could stay together. [They] realized that the baskets would serve as the symbol of why and how they came. They held on to [basket making] so that the generations that came would always have and keep their identity with Africa" (Shaw, 197).

Jennifer Hildebrand

See also: Gullah; Pottery; Wood Carving

Further Reading

Chase, Judith Wragg, 1971, *Afro-American Art and Craft* (New York: Van Nostrand Reinhold Co.); Coakley, Joyce V., 2005, *Sweetgrass Baskets and the Gullah Tradition* (Arcadia Publishing); Davis, Gerald L., "Afro-American Coil Basketry in Charleston County, South Carolina," in *American Folklife*, ed. Don Yoder (Austin: University of Texas); Georgia Writers' Project, 1986 [1940], *Drums and Shadows* (Athens: University of Georgia); Halfacre, Angela, Patrick T. Hurley, and Brian Grabbatin, 2010, "Sewing Environmental Justice into African-American Sweetgrass Basket-Making in the South Carolina Lowcountry," *Southeastern Geographer* 50 (1): 147–68; Herskovits, Melville, 1958, *Myth of the Negro Past* (Boston: Beacon Press); Heywood, Duncan Clinch, 1937, *Seed from Madagascar* (Chapel Hill: University of North Carolina Press); Hurley, Patrick T., and Angela C. Halfacre, 2011, "Dodging Alligators, Rattlesnakes, and Backyard Docks: A Political Ecology of Sweetgrass Basket-Making and Conservation in the South Carolina Lowcountry, USA," *Geojournal* 76 (4): 383–99; Johnson, Jessica, 2008, "Basket Weaving Endures From African Tool to American Art," *The Post and Courier* (postandcourier.com), August 28; Jones-Jackson, Patricia, 1987, *When Roots Die* (Athens: The University of Georgia Press); Rosengarten, Dale, Theodore Rosengarten, and Enid Schildkrout, eds., 2008, *Grass Roots: African Origins of an American Art* (New York: Museum for African Art); Schildkrout, Enid, Dale Rosengarten, Theodore Rosengarten, and Ted Rosengarten, 2009, "Grass Roots: African Origins of an American Art," *African Arts* 42 (2): 44–55; Shaw, Robert, 2000, *American Baskets* (New York: Clarkson Potter/Publishers); Vlach, John Michael, 1990, *The Afro-American Tradition in Decorative Arts* (Athens: The University of Georgia Press); Vlach, John Michael, 1999 [1991], *By the Work of Their Hands* (Charlottesville: University Press of Virginia); Wardi, Anissa Janine, 2011, *Water and African American Memory: An Ecocritical Perspective*, 1st ed. (Gainesville: University Press of Florida).

BIBLICAL CHARACTERS

Men and women of the Bible have a profound presence in African American folk-lore. In their **spirituals**, **jokes**, **sermons**, and literature, African Americans recast their struggles in the contexts of biblical patriarchs, kings, and prophets. Enslaved African Americans compared their experiences to the biblical Israelites. To a captive people awaiting their freedom, their spirituals carried double meanings. The lyric "Go down Moses / Way down in Egypt land / And tell ol' Pharaoh / To let my people go" was as much about Harriet Tubman, an African American Moses figure leading her people North, as it was about the Hebrew Moses leading his people out of Egypt. The titles of other spirituals also attest to the link the enslaved Africans saw between themselves and biblical heroes and heroines: "We Are Climbing Jacob's Ladder," "Ezekiel Saw de Wheel," "Little David, Play on Your Harp," "Didn't My Lord Deliver Daniel?" "Oh, Mary Don't You Weep, Oh, Martha Don't You Mourn," "Steal Away, Steal Away to Jesus." Communities of enslaved African Americans identified with the general motifs of exodus and deliverance, raising the question, "What did it mean 'to steal away to Jesus' when one had been stolen from Africa and enslaved in white America? . . . What did it mean to be a 'child of God' and a black slave in a white society?" (Cone, 3).

Similar to the spirituals that speak of biblical characters, African American folk-tales are full of references to biblical prophets. These folk jokes usually center on mules that bear the names of major and minor prophets. Although mules often represent the tenacity of people, mules named Hezekiah, Jeremiah, and Malachi often complain about carrying too much of a burden. Other folk jokes involve John, who in scripture is the beloved disciple. In African American folklore, Ol' Massa thinks that John is his beloved slave and repeatedly tries to engage John in some argument. A popular joke tells of when Ol' Massa and John swap dreams about heaven. Massa dreamed of a white heaven that was glorious and clean and a black heaven that was dirty and noisy. John says that he too dreamed of a white heaven that was glorious but had one problem—there were no people there. Other folk jokes describe a Peter who is standing at heaven's gates with his own set of **Jim Crow** laws, which mock the notion that there are separate white and black heavens. Some of these jokes describe white bigots who want to enter a white-only heaven. When Peter insists that there is only one "heben," the bigots are shocked to hear a voice say, "I'se the Lord."

One biblical character who almost always has a different role in African American folklore than the one that he has in the Bible is the **devil**. The Bible's devil is a "roaring lion, [who] walketh about, seeking whom he may devour" (1 Peter 5:8). He is a dragon, an old serpent, a deceiver (Revelation 20:2, 10). Contrastingly, the "debbil" in African American lore poses no threat to **bad men** such as **Stagolee** (Stakerlee):

> Stackerlee he told de debbil
> Say, "Come on, les have some fun,
> You stick me wid yo pitchfork,
> I shoot you wid mah .41.
> Take dat pitchfork, Tom Debbil
> An lay it on da shef;

I'm dat bad man, Stackerlee
An I'm gonna rule Hell by myself."

(Barksdale and Kinnamon, 460)

Throughout history, black ministers have preached a gospel that imagines selected biblical characters to be black men and women. Solomon, the wisest person
ever to live, becomes a black king in love with a Shulamite woman who is "black,
but comely" (Song of Solomon 1:5, King James Version). Queen Esther is a young
woman who is "passing," hiding her Jewish descent from the Persian king. The day
comes when she must claim her identity to save her people. In the mouths of black
preachers, the three Hebrew boys, Shadrach, Meshach, and Abednego, become
Shadrach, Meshach, and "a bad Negro." Historically, **black church** traditions have
interpreted biblical heroes in the context of black experience. Rather than accepting that blacks were the cursed children of Cain or Ham, as taught in some white
theological traditions, many black religious traditions reclaim an Africanist presence throughout the scriptures, pointing to Simon of Cyrene, who helped carry the
cross of Christ; Zipporah, Moses' Ethiopian wife; and Hagar, the Egyptian woman
by whom Abraham bears Ishmael. Cast out from the family by a jealous wife,
Hagar and Ishmael must eke out a life in the wilderness. Throughout the slavery
era and the early part of the 20th century, blacks often referred to themselves as
"Aunt Hagar's children"—children who are relegated to less desirable landscapes,
given meager resources, and expected to survive.

Given the popularity of biblical characters in spirituals and the black religious
experience in general, it is not surprising that biblical characters also populate African American literature. Toni Morrison's *Song of Solomon* parodies a number of
biblical characters, including Ruth, Pilate, Rebecca (Reba), and Hagar, as well as
naming a character after a well-known biblical book: "First Corinthians." James
Baldwin's *Go Tell It on the Mountain* has Gabriel, Esther, Ruth, John, and a Roy[al],
as in royal priesthood. Gloria Naylor's *Bailey's Café* is peopled by Eve, Esther, Mariam, Gabriel, Jesse, Eli, and Mary.

In African American folklore, life, and literature, biblical characters are black
men and women who are resilient, resourceful, and reverential of a "God who will
make a way out of no way."

Valerie Lee

Further Reading

Abrahams, Roger D., ed., 1985, *Afro-American Folktales: Stories from Black Traditions in the
New World* (New York: Pantheon Books); Barksdale, Richard, and Keneth Kinnamon,
1972, *Black Writers of America: A Comprehensive Anthology* (New York: The Macmillan
Company); *The Bible, King James Version*; Callahan, Allen Dwight, 2006, *The Talking
Book: African Americans and the Bible* (New Haven: Yale University Press); Cone, James
H., 1972, *The Spirituals and the Blues* (New York: The Seabury Press); Dance, Daryl
Cumber, 2002, *From My People: 400 Years of African American Folklore* (New York:
W. W. Norton & Company); Harvey, Paul, 2011, *Through the Storm, through the Night:
A History of African American Christianity* (Lanham, MD: Rowman & Littlefield Pub-
lishers); Watkins, Mel, 2002, *African American Humor* (Chicago: Lawrence Hill Books).

BITCH

At its origin, the term "bitch" was meant to define a female dog, but it was also used as early as the 14th century as a pejorative term for women. Geneva Smitherman's book *Black Talk: Words and Phrases from the Hood to the Amen Corner* explores the myriad dimensions of the word in African American vernacular culture:

> A generic term for a female. Women of varying ages use the term among themselves in a generic, neutral way. . . . Men also use the term in this generic way. . . . However use of the term by males may not be accepted by all women. . . . Used by males and females to refer to a weak or subservient male. . . . May be used in reference to objects and things. (Smitherman, 69)

Whatever its use, "bitch" remains a controversial but useful idiom in black folklore traditions such as music and comedy. "It's gettin' hot up in dis bitch" is one example of how the term refers to objects or things. It could also mean a person who rides specifically in the middle of the front seat of a car only meant for two passengers: "Skee-lo is ridin' bitch again." In addition to these meanings, bitch also denotes situational status, temperament, and behavior. For instance African American **blues** singer Johnny "Guitar" Watson uses the term to refer to a bad economic situation, as opposed to a person, in his 1976 song "Ain't That a Bitch."

Many times the word becomes liberally applied to either gender, but it still implies an association with stereotypical characteristics such as nagging or complaining that are usually ascribed to women. In traditions of **toasts** and "bad n*gger" tales, the word becomes more associated with gender status, and this is the way it is most commonly used in the folk-derived, male-oriented art form of **rap**. The use of "bitch" in gangster rap was meant to be negative in the cultural imagination of the African American male during the 1990s. Traditionally, males have consistently used gender-specific epithets as a way to control and dominate females. The creators of gangster rap were no different. When N.W.A's Ice Cube rapped about the controversial word in "A Bitch Iz a Bitch" on that group's 1998 album *Straight Outta Compton*, the use of "bitch" developed as a way to demean women and applied to confident and assertive black women, too.

Some female lyricists fought back in an explicit rejection of the term. Queen Latifah's 1993 song "U.N.I.T.Y." became a well-known hit, and the lyric, "Who you calling a bitch?" became an anthem for females disenchanted with the excessive use of the term. However, in what some critics deemed a response to the overt masochistic and sexist undertones of the use of the word, female rappers appropriated the term and semantically inverted it in an effort to remove the control and power males wielded in their uses of the term. Lil' Kim's nickname of "Queen Bitch," Mia X as "Boss Bitch," and Trina as "The Baddest Bitch" all came about as females wanted to assert their autonomy, tenacity, sexuality, fierceness on the mike, and role as social beings producing a distinct culture unafraid of those "g's" and thugs.

Over the years, the various meanings and uses of the term occurred in comedy routines by Richard Pryor, Chris Rock, Dave Chappelle, Sommore, Adele Givens, LaWanda Page, Eddie Murphy, Whoopi Goldberg, Mo'Nique, and Redd Foxx. Still, the term continues both to be a point of contention and shows no sign of being used less often in the black folk tongue anytime soon.

LaMonda Horton-Stallings

Further Reading

Dunn, Stephane, 2008, *"Baad Bitches" and Sassy Supermamas: Black Power Action Films* (Urbana: University of Illinois Press); Majors, Clarence, 1994, *Juba to Jive: A Dictionary of African-American Slang* (New York: Viking); Meyers, Marian, 2013, *African American Women in the News: Gender, Race, and Class in Journalism* (New York: Routledge); Schneider, Christopher J., 2011, "Culture, Rap Music, 'Bitch,' and the Development of the Censorship Frame," *American Behavioral Scientist* 55 (1): 36–56; Smitherman, Geneva, 2000 [1994], *Black Talk: Words and Phrases from the Hood to the Amen Corner* (Boston and New York: Houghton Mifflin); Stephens, Dionne P., and April L. Few, 2007, "The Effects of Images of African American Women in Hip Hop on Early Adolescents' Attitudes Toward Physical Attractiveness and Interpersonal Relationships," *Sex Roles* 56 (3): 251–64; Stephens, Dionne P., and April L. Few, 2007, "Hip Hop Honey Or Video Ho: African American Preadolescents' Understanding of Female Sexual Scripts in Hip Hop Culture," *Sexuality & Culture* 11 (4): 48–69.

BLACK CAT BONE

The black cat bone is one of the most marvelous amulets in the African American **conjure** tradition. Some advocates assert that the properly acquired bone can grant any desire, including the ability to fly or shift shape. The bone often functions as a general talisman to ward off evil and attract good luck, especially in affairs of love or gambling. However, the black cat bone is best known for its power to render one invisible, thus allowing one to rob banks unseen.

The ceremony for procuring the magical bone is elaborate and precise. Usually, the cat must be entirely black, without a single white hair. Other stipulations include a cat that is male, stolen, or lactating. The unfortunate animal is boiled alive, usually in a kettle with a tight-fitting lid. Water is the typical medium, but oil or even milk from a black cow (obtained in darkness), might be required. The full moon is the favored time of the month and midnight the popular hour. The ceremony typically is performed in some isolated spot, such as the woods, particularly at the fork of a road or a **crossroads**. While not always stated directly, the need for secrecy is implicit. Performers of the ritual also might be instructed to remain silent and not look back.

During the ceremony, God and the **devil** may be invoked with equal facility and no apparent contradiction, but the pervading sense is that the practitioner is casting his lot with the devil. Cursing and swearing as well as the receipt of a new title such as "witch," "wizard," or "evil fortune-teller," are verbal affirmations of this acceptance of the devil. If the devil makes an appearance, his presence may be signaled by wind and rain, thunder and lightning, feared animals including snakes and lions, or supernatural creatures such as imps and demons.

The cat is boiled until its flesh softens and separates from the bones, which signals the crucial part of the ceremony: identifying the magical bone. When the power of invisibility is sought, the practitioner stands before a mirror while passing each bone through his (or her) teeth or mouth. The magical bone causes his image, and presumably, his corporeal body, to disappear. To become visible again, one simply removes the bone from one's mouth. After a woman from Louisiana described this part of the ritual, she was asked if she had ever tried it herself. She answered no, explaining that she was afraid that if she accidentally swallowed the bone, she would never be visible again. An alternative method for finding the proper bone is to throw all of the bones into running water and select the only one that floats upstream. Some advocates claim that the magic bone will rise to the surface of the boiling medium. Once the right bone is identified, the devotee usually is instructed to carry it or wear it around the neck, perhaps sewn or wrapped in red flannel or some other kind of conjure bag.

Amulets of animal bone appear to be both ancient and worldwide. The magical powers of the black cat bone and its associated rituals have been documented, in nearly identical forms, in Hungary, Finland, and Ireland, as well as countries colonized by Europeans, including the United States, Canada, the Philippines, and the Cape Verde Islands. The English "Toadmen" tradition is strikingly parallel. When the proper bone from a toad is recovered through rituals very similar to those of the black cat, its owner acquires a variety of uncanny powers, including the abilities to become invisible, cure various ailments, and attract good fortune.

Michael E. Bell

Further Reading

Anderson, Jeffrey E., 2007, *Conjure in African American Society* (Baton Rouge: Louisiana State University); Chireau, Yvonne Patricia, 2003, *Black Magic: Religion and the African American Conjuring Tradition* (Berkeley: University of California Press); Covey, Herbert C., 2007, *African American Slave Medicine: Herbal and Non-Herbal Treatments* (Lanham: Lexington Books); Hand, Wayland D., ed., 1964, "Popular Beliefs and Superstitions from North Carolina," in *Frank C. Brown Collection of North Carolina Folklore*, vols. 6–7 (Durham, NC: Duke University Press); Hazzard-Donald, Katrina, 2013, *Mojo Workin': The Old African American Hoodoo System* (Chicago: University of Illinois Press); Hurston, Zora Neale, 1935, *Mules and Men* (Philadelphia: J. B. Lippincott); Hyatt, Harry Middleton, 1970, *Hoodoo—Conjuration—Witchcraft—Rootwork, vol. 1, Memoirs of the Alma Egan Hyatt Foundation* (Hannibal, MO: Western Publishing); Mitchem, Stephanie Y., 2007, *African American Folk Healing* (New York: New York University Press).

BLACK INDIANS

See Mardi Gras; Native American and African American Folklore

BLACKSMITHING

The process of blacksmithing involves forging and shaping both wrought iron, a hand-crafted malleable medium, and cast iron, a nonmalleable medium. The creation of both was done by hand with an anvil and hammer.

In the 17th century most African American blacksmiths worked as slaves and fewer as free men. They could draw from a more than 200-year history of the tradition in **Africa**. Smiths, along with griots, were a closed, male-dominated caste in West and Central Africa (Kriger, 1999) that garnered prestige, wealth, fear, and reverence for their specialized knowledge, skills, and connection with the mystical. Events narrated in the epic of Sunjata, which is set during the 13th and 14th centuries, identify Sujmanguru, the Sosso magician-king, as a blacksmith. European accounts from the 15th century describe blacksmiths in coastal West Africa. Slave blacksmiths in the United States drew on this heritage. A wrought-iron sculpture discovered during the excavation of the site of a blacksmith shop and slave quarters in Alexandria, Virginia, is similar to a wrought-iron sculpture from the Bamana in Mali and also carved wood figures from Mali (Vlach, 1981).

During the era of slavery in the United States, slave owners in rural and urban areas saw that their blacksmiths were trained. Slave smiths were employed as individuals and in groups to complete utilitarian objects for the farm, such as plows, bridle bits, spurs, and other farming implements. They also shod the masters' horses and mules. Decorative objects included iron gates, hinges, and the decorative railings and balconies that were notable in New Orleans, Mobile, Alabama, and other places. In New Orleans blacksmithing combined wrought iron and cast iron (Vlach, 2002). Many references to blacksmiths appear in the 18th century, and their sheer number points to their significance as important, skilled tradesmen. It appears as though African American blacksmiths practiced their craft in many parts of the United States and, in particular, the urban and rural **South**. Notable urban areas where African American blacksmiths were documented included Charleston, Savannah, Mobile, Natchez, and New Orleans, as well as New Bedford, Massachusetts, and New York. Blacksmiths were found on many rural farms.

James William Charles Pennington, a former slave and author of the **slave narrative** *The Fugitive Blacksmith*, recounts how he and other slave blacksmiths learned their trade. To make the plantation self-sufficient, his slaveholder hired out the younger slaves to nonslaveholders to learn trades such as blacksmithing. After the slaves learned the trade, they worked on their master's plantation and were also hired out. Antebellum Charleston in 1848 boasted of 89 blacksmiths: 45 were white, 40 were slaves, and four were listed as "free persons of color" (Vlach 1981, 14). The high purchase price of blacksmiths indicated their elevated role and status in slavery. In 1842, the price of a slave blacksmith was $1,500. A slave blacksmith sold for $2,000 in 1856 (Christian).

The blacksmith trade offered its slave practitioners many advantages, such as money to purchase their and/or their family's freedom, the chance to invent tools, or opportunities to make weapons to use in revolts. Many slave blacksmiths used these advantages. For example, Virginia-born Lewis Temple of New Bedford, Massachusetts, invented a whaling harpoon in the 1840s that became the industry standard.

After emancipation, many African American blacksmiths opened successful businesses. New Orleans–based Elisha Dillon, a recognized blacksmith and wheelwright, operated two horseshoeing and wagon-building shops. Outside New Orleans in neighboring Houma at least four African American blacksmiths operated shops in the early 1900s. Mike Brown from Henderson, Tennessee, started a blacksmithing business in 1866 that would last until 1959. In the early 20th century blacksmiths were pivotal craftsman. Many father-and-son blacksmithing operations, such as that of James and Pete Goudeau in east Texas, also existed in other parts of the South.

Blacksmithing was also common on small farms. Farm blacksmiths made tools, repaired farm implements and maintained wagons and plows.

By the latter part of the 20th century, the number of blacksmiths of various ethnicities in the United States had diminished, and so had the number of African American blacksmiths. There were 220,000 blacksmiths in 1900 and only 10,000 in 1970. While there are no reliable statistics of how many African American blacksmiths are practicing now, it's clear that the trade in the early 21st century is almost a lost art. One notable exception is Philip Simmons of Charleston, South Carolina.

Simmons is the only African American blacksmith who has been studied extensively (Vlach, 1981). As of 2004, he had worked as a blacksmith for more than 76 years. He was born in 1912 on Daniel Island, one of the Sea Islands off the Carolina coast, and he moved to Charleston at the age of eight to live with his mother, and later learned blacksmithing. Simmons also learned the related jobs of forger, boatwright, cartwright, and farrier. After he opened a shop on Alexander Street in 1937, Simmons realized that his future would be to specialize in decorative blacksmithing. Simmons had repaired decorative gates, but the transition to making them took a year. A long list of commissions followed, including stair rails, gates, porch railings, and window and doorway grills.

Simmons was a recipient of the National Endowment for the Arts National Heritage Fellowship in 1982. His decorative iron works can be seen at the Smithsonian Institution, the South Carolina State Museum, Charleston International Airport's Visitor Reception and Transportation Center, and many buildings and places in the city of Charleston. In 1991, Simmons's friends formed the Philip Simmons Foundation, a nonprofit association to develop and maintain a commemorative garden and to preserve Simmon's legacy.

Willie Collins

Further Reading

Bishir, Catherine W. 2013, *Crafting Lives: African American Artisans in New Bern, North Carolina, 1770–1900* (Chapel Hill: The University of North Carolina Press); Christian, Marcus, 1972, *Negro Ironworkers of Louisiana, 1718–1900* (Gretna, LA: Pelican); Kriger, Colleen, 1999, *Pride of Men: Ironworking in 19th Century West Central Africa* (Portsmouth, NH: Heinemann); Pennington, James William Charles, 1849, *The Fugitive Blacksmith; or, Events in the History of James W. C. Pennington, Pastor of a Presbyterian Church, New York, Formerly a Slave in the State of Maryland, United States*, electronic edition, University of North Carolina Web site, http://docsouth.unc.edu/neh/penning49/penning49.html; Pursell, Carroll W., and Lemelson Center, 2005, *A Hammer in their Hands: A Documentary History of Technology and the African-American Experience* (Cambridge, MA: MIT Press); Vlach, John Michael, 1981, *Charleston Blacksmith: The Work of Philip Simmons* (Columbia: University of South Carolina Press); Vlach,

John Michael, 2002, "Precious Work: Creativity in the Building Trades of New Orleans," in *Raised to the Trade: Creole Building Arts of New Orleans*, ed. John Ethan Hankins and Steven Maklansky (New Orleans: New Orleans Museum of Art); Zaborney, John J., 2012, *Slaves for Hire: Renting Enslaved Laborers in Antebellum Virginia* (Baton Rouge: Louisiana State University Press).

BLUES

Blues music has been the most influential popular music genre in the United States for more than five decades. It has been defined as a 12-bar form in common time, in which each stanza comprises three phrases, each four measures long. Lyrically, the first line of each stanza is repeated as the second and followed by a third that responds to the first two and rhymes with them, as in this excerpt from Gertrude "Ma" Rainey's "Traveling Blues":

> Train's at the station, I heard the whistle blow.
> Train's at the station, I heard the whistle blow.
> I done bought my ticket but I don't know where I'll go.

The blues also uses certain characteristic chord progressions, keys, and "blue notes," which are quarter tones that lie between the minor and major third notes of the scale or between the minor and major seventh. There are clear African influences in the call-and-response pattern of the stanzas, elements of the vocal style, and the use of instruments to imitate and sometimes substitute for the human voice. However, any of these "rules" may be breached if the blues attitude and tone are maintained. The spirit of the blues, it is said, cannot be contained in any musical notation or adequately described by any words. In her landmark book, *Black Pearls: Blues Queens of the 1920s*, Daphne Duval Harrison cites composer Willie Dixon as saying, "The blues ain't nothing but the facts of life."

Origin of the Blues

Rainey said that she first heard the blues being sung by a young woman in a town in Missouri in 1902. W. C. Handy heard his first blues song in Mississippi in 1903. The music clearly predated these first "sightings," but by how much is unknown. No one is absolutely sure where the blues came from or how it evolved, but there are indications in the music itself of its origins. In **Africa** and in the United States during and after the era of slavery, singing was frequently used to inspire and direct work. While there are elements in the blues of various African and African American forms, its most direct antecedent is probably the "**field holler**," a form of **work song**. Musicologist John Storm Roberts suggests that it would be difficult to draw the line between a holler that is moving toward a blues song and a blues song that is simply a complex holler.

It is probably unimportant to decide just what degree of repetition and musicality tips the balance. What is important is that the blues arose toward the end of the 19th century, during the worst of the **Jim Crow** era, when African Americans were in need of a way to express their profound feelings of pain and anger and their sense of living in a hostile and unjust world. The blues gave them that. It was music of the folk, identified with the feelings of individual members of its audience. It developed in at least three separate geographical regions: East Texas (where practitioners included Leadbelly and Blind Lemon Jefferson), the Mississippi Delta (Robert Johnson, Willie Brown), and the Piedmont area (Josh White, Blind Boy Fuller). Soon picked up by traveling entertainers, it spread throughout the South and, during the Great Migration, into the urban North.

The codification of the blues form happened during the first decades of the 20th century, as it began to be performed by groups. An individual blues singer might use a verse of eight, 10, or 11 bars with no difficulty, but as small instrumental groups began to provide accompaniment to singers and as songs were recorded and passed from singer to singer, the structure became more uniform. Still, as Roberts points out, "Bessie Smith probably sang more songs that were not twelve-bar than ones that were."

Classic Blues

Bessie Smith and Ma Rainey were among the first group of singers to perform the blues in professional entertainment venues and later to record them: the "classic blues" singers. These were women, for the most part, who began singing the blues on the black tent-show and vaudeville circuit. The first to perform in the genre professionally was apparently Rainey, who had a powerful, earthy style and sang blues about rural southern life. A star of the Theatre Owners Booking Association circuit, she began singing the blues in her act shortly after hearing a young woman in Missouri in 1902. Both Smith and Rainey emerged into stardom in the mid-1920s after they began recording.

The first blues recording was made by Mamie Smith for OKeh Records in August 1920. "Crazy Blues" was so successful that other blueswomen were immediately enlisted to record by such companies as Paramount and the Black Swan label of Pace Records. Soon, Ethel Waters, Trixie Smith, Gladys Bryant, Ida Cox, Sippie Wallace, and many others were making "race records" a highly lucrative proposition for the first time. They also brought the blues to the attention of a national, and white, audience.

Although these "blues queens" dressed in satin and sequins, fulfilling their black audience's need for glamour, their songs were about the harsh realities of life—not only infidelity and lost love, but also poverty, violence, and prison. The blues would have been of no use to the black community if the lyrics had been softened, if the singers had flinched from the authentic experience of African Americans both in the fields of the **South** and in the densely crowded urban ghettos of both the North and South. One of those urban ghettos, the south side of Chicago, became the center of blues performance and recording. There, the blues went into another stage.

Country Blues

While the classic blues singers were mostly women backed by small ensembles, the country blues singer was usually a solitary man with a guitar, sometimes a harmonica. Other instruments in very early blues music included the panpipe, fiddle, fife and drum, diddly bow, and percussive instruments such as tin cans and empty bottles. Although the record companies had occasionally gone into the South to record the blues on location during the early 1920s, it was not until 1926 that Blind Lemon Jefferson was brought to Chicago to record "Got the Blues." When he died three years later, he had recorded 90 country blues songs, and record companies had begun scouring the South for other blues singers. During these field trips, Columbia Records found Peg Leg Howell and his string band and Blind Willie McTell. Paramount found Son House and Charlie Patton and brought them north to record. Different styles of country blues developed in different parts of the South, and each region can be said to have had its own lineage of artists. For example, in the Mississippi Delta, Charlie Patton influenced the likes of Son House and Robert Johnson, who then influenced bluesmen such as Muddy Waters, Johnny Shines, and John Lee Hooker. In Texas blues, Henry Thomas and Blind Lemon Jefferson influenced Lightnin' Hopkins, and both of these generations were an important inspiration for later musicians such as Aaron "T-Bone" Walker. Other regional styles included the Piedmont, where artists such as Elizabeth Cotten, Pink Anderson, Blind Boy Fuller, and Reverend Gary Davis. Each region also employed somewhat different approaches to their instruments, and had different basic song repertoires.

Urban Blues

In the first decade of the 20th century, blues singers began moving to northern (and western) cities as a part of the black migration out of the South. Areas such as Kansas City, St. Louis, Detroit, Harlem, and especially Chicago became centers of blues music. Blues clubs became as common as storefront churches, bringing the culture of the rural South into northern and western cities. Chicago saw the arrival of Memphis Minnie, Tampa Red, and John Lee "Sonny Boy" Williamson (a.k.a. Sonny Boy Williamson I), among many others. John Lee Hooker found his way to Detroit. T-Bone Walker became one of the mainstays of the Los Angeles blues community. Among the Delta blues musicians who went north were Big Bill Broonzy, Frank Stokes, and J. D. Short. These singers even encouraged the migration through their music, as in Arthur "Big Boy" Crudup's "Chicago Blues."

Blues lyrics began reflecting the new urban experience of the style's performers and audience. Having traveled north to escape the violence and poverty of the Jim Crow South, African Americans often found a world that offered them little more than they had left behind. The only work they could find was of the meanest and most difficult sort, in stockyards and automobile factories. Women frequently found only domestic work. The racism of the North, although not always so overt as that of the South, could be equally brutal. The disappointments and disillusion-ment found expression in the blues.

In order to be heard over the crowds at social events in clubs and house parties, and because of influences from other forms of popular music, blues musicians in urban areas began amplifying their instruments. Perhaps the most influential sound came out of Chicago, where the style that came to be called "Chicago blues" developed after World War II. Artists like Muddy Waters, Chester Arthur Burnett (Howlin' Wolf), Elmore James, Little Walter (Jacobs), and Otis Spann horrified blues purists but revitalized the Chicago blues scenes with their electric blues. They were later joined by singers such as Bobby "Blue" Bland and the queen of Chicago blues, Koko Taylor. As in classic blues, solo performers were replaced by small musical ensembles, usually an electric guitar or two, an electric bass, drums, harmonica, and a piano or organ. Occasionally, a trumpet or saxophone was added. The slow cadences of earlier country blues were transformed into intense, hard-driving instrumentals and raw, shouted vocals that reflected the urgency of life in the city.

The sound spread over the airwaves, on stations such as WAOK in Atlanta, WHAT in Philadelphia, KXLW in St. Louis, and WDIA in Memphis. It was also recorded by two Chicago record companies, Chess and Vee-Jay Records, and began to influence the next major developments in American popular music: rhythm and blues and its sibling, rock and roll.

The Influence of the Blues

The importance of the blues during the second half of the 20th century and into the 21th century lies in the music it inspired. The line of development, however, is not a simple and clear one. At the same time that Chicago blues music was coming into existence, other kinds of blues music in other places were changing as well. A significant element in these changes was **dance**.

It is virtually impossible to separate movement from music in African America. Whether in the church or the **juke** joint, black music was designed to incite mo-tion, from jubilant handclaps to low-down shimmying. In the early decades of the 20th century, black dance music was primarily **jazz**. Then, jazz began to go in a different, more abstract, less rhythmically regular direction. That's when the blues moved into the vacuum and became rhythm and blues. In the 1930s, Louis Jordan, for example, began recording blues numbers with upbeat rhythms and funny lyr-ics, incorporating boogie woogie. The result is sometimes called jump blues, and it was performed by Amos Milburn, Wynonie Harris, Big Joe Turner, and others.

By the early 1950s, rhythm and blues was a recognized form, and such vocalists as Ruth Brown and LaVern Baker became stars within the genre, which was also deeply influenced by gospel. Of course, gospel itself had grown out of the blues experience. The father of gospel, Thomas A. Dorsey, was once the accompanist for Ma Rainey and had performed the blues under the name Georgia Tom.

When rhythm and blues caught on among white youth who were bored by mainstream popular music, rock and roll was born. It became the dominant popular music for the rest of the century. Periodically, it received another infusion of the blues. Janis Joplin, for example, was a disciple of "Big Mama" Thornton. The British Invasion of the 1960s brought musicians whose adulation of blues performers bordered on idolatry. The **soul** music of the 1970s brought another dose of blues into rock and roll, as did the "surge singing" style of Whitney Houston and her successors. The blues inspired, nourished, and maintained American popular music over all these years.

Blues has also been important because of the emotional terrain that it has covered. The response of African Americans to their suffering seems to have captured an emotional space that all Americans in general have gravitated toward as an anchor in the midst of their postmodern angst. This emotional space has been as much of the appeal of blues as the actual structure of the music. The space is an Africanized one, in which emotional, spiritual, corporeal, and intellectual modalities can coexist in a way that is somewhat foreign to the sensibilities of the dominant society. When interviewed, older country blues artists would often respond to the question, "What is the blues?" with, "The blues is a feeling." A spirit perhaps. Such images are called to mind by traditional lines such as, "The blues chase a rabbit / Chased him for a quarter mile / The blues caught that little furry bunny / And he screamed just like a baby child." As such, the blues can be thought of as a New World loa (lwa), and one that has captured the heart of America.

Many scholars have looked at the significance of the blues in African American culture, including Angela Y. Davis, Hazel Carby, Amiri Baraka, and Ralph Ellison. All of them argue, in different ways, that this musical form has produced important cultural works. Together, their explorations of the form make it clear that the symbolic meaning of the genre, its ability to serve as a metaphor for black cultural resistance, cannot be underestimated. It is a very African form that, with limitless creativity from its artists, transforms European musical resources with limitless creativity to express the deepest feelings of black America.

Kathleen Thompson

Further Reading

Baraka, Amiri, 1963, *Blues People: The Negro Experience in White America and the Music That Developed from It* (New York: William Morrow); Bromell, Nick, 2000, "The Blues and the Veil: The Cultural Work of Musical Forms in Blues and Sixties Rock," *American Music*, July 1; Ferris, William R., 2009, *Give My Poor Heart Ease: Voices of the Mississippi Blues* (Chapel Hill: University of North Carolina Press); Gioia, Ted, 2008, *Delta Blues: The Life and Times of the Mississippi Masters who Revolutionized American Music* (Jackson: University of Mississippi Press); Harrison, Daphne Duval, 1988, *Black Pearls: Blues Queens of the 1920s* (New Brunswick, NJ: Rutgers University Press); Roberts, John Storm, 1972, *Black Music of Two Worlds* (Tivoli, NY: Original Music); Thompson, Gordon E., 2014, *Black Music, Black Poetry: Blues and Jazz's Impact on African American Versification* (Burlington, VT: Ashgate); Wald, Elijah, 2010, *The Blues: A Very Short Introduction* (New York: Oxford University Press); Zack, Ian, 2015, *Say No to the Devil: The Life and Musical Genius of Rev. Gary Davis* (Chicago: The University of Chicago Press).

BOTTLE TREES

A bottle tree is an African American folk talisman consisting of a base (generally a tree) that is adorned with discarded bottles. Its function is to capture and contain negative forces of the metaphysical world that would otherwise take up residence in one's home. Bottle trees are built around a central trunk or pillar, from which branches or inserted stakes extend outward and upward. Colorful bottles of various sizes and shapes, generally of glass but sometimes of plastic, are then placed mouth first onto the branches. Either a dead tree or a tree from which all foliage has been clipped and the branches trimmed short is used to build the bottle tree. Because of their straight and central trunks surrounded by numerous, evenly distributed branches that radiate upward, cedars and cypress trees have been popular choices for the construction of bottle trees.

Bottle trees have traditionally been found in the rural **South** of the United States and in the Caribbean, where peoples of African descent constructed them as guards against evil spirits. They have since been ascribed value as folk art objects and nowadays are created more frequently for their intrinsic, luminous beauty rather than for the spiritual and medicinal purposes that generated their original use.

Ideally, a bottle tree is placed a distance away from the home, in a space in the yard where it will attract any passing evil spirits or wandering ancestral forces. The brightly colored glass of the tree lures the spirits up inside the bottles, where they are trapped and thus unable to enter the house and do its inhabitants harm. According to African American folk tradition, the color blue possesses strong power to control evil, and spirits are purported to be especially charmed by cobalt blue bottles. For this reason, they have been popularly used in the construction of bottle trees (milk of magnesia bottles have been a common choice to this end). Proof that the evil spirits are successfully trapped is provided when the wind blows and one can hear them howling and whistling in lament of their capture.

The belief that spirits are attracted to the play of light on glass may extend as far back as the ninth century in Kongo, where inhabitants hung handblown glass in the trees to keep their homes free of evil. Bottle trees may also have evolved from the African tradition of the tree altar, used to pay homage to the dead. Tree altars were constructed by attaching porcelain plates to the tips of tree branches at gravesites. Fully elaborated bottle trees were documented in Angola and the southern United States as early as the late 18th century. Their function as talismans over more than two centuries has more recently given way to their role as **yard art**.

Southern folk art historian William Arnett has photographed and studied bottle trees along with contemporary sculptures inspired by them. An exhibit at the Aldrich Contemporary Art Museum in Ridgefield, Connecticut, titled *Bottle: Contemporary Art and Vernacular Tradition* (September 19, 2004–January 2, 2005) included photographs of southern bottle trees and their influence on sculptural media.

Margaret M. Olsen

Further Reading

Arnett, Paul, and William Arnett, 2000, *Souls Grown Deep: African American Vernacular Art of the South* (Atlanta: Tinwood Books); Bernier, Celeste-Marie, 2009 [2008], *African*

American Visual Arts: From Slavery to the Present (GB: Edinburgh University Press); Crown, Carol, and Charles Russell, 2007, *Sacred and Profane: Voice and Vision in Southern Self-Taught Art* (Jackson: University Press of Mississippi); Crown, Carol, Cheryl Rivers, and Charles Reagan Wilson, 2013, *The New Encyclopedia of Southern Culture: Volume 23: Folk Art.* (Chapel Hill: The University of North Carolina Press); Ferris, William R., 1986, *Afro-American Folk Art and Crafts* (Jackson: University Press of Mississippi); James, A. Everette, 2000, *Essays in Folk Art* (Chapel Hill, NC: Professional Press); Nelson, Louis P., 2006, *American Sanctuary: Understanding Sacred Spaces* (Bloomington: Indiana University Press); Russell, Charles, 2001, *Self-Taught Art: The Culture and Aesthetics of American Vernacular Art* (Jackson: University Press of Mississippi); Tullos, Allen, ed., 1977, *Long Journey Home: Folklife in the South* (Chapel Hill, NC: Southern Exposure); Young, Jason, 2006, "Through the Prism of Slave Art: History, Literature, Memory, and the Work of P. Sterling Stuckey," in *The Journal of African American History* 91 (4): 389–400.

BREAK DANCING

Originated by teenage African American males in the South Bronx of New York City, ca. 1970, break dancing began as an expressive response to emergent **hip-hop** music. First known as "b-boying," breaking quickly became a ritualized form of youth gang fighting, one that mixed physically demanding movements that exploited the daredevil prowess of their performers with stylized punching and kicking movements directed at an opponent. Clearly related to *capoeira*, the Brazilian form of martial arts dance, breaking developed as the movement aspect of **rap** music when break dancers—b-boys—filled the musical breaks between records mixed by disc jockeys at parties and discotheques. Break dancing emerged as part of a young urban culture built upon innovations in language, hip-hop music, fashion (e.g., unlaced sneakers, hooded sweatshirts, nylon Windbreakers), and visual arts (e.g., graffiti).

Practicing in a circle, like the *roda* of capoeira, break dancing groups, or "crews," met on street corners, in subway stations, or

A break dancer performs on a street in New York City, 2008. (snezana13/iStockphoto.com)

on the dance floors in nightclubs to battle other groups, with virtuosity, style, and wit determining the winner. Peppered by elaborate spins, balances, flips, contortions, and freezes, the dance required extreme agility and coordination by its young practitioners. Real physical danger surrounded movements, including the "windmill," in which dancers spun on the ground supported only by the shoulders, or the "suicide," in which an erect dancer threw himself forward to land flat on his back. The competitive roots of break dancing as a sport encouraged these sensational movements and others, such as multiple spins while balanced on the head, back, or one hand.

Break dancing quickly evolved into distinct movement idioms that included "breaking" (acrobatic flips and spins with support by the head, arms, or shoulders as point of balance), "uprock" (fighting movements directed at an opponent), "webbo" (extravagant footwork that connected breaking movements), and "electric boogie" (robot-like movements). The electric boogie style, reminiscent of a long tradition of eccentric African American dances, developed in Los Angeles concurrent with electronically produced disco music. In this style, dancers appeared to be weightless and rubber-limbed, to execute baffling floating walks and precise body isolations, and to pantomime robotic sequences. This form included the "moonwalk," popularized on national television by Michael Jackson, in which the dancer's feet appeared to be floating across the floor without touching it. Other boogie moves included the "wave," in which the body simulates an electric current passing through it, and "poplocking," a series of tightly contained staccato movements separated by freezes. An "Egyptian" style, which imitated popular conceptions of ancient wall paintings, was briefly popular in the 1980s.

Among break dancing's many movement innovations, the "freeze," common to both breaking and boogie styles, provided posed punctuation to the dancer's brief display and suggested the body as capable of unlikely physical transformation. Although break dancers typically danced one at a time, the performance of group movements, such as a balance and spin on a partner, became popular as competitive breaking evolved. Although less well-documented, young women, or "b-girls," began breaking almost concurrently with men and participated in dance battles in New York and Los Angeles.

In a typical uprock battle, dancers connected pantomime sequences of movement that acted as mockery and signified on an opponent's shortcomings with kicking, jabbing, and punching gestures toward the rival's face. The battlers never touched. Distinctive break dancing tied personal style to eloquence of motion and presented overlapping levels of movement as metaphor. Break dancing became widely recognized by cultural anthropologists when the New York City Breakers performed at the Kennedy Center Honors ceremony for prominent African American dancer and anthropologist Katherine Dunham in 1983.

Break dancing found a mainstream audience through several films that cashed in on its sensational aspects while minimizing its competitive format. Charlie Ahearn's *Wild Style* (1982), the first film to document emergent hip-hop culture, was eclipsed by a 30-second breaking sequence in *Flashdance* (1983) that pushed the form to international attention. Other break dancing films included *Breakin'*

(1984), which starred Shabba Doo (Adolfo Quinones), an important break dance choreographer from Chicago; and Harry Belafonte's *Beat Street* (1984), which featured the New York City Breakers. Break dancing dropped out of the public limelight in the late 1980s only to reemerge as a social dance form practiced by teenagers in nightclubs across the country in the 1990s. By the 2000s, formalized break dancing competitions, sponsored by corporate entities, occurred as annual events in many international arenas.

Thomas F. DeFrantz

Further Reading

Asante, Molefi K., 2008, *It's Bigger Than Hip Hop: The Rise of the Post Hip-Hop Generation* (New York: St. Martin's Press); Banes, Sally, 1985, "Breakdancing," in *Fresh: Hip Hop Don't Stop*, ed. Nelson George et al. (New York: Random House), pp. 79–112; De-Frantz, Thomas F., 2004, "The Black Beat Made Visible: Body Power in Hip Hop Dance," in *Of the Presence of the Body: Essays on Dance and Performance Theory*, ed. Andre Lepecki (Middletown, CT: Wesleyan University Press), pp. 64–81; Hazzard-Donald, Katrina, 1996, "Dance in Hip Hop Culture," in *Droppin' Science: Critical Essays on Rap Music and Hip Hop Culture*, ed. William Eric Perkins (Philadelphia: Temple University Press), pp. 220–235; Katz, Mark, 2012, *Groove Music: The Art and Culture of the Hip-Hop DJ* (New York: Oxford University Press); Rajakumar, Mohanalakshmi, 2012, *Hip Hop Dance* (Santa Barbara, CA: Greenwood); Schloss, Joseph Glenn, 2009, *Foundation: B-Boys, B-Girls, and Hip-Hop Culture in New York* (New York: Oxford University Press); Thompson, Robert Farris, 1986, "Hip-hop 101," *Rolling Stone*, March 27, pp. 95–100; Walter, Carla Stalling, 2007, *Hip Hop Dance: Meanings and Messages* (Jefferson, NC: McFarland & Co).

BRIAR PATCH

The briar patch in African American folklore is both a real place and a metaphoric one. Joel Chandler Harris gave this impenetrable, thorny locale its fame in his 1880 rendering of the traditional "stick-fast" tale of **Brer Rabbit's** encounter with the tar baby. Brer Rabbit uses one of the world's most famous examples of reverse psychology to plant the idea in his captor, **Brer Fox**, that being thrown into the briar patch is a much more brutal way of dying than being roasted, hanged, drowned, or having one's ears and eyeballs ripped out. "Do for de Lord's sake don't fling me in that brier-patch," pleads Brer Rabbit, again and again. So Brer Fox hurls Brer Rabbit into the briar patch—only to hear the rabbit's saucy response, as he cleans the tar off his limbs with a wood chip: "Bred en bawn in a brier-patch, Brer Fox—bred and bawn in a brier-patch!"

The briar patch is the rabbit's safe haven, his neighborhood, where he can live and raise his offspring in relative security from the larger, predatory animals such as Brer Fox and Brer Wolf, who regularly symbolize white masters and overseers in these slave stories. However, the briar patch has also become a metaphor that represents native space, home, retreat, and racial and ethnic identity in the iconography of the African American **folktale**. Briar patches can be pre- and post-emancipation locales; rural and urban; the slave quarters or a small town in wiregrass country; the woods or the 'hood. Yet the briar patch can also be a thorny place for its native inhabitants at times, a place of recycled grief and continuing internal struggle. In the century-and-a-quarter since Harris made this domain famous, the term has also entered the languages of literary and popular culture and of politics and trade. In a controversial essay titled "The Briar Patch" from the agrarian manifesto *I'll Take My Stand*, Robert Penn Warren affirmed his sense of place, racial identity, and rural values in the southern briar patch. William Faulkner included a passing reference to trying to flush a rabbit out of a briar patch in *Absalom, Absalom!* Protesting ironically about not wanting to be thrown into the briar patch has turned up everywhere from Interstate Commerce Commission deregulation hearings to British House of Commons debates. The Briar Patch is the name for a national gift shop franchise; for dozens of individually owned restaurants, inns, and bed-and-breakfasts from Winter Park, Florida, to Middleton, Rhode Island; for separate lines of children's furniture and toddlers' clothes; for an Atlanta apartment complex a few miles east of Harris's house (now a museum), The Wren's Nest; for various political columnists' op-ed corners; and for an online stock market newsletter. Punching up "the briar patch" on the Google computer search engine in the summer of 2004 produced 51,000 allusions and Web sites. Almost everyone is trying to call Brer Rabbit's briar patch home these days, including some wolves and foxes, too.

R. Bruce Bickley Jr.

See also: Remus, Uncle; Trickster

Further Reading

Bickley, John T., and R. Bruce Bickley, eds., 2002, *Nights with Uncle Remus* (New York: Penguin Classics); Chase, Richard, ed., 1955, *The Complete Tales of Uncle Remus* (Boston: Houghton Mifflin); Faulkner, William, 1936, *Absalom, Absalom!* (New York: Random House); Jarmon, Laura C., 2003, *Wishbone: Reference and Interpretation in Black Folk Narrative* (Knoxville: The University of Tennessee Press); M'Baye, Babacar, 2009, *The Trickster Comes West; Pan-African Influence in Early Black Diasporan Narratives* (Jackson: University Press of Mississippi); Sperb, Jason, 2012, *Disney's Most Notorious Film: Race, Convergence, and the Hidden Histories of Song of the South* (Austin: University of Texas Press); Warren, Robert Penn, 1930, "The Briar Patch," in *I'll Take My Stand: The South and the Agrarian Tradition, by Twelve Southerners* (New York and London: Harper & Brothers).

C

CAUL

This term refers to the uncommon occurrence when a membrane or facial mask covers an infant's head at birth. The amniotic fluid that forms the mask is more popularly called a veil. Various societies have different beliefs about what should be done with cauls. Many believe that cauls should be delicately removed and hung out to dry. In general lore, cauls are supposed to protect against drowning. In African American lore, the most common belief is that those born with cauls have visionary powers, including the power to see ghosts. Toni Morrison's *Song of Solomon* (1977) makes use of caul lore. The community of women in the novel see Ruth Foster's baby as "mysterious" and "deep," prompting them to ask her if the baby came with a caul. Upon discovering that he was, they admonish her that she "should have dried it and made him some tea from it to drink. If you don't he'll see ghosts" (Morrison, 10). When the baby, "Milkman" Dead III, grows older, he must confront family ghosts.

Another prominent literary example that demonstrates caul lore is Tina Ansa's *Baby of the Family* (1989). When Lena is born, the doctor remarks, "This one came with a veil over her face. Yes indeed, it's a sure sign that she's a lucky one, yes indeedy." The mother is amazed that the baby is able to cry because "over her entire head, as if draped there by a band of angels, lay a thin membrane that rose and fell away from the child's sweet face with each breath she took" (Ansa, 2–3). A nurse who believes in all the old rituals preserves the caul and makes a tea from it to protect Lena from evil. A special child, Lena can see ghosts and predict the future.

Valerie Lee

Further Reading

Anderson, Jeffrey, 2007, *Conjure in African American Society* (Baton Rouge: Louisiana State University Press); Ansa, Tina McElroy, 1989, *Baby of the Family* (San Diego: Harcourt Brace Jovanovich); Hazzard-Donald, Katrina, 2013, *Mojo Workin': The Old African American Hoodoo System* (Urbana, IL: University of Illinois Press); Lee, Valerie, 1996, *Granny Midwives & Black Women Writers: Double-Dutched Readings* (New York: Routledge); Morrison, Toni, 1977, *Song of Solomon* (New York: Knopf); Young, Jason R., 2007, *Rituals of Resistance: African Atlantic Religion in Kongo and the Lowcountry South in the Era of Slavery* (Baton Rouge: Louisiana State University Press).

CHARMS

Also known as amulets, gris-gris, juju bags, jacks, and protective hands, these devices formed a unique category of spiritual implements used by African- and

American-born conjurers, root doctors, and diviners throughout North America. Typically worn around the neck, wrist, or ankle and used for a variety of purposes, charms played an important role in the lives of enslaved and free blacks from the 17th through the 20th centuries. Because of specific African beliefs regarding causality in which "accidents" or bad fortune were understood to be caused by malevolent actions on the part of the living or the dead, protective charms became a central element in the folk culture that developed among African Americans. Notably, the use of protective charms in slave conspiracies, revolts, and other modes of resistance created a significant amount of concern among colonial- and antebellum-era whites.

Perhaps the best-documented example of charms used in an act of slave resistance is the 1822 Charleston, South Carolina, plot initiated and led by Denmark Vesey. His plan to destroy Charleston was greatly bolstered by an African-born conjurer named **Gullah** Jack. Having served as a "doctor" in Charleston for 15 years, Jack was a mystic whose renown allowed him to sway enslaved Africans of all ethnic backgrounds who respected him as both conjurer and "General" of the plot. Not only was Jack believed to have a "charmed invulnerability" that would prevent him from being harmed at the hands of whites, but he also produced and distributed charms for slave combatants that were said to render them invincible. For Gullah Jack's protective charms to work, conspirators first had to fast the night before the planned revolt. To be fully protected from harm, the following morning they were to place the charms, made of crab claws, in their mouths. The fact that not one slave questioned the validity of Jack's powers during the course of the trials is a singular testament to the continuing connection they had to African spiritual beliefs and values.

Another example of the use of protective charms or hands in an act of slave resistance is recounted in the story of William Webb. In this case, Webb—a conjurer living in Kentucky during the 1840s—became concerned about the abusive treatment faced by slaves on a neighboring plantation. After secretly meeting with this group, he urged them to gather roots, which were then placed into bags. The slaves were then instructed to walk around their own quarters a few times and were told to position the **conjure** bags in front of their owner's house during the early morning hours. These steps were taken to cause their owner to have disturbing nightmares about the slaves gaining retribution for past wrongs. In the following weeks, the owner reportedly began to treat the slaves decidedly better, and Webb's influence over them increased dramatically as a direct result.

Items placed into bags and used as protective charms were generally known as "hands" or "jacks" and were either worn or buried to work properly. A hand or jack would typically contain a variety of objects, including roots, tree bark, human hair and fingernail clippings, graveyard dirt, horseshoe nails, hog bristles, animal and insect parts, red pepper, gunpowder, and other substances. In this regard, the finding of a "conjure's cache" in an Annapolis, Maryland, house in 1996 proves instructive. Buried sometime during the 18th century in the northeast corner of this home, the items in the cache included beads, pins, buttons, a coin with a hole in it, rock crystals, a piece of crab claw, a brass ring and bell, and pieces of bone and glass. This was one of 11 such findings in Virginia and Maryland, which indicates a clear pattern—especially given the fact that the caches were always buried in the northeast corners of rooms or slave quarters. In all likelihood, these items were protective jacks buried by enslaved blacks to elicit the aid of powerful spiritual forces.

According to a number of African spiritual systems, certain items found in nature are imbued with an innate amount of spiritual force, which becomes even more potent when prepared by a conjurer. The frequent presence of charms in enslaved and free African American communities from as early as the 17th century exemplifies the perseverance of important African religious concepts. It should be mentioned that charms were not always used for benevolent purposes. A charm could also be used to harm, inhibit, or kill others, particularly if it contained the intended victim's hair or nail clippings. In this case, "frizzled" chickens were often used to find evil charms and gris-gris that were buried by conjurers. In addition to frizzled chickens, a number of countercharms were used to ward off the effects of evil. Red pepper, salt, grave dirt or goofer dust, and strips of red flannel cloth were frequently used in countercharms for a variety of reasons, and countercharms were believed to prevent anything from insanity to death caused by evil charms.

Walter Rucker

Further Reading

Anderson, Jeffrey E., 2007, *Conjure in African American Society* (Baton Rouge: Louisiana State University Press); Blassingame, John, 1972, *The Slave Community: Plantation Life in the Antebellum South* (New York: Oxford University Press); Covey, Herbert C., 2008, *African American Slave Medicine: Herbal and Non-herbal Treatments* (Lanham: Lexington Books); Georgia Writers' Project, 1940, *Drums and Shadows: Survival Studies among the Coastal Negroes* (Athens: University of Georgia Press); Mitchem, Stephanie Y., and New York University, 2007, *African American Folk Healing* (New York: New York University Press); Puckett, Newbell Nile, 1926, *Folk Beliefs of the Southern Negro* (Chapel Hill: University of North Carolina Press); Raboteau, Albert J., 1978, *Slave Religion: The "Invisible Institution" in the Antebellum South* (New York: Oxford University Press); Rucker, Walter, 2001, "Conjure, Magic, and Power: The Influence of Afro-Atlantic Religious Practices on Slave Resistance and Rebellion," *Journal of Black Studies* 32: 84–103.

CHEERLEADING

The African American play tradition of cheering evolved as an offshoot of the earlier 20th-century school-based cheerleading tradition that developed with the rise of sports programs in American colleges and high schools. These traditions were a part of high school and college cultures at all-black schools throughout the country. Across the country, schools recruited student cheer (or yell) leaders to guide fans in enthusiastic cheering in support of their school's athletic teams during football and, later, basketball games. Through cheerleading, these student leaders began to build and control strong fan allegiances to the schools and local community. In turn, these allegiances developed a loyal volunteer, alumni, and economic base for the support of a particular educational institution.

In the earliest days of American cheerleading, a few male students led football fans in shouting cheers with megaphones and sparse arm motions at games. Cheers initially were song-based odes or short, repetitive poems. With the shortage of males during World War II, young women moved into roles as school cheerleaders, just as they took advantage of newly opened opportunities in other arenas of American life. At first they cheered with men, but by the 1950s cheerleading had been relegated to a predominantly female activity. Female cheerleaders transformed the tradition by moving it toward entertainment through the addition of dance steps and rhythmic movement and performance in squads.

The tradition of African American cheerleading first gained the attention of folklorists during the mid-1970s as a component of African American children's folklore. Urban black girls mixed the performance of cheers with hand-clapping games, **jump rope** rhymes, and other rhythmic, chanted play activities during their recesses on school playgrounds. Many of the same aesthetics that characterized black dance and musical performances in general were also important elements of cheering; for example, call-and-response, rhythmic movement, and an emphasis on a percussive style of performing. This predominantly female play and performance tradition seems to have emerged after the 1972 Olympics and features the collective chanting of short, snappy rhymes that are coordinated with rhythmic steps and hand clapping. Kate Rinzler's fieldwork and her gathering of others' fieldwork for the children's section of the Festival of American Folklife in 1975 and 1976 offers some of the earliest documentation and public presentation of this play tradition.

Cheering as play is one of several African American cheering traditions engaging girls from preschool through college. As play, girls occasionally performed cheers before mostly informal audiences for the mere satisfaction of group rhythmic interaction, integrating African-derived traditional and popular music and **dance** styles into the activity. However, by the late 1970s, girls also began to view cheerleading as a sport requiring the mastery of athletic and performance skills. As girls transformed this playground tradition into a competitive form of sport and display, they formalized the criteria for participation and performance, and added expensive uniforms and gymnastic skills to performance requirements. By the 1980s and 1990s, cheering had grown in popularity and expanded beyond school playgrounds to become a community-based, sponsored activity, generating neighborhood- and school-based squads that performed at local, regional, and even national celebrations and competitions. Cheerleading has been popularized through such media images as televised competitions, elaborate productions of halftime performances, and films focused on cheerleading.

Within the context of athletic events, cheerleaders have cheered strategically to support a **sports** team, rally the fans, and comment on the team's and the opponent's actions during games. Cheerleading squads strive to create a unique identity for their team and their school through their cheers, one that demonstrates the prominence of the team and school in comparison to that of their opponents. The squads draw on school, local, and ethnic traditions to express these unique identities through their combinations of movement, language, and imagery.

Within the context of cheering as sport, cheerleading squads competitively display their performative competence to audiences and judges. They demonstrate their mastery of fundamental cheerleading skills and their ability to communicate creatively with their audiences. The African American aesthetic emphasizing skillful performance is celebrated in these competitive events.

As a performance genre, the African American cheering tradition emphasizes multichanneled communicative competence and draws resources from African American vernacular language, popular dance, and music traditions as well as African American traditional culture and American popular culture. Among the artistic characteristics that are valued in skillful cheerleading in the African American aesthetic are the following: antiphony, repetition, improvisation, polyrhythmic structure, segmentation of form, the complementarity of movement and text, an increasing emotional intensity, and effective delivery.

Phyllis M. May-Machunda

Further Reading

Adams, Natalie G., and Pamela Bettis, 2003, *Cheerleader! Cheerleader!: An American Icon* (New York: Palgrave Macmillan); Gaunt, Kyra, 1997, "The Games Black Girls Play: Music, Body and Soul," PhD dissertation, University of Michigan, Ann Arbor; Gaunt, Kyra Danielle, 2006, *The Games Black Girls Play: Learning the Ropes from Double-Dutch to Hip-hop* (New York: New York University Press); May, Phyllis M., and Jean Kaplan, 1975–1976, "Children's Handclapping Games" (field collection and documentation of fieldwork in Indiana), unpublished, Archives of Traditional Music, Indiana University; May-Machunda, Phyllis M., 1989, "Cheerleading and Baton-Twirling" in ed. William Ferris, Charles R. Wilson, *Center for Southern Culture* (Jackson: University of Mississippi Press); May-Machunda, Phyllis M., "'Ain't It Funky, Now?': African American Cheerleading as Traditional Play and Performance in Washington, D.C.," PhD dissertation, Indiana University, Bloomington; Soileau, Jeanne, 1980, "Children's Cheers as Folklore," *Western Folklore* 39 (July): 232–247; Swanson, Catherine, 1980, "We're Gonna Win Tonight: The Rhythm of School Spirit," *Center for Southern Folklore* Magazine 3:11; West, Emily, and Laura Grindstaff, 2010, "'Hands on Hips, Smiles on Lips!' Gender, Race, and the Performance of Spirit in Cheerleading," *Text and Performance Quarterly* 30 (2): 143–162.

CHITTERLINGS

Also called chitlins, chitterlings are a delicacy in the African American **soul food** tradition. They are the intestines of young pigs that are often cleaned and prepared a number of ways. They can be battered, fried, grilled, stewed, stir-fried, or stuffed like sausages.

Chitterlings are seen as a dish that had its beginnings in the 19th-century slave culture of southern U.S. plantations. When slaves became the cooks and agricultural labor force on many plantations, they learned to slaughter and clean many kinds of animals, from chickens to pigs. It was the denial or small allotment of food that inevitably led to slaves' ingenuity in using discarded parts from slaughtered animals to feed themselves. While white families dined on select, choice cuts of animals, such as chops, ribs, and ham, slaves received the lean or fat. In Virginia, pigs were usually slaughtered during the month of December. In that particular part of the country, slaves featured chitterling dishes at **Christmas** and on New Year's Eve. After emancipation, chitterlings remained a staple of the African American diet because of the taste but also because of economics. Although no longer enslaved, African American families could rarely afford to spend money on higher-priced meats. Pork remains such as pig's feet, fat back, hog's maw, and chitterlings continued to be a supplement to the mostly vegetarian diet of poor emancipated blacks.

The preparation of chitterlings is a folk ritual in itself that often leads to communal acts associated with the aesthetics of traditional **folk foods**. Whereas today chitterlings can be bought frozen and partially or fully cleaned, the making of fresh chitterlings means a long, arduous process in which people can often find themselves spending a great deal of time together as they wait to eat the finished dish. A game of cards, a conversation about politics and daily events, or the simple, humorous discussion of the oxymoronic reality that something that tastes so good could smell so bad often occurs while people are sitting and waiting for the dish to be done. Traditionally, chitterlings soak in cold water for at least six hours in a covered pot. Cooks then drain the pot and strip as much fat as possible from each piece and then wash the intestines thoroughly in cold water to make sure they are entirely free of dirt. It is the time-consuming effort that has led to myths about chitterlings being a food of death and destruction for the body. Undoubtedly, rushing while cleaning the intestines allows waste, fecal matter, or bacteria to remain, and the result can be food poisoning. However, as many African Americans can attest, "clean chitlins never killed nobody." After cleaning, the chitterlings are usually cut into small pieces (about one inch) and placed in a full pot of water with salt and pepper or other spices and ingredients. Hog maws are often cooked with chitterlings. The cooking time usually ranges from three to three and one-half hours, or until tender. They are often served with vinegar or hot sauce. The texture can range from soft to gristle-like, but the dish remains a filling substitute for other meat products. The preparing and cooking of the dish has also been the cause of much folklore. The smell of the food can linger for days, and as many connoisseurs note, you can often tell when someone is cooking them from blocks away.

Even as chitterlings are considered a cultural mainstay, they are also a taboo among some members of the African diasporic community. Since they are from the belly of a pig, Islamic thought considers the dish to be one of the foulest meals that could be conceived or taken into the human body. The fact that one is not simply eating the pig, but inevitably symbolically digesting what that pig may have eaten is seen in many ways as defiling the body, which serves as a temple for the spirit. In recent years, concerns over the high rates of high blood pressure, obesity, and heart disease suffered by many African Americans has also caused some dietitians to suggest that consumption of chitterlings be reduced or the dish removed from the diet of black people.

LaMonda Horton-Stallings

Further Reading

Angelou, Maya, and Jessica B. Harris, 2011, *High on the Hog: A Culinary Journey from Africa to America* (New York: Bloomsbury); Bowser, Pearl, and Jean Eckstein, 1970, *A Pinch of Soul* (New York: Avon); Brown, William Wells, and John Ernest, 2011, *My Southern Home: Or, the South and Its People* (Chapel Hill: University of North Carolina Press); Counihan, Carol, and Penny Van Esterik, 1997, eds., *Food and Culture, A Reader* (New York: Routledge); Crawford, Willie, The Chitterling Site, http://www.chitterlings.com; Harris, Jessica, 1996, *The Welcome Table–African American Heritage Cooking* (New York: Simon and Schuster); Miller, Adrian, 2013, *Soul Food: The Surprising Story of an American Cuisine, One Plate at a Time* (Chapel Hill: University of North Carolina Press); Opie, Frederick Douglass, 2010, *Hog and Hominy: Soul Food from Africa to America* (New York: Columbia University Press); Puckett, Susan, 1997, "Restaurant and Institutions," *Soul Food Revival* 107 (February 1): 64; Williams-Forson, Psyche A., 2006, *Building Houses Out of Chicken Legs: Black Women, Food, and Power* (Chapel Hill: University of North Carolina Press); Witt, D., 1999, *Black Hunger: Food and the Politics of US Identity* (New York and London: Oxford University Press); Witt, D., 1998, "Soul Food: Where the Chitterling Hits the (Primal) Pan," *Eating Culture*, eds. Ron Scapp, Brian Seitz (Albany: State University of New York Press).

CHRISTMAS

The date of the earliest celebrations of Christmas varied. The eastern branch of the Catholic Church focused its observances on January 6, now known as the Feast of the Epiphany, which commemorates the visit of the Magi (the three Wise Men) to the infant Jesus. The western branch of the Catholic Church selected December 25 to commemorate the nativity, perhaps because the date coincided with winter solstice celebrations. Throughout the United States, the story of Christmas is told visually in a tableau. It is said that St. Francis first brought the crèche or representation of the birth of Jesus Christ with the Holy Family and the ox and ass into the church. Today, nativity scenes placed in private homes and on church grounds depict the Christmas story of travelers seeking shelter among the animals in the stable, the child lying in the manger, and the three Magi being led to Bethlehem by the light of a star.

Popular celebrations of Christmas in the Americas may vary considerably based on different ethnic, regional, and familial traditions. Religious and secular traditions have developed for all, giving Christmas a unique significance for each group. For African Americans in particular, the meaning of Christmas traditions must be understood within the historical context of slavery. Within this context, Christmas emerges as a time to assert African identity through performance. Important traditions such as the presentation of mummers' plays or the performances of John Canoe, although on the surface appearing to mimic European practices, may actually communicate subversive messages. Within this historical context, therefore, the emergence and increasing popularity of **Kwanzaa** celebrations in the United States that allow African Americans to assert their own identity seem a natural part of this holiday period.

During the days of slavery, Christmas provided a time of greater social and physical freedom for the slaves; in fact, it was the most important festival in the lives of most slaves. The journals and travel literature written in the late 18th and early 19th centuries describe the various activities of the slaves during this time. Given a few days off, they would attempt to procure provisions to help in their celebrations. They might be able to kill poultry or a hog for their holiday meal, and they would dress in their finest clothes. Many of the traditions that are practiced currently were observed on many plantations. For example, slaves greeted slave owners with shouts of "Christmas Gift!" and the owners often assembled their slaves and passed out gifts such as coins and handkerchiefs. Slave children were sometimes given apples, oranges, candies, or nuts. Commonly slave owners gave their slaves a week-long rest, in which a variety of activities were enjoyed, including fishing, handicrafts, hunting, boxing, and running contests. Most owners permitted slaves to visit family and friends on nearby plantations. And as in other parts of the diaspora, the spirit of revelry characterized Christmas on plantations in the southern United States. Drinking and dancing were popular activities, and on some plantations there were parties in the slave quarters each night, with fiddles, **banjos**, and other instruments, including drums. Plantation owners often provided slaves with an abundance of food, which was supplemented by game hunted by the slaves. In many cases, slaves held a Christmas dinner, which included, at times, turkey, **barbecue** pork, catfish, and rice. Descriptions of festivities in the United States are similar to those in parts of the Caribbean. One writer notes:

> The negroes are out in great numbers arrayed in their best and their ebony faces shine with joy and happiness. Already they have paraded with a corps of staff officers with red sashes, mock epaulettes & goose quill feathers, and a band of music composed of 3 fiddles, 1 tenor & 1 bass drum, 2 triangles & 2 tamborines and they are marching up & down the streets in great style. They are followed by ohers [sic], some dancing, some walking & some hopping, othrs [sic] singing, all as lively as can be. (Whipple, 51)

Although play occurred during other festive occasions throughout the year, playing, or the assertion of black identity through performance, became most pronounced during the Christmas season during slavery. This "nonsense" or unruly behavior threatened plantation owners who feared the possibility of insurrections and rebellions, especially during this time. In response, plantation owners sought ways to minimize the threats and to exploit the freedom permitted during the Christmas season. For example, the promise of Christmas gifts or freedoms was invoked as much as six months in advance to discipline slaves, in much the same way that adults use such promises with children. When the holidays arrived, slaves were customarily given large quantities of alcohol along with verbal encouragement to stay drunk (Folly, 122). Keeping slaves inebriated helped to lessen the plantation owners' fear of insurrections. The travel and journal literature repeatedly comments on these fears, adding that to stop such performances would definitely lead to insurrection. These comments point to the importance of the Christmas playful practices that developed. Even when these Christmas traditions appeared to mimic European practices, they always involved "play." The performances of John Canoe **festivals** exemplify this.

Performances of John Canoe (also known as John Kuners, jonkunnu, or junkanoo festivals) took place throughout the southern United States and the Caribbean. In Wilmington, North Carolina, slaves dressed in colored, tattered costumes and donned grinning masks, horns, and beards. They went from house to house singing and dancing and playing an assortment of handmade musical instruments, including bones, triangles, and cow's horns. Those in the houses made small donations in exchange for the entertainment. Improvised satirical songs were sung for any who failed to be generous. This tradition continued after emancipation in North Carolina, reaching the peak of its popularity in the 1880s. By 1900, the tradition seemed to have disappeared. Lawrence W. Levine writes that a growing opposition by African American clergy and the African American middle class developed, denigrating the traditions for being lower class. The relevancy of its "playfulness" declined in these changing social contexts.

Although the secular activities seem to have far outweighed the religious ones, there were a few religious activities practiced by slaves. Some slaves regarded the holiday season as an opportunity for prayer meetings and other spiritual celebrations. There are reports of "Watchnight meetings" which took place on Christmas Eve, but there is little description of what the meetings were like. We can speculate that such meetings bore a resemblance to religious gatherings held in **hush harbors**.

Christmas traditions throughout the African American community continue to have many similarities to Christmas celebrations throughout the Christian community. Certainly, Christmas itself as the celebration of the birth of Jesus Christ defines Christian identity, and this component of the holiday has gained more importance over time. But paradoxically, the commercial aspects of the Christmas holiday also have become increasingly pronounced. The basic notions of Christmas among many in the diaspora today mirror the practices of the religious and commercial mainstream, although traditional culturally specific events still occur. For example, the ideas of buying and giving gifts and renewing family bonds are the main components. The celebration of Kwanzaa adds dimensions to the Christmas holidays that appeal to more and more people of African descent, for example, the conscious celebration of African heritage and the commitment to building strong communities. The historical context of slavery in which holiday performances have emerged gives them added significance. African Americans have, through "play" and other means, made the celebration of Christmas an extremely important part of their own traditions.

Michele A. Goldwasser

Further Reading

Folly, Dennis W. (Anand Prahlad), 1983, "Christmas Gif': Afro-American Celebration of Christmas," in *International Folklore Review: Folklore Studies from Overseas*, vol. 3 (London: New Abbey Publications), pp. 120–130; Gay, Kathlyn, 2007, *African-American Holidays, Festivals, and Celebrations: The History, Customs, and Symbols Associated with Both Traditional and Contemporary Religious and Secular Events Observed by Americans of African Descent* (Detroit, MI: Omnigraphics); Whipple, Benjamin Henry, 1937, *Bishop Whipple's Southern Diary, 1843–1844*, ed. Lester B. Shipee (Minneapolis: The University of Minnesota Press).

CHURCH, THE BLACK

The black church refers to communities centered around black Christian-based religion. As the foundation of African American culture, an agency of social control, a place of political activity and economic cooperation, and a sanctuary from the horrors of racism, the black church has formed the cornerstone of African American culture. As with African folk songs, tales, beliefs, and customs, the enslaved peoples of **Africa** transformed religion in the New World. African gods made the transatlantic journey and were worshipped in the New World in Candomblé, Santería, Shango, Vodou, and various lesser-known groups, as well as in Catholicism. African theology was flexible and universal enough to embrace the Bible and Christianity without denying basic African assumptions. One of those assumptions was that the spirit world and humankind exist and interact with each other. Spiritual power was believed to be morally neutral and could be used for good or evil.

The tendency of religion to unite its followers made the threat of slave rebellions much more likely; thus, slaveholders in the American **South** were vigilant regarding the appearance of anything that resembled religious "cult" practice. They had seen the role that religion played in Haiti, where Hyacinthe led a group of 15,000 slaves into battle united under the religious belief that if they died in battle they would go back to Africa. Still, whites could not control slave religious belief. **Conjure**, which included **herbalism**, ghost stories, fortune-telling, and root working, was practiced in slave quarters. Christianity, with its teachings of meekness and otherworldly rewards, proved to be a double-edged sword that also demonized slaveholders and incited some to rebellion. Paul Vesey, Denmark Vesey, and Nat Turner led dangerous insurrections. Many of the African Americans executed for these rebellions were members of the African Methodist Episcopal Church, or otherwise inspired by Christian texts.

According to Raboteau, as early as 1774, African Americans were pointing out the contradictions between slavery and Christianity. For the enslaved African American the incongruity did not lie between Christian doctrine and African theology; rather it lay in the blatant difference between theory and practice. Whereas the Bible taught the loving kindness of Jesus Christ, the enslaved witnessed daily the evil hypocrisy of those who claimed to be Christians. They understood Christian love and forgiveness but struggled internally with these troubling questions: how not to hate white people and how to forgive them. The **spirituals** reflected the religious ideologies of the slaves. The ups and downs, the trouble in mind, and the experiences of the lonesome valley were biblical allusions that mirrored their daily lives.

The development of the black church resulted from the racism of whites, which dictated the segregation of African American worshippers from the white congregation, and it also resulted from the refusal of black Christians to accept these insults. Richard Allen and Absalom Jones's departure from St. George's Methodist Episcopal Church in 1787 and their founding of Bethel African Methodist Episcopal Church in 1794 is an example of the development of the black church in the

Northeast. In the South, a separate system was arranged for the slaves in order to prevent integrated congregations. Some slaveholders rejected the idea of religious instruction for their slaves, and other slaveholders thought that communal worship would destroy the social hierarchy they sought to maintain between blacks and whites. However, others, mainly missionaries, argued that church discipline would be useful in teaching the enslaved their place in society. The plantation **preacher** came between the enslaved community and the plantation owners—a precarious position, but one that many were able to manipulate and use to the advantage of the enslaved by preaching liberation theology thinly disguised as the story of the Hebrew children.

Following emancipation, African Americans used the church as their institution of social uplift and economic development. Church schools were opened and supported by African American congregations. The separateness of African American congregations enabled them to develop distinctly African characteristics, one of the most notable being the folk expressions of black sermons and sermonizing.

Zora Neale Hurston accurately identifies drama as a unique characteristic of black expression. The black sermon is highly dramatic and is made so by the ample use of metaphor and simile, the double descriptive ("high-tall," or "low-down"), and verbal nouns ("funeralize"). This dramatic oratory is part and parcel of the African oral tradition. The use of a stylized method of breathing by the preacher that results in the characteristic "ha!" is, according to Hurston, the expulsion of air just before inhalation. Chants and hums also are characteristic of African American church services, as are **shouts**, being filled with the spirit, praying and **testifying**, and singing praise songs such as **gospels**. The aesthetic discourse of the church service is the core around which most other forms of black expression revolve, including **dance**, music, speech styles, dress, gestures, and aesthetics. The spirit and performance styles of the church permeate black expressive form to such an extent that one can imagine the church as a modality, not just simply as a physical place. For example, musicians and other artists invoke the spirit of the church in contexts that are well beyond the physical spaces of the church building.

Another aspect that developed in the church after emancipation was the will to adorn. The desire for beauty and the need to embellish resulted in the Sunday-go-to-meeting dress. Sunday hats worn by women parishioners were not unlike African headwraps. Formal attire for church service was part of ritualized church etiquette. During the civil rights movement, when white movement workers appeared in black churches not dressed in their Sunday best, many church members were insulted but too polite ever to tell their guests that they were dressed inappropriately.

Other parts of ritualistic church worship include conversion, visions, call-and-response singing, and shouting. Conversion experiences and visions are closely connected. One does not usually occur without the other, and together they frequently constitute a call to preach. In the vision the nonbeliever asks for a sign from God as a proof. Often it takes three (a holy number) before the neophyte is convinced.

Hurston maintains that shouting is a survival of African spirit possession. The African tradition is sacred to the priesthood. In the African American church it became generalized; however, the meaning is the same. The person loses individual consciousness, and the spirit temporarily uses the body for its expression. The urge to shout is triggered by rhythm, whether it is sung, spoken, hummed, foot-tapped, or hand-clapped. Women shout more frequently than men. Hurston identifies two kinds of shouters: silent and vocal, with the vocal type being the most frequent. Singing, shouting, rhythmic music that is possible to dance to, and dramatic sermons punctuated by "ha!" are associated with traditional African American churches.

Nagueyalti Warren

See also: Conversion Narratives

Further Reading

Hayes, Diana L., 2012, *Forged in the Fiery Furnace* (Maryknoll, NY: Orbis Books); Hurston, Zora Neale, 1983, *The Sanctified Church* (Berkeley, CA: Turtle Island); Nelson, Timothy Jon, 2005, *Every Time I Feel the Spirit: Religious Experience and Ritual in an African American Church* (New York: New York University Press); Raboteau, Albert J., 1978, *Slave Religion* (New York: Oxford University Press); Whelchel, L. H., 2011, *The History and Heritage of African-American Churches: A Way Out of No Way* (St. Paul, MN: Paragon House).

CONGO SQUARE

This is a public space in New Orleans where slaves gathered to sing and **dance** in ways that allowed them to recall their African heritage. These public expressions of African and African American culture began in the early 19th century and continued through the 1880s. In 1817 the mayor of New Orleans mandated that these public performances take place only on Sundays and always at Congo Square (a very public venue); slave gatherings outside of the public eye had become dangerous. Assembling on any other day or dancing together after sunset on Sunday would earn violators 10 to 25 lashes. The number of participants at Congo Square reached the hundreds and even thousands, and the dances attracted white audiences. Although most of these observers did not realize the African influence on what they saw, their accounts are detailed enough to allow scholars familiar with African song and dance patterns to discern the similarities.

Initially called "Place Publique," the area went by many names, including "Circus Public Square" because it frequently hosted traveling circuses, "Beauregard Square" for the confederate general from New Orleans, and "Louis Armstrong Square" in honor of the **jazz** trumpeter. Although the area never officially received the appellation "Congo Square," that was how it was known to most people before the Civil War. Congo Square sat amidst Congo Plains, near Orleans and Rampart streets on the back side of the French Quarter. Congo Plains refers to the open grounds surrounding Congo Square, and the latter was by far the most widely used part of the plot.

The slaves of New Orleans, like those throughout the United States, found numerous ways to maintain their sense of community and their African heritage. Spanish records from 1786 show that the army outlawed the "dances of colored people" that had apparently become disruptive to some. Their edict apparently went unheeded: a traveler in 1799 described what now might be referred to as nation dances, recalling that the performers, men, women, and children, "assembled together on the levee, drumming, fifing and dancing in large rings" (Donaldson, 64). Benjamin Henry Latrobe, an architect, provided this early 19th-century description of a gathering of Africans and African Americans in Congo Square:

> They were formed into circular groups, in the midst of four of which that I examined (but there were more of them) was a ring, the largest not ten feet in diameter. In the first were two women dancing. They held each a coarse hand-kerchief, extended by the corners, in their hands, and set to each other in a miserably dull and slow figure, hardly moving their feet or bodies. The music consisted of two drums and a stringed instrument. An old man sat astride of a cylindrical drum, about a foot in diameter, and beat it with incredible quickness with the edge of his hand and fingers. The other drum was an open-staved thing held between the knees and beaten in the same manner. They made an incredible noise. The most curious instrument, however, was a stringed instrument, which no doubt was imported from Africa. On the top of the finger board was the rude figure of a man in a sitting posture, and two pegs behind him to which the strings were fastened. The body was a calabash. It was played upon by a very little old man, apparently eighty or ninety years old.

In the next circle, Latrobe observed much of the same. This circle was larger, and "a ring of a dozen women walked, by way of dancing, round the music in the center. But the instruments were of different construction." There, "[a] man sung an uncouth song to the dancing, which I suppose was in some African language, for it was not French, and the women screamed a detestable burden on one single note" (quoted in Southern 1971, 50–51). These references to "a miserably dull and slow figure" and women who "walked, by way of dancing" suggest that the performers danced the shuffle step so widely known throughout West Africa.

The instruments used by the performers also suggest West African connections. Specifically, Latrobe observed "a block cut into something of the form of a cricket bat with a long & deep mortice down the center," which Harold Courlander suspects has Yoruban origins. Latrobe also described "a square drum, looking like a stool," to which Courlander imputes an Ashanti connection (quoted in Stearns, 52). Other instruments seen in Congo Square that are emblematic of West Africa include calabash rattles, the triangle, animal jawbones for scraping, and the **banjo** (Emery, 159). The African nature of such performances might also be inferred from the reactions of white observers. A New Orleans guidebook, *Paxton's Directory of 1822*, warned its readers about Congo Square, a place where "the Congo and other negroes DANCE, CAROUSE, AND DEBAUCH ON THE SABBATH, to the great injury of the morals of the rising generation," concluding that "it is a foolish custom, that elicits the ridicule of most respectable persons who visit the city." In 1846 a reporter for the New Orleans *Daily Picayune* called the activities "novel, interesting, and highly amusing" and noted that he saw, among other things, "the most grotesque African dances." George Washington Cable observed dance at Congo Square in 1886, and termed it "frenzy," "furious," "frantic," "wild," and "madness" (Emery, 160, 163). Although the authors' opinions regarding the value of such performances differed, the sentiment was the same: the performances seen in Congo Square were something unique to white observers, something almost certainly reflecting the slaves' African heritage.

Such gatherings created a dual opportunity for African slaves: they could recall their individual ethnic heritage while creating a sense of pan-African nationalism based on complementary although not identical cultures. William Wells Brown, in *My Southern Home*, informed his readers that at least six different African peoples had come together to dance at Congo Square—the "Kraels, Minahs, Congos and Mandringas, Gangas, Hiboas, and Fulas" (Southern, 1983, 137). The gatherings at Congo Square became a cultural root that fed religious traditions such as **Hoodoo**, musical traditions such as jazz, and celebratory performances of festivals such as Mardi Gras.

Jennifer Hildebrand

Further Reading

Donaldson, Gary A., 1984, "A Window on Slave Culture: Dances at Congo Square in New Orleans, 1800–1862," *The Journal of Negro History* 69 (2): 63–72; Emery, Lynne Fauley, 1988, *Black Dance from 1619 to Today* (Princeton, NJ: Princeton Book Company); Evans, Freddi Williams, 2014, *Congo Square: African Roots in New Orleans* (Lafayette, LA: University of Louisiana Press); Southern, Eileen, 1983, *The Music of Black Americans* (New York: W. W. Norton & Co.); Southern, Eileen, 1971, *Readings in Black American Music* (New York: W. W. Norton & Co.); Stearns, Marshall, 1958, *The Story of Jazz* (New York: Oxford University Press).

CONJURE

A general term used to describe African American magic throughout the 19th and early 20th centuries, conjure is less common today than it once was, although it has not totally faded from use. Synonyms are **Hoodoo**, tricking, goofer, mojo, and rootwork, with certain terms predominating in particular regions of the country. For instance, Hoodoo is popular along the banks of the Mississippi River, as is **mojo**. Rootwork, on the other hand, is most popular along the Atlantic coast, as are goofer and tricking. Many also use the word "Voodoo" interchangeably with conjure, though scholars typically shun this term. Practitioners of conjure are known by many names, including but not limited to conjure men and women, conjure doctors, conjurers, Hoodoo doctors, trick doctors, "two-headed doctors," goofer doctors, and rootworkers.

Conjurers have been an ever-present feature of African American society since the colonial period. One of the first recorded instances of Hoodoo in the United States took place in Salem, Massachusetts, when a slave by the name of Tituba instructed some young girls in the art of fortune-telling, prompting the girls to accuse Tituba and several other townsfolk of witchcraft. Remains of magical materials have also been unearthed from former slave dwellings throughout the **South**, dating from colonial times to the late antebellum period. The practice survived emancipation and continues to be a significant feature of African American life in many communities.

Traditional conjurers told fortunes, performed spells, located lost items and buried treasure, and in parts of the Mississippi Valley and along the Gulf Coast, acted as priests of African American syncretic faiths. Their chief business, however, consisted of the manufacture of **charms**, variously known as hands, gris-gris bags, mojos, tobies, jacks, conjure bags, conjure balls, and conjure bottles. Clients approached practitioners for virtually any need that they felt unable to satisfy by normal means. These concerns have always ranged from winning love to bringing luck. Before the Civil War, many slaves also relied on conjurers' charms for protection against the brutal whippings inflicted by cruel slave masters. Following emancipation, Hoodoo practitioners increasingly produced charms to aid free blacks in court cases, to bring success in business, to attract luck at gambling, and to curb the behavior of unruly teenagers.

Not all charms were designed for good ends; many had the express purpose of harming others. Clients frequently purchased such items to drive away, sicken, or kill their enemies. Two of the most common and disturbing deaths that struck conjurers' victims were locked bowels and living animals in their bodies. Locked bowels resulted in terminal constipation that supposedly caused an exquisitely painful death. Having animals in one's body was worse. Sufferers reported that snakes or insects could be seen crawling under their skin or issuing from their mouths. In most cases, only the speedy intervention of another conjurer could save a victim of evil Hoodoo.

Charms have traditionally used a wide range of materials, most of which would have been obtainable from nature or would already be common in most households. For example, one mojo hand described by amateur folklorist Harry Middleton Hyatt consisted of a **John the Conqueror** root (most likely *Polygonatum multiflorum*, *Arum triphyllum*, and/or *Ipomea jalap*) and an Adam-and-Eve root (*Aplectrum hyemale*) worn in a bag around the neck. This particular charm was designed to help its possessor hold a steady job. Some other materials commonly found in conjure bags were graveyard dirt, pins and needles, human hair and blood, bones, powdered reptiles and amphibians, and a virtually inexhaustible array of botanical items.

Conjure grew out of African spiritual beliefs. The Yoruba, Fon, Ewe, and related peoples of northern West Africa and the Kongo of western Central Africa contributed the most to American conjure. Practitioners of New Orleans Hoodoo addressed a spirit named Agoussou when dealing in matters of love. Agoussou was derived from the Fon deity Agasu, an ancestral spirit and founder of the royal line of Abomey. In the same area, the gris-gris bags carried by conjurers and their clients developed from northern West African charms known as gregory bags. Outside the Mississippi Basin, the Kongo legacy proved more enduring. As had been true in western Central Africa, conjure in the Atlantic South was particularly tied to the dead. Many—by some accounts most—charms used graveyard dirt, often called goopher dust. This term was likely a corruption of the Kongo word *kufwa*, which means "to die."

If African beliefs were the root of conjure, many of the branches were European and Native American. Conjurers quickly grafted Christian elements onto their practices. Bibles were commonly used in the manufacture of charms and the telling of fortunes, as were **prayers** and psalms. European folk supernaturalism, including Quaker magic and Jewish Kabbalah, rapidly entered Hoodoo as conjure doctors pragmatically picked and chose what worked best for them. Practitioners also borrowed widely from Native Americans; Amerindian herbal medicine had found its way into African American magic well before the Civil War. Some of the best-known conjure items originated with Native Americans, including Adam-and-Eve root, particularly common in love charms, and puccoon root, used to produce good luck. Indians also seem to have introduced the concept of magical stones into Hoodoo. Practitioners in the 19th and early 20th centuries commonly carried such "conjure stones" to gain or amplify their power.

Conjure has undergone many notable changes since the Civil War. Perhaps the most visible of these has been the rise of the spiritual supply industry. Spiritual supplies are manufactured items that serve the same purposes as old-fashioned charms and spells. Although most of the botanical and many of the zoological items used in traditional African American magic are still available, their popularity has declined in favor of various oils, incenses, bath crystals, soaps, aerosol sprays, and the like that promise identical results. By the late 19th century, such items were readily available from large manufacturers, who sold their goods across the country by mail order and from local conjure shops. Spiritual supply businesses, especially the manufacturers, often had white (especially Jewish) owners, although their clientele largely remained black. Today, Hoodoo continues to undergo many changes, most notably by incorporating features of Santería and other Afro-Caribbean faiths, Eastern mysticism associated with the new age movement, and scientific and pseudoscientific explanations for paranormal activity.

At heart, conjure has comprised both folklore and business. Supernatural skills allowed successful conjurers to amass great wealth and power, making them important leaders in the African American community. Marie Laveau, the famed New Orleans "Voodoo Queen," was one of the best-known black women of the late 19th century. Following her death in 1881, the New Orleans *Daily Picayune* carried a lengthy obituary, describing her good works and ignoring persistent **rumors** that much of her activity was less than benevolent. At least one reader felt provoked enough to write to the newspaper, questioning the author's good sense. Whatever her contemporaries' evaluations, some modern practitioners regard her as a goddess. Stephaney (Stephany) Robinson, better known as "Dr. Buzzard," a rootworker from near Beaufort, South Carolina, became a living legend during his career, which stretched from the late 1800s to his death in 1947. He was known and respected throughout the state and nation, attracting clients from hundreds of miles away and inspiring a succession of imitators. He amassed such a fortune that he reportedly once destroyed $1,500 in postal money orders simply because he feared that police might use it as evidence to prosecute him for practicing medicine without a license. James Spurgeon Jordan became so rich from his conjure practice that he used his income to support a small community, called Jordanville; created a sandlot baseball team; and purchased other businesses, including a country store, multiple farms, and a logging company. Folklorist Elon Kulii also has testified to the recent strength of the spiritual supplies business. According to his estimates, the industry generated approximately $3 billion annually during the late 1970s. The figure would likely be higher today.

While conjure often gave its practitioners fame, wealth, and power, its most important legacy has been the hope that it has given African Americans. Historically, conjure provided blacks with magical protection, redress, and success in an often-hostile world dominated by whites. As such, it is the most important African feature of black society to survive slavery and the legacy of racial discrimination and injustice that has been an ever-present feature of African American history.

Jeffrey E. Anderson

See also: Black Cat Bone; Herbalism; Hoodoo

Further Reading

Anderson, Jeffrey Elton, 2007, *Conjure in African American Society* (Baton Rouge: Louisiana State University Press); Anderson, Jeffrey E., 2008, *Hoodoo, Voodoo, and Conjure: A Handbook* (Westport, CT: Greenwood Press); Covey, Herbert C., 2008, *African American Slave Medicine: Herbal and Non-herbal Treatments* (Lanham: Lexington Books); Hazzard-Donald, Katrina, 2013, *Mojo Workin': The Old African American Hoodoo System* (Chicago: University of Illinois Press); Hurston, Zora Neale, 1931, "A Hoodoo in America," *Journal of American Folklore* 44: 318–417; Hyatt, Harry Middleton, 1970, *Hoodoo—Conjuration—Witchcraft—Rootwork; Beliefs Accepted by Many Negroes and White Persons, These Being Orally Recorded among Blacks and Whites*, vols. 1–5 (Hannibal, MO: Western Publishing Company); Long, Carolyn Morrow, 2001, *Spiritual Merchants: Religion, Magic, and Commerce* (Knoxville: University of Tennessee Press); Murray, David, 2007, *Matter, Magic, and Spirit: Representing Indian and African American Belief* (Philadelphia: University of Pennsylvania Press); Puckett, Newbell Niles, 1968 [1926], *Folk Beliefs of the Southern Negro* (New York: Negro Universities Press); Young, Jason R., 2007, *Rituals of Resistance: African Atlantic Religion in Kongo and the Lowcountry South in the Era of Slavery* (Baton Rouge: Louisiana State University Press).

CONVERSION NARRATIVES

These are colorful narratives depicting dreamlike scenarios and leading to a conversion to Christianity. In many parts of the southern United States, during slavery and well into the postbellum period, converting to Christianity and becoming a member of the **black church** community were highly ritualized processes. Someone wanting to join the church was often expected to go through a rite of passage, which would begin with a period of "seeking," in which he or she would spend time alone. At some point, the seeker would be "struck dead," and while lying in a coma or trancelike state, have a visionary experience in which they would travel to heaven and interact with God. After this mystical encounter, the seeker would narrate his or her experience to church elders, and could then be baptized. After

baptism by immersion in water, the person would become a member of the church community.

Conversion narratives tended to follow similar structures and to include a traditional set of motifs, although some were more elaborate than others. The motif of being struck dead is consistent but is sometimes preceded by occasions in which the seeker experiences other visions, all sent by God as a way of calling the seeker away from a life of sin. Typically, after being struck dead, the person would follow a path and encounter a number of obstacles. Sometimes they encountered large, ferocious dogs and inclement weather, such as snow. Often, they would have to walk on a thin rope over hell, and could hear the voices of the damned crying and screaming. They would sometimes see the **devil** and feel the heat of hell. A mediator would often appear "in the form of an angel or a mysterious 'little man.'" He would reassure the person and lead them to heaven. They would see God, sitting on his throne or in a big chair. God would tell them that they were saved and that they should go back into the world and testify and carry His message. The seeker would awake, filled with joy.

Conversion narratives for many people marked the most momentous event in their lives. Besides playing a central role in the initiation process of converting to the church, these narratives also suggest some of the psychological stresses that weighed upon slaves and later generations of African Americans. They are deeply personal and provide descriptions of the interior, emotional landscapes of black people, reflecting some of the most intimate and vulnerable moments in black folklore. It is no coincidence that the conversion process was marked by intense anxiety and hyperawareness of one's mortality. In the day-to-day life of slavery, African Americans had every reason to be anxious and fearful that their lives might end abruptly and prematurely. One can see reflections of slave life in the seeker's visionary journey and in the symbols that appear in the narratives. For example, walking on a path beset with obstacles, hanging by a thread over hell, or being confronted or pursued by dogs could easily be descriptions of common experiences in the lives of slaves. Forms of conversion narratives still exist in some African American churches, although most of them have different motifs and structures than the narratives told during the slavery period and in the first part of the 20th century. These narratives suggest the continued importance of religious rites of passage and of public testimonies describing one's conversion as precursors to becoming members of spiritual communities.

Anand Prahlad

See also: Testifying

Further Reading

Johnson, Clifton H., ed., 1969, *God Struck Me Dead: Religious Conversion Experiences and Autobiographies of Ex-Slaves* (Philadelphia: Pilgrim Press); Lee, Pamela Chandler, 2008, "Christian Conversion Stories of African American Women: A Qualitative Analysis," *Journal of Psychology and Christianity* 27 (3): 238; Moore, Cecilia Annette, 2010, "Conversion Narratives: The Dual Experiences and Voices of African American Catholic

Converts," *U.S. Catholic Historian* 28 (1): 27–40; Raboteau, Albert J., 1978, *Slave Religion: The "Invisible Institution" in the Antebellum South* (New York: Oxford University Press).

COOL

The term denotes an attitude; a way of being in the world exemplified by a calm demeanor—a kind of casual smoothness and quiet confidence—accompanied by an impeccable sense of style meant to signify profound dignity and pride in the face of extreme oppression. For decades, black men have been the primary purveyors of this performative stance as they have struggled to develop a manner designed to both preserve and exhibit their manhood, even as it has constantly been under attack by an oppressive society. According to psychologist Richard Majors and sociologist Janet Billson, this stance or attitude, which they have referred to as "Cool Pose" in their book with the same title, can be traced back to ancient West African cultures (Majors, 57). Contemporary manifestations of "cool" serve to provide "the black male with a sense of control, inner strength, balance, stability, confidence, and security. . . . Cool helps him deal with the closed doors and negative images of himself that he must confront on a daily basis" (Majors, 9). Understood in this way, "cool" or "cool pose" is a kind of mechanism purposefully used by black men to help shield them from the harsh humiliation of their everyday existence in a world that, at the very least, undervalues them as human beings.

In black expressive culture then, the idea of "cool" acquires significance as a defining trait of the folk hero and of black folkloric performance. Many important figures in black folklore embody this characteristic and serve as models of "cool" behavior; the image of the black male as simultaneously quiet, contemplative, and dangerous is one that has been such a staple of black culture that it has become a stamp of racial authenticity (picture the cool demeanor with which **Stagolee** shoots Billy Lyons and launches himself as a black folk icon). The idea of "cool" has become a requisite for a kind of masculinity exemplified by the **bad man**, the **pimp**, the hustler, the bluesman, the jazzman, and most recently the **hip-hop** youth. One can witness "cool" in the style of Billy Dee Williams, Eddie Murphy, Samuel L. Jackson, Denzel Washington, John Coltrane, Rakim, Ice Cube, Snoop Dogg, and others. Musicians and entertainers alike subscribe to this performative pose as a way of demonstrating their authenticity as black men.

Robin Kelley's portrait of **jazz** great Miles Davis highlights the power of controversial black male figures who both fascinate and frighten with their silent, threatening presence: "[Miles] was the product of a masculine culture that aspired to be like a pimp, that embraced the cool performative styles of the players (pronounced 'playas'), the 'macks,' the hustlers, who not only circulated in the jazz world but whose walk and talk also drew from the well of black music. . . . Like the coolest pimps on my block while I was growing up in Harlem, Miles was constantly posing; he knew how to stand, how to move, how to compose himself in space so that the world revolved around him" (2001:2.1). This "cool" that Miles exuded—part of what Kelley calls "The Pimp Aesthetic"—has been coveted by black and white men alike (recall Norman Mailer's notorious apotheosis of blackness, "The White

Negro"); for black men it announces the resiliency of their oft-assaulted manhood and for whites it is often used as a way to declare a rejection of staid, middle-class values. For both, the performance of "cool" serves to venerate and perpetuate popular constructions of black masculinity.

David Todd Lawrence

See also Bad Man, The

Further Reading

Brown, Cecil, 2004, *Stagolee Shot Billy* (Boston: Harvard University Press); Hall, Ronald E., 2009, "Cool Pose, Black Manhood, and Juvenile Delinquency," *Journal of Human Behavior in the Social Environment* 19 (5): 531–539; Henry, David, and Joe Henry, 2013, *Furious Cool: Richard Pryor and the World That Made Him* (Chapel Hill, NC: Algonquin Books of Chapel Hill); Kelley, Robin D. G., 2001, "A Jazz Genius in the Guise of a Hustler," *New York Times*, May 13, 2001, late ed., 2.1; Mailer, Norman, 1959, "The White Negro," in *Advertisements for Myself* (New York: G. P. Putnam's Sons), pp. 331–358; Majors, Richard, and Janet Mancini Billson, 1992, *Cool Pose: The Dilemmas of Black Manhood in America* (New York: Lexington Books); Thomas, Alvin, Wizdom Powell Hammond, and Laura P. Kohn-Wood, 2015, "Chill, Be Cool Man: African American Men, Identity, Coping, and Aggressive Ideation," *Cultural Diversity & Ethnic Minority Psychology* 21 (3): 369–379; Thompson, Robert Farris, 1983, *Flash of the Spirit: African and Afro-American Art and Philosophy* (New York: Random House).

CP TIME

Colored People's time or CP time is a reference to the notion that people of African descent are allegedly always late. Colored People's time emphasizes a different relationship to time than the precision of hours, minutes, and seconds. During the era of slavery, many enslaved Africans lived by more natural time divisions, counting the time in broad strokes—seed time, planting time, and harvest time. Enslaved Africans had no control over their time. Thus, time was a commodity controlled and measured by masters and overseers. In Richard Wright's short story "Long Black Song," a white college student is trying to sell a rural black woman a gramophone with a clock built into it so that she will have music and time. While talking to her, however, he notices that her baby is beating and banging on an old clock. The salesman is dumbfounded that the mother could let the baby destroy such a useful item. He does not see how it is possible to live without a clock and questions the mother, asking her how in the world she can live without clocks. How is it that she knows when to wake up? Her reply is "We git up wid the sun." And when he asks how it is that she knows when it is night, her reply is "It gits dark when the sun goes down" (Wright, 423).

Those who live by CP time view time as a European construction and therefore expect such occasions as weddings, church services, **funerals**, picnics, and parties to start late. Blacks missing out on heaven or some other benefit because of CP time have become a source of folk **jokes**.

Valerie Lee

Further Reading

King, J. L., 2007, *CP Time: Why Some People Are Always Late* (New York: Strebor Books); Streamas, John, Robin Lucy, and Deirdre H. McMahon, 2010, "Closure and 'Colored People's Time,'" *Study of Time* 13 : 219–235; Wright, Richard, 1995, "Long Black Song," in *Voices from the Harlem Renaissance*, ed. Nathan Irvin Huggins (New York: Oxford University Press).

CROSSROADS, THE

This is a site of mystical, concentrated power. Probably one of the most popular and enduring motifs in the history of **blues** is that of the crossroads. This motif is also prevalent in black religious traditions of the Caribbean and South America. It was at the crossroads where bluesmen Tommy Johnson and Robert Johnson (no relation) were said to have traded their souls to the **devil** for guitar skills. The crossroads motif is but one of many that have become part of the lexicon of African American folklore and that have a lineage from West African culture.

African and Afro-diasporic cultures have "**trickster** gods" whose responsibilities and characteristics directly relate to the themes found in the crossroads motif. The trickster gods "either tend to be associated with animal spirits or are Promethean figures, archetypal 'humans' who interact with and upset the world of the gods" (Davis). The names for these orishas (deities) are many: Esu, Eshu, Legba, Elegbara, Eshu-Elegbara. They are responsible for communication and are able to speak in a spiritual language. Additionally, these deities can affect one's future. "Legba is responsible for communicating human destinies" (Davis). Legba's involvement is required for any interaction between the vodun, priest, and any other spiritual representative to perform rituals successfully. Because of this, Elegbara is seen as standing at a metaphysical gate, or crossroads. To further link Eshu to the crossroads, places of respect and worship are often found there and at markets. "In all Yoruban-based ceremonies, Elgeba is greeted first because it is he who stands at the crossroads between man and spirit" (Cole).

The orisha came to the New World by way of the Middle Passage. Here they were incorporated into Christianity. "The world's most vibrant form of syncretism emerged, where Catholic saints and the orisha blended into one another, and the worldly wisdom of West Africa continued disguised in song, drum, and celebration" (Davis). Afro-Haitians referred to the orisha Legba as the loa (lwa), Papa Legba. As is the case with most human representations of gods, the deity takes on the characteristics of the rural, peasant people. "Papa Legba is often pictured with typical attire—jeans and work shirt. He is also understood as having a crutch or cane and smoking a pipe, with a peasant bag in tow" (Laguerre). The Haitian expression of Legba has a duality. He is both good and evil, a Rada and a Petro. "Legba's Petro aspect is called Carrefour, the crossroads, and he is lord of black magic" (Davis).

In the South, one syncretization of **Africa** and Europe was called "**Hoodoo**." Although many embraced the continuity between African-based religious systems and their offshoots in the southern United States, just as often such practices as Hoodoo were demonized. One clear reason for this is the impact of Christianity, which in some situations left little room for polytheistic worship, or the holding to two forms of worship at the same time. Yet many reports affirm the continued presence of the crossroads motif in African American culture.

> American beliefs about the crossroads are many and they come in numerous variations. There are two major themes regarding crossroads rituals in the African-American hoodoo tradition. While these customs may contain an admixture of European folklore, they are primarily derived from African antecedents. (Yronwode)

The most common expression of the motif in the United States is certainly as a site for meeting with the devil to obtain some kind of magical gift. The portrayal of the devil in these narratives suggests a syncretism between the European devil and African orishas such as Elegba. In 19th-century African American culture, the "devil" was petitioned for skills, good fortune, fame, and even health. It is curious that for some it is the devil that is deemed capable of bestowing these gifts, not the Christian God.

> Take a **black cat bone** and a guitar and go to a lonely fork in the roads at mid-night. Sit down there and play your best piece, thinking of and wishing for the devil all the while. . . . You will be able to play any piece you desire on the guitar and you can do anything you want to in the world, but you have sold your eternal soul to the devil and are his in the world to come. (Puckett)

St. Louis bluesman Peetie Wheatstraw went even further and used the stage name "the Devil's Son-in-Law." According to Wheatstraw,

> If you want to learn how to make songs yourself, you take your guitar and you go to where the road crosses that way, where a crossroads is. Get there, be sure to get there just a little 'fore 12 that night so you know you'll be there. You have your guitar and be playing a piece there by yourself. . . . A big black man will walk up there and take your guitar and he'll tune it. And then he'll play a piece and hand it back to you. That's the way I learned to play anything I want. (Evans)

The crossroads is an example of a motif embodying syncretism between European and African elements. It suggests that although the original meanings behind many African elements were transformed, they continued to resonate in cultures of African heritages in the New World.

Yolanda Y. Williams

Further Reading

Calt, Stephen, 2001, *Hellhound on My Trail: The Life and Legend of Robert Johnson* (New York: Grove Press); Davis, Erik, 1991, "Trickster at the Crossroads," *Gnosis* (Spring); Desmangles, Leslie Gerald, 1992, *The Faces of the Gods: Vodou and Roman Catholicism in Haiti* (Chapel Hill: The University of North Carolina Press); Groom, Bob, 1976, "Standing at the Crossroads: Robert Johnson's Recordings," *Blues Unlimited*, March and October, pp. 118–121; Hazzard-Donald, Katrina, 2013, *Mojo Workin: The Old African American Hoodoo System* (Urbana, IL: University of Illinois Press); Johnson, Robert, 1936, *King of the Delta Blues* (1936–1937) (Columbia Records C-30034); Laguerre, Michel S., 1980, *Voodoo Heritage* (Beverly Hills, CA: Sage Publications); Pelton, Robert D., 1980, *The Trickster in West Africa: A Study of Mythic Irony and Sacred Delight*

(Berkeley: University of California Press); Puckett, Newbell Niles, 1968 [1926], *Folk Beliefs of the Southern Negro* (New York: Negro Universities Press); York, Jake Adam, 2002, "Southern Crossroads in Myth, Legend and Life," *StorySouth: Best from New Southern Writers* (Summer); Yronwode, Catherine, Copyright by Catherine Yronwode, 1995–2003, *Hoodoo in Theory and Practice: An Introduction to African-American Rootwork.*

D

DANCE

One of the most pervasive features of African American folklore is dance. Dance conjoins a rich constellation of physical memory, individual expression, and social presence within African American life. Because it is always intertwined with traditions of music—Harlem Renaissance art critic Alain Locke termed dance "the cradle of Negro music"—dance affirms, for the individual and the group, physical opportunities to express pleasure, pain, desire, and aesthetic excellence. Learned by youngsters as an integral aspect of identity formation and social interaction, dance connects long-standing African traditions of body talking, musicality, and individual expression. Dance also articulates group experiences for African Americans, as each generation produces its own particular musical and dance structures suited to its temperament and the current social climate.

Many folklorists and historians concur that dance and music bring African characteristics and traditions into the New World to a greater degree than other constituent cultural traits. Stylized movement has long been important to African Americans, who transform everyday gestures into choreographed movements, as in the "high five" of basketball players or the complex handshake greetings that end with a snap of the fingers preferred by contemporary youth. This tradition of movement innovation is doubtless African in origin. Anthropologist Katrina Hazzard-Gordon writes that from its beginnings, African American dance "has served its participants as an instrument of aesthetic, intellectual and emotional expansion and enjoyment, as well as a source of self-awareness." Dance has also served ritual and ceremonial purposes and been thought of by many as a medium that links people and the worlds of the gods.

As if to agree with the adage that, in African American culture, the act supersedes its discussion, dance has received little scholarly attention, and the literature on its history, theory, and practice remains small. Reliable documentation of dance events predating the mid-20th century is slight. Before the 1800s, slave society strictly regulated public dancing by African Americans. Drum dancing solidified connections among the slaves' varied West African cultures, so to minimize these powerful affinities, slave owners legislated performance and carefully mediated dancing affairs that might provide opportunities "to exchange information and plot insurrections." The dancing body, after slave uprisings such as the South Carolina Stono insurrection of 1739, was linked with rebellion in the minds of whites. The resultant slave laws of 1740 prohibited any Negro from "beating drums, blowing horns or the like which might on occasion be used to arouse slaves to insurrectionary activity." According to Hazzard-Gordon, public dancing came "under the strict governance and supervision of whites who legitimized violence as a means of controlling the slave population." Eventually, the most important idioms of African American dancing went underground, and dances that carried significant aesthetic information became disguised or hidden from public view.

The earliest codified and documented dances of slaves combined ritual, play, and communal rebirth within the provisional safety of the Christian church. The **ring shout**—a circle dance of praise that allowed for bits of individual expression—emerged in Georgia, Virginia, and the Carolinas. Although the Protestant church frowned upon rhythmic fiddle music and dance, "marching praise services" were allowed in some congregations in the 19th century. As these marching services developed complex rhythmic structures, worshipers developed rules to satisfy the stringent church restrictions: the feet must not leave the floor or cross each other. Technically, this made the ring shout "not a dance." Like later group dances, including the big apple, the ring shout encouraged individual expression and innovation such as body patting, slapping, clapping, and stomping within the repeated slide-together-slide movement of the group. The ring shout continued as a central feature of many **black church** denominations and probably led to the rise in liturgical praise dancing of the many latter 20th-century denominations.

Outside of the slave master and repressive clergy's controlling eye, however, dance flourished among African Americans. Three distinctive solo performance forms emerged in the 19th century: buck dances that featured weighted, percussive foot work; wing dances that focused on flapping gestures of the arms and knees; and jig dances that emphasized speed and agility of the body, especially in the legs and feet. All of these plantation-era movement idioms found their way into the cakewalk, a partnered competition and parody dance that began among African Americans in the South but grew in popularity to reach an international public. Like nearly every other African American social dance that followed it, the cakewalk became an international sensation practiced and appreciated by dancers around the world. Its basic features involved exaggeration, improvisation by individuals, comic allusion, virtuosity, complex meter, and percussive attack, all features noted a century later by African American art historian Robert Farris Thompson in his seminal research article "Dance and Culture: An Aesthetic of the **Cool**."

The cakewalk began as a social ritual of competitive play and parody but became a theatrical form inseparable from the minstrel show, which was a 19th-century phenomenon initially performed by men in blackface aping the plantation manners and **festival** dances of southern slaves. The minstrel show solidified around 1840 and remained popular until the turn of the century. Its preferred format featured competitive and eccentric dances, boastful struts and cakewalks, and freakishly stylized characters, including stock types Zip Coon and **Jim Crow** as well as African American dancer William Henry Lane's stage persona, Master Juba. The cakewalk's ascendancy on Broadway set in motion the undeniable importance of African American social dances and music for all of American popular entertainment.

Dance as an aspect of religious worship flourished in the Caribbean, where African traditions melded in the syncretic practices of Santería, Candomblé, and

Vodou. Fused primarily from spiritual practices of the enslaved Yoruban people, which included divination knowledge of natural forces and a relationship to the ancestral realms, these religions value dance as a foundational form of worship. Here, dancing and drumming explicitly serve to enhance the spiritual well-being of African Americans in traditions that include dances of ritual, possession, and transcendence.

Even under slavery, African Americans convened frequently to celebrate and share movements, compete in dance challenges, and consecrate a common artistic heritage of dance. In New Orleans, **Congo Square** became the site of a large festival dance that convened regularly from the early 1800s until at least the 1880s. Here, African drumming accompanied dances practiced by the many Caribbean immigrants, including the chica, the bamboula, and the calenda. At Congo Square, and contemporaneously at competitions in the Five Points district of New York City, intense competitions pitted dancers against each other in challenges of style, agility, and innovation.

At the turn of the 20th century, amid increasing northern migration and industrialization, individual expression became more possible for African Americans, and social dances reflected the hard-won expansion of personal freedoms. By the 1920s, New York, and especially Harlem, became a mecca for a cohesive black community, and "eccentric dances" accompanied the emergent **jazz** age. These dances, including the black bottom and the Charleston, featured extravagant body-part isolations, especially in sinewy or sudden motions of the pelvis and spine and in rolling of the torso, shoulders, elbows, and knees in unexpected, continuous waves or accented, rhythmic jerking. The snakehips dance, popularized by impressive performances of Earl "Snake Hips" Tucker, a soloist with the Duke Ellington Orchestra, emphasized successional movements clearly derived from religious dances retained by black Americans in the Caribbean, including the movements of Damballa, a snake deity of the Vodoun. While some found these dances to be sexually explicit, others recognized them to be African American versions of African fertility, kinship, and possession dances.

After the cakewalk declined, the Charleston and its affiliated eccentric dances took center stage in Broadway musicals, and a cycle began in which social dances emerged in regional locations, traveled to New York where they were further refined, were transmitted to the New York stage where they became the toast of the town, and then were performed abroad to international acclaim. The Savoy Ballroom in Harlem allowed dancers the space to codify a great many social dances that gained international currency, including the lindy hop, the Harlem stomp, the big apple, peckin', and versions of dances from the South, including the turkey trot and the bunny hug.

Broadway also codified folk forms of rhythmic dance that became known as tap dance. Developed among the social crucible of dance competitions among African, Irish, and British immigrants in downtown New York, tap emerged as a distinctive form in the 1910s. It was a hybrid of African American buck-and-wing dances, English clog dances, and Irish jigs. Outstanding African American tap artists including Bill "Bojangles" Robinson, the "class act" team of Honi Coles and Cholly

Atkins, and the expertly virtuosic Nicholas Brothers achieved fame and acclaim for their mastery and advancement of the idiom on stage and film, as did latter-day artists Sammy Davis Jr., Dianne Walker, Gregory Hines, and Savion Glover.

African American dancers who aspired to the concert stage also achieved success by transforming black social dances into theatrical fare. While ballet and modern dance remained the realm of white dancers in the 1930s and 1940s, some black artists managed to break the "color line" by creating dance programs that featured African American artists in works with African American themes. In New York, Edna Guy and Hemsley Winfield organized the "First Negro Dance Recital in America" in April 1931; years later, Guy organized the 1937 "Negro Dance Evening" with Alison Burroughs at the 92nd Street YM-YWHA. Sierra Leonean émigré Asadata Dafora created opera-styled dance-dramas with African themes in *Kykunkor* (1934) and *Zunguru* (1938), works that employed African and African American musicians and dancers to great theatrical effect. During this era, some prominent white choreographers also turned to African American themes in works set to Negro spirituals or Caribbean religious rituals, placing African American folklore at center stage.

Two African American women gained unequivocal celebrity status as pioneers of African American modes of concert dance performance. Katherine Dunham and Pearl Primus each surrounded her artistic innovations with graduate work in anthropology, a strategy that ensured attention respectful of the effort to catalog deep structures of African American performance. Dunham achieved her greatest performing success within the commercial arenas of Broadway and Hollywood. She based much of her stage choreography on her research in Afro-Caribbean traditions and developed a dance technique from aesthetic features of African movement retentions that were visible in the Americas. In 1931 Dunham founded the Negro Dance Group in Chicago, and after traveling extensively in the West Indies, she choreographed one of her most famous works, *L'Ag'Ya* (1938), which was based on a fighting dance of Martinique. She made Haiti a principal site of her research before moving to East Saint Louis in 1967, where she created a museum and center for dance and culture.

Primus understood dances to be compelling documents of culture in their own right and synthesized extensive fieldwork in Africa to create structures of bodily memory—cultural memories residing not just in the psyche but deeply embedded in the physical body. In her essay "Primitive African Dance (and Its Influence on the Churches of the South)," which was written for the 1949 *Dance Encyclopedia*, Primus argued an aesthetic connection between African American dance practice and African musicality; she also pointed out the absence of audience in the African and African American traditions where call-and-response requires that everyone participate in the dance. Her choreography of African and African American themes included solo dances that expressed rage at racial indignity, as in *Strange Fruit* (1945), and introduced African rituals to American audiences, as in *Fanga* (1949).

Other dance companies incorporated elements of African American life in their stage choreographies, with special success achieved by Alvin Ailey, whose *Revelations* (1960) depicted a spectrum of black spiritual practice. Also, Louis Johnson's ballet *Forces of Rhythm* (1972) was created for ballet dancer Arthur Mitchell's company, Dance Theatre of Harlem, to depict the synthesis of ballet and black social dance, and Talley Beatty's *The Stack Up* (1983) melded theatrical jazz dance, ballet, modern dance technique, and contemporary social dance. At the close of the 20th century, Jawole Willa Jo Zollar's *Batty Moves* (1995), Donald Byrd's *Harlem Nutcracker* (1996), and Ronald K. Brown's *Grace* (1999) each reconfigured the theatrical possibilities of African American social dance for contemporary opera house stages.

The place of dance as a political strategy shifted when civil rights activism in the 1950s and 1960s precipitated a neo-African movement that valued African dance forms that had been transformed for African American dancers and audiences. "African dance" classes sprang up first at cultural centers across the country and later in college dance curricula. Following the lead set by Pearl Primus, Baba Chuck Davis, from Raleigh, North Carolina, founded the African American Dance Ensemble in 1968, and spearheaded an annual festival event, Dance Africa, that includes music making, food and crafts sales, dance workshops and performances, and ceremonies for elders in the dance community. Simultaneous with the rise of neo-African forms, **stepping** emerged with vigorous followings first in college fraternities and sororities and later in community centers and youth programs, where it was designed to engage concepts of physical discipline, aesthetic expression, and group cooperation. Step routines are part of an entertainment ritual that includes chanting, singing, speaking, dancing, and a synchronized group dynamic that promotes solidarity and cooperation.

Dance studios helped professionalize social dances by standardizing them, and dance schools often serve as important sites for community gatherings. The affiliated schools of the Philadelphia Dance Company, Lula Washington Dance in Los Angeles, Denver's Cleo Parker Robinson Dance School, the Dallas Black Dance Academy, and Jeraldyne's School of Dance, which is affiliated with the Dayton Contemporary Dance Company, all number among the many professional dance academies that have deeply influenced social life for African Americans through dance study. On the social front, discotheques, which became popular in cities during the 1960s, pushed a range of African American social dances into the mainstream, including the mashed potato, the frug, the swim, the skate, the watusi, and the twist.

Although dances are typically learned body-to-body, by imitation and repetition, technologies of mass distribution, and especially musical recordings and television programs, have quickened the movement of African American social dances from local communities to an international populace. The rise of **hip-hop** and its affiliated movement components, "b-boying," "b-girling," and break dancing, signaled a return to dance as metaphorical communication. Rife with intimations of taunting and boasting, b-boying became a competitive strain that inspired the 2005 television show *Dance 360*, in which dancers competed through highly personal styles with virtuosity, surprise, charismatic presence, and coolness, helping the audience to determine the winner. Dances of the 1980s and 1990s often made reference to technology and to consumer culture, and include the bump, the freak, the rock, the robot, the cabbage patch, the running man, the roger rabbit, and the butt. Now, as never before, African American social dances are transmitted to a mass populace with decreased reference to the social contexts in which they are invented. Dance remains central to African American life, even as its deeper implications of religious, aesthetic, and holistic meaning often go unremarked.

Thomas F. DeFrantz

Further Reading

Abrahams, Roger D., 1992, *Singing the Master: The Emergence of African American Culture in the Plantation South* (New York: Pantheon Books); Amin, Takiyah Nur, 2011, "A Terminology of Difference: Making the Case for Black Dance in the 21st Century and Beyond," *Journal of Pan African Studies* 4 (6): 7–15; Banks, Ojeya Cruz, 2012, "Katherine Dunham: Decolonizing Anthropology Through African American Dance Pedagogy," *Transforming Anthropology* 20 (2): 159–168; DeFrantz, Thomas F., ed., 2002, *Dancing Many Drums: Excavations in African American Dance* (Madison: University of Wisconsin Press); DeFrantz, Thomas, 2004, *Dancing Revelations: Alvin Ailey's Embodiment of African American Culture* (New York: Oxford University Press); DeFrantz, Thomas F., 2011, "Theorizing Connectivities: African American Women in Concert Dance," *Journal of Pan African Studies* 4 (6): 56–74; Emery, Lynne Fauley, 1972, *Black Dance in the United States from 1619 to 1970* (Palo Alto, CA: National Press Books); George-Graves, Nadine, 2010, *Urban Bush Women: Twenty Years of African American Dance Theater, Community Engagement, and Working It Out* (Madison: University of Wisconsin Press); Gittens, Angela Fatou, 2012, "Black Dance and the Fight for Flight: Sabar and the Transformation and Cultural Significance of Dance from West Africa to Black America (1960–2010)," *Journal of Black Studies* 43 (1): 49–71; Glass, Barbara S., 2007, *African American Dance: An Illustrated History* (Jefferson, N.C: McFarland & Co.); Gottschild, Brenda Dixon, 2003, *The Black Dancing Body: A Geography from Coon to Cool* (New York: Palgrave Macmillan); Hazzard-Gordon, Katrina, 1990, *Jookin': The Rise of Social Dance Formations among African-Americans* (Philadelphia: Temple University Press); Malone, Jacqui, 1996, *Stepping on the Blues: The Visible Rhythms of African American Dance* (Urbana: University of Illinois Press); Marcus, Kenneth H., 2014, "Dance Moves: An African American Ballet Company in Postwar Los Angeles." *Pacific Historical Review* 83 (3): 487–527; Phillips, Susan A., 2009, "Crip Walk, Villain Dance, Pueblo Stroll: The Embodiment of Writing in African American Gang Dance," *Anthropological Quarterly* 82 (1): 69; Stearns, Marshall, and Jean Stearns, 1979 [1968], *Jazz Dance: The Story of American Vernacular Dance* (New York: Schirmer Books); Thompson, Katrina Dyonne, 2014, *Ring Shout, Wheel About: The Racial Politics of Music and Dance in North American Slavery* (Urbana: University of Illinois Press); Thompson, Robert Farris, 1966, "Dance and Culture, an Aesthetic of the Cool: West African Dance," *African Forum* 2 (2): 85–102; Winter, Marian Hannah, 1996 [1947], "Juba and American Minstrelsy," in *Inside the Minstrel Mask: Readings in Nineteenth-Century Blackface Minstrelsy*, ed. Annemarie Bean, James V. Hatch, and Brooks McNamara (Hanover, NH: Wesleyan University Press), pp. 223–241.

DEVIL, THE

In African American folklore, the devil is a central figure but one that is viewed with ambivalence. For slaves to accept the devil of white Christianity would have been to accept the demonization of many core elements of their culture—their love of dance and music, for example. Yet rejecting the demonization meant having to serve two gods at the same time, understanding the realm of power in which each one was the master. In African American folklore, the devil is sometimes portrayed in the Christian tradition as evil, as the antihero, or as the antithesis of God and good. At other times he is portrayed more in the African tradition of a trickster, a mischief maker, or an antihero in the positive sense, that is, someone who is outside of the norms of the dominant white society.

The devil in African American folklore has been depicted in a variety of ways, reflecting social influences of different historical periods and the interactions among multiple theologies. In commenting on the devil of slave **spirituals**, Lawrence Levine wrote, "Their songs of the Devil pictured a harsh but almost semi-comic figure (often, one suspects, a surrogate for the white man), over whom they triumphed with reassuring regularity" (Levine, 40). Such stanzas as the following reflect these depictions:

Ole Satan thought he had a mighty aim;
He missed my soul and caught my sins.
He took my sins upon his back;
Went muttering and grumbling down to hell
Old Satan's church is here below.
Up to God's free church I hope to go
Cry Amen, cry Amen, cry Amen to God!

(Levine, 40)

It is clear that in some instances the devil stood for the evils of slavery and colonialism, more specifically, for white slave owners. It is certainly understandable that slaves would draw parallels between the biblical hell and their own condition of servitude. However, the devil also seemed to symbolize the general danger of life in the slave culture and the psychological temptation to give in, to stop fighting for dignity and freedom.

The devil also became associated with African-derived elements of African American culture. The tendency on the part of Europeans and white Americans to demonize Africans often influenced the way in which African Americans related to their own heritage. Reflecting the puritanical impulse in American Christianity, African Americans often associated secular music and activities such as dancing and fiddling with the devil, hence the term "the devil's music." African-derived religious practices, such as **Hoodoo** and **herbalism**, were also sometimes associated with the devil. Lines from a spiritual capture these sentiments: "Old Satan is a liar and a conjurer, too / If you don't mind, he'll **conjure** you" (Levine, 57). This association with conjuring reveals the complexity of the devil motif in African American culture, for conjurers were respected for their powers (which could come either from God or the devil) and valued for the roles that they played in their communities. As such, the connection that some made between conjurers and the devil reflected ideas about supernatural power without necessarily including strict categories of good or bad.

Beliefs about the devil from the slavery period carried over into the postbellum and modern eras. As Levine notes, "In freedom as in slavery, the Devil—over whom blacks generally triumphed in their songs—often looked suspiciously like a sur-rogate for the white man" (Levine, 160). When African Americans sang, "Why doen de debbil let me be?" "What makes Satan hate me so?" or "Ole Satan thought he had me fast / Broke his chain and I'm free at last" (Levine, 160), it is difficult to miss the connections between oppressive, white society and the devil. As Daryl Cumber Dance writes, "The white devil in Black folklore remains the cruel, racist, white Southerner: the harsh slave master, the unfeeling white boss, the brutal, sa-distic white sheriff, the unjust white judge, and the ordinary, all-American, white Christian who visits all manner of persecution onto his Black brother" (Dance, 165). Hence, the initial emphasis by Elijah Mohammed and the Nation of Islam that the white man is the devil was not by any means a new idea in African Ameri-can culture but was instead a new chapter in the life history of a motif that dated back at least to the period of slavery and colonialism.

African-influenced ideologies continued to be mediated through references to the devil in folklore in the 20th century. Jon Michael Spencer, a contemporary scholar of African American music, argues convincingly that a separate theology existed in African American culture alongside that of Christianity. The **mythology** of this other theology was expressed primarily through **blues** music, which can therefore be considered sacred. According to Spencer, the devil of blues theology is linked to the African **trickster** deity, Legba. Folklorist Melville Herskovits argued similarly for a different concept of the devil among African-derived people in the United States. Herskovits writes:

> That this Devil is far from the fallen angel of European dogma, the avenger who pre-sides over the terrors of hell and holds the souls of the damned to their penalties, is apparent. So different is this tricksterlike creature from Satan as generally conceived, indeed, that his is almost a different being. To account for the difference, therefore, we turn again to that character in Dahomean-Yoruba mythology, the divine trickster and the god of accident known as "Legba." It is of some importance to note that, in West Africa, this deity is identified with the Devil by missionaries. (Spencer, 32–33)

In this form, the devil plays a central role in blues mythology. He is beseeched for "the acquisition of magical powers, specifically musical talent" (Spencer, 33). The devil also becomes an ideological mechanism through which members of the blues congregation can move beyond simplistic dichotomies of good and bad (which often operate as signifiers of race), and embrace a more holistic sense of self. The blues self, then, is able to incorporate and integrate cultural and psycho-logical elements often opposed in the rhetoric and practice of the dominant society, and even those within African American culture. The devil in the blues context also functions as a trickster figure who facilitates a mediation of racial and gen-dered conflicts. Spencer writes that the devil in blues

> was not so much unequivocally evil as he was highly unpredictable. He was, for in-stance, the no-good city slicker of Clara Smith's "Done Sold My Soul, Sold it to the Devil." She took him up on his offer to make her happy and he gave her a lot of gold, but then, sang Smith, he would not leave her be. Thus the trickster-like "devil" of African American lore of the old South (and country blues) was often portrayed as a

conjurer; the trickster-like "devil" in the new North (and in city blues) was often portrayed as a pimp. (Spencer, 33)

The urbanized devil mentioned here is also encountered in "**bad man**" narratives such as songs or **toasts** (another tradition associated with life outside of the church and often connected to **pimp** subculture). In some versions of the "**Stagolee**" story, for example, Stagolee is executed for killing Billy the Lyons and ends up going to hell. He is so bad, though, that even the devil feels threatened by his rebellious nature and forces Stagolee to leave.

The devil in African American culture has historically encompassed very Christian ideas of an evil force or personality. He tempts people to commit sins that ultimately lead to their being cast into hell. Yet his nature tends to be more multidimensional. The devil has also been seen both as a symbol for white society and a trickster figure who negotiates different realms of power.

Anand Prahlad

See also: Biblical Characters; Church, The Black; Conjure

Further Reading

Dance, Daryl C., ed., 1978, *Shuckin' and Jivin': Folklore from Contemporary Black Americans* (Bloomington: Indiana University Press); Lawless, Elaine J., 2013, "What Zora Knew: A Crossroads, a Bargain with the Devil, and a Late Witness," *The Journal of American Folklore* 126 (500): 152–173; Levine, Lawrence W., 1977, *Black Culture and Black Consciousness: Afro-American Folk Thought from Slavery to Freedom* (Oxford and New York: Oxford University Press); Pinn, Anthony B., 2010, *Understanding & Transforming the Black Church* (Eugene, Or: Cascade Books); Raboteau, Albert J., 1978, *Slave Religion: The "Invisible Institution" in the Antebellum South* (New York: Oxford University Press); Spencer, Jon Michael, 1993, *Blues and Evil* (Knoxville: University of Tennessee Press).

DICY, AUNT

Aunt Dicy was a figure created by African Americans, for African Americans, in the oral literature tradition. It was not until the late 1800s that folklorists such as William Wells Brown and J. Mason Brewer documented this rich heritage. Like the **trickster** figures **Brer Rabbit** and John, otherwise known as **John the Conqueror**, Aunt Dicy outsmarts other characters. Most of her tales include humor and reflect the life and experiences of the African Americans who created her. Aunt Dicy emerges as an independent and intelligent woman. She is also notorious for her snuff-dipping habit, and the majority of her stories revolve around this vice. This is also what makes her so human and endearing. Furthermore, Aunt Dicy tales provide a glimpse of life after the slavery era. They also reflect issues, persons, and traditions that are significant to African Americans.

Aunt Dicy shares many traits of most trickster figures in African American **folktales**. Aunt Dicy becomes a **legend** in her own right when her neighbors name their town in her honor in "Aunt Dicy and the Mailman." In this story, Aunt Dicy, her husband, and their three children move to a Texas town after slavery ends.

When she gives the mailman ten cents every week to buy her a dime box of snuff, the neighbors name their new community Dime Box. Aunt Dicy can outwit anyone, as illustrated in various stories. In "Aunt Dicy and the Snuff Salesman," Aunt Dicy outsmarts the salesman when she, blindfolded, distinguishes between her favorite snuff and an imitation brand. She subsequently wins five jars of snuff. In "Aunt Dicy in the Courtroom," Aunt Dicy prepays a fine for spitting her snuff on the floor. In "Aunt Dicy and Rev. Jackson's Sermon," Aunt Dicy challenges the reverend when he rebukes her snuff-dipping habit. She jumps "up from the bench she was sitting on and [yells], 'Look ahere, Reverend, you've done stopped preaching and gone to meddling!'" (Spalding, 121).

Aunt Dicy tales reflect the real-life figures, locations, traditions, and experiences of African Americans after the era of slavery. Prominent African American figures of her time are integrated in these tales, including Booker T. Washington. Many Texans, even today, can recognize what is now Prairie View A&M University, which Aunt Dicy's two daughters attended. Also familiar to African American traditions is the pomp in which Aunt Dicy's husband enjoys carrying his family to church and public meetings. Aunt Dicy tales also address pertinent issues, such as the shame and frustration young educated African American youth felt concerning their past. Aunt Dicy's college-educated daughters "look down on their community Dime Box" (Spalding, 123). At one point, they decide not to celebrate **Juneteenth**, to Aunt Dicy's disappointment (Spalding, 123). Nevertheless, Aunt Dicy does not say anything to her daughters or do anything to remedy the situation until they begin complaining about her snuff-dipping. Then, "with hands akimbo on her hips," Aunt Dicy destroys the family's will and announces, "Now I'll spit where I please!" (Spalding, 123).

Gladys L. Knight

Further Reading

Brewer, J. Mason, ed., 1968, *American Negro Folklore* (Chicago: Quadrangle Books); Brewer, J. Mason, ed., 1956, *Aunt Dicy Tales: Snuff-Dipping Tales of the Texas Negro* (Austin, TX); Harris, Trudier, 2009, "The Yellow Rose of Texas: A Different Cultural View," *Callaloo* 32 (2): 529–539; Spalding, Henry D., ed., 1972, *Encyclopedia of Black Folklore and Humor* (Middle Village, NY: Jonathan David Publishers); Untiedt, Kenneth L., 2009, *Celebrating 100 Years of the Texas Folklore Society, 1909–2009* (Denton: University of North Texas Press).

DOUBLE DUTCH

Jumping double dutch is an activity wherein one jumps through two alternating ropes turning at the same time. More complex than one person using one rope to skip, jumping double dutch requires two rope turners and can have multiple rope jumpers hopping up and down in the same space at the same time. Although a popular activity in many cultures, in the United States double dutch jumping has been especially associated with the growing-up experiences of African American girls. Segregated black schools often had very few resources to equip their playgrounds, and jumping double dutch required only two ropes. When ropes were not handy, clotheslines could be substituted.

Jumping double dutch is often accompanied by the recitation of folk rhymes. Jumpers measure their skills by how well they recite and jump in and out of the ropes at the same time. The folk rhymes and songs tell the jumper what action to take. Several of the jumping games ask a question that can be answered numerically. How many times the jumper can jump without getting her feet entangled in the ropes becomes the answer to the posed question. These questions often deal with coming-of-age predictions: How many babies will I have? How many years before I marry? How many boyfriends do I have?

Persons turning the ropes are as important as those doing the jumping. Those who cannot turn the ropes properly are referred to as "double-handed." Advanced jumpers are able to do gymnastic feats while jumping, such as picking up an item before landing back on the ground, doing a jumping jack, doing a cartwheel, turning all the way around, and jumping side by side with a partner. Double dutch teams compete in national competitions.

Given its identification with African American girls' experiences, double dutch has been proposed as a metaphor for understanding the multilayered, interdisciplinary field of African American women's studies. In *Granny Midwives and Black Women Writers: Double-Dutched Readings*, the author explains how one can understand the simultaneous interplay of dual cultural performances through a methodology of reading double dutch: "Two sets of meanings interacting with each other . . . mov[ing] easily between two performances, much like young black girls do when jumping double dutch. . . . The greater sophistication and creativity demanded by jumping and reading double-dutch result in a more integrated performance" (Lee, 3).

Valerie Lee

See also: Games, Folk; Jump Rope Rhymes/Games

Further Reading

Gaunt, Kyra Danielle, 2006, *The Games Black Girls Play: Learning the Ropes from Double-Dutch to Hip-Hop* (New York: New York University Press); Lee, Valerie, 1996, *Granny Midwives and Black Women Writers: Double-Dutched Readings* (New York: Routledge).

DOZENS, THE

The dozens is a game of ritual insult that is played most often by African American males, though females are also quite adept at exhibiting their verbal skills in this activity. The game's insults usually target a victim's relative, especially one's mother. Showing off one's verbal skills is one of the genre's most salient features. The verbal exchange goes by several names, depending on the part of the country in which the participants live. In Chicago it is sometimes called "sigging" or "**signifying**," and in Washington, D.C., it is referred to as "joning." Philadelphia adolescents may call it "woofing"; on the West Coast, the common term is "capping." Young Jacksonville, Florida, black people refer to it as "ranking." Another variation on the term is "sounding," but sounding often refers more specifically to the initial act of insulting another (i.e., "sounding" on somebody). No matter what it's called, there are features of this activity that have attracted a number of scholars of African American speech play and verbal art, and they have offered interesting interpretations about the functions this type of verbal dueling tends to have among participants.

The term "dozens" may have originated from the slavery era, when a "dirty dozen" of the most undesirable-looking black captives surviving the trans-Atlantic crossing were sold on the auction block at a discount. Says Quincy Jones in his foreword to *Snaps*, "The only thing even more degrading than slavery was to be part of this group. Insulting your mama was meant to make you feel as low as one of the dirty dozens" (Percelay, Ivey, and Dweck, 1994, 8). Another explanation for the term "the dozens" relates to the slinging of a dozen insults from each of the contestants. Roger D. Abrahams cites other possible sources that suggest the term "the dozens" may have originated in reference to the misfortune of rolling a 12 in craps; he also cites Mack McCormick, in the liner notes "to his record *Unexpurgated Folk Songs of Men* [who] gives the most compelling source, a formulaic song routine about the subject which began 'I f*cked your mother one, . . .' going up to twelve" (Abrahams, 261).

This explanation concerning the mother as a target has African antecedents, and ethnographic data bear witness to the prevalence of an affinity that Igbo (Ibo) boys have toward hurling insults about one's mother. To reach manhood, a male must break his ties from his mother's protection, increasingly detaching himself from hearth and home as he prepares to enter the unpredictable world of men. Similarly, the Ashanti enjoy such verbal dueling, and others have reported that it is part of an initiation ceremony among adolescent males who target one another's mother in pornographic terms. Besides targeting a person's close relative, the dozens requires an audience for the verbal dueling to succeed, and listeners do not hesitate to join in the fun by either praising an especially creative "snap" (as a one-liner is sometimes called in the United States) or ridiculing a lame response to an initial insult.

There is a definite pattern that marks the ritual, one that New York City adolescents displayed to William Labov. He succinctly outlined the pattern in an article that appeared in *Rappin and Stylin' Out*, edited by Thomas Kochman in 1972. Labov summed up a general rule for ritual "sounding" in the following formula: T(B) is so X that P, where T is the target of the sound, X is the attribute of T which is focused on, and P is a proposition that is coupled by the quantifier "so . . . that" to express the degree to which T has X. The target T(B) is normally B's mother or other relative.

Labov then provides examples, such as "Your mother [T(B)] so old [X] she fart dust [P]" (Labov, 299–300). (Note that, as in nearly all African American oral traditions, black dialect is an important feature of the dozens. Accordingly, verbs are either missing or, like many nouns, do not require plurality.) Most sounds, then, follow this T(B) is so X that P model, but a sounding situation also requires an audience, which Labov designates as "C" in the following rule:

> If A makes an utterance S in the presence of B and an audience C, which includes reference to a target related to B, T(B), in a proposition P, and (a) B believes that A

believes that P is not true and (b) B believes that A believes that B knows that P is not true . . . then S is a *sound*, heard as *T(B) is so X that P* where X is a pejorative attribute, and A is said to have *sounded* on B. (Labov, 302, italics in original)

In other words, if Sam says to Joe, "Your mother is so old she fart dust," in the presence of an audience, and everyone understands that the statement is not true, then Sam is "sounding" on Joe. The audience's role is essential. The initial sounding situation is a remark that A makes in a loud voice so that others can hear, and everyone present interprets it as a ritual insult and knows that the proposition P is not true. The original sound is usually followed by a similar response, for example, Joe might say, "Your mother so old she got spider webs under her arms." The exchanges go back and forth, with each contestant trying to outdo the other. If either contestant loses his temper, then the ritual ends, and audience members will proclaim the other the winner.

However, young African American children may not always understand the rules for ritual insults and do not take the exchanges as a game, and second and third graders may even feel compelled to tell the teacher on their classmates. When considering the themes that the dozens often include, it is not difficult to understand such a misunderstanding among young children.

Some major themes of the dozens, those Labov might call attributes in the above model, include: poverty ("Your mother is so poor, I saw her on the street selling loose M&Ms" [Percelay et al., 1994, 133]), ugliness ("Your mother is so ugly, police artists are afraid to sketch her" [Percelay et al., 1995, 73]), stupidity ("Your mother's so stupid that she can't walk and chew gum at the same time" [Jemie, 181]), sexual promiscuity ("Your mother and father were so happy when you were born that they ran out and got married" [Jemie, 182]), and many others that appear in such recent collections as Onwuchekwa Jemie's *"Yo' Mama!": New Raps, Toasts, Dozens, Jokes & Children's Rhymes from Urban Black America* (2003), and James Percelay, Stephen Dweck, and Monteria Ivey's *Snaps* (1994) and its sequel *Double Snaps* (1995). The latter two volumes also include a brief history of the dozens, but, unlike Labov's earlier discourse analysis of the dozens, they devote their collections to one-liners with no contexts in which they are performed. However, they do provide a sense of the general social setting in which snaps are typically performed, and the authors offer several quotes from popular comedians who grew up playing the dozens.

Jemie's collection includes many snaps that he and his students collected from 1969 to 1973, so they may seem a bit dated, but his introduction provides an insight into the function of the dozens in light of some of the earliest scholarship on this type of verbal art. John Dollard argued that the dozens exist as a result of race relations and displaced aggressions among African Americans, while Abrahams viewed them as a reflection of tensions emerging from the black family structure, from which eventually "black males find themselves in a totally male environment in which the necessity to prove one's masculinity [and to reject the feminine principle] recurs constantly" (Dundes, 54). Because the young boy cannot openly attack his own mother either to himself or to others, he creates a play situation which enables him to attack some other person's mother, thereby exorcising his mother's influence (Dundes, 55).

By playing the dozens, the combatants not only develop defense mechanisms but also build up their self-images and affirm their masculinity. Building on his predecessors, Jemie explains why such disrespect is shown the mother in the dozens, suggesting that, while a mother's intimacy is a child's source of comfort, a boy eventually must disengage himself from that embrace. Jemie compares this African worldview with that of the African American male, who must "achieve *detachment* of a higher, deeper, tougher quality than his cousin in the homeland, or his counterparts elsewhere in the world," particularly given the abuse black males suffered in this country and their subsequent inability to protect family members (Jemie, 25–27, italics in original).

In short, the dozens introduces a boy to manhood and the ability to deal with verbal abuse. Despite these compelling arguments and observations, such explanations do not provide an explanation for how the dozens might function among females. Nevertheless, Dollard, Abrahams, Jemie, and the references that follow demonstrate the significance of the dozens and related African American folklore forms (e.g., **toasts**) as part of a vibrant part of traditional black culture. And, as Wald demonstrates, the lasting legacies of the dozens are evident throughout American popular culture, for example, in lyrics and performance styles of **rap** and **hip-hop**, and in spoken word poetry.

Richard Allen Burns

Further Reading

Abrahams, Roger, 1970 [1963], *Deep Down in the Jungle: Negro Narrative Folklore from the Streets of Philadelphia* (Chicago: Aldine Publishing Company); Dundes, Alan, ed., 1990 [1973], *Mother Wit from the Laughing Barrel: Readings in the Interpretation of Afro-American Folklore* (Jackson: University Press of Mississippi); Jackson, Bruce, 1974, *"Get Your Ass in the Water and Swim Like Me": Narrative Poetry from Black Oral Tradition* (Cambridge, MA: Harvard University Press); Jemie, Onwuchekwa, ed., 2003, *"Yo' Mama!": New Raps, Toasts, Dozens, Jokes & Children's Rhymes from Urban Black America* (Philadelphia: Temple University Press); Kochman, Thomas, 1970, "Toward an Ethnography of Black American Speech Behavior," in *Afro-American Anthropology: Contemporary Perspectives*, ed. Norman E. Whitten Jr. and John F. Szwed (New York: The Free Press), pp. 145–162; Labov, William, 1972, "Rules for Ritual Insult," in *Rappin' and Stylin' Out: Communication in Urban Black America*, ed. Thomas Kochman (Chicago: University of Illinois Press), pp. 265–314; Levine, Lawrence, 1980 [1977], *Black Culture and Black Consciousness: Afro-American Folk Thought from Slavery to Freedom* (Oxford and New York: Oxford University Press); Majors, Richard, and Janet Mancini Billson, 1992, "Playing the Dozens," in *Cool Pose: The Dilemmas of Black Manhood in America* (New York: Lexington Books), pp. 91–102; Percelay, James, Monteria Ivey, and Stephen Dweck, 1995, *Double Snaps* (New York: William Morrow); Percelay, James, Monteria Ivey, and Stephen Dweck, 1994, *Snaps: "If Ugliness Were Bricks, Your Mother Would Be a Housing Project" . . . and More Than 450 Other Snaps, Caps, and Insults for Playing the Dozens* (New York: William Morrow); Wald, Elijah, 2012, *The Dozens: A History of Rap's Mama* (New York: Oxford University Press); Wepman, Dennis, Ronald B.

Newman, and Murray B. Binderman, 1976, *The Life: The Lore and Folk Poetry of the Black Hustler* (Philadelphia: University of Pennsylvania Press); Wald, Elijah, 2014, *Talking 'bout Your Mama: The Dozens, Snaps, and the Deep Roots of Rap* (New York: Oxford University Press).

DRYLONGSO

This African American vernacular term means ordinary, customary, plain, or everyday. "Drylongso" is a term adopted from the **Gullah** dialect. Often it has the particular meaning of something previously rare becoming commonplace. It may have originally referred to extended periods of drought that went on so long as to appear ordinary. The land was "dry so long" that it became an everyday reality. A sense of endurance before the forces of nature came to be associated with the term.

"Drylongso" is a compelling example of the linguistic variety to be found among the Gullah people. They reside in the islands off the coasts of South Carolina and Georgia. Geographically isolated, the Gullah people have maintained stronger African cultural retentions than other black communities in the American **South**. This includes a distinctive dialect. Lorenzo Dow Turner, the father of African American linguists, offered the first formal research of the Gullah people and their language in his landmark 1949 study, *Africanisms in the Gullah Dialect*.

"Drylongso" has since been employed as a folk idiom outside of its etymological roots in a range of contexts within the arts and the academy. In 1980 folklorist and anthropologist John Langston Gwaltney published his prizewinning work *Drylongso: A Self-Portrait of Black America*. The book reflects the essence of the term by presenting an oral history of black American culture as told by those who constitute it—the "core black people" living it every day. Gwaltney calls attention to the insight and value in "common" perspectives on culture. It is now a recognized classic in African American studies.

Adam Bradley

Further Reading

Gwaltney, John Langston, 1980, *Drylongso: A Self-Portrait of Black America* (New York: Random House); Hamilton, Virginia, 1992, "Hagi, Mose, and Drylongso," in *The Zena Sutherland Lectures*, 1983–1991, ed. Betsy Hearne (New York: Clarion), pp. 75–91.

E

ELECTION DAY

Election Day was a social and political gathering of African Americans that occurred during the 18th and early 19th centuries, when New England slaves and free blacks assembled for a four-day holiday. Slave masters gathered on this day in major cities to witness their governor's inauguration (General Election Day) or to watch Training Day, a ceremonial drill conducted on parade grounds. Many brought their slaves with them, and the slaves took advantage of the opportunity to gather en masse. These gatherings, held in open, public spaces, began roughly in the mid-18th century and occurred throughout the New England colonies on the dates corresponding with each colony's own Election Day, generally during May and June. The number of slaves and freedmen and women who took part was significant: one source observed that they "swarmed over the Common" (Greene, 248).

At such gatherings, the collected multitude would elect their own kings, governors, and other officials, and then hold an inauguration celebration. According to custom, the defeated candidate "drank the first toast to his successful opponent. In the conviviality of the inaugural banquet all animosities were forgotten" (Greene, 250–251). Scholars of an earlier era tended to attribute African American Election Day to a desire among slaves to mimic the electoral behavior of their superior owners. More thorough research and interpretation indicates that there was a blending of European American and African cultural practices at such events.

These meetings provided a valuable opportunity for persons of African descent, both free and enslaved, to share stories about **Africa**, regale one another with **folktales**, produce music communally (especially with fiddles or **banjos**), and **dance** together. The talent of these musicians was such that "numerous advertisements called attention" to their performances. The opportunity to sing, play music, and dance using African and African-inspired rhythms was not wasted: a book surveying colonial homes of Darien, Connecticut reported that such dances were so frequent at the town's Middlesex Inn that "in one room of the house the heavy hardwood floor is now thin in places from the movement of the merry dancers" (Greene, 249, 251). In Newport, Rhode Island, one observer commented that "all the various languages of Africa, mixed with broken and ludicrous English, filled the air accompanied with the music of the fiddle, tambourine, the banjo, drum, etc." (Wade, 176).

Like other public gatherings, Election Day allowed slaves and freedmen and women to recall their ethnic heritage while they created a new African American identity. Scholars have indicated that Negro Election Day ceremonies have a distinct Fanti and Ashanti influence (Wade, 174–176). Slaves from those backgrounds would have especially enjoyed the celebrations, but the fusion of cultures and the apparent openness of the festivities would have allowed all persons of African descent access and would have fostered the creation of a sense of African American communality.

Much like **Pinkster** in the North and **Christmas** celebrations in the **South**, the African and African American participants used this opportunity to be free in ways that they could not under the usual practices of slavery. At Election Day, one expression of this freedom was their attire: dressing in castoffs from their masters, including even pomaded wigs, the participants arrived in style. On occasion a master might lend his horse or even his carriage to facilitate his slave's (or slaves') grand entrance (Greene, 250).

The representatives elected by the black populace had clearly earned their position as respected leaders in the black community. Many, including Guy Watson, Peleg Nott, Tobiah, and his son Eben Tobias, served during the American Revolution. Their respect within the black community most likely came from another position of leadership, however. Numerous kings or governors, including Tobiah and Eben Tobias, were descended from African royalty. Many others could trace their African heritage back several generations. Melvin Wade concludes that at least 16 of the 31 kings and governors came from a well-defined African lineage (Greene, 252; Wade, 174–175). This connection would have been especially powerful to Ashanti-descended slaves and freedmen and women, because the Ashanti chief was both the "civil ruler who is the axis of the political relations of his people" and "the symbol of their identity and continuity as a tribe and the embodiment of their spiritual values" (Wade, 175).

Like most public events that allowed the mixture of slaves and free individuals, the mixture of black and white, the recollection of Africa, and the empowerment of the slave, Negro Election Day came under attack from whites in power. Some complained that such public festivities invited vice, others pointed to the availability of alcohol, and some worried that lower-class whites enjoyed too much freedom on such occasions. The majority, however, recognized the danger in allowing persons of African descent this opportunity to create a shared sense of identity and a shared desire to resist slavery, and these gatherings were gradually legislated out of existence.

Jennifer Hildebrand

See also: Congo Square; Festivals

Further Reading

Fabre, Genevieve, 2001, "Negro Election Celebrations as Political and Intellectual Resistance in New England, 1740–1850," in *Celebrating Ethnicity and Nation*, ed. Jurgen Heideking Fabre and Kai Dreisbach (New York: Berghahn Books); Gay, Kathlyn, 2007, *African-American Holidays, Festivals, and Celebrations: The History, Customs, and Symbols Associated with Both Traditional and Contemporary Religious and Secular Events Observed by Americans of African Descent* (Detroit, MI: Omnigraphics); Greene, Lorenzo, 1942, *The Negro in Colonial New England, 1620–1776* (New York: Columbia University Press); Miller, Monica L., 2009, *Slaves to Fashion: Black Dandyism and the Styling of Black*

Diasporic Identity (Durham, NC: Duke University Press); Stuckey, Sterling, 2013, *Slave Culture: Nationalist Theory and the Foundations of Black America.* 25th anniversary ed. (New York: Oxford University Press); Wade, Melvin, 1988, "'Shining in Borrowed Plumage': Affirmation of Community in the Black Coronation Festivals of New England, ca. 1750–1850," in *Material Life in America, 1600–1860*, ed. Robert Blair St. George (Boston: Northeastern University Press).

F

FABLES

Fables are usually defined as animal tales with a moral, although many fables contain human characters. Fables are a subgenre of **folktales**. The most essential element of fables is the moral or lesson, which usually comes at the end and is often in the form of a proverb. Perhaps the most widely known fables in the Western world are from Aesop (ca. 600 BC), the legendary Greek writer and collector of these tales. Fables often share aesthetic qualities with the genre of parables, which are generally associated with spiritual teachings. In both cases, there is a lesson being taught through the symbols of the story, something to be taken seriously and pondered. In the case of fables, though, there is a lighthearted quality about the lessons.

Fables in Africa

The fable is part of the folktale, which is the most common genre in African traditional literature, verbal arts, and folklore, and most African societies have had strong traditions of fables. It is essential to point out that in African societies the folktale has a highly performative, multidimensional aspect and is composed of narration, songs, drums, hand clapping, foot thumping, and so forth. The underlying mode of the folktale is **storytelling**. As a rule, fables are told only at night because it is a time when people do not work, but also, with the onset of darkness, easy associations can be made with the spirits, the ancestors, and the animal world. The themes are numerous and the roles are distributed according to age, status in society, and gender.

The **trickster** tale is a favorite in African societies, in part because it involves animals. Animals are invoked to point to human failings and to satirize and mock bad behavior. There is always a moral in trickster tales, and they are used as devices to encourage listeners to mend their behaviors as well as to bring about changes in societies. One aim of the fable is to discourage selfishness and encourage solidarity and community spirit.

In West Africa, the hare and the spider are well-known protagonists of the trickster fables. The hare is very famous in Senegal and the Senegalese author Birago Diop has translated Wolof tales into French, a collection known as *Tales of Amadou Koumba* (1947). The hare is also a major and recurring motif in New World African folklore and there are versions of tales featuring the hare in Haiti and other parts of the diaspora. In African versions, the hare's chief rival is the hyena, although this identity changes in different parts of the diaspora. In fables involving the hare, the moral is usually that cunning is always victorious over force. In one of Diop's stories, for example, an orphan girl is sent with her stepsister by her mean stepmother to get water from the sea far away. In the process, the girl overcomes all the hurdles and finds happiness at the end. The stepmother's own daughter, however, finds only misfortune on her way because she is spoiled by her mother. The moral is that when one does good, one reaps good, and that when one does bad, one reaps bad. Anancy the spider is another popular figure in African fables who was transplanted from West Africa to Jamaica, Trinidad, and other parts of the diaspora during the transatlantic slave trade.

Fables in the Americas

Although the form of the fable in which it ends in a **proverb** or a moral is not found frequently throughout the diaspora, it has been noted in certain regions, for example the coastal area of Georgia. In the tale "The Dying Bullfrog," the bullfrog gathers his friends and asks, "Who is going to take my wife when the breath leaves this here body?" Many voices yell "Me, Me!" But when the bullfrog asks who will be willing to take care of his children, the crowd is silent. The tale ends with, "A heap of people are willing to notice a pretty young widow, but they don't want to bother themselves with another man's children" (Courlander, 487). In "Buh Lion and Buh Goat," Buh Lion comes across Buh Goat lying on a big rock, chewing. He is puzzled about what Buh Goat is chewing and comes closer and closer to try to figure it out. Eventually he asks Buh Goat, and Buh Goat is frightened, but keeps his composure. He responds, "I'm chewing on this rock, and if you don't get out of here, when I'm through I'm going to eat you." Frightened, Buh Lion leaves. The story ends with the moral, "A bold man gets out of his difficulties, a coward loses his life" (Courlander, 491). Other examples include "Buh Fox Says Grace," which ends with, "The best thing for a man is to make sure of his vittles before he says thank you for them," and "Buh Turkey Buzzard and the Rain," which has as its proverbial lesson, "A careless man is just like Buh Turkey Buzzard" (Courlander, 490–491).

Versions of **Brer Rabbit** (Buh Rabbit) tales told as fables have also been collected. A version of "Buh Fox's Number Nine Shoes" collected by Harold Courlander in the 1950s is a good illustration. The tale begins with the narrator's elaboration on why Buh Rabbit is such a successful trickster; it is because he never does the same trick twice. From there it moves to Buh Rabbit being cornered in a log by Buh Fox (**Brer Fox**), and offering to help Fox trick Buh Bear out of his daily catch of fish if Fox will let Rabbit go. Buh Fox agrees and Buh Rabbit leaves one of his shoes in the road as Buh Bear is coming along with his fish. Buh Bear notices the shoe but keeps going. Buh Rabbit then runs ahead and leaves his other shoe in the road. When Buh Bear sees the second one, he sets his fish down and goes back to get the first shoe. Buh Rabbit takes the fish and divides them with Buh Fox. The next day Buh Fox attempts the same trick, but Buh Bear doesn't fall for it this time—he picks up the shoes but doesn't set down the fish. Shoeless, Buh Fox approaches Buh Bear to ask for his shoes and gets a severe beating instead. The narrator ends with, "Like I said before, the moral is—it don't do you no good to learn the right trick at the wrong time" (Courlander, 494). Other Brer Rabbit tales told as fables have also been collected in the southern United States, and fables are not uncommon in areas of the Caribbean, for example in Jamaican storytelling traditions, where characters like Anancy are often central protagonists.

The decline in popularity of fables is related to social changes that make the telling of tales in general less a part of the everyday lives of African Americans. However, the fable is still one type of tale found in contemporary traditions. At times, the convention of a moralizing ending emerges as a part of other narrative traditions, which raises the question of whether some of the functions served by fables are now being served by other genres. For instance, **toasts** occasionally end with moralistic or prescriptive advice. "The Sporting Life" reflects on the pitfalls of the **pimp** lifestyle, almost in a mentoring vein, and ends with "Just bear in mind that you must do time / When-ever you pull a bone / So don't cry in terror when you make an error / Just do your bid and go home" (Wepman, Newman, and Binderman, 68–70). Most often, however, although toasts may offer implicit suggestions for behavior, through the exploits of characters such as Monkey and Lion, they do not end with explicit moralizing statements. Prescriptive endings can also be found in song traditions, such as **blues**, reggae, **gospel**, **rap**, and calypso. Missing from these modern contexts, however, are the dramatic scenarios involving animal characters for which the fable is most commonly known.

Samba Diop

Further Reading

Bojang, Sukai Mbye, 2013, *Folk Tales and Fables from the Gambia.* Volume 3 (Banju, GMB: Educational Services); Courlander, Harold, ed., 1976, *A Treasury of Afro-American Folklore* (New York: Crown Publishers); Dance, Daryl C., ed., 2002, *From My People: 400 Years of African American Folklore* (New York: W. W. Norton); Diop, Birago, ed., 1966, *Tales of Amadou Koumba* (French), trans. by Dorothy S. Blair (London: Oxford University Press); Dorson, Richard, ed., 1967, *American Negro Folktales* (Greenwich, CT: Fawcett Publications, Inc.); Green, Thomas A., 2009, *African American Folktales* (Westport, CT: Greenwood Press); Hurston, Zora Neale, 1995, *Folklore, Memoirs, and Other Writings* (New York: Library of America); Jarmon, Laura C., *Wishbone: Reference and Interpretation in Black Folk Narratives* (Knoxville: University of Tennessee Press); Offodile, Buchi, ed., 2001, *The Orphan Girl and Other Stories: West African Folk Tales* (New York: Interlink Books); Yenika-Agbaw, Vivian S., Ruth McKoy Lowery, and Laretta Henderson, 2013, *Fairy Tales with a Black Consciousness: Essays on Adaptations of Familiar Stories* (Jefferson, NC: McFarland & Company).

FAMILY REUNIONS

This term refers to annual and semiannual gatherings of consanguineous and conjugal kin. Although family reunions are common among many cultural and ethnic groups in the United States, for African Americans these celebrations play an important role in establishing family and cultural identity and preserving family history. African American family reunions typically involve two or three family names, usually the names of an ancestor and his or her spouse, and the kinship connections among the participants are much looser than those of their European American counterparts (or even nonexistent). The inclusiveness of such reunions reflects the history of African American family structure and the definition of family, with a core family consisting not only of parents (or one parent) and children, but grandparents and aunts and uncles as well as family friends. Although the development of this definition of family can be traced to West African traditions of family organization, the modern African American definition of family is the result of the legacy of slavery and later the mass migration of southern African Americans to the North. Within this expanded notion of family, African American reunions serve to celebrate family and ancestral connections. These reunions are a vital part of the survival of African American traditions and the family histories of individual African American kin groups and are seen by the reunion participants as an extremely significant part of their lives, their histories, and their identities.

African American family reunions—both formal and structured, and informal, unstructured get-togethers—have existed possibly as far back as emancipation. The popularity of reunions expanded in the late 1970s to mid-1980s. Several factors account for this blossoming of reunions, not the least of which was the popularity of the book and miniseries *Roots* and the national interest in genealogy it spawned. This growing interest in reconnecting family ties was spurred on by an initiative put forth by the National Council of Negro Women, who in 1986 launched the Black Family Reunion Celebrations in response to negative projections of African American families in mainstream media, and as means of promoting the positive educational and cultural values the Council associated with the African American family and its history. In the 1990s and through the turn of the 21st century, reunions have grown in size and popularity, often to the point where they resemble business conventions.

Types of reunions range from fish fries and **barbecues** at a family member's home or at a family homesite, to more formal gatherings at extravagant hotels. The responsibility for organizing and planning these events can vary from a group of siblings or cousins who gather informally as an ad hoc planning committee, to the establishment of formal organizations complete with bylaws and officers. However, most African American reunions typically follow the same pattern: a three-day format centered around a series of meals. While these meals may be typical banquet fare, reunion organizers often include traditional family dishes in at least one of the meals. Often reunion events include religious services, family contests and competitions, amateur family or professional entertainment, and ceremonies designed to honor ancestors and the recently deceased. Most reunions are held in the summer months; Labor Day weekend and weekends near the Fourth of July are the most common reunion dates. Although many reunions are held at a rural family homesite (particularly one associated with a family's matriarch or patriarch), others are held at amusement parks or near large cities where shopping, air travel, and other modern conveniences are more easily accessible. Regardless of where they are held, these family celebrations serve to keep family history alive and family members in touch.

A key component of African American family reunions is the commemoration of ancestors and the retelling of the family's history. The reunions serve to tell the family story, not only through narratives but also through family memorabilia, photographs, songs, food traditions, and worship services. The participants, the context, and the narrative event are all part of the performance created to bind the family together and remind its members of who they are. African American family reunions function as sites where both the family's story and its identity are made and remade as its members reconnect with one another over food, formal events, and informal fellowship.

Stephen Criswell

Further Reading

Ayoub, Millicent R., 1966, "The Family Reunion," *Ethnology: An International Journal of Cultural and Social Anthropology* 5 (4): 415–433; Chadiha, Letha A., Julie Miller-Cribbs, Jane Rafferty, Portia Adams, Robert Pierce, and Swapna Kommidi, 2012, "Urban and Rural African American Female Caregivers' Family Reunion Participation." *Marriage and Family Review* 37 (1–2): 129–146; Criswell, Stephen, 2003, "'You've Got Family Here': Family Reunions in Lower Alabama," *Tributaries: Journal of the Alabama Folklife Association* 1 (6):17–33; McCoy, Renee, 2011, "African American Elders, Cultural Traditions, and the Family Reunion," *Generations* 35 (3): 16–21.

FESTIVALS

Festivals are recurring celebrations that hold special significance for a particular group. They are found among people across the globe, and usually mark special occasions such as rites of passage, birthdays or deaths, or historical events. A distinguishing feature of festivals is that they consist of many genres, such as music, **dance**, **games**, narrative traditions, dress and costuming, rituals, and so on. In his discussion of festivals, Robert Smith lists several categories, including seasonal festivals (usually held in spring, midsummer, and midwinter), Christian calendar festivals, and limited participation festivals (celebrations limited to small groups, such as occupational groups or clubs, family festivals, weddings, conventions, **funerals**, barn raisings, rodeos, and fairs).

Although the traditional festivals found in African societies differ from those in Europe or the Americas, they can be divided into comparable categories. However, traditional African festivals tend to incorporate religious elements, and so it is more difficult to fit them into just one of these categories. For example, the Yam Festival is held in parts of Ghana and Nigeria in the beginning of August at the end of the rainy season. During the Yam Festival, yams are offered to ancestors and deities as a way of giving thanks. The festival consists of cleansing pots and bowls, music, dancing, and feasting. But the festival is not just seasonal; it is also religious. This is true as well for the Homowo harvest festival, also celebrated in Ghana, in the Accra region. This festival corresponds with the first planting of millet in May by priests. The Adae festival celebrated by the Akan people of Ghana is another illustration, exemplifying the merging of calendar, seasonal, state, and religious elements. As one would expect, since the slavery period, festivals have been an important element of life among people of African heritages in the Americas.

Festivals during the Slavery Period

There is ample evidence that during the slavery period African-style festivals were celebrated in the United States. These festivals occurred primarily in the North, where there was less fear of large groups of black people assembling, and where more positive relationships existed between whites and black leaders. Eileen Jackson Southern writes that "black men in the English colonies found ways to carry on some of their traditional African practices despite the bonds of slavery. Perhaps the most spectacular of these practices occurred in the slave gatherings and festivals that took place throughout the colonial period in northern cities where there were large concentrations of blacks" (Southern, 48). One such festival was **Election Day** ('Lection Day). Although the slave festival paralleled the white celebration of the same name, it was decidedly African when practiced by the slaves in New England cities and towns. Based on descriptions from journals, newspapers, and the like, Election Day, which was celebrated in May or June, was quite similar to the contemporary New Orleans **Mardi Gras**, or to other Carnival traditions throughout the diaspora. It involved a parade with music, singing, elaborate costuming, and dancing, the election of "governers" or "kings," as well as playing games, wrestling, and so on. The **Pinkster** Day festival was another large celebration, held in New York, Pennsylvania, and Maryland. Pinkster Day was derived from the Dutch and British and celebrated for a day by whites, after which blacks took over and celebrated for up to a week. The festival, which drew thousands, was referred to even in the 18th century as "the Carnival of Africans," and included fair-like activities, drumming, and dancing that centered on a costumed African King. Other, smaller-scale festivals were held in other parts of the North, and were often called "jubilees" (Southern, 54–55).

The closest southern parallel to the large-scale festive events of the North were the Sunday slave gatherings in **Congo Square**, or Place Congo, in New Orleans. These weekly gatherings featured up to 600 slaves, who came from several African groups, including the Kongos, Mandringas, Gangas, Hiboas, Fulas, Minahs, and Kraels. Each group was accompanied by its own drummers and other musicians, and the music and dancing lasted until nine o'clock at night. Among others, one common thread among all of these festivals was the practice of people dancing until they would go into trance states and fall to the ground (Southern, 135–137).

Christmas celebrations were probably the most widespread southern festival during slavery in the United States. Christmas celebrations provided an opportunity for slaves to visit family and friends on nearby plantations, to make music, dance, and feast together. Mirroring the practices of the slaveholding culture, African Americans consumed abundant amounts of alcohol, played cards and other games, and shot off firecrackers. There were also antecedents of contemporary Mardi Gras festivals found on some plantations in parts of Louisiana.

Festivals were also an important part of life for slaves in the Caribbean, where Carnival traditions have always been abundant. In most cases, Carnival festivals were brought to the islands by the colonizing nation and quickly adopted and adapted by slaves. For example, Carnival celebrations were brought to Trinidad and Tobago by the French ca. 1785, and were picked up by slaves, later becoming associated with the lower classes. In every instance, African traditions and aesthetics merged with European structures to birth festivals among the black populations, and these celebrations were infused with meanings relevant to the lives and social conditions of black people. The Junkanoo festival of the Bahamas is another celebration involving parades, costuming, and music, dating back at least to the 19th century. Like many others, it takes place during the Christmas season. Another festival of the Christmas/New Year's season is the mumming tradition, practiced in countries such as Saint Kitts, Nevis, Jamaica, and in parts of the United States. Mumming traditions were also brought to the colonies by Europeans, the British in this case. Key elements of mumming celebrations include the performances of plays, songs, dances, and comic routines, and masking and costuming.

Smaller-scale festive events were also practiced in the slavery era. These included weddings, which were more elaborate in some locales than in others. For instance, the wedding traditions of Carriacou were much more involved than the simpler customs of **jumping the broom** found in some communities in the United States. **Wakes** and other funeral observances constituted another kind of festive event, which also varied from one region to another. Accompanying most funeral observances though, was some kind of large meal. Church revivals would also qualify as a kind of festival practiced during this period.

Festivals during the slavery period served a number of critical functions for black people in the Americas. They helped to reaffirm cultural identity and became forms for asserting cultural pluralism, in some cases in very public ways. Thus, festivals not only strengthened the spirits of people of African heritages, but also aided them in publicly claiming cultural space. Festive events were public parties, which can be viewed as parallels of secret meetings in **bush harbors**; gatherings in which slaves could celebrate in their own way without the interference or imposition of mainstream white ideas or norms. Whites frequently commented on the loudness and other elements of black festive events, but they were also drawn to them in large numbers as spectators, and during certain historical periods gave them free license. But not only did festive events provide opportunities for the expression of African-derived cultural practices, they were also socially acceptable forums in which black people could offer social commentary. Through masking, and playful and sardonic imitation of whites in certain festive events, for example, black people were able to enact carnivalesque dramas that gave vent to some of their anger and other emotions that would otherwise have had to be repressed or communicated only in private.

Festivals in the Modern Age

Many of the festivals from the slavery period in the Caribbean and the United States have continued, although in modified forms, and numerous new festivals have arisen. The modern festival, though, is often more complex than earlier ones, or at least it is complex in different ways. For example, modern celebrations often contain elements of both the religious and secular, and have commercial and traditional components. Christmas celebrations are a good illustration. At the same time that mainstream, commercial Christmas customs are practiced (Christmas trees and buying presents), so are religious events such as **prayer** meetings, and contemporary observances such as **Kwanzaa**. Also, while Kwanzaa is sometimes observed simply within individual households, there are also community celebrations of this festive event, not to mention the commercial aspect involving the sale of Kwanzaa-related items. Similar complexities can be found with festive events such as jumping the broom, **Juneteenth**, and other festive events celebrating historical or cultural elements of black heritage, or marking transitional points in individual lives. **Family reunions**, church revivals (big meeting), funeral observances, Thanksgiving, and wedding celebrations are also characterized by the convergences of multiple interests. In this way, modern festive events often contain opposing elements of resistance and accommodation to mainstream norms.

These contradictory impulses are sometimes found in heritage festivals, which are organized and sponsored events devoted to celebrating the cultural heritage of particular groups, for instance the **Gullah**. Unlike festivals that are devoted primarily to celebrations among and within groups, heritage festivals are open to all, and serve not only the functions of community celebration and connection, but also educate outsiders to the traditions of the given group. In some cases, they represent a renewed pride in the group's heritage and recognition of the uniqueness and richness of their culture. Festive events such as the big drum ceremonies of Carriacou, or Carnival in many countries would fit this kind of model. The modern context, then, changes some of the dynamics of festive events that date back to earlier periods. Rather than being isolated and meaningful only to members of selected communities, festivals have become more and more open and celebrated as a part of a diasporic consciousness and pan-African identity. Of course, this has been more the case with some festive events than with others, and one factor seems to be the extent of media coverage and advertising given to particular events. These factors have also influenced changes in the nature of some festive events, and even the decline of events or core elements that were once associated with them.

There are numerous other significant festive events that mark the lives of African Americans, but that involve fewer people; for instance, birthday celebrations, graduations, homecomings, and events put on by various community clubs, schools, and other organizations. Although such events can be important as celebrations of ethnic pride, they also provide links to the larger society; birthday celebrations and graduations, for instance, are very American. Because such events tend to receive less attention, little has been written about them, and so we know less about their richness and diversity. It is clear that festivals and festive events play a major role in fostering familial, community, and national pride and solidarity among people of African heritage in the Americas, as well as functioning as bridges to the institutions of the mainstream society.

Anand Prahlad

Further Reading

Abrahams, Roger D., 1983, *The Man-of-Words in the West Indies: Performance and the Emergence of Creole Culture* (Baltimore: John Hopkins Press); Gay, Kathlyn, 2007, *African-American Holidays, Festivals, and Celebrations: The History, Customs, and Symbols Associated with Both Traditional and Contemporary Religious and Secular Events Observed by Americans of African Descent* (Detroit, MI: Omnigraphics); Smith, Robert J., 1972, "Festivals and Celebrations," in *Folklore and Folklife: An Introduction*, ed. Richard M. Dorson (Chicago: The University of Chicago Press), pp. 159–172; Southern, Eileen, 1971, *The Music of Black Americans: A History* (New York: W. W. Norton & Company).

FIELD HOLLERS

This is a genre of seemingly spontaneous, a cappella songs associated with contexts of manual labor. The name of this important genre of African American music is a misnomer. Hollers were not confined to the fields; street vendor cries sung in southern port cities to advertise wares are also subsumed under the definition of holler. Hollers and cries are used interchangeably in the literature. There are several names for field hollers, including cornfield holler, arwoolie (arhoolie), "n*gger squall," field cries, cornfield whoops, piney-woods whoop, roustabout drunk-yell, and loudmouthing. According to Chris Strachwitz, owner of Arhoolie Records in El Cerrito, California, the name hoolie has been heard of but "arwhoolie" may have come from a Library of Congress recording of a cornfield holler by Mississippi resident Thomas J. Marshall. When asked what he called the selection, Marshall hesitated in his response, with the "ah rah" common among many black speakers from the **South**, and the interviewer thought he said "arhoolie." Several field hollers were recorded under the auspices of folklorist and ethnomusicologist Alan Lomax, among others, for the Library of Congress between 1933 and 1942, and in subsequent years at prisons.

Typically, an African American voiced these high and lonesome declarations while working. The hollers were sung solo, not as a group, often in one to two lines of a musical phrase or stanza, sometimes repeating the lines and sometimes stringing a series of lines to form a narrative. They were sung both in antebellum slavery and postbellum times. Frances Anne Kemble described a holler heard in 1839 on a coastal Georgia plantation: "Oh! My massa told me, there's no grass in Georgia" (Evans, 1999). These hollers associated with work served to vent and relieve the tension and drudgery of the labor. Sometimes the singers—whether mule skinners, levee workers, corn pickers, or other workers in the field—sang of dissatisfaction with the work conditions, love life, or calls to God for relief of their condition.

Musically, the hollers were characterized by spontaneous, free flowing, melismatic, and improvised expression with the use of the flatted third and seventh, or the so-called "blue notes" that appear so frequently in **blues**, **jazz**, and **gospel** music. The phrases of hollers many times end with humming, that is, the lips are closed without the articulation of syllables. The voice of some hollers would seem to snap or break, sliding from note to note and from a lower to upper register.

Later writers called this technique falsetto voice or falsetto break. According to folklorist Willis James, the florid cries were the most prevalent and the most favored.

The melodic, timbre, and thematic content of the holler served as raw material for the evolution of early country blues. Also, a number of hollers were probably moans, groans of the invisible church sung in the field (Collins, 1988). The slaves carried their religion in the field and everywhere they went. Several bluesmen attribute the creation of the blues to the holler; these include Mississippi Delta bluesman Eddie "Son" House, and Booker White. Texas Alexander's blues can be described as a field holler style because of its florid and decorative quality. Likewise, the sounds of one of the moaners at an Alabama church where this writer did research could be described as a field holler–style moan, although the moan may have preceded the holler in terms of chronology.

The southern white folk singing tradition has embraced hollering, and hollers were recorded in Alabama among white farmers who called their tradition "n*gger hollers." As to origin, recent research has linked the melody of the "Levee Camp Holler" on the Negro Prison Blues and Songs CD to the religion of Islam and the muezzin's call to **prayer** (Diouf, 1998). However, more recorded examples and documentation would provide a better argument for and substantiation of the African Islamic basis for the holler.

Willie Collins

Further Reading

Berry, Charles, 1997, "Cornfield Hollers," on *Negro Blues and Hollers* (Rounder, 1501); Burton, J. Bryan, and Ann L. McFarland, 2009, "Celebrating African-American History Through Plantation Songs and Folklore," *General Music Today* (Online) 22 (2): 31; Chiriacò, Gianpaolo, 2011, "The Legacy of Field Hollers: A Research Framework," *CBMR Digest* 24 (2): 7–8; Collins, Willie R., 1988, "Moaning and Prayer: A Musical and Contextual Analysis of Chants to Accompany Prayer in Two Afro-American Baptist Churches in Southeast Alabama," dissertation, University of California at Los Angeles; Courlander, Harold, ed., 1963, *Negro Folk Music, U.S.A.* (New York: Columbia University Press); Diouf, Sylviane A., 1998, *Servants of Allah: African Muslims Enslaved in the Americas* (New York: New York University Press), pp. 197–198; Evans, David, 1999, "Folk and Popular Blues," in *Write Me a Few of Your Lines: A Blues Reader*, ed. Steven C. Tracy (Amherst: University of Massachusetts Press); Gioia, Ted, 2006, *Work Songs* (Durham, NC: Duke University Press); House, Son, and Willie Brown, 1997, "Camp Hollers," on *Negro Blues and Hollers* (Rounder, 1501); James, Willis Laurence, 1955, "The Romance of the Negro Folk Cry in America," *Phylon* 16: 16; "Levee Camp Holler," on *Negro Prison Blues and Songs: Recorded Live* (Bescol); Marshall, Thomas J., 1999, "Arwhoolie (Cornfield Holler)," on *Negro Work Songs and Calls* (Rounder, LC AFS L 8); Peretti, Burton, 2009, *Lift Every Voice: The History of African American Music* (Lanham, MD: Rowman & Littlefield Publishers); Southern, Eileen, 1971, *The Music of Black Americans: A History* (New York: W. W. Norton); White, Shane, and Graham J. White, 2005, *The Sounds of Slavery: Discovering African American History through Songs, Sermons, and Speech* (Boston: Beacon Press).

FIELD NEGRO/HOUSE NEGRO

An expression used to designate a person's position or social caste relative to black and white societies. The term "field Negro" refers historically to the slaves who worked in the fields, who did the grueling, long hours of manual labor that kept the plantation economy and hence the economy of the **South** flourishing and afloat. Such labor included picking cotton; planting and harvesting tobacco; plowing, sowing, and harvesting a variety of other crops; digging and providing the labor for the construction of buildings, and so on. It also included the common experience of being "driven" by an overseer who lashed those that seemed to be moving too slowly or getting too little done, or for whatever reason he deemed they needed it. By contrast, the "house Negro" was the domestic laborer, whose work included cooking, cleaning, and taking care of children. According to folklore, the house Negro has it good compared to the field Negro. Not only did the house Negro not have to labor as hard or in the heat of the southern sun, but he or she did not have to worry about being whipped, and proximity to the slave owner and his family yielded social advantages.

In the vernacular, house/field Negro suggests a difference of class status within slave society, the house Negro being higher on the social ladder than the field Negro. Political and social orientations are also connected to the two. For instance, the house Negro becomes suspect in the eyes of the black majority, and his or her allegiance to the black community is questioned. In folklore, the psychology of the house Negro is that of someone who despises his/her own race and who will do whatever is necessary to look good in the eyes of the slave owner and other whites. Hence, the house Negro is a symbol of the black person who suffers from internalized racism, who desperately wants to be loved by his/her white family, and who cannot imagine black autonomy. By contrast, the field Negro symbolizes the black majority, the working class who is still oppressed but whose identities and loyalties are grounded in the black community. The terminology enjoyed a resurgence of popularity after being used as a central motif in Malcolm X's 1963 speech, "Message to the Grassroots," in which he makes it clear that black revolutionaries are field Negroes.

The uses of these expressions are particularly fraught with the dangers of ingroup stereotyping and reflect polemical positions within African American culture. They were not uncommon in the political rhetoric of activists in the 1960s, and are still heard contemporarily, as in KRS One's song, "House N*gga's" (1989) and Luther Campbell's "Pussy Ass Kid and Hoe Ass Play" (1992). Arguments involving these two reductionist poles of black identity and politics resurface periodically, for example, in the opinions about Quentin Tarantino's 2013 film, *Django Unchained.* When black filmmaker Spike Lee objected to what he perceived as stereotypical and demeaning portraits of African Americans in Tarantino's film, another black celebrity responded by referring to Lee as "Hollywood's resident house Negro." The determination of what constitutes race loyalty is often a subjective judgment, and therefore people may be labeled a house Negro, or an "**Uncle Tom**" based on characteristics or affiliations that, in fact, are not in conflict with a very positive embrace of and commitment to black culture. For instance, belonging to white organizations, declaring oneself a Republican, or dressing conservatively may be enough in some circumstances to invite one of these labels. Rather than encouraging an understanding of the diverse social circumstances and political positions that exist among African people, these expressions tend to endorse a simplistic and polarized perspective.

Anand Prahlad

Further Reading

Cleaver, Eldridge, accessed July 2005, "The Fire Now: Field N*gger Power Takes Over the Black Movement," www.nathanielturner.com/eldridgecleaverfirenow.htm; Darryl, James, accessed July 2005, "The Bridge: In the House," www.blacknla.com/news /articles/djinthehouse.asp; Intended, Malice, January 24, 2013, "Django Unchained Has Renewed the House Negro Vs. Field Negro Conflict," http://planetill.com/2013/01 /the-neverending-war-the-discourse-surrounding-django-unchained-has-brought -the-house-negro-vs-field-negro-conflict-to-the-forefront/. (accessed November 28, 2015); Kazi, Lynn, 2001, *Cottonland Songstress* (Frederick, MD: Publish America).

FILM

Black folklore has been incorporated into film in a number of ways, and is influenced by the film genre in which the folklore appears. Generally speaking, the types of film that include folklore are Hollywood entertainment films, low-budget (sometimes independent) films, documentaries, and ethnographic films.

The uses of black folklore in Hollywood entertainment films have historically tended toward presentations of black traditions as spectacle, or as background motifs to lend a kind of exoticism to the entire film or to particular scenes. The types of folklore that have been used most often in these ways involve those incorporated into music, **dance**, and religion. A common practice in Hollywood films, for instance, has been the use of **blues** or **jazz** as part of the soundtrack. In much the same way that black bodies have been historically used in European and mainstream American visual culture to signify sexuality, soundtracks containing blues and jazz have customarily played this role in Hollywood film. In most cases, the soundtrack accompanies visual displays of white characters, indicating a sexually charged moment. Such instances might include, for example, a fragment of a B. B. King or Muddy Waters song, or the sound of a jazz saxophone. It is also common to have short visual moments in which black jazz or blues musicians are performing in the background as dramatic scenes between white characters unfold.

The use of black folk traditions as spectacle is one of the most prevalent filmic formulas in Hollywood. Stock scenes include short clips of **gospel** choirs; blues and jazz musicians; scenes from black Baptist churches; **pimps**; drug-dealing Rastafarians; evil Santería or Vodou worshippers; dangerous zombies; dancers of all kinds; and buffoonish characters who can only communicate in exaggerated black dialects. D. W. Griffith initiated this tradition in his 1915 film *Birth of a Nation*. Other early examples of films in this tradition include *Dixiana* (1930), *White Zombie* (1932), *Judge Priest* (1934), and *Gone with the Wind* (1939). Contemporary examples would include *The Serpent and the Rainbow* (1988), *The Blues Brothers* (1980), *The Cotton Club* (1984), *Angel Heart* (1987), *Candyman* (1992), *and Marked for Death* (1990). In many such films, distorted spectacles of black religious groups and sometimes their worship practices, musical and dance performances, and other community traditions become the background visual and thematic points of interest that add meaning to the drama between white characters in the foreground. In each instance, elements of black folklore are taken out of their natural cultural contexts and often function to reinforce negative and stereotypical notions of black people. Another kind of Hollywood film takes an element of black folklore as the central focus of the film, but distorts it in much the same way as in the films mentioned earlier. Disney's 1946 *Song of the South* is an example. Disney takes Joel Chandler Harris's **Uncle Remus** and translates it into film, but reemphasizes the stereotypical and racist elements contained in the book.

Many critics would argue that "blaxploitation" films suffer some of the same problems that characterize mainstream productions such as the aforementioned ones. The term "blaxploitation" is usually applied to Hollywood films of the late 1960s and early 1970s that featured black casts. Most of these 60 or so films were cheaply made, set in the black ghetto, and geared toward primarily inner-city, young, black audiences. Such films reflected, to some degree, pressures by newly politicized black audiences for less derogatory cinematic images and the desire to see some of the emerging attitudes of racial pride and defiance reflected on the screen.

The period also saw not only a surge in films with black casts, but the entrance of black filmmakers, for example Gordon Parks and Melvin Van Peebles, into the mainstream. Because these films were usually set in the ghetto, they depict instances of urban folklore such as pimps, gambling, storefront churches, and bar scenes. They also often feature black music on their soundtracks. One of the films that set the tone for this period was Van Peebles' *Sweet Sweetback's Baadasssss Song* (1971), an independently made film that was a megahit. Other hits included *Shaft* (1971), *Superfly* (1972), *The Mack* (1973), *Trick Baby* (1973), and *Foxy Brown* (1974). Criticisms of these films include their romanticization of ghetto life and the glorification of pimp culture and black machismo in general. A central folk motif in blaxploitation films is the black **trickster/Bad Man** figure who, like the characters in **toasts**, relies on his wits to win against the system. While the victories of these characters were celebrated by many black audiences of the times, they also drew criticism for perpetrating some of the same stereotypes about black people as those commonly found in mainstream films.

Until the 1990s, when there was a surge of films by black filmmakers, only a few Hollywood movies rose above the conventional formulas in portraying elements of black folk culture. One of these was Gordon Parks's *Learning Tree* (1969), a coming-of-age story set in the **South**. Another was *Sounder* (1972), also set in the South. Starring Cicely Tyson, Paul Winfield, and Taj Mahal, *Sounder* renders humanistic and believable portraits of southern folk culture among a black family of sharecroppers.

The 1990s saw a wave of new black filmmakers whose films portrayed folk elements in more realistic and humanistic ways than had previous Hollywood films. Some of these filmmakers were able to get their works distributed by major companies, but many were not. Spike Lee explores the inner dramas of black fraternity life in *School Daze* (1988), a film with many reflections of **fraternity** traditions. In *Daughters of the Dust* (1991), Julie Dash explores the tensions within a **Gullah** family leaving their island home to move to the mainland in search of better opportunities. In Charles Burnett's *To Sleep with Anger* (1990), a relative turns up in the Los Angeles home of a family who had moved away from the South, bringing with him a host of superstitions and other elements of southern folk culture that the family would rather leave behind. Another film of this period is John Singleton's *Boyz N the Hood* (1991), which offers glimpses into the folklore of South-Central Los Angeles gangs. Of course, the emergence of black filmmakers did not mean the end of stereotypical images of black folklife in films, but it did help to create more space for realistic portrayals of black folk culture in Hollywood.

Besides Hollywood entertainment films, there are abundant documentary and ethnographic films focusing on black folk artists and folk traditions throughout the diaspora. While some of these may suffer from a different kind of romanticization, their intent is clearly to depict these traditions in informative and positive ways. Films have been made on almost every kind of black folkloric tradition imaginable, including **pottery**, **blacksmithing**, basketry, **quilting**, instrument-making, dance, most musical traditions, **folk foods**, Carnival and other **festivals**, and many different kinds of religious worship. Undoubtedly, most films focus on rural traditions to which substantial scholarship has been devoted. Most often, anthropologists or folklorists who are employed in academic positions or who work for state or regional centers or folk arts programs make such films. These films tend to be housed in either university or regional folk centers, or in state folklife or folk art programs. Less frequently, independent filmmakers devote their lives to making films that explore the folk traditions of diverse groups. One such filmmaker is Les Blank, who founded his company "Flower Films" in 1967, and has since made films on the black traditions of **Mardi Gras**; Lightnin' Hopkins; Texas songster Mance Lipscomb; Dizzie Gillespie; Afro-Cuban master drummer and percussionist Francisco Aguabella; "**Zydeco** King" Clifton Chenier; black Creole musician Bois-Sec Ardoin (and the culture surrounding him); and Oakland blues guitarist and singer Sonny Rhodes as well as films on Latin, African, Cajun, Hawaiian, Tex-Mex, and other ethnic musical traditions.

Debates such as those surrounding the recent film *Django in Chains* by filmmaker Quentin Tarantino must be viewed in the context of this long history of distorted and demeaning portraitures of black people and their folklore in American film.

Anand Prahlad

Further Reading

Barker, Deborah E., and Kathryn McKee, 2011, *American Cinema and the Southern Imaginary* (University of Georgia Press); Bogle, Donald, 2001, *Toms, Coons, Mulattoes,*

Mammies, and Bucks: An Interpretive History of Blacks in American Films, 4th. Edition, (Continuum International); Chandler, Karen, 1999, "Folk Culture and Masculine Identity in Charles Burnett's 'To Sleep with Anger,'" *African American Review* 33 (2): 299–311; Diawara, Manthia, 1993, "Noir by Noirs: Towards a New Realism in Black," *African-American Review* 27: 525–537; Greene, Dennis, 1994, "Tragically Hip: Hollywood and African-American Cinema," *Cineaste* 20 (4): 28–29; Guerrero, Ed, 1993, *Framing Blackness: The African American Image in Film* (Philadelphia: Temple University Press); Hamlet, Janice D., and Robin R. Means Coleman, eds., 2009, *Fight the Power: The Spike Lee Reader* (New York: Peter Lang); hooks, bell, 1992, *Black Looks: Race and Representation* (Boston: South End Press); hooks, bell, 1996, *Reel to Real: Race, Sex, and Class at the Movies* (New York: Routledge); Jones, Jacquie, 1993, "The Black South in Contemporary Film," *African American Review* 27 (1): 19–24; King, Jeannine, 2010, "Memory and the Phantom South in African American Migration Film," *Mississippi Quarterly* 63 (3–4): 477–491; Massood, Paula, 2003, *Black City Cinema*, (Philadelphia: Temple University Press); Nama, Adilifu, 2008, *Black Space: Imagining Race in Science Fiction Film* (Austin: University of Texas Press); Rhines, Jesse Algeron, 1995, "The Political Economy of Black Film," *Cineaste* 21: 38–39; Rocchio, Vincent F., 2000, *Reel Racism: Confronting Hollywood's Construction of Afro-American Culture* (Westview Press); Weisenfeld, Judith, 2007, *Hollywood be Thy Name: African American Religion in American Film: 1929–1949* (University of California Press); Yearwood, Gladstone L., 2000, *Black Film as a Signifying Presence: Cinema, Narration and the African-American Aesthetic Tradition* (Trenton, NJ: Africa World Press).

FLYING AFRICANS

The flying Africans are a legendary group of enslaved Africans who used magic to escape slavery by flying back to **Africa**. The legend is common to the **Gullah** people of the South Sea Islands, but has also been found among groups of African Americans on the mainland. The flying Africans legend is often associated with two other folk motifs: the tale of the independent hoe—and other iron tools that work by themselves—and the tale of the magic dish dispensing unlimited quantities of food.

The general outline of events in the legend is that during the period of American slavery some Africans were brought to the islands as slaves, but they were not suited to the role and used magic to escape. In one variant of the legend these Africans had magic power and refused to work as slaves. They could neither speak nor understand English. They were put into the fields with hoes to chop cotton but could not do it well. The white overseer approached them to whip them, and they uttered a magic incantation, arose, and flew back to Africa. They left their hoes standing in the field, continuing to work by themselves. Some variants of the legend say that the Africans enacted as part of their escape a ritual in which they joined hands and moved in a circle steadily more rapidly until they were aloft, all the while chanting in unison. Some tellers use the simile "like a bird," and some identify the bird as a buzzard. In some variants, they actually change into birds. Some variants hold that the leaders were a man and his wife who had magical power, but they also had children who did not have such power and were not able to fly away to Africa. Because the children were left behind, their parents had to return to the islands from time to time to visit them. One variant explains that one of the children left behind was a daughter who wanted to learn to **conjure** but was told that she had to undergo a sort of formal apprenticeship to gain such ability.

One of the core motifs in the legend, which is sometimes found in other tales, is the magical tool that has special powers that are accessible to anyone who knows how to wield it. The tool may be an ax, a sword, a spear, a nail, a needle, or a knife, and this motif occurs commonly in some African tales. In an Ashanti narrative, for example, Porcupine, the hoe's owner, uses it daily and hides it when he stops work. But Spider watches him, steals the hoe, and sets it to work but cannot stop it because he does not know the halt command. Likewise, on Wilmington Island, Georgia, the tale is that **Brer Rabbit** steals Brer Wolf's magic hoe, but although Wolf informs Rabbit of the magic word to start the hoe, he neglects to tell him the formula for stopping it, and it continues chopping until it ruins Rabbit's crop. In another variant in which Brer Rabbit is the owner and **Brer Fox** is the thief, the hoe works Fox to death because he is too stupid to remember the halt command. Among the Bambara, an African group, the narrative juxtaposes Hare as the owner and Hyena as the character who borrows the hoe to work a field and earn a wife. Hare does not reveal the halt command and lets Hyena die from exhaustion so he can take the wife for himself. The iron in the hoe and other such objects is the source of magical power that enables transformation to occur. The flying Africans use the hoe that works by itself as a tool in their ritual of transformation and escape.

The legend has come to symbolize the ability of enslaved Africans to maintain cultural and psychological connections to Africa and an Afrocentric identity and value system. As such, it represents cultural resistance to enslavement. Allusions to the legend surface in various forms in African American oral tradition, literature and visual art. For example, "I'll Fly Away" and "If I had Two Wings" are two common spirituals in which the motif is found. It also plays a central role in Toni Morrison's novel, *Song of Solomon*, and in filmmaker Julie Dash's *Daughters of the Dust*.

Laura C. Jarmon

Further Reading

Barnes, Paula C., 2009, "Pearl Ceage's Flyin' West and the African American Motif of Flight," *Obsidian III: Literature in the African Diaspora* 10 (1): 68; DeFrantz, Thomas, and Anita Gonzalez, 2014, *Black Performance Theory* (Durham: Duke University Press); Fauset, Arthur Huff, 1927, "Negro Folk Tales from the South (Alabama, Mississippi, Louisiana)," *Journal of American Folklore* 40 (157): 213–303; Georgia Writers' Project, Works Progress Administration, 1986 [1940], *Drums and Shadows: Survival Studies among the Georgia Coastal Negroes* (Athens: University of Georgia Press); Green, Thomas A., 2009, *African American Folktales* (Westport, CT: Greenwood Press); Jarmon, Laura C., 2003, *Wishbone: Reference and Interpretation in Black Folk Narrative* (Knoxville: University of Tennessee Press); Radin, Paul, ed., 1983 [1952], *African Folktales* (New York: Schocken Books); Zahan, Dominique, 1979, *The Religion, Spirituality, and Thought of Traditional Africa*, trans. Kate Ezra and Lawrence M. Martin (Chicago: University of Chicago Press).

FOLK FOODS

In many ways folk food mirrors the more popular **soul food**, in that folk food was based on the utilitarian needs of black people. It was created from food that enslaved and emancipated blacks had access to, or rations provided by the slave master, combined with African foods and spices that were smuggled over on the slave ships (okra, yams, black-eyed peas, sorghum, sesame seeds, and greens) as well as those foods harvested by the slaves in the New World (sugarcane, rice, and corn). Kale, cress, mustard, and pokeweed greens replaced the turnips and beets of **Africa**. The sweet potato replaced the yam of Africa and the white potato of U.S. Southerners. Cornmeal became an ingredient for creative breads as well as desserts when used with molasses. Food cooked in a big pot came to be known as a one-pot meal, with pork remains as a major meat. Blacks planted, harvested, cooked, canned, and preserved apples, peaches, berries, nuts, and grains from the land on which they toiled, and these ingredients soon became puddings and pies. It was a cycle of utilization and renewal through which they gave and took from the earth, taking pride and satisfaction in their work.

Folk foods are ritualistic, cyclic, and life-sustaining for blacks in the African diaspora. They play a central role in unifying African American families and communities. Cultural knowledge about folk foods is passed through recipes as well as through other forms of folklore, such as **proverbs**. This knowledge is reinforced by the communal value attached to activities such as the shucking of the corn, the peeling of the yam, the cleaning of the chitlins, the descaling of the fish, or a weekly fish-fry night. While these foods are learned informally as a part of everyday life, they are also often tied to cultural events like the yam festivals in Nigeria or Jamaica, the chitlin circuit entertainment venues, and rice **festivals** in Georgia and South Carolina. They can be associated with specific African and African American spiritual traditions or evoke their own superstitions or **myths**.

There are often tales, myths, and **fables** about these foods and sometimes a folk food spawns its own proverbial wisdom. For example, the Yoruban saying, *Obu ko to iyo* ("Obu [or 'salt earth'] is not to be compared with real salt"), is spoken to someone pretending to be something other than he is. Likewise, Trinidadians, black Americans, and other African-derived groups have a saying that addresses doing what needs to be done: "Hard times made even the monkey eat red pepper." The monkey is a traditional folklore figure known for his cunning deceptiveness, whereas red pepper enjoys a folk reputation of extreme taste and is often used as a way to drive away unwanted persons or things. In African American lore, the proverb "a sweet plum might contain a worm" uses food to serve as a pedagogical tool to explain how deceptive physical appearance can be in regard to human nature. The cooking and eating of folk foods can easily enhance the remembering and passing on of wisdom from generation to generation.

Folk food is also about performance and expression; perhaps this is why so many traditions in African American music return again and again to folk foods as a creative source to express ideas. Folk idioms such as "gravy with my grits," "put

Barbecue is culturally significant to African Americans and plays a central role in celebrations, community organizing, and political gatherings. (Kim Karpeles /Alamy Stock Photo)

a little sugar in my bowl," and "jelly in need of a roll" can be found in various **blues**, **jazz**, **soul**, rhythm and blues, and **hip-hop** lyrics. Black peoples' multiple usages of folk foods continuously explores the rich dimensions of the shared connection between language and food in African American cultural traditions stemming from long-held beliefs and the use of food as part of rites and rituals.

Folk food in the African diaspora has a varied tradition that dates back to African origins. Its use changes with time and geographical location. In his classic slave narrative, Olaudah Equiano (or Gustavus Vassa) explained that food and beverage were essential parts of honoring ancestral presences: "After washing, libation is made, by pouring out a small portion of the drink on the floor, and by tossing a small quantity of the food in a certain place, for the spirits of departed relations, which the natives suppose to preside over their conduct, and guard them from evil" (Equiano, 15). Yams, eddoes, plantains, and nuts were foods believed to sustain the dead in their transition from the human world to the spirit universe. Many other slave rituals involved food, such as leaving food and water out for the spirits of the dead, or placing spoons, cups, or other personal possessions on a new grave. Based on West African cultural tradition, these examples are still practiced today in different evolved forms.

Folk foods are also important as ingredients for **Hoodoo**. In many Hoodoo potions and healing rites, folk food becomes the secret way to lay a trick. As Zora Neale Hurston notes in *Mules and Men*, most Hoodoo features foods such as rice, figs, sycamore bark, **High John the Conqueror** root, vinegar, livers, hearts, or other organs that might be cooked in a potion. Other Hoodoo rituals gravitate toward folk foods because they are associated with comfort, or their texture makes it easy to hide other ingredients of the Hoodoo. For example, dumplings might be used to feed a victim spider eggs, to cause the esoteric illness called "Live Things in You." Foods are also essential and central elements on altars in many religious settings, for example in Vodou. In these cases they represent sincere and symbolic offerings to ancestors, orishas, loas (lwas), or other divine beings.

In addition to Hoodoo-related practices, foods are associated with luck and material fortune. Many culinary dishes thought to bring good luck to those who eat them contain folk foods such as those harvested by slaves in earlier times. Benne cakes are a food from West Africa introduced to southern coastal parts of the United States by slaves. "Benne" means sesame seeds. The sesame seeds are eaten for good luck, and wafers and cookies made from benne are now a part of **Kwanzaa**. Slaves are also said to have introduced the New Year's dish Hoppin' John, a casserole of rice and black-eyed peas. The dish was traditionally served with a shiny dime buried deep within it. The person whose portion had the coin was guaranteed good luck in the new year. Black-eyed peas alone are thought to be the key to good fortune. Eating rice, greens, and fish on the first day of the year is also believed to bring financial wealth.

Perhaps more than any other item of folklore, food tends to symbolize group identity, and perhaps because of the close association between eating and a sense of being, foods can signify the essence of a particular group. Such symbolism can apply at national, regional, or familial levels. For example, Jamaicans proudly boast about akee and salt fish, rice and peas, or callaloo, conveying to others the sentiment that they have not really experienced or understood Jamaican culture until they have eaten these dishes. Within Jamaican society, Rastafari might express similar feelings about Ital cooking. For Afro-Brazilians the dishes might be *feijoada*, or rice and beans. In the United States, **barbecue** and fried chicken are examples of foods that signify ethnic pride. Beyond the larger scale of ethnic symbols, versions and varieties of foods are found within specific regions and among different families. When one thinks of New Orleans, one thinks of **gumbo**, whereas other locales are known for smoked ham, biscuits and gravy, or sweet potato pie. Understandably, foods become linked to survival, and to some extent their symbolic significance encapsulates the entire history of struggle, endurance, and progress that marks most African-derived populations.

LaMonda Horton-Stallings

Further Reading

Byars, D., 1996, "Traditional African American Foods and African Americans," *Agriculture and Human Values* 13: 74–78; Carney, J., 2001, *Black Rice: The African Origins of Rice Cultivation in the Americas* (Boston: Harvard University Press); Dance, Daryl Cumber, ed., 2002, *From My People: 400 Years of African American Folklore* (New York: W. W. Norton & Company); Equiano, Olaudah, 1987 [1789], "The Interesting Narrative of the Life of Olaudah Equiano, or Gustavus Vassa, the African," in *The Classic Slave Narratives*, ed. Henry L. Gates (New York: Penguin Books), pp. 1–182; Ferris, Marcie Cohen, 2014, *The Edible South: The Power of Food and the Making of an American Region* (Chapel Hill: The University of North Carolina Press); Opie, Frederick Douglass, 2010, *Hog and Hominy: Soul Food from Africa to America* (New York: Columbia University Press); Witt, D., 1999, *Black Hunger: Food and the Politics of US Identity* (New York and London: Oxford University Press).

FOLKTALES

Folktales are multifaceted stories told among African Americans throughout the diaspora. They reflect an African cultural background as well as the American reality of slavery and racism. Africans and their descendants in the United States found many ways to record their history, but writing was not their primary format. Because of the emphasis on orality in **Africa** and the limitations on slaves' access to literacy, African Americans looked for their self-expression in other areas, including music, song, and **dance**.

Folktales serve many purposes, including education: "While you Whites have schools and books for teaching your children," a Dahomean interviewee explained to Melville and Frances Herskovits, "we tell them stories, for our stories are our books" (Levine, 90). This quote suggests the importance of orality to African and African American cultures. Educational tales might explain something in the natural world, such as why alligator's back was covered in scales ("De Reason Why de 'Gator Stan' So," Christensen, 54–57), or they might teach morality, "how to act, how to live" (Heli Chatelain, quoted in Levine, 91).

In Africa and throughout the diaspora, folktales provided a socially sanctioned psychic release. Frustrations about the behavior of a powerful figure—an African chief, a slave master—might be shared without bringing reprisals. The misbehavior of the powerful person was transferred to a **trickster** figure, and through his behavior, taletellers could voice frustration at specific individuals in society or at circumstances beyond their control. Anthropologist R. S. Rattray's informant explained the significance of these tale types in Africa: "These occasions gave everyone an opportunity of talking about and laughing at such things; it was 'good' for everyone concerned, he said" (Rattray, 7). It gave those who felt mistreated an opportunity to express their frustrations and a way to disparage those whose behavior offended them, free from the fear of vengeance.

Folktales also took many forms. Animal tales were perhaps the most ubiquitous, and in these the connection to Africa was quite strong. Folklorist Harold Courlander observed that "a considerable number" of **Brer Rabbit** tales collected in the diaspora have "recognizable African antecedents." In these tales, Brer Rabbit subsumed other African tricksters, including hare, **tortoise**, and spider. The trickster's antagonists, both in Africa and the diaspora, were "physically stronger and usually predatory creatures," such as lion, leopard, and elephant in Africa and fox, wolf, and alligator in the United States. In some cases,.the smaller protagonist was a thinly veiled stand-in for the slave. His victory over his larger, stronger foe, usually the result of his cunning, would have resonated with slaves whose masters did not understand the deeper meaning of the tales, believing instead that their slaves were simply entertained by the animals' exploits (Courlander, 466–467). The animals that people these tales do so quite literally. Although they are identified as animals, and each animal character retains the traits that he would have in the natural world, they are also quite human, sharing the weaknesses, desires, and emotions of humans.

The Old Master and John cycle also represented a large body of tales. John was subservient to Old Master, and was usually portrayed as his slave, although sometimes he was represented as a plantation servant "liberated" by the Civil War. Courlander found in John a "combination of traits." Sometimes he was quick-witted, other times he seemed rather slow. Though often "tolerant" of Old Master and "eager to please," John could also be "stubborn, contemptuous, or rebellious." John could be a trickster, finding "sly ways to chastise [Old Master] or put him down." Old Master, on the other hand, was "likely to be firm and demanding, even harsh and arbitrary, but he [was] also paternal and protective." Sometimes, Courlander observed, the Old Master and John cycle of tales appeared to be "a human version of the war of wits between Brother Rabbit and Brother Fox," but this human version was "far more subtle and contain[ed] endless social nuances." Nonetheless, the stories were always told from John's perspective (Courlander, 419–420).

Telling folktales was more than the sharing of a story; it was a performance. There was a rhythm to the telling of a story: "I don't know how they do it," wrote Emma Backus, "but they will say 'lipity clipity, lipity clipity,' so you can almost hear a rabbit coming through the woods" (Levine, 88–89). Adding to the performative aspect, it was not at all unusual for the storyteller to act out the story. "To indicate continuous running, rather than a sudden sharp spurt," reported Richard Dorson, "[the storyteller] drops his hands to his sides, spreads the fingers, and wriggles his wrists in a sideways motion, thus suggesting steady movement. Sometimes the reciter gets to his feet and weaves, writhes, gestures, and groans, to simulate the **preacher** exhorting his flock, or a witch straddling her victim" (Levine, 89). "An accomplished storyteller brings to his narration imagination and the arts of theater," wrote Harold Courlander. "He may dramatize his characters, innovate and embellish, and the mere words of his narration in print seem impoverished by comparison with his original live performance" (Courlander, 467).

Moreover, taletelling was done communally. Communalism was an important element in most African cultures, producing in Africa and throughout the diaspora an emphasis on "interconnectedness, community and communalism" (Jefferson, 113). This "interconnectedness" pervades the telling of stories, with the call-and-response pattern of singing finding its way into **storytelling**. According to Joel Chandler Harris, the audience responded to the tales constantly with shouts of "Dar now!" "He's a honey, mon!" and "Git out de way, an' gin 'im room!" (Levine, 89). Folktales are told far less frequently in oral forms in today's society, however, traditional tales continue to be incorporated into literature, visual arts, and film.

Jennifer Hildebrand

See also: Fables; Fox, Brer

Further Reading

Adams, E. C. L., 1987, *Tales of the Congaree* (Chapel Hill: University of North Carolina Press); Christensen, Abigail M. H., 1969 [1892], *Afro- American Folk Lore* (New York: Negro Universities Press); Courlander, Harold, 1996 [1976], *A Treasury of Afro-American Folklore* (New York: Marlowe & Company); Faulkner, William, 1993, *Days When the Animals Talked* (Trenton, NJ: Africa World Press, Inc.); Green, Thomas A., 2009, *African American Folktales* (Westport, CT: Greenwood Press); Jarmon, Laura C., 2003, *Wishbone: Reference and Interpretation in Black Folk Narrative* (Knoxville: University of

Tennessee Press); Jefferson, Antonette, 2010, *Essays on Social Issues & How They Impact African Americans and Other People of Color: Law, Literature, and Social Work* (Xlibris, Corp Publishers); Jones, Charles C., 2012 [2000], *Gullah Folktales from the Georgia Coast* (Athens: University of Georgia Press); Levine, Lawrence, 1977, *Black Culture and Black Consciousness* (New York: Oxford University Press); M'Baye, Babacar, 2009, *The Trickster Comes West: Pan-African Influence in Early Black Diasporan Narratives* (Jackson: University Press of Mississippi); Rattray, R. S., 1928–1929, "Some Aspects of West African Folklore," *Journal of the African Society* 28 (109): 1–11; Washington, Teresa N., 2012, "Mules and Men and Messiahs: Continuity in Yoruba Divination Verses and African American Folktales," *Journal of American Folklore* 125 (497): 263–285.

FOODS
See Folk Foods

"FORTY ACRES AND A MULE"

The phrase "Forty Acres and a Mule" has both a historical meaning and a meaning within the context of the debate over slavery reparations. Historically, the phrase refers to a promise made by an agency of the federal government and by General William Tecumseh Sherman. In the closing weeks of the Civil War, Congress created a government agency, the Bureau of Refugees, Freedmen, and Abandoned Lands. The agency, among other duties, had responsibility for issues arising from the vast number of freed slaves and "loyal" refugees. The agency's charter also authorized the distribution of land abandoned or seized in the former Confederacy. Notably, the agency's charter indicated that the land grants not exceed 40 acres. The agency's policy, which had been implemented in part, was put forward as a bill in the U.S. Congress and was subsequently defeated in February 1866. The government returned the seized lands to their original owners, displacing without compensation those freedmen and loyal refugees who had been given the land in the months before the bill's defeat. In late 1864 through early 1865, General Sherman advanced into the heart of the Confederacy, determined to break the rebelling states' will to fight.

To gain the support of liberated slaves, General Sherman issued Special Field Order No. 15 in January 1865. Significantly, although the Emancipation Proclamation carried no legal weight for slaveholding states that remained loyal to the Union and had no possibility for adoption in states under Confederate jurisdiction, once the Federal army took control of a formerly rebellious territory, the Emancipation Proclamation took full force. In effect, Sherman's march was one of liberation for numerous slaves. Clearly, then, his field order sought to give newly freed slaves a further incentive to fight against their former masters and to break the will of former slaveholders and supporters of slavery. Sherman could consequently claim that his was a battle not for retribution but for freedom. In short, Sherman's order gave moral weight to his "March to the Sea." The field order specified that freedmen who assisted the Federal army should be given tracts of land in the former Confederacy. The field order promised land in 40-acre parcels, from northern Florida through

Georgia and into South Carolina, to be set aside for the freedmen. Sherman's order, when implemented, resulted in the distribution of 400,000 acres of land. The general further ordered that each family be granted legal title to the 40-acre plots and be given animals to assist in the cultivation of the land.

However, in September 1865, President Andrew Johnson rescinded Sherman's order, retracted the land grants and titles, and ordered the land returned to the original owners. The government then seized the freedmen's lands, displacing them with no compensation. Supporters of the freedmen's right to be compensated for the seized lands then put forward a number of proposals designed to make good on General Sherman's promises, on behalf of the federal government. The proposals included land surrounding the railroads and other land in the **South**. Other proposals came forward suggesting that former slaves might be granted land in Texas or in the unsettled Western territories. President Johnson rejected each proposal. Johnson's motivation, probably, was to enable a smoother transition from war to peace in the former Confederate territories. However, in rejecting the repeated calls for compensation to freedmen, Johnson in effect dismissed the moral right many freedmen had to lands and property in the South, a moral right used, to great effect, by General Sherman in the final months of the war. Clearly then, although no law promised or guaranteed freedmen compensation (reparation or restitution), many prominent Americans thought and felt that reparations were due to former slaves and their families. Furthermore, government agencies and representatives of the federal government had given their word that land would go to freedmen.

Bernard McKenna

Further Reading

Bardolph, Richard, 1970, *The Civil Rights Record: Black Americans and the Law 1849–1970* (New York: Crowell); Bell, Derrick, *1992, Race, Racism & American Law* (Boston: Little, Brown, and Company); Copeland, Roy W., 2013, "In the Beginning: Origins of African American Real Property Ownership in the United States," *Journal of Black Studies* 44 (6): 646–664; Darity, William, 2008, "Forty Acres and a Mule in the 21st Century," *Social Science Quarterly* 89 (3): 656–664; Finney, Carolyn, 2014, *Black Faces, White Spaces: Reimagining the Relationship of African Americans to the Great Outdoors* (Chapel Hill: The University of North Carolina Press); Henry, Charles P., 2007, *Long Overdue: The Politics of Racial Reparation,* 1st ed. (New York: New York University Press); Hollis, Shirley A., 2009, "Neither Slave nor Free: The Ideology of Capitalism and the Failure of Radical Reform in the American South," *Critical Sociology* 35 (1): 9–27; Oubre, Claude, 1978, *Forty Acres and a Mule: The Freedmen's Bureau and Black Land Ownership* (Baton Rouge: Louisiana State University Press); Reid, Debra Ann, and Evan P. Bennett, 2012, *Beyond Forty Acres and a Mule: African American Landowning Families Since Reconstruction* (Gainesville: University Press of Florida).

FOX, BRER

Brer Fox, Br'er Fox, Ber Fox, or Bruh Fox (all short for Brother Fox), appears frequently as a predator or protagonist in African American oral and written folklore. The fox has adapted to most of the world's climates and terrains, and storytellers from **Africa** to Europe and North America have long noted the species' trickery, resourcefulness, speed, and elusiveness. In Aesop's **fables** and other European folklore, especially in *La Roman de Renard*, the Reynard tale cycle, the fox appears as a crafty and selfish predator, trying to gain an advantage over his adversary by his seductive talk and other ruses. Brer Fox is **Brer Rabbit**'s chief adversary in Joel Chandler Harris's African American **Uncle Remus** tales from the 1880s and 1890s. In the celebrated tar baby story, for example, Brer Fox fashions a female figure out of pitch and puts her on a log on the Big Road; then he "lay low." When the tar baby won't talk "spectubble" to Brer Rabbit, the rabbit begins to punch her, until all four of his feet and his head are stuck to her adhesive body. But the **trickster** fox is out-foxed by the even wilier rabbit, who uses reverse psychology to urge Brer Fox to kill him any way he wants, so long as he does not throw him in the **briar patch** (which turns out to be Brer Rabbit's natural habitat).

In the iconography and sociology of African American slave folklore, Brer Fox and his kin typically represent the stronger, predatory white slave master or overseer, eager to catch and eat Brer Rabbit, his children, and his cousins. In the subtext of these animal stories and related cycles, Brer Rabbit, the black slave's hero, is resented by the stronger animals like Brer Fox because the rabbit is a nuisance who raids the higher-class animals' food supply and embarrasses the fox in full view of Miss Meadows and the gals. Moreover, the so-called dominant animals are irritated by Brer Rabbit's cockiness and one-upmanship. All the more reason to catch him and silence him forever.

In the oral traditions of the southeastern United States, Brer Fox is more famous for his failures as an adversary than for his successes. In an etiological tale, which appears in numerous versions across folklore traditions, Brer Fox does successfully trick Brer Rabbit into fishing with what was then his long bushy tail, only to find it eaten off by the fish he had sought to catch. But Brer Rabbit gets even in story after story: tricking Brer Fox into being the rabbit's riding horse, running him into a hornets' nest, and even tricking him into fatal encounters with other animals or with Mister Man. The motif of the supposedly weaker animal riding on the stronger one is a major theme in hundreds of variants across the diaspora, in European **folktales**, and in American lore.

Brer Fox has endured into modern times. Julius Lester keeps his misadventures alive in his four-volume set of modern retellings of the Brer Rabbit tales (published 1987–1994); Brer Fox and his tar baby trap regularly surface in political cartoons and editorials; and Brer Fox is the alias for a player in at least one military strategy game on the Web.

R. Bruce Bickley Jr.

Further Reading

Abrahams, Roger D., ed., 1985, *Afro-American Folktales. Stories from the Black Traditions in the New World* (New York: Pantheon Books); Baer, Florence E., 1980, *Sources and Analogues of the Uncle Remus Tales* (Helsinki, Finland: Folklore Fellows Communications); Bascom, William, 1992, *African Folktales in the New World* (Bloomington: Indiana University Press); Bickley, John T., and R. Bruce Bickley Jr., eds., 2003, *Nights with Uncle*

Remus, with a critical introduction, "Folklore Performance and the Legacy of Joel Chandler Harris" (New York: Penguin Classics); Bickley, R. Bruce, Jr., 2000, *Joel Chandler Harris: A Biography and Critical Study* (Lincoln, NE: Authors Guild/Iuniverse); Carpio, Glenda, 2008, *Laughing Fit to Kill: Black Humor in the Fictions of Slavery* (New York: Oxford University Press); Chase, Richard, ed., 1955, *The Complete Tales of Uncle Remus* (Boston: Houghton Mifflin); Green, Thomas, 2009, *African American Folktales* (Westport, CT: Greenwood Press); Harris, Joel Chandler, 1982 [1880], *Uncle Remus: His Songs and His Sayings, with a critical introduction*, "Author, Teller, and Hero," by Robert Hemenway (New York: Penguin Classics); Okepewho, Isidore, 1994, "The Cousins of Uncle Remus" in *The Black Columbiad: Defining Moments in African American Literature and Culture*, ed. Werner Sollors and Maria Diedrich (Cambridge: Harvard University Press); Sperb, Jason, 2012, *Disney's Most Notorious Film: Race, Convergence, and the Hidden Histories of Song of the South* (Austin: University of Texas Press).

FRATERNITY FOLKORE

The beliefs, practices, and symbols found among black college fraternities are what constitute fraternity lore. Although the folklore of black fraternities is ever evolving, changing in form and style, consistent categories of practices have persisted over time. These practices play important roles in group identity and cohesiveness as well as providing a sense of community support and bolstering self-esteem. Some of the most critical traditions are those associated with rites of passage. Although many fraternity traditions are secret, many are also public and help to mediate between these groups and outsiders. This function of the fraternities is especially important for black students on predominantly white campuses, where the experiences of isolation and being under assault can be so pervasive.

Efforts to form black fraternities began in 1903, with the Kappa Alpha Nu (later changed to Kappa Alpha Psi) fraternity at Indiana University. Sigma Pi Phi, or *Boulé*, was organized in 1904 as a fraternity of graduate students. *Boulé* was a secret, elite, and professional organization that was criticized by scholars such as E. Franklin Frazier and W. E. B. Du Bois for its exclusivity and conservatism. The oldest black fraternity, *Boulé* is still an active organization, boasting a membership that has included James Weldon Johnson, Carter G. Woodson, Martin Luther King Jr., Vernon Jordan, and Benjamin E. Mays. In addition to professionals such as medical doctors, and others of considerable wealth, "the vast majority of Black mayors and college presidents, represent the current ranks of the organization" (Kimbrough, 28). *Boulé* was so successful in maintaining its secrecy that it was not until the early 1980s, when its members decided to announce its existence, that the general public (including African Americans) became aware of the fraternity. Responses among African Americans included **rumors** that the group was committed to maintaining white supremacy, and that they controlled other black fraternities who, under the influence of the *Boulé*, also supported white supremacy.

The most critical period in the emergence of black fraternities was between 1905 and 1930 (Kimbrough, 29). During these years a number of fraternities were organized that did not last, and most of those that would become the major, lasting organizations were also formed. For example, Gamma Phi was formed in 1905 at Wilberforce University in Ohio, but after approximately three decades of existence it seemed to disappear (Kimbrough, 30). Several fraternities were formed at Howard University during this period, including Omega Psi Phi and Phi Beta Sigma. Alpha Phi Alpha was organized at Cornell University in 1906, and Kappa Alpha Psi was formed at Indiana University in 1911.

The period of the 1960s, which was framed by such historic events as the civil rights and black power movements, saw the emergence of many black fraternal groups on college campuses. Some of these, for instance Nun Phi Nun and Hound Phi Hound, were intended to parody the major fraternal organizations. Others were more serious efforts to establish alternative fraternal groups that embraced ideals of black power and honored the desire to form groups that would reflect the members' African heritage rather than identifying with Greek (or European) culture. One such organization was Iota Phi Theta, which was formed at Morgan State in 1963. Another was Malik Sigma Psi, formed in 1977 at C. W. Post College on Long Island. Malik Sigma Psi consciously embraced African culture and adopted an ideological stance against the idea of "Black Greek" organizations.

There was another wave of new fraternities in the late 1980s and 1990s, a period marked by several social factors, including multiculturalism, Afrocentrism, Web-based organizations, and the popularity of groups that emphasized their Christianity in the ways in which they identified and represented themselves. Examples of Christian-oriented fraternities included the Alpha Nu Omega fraternity organized in 1988 at Morgan State, and Gamma Phi Delta, formed at the University of Texas in 1988. Such fraternities were responding in part to the stereotypical "partying" and other activities involving drugs and sex that have often been associated with the fraternity lifestyle. The Gamma Alpha Chi group, founded by black and white students at Louisiana State University in 1990, exemplified fraternities that hold multiculturalism as a part of their ideology. Delta Phi Upsilon was organized in 1985 at Florida State University and is devoted in part to fostering community and solidarity among gay black men. A natural development of the growing interest among black students in African and African-derived cultures was the formation of fraternities with Afrocentric ideologies. Such groups included Kemet, formed in 1988 at Atlanta University; Ndugu, organized ca. 1995 at Clark Atlanta University; Malika Kambe Umfazi, organized in 1995 at the State University of New York at Buffalo; and Hetheru, formed at Tuskegee University.

Despite the advent of other fraternities and sororities in the 1960s, which continues to the present, the first eight are still considered the major black fraternal groups, and are referred to as "The Great Eight," "The Big Eight," or "The Elite Eight" (Alpha Phi Alpha, Kappa Alpha Psi, Omega Psi Phi, Phi Beta Sigma fraternities, and Alpha Kappa Alpha, Delta Sigma Theta, and Zeta Phi Beta sororities). Of the newer organizations, only Iota Phi Theta has gained membership in the National Pan-Hellenic Council (NPHC; the council of black fraternities), and in the North American Interfraternity Conference (NIC). Although the major black fraternities and sororities are now referred to as "The Noble Nine," or "The Divine Nine," many members and officials of the original eight groups refuse to accept

Iota Phi Theta as worthy of their notice or respect. Those groups that have not gained official entrance into the NPHC are also regarded dismissively, in part because it is assumed that they will lose momentum and disappear before they achieve the numbers and organizational stature that would gain them membership in the NPHC, and in part due to the belief in the superiority of the well-established fraternities.

Traditions

Although some of the folklore of black fraternities is revealed only to those in the group, many traditions are publicly displayed. For example, fraternities have symbols that identify and are sacred to the group, such as colors. The colors of Alpha Phi Alpha are black and gold. Black symbolizes the black man in Western history, and gold signifies the soul. The fraternity's symbols are the sphinx and the pyramid, both allusions to an African heritage. The fraternity colors of Kappa Alpha Psi are crimson and cream, and its symbols are diamonds and the cane. The colors of Omega Psi Phi are purple and gold. Phi Beta Sigma's colors are blue and white, and its symbols are the crescent moon and the torch. Iota Phi Theta's colors are charcoal and brown, and its symbol is the centaur. Although the colors and symbols have special meaning for fraternity members, they are displayed in a variety of ways to the public; for instance, on articles of clothing. Hand signs are another element of fraternity traditions that outside observers may notice, but that have special significance for members of the groups. Hand signals are especially prominent as nonverbal accompaniments to calls during **stepping** shows.

Stepping is a key practice among black fraternities, and it includes a complex set of elements. First, members of separate fraternities performing in stepping shows are customarily dressed identically. Step routines incorporate components of marching bands, military jodies (traditional military songs with "Jody" as a central figure), drill teams, minstrel routines, handclapping games, **cheerleading**, street parades, African **dance**, African American dance (for example, tap and **break dancing**), theater, acrobatics, and pantomime. Routines are orally created, and whereas new routines are regularly developed, certain traditional elements are maintained. Traditional dances are encoded with mythological and legendary significance. For instance, for members of Iota Phi Theta, the symbol of the Centaur, half man and half stallion, is central to the group's identity. The Centaur is displayed on the fraternity's shield, and is armed with a bow and arrow. The Centaur is also a key component of the group's dance routines. In 1966, Brother Robert Young invented the "Centaur Walk," which became a part of the fraternity's stepping performances, during which fraternity members enact the mythological drama of the Centaur about to release an arrow from his bow.

Oral forms are also a part of stepping routines. Chants, songs, or other oral performances are often based on call-and-response patterns. For example, a leader may yell out lines that are then repeated by the group. **Signifying** is another common element of stepping shows, and may be done verbally or through movements and mime. In the context of stepping, signifying is referred to as "cracking."

Because stepping shows are competitive performances between fraternities and sororities, signifying functions to mock, challenge, and assert superiority over rivals. Verbal instances of signifying contain components of **the dozens**, **rap**, marking, and sounding. Steppers also frequently signify or crack nonverbally through dance.

Perhaps the most intense occasions involving folklore in black fraternities are connected with the pledge process. Authors writing about black fraternities, and fraternities in general, have invariably identified the pledge process as a rite of passage. As with fraternities in general, those wishing to become members must suffer through a period of tests and trials, and successfully rise above them before gaining entrance into the fraternal community. Hazing or pledging rituals strip away the formerly constructed identities of the pledges, reducing them to symbolic infancy through physical pain and psychological humiliation. Pledges either pass the tests and are symbolically reborn into the fraternal community with a new identity, or they fail. Pledging rituals take place in the larger social context of the ritualized assaults on black manhood in America, and the perceived necessity to adopt hypermasculine personas to survive and meet the challenges of manhood in American society. Hence, some have suggested that pledging rituals within black fraternities are among the most severe on many college campuses. Some rituals noted for black fraternities are similar to those practiced among other college groups; for instance walking in line, carrying bricks, saluting, speaking in unison with other pledges, and running errands (Kimbrough, 66). However, others that include "paddling, slapping, beatings with a folding chair, and having cigarette ashes dropped in his mouth" (Kimbrough, 74) have led to numerous serious injuries and deaths, and have been a great cause of concern for many. On several occasions over the last several decades the NPHC has met to deliberate pledge-related issues, and has even passed measures against hazing and pledging. Nevertheless, because the ritual process is so integral to the identity of the groups, measures enacted against it simply tend to move the rituals underground. Similarities between many pledging rituals and the experiences of slaves make this phenomenon all the more disturbing.

Besides practices such as beatings (the paddle is a major fraternity symbol and is apparently used frequently and with great severity), another tradition evoking plantation experiences is that of branding. Although there are reports of branding as far back as the 1930s, its popularity has presumably increased since the 1970s. Comments from one fraternity member suggest common attitudes toward the practice: "It's all about how hard did you pledge, you know, how long did it take you to be made, you know, what did you go through? And for an individual now not to have a brand, it's like you didn't go through anything" (Kimbrough, 133). Allusions to slavery are also suggested by the "line"; the practice of pledges walking in single file across campuses. The line evokes images of slaves chained together, of slaves escaping to the North on the Underground Railroad, of slaves packed into slave vessels, and of African rites-of-passage ceremonies. The term "shippie" has often been used to describe pledge classes, and at times classes have been referred to, for instance, as "the Zeta ship" or "the Sigma ship" (Kimbrough, 114–115).

Undoubtedly, the connections between experiences of enslavement and fraternal traditions are complex and worthy of serious study.

Other folk traditions of black fraternities have been implemented in rituals of community support and service. More so than their white counterparts, black fraternities have reputations for their focus on performing civic duties that involve providing aid to black communities. Such aid might include food drives, mentor programs, voter registration drives, and fund-raising activities. Because fraternities evolved out of the historical context of black oppression, they have embodied the long-standing belief that those who are successful in achieving better educations or professional careers should give back to black communities. Besides providing support to communities, an important aspect of fraternities is the lifelong brotherhood and support offered to members. In essence, the fraternity becomes a second, extended family whose support is available for members throughout their lifetimes. Thus, beyond the specific folkloric elements found among fraternal groups, fraternities are contemporary examples of folk communities, characterized by strong emotional bonds and commonly shared beliefs and values. Besides black churches, fraternal communities are perhaps the most important social institutions in African American culture.

Anand Prahlad

See also: Church, The Black

Further Reading

Brown, Tamara L., Gregory Parks, and Clarenda M. Phillips, 2005, *African American Fraternities and Sororities: The Legacy and the Vision* (Lexington: University Press of Kentucky); Dancy, T. Elon II, and Bryan K. Hotchkins, 2015, "Schools for the Better Making of Men? Undergraduate Black Males, Fraternity Membership, and Manhood," *Culture, Society and Masculinities* 7 (1): 7; Fine, Elizabeth C., 2003, *Soulstepping: African American Step Shows* (Urbana: University of Illinois Press); Jones, Ricky L., 2015, *Black Haze: Violence, Sacrifice, and Manhood in Black Greek-Letter Fraternities* (Albany: State University of New York Press); Kimbrough, Walter M., 2003, *Black Greek 101: The Culture, Customs, and Challenges of Black Fraternities and Sororities* (Madison and Teaneck, NJ: Fairleigh Dickinson University Press); Malone, Jacqui, 1996, *Steppin' on the Blues: The Visible Rhythms of African American Dance* (Urbana: University of Illinois Press); McClure, Stephanie M., 2006, "Improvising Masculinity: African American Fraternity Membership in the Construction of a Black Masculinity," *Journal of African American Studies* 10 (1): 57–73; Parks, Gregory, 2008, *Black Greek-Letter Organizations in the Twenty-First Century: Our Fight Has Just Begun* (Lexington, KY: University Press of Kentucky); Parks, Gregory S., and Stefan M. Bradley, 2011, *Alpha Phi Alpha* (Lexington: University Press of Kentucky).

FUNERALS

These are crucial rites that must be performed after the death of the body to ensure the continued life of the soul or spirit. In traditional African American funerals, immediately after the death of the individual, a "settin' up" would be held in which friends and family would sit with the body of the dead as it began its journey to the next world. The settin' up would be followed by as proper a burial as slaves or free (but poor) blacks living during the slavery era could afford. Africans of almost every ethnicity as well as black Americans held (and still hold) strong beliefs about the significance of a proper burial.

The Igbo in West Africa, for example, believed that two burials were required to ensure the longevity of the soul; a physical one, in which the body was laid to rest, and a spiritual one. The spiritual burial was perhaps the more important of the two; it functioned as "the connecting link between this world and the next, as well as the passport, so to speak, of the soul . . . through the hands of the Creator into the land of spirits. Without it . . . the soul, when it leaves the dead body that has been its tenement for so long, cannot pass along the road that leads to its destination" (Leonard, 154). Although the institution of slavery interfered with slaves' ability to perform proper burials, they did find ways to subvert the system and maintain the tradition of a second burial. Their success is proven by contemporary accounts as well as documentation indicating the continued importance of proper funeral rites well into the 20th century. Rosa, a former slave living in Harris Neck on the Georgia Sea Islands, informed a WPA interviewer that "Folks alluz hab two fewnuls. We hab one wen dey die an den once a yeah we hab a suhvice fuh ebrybody wut died durin duh yeah. Duh preachuh say a prayuh fuhrum all." Jane, another former slave living in Darien on the islands, observed, "We ain preach duh suhmon wen we bury um but we waits a wile so's all duh relations kin come. . . . We alluz hab two fewnul fuh duh pusson. We hab duh regluh fewnul wen yuh die. Den once a yeah we hab one big preachin fuh ebrybody wut die dat yeah" (Georgia Writers' Project, 131, 147). In his research, John Blassingame also found that slaves often held services several weeks after the physical burial, although he concluded that the practice reflected demanding labor requirements rather than a preference of the slaves (Blassingame, 33).

A significant number of Dahomeans, a West African people, were brought forcibly to the United States, and they brought their own intricate funerary traditions. They believed that the spirit must follow a long path to reach the spirit world, and to traverse it successfully it would need money, clothes, and tobacco to pay various people that it would meet along the way. Such items must be provided by those the deceased had left behind. Most importantly, however, to cross the river, which was the final boundary dividing the living world from the spirit world, the spirit had to rely on family and friends, because here "neither gifts nor money prevail; he can only be ferried if the boatman is called by the living [through the proper completion of funeral customs] who have been left behind. It is for this reason that the final ceremonies . . . must be so meticulously carried out" (Herskovits, 240). Should the survivors fail in their duties, the spirit would not be able to enter the spirit world; instead he would become a ghost, "doomed to wander between the worlds." In this case, survivors would be punished: "wandering restlessly," ghosts soon "become evil spirits, wreaking their vengeance on their neglectful children" (Herskovits, 240). Such beliefs likewise persisted in the United States, as the numerous spirits wandering throughout African American **folktales** can attest.

Indeed, fear of angry spirits may have been the most powerful motivation for preserving African burial traditions among Africans and their descendants in the United States, because it was a cultural trait shared by Africans of many ethnic backgrounds. Southern Nigerians shared Dahomeans' belief that an improperly buried spirit would be prohibited from entering the spirit land. That spirit would become a trapped ghost, and resenting that position, would blame its family and neighbors. They therefore did "all in their power to humour and appease [spirits'] inveterate hate and insatiable greed" (Leonard, 155). Another ethnic group, the Ashanti, might have found in agreement about the importance of proper burial ceremonies a common ground from which to build a shared sense of black nationalism. They likewise feared the spirits of the improperly buried: R. S. Rattray noted that their motive for carefully completing funerary rites "seems to have been pure fear; fear of the harm the ghost could do." He further observed that it was "the bad, revengeful, and hurtful element in a spirit" that must "at all costs . . . be 'laid' or rendered innocuous. The funeral rites which are now being dealt with are really, I believe, the placating, appeasing, and the final speeding of a soul which may contain this very dangerous element in its composition" (Rattray, 153, 183).

The persistence of strict rules for burial in the United States is evidenced by Charles Ball's *Slavery in the United States*. Ball described a man who came from "a country far in the interior of **Africa**" who said that "he had been a priest in his own nation." When this father lost a child to illness, he insisted on approximating, as closely as possible, a proper burial. The grieving father buried his child with

> a small bow and several arrows; a little bag of parched meal; a miniature canoe, about a foot long, and a little paddle (with which he said it would cross the ocean to his own country), a small stick, with an iron nail, sharpened, and fastened into one end of it and a piece of white muslin, with several curious and strange figures painted on it in blue and red, by which, he said, his relations and countrymen would know the infant to be his son, and would receive it accordingly, on its arrival amongst them. . . . He cut a lock of hair from his head, threw it upon the dead infant, and closed the grave with his own hands. He then told us the God of his country was looking at him, and was pleased with what he had done. (Ball, 374)

Ball also observed that native Africans were "universally of the opinion, and this opinion is founded in their religion, that after death they shall return to their own country, and rejoin their former companions and friends, in some happy region, in which they will be provided with plenty of food, and beautiful women, from the lovely daughters of their own native land" (Ball, 355). Although Ball's presentation of this belief does not make the connection between burial and reincarnation explicit, Africans and their descendants understood that the proper observance of funerary traditions was the key that unlocked the possibility of rebirth. Ball's narrative makes it clear that the burial rites of slaves in the United States had African origins.

The bereaved father's deposit of so many objects in his son's place of burial was common in Africa and among people of African descent in America. "Broken earthenware adorns the surface of the graves of some Afro-Americans in remote areas of

Mississippi, Georgia, and South Carolina," observed art historian Robert Farris Thompson. "[C]arved wooden gravemarkers" have also been found near some of these burial places. Thompson traces this practice back several centuries, noting that "earthenware images were placed on the top of graves along the coast of what is now Ghana in the early eighteenth century." Another of Thompson's sources observed that among the Kwahu of Ghana, the items buried with the dead include "wooden utensils, including a wooden pestle spoon, earthenware, and . . . terra-cotta images." Between the areas now known as Cameroon and the Republic of Congo, "the dead man's goods, cloth, hardware, crockery, and so forth [are] laid by the body . . . on the top of the ground." The placement of household goods, wooden sculpture, and other markers have been observed in the Kongo-Angola area, from where many slaves later sold in South Carolina originated. Items observed on African American graves include "bleached sea shells, broken glassware, broken pitchers, soap dishes, lamp chimneys, tureens, coffee cups, syrup jugs, ornamental vases, cigar boxes, gun locks, tomato containers, teapots, fragments of stucco, plaster images, fragments of carved stonework, glass lamps, and tumblers" (Thompson, 149–150).

As indicated earlier, the emphasis placed on proper burial by Africans and their descendants did not decline after slavery; indeed, Thompson's evidence and the testimony of former slaves collected by Works Progress Administration (WPA) writers demonstrate that an African interpretation of the necessary funerary rites remained strong in America more than a century after the legal importation of Africans ended. The placement of such objects on the grave was a crucial rite. After insisting that dishes, bottles, and other possessions of the deceased must be buried with the person, narrators from the Georgia Sea Island, interviewed ca. 1939, explained the necessity. "The spirit needs these—just like when they's alive," said one informant. Another explained that the objects were placed on the grave "for the spirit to feel at home." Two other informants associated the practice with keeping the spirit happy and preventing death from taking friends and family members. One explained that the items left for the dead must be broken "so that the chain will be broke"; that is, so no one else will follow the departed to the grave. Another individual's testimony explained that leaving the things last used by the deceased on the grave "was supposed to satisfy the spirit and keep it from following you back to the house" (Georgia Writers' Project, 151).

Altogether, the continuance of African-influenced funeral traditions throughout the United States remains among the strongest ties between Africans and their descendants in this country.

Jennifer Hildebrand

See also: Wakes

Further Reading
Atkins, Jennifer, 2012, "Class Acts and Daredevils: Black Masculinity in Jazz Funeral Dancing," *Journal of American Culture* 35 (2): 166; Ball, Charles, with Isaac Fisher, 1999, "Slavery in the United States: A Narrative of the Life and Adventures of Charles Ball, A Black Man," in *I Was Born a Slave*, vol. 1, ed. Yuval Taylor (Chicago: Lawrence Hill

Books); Blassingame, John, 1972, *The Slave Community* (New York: Oxford University Press); Bordere, Tashel C. 2008, "To Look at Death Another Way: Black Teenage Males' Perspectives on Second-Lines and Regular Funerals in New Orleans," *Journal of Death and Dying* 58 (3): 213–232; Collins, Wanda, and Amy Doolittle, 2006, "Personal Reflections of Funeral Rituals and Spirituality in a Kentucky African American Family," *Death Studies* 30 (10): 957–969; Georgia Writers' Project, 1940, *Drums and Shadows* (Westport, CT: Greenwood Press); Herskovits, Melville, 1938, *Dahomey: An Ancient West African Kingdom*, vol. 2 (New York: J. J. Augustin); Leonard, Major Arthur Glyn, 1906, *The Lower Niger and Its Tribes* (New York: The MacMillan Co.); Rattray, Captain Robert Sutherland, 1959 [1927], *Religion and Art in Ashanti* (New York: Oxford University Press); Smith, Suzanne E., 2010, *To Serve the Living: Funeral Directors and the African American Way of Death* (Cambridge, Mass: Belknap Press of Harvard University Press); Thompson, Robert Farris, 1969, "African Influence on the Art of the United States," in *Black Studies in the University*, ed. Armstead Robinson, Craig Foster, and Donald Ogilvie (New Haven: Yale University Press).

G

GAMES, FOLK

Like any cultural group, African Americans from early childhood to old age play a range of games. Most research on games by folklorists, however, has concentrated on play among children. Technically, games are defined as structured forms of recreational competition or imaginative, mimetic play. These play activities usually involve the element of winning or losing and a recognizable structure with rules. Games are distinguished from other kinds of play, sometimes referred to as "pastimes," that lack these elements. For instance, skipping rope or dribbling a basketball would be pastimes, whereas "Hide and Seek" or "Tag" would be considered games. Games have been further divided into three basic categories, reflecting the main emphasis of the play involved. The first category includes games of physical action, such as "Tag" or "Hopscotch." The second category includes games that focus on the manipulation of objects, such as marbles or jacks. The third category includes games that rely on mental activity, such as "Tic-Tac-Toe" or "Charades" (Brunvand, 226–235).

Games teach many different kinds of physical and mental skills. Through socialization, they also help children develop values, beliefs, and proper conduct within society, as well as cultural, racial, and gendered identities. Games and play activities in general tend to involve active imagination, mimicry, and drama, and they are generally recognized as arenas for children, especially, to learn and practice the values that are important to the group to which they belong.

African American games include, among others, song and ring games, imitation games, word games, jump rope games, guessing games, and counting-out games. As with other genres of African American folklore, games include elements of European and African traditions. For example, games containing songs very often may have the combination of European-derived lyrics and melodies with African-influenced physical elements. Recurring aspects of African American games that have been most written about include call-and-response interactions, clapping, **dance** movements, and the use of circles or rings. Unfortunately, most researchers do not specify whether the games are played by boys, girls, or by both, but many of the descriptions of ring, clapping, and song games suggests that these are activities engaged in primarily by girls.

One of the oldest known games is a clapping and song slave game called "Juba." Verses of the song were sung while patting the thigh or feet, or clapping, and sometimes dancing.

> Master had a yaller man.
> Tallest n*gger in de land.

Juba was dat feller's name.
De way he strutted was a shame.
Juba, Juba, Juba, Juba (repeat several times).

(Dance, 507)

"Hambone" and "Jump **Jim Crow**," (which became a theme song of the minstrel tradition) are two other patting or dancing game songs from the slavery period. Other popular ring or circle games that also involve dance and handclapping—and which date back to at least the postbellum period—include "Mary Mack," "Lil Liza Jane," "Little Sally Walker," "Rosie, Darling Rosie," and "Aunt Dinah's Dead." In one version of "Mary Mack," an "It" kneels in the middle of the ring while the group sings and claps, and the "It" performs as the lines of the song direct. Whomever the "It" points her hip toward at the end of the song becomes the next "It."

One version of "Little Sally Walker" goes like this:
Little Sally Walker,
Sitting in the sand,
Crying and a weeping for a nice young man.
Rise, Sally, rise,
Wipe your eye.
Shake it to the east,
Shake it to the west,
Shake it to the one
That you love the best.

(Dance, 503)

These ring games have been popular among African Americans in rural and urban areas throughout the United States and have been common in parts of the Caribbean as well. The game "Watch that Lady," for instance, is found in the United States, Jamaica, Trinidad, Martinique, and Haiti (Courlander, 536). The game is played with one child in the middle of the ring, holding an imaginary key. As the group sings, the "It" enacts various activities such as combing her hair, standing on one foot, shaking, dancing, and so on, and the group has to imitate her. The children also clap during the game.

Clapping games are also prominent in the African American tradition. Most commonly, clapping games consist of two or more people facing each other, patting both each other's open palms and their own in complex rhythmic patterns. Jump rope games are also highly popular among African American children. Often two ropes are used, swung by two players, while a third does the jumping (this is called **double dutch**). Again, there is an emphasis on agility, creativity, and rhythm as the jumper displays elaborate footwork, dance moves, and sometimes flips and other gymnastics. Both jump rope and clapping games are accompanied by song. At times older songs such as "Mary Mack" accompany these games, and at other times more recent lyrics are sung, as with the clapping game, "Grandma, Grandma" (Dance, 510).

Word games are also popular among African American children. One type of word game is counting-out rhymes. The familiar rhyme "Eeny Meeny" has been a part of the black tradition, although the words, at least in collections, have been quite different than those of the stereotypically racist version widely known by many Americans:

Eeny, meeny, miney-mo,
Catch a boy by his toe.
If he hollers let him go.
Eeny, meeny, miney-mo.
Out goes you.

(Hughes and Bontemps, 422)

Riddles are another kind of word game, although riddling is much more popular in the Caribbean than in the United States. The most popular kind of word game in the United States is the game of insult, or verbal dueling, known by such names as the **dozens**, sounding, **signifying**, toasting, rapping, capping, or chopping. In games of verbal dueling, players typically exchange creative insults. The games are most frequently associated with boys, especially adolescents. This type of play has been discussed in terms of honing improvisational, extemporaneous speaking skills and verbal acuity as well as teaching players the value of remaining "**cool**" under assault, a generally valued personality trait for African Americans in the context of a racist society.

Besides the many games that combine African and European elements, some games are believed to be of African origin. A number of games have close parallels with ones found in **Africa**. One of these is "hull-gull," a counting, guessing game. "Hull-gull" is played with two players who sit facing each other. One of them holds a number of dried seeds or similar objects in a fist, while the second player guesses how many the first has. If the second player guesses high, he has to pay the difference between his guess and the actual number of seeds in the first player's hand. If he guesses low, the first player repeats the initial action of picking seeds and holding them in a fist. If the second player guesses correctly, the first player gives away all of the seeds in his hand, and the second player takes his turn at holding seeds in a fist, while the first player guesses. The game ends when one of the players runs out of seeds. This same game also is played in Ghana, where it is known as *owari*, and throughout West Africa, where it is known by a variety of other names (Dance, 504).

Another game that may be derived from African origins is "Chick-a-My, Chick-A-My Crainy Crow," or "What Time, Old Witch?" Players, pretending to be a hen and her chickens, walk around a "witch," who is in the middle of the circle. As they walk, they chant:

Chick-a-my, chick-a-my Crainy Crow,
I went to the river to wash my toe.
When I got back
My black-eyed Susan was gone.
What time, Old Witch?

(Dance, 506)

The witch responds with a number between one and 12, but when she responds by saying "twelve," she jumps up and tries to catch one of the chickens. The captured chicken becomes the next witch. The game exemplifies the difficulty in determining the origin of some games, as the structure of this one is found internationally, resembling such games as the American "Goose, Goose."

African American children's games often contain social commentary on quite serious topics. Improvisation is as much an element of children's games as it is of so many adult genres of African American folklore. For example, the "did-you" game is structured with a leader posing a question and the group responding in unison. Traditional questions include "Did you go to the hen house?" "Did you get any eggs?" "Did you put 'em in the bread?" "Did you bake it brown?" and "Did you hand it over?" After each question, the group responds, "Yes, M'am!" However, one version of the game includes the following lines:

Did you go to the lynchin?
Yes, M'am!
Did they lynch that man?
Yes, M'am!
Did that man cry?
Yes, M'am!
How did he cry?
Baa, baa!
How did he cry?
Baa, baa!

(Hughes and Bontemps, 423)

A more contemporary example, sung as a group line dance, comments on the tragedies caused by drug use in many urban communities:

Yo' momma, yo' daddy, they betta leave that pipe alone.
Yo' sista, yo' brotha, they betta leave that crack alone.
Yo' antee, yo' uncle, they betta leave that pipe alone.
Yo' family, yo' friends they betta leave that crack alone.
Do wha'cha wanna. Do wha'cha wanna.
Do wha'cha wanna. Do wha'cha wanna.

(Saloy)

Such games suggest how important play traditions are in reinforcing community values and providing psychological release for anxieties resulting from difficult and sometimes horrifying realities.

Adults also play many traditional games. One of the most popular is basketball. Although based on the game as played by professionals, "street ball," or "playground basketball," typically emphasizes elements that are often discouraged at the professional level. For instance, verbal dueling, commonly known as "trash talking," is one such prominent element. Elements of verbal dueling tend to be a part of many male-centered games. "Craps," or dice, is another game that has been popular among African American men, going back at least to the postbellum period. Aspects of verbal dueling along with traditional crap-shooting rhymes are often integral parts of the game. One such rhyme is as follows:

Look down rider, spot me in the dark,
When I calls these dice, break these n*ggas' hearts.

Roll out, seven, stand back, craps,
If I make this pass, I'll be standin' pat.

(Dance, 501)

Card games such as poker and table games such as pool and billiards have also held a special place among African American men. Finally, dominoes have historically been a popular game among adult men throughout the African diaspora, and gatherings to play dominoes have taken on similar associations as those made with the social sphere of **barbershops**. One can find men in many parts of the diaspora relaxing while drinking and playing dominoes.

Anand Prahlad

See also: Jump Rope Rhymes/Games; Rap; Toasts

Further Reading

Abrahams, Roger D., 1992, *Singing the Master: The Emergence of African American Culture in the Plantation South* (New York: Pantheon Books); Brunvand, Jan Harold, 1968, *The Study of American Folklore: An Introduction* (New York: W. W. Norton & Company); Courlander, Harold, 1976, *A Treasury of Afro-American Folklore* (New York: Crown Publishers); Dance, Daryl Cumber, ed., 2002, *From My People: 400 Years of African American Folklore* (New York: W. W. Norton & Company); Gaunt, Kyra Danielle, 2006, *The Games Black Girls Play: Learning the Ropes from Double-Dutch to Hip-Hop,* 1st ed. (New York: New York University Press); Genovese, Eugene D., 1972, *Roll, Jordan, Roll: The World the Slaves Made* (New York: Random House); Hopson, Darlene Powell, and Derek S. Hopson, 1996, *Juba This and Juba That: 100 African American Games for Children* (New York: Fireside); Hughes, Langston, and Arna Bontemps, eds., 1958, *Book of Negro Folk-Lore* (New York: Dodd, Mead & Company); Jones, Bessie, and Bess Lomax Hawes, 1972, *Step It Down: Games, Plays, Songs, and Stories from the Afro-American Heritage* (New York: Harper & Row); Levine, Lawrence W., 1977, *Black Culture and Black Consciousness: Afro-American Folk Thought from Slavery to Freedom* (Oxford: Oxford University Press); Saloy, Mona Lisa, 1998 (accessed January 3, 3005), "African American Oral Traditions in Louisiana," http://www.louisianafolklife.org/LT /Articles_Essays/creole_art_african_am_oral.html.

GAY AND LESBIAN FOLKLORE

There have always been lesbian, gay, bisexual, transgendered, and queer (LGBTQ) people in the African American community. Since slavery, homosexuality and heterosexuality have enjoyed relatively unencumbered proximity to each other in African American communities. Professor Roderick Ferguson of the University of Minnesota notes, "Black slaves in North America engaged in a range of sexual practices and elaborated a variety of family structures." Because enslaved African Americans did not have legal marriages that white slaveholders were bound to respect or legal possession of their children, black slave societies consisted of a number of alternative sexual and familial arrangements, some of which included same-sex partnerships. Since the abolition of slavery, many African Americans have worked to improve their public image as moral, law-abiding citizens by adopting the norms of the wider culture in the United States.

With the legalization of black marriages in the 19th century, the institution and strong influence of the black church, and the constant struggle for equal access and recognition in politics and culture, black Americans have become increasingly committed to developing strong, traditional family units. This has led to stringent religious and cultural condemnation of homosexuality. Although some members of the LGBTQ community have found acceptance among their families, political organizations, and religious institutions, homosexuality currently exists in the black community alongside virulent homophobia for the most part.

Homophobia in the black community has been tied in the latter half of the 20th century to radical black politics, such as the views espoused by proponents of black nationalism and black power movements in the 1960s and 1970s. Instead of recognizing homosexuality as intrinsic to individuals within all communities, homosexuality was described primarily in terms of white racial violence against black men in the segregated South. In other words, throughout much of the 20th century, homosexuality was associated with white sexual deviance and black men's emasculation. In his largely autobiographical novel, *Go Tell It on the Mountain*, black, gay writer James Baldwin comments on the subordinate and vulnerable position of black men in the South with the poignant question, "Who had not been made to bend his head and drink white men's muddy water?" In his biography, musician Little Richard recalls, "Sometimes white men would pick me up in their car and take me to the woods and try to get me to suck them. A whole lot of black people have had to do that. It happened to me and to my friend, Lester" (White, 11). For many black cultural nationalists, homosexuality is associated with white sexual depravity and white racial violence.

Even though both Baldwin and Little Richard made a point of describing white sexual violence against black men, both men also experienced attacks by members of the black community for being gay. Perceiving that homosexuality is fundamentally contradictory to the aims of black nation building, black nationalists also disparaged black gays and lesbians for engaging in sexual practices that do not result in the propagation of black generations to preserve, bolster, and defend the race. The cultural injunctions against same-sex relationships that characterize black nationalist politics have corollaries in black churches and in individual black families. Homophobia in the black community reduces LGBTQ people to stereotypes summed up in a series of derogatory folk names, including sissy, punk, f*ggot, and bull dyke, among others. Whereas these offensive terms, and similar vernacular, have historically designated a person who does not fulfill normative gender requirements, they have taken on greater resonances. For example, the word "punk" has entered common parlance as the verb "to punk." To punk someone is to mislead someone, to take advantage of them, or more generally, to make a fool of them. Despite the prevailing antigay sentiment in African American culture, however, strong black LGBTQ subcultures exist and thrive, and include many forms of folklore.

For African American members of the LGBTQ subculture, identifying other nonheterosexual people is key, not only for pursuing romantic partnerships but also for cultivating a community within a community and for developing social networks of support. Festivals are one type of folk event that contributes to a sense of social cohesiveness and pride. For instance, many black LGBTQ individuals participate in annual Gay Pride parades and marches that occur in major American cities in late June, often creating their own smaller gatherings and celebrations as well. Such events also expose the straight community to the diversity of groups that exist within the LGBTQ culture.

For LGBTQ African Americans, the need for community is heightened because they possess at once two stigmatized identities and are subject to both physical violence and social exclusion as a result of both. Furthermore, many LGBTQ African Americans experience pressure to fragment themselves and pledge allegiance to one aspect of their identity over another. Finding safe cultural spaces to proclaim their sexual identity and form cohesive bonds with other LGBTQ people is important for black members of the LGBTQ community. These concerns are reflected not online public events, such as festivals, but also in **folk speech**, dress styles, **storytelling** traditions, and other nonverbal forms of communication. Members of the LGBTQ community sometimes claim to have "gaydar," the ability to recognize other LGBTQ people who may not appear as such. People who engage in same-sex eroticism are sometimes said to be "in the life" or "fam," an abbreviation of the word "family." Both of these terms invoke pride, community, and cohesion. With bars, bookstores, Internet Web sites, community centers, and spiritual organizations that cater to the unique desires and needs of LGBTQ people, it is no longer as difficult as it once was to find and participate in the LGBTQ community.

Although homosexuality is not scripted onto the body directly, there are certain mannerisms, aspects of bodily style, coded gestures, social environments, and linguistic expressions that people believe make homosexuality visible, if not to the straight community then certainly to the gay one. Some of the dress styles and mannerisms enable others to label LGBTQ individuals according to their desires and sexual practices. A man who is very masculine and who dresses according to the latest urban fashions may be called a "homothug." A woman who does the same may be called "aggressive." A man who is effeminate in his manner may be called a "queen" and may be described as "flaming," which denotes one who is flamboyantly and demonstratively gay. An effeminate lesbian may be called a "femme." Black men who prefer to date white men are often designated "snow queens." Those who prefer dating Asian men are designated "rice queens." In order to get away from Eurocentric definitions of their sexual identity, many black LGBTQ people prefer to call themselves "same-genderloving."

For many LGBTQ African Americans, declaring publicly their sexual identity put them at risk of religious condemnation, social alienation, family rejection, and homophobic violence, also known as "gay bashing." Despite these risks, many black members of the LGBTQ community disclose their sexual orientation to their families, friends, and coworkers. This process is called "coming out." Members of the LGBTQ community often share their coming out stories with one another. Although each story is different, coming out stories typically include descriptions of: (1) one's dawning awareness of same-sex desire, (2) first sexual experiences, (3) family members' and peers' reactions, and (4) final acceptance of his or her sexual identity. Because most people dwell within a number of social networks simultaneously, coming out is a continual process of disclosure, and it is not uncommon for people to come out first to family and then to colleagues or coworkers, or vice versa.

There is more pressure currently in the black community for people to disclose their sexual practices since the advent of the "Down Low brother." The phrase "living on the Down Low," or "DL," has been popularized by the media in discussions of HIV transmission among heterosexuals in the black community. The term is used to describe black men who have sex with other men but do not consider themselves gay or bisexual. These men are not effeminate, do not participate publicly in the gay subculture, and have wives and girlfriends who are unaware of their partner's same-sex practices. Whether pressured to do so by a homophobic community that holds them responsible for the spread of disease or inspired by an internal wish to share an otherwise private aspect of their identity, coming out is an empowering experience for many LGBTQ people because it allows them to get beyond shame and repression to live their lives and celebrate their desires "out loud."

Aliyyah I. Abdur-Rahman

Further Reading

Baldwin, James, 1995 [1953], *Go Tell It on the Mountain* (New York: The Modern Library); Beam, Joseph, 1988, *In the Life: A Black Gay Anthology* (Boston: Alyson Publications); Boykin, Keith, 1996, *One More River to Cross: Black and Gay in America* (New York: Anchor Books); Carbado, Devon W., et al., eds., 2002, *Black Like Us: A Century of Lesbian, Gay, and Bisexual African American Fiction* (San Francisco: Cleis Press); Constantine-Simms, Delroy, 2001, *The Greatest Taboo: Homosexuality in Black Communities* (Boston: Alyson Publications); Ferguson, Roderick, 2004, *Aberrations in Black: Toward a Queer of Color Critique* (Minneapolis: University of Minnesota Press); Goodwin, Joseph P., 1989, *More Man Than You'll Ever Be: Gay Folklore and Acculturation in Middle America* (Bloomington: Indiana University Press); Hemphill, Essex, and Joseph Beam, eds., 1991, *Brother to Brother: New Writings by Black Gay Men* (Boston: Alyson Publications); Jay, Karla, ed.,1995, *Dyke Life: From Growing Up to Growing Old, a Celebration of the Lesbian Experience* (New York: Basic Books); Lorde, Audre, 1984, *Sister Outsider: Essays and Speeches* (New York: Crossing Press); Reid-Pharr, Robert F., and Samuel R. Delany, eds., 2001, *Black Gay Man: Essays* (New York: New York University Press); White, Charles, 1984, *The Life and Times of Little Richard: The Quasar of Rock* (New York: Harmony Books).

GEECHEE
See Gullah

GESTURES
See Nonverbal Communication

GOSPEL MUSIC
Gospel music is a sacred composed music that is a product of the black folk church in the early 20th century. It is a synthesis of music, **dance**, poetry, and drama dis-

tilled into a unified whole. Rooted in **spirituals**, sanctified tunes, early congregational and urban revival songs, **blues**, and ragtime, gospel emerged as an innovative popular style of sacred music. Today, because of stylistic changes, gospel is divided into and recognized as traditional and contemporary forms; however, the genre is still evolving.

Gospel music represents a strong link to African roots in both subtle and sometimes obvious ways. African American slaves in the 18th century created the spiritual, which was strongly influenced by African musical concepts. The spiritual served as the most important musical tradition until the Civil War. After the war, that sacred music of sorrow, rebellion, and hope was transformed along with the slave populace. There is a conceptual link between the spiritual and gospel music, and the aesthetic values and performance practices intrinsic to the gospel music tradition do not represent a break with the traditional past.

With the outbreak of World War I and later World War II, many southern rural blacks migrated to urban centers, which seemed to hold promises of economic and social opportunities and personal freedom. Unfortunately, life in the cities often did not meet the expectations of the migrants. The practice of discrimination in employment, housing, and education forced African Americans to create an alternate lifestyle.

Gospel, a new sacred music reflecting the concerns of urban life, replaced the rural spiritual and gave a sense of pride and hope to those who had recently uprooted themselves in pursuit of a dream that seemed increasingly difficult to attain. The new gospel was a highly emotional and spirit-filled music that evolved from the dynamics of "**praise houses**," which were slave-quarters church congregations. Gradually, the gospel style spread throughout northern cities through worship services in Pentecostal and Baptist "storefront churches" that held services in buildings that were formerly stores or warehouses.

In these sacred spaces, musical practices played a very significant role in the ritual services. Many West African musical concepts contained in the spiritual were used in forming the foundation of gospel music. Hand clapping, foot stomping, and other body movements were incorporated in the gospel music performance style. Freedom of expression was manifested in call-and-response structures and layered rhythms as well as spontaneous testimonies, prayers, and praises from individuals. In time, many different kinds of churches across the country were using the exciting sounds of gospel in their services.

Charles A. Tindley, renowned during his lifetime as an eloquent Methodist minister, pioneered gospel music in Philadelphia during the early 1900s. He is credited with being the first African American to compose both music and words and publish the first gospel prototype, also referred to as the "gospelhymn." His compositions include such standards as "Stand By Me," "Leave it There," "Nothing Between," and "We'll Understand It Better By and By." Tindley composed about 50 songs, and his most prolific writing period was from 1900 to 1906. However, the songs did not become popular until Pentecostal church congregations began to use them in the 1920s. These congregations were considered the primary influence on the emergence of gospel music during this era.

In Chicago, an ex-blues pianist by the name of Thomas A. Dorsey was influenced by Tindley's work, and during the Great Depression he became a major catalyst in bringing gospel music to the forefront. During his blues years, Dorsey, known as "Georgia Tom," composed blues music and accompanied performers including Gertrude "Ma" Rainey and Tampa Red. However, after surviving a serious illness and seeing the death of his wife and child, Dorsey dedicated his musical talents to the service of God and the church. His songs were not accepted at first because of his background and the obvious influence of the blues on his music. However, while working to develop and popularize the form, he established his own publishing company, used persistent promotional and distribution methods aimed at church congregations, and was one of the founders of the National Convention of Gospel Choirs and Choruses. These feats, along with composing songs that communicated hope to the masses in difficult times, eventually led to his acceptance. He also engaged the services of Roberta Martin, Sallie Martin, and Mahalia Jackson to perform his songs for congregations and at conventions. Dorsey, now commonly recognized as "the Father of Gospel Music," established the foundation and style for an original 20th-century genre of black sacred music. He captured the spirit of the urban lifestyle and gave blacks a source of hope and inspiration through his musical style and in the lyrics to his songs. "Precious Lord, Take My Hand," "There Will Be Peace in the Valley," and "The Lord Will Make a Way Somehow" are some of his best-known tunes.

Most of these early gospel songs have verse-chorus structure, called the strophic form. They are based on primary triads and seventh chords with the third and seventh degrees of the scale often varied to create "blue notes." Although these characteristics are usually present in a song's written form, gospel songs are rarely performed as written; they leave room for improvisation. Since the songs are usually transmitted orally, they are classified as "composed folk songs" and are interpreted individually by singers as well as instrumentalists.

One of the main elements in black gospel performance is that of contrast in both the vocal and instrumental parts. Since the 1920s, instrumental accompaniment has been added to the traditional hand clapping and foot stomping. Instruments that are commonly found in gospel music performances include pianos, organs, drums, a variety of horns, and even synthesizers. The use of these instruments can create many tonal contrasts within a single piece.

During the 1930s and 1940s, male quartets, female quartets, and mixed groups were prominent. Tindley, Dorsey, Lucie E. Campbell, Theodore Fry, Herbert W. Brewster, Kenneth Morris, and other early pioneers in the field tended to compose especially well for the four-part harmony style used in quartet and small-group arrangements. The quartets and groups toured outside of their home communities as professionals or semiprofessionals, and the market for the music was very high. Therefore, expansion of the repertoire was necessary to please different audiences. In fact, the four-part harmonies in many old, secular "doo wop" songs from the 1950s evolved directly from the sound of gospel quartets.

Other elements contribute to the excitement of a gospel music performance. One key feature is audience participation. People in the audience are encouraged to add their voices to the sounds of the choir and soloists whether in a call-and-response

The choir of St. Charles Borromeo Catholic Church sings for mass. Once only associated with Baptist churches, gospel choirs now perform in many different denominations, as well as at secular events. (Andrew Burton/epa/Corbis)

situation or all together as one big chorus. The colorful robes worn by small ensembles and choirs and the uniform suits and tuxedos worn by quartets, as well as the bouffant hairstyles, long flowing gowns, and other dramatic clothing worn by female groups, are all part of the gospel music aesthetic tradition. Both audience participation and the wearing of colorful and dramatic clothes represent a continuation of performance practices that grew out of African musical customs.

The Great Depression ended with the start of World War II, and with the war brought affluence came an increase in purchasing power, high-volume record sales, and *Billboard* magazine top-seller lists. Since the late 1940s, gospel music has become big business, and this factor, perhaps more than any other, has influenced changes in its performance. Numerous independent record companies were set up immediately following the war to serve the renewed demand for gospel "race records," records targeted for the African American community. Radio also served as an outlet for the promotion of gospel music. The major radio networks featured quartets and groups on live broadcasts, and the groups began to tour on a large scale. Quartets like the Soul Stirrers, the Fairfield Four, the Blind Boys of Alabama, the Dixie Hummingbirds, the Zion Harmonizers, and the Spirit of Memphis were in great demand by promoters. They competed with each other, and in this strong competitive atmosphere, versatility and virtuosity became even more necessary.

Although congregational singing was still prevalent in the churches, church and community choirs began to proliferate in the 1950s with the advent of the civil rights movement, the development of a new African American consciousness, and the subsequent uniting of religious institutions for a common cause.

In the late 1960s, gospel music crossed over to the secular charts for the first time. "Oh Happy Day," recorded in 1969 by the Edwin Hawkins Singers, reflected the secular style of **soul** music and launched gospel music into a new era. It was the first gospel song to cross over to the soul charts. Since then other innovations have occurred, including the use of full orchestras, the increase in gospel songs arranged from secular compositions, and the production of gospel-based musicals.

In the late 1980s, yet another form, "**rap** gospel," emerged as an outgrowth of the cultural phenomenon of rap music that is still making an impact on not only African American communities but also the world. In the same vein, Caribbean communities have developed hybrid gospel styles referred to as "reggae gospel" and "gospelypso." Gospel songs that are derived from existing genres often employ the form associated with that source. The improvisatory nature and the lack of a predetermined song length allow gospel performers to expand, contract, and make other changes to established forms at will.

Over the years, gospel music has evolved to encompass many traditions and styles of music, from **spirituals**, hymns, and blues to contemporary **jazz** and soul. It has had a great impact on contemporary music, providing a reservoir of musical styles and practices. Many black popular music performers served their musical apprenticeships in the field of gospel music, as members of church or community quartets, groups, or choirs. These singers include Sam Cooke, Aretha Franklin, Lou Rawls, Dionne Warwick, Gladys Knight, and Whitney Houston.

Performers of the traditional style are Rev. James Cleveland, Shirley Caesar, the Fairfield Four, and Mahalia Jackson. The contemporary style of gospel mixes in more elements from popular music, soul, rhythm and blues, and musical technology such as synthesizers and music videos. The Winans, Yolanda Adams, Kirk Franklin, and Donnie McClurkin lead this style. It also mixes in elements from rap, **hip-hop**, stage plays, and musical theater, including changes in dress attire that distinguish some of the most recent gospel from earlier periods. Further, recent gospel has seen the emergence of more women playing a more prominent role in gospel; for example, as gospel announcers (Pollard). Despite changes in musical style and content, gospel continues to serve a vital cultural function in the black community, succeeding spiritually, artistically, and commercially.

Joyce Marie Jackson

Further Reading

Abbington, James, 2014, *Readings in African American Church Music and Worship, Volume 2* (New York: W. W. Norton & Co.); Boyer, Horace Clarence, 2000, *The Golden Age of Gospel Music* (Urbana: University of Illinois Press); Burnim, Mellonee, 1988, "Functional Dimensions of Gospel Music Performance," *Western Journal of Black Studies* 12 (2): 112–121; Costen, Melva Wilson, 2004, *In Spirit and in Truth: The Music of African American Worship* (Louisville: Westminster John Knox Press); Jackson, Joyce Marie, 1995, "The Changing Nature of Gospel Music: A Southern Case Study," *African American Review* 29 (2): 185–200; Jones, Pearl Williams, 1975, "Afro-American Gospel Music: A Crystallization of the

Black Aesthetic," *Ethnomusicology* 19 (3): 373–385; Pollard, Deborah Smith, 2008, *When the Church Becomes Your Party: Contemporary Gospel Music* (Detroit: Wayne State University Press); Price, Emmett George, 2012, *The Black Church and Hip Hop Culture: Toward Bridging the Generational Divide* (Lanham, MD: Scarecrow Press); Reagon, Bernice Johnson, ed., 1992, *We'll Understand It Better By and By: Pioneering African American Gospel Composers* (Washington, DC: Smithsonian Institution Press).

GRAFFITI
See Aerosol Art

GRAPEVINE, THE
"The grapevine" is the informal network of communication that exists in African American communities. Because of white control of the more formal outlets for disseminating information, the grapevine has always been of great importance in African American culture.

The term "grapevine telegraph" came into common use in the United States in the late 1840s or early 1850s to denote a form of communication that was different from the straight lines of the telegraph wire. Jonathan Lighter in *The Random House Historical Dictionary of American Slang* states that the first recorded usage was in a political dictionary of 1852, which included the sentence, "By the Grape Vine Telegraph Line . . . we have received the following." In the white community it came to mean an unsubstantiated **rumor**. *The Oxford English Dictionary* cites this 1867 usage: "Just another foolish grapevine," from B. F. Willson's *The Old Sergeant*.

In the black community, on the other hand, the grapevine, or the grapevine telegraph, referred to a more authentic source of information than racist white newspapers, official statements, and words from slaveholders. It existed long before the term became familiar in white culture and consisted of information passed from person to person, from plantation to plantation. **Spirituals**, with their hidden messages, were part of the grapevine, as were drums. Enslaved Africans were adept at communication over long distances without written material or telegraph wires because of the primarily oral tradition most of them came from. The grapevine was crucial to the security of the black community, providing an alternative to the great danger of letting the world be defined and limited by white information.

Booker T. Washington, in his autobiography, said that he often heard his mother talking with other slaves about events before and during the Civil War. "These discussions showed that they understood the situation, and that they kept themselves informed of events by what was termed the 'grape-vine' telegraph," he wrote. This same sort of information network persisted long after slavery was abolished and was used for more ordinary purposes, such as keeping up with black fashions and hair care methods that were not covered in white women's magazines. The term "grapevine," is connected to the proverbial expression, "to hear something through the grapevine," suggesting that one learns about something through word of mouth or rumors. In 1967 Gladys Knight and the Pips gave the expression new life with her song "I Heard It through the Grapevine," followed by Marvin Gaye's version in 1968. Although alternate origins of the expression have been suggested, it is indisputable that it enjoyed currency among African Americans going back to the slavery period. It continues to be widely used, not just among African Americans, but in American culture in general.

Kathleen Thompson

Further Reading

Heacock, Paul, 2003, *Cambridge Dictionary of American Idioms* (Cambridge: Cambridge University Press); Hine, Darlene Clark, and Kathleen Thompson, 1998, *A Shining Thread of Hope: The History of Black Women in America* (New York: Broadway Books); Stevenson, Brenda E., 1996, *Life in Black and White: Family and Community in the Slave South* (New York: Oxford University Press); Washington, Booker T., 1963, *Up from Slavery: An Autobiography* (New York: Doubleday).

GRAVE DECORATIONS

Grave adornments of various sorts were part of the complex set of African American **funeral** practices in North America. Decorations could include carvings and symbols on coffins and items placed on top of graves or interred with the deceased. The African origins of these practices have been demonstrated by a number of scholars, including Robert Farris Thompson, John Michael Vlach, and Michael Blakey. While the influences on the funeral practices of African Americans originated in a number of African cultures, the Kongo region of western Central **Africa** provided the most important burial retentions. This is true of South Carolina and Georgia, where western Central Africans accounted for the majority of slave imports. In this regard, the African ethnic groups imported into Virginia and New York City determined the funeral practices in those regions also.

Surviving well into the 20th century, the Kongo influences on African American burial practices are the most significant, though it is likely that certain customs were found among a number of African groups. Of particular note is the practice of placing earthenware, broken **pottery**, and other possessions on top of graves. Traced to both the Gold Coast and western-Central Africa, the use of burned terracotta images or wood sculptures and broken pottery symbolized the human form destroyed by death. Another interpretation, offered by former slaves living in coastal Georgia, was that pottery and glass were broken to symbolize the broken chain of life. If the items were not broken, then others in the family of the deceased might die also.

These items were also meant to reinforce the idea that the dead should be honored by having favored possessions placed on top of their eternal resting places. Black cemeteries in Texas, Missouri, Georgia, South Carolina, and Delaware showed striking representations of Kongo influences. At these specific sites, conch shells were among the items placed on top of graves. In western Central Africa, emblematic conch shell spirals were painted on red cloth to represent the Kongo cosmogram (a symbol or pictograph of the cosmos) and to indicate the point of spiritual return. Though the forms are obviously different in these examples, the use of the conch shell as a symbol of spiritual transmigration demonstrates the perseverance of ancient Atlantic African customs in 19th- and 20th-century North America. In certain cases, shells accompanied a burial mound. Again, this reflects a practice that resonated in Kongo culture. In this specific regard, building a burial mound and placing a fence of shells around it was a means of conveying a message of protection and concern to the departed spirit. African American burial mounds, with or without embedded conch shells, are most notable in Georgia, Alabama, South Carolina, and other parts of the **South**.

At times, the last object used by the deceased was placed on top of the grave in an effort to arrest or comfort the spirit. In this case, the gravesite itself becomes a kind of **charm**. Items placed on top of burial sites were meant to both enclose and appease the spirits of the deceased. The act of enclosing the spirit in earth perhaps explains the importance of goofer dust, also known as graveyard dirt, in the creation of charms in African American folk culture. While interpretations may vary, it is clear that burial sites were seen as places of enormous spiritual power and ancestral protection. This view may explain the use of ceramic white chickens at African American gravesites. Reflecting a Kongo belief in which white chickens symbolized the protective power of ancestral spirits, this practice is possibly linked to the sacrifice of white chickens over graves in western Central Africa, the Caribbean, and the American South.

At the Utopia Quarter slave cemetery in James City County, Virginia, grave decorations demonstrate another strong hint of African influence. In this particular case, goods were placed inside graves as gifts to the ancestral spirits or as means to provide comfort to the deceased in their spiritual journeys. The burial site of an adolescent at Utopia Quarter included a bead necklace of amethyst-colored glass. Clay tobacco pipes were interred at other sites in this burial ground, representing a connection to Igbo culture. During the 18th century, the Igbo of the Niger River delta buried spiritual leaders and distinguished elders with tobacco and pipes to comfort them in the afterlife.

In addition to the many examples in the South, the recently discovered African Burial Ground in New York City demonstrates the continuity of African religious beliefs. As the oldest and largest colonial-era African American graveyard in North America, the African Burial Ground dates back to the late 1630s and was in active use until 1796. Though only 427 of approximately 20,000 graves were excavated by November 1993, it is clear from this small sampling of remains that certain African cultural practices were frequently carried out at the burial ground. Of particular note is the coffin lid on Burial 101, which has 51 metal tacks arranged in a heart-shaped pattern. This unique symbol on the coffin, which dated from the early 18th century, could be a representation of the Akan (Gold Coast) *Adinkra* known as *sankofa*. *Adinkra* refers to a group of symbols used frequently as stamped patterns on cloth. The symbols denote folktales, proverbs, animals, virtues, and historical events. At the time, *Adinkra* cloth was only worn at funerals, but is now worn on many occasions. The term *Adinkra* is also sometimes used to refer to this type of cloth. The *sankofa* symbol, one of *Adinkra*, would be quite appropriate on a coffin or grave marker because it symbolizes the concept of spiritual transmigration among Akan speakers. *Sankofa* means to look to the past in order to understand the present—a notion fully intertwined with the belief that every human being has lived many past lives.

Other tangible connections to Africa were found at the African Burial Ground. Burial 340, which contained a clay pipe and 111 beads of various types, also points to a strong connection to African cultural vectors. Michael Blakey, anthropologist and scientific director of the African Burial Ground Project, claims, "The string of 111 glass beads and cowrie shells around the waist of one woman's burial . . . suggest that she belonged to an Akan-speaking society in which such beads are buried with their owner. A quartz crystal and examples of shells buried with human remains point to a variety of African burial customs" (Blakey, 55–56). In addition, large amounts of broken pottery were also found at the burial ground, though this could have been the kiln refuse from two nearby pottery factories.

Walter Rucker

Further Reading

Arnett, Paul, and William Arnett, 2000, *Souls Grown Deep: African American Vernacular Art of the South,* Volumes 1 and 2 (Atlanta, GA: Tinwood Books); Blakey, Michael, 1998, "The New York Burial Ground Project: An Examination of Enslaved Lives, A Construction of Ancestral Ties," *Transforming Archaeology: Journal of the Association of Black Anthropologists* 7: 53–58; Cartwright, Keith, 2013, *Sacral Grooves, Limbo Gateways: Travels in Deep Southern Time, Circum-Caribbean Space, Afro-creole Authority (The New Southern Studies)* (Athens: University of Georgia Press); Fenn, Elizabeth A., 1984, "Honoring the Ancestors: Kongo-American Graves in the American South," *Southern Exposure* 13: 42–47; Ferguson, Leland, 1992, *Uncommon Ground: Archaeology and Early African America, 1650–1800* (Washington, DC: Smithsonian Institution Press); Holloway, Joseph, ed., 1991, *Africanisms in American Culture* (Bloomington: Indiana University Press); Jabbour, Alan, and Karen Singer Jabbour, 2010, *Decoration Day in the Mountains: Traditions of Cemetery Decoration in the Southern Appalachians* (Chapel Hill: University of North Carolina Press); Jamieson, Ross, 1995, "Material Culture and Social Death: African-American Burial Practices," *Historical Archaeology* 29: 39–58; McClusky, Pamela, 2002, *Art From Africa: Long Steps Never Broke a Back* (Seattle Art Museum. Princeton, NJ: Princeton University Press); Samford, Patricia, 1996, "The Archaeology of African-American Slavery and Material Culture," *William & Mary Quarterly*, 3rd Series, 53: 87–114; Thompson, Robert Farris, 1991, "Kongo Influences on African-American Artistic Culture," in *Africanisms in American Culture*, ed. Joseph Holloway (Bloomington: Indiana University Press), pp. 148–184; Vlach, John M., 1977, "Graveyards and Afro-American Art," *Southern Exposure* 5: 61–65; 2014, "African American Grave Decoration," www.http/southernart.ua.edu (accessed November 1, 2015).

GULLAH

Gullah, or Geechee, refers to both the culture and language of African Americans who have historically resided on the South Sea Islands, also known as the "Gullah Coast" or the "Gullah Corridor." The Gullah Corridor encompasses an "area along the southeastern coast of the United States from the northern border of Pender County, North Carolina to the southern border of St. Johns County, Florida and 30 miles inland (http://www.gullahgeecheecorridor.org)." This area includes roughly 79 barrier islands, among them, Saint Helena, Hilton Head, and James Island, of South Carolina; Sapelo Island, Georgia; and Amelia Island, Florida.

Gullah Culture

The Gullah are a unique group of African American descendants of enslaved Africans who were shipped from West Africa's Rice (West) Coast more than two centuries ago. They brought with them many of their indigenous African skills in agricultural production, such as rice cultivation, which was a desirable skill among 18th-century Georgia and Carolina slave owners and planters (Wood; Littlefield), and "the knowledge of how to make tools needed for rice harvesting" (http://www .georgiaencyclopedia.org) and tools for other forms of agricultural and domestic labor, such as larger mortars and pestles. They also brought many other West African cultural traditions: for example, the style of sweetgrass **basket weaving** which is also found in Sierra Leone (Opala); Gullah fishing, crabbing, and shrimping traditions; and some favorite Gullah cuisines that are similar to West African recipes for foods such as rice, stewed vegetables, gumbo, red rice and okra soup, and greens. Folklorists and other observers have documented African influenced religious rituals, such as the **ring shout** and worship services in **praise houses, games,** songs, **dance, funeral** traditions, **trickster** narratives such as **Brer Rabbit** tales, **herbalism** and traditional healing practices, **wood carving,** and performance styles in music and **storytelling**. Because of their geographical isolation on the islands, and because there was less effort on the part of slave owners to strip them of their African culture, the Gullah were able to maintain more African traditions and cultural perspectives than other African Americans on the mainland. This led to their often being stigmatized by other African Americans, who saw them as "backward," and used terms such as "rice field Negroes," or "rice eater." Even the term "Geechee," which is sometimes used interchangeably with "Gullah," has often been used as a slur.

When it comes to Africanisms and the continuity of African cultural traditions, the Gullah Corridor and its people are recognized as one of the most culturally rich areas and groups in the United States. The strong African influence on their culture has enabled scholars to theorize and substantiate African survivals and to better understand the hybridization of African folk forms in the New World. Examples of Gullah folklore in many genres have become emblematic—for example, basket making, spiritual beliefs, herbalism, grave decorations, and religious rituals. It is no accident that the language of **Uncle Remus** tales is influenced by Gullah folk speech. Representatives of Gullah culture have been visible at folk festivals, such as the Smithsonian Folklife Festival, since the folk revival of the 1960s, and they have toured and appeared in many other educational and cultural venues as well.

Gullah Language

Much scholarship has been devoted to the origins and linguistic features of the Gullah language. It has been argued that the word "Gullah" itself is a derivative of Angola and the Gola tribe. The word "Gola" (or "Goulah") is the name of an ethnic group found in parts of Sierra Leone and Liberia, an area historically known for slaving and rice agriculture (Turner; Sengova). The Gola also speak a West Atlantic language called *Gola*. Also, the country of Angola, located further down the western African coast, is home to another African group of people, the Ngola, who also speak a language by that name. Historian Peter Wood brought an American angle to the issue by suggesting a possible Native American influence, citing "Ogeechee," the Native American name for Georgia's tidal water area, as the origin of "Geechee."

While scholars disagree on the origins of the language, they agree that Gullah is a Creole language that developed from a mixture of English dialects and African languages. The language has historically been maligned by folklorists and writers. For instance, Krapp (1924) called Gullah speech "a form of baby-talk" or "infantile English," that is, not a so-called real language like English with unique sound features, grammar, and vocabulary. For folklorist Ambrose Elliott Gonzales (1922), it was "peasant English" adopted as a favorite vehicle of communication between slave masters and their slaves because it was easier for the enslaved Africans to understand than English. Methodist Episcopal clergyman William Pope Harrison thought he heard Gullah speakers speaking "English in a broken way"; in Harrison's exact words, "hundreds still jabbered unintelligently in their Gullah and other African dialects." Like Harrison, another Charleston cultural writer, Samuel G. Stoney, in his preface to Ambrose Gonzales's classic book *Black Border*, makes a demeaning remark about Gullah speech, which in some ways reminds one of early European attempts to figure out the nuances of hundreds of African languages:

> Their speech was a guttural staccato that made a Dutchman name them the "Qua-Quas," because they gabbled like geese. A Gola negro on a plantation was a marked man, his quacking tongue would betray him; and his speech was "gullah" (uncouth) to the other negroes. With dramatic justice, their general jargon became "Gullah" to the white man.

Lorenzo Dow Turner, the first black linguist, was also the first to seriously challenge early assumptions about Gullah in his studies from the 1940s. He showed that Gullah speech derived from more than 30 different sub-Saharan Niger-Kongo languages. In his book *Africanisms in the Gullah Dialect*, Turner tried to show that Gullah was not only derived from substandard dialects of British English but also from several major African Niger-Kongo languages. He used approximately 4,000 African words, phrases, and expressions found in conversations, stories, **prayers**, and songs to describe Gullah as "a creolized form of English," a mixed language of English and African origins. He found what he called "survivals from many of these African languages spoken by the slaves who were brought to South Carolina and Georgia during the 18th and first half of the 19th century" (Turner).

Turner argued that he had found many striking similarities between Gullah and the African languages in the speech sounds or pronunciation and the way in which words are formed and arranged in sentences and phrases. However, according to him, the African retentions or "survivals" were most numerous in the vocabulary of Gullah (see Turner; Sengova).

Other linguists have noted similarities between Gullah, Sierra Leonean Krio, and other Atlantic Creole languages spoken by descendants of enslaved Africans in the New World, including those spoken in Jamaica, Trinidad, Suriname, and Barbados. Compare these Gullah, Krio, and English examples:

Gullah: "Anytime . . . where you see a big fire, they killin' hog."
Krio: "Eni tem wey you see big fire, them de kill hog."
English: "Anytime you see a big fire going, someone's slaughtering a hog."

In literary and folklore texts, Gullah dialect lives on in such works as Joel Chandler Harris's Brer Rabbit tales and in the fiction of South Carolina's Ambrose E. Gonzales.

Gullah Today

Many elements of traditional Gullah culture and language have been affected and threatened by forces such as migration to the mainland, lack of jobs, encroaching development, and real estate development. The Gullah Corridor officially became the Gullah Geechee Cultural Heritage Corridor in 2006, through an act of Congress, which was created to help preserve Gullah Geechee culture. At that time, Congressman James E. Clyburn wrote: "Stories and traditions of this fusion of African and European cultures brought long ago to these shores have been slipping away along the marsh and sand that are disappearing because of the encroachment of developments and pressures to assimilate into the 'modern' world." But he also noted that small enclaves remained, continuing to practice traditions from 400 years ago. Prior to this legislation, Gullah people had come together and declared themselves a nation on July 2, 2000. They elected Queen Quet, Chieftess and Head-of-State for the Gullah/Geechee Nation (www.QueenQuet.com). The nation drafted a constitution, and a declaration of goals that included the protection and continued development of their culture, and their right to self-determination. The Gullah/Geechee nation is a strong and determined culture that continues to thrive and to confront the challenges that have threatened their ways of life (www.gullahgeecheenation.com). They have become for many African Americans a cultural symbol of African centered aesthetics and lifestyles, as evidenced by filmmaker Julie Dash's now-classic *Daughters of the Dust*, by the numbers of African Americans who have become interested in learning more about the Gullah, and in events such as the annual Heritage Day Celebrations.

Joko M. Sengova

Further Reading
Adams, Dennis, and Hillary Barnwell, 2002, *The Gullah Dialect and Sea Island Culture. Part 1: The Gullah Dialect* (Beaufort, SC: Beaufort County Public Library), http://www

.co.beaufort.sc.us/bftlib/gullah.htm; Cross, Wilbur, 2008, *Gullah Culture in America* (Westport, CT: Praeger); Dalgish, Gerard M., 1982, *A Dictionary of Africanisms: Contributions of Sub-Saharan Africa to the English Language* (Westport, CT: Greenwood Press); Gonzales, Ambrose, 1922, *Black Border: Gullah Stories of the Carolina Coast* (Columbia, SC: state co.); Hamilton, Kendra, 2012, "Mother Tongues and Captive Identities: Celebrating and 'Disappearing' the Gullah/Geechee Coast," *Mississippi Quarterly* 65 (1): 51–68; Hancock, Ian F., 1980, "Texas Gullah: The Creole English of the Brackettville Afro-Seminoles," in *Perspectives on American English*, ed. J. L. Dillard (The Hague: Mouton) pp. 305–333; Harrison, William Pope, 1893, *The Gospel among the Slaves* (Nashville: Publishing House of the Methodist Episcopal Church); Krapp, George Phillip, 1925, *The English Language in America*, 2 vols. (New York: Frederick Ungar); Littlefield, Daniel C., 1981, *Rice and Slaves: Ethnicity and the Slave Trade in Colonial South Carolina* (Baton Rouge: Louisiana State University Press); National Park Service, 2005, "Gullah Geechee Special Resource Study, Low Country Gullah Geechee Culture," http://www.nps.gov/sero/planning/gg-srs/gg-process.htm; Opala, Joseph, 1986, *The Gullah: Rice, Slavery and the Sierra Leone-American Connection* (Freetown Sierra Leone: United States Information Service); Sengova, Joko, 1994, "Recollections of African Language Patterns in an American Speech Variety: An Assessment of Mende Influences in Lorenzo Dow Turner's Gullah Data," in *The Crucible of Carolina: Essays in the Development of Gullah Language and Culture*, ed. Michael Montgomery (Athens: University of Georgia Press), pp. 175–200; Smalls, Krystal A., 2012, "'We Had Lighter Tongues': Making and Mediating Gullah/Geechee Personhood in the South Carolina Lowcountry," *Language and Communication* 32 (2): 147–159; Stewart, Thomas J., and Joko Sengova, 1993, "Genesis of Gullah: Some Early and Contemporary Accounts of African-American Ethnicity and Provenance in the South Carolina–Georgia Low Country" (unpublished paper); Turner, Lorenzo, 1949, *Africanisms in the Gullah Dialect* (Ann Arbor: The University of Michigan); Wood, Peter H., 1974, *Black Majority: Negroes in Colonial South Carolina from 1670 through the Stono Rebellion* (New York: Knopf).

GUMBO

Gumbo is a thick soup or stew that is usually thickened with okra. Sometimes filé powder, or ground sassafras root, is used as an alternative thickener. The English word "gumbo" comes from the African Kongo word *quingombo*, which means okra. The term is sometimes used to refer to just the vegetable okra, *Hibiscus esculentus*, to either the plant or its pods. Gumbo stew can feature ingredients like chicken, duck, seafood (e.g., shrimp, crabs, oysters), andouille sausage, crawdads, and/or turkey. Other additions might be celery, onions, tomatoes, peppers, beans, and, of course, okra. Gumbo is sometimes served over rice. Herbs, chili powder, and broth or stock help provide flavor for gumbo.

Roux, a mixture of fat and flour cooked together in equal amounts, forms a flavorful base for most gumbo and also helps to thicken it. The flour contributes to the thickness of the gumbo, while the fat—lard, oil, or butter—smoothes the flour and prevents lumps from forming. A roux is formed by melting the fat and adding the flour, then cooking the mixture over low heat. To prevent the roux from scorching, it must be stirred during this process. There are three varieties of roux: white, blond, and brown. Brown roux is the type used in Cajun and Creole cooking, and it is cooked the longest. Although the words "Creole" and "Cajun" are often used interchangeably, they describe two separate cultures, traditions, and cooking styles. Creole is a blend of Spanish, French, African, Portuguese, and West Indian styles. Cajun is French Canadian in origin. Okra is a staple in Creole cooking, and gumbo is possibly the most famous Creole dish.

At least two well-known New Orleans–based musicians have named their recordings after gumbo. In 1972, Dr. John, who took the name of a 19th-century Vodou healer as his stage alias, released his album *Dr. John's Gumbo*, featuring the song "Iko Iko." Rhythm and blues artist Professor Longhair followed with *Rock 'n Roll Gumbo* in 1974.

"Gumbo" is also a term for a French patois spoken by Creoles. A patois is the spoken dialect of a region, which often differs fundamentally from the official, written, or literary language. Patois results from the mixing of two or more cultures and languages. Gumbo patois is spoken by black and Creole people in Louisiana, Bourbon, Mauritius, and the French West Indies. New Orleans writer Sybil Kein explores Creole language and culture in her poems. One of Kein's books of poetry is titled *Gumbo People*. Gumbo may also refer to the mud of the prairies or the lower portion of the Mississippi Valley.

M. J. Strong

See also: Folk Foods

Further Reading

Broussard, James F., 1972, *Louisiana Creole* (London: Kennikat Press); Harris, E. Lynn, and Marita Golden, eds., 2002, *Gumbo: A Celebration of African American Writing* (New York: Harlem Moon); Kein, Sybil, 1999, *Gumbo People* (New Orleans: Margaret Media); McKee, Gwen, 1986, *The Little Gumbo Book* (Brandon, MS: Quail Ridge Press); Opie, Frederick Douglass, 2010, *Hog and Hominy: Soul Food from Africa to America* (New York: Columbia University Press); Saxon, Lyle, Edward Dreyer, and Robert Tallant, eds., 1987, *Gumbo Ya-Ya: A Collection of Louisiana Folk Tales* (Gretna, LA: Pelican Publishing).

H

HENRY, JOHN

The legend of John Henry is about a black railroad worker who dies winning a contest with a steam drill. Its most common form is a **folktale** or folk song. It is usually set at the Big Bend Tunnel in West Virginia around 1870 or at a similar point in the Industrial Revolution, and John Henry is almost always a character of lauded physical prowess who works as a steel driver for the C&O Railroad.

However, as would be expected of any folktale, dozens of documentations of the John Henry text give us almost as many versions of it. Furthermore, and much more remarkably, the text of the John Henry story has been found in several folklore genres, from verse to material art. The versatility, tenacity, and long history of this text in all its versions and genres best attest to its importance in African American folklore and American folklore in general. To appreciate the meaning and functions of all these different versions and genres, we must study them in context by tracing the John Henry text through its rich history.

The earliest documentation of the John Henry text was by an Appalachian ballad collector, Louise Bascom, in 1909. From this account, only the first two lines are preserved: "John Henry was a hard-workin' man / he died with a hammer in his hand." E. C. Perrow collected John Henry verse from southern railroad workers who spoke of a "steel-driving man." These early ballads told by railroad workers to other railroad workers emphasize John Henry's supernatural physical strength and prowess, idealizing him as a railroad hero. Further idealizing him, the most common lines in this genre refer to John Henry being the most attractive man to "all de women in de wes."

The 1920s in America saw a flurry of scholarship about African American folklore and folk song, especially African American song. Many folk song collectors, including John Avery Lomax, Newman I. White, and Howard Washington Odum, published bits of John Henry songs collected in a traditional context. These collections provided the material for some commercial and semitraditional musicians, including Aaron Copeland, John Wesley Work III, W. C. Handy, Charles Seeger, Bob Gibson, and Leadbelly to record popular versions of the John Henry song to sate the public's ravenous appetite for nostalgic Americana that peaked during the Great Depression. Here we have a perfect illustration of the process by which a folklore text, such as folk song, weaves in and out of other contexts (such as mainstream, popular, or commercial contexts).

In the late 1920s and early 1930s, the scholars who published the first two full-length volumes on John Henry folklore, sociologist Guy Benton Johnson and folklorist Louis Chappell, laid the groundwork for a rush of collectors of narrative folklore and fiction writers who use folklore to take interest in the John Henry folk narrative. Beginning with the book *Here's Audacity! American Legendary Heroes* by Frank Shay (Books for Libraries Press, 1930), a juvenile audience was targeted to construct John Henry as an American folk hero, often as the black Paul Bunyan. In the more protracted artistic form of the children's book, the John Henry text enjoys its greatest embellishments. Just as folklore texts are recreated in popular contexts, as is the case with the John Henry folk song, here we see how folklore is recreated in the context of high art: in the 1930s, these unprecedented full narratives gave Palmer Hayden the material to tell a complete life story of John Henry in the form of a collection of twelve oil paintings.

As John Henry was fleshed out in full-length literary treatments in the 1930s, a wide range of common African American folk types stuck to this now-popular folk hero. In James Cloyd Bowman's 1942 book, *John Henry, The Rambling Black Ulysses*, the title character receives his fullest embellishment as a **trickster** who outsmarts con men and gamblers. In other children's books, John Henry resembles **Uncle Tom** as a selfless, fulfilled worker who dies a martyr for the cause of American progress.

In contrast, it was in the 1950s with the John Henry **toast**, part of a genre of verse commonly exchanged between adult black men, and with the many folk songs collected by Alan Lomax, that we see John Henry as a **bad man**. In these versions, the sexual imagery underlying John Henry's contest is exploited, and Lomax reads it through a specifically Freudian lens that casts the hammer as phallic, and the journey through the tunnel as intercourse. In these versions, John Henry's relationship to a Polly Ann or Julie Ann is filled out as the female character he notoriously loves and leaves. Also in these versions, John Henry often dies not of man-against-machine struggle, but of lovemaking. The first fictional retelling of John Henry for adult audiences by Roark Bradford in 1931 casts John Henry as a monstrous demon with hideous features and terrifyingly supernatural powers.

Because of the ambiguity at its heart—its setting being the anxiety-ridden time between slavery and industrialism, its hero being a member of a politically demonized group, and its resolution being simultaneously a remarkable victory and a tragic defeat—the John Henry text is especially ripe for a wide range of theoretical applications and critical readings. Besides the Freudian analysis already treated, the text is tapped for its Marxist potential in the 1953 book *American Folksongs of Protest*, when John Henry is cast as the labor martyr of preunion times. Alan Dundes insightfully places John Henry in a genealogy of African American folklore in which the less powerful outwits the more powerful, a tradition starting with **Brer Rabbit** and progressing with John and Old Marster. In addition to these especially germane postcolonial readings, also available are absurdist, nihilist, and Lacanian readings.

In popular and high art, for example in contemporary musicals targeting a young, multicultural audience, the text is most often read didactically: John Henry's work ethic, perseverance, and talent immortalize him as a role model for young black people facing discrimination and oppression, and in these forms, John Henry's type resembles the **preacher**. Besides souvenirs, posters, adult fiction books, a sculpture, ceramics, and fine wood carvings, two notable contemporary examples of other nonfolkloric incorporations of the John Henry text are Julian Schnabel's 1996 **film** *Basquiat* and Colson Whitehead's 2001 novel *John Henry Days*, but other noteworthy popular and high art representations of John Henry are too numerous to mention. This sheer wealth of contemporary representations of this character in such a wide range of versions, genres, and contexts expresses the enduring relevance of John Henry folklore.

Lucia Pawlowski

Further Reading

Bicknell, J. 2009, "Reflections on 'John Henry': Ethical Issues in Singing Performance," *The Journal of Aesthetics and Art Criticism* 67 (2), 173–180; Dorson, Richard, 1965, "The Career of John Henry," *Journal of American Folklore* 24: 155–163; Garst, John 2006, "On the Trail of the Real John Henry," *History News Network* (George Mason University); Green, Archie, 1978, "John Henry Depicted," *JEMF Quarterly* 14: 126–143; Nelson, Scott Reynolds, 2006, *Steel Drivin' Man: John Henry, the Untold Story of an American Legend* (Oxford: Oxford University Press).

HERBALISM

Herbalism is the practice of using herbs medicinally to treat various ills of a physical, spiritual, or psychological origin. When we consider African botanical medicine, one of the first obstacles to overcome is the scarce use of the term "herbalism" as it formed from a European conceptual basis rather than African tradition. Most African healers are specialists from various professions who use herbalism along with other forms of natural therapy within the community. Priests and priestesses, shamans, witch doctors, hunters, medicine men, midwives, and diviners are all adept herbalists. Within their respective communities there is more of an emphasis on the practitioners' larger role in society than a specific focus on how they use herbs (Bird 2003).

In traditional West Africa, a holistic approach to health has existed for thousands of years, continuing in most areas to the present day. The tradition continues in the Americas (Bird 2003). Africans brought in-depth knowledge of the environment, farming, and sustainability with them, and this knowledge is essential to survival. They also brought indigenous West African plants. The plants carried include licorice, which was used on the boats of the Middle Passage to deter seasickness; grasses; sesame (benne); okra; melon seeds; and black-eyed peas (Fett, 63).

From the earliest history of enslaved Africans in the Americas and Caribbean, people of African descent were directly involved in health care on plantations. Mostly, herbs and other natural ingredients (like honey, salts, and clay) were used as medicine (Mitchell, 27). By the 18th century, herbal medicines of enslaved Africans began to incorporate indigenous American plants like Jerusalem oak and capsicum (Fett, 63).

In the United States, practitioners of herbalism in the African American community were often called "rootworkers." Illnesses (whether of the mind, body, or spirit) are cured with roots (used here as a synonym for herbs), by a rootworker, also known as an herbalist. Materials called medicines or roots include barks, berries, roots, leaves, flowers, and herbs, and are used for physical and spiritual illness (Mitchell, 33). African American rootworkers do not simply heal a sore throat; they examine environmental issues, spiritual matters, overall health, and the psychological state of their clients before making any diagnosis (Bird 2003, 46).

Objective use of the phrase "witch doctor," stripped of religiosity and negative stereotypes, aptly fits African herbalism because it suggests a magical–spiritual and physical connection (Bird 2003, 46). Slaves who were specialists in herbal healing were commonly called "doctor" or "doctress" (Mitchell, 30). These local doctors offered what the white (allopathic) doctors did not—a community-based, African-influenced healing paradigm.

The local rootworkers or doctors were healers of choice on the plantations, a tradition that continued well after emancipation. In the book *Ain't You Got a Right to the Tree of Life? The People of Johns Island, South Carolina—Their Faces, Their Words and Their Songs*, informant Mrs. Janie Hunter describes the self-sufficiency herbalism offers: "We don't go to no doctor. My daddy used to cook medicine-herbs medicine: sea muckle, pine top, life everlasting, shoemaker root, ground moss, peach tree leaf, big-root, bloodroot, red oak bark, terrywuk." Mrs. Hunter also describes a few **Gullah** remedies: "Now when my children have fever, I boil life everlasting; squeeze little lemon juice in it." For children with parasites, Mrs. Hunter reports, "we get something call Jimsey weed. You put it in cloth and eat [chew to soften] it. And when you done beat it, you squeeze the juice out of it and you put four, four drop turpentine in it, give children that to drink. You give a dose of castor oil behind 'em. You don't have to take 'em to no [allopathic] doctor" (Carawan and Carawan, 27).

According to indigenous African philosophy, you cannot just give an aspirin or cook up an herbal recipe for healing. Among other things, the knowledge of the energetic configuration and the identity and purpose of the person being treated is essential (Some Patrice). Elsewhere in the diaspora, practitioners called Obeah men of Jamaica are also herbalists and root doctors. Understanding their view of herbs as being spiritual and imbued with healing powers sheds light on herbalism within the African diaspora. According to Joseph McCartney, Obeah practitioners believe "plants absorb the cosmic properties of the sun, moon and planets, whether they are taken internally or used as a fetish or amulet [like a **mojo** bag]" (McCartney, 98).

The job of the Obeah man is steeped in herbalism. Obeah men need to be skilled in the knowledge of the pharmaceutical qualities and medicinal applications of certain plants and herbs to treat common ailments, the methods of preparation of particular medicines, and their administration, including dosage and potential side effects. Preparations are similar to those used in folk medicine all over the world, including Chinese herbalism, Western (European-based) herbalism, and East Indian Ayurveda. These preparations include poultices, teas, and baths used to treat a variety of ills from kidney disease to boils, fevers, and AIDS (Olmos and Paravisini-Gebert, 137).

The foundation of African American herbalism was self-determination and empowerment. From the gathering of plants in the forests (what is today called "wildcrafting") to the transmission of applications of herbal knowledge from one generation to the next, southern black herbalism reflected a sacred, parallel relationship between health, community identity, and healing (Fett, 62). Knowledge of herbs enriched many aspects of life and was not limited to applications for physical illnesses. Enslaved African Americans used botanical knowledge to make clothing dyes, clothing and accessories, **games**, arts and crafts, food, and of course medicines, all using local plants (Fett, 70). Names of the herbs, like Little John, Heart Root, Blood Root, Sacred Root, and **High John the Conqueror** root, attest to an animistic vision of plants. Colloquial names of the plants also encapsulate the stories, ethos, and beliefs of African people in various locations throughout the diaspora.

Passing down herbal knowledge from generation to generation, the "doctors" also served as griots, preserving heroic epics and survival stories that can be traced to West African origins. Root doctors were generally conversant not only with natural medicine but also with everyday, acute, and chronic conditions (Mitchell, 30). According to Mrs. Hunter, "the older generation, those old people, died out now, but they worked their own remedy and their own remedy came out good" (Carawan and Carawan, 27).

Herbalism is not a tradition limited to **Africa**, plantations, or rural practice. As early as the 1930s, folklore interviewers were recording herbal healing practices directly from practitioners in major metropolitan areas like New York City. The interview of Sagwa by Works Progress Administration (WPA) writer Vivian Morris (October 31, 1938) called "Harlem **Conjure** Man" is an example. Vivian Morris reports that if she were a believer in fantasy, Harlem would now appear to be a distant land, intriguing as the activity in a conjure man's den after dark. She goes on to say that she is almost convinced that no matter what the ailment, there is an herbal treatment in Harlem that could cure it.

Morris' interview also sheds light on the early manifestation of stores that successfully blend herbalism with allopathic medicines within a pharmacy setting, a tradition that continues in neighborhood "spiritual" shops and botanicas from San Francisco to Harlem. To illuminate the point there is a brief discussion of the respected root doctor William Weiner, known as Jupiter Man, who was also a registered pharmacist (Works Progress Administration [WPA] Writers Project interview, October 31, 1938).

Today black herbalists like Brooklyn-based Lisa Price of Carol's Daughter and author/manufacturer Queen Afua (*Sacred Woman* and *Heal Thyself*) continue to offer herb-based natural products to treat a variety of health and beauty concerns specific to the African American community.

Blues, "American Roots" music, such as that by Robert Johnson and Muddy Waters, preserves the traditions of the root doctor and conjure man's practices in the United States in the 20th century. Olu Dara, a Southerner transplanted from Mississippi to Harlem, is a contemporary singer/songwriter whose lyrics succinctly describe African American "roots" medicine (herbalism) in his song "Herb Man" on the CD titled *Neighborhoods* (Bird 2003, 44–45). Blues songs that feature stories of conjure men, mojo bags, and **Hoodoo**, as well as Olu Dara's "Herbman" serve as a materia medica of African American folk healing using African traditional oral transmission.

Stephanie Rose Bird

Further Reading

Anderson, Jeffrey E., 2008, *Hoodoo, Voodoo, and Conjure: A Handbook* (Greenwood); Bird, Stephanie Rose, 2009, *A Healing Grove: African Tree Remedies and Rituals for Body and Spirit* (Chicago, IL: Lawrence Hill Books); Bird, Stephanie R., 2003, "African-American Herbal Traditions," *Herb Quarterly* (Winter): 44–48; Bird, Stephanie, 2004, *Sticks, Stones, Roots and Bones: Hoodoo, Mojo and Conjuring with Herbs* (St. Paul, MN: Llewellyn Worldwide Publishers); Carawan, C., and G. Carawan, 1989, "They Worked Their Own Remedy," interview of Mrs. Janie Hunter in *Aint You Got a Right to the Tree of Life? The People of Johns Island, South Carolina, Their Faces, Their Words and Their Songs* (Athens and London: The University of Georgia Press); Covey, Herbert C., 2007, *African American Slave Medicine: Herbal and Non-herbal Treatments* (Lanham: Lexington Books); Dara, Olu, 2001, "Neighborhoods" (Atlantic Records, Audio CD 83391); Fett, Sharla, 2002, *Working Cures: Healing, Health and Power on Southern Slave Plantations* (Chapel Hill and London: The University of North Carolina Press); Hazzard-Donald, Katrina, 2013, *Mojo Workin': The Old African American Hoodoo System* (Urbana, IL: University of Illinois Press); McCartney, Joseph, 1976, *Ten, Ten the Bible Ten: Obeah in the Bahamas* (Nassau, Bahamas: Tom Paul Publishing); Mitchell, Faith, 1999, *Hoodoo Medicine: Gullah Herbal Remedies* (Columbia, SC: Summerhouse Press); Mitchem, Stephanie Y., 2007, *African American Folk Healing* (New York: New York University); Morris, Vivian, 1938, "Conjure Man," personal interview with Sagwa, West 141 Street near Lenox Avenue, Harlem, New York, October 31, *American Life Histories: Manuscripts from the Federal Writer's Project, 1936–1940*; Olmos, Margarite Fernandez, and Lizabeth Paravisini-Gebert, 2003, *Creole Religions of the Caribbean: An Introduction from Vodou and Santeria to Obeah and Espiritismo* (New York and London: New York University Press); Some Patrice, Malidoma, 1998, *The Healing Wisdom of Africa: Finding Life Purpose through Nature, Ritual and Community* (New York: Jeremy P. Tarcher/Putnam).

HIGH JOHN THE CONQUEROR

See John the Conqueror, High

HIP-HOP

Originally an African American urban musical style, hip-hop is characterized by **rap** (a rhyming spoken-word performance) and disc jockeying (the mixing and sampling of recorded music).

Hip-hop arose as a folk style among African American New Yorkers in the 1970s, on the heels of **soul**, funk, and disco. Seeking relief from the mainstreaming and sanitizing of black musical genres, nightclub and block-party disc jockeys, chief among them Jamaican Kool DJ Herc of the Bronx, developed the techniques of both isolating percussion elements from **dance** music and talking to audiences between or during songs in a rhythmic and movement-inspiring manner. Eventually, the practice of mixing samples from records on separate turntables became commonplace and merged with lyrical spoken vocals, the predecessors of which appear in West African praise singing, Jamaican dub music, and African American rhyming traditions. A hip-hop subculture emerged, marked visually by the spread of graffiti art and the prevalence of loose-fitting, casual clothes accessorized with baseball caps and ostentatious gold medallions.

The first major recorded rap/hip-hop single, the 1979 "Rapper's Delight" by the Sugarhill Gang, was followed in the early 1980s by the popularization of **break dancing**, the style of street dance that often accompanied hip-hop, and a surge in rap recordings by artists including Afrika Bambaataa, Fatback Band, Kurtis Blow, LL Cool J and Run DMC. Musicians varyingly used synthesizers, samples, and instrumental performances, and the lyrics began to expand beyond self-referential discourse into socially conscious commentary, initiated by the song "The Message," released by Grandmaster Flash and the Furious Five in 1982. By 1985, black women had hit the hip-hop scene, led by the trio Salt-N-Pepa, and the 1980s saw the emergence of the first mainstream white rappers, the Beastie Boys and Vanilla Ice.

The end of the 1980s brought the beginning of both the political hip-hop style known as "gangsta rap," in the work of artists such as Ice-T, Public Enemy, and N.W.A (N*ggaz with Attitude), and, through many of the same artists, the explosion of a West Coast hip-hop scene. Controversies arose from both developments. Gangsta rap, with its often violent, sexually explicit, profane, and politically subversive lyrics, drew the attention of censorship advocates, including Senator (later Vice President) Al Gore's wife Tipper Gore. With others, she formed the Parents Resource Music Center and helped to make mandatory the use of parental-advisory warning labels on albums featuring lyrics about sex, drugs, or violence. Rap group 2 Live Crew's music was banned from retail outlets nationwide, and cities passed new ordinances to impede 2 Live's concerts; eventually the group fought obscenity charges in court. N.W.A's "F*ck Tha Police" irritated the FBI and helped spread in mainstream American culture the myth that rappers presented a danger to law enforcement as well as to the general public.

In truth, the dangers were internal, arising from the second major development in late-1980s rap: the West Coast scene, from which arose the infamous East Coast/West Coast rivalry of the 1990s. West Coast hip-hop, featuring a funkier sound, was dominated by Marion "Suge" Knight's Death Row Records and hip-hop artists such as Snoop Dogg, while the East Coast scene revolved around Bad Boy Records, led by multitasking culture-maker Sean "Puffy" Combs (Puff Daddy/P. Diddy) and featuring rappers including Busta Rhymes. Dozens of rappers found opponents to "dis" (disrespect), with most criticisms concerning selling out (appealing to white mainstream culture), imitating other rappers' styles, or otherwise being unoriginal. Some known squabblers in hip-hop have included Dr. Dre and Eazy-E; LL Cool J and Canibus; Eminem and Everlast; Fat Joe and Jay Z; Foxy Brown and Lil' Kim; and Ja Rule and DMX.

Although the taunting of rivals in performances had been a long-standing component of hip-hop, as an evolution of the African American tradition of "playing the **dozens**," the conflicts grew serious in the mid-1990s. At the peak, the young Death Row Records artist 2Pac (Tupac Shakur), after claiming to have slept with the wife of Bad Boy Records' Notorious B.I.G. (Biggie Smalls), was murdered in the fall of 1996, and B.I.G. was killed in the spring of 1997; both were shot to death while riding in cars. Neither murder was solved, and the hip-hop world exploded with lore. A popular urban legend, circulated through print and electronic media, was that Tupac had faked his death to boost record sales; several new Tupac albums and music videos, in which he appeared, were released after the shooting, and fans found "hidden messages" in the titles and lyrics to suggest that the rapper was still alive. Other theories include (1) that Notorious B.I.G. ordered Tupac's murder and Death Row Records retaliated, with members of the Bloods gang carrying out B.I.G.'s murder; and (2) that the intended targets were actually Knight and Combs, who were with the victims at the times of the shootings. Combs's ability to attract controversy did not end when Tupac was laid to rest. In December of 1999, while purportedly flaunting his wealth, popularity, and girlfriend (singer/actress Jennifer Lopez) at a New York nightclub, Combs angered and provoked a verbal assault from Brooklyn felon Matthew "Scar" Allen, and shots were fired, including some from Puffy's protégé, rapper Jamal "Shyne" Barrow. Combs eventually was acquitted of charges related to the incident, but tales continued to circulate that Combs had fired a gun and/or bribed his driver to claim possession of his weapon. Shyne went to prison.

Such incidents and resulting **rumors** in the late 1990s helped cement the myth of the hip-hop artist as street savvy, potentially thuggish, armed, and willing to kill to protect personal interests and/or settle an argument. For example, rapper Jay Z, widely lauded for his talent, pled guilty to stabbing record producer Lance "Un" Rivera in 1999. Closely tied to—and possibly inextricable from—this aspect of hip-hop lore is the notion that hip-hop artists are expected to have led difficult lives, which both excuse their legal troubles and enable them to achieve authenticity in their work, helping them connect with urban youth from tough neighborhoods. Rapper 50 Cent has boasted about having been shot nine times. Grammy-winning white rapper Eminem (Marshall Mathers/Slim Shady), notorious for misogynistic and antigay lyrics, raps about a childhood full of poverty, abuse, and parental neglect. These images, embraced by the urban audiences they're expected to reach, also have gained appeal among middle-class white listeners, for whom the hip-hop lifestyle holds danger and glamour, which makes the music more appealing and marketable. The marketing, meanwhile, expands beyond the music itself and into attire; in hip-hop culture, fashion equals status. Along with the work of white designer Tommy Hilfiger, rappers and fans have embraced labels such as Phat Farm (from rap mogul Russell Simmons), FUBU (a.k.a. For Us By Us) and Sean Jean (Combs's clothing line), as well as sportswear by Nike. Priced beyond the expected reach of the working class, the clothes and their accompanying image attract a middle-class youth following.

While hip-hop has permeated the borders of all American communities, it also has reached international audiences of various socioeconomic levels, appealing most overtly to members of oppressed groups. Shantytowns of South Africa produced hip-hop artists during and after apartheid, including groups such as Black Noise and Brasse Vannie Kaap. Cuban group Cypress Hill has met with success both in Latin America and in the United States. From the Maori people of New Zealand, a disenfranchised indigenous nation seeking sovereignty from the white-dominated government, have arisen hip-hop artists such as Upper Hutt Posse and Dalvanius Prime. Caribbean musicians have merged reggae, a hip-hop predecessor, with contemporary hip-hop to create sounds made famous by the likes of Shaggy and Sean Paul.

Tied to the internationally embraced music, fashion, and sensational rap rumors, an associated slang sown in the hip-hop subculture has spread into mainstream language in the United States and abroad. Early hip-hop slang of the 1980s— "homie" (home boy/friend), "phat" (**cool**)—gave way to "bling bling" (flashy, expensive jewelry) by the end of the 1990s and was supplanted in the 2000s by a more complicated vocabulary and grammar. California rapper E-40 coined terms such as "po-po" (police) and "skrilla" (money) as well as a means of injecting "illy" and "izzle" into commonplace language, a vernacular style made popular by the better-known rapper Snoop Dogg (Calvin Broadus). Terms such as "f'shizzle" (for sure) soon became a fixture of the mainstream youth lexicon, bolstered by Snoop's 2003 MTV variety series "Doggy Fizzle Televizzle" and multiple advertisements.

However, on the flip side of fun-loving linguistic play is a long-standing tendency toward sexist and misogynistic language in hip-hop—including references to women as "**bitches**" or "**hos**" (whores) and the condoning of violence against women—language often paired with music videos showing male rappers amid a bevy of barely clad, sexually generous, silent women. By the end of the 1990s and the early 2000s, the trend had sparked a backlash among women in hip-hop culture and a surge in the popularity of women hip-hop artists promoting images of strength and independence, including Queen Latifah, Eve, Lauryn Hill, and Missy "Misdemeanor" Elliott.

Hip-hop has continued to evolve, both musically and culturally, splitting into smaller "alternative" hip-hop subcultures.

Karen Pojmann

Further Reading

Ayanna, s.v. "The Exploitation of Women in Hip-Hop Culture," MySistahs.org, http://www.mysistahs.org/features/hiphop.htm; Bakari, Kitwana, 2002, *The Hip Hop Generation: Young Blacks and the Crises in African American Culture* (New York: Basic Civitas); Court T.V.'s Crime Library, s.v. "Hip-Hop Homicide: East Coast vs. West Coast," http://www.crimelibrary.com/notorious_murders/celebrity/shakur_BIG/2.html?sect=26; Davey D.'s Hip Hop Corner, s.v. "The History of Hip Hop," http://www.daveyd.com/raptitle.html; Edwards, Paul, 2015, *The Concise Guide to Hip-Hop Music: A Fresh Look at the Art of Hip-Hop, from Old School Beats to Freestyle Rap* (New York: St. Martin's Griffin); illseed, "Hip Hop's Love of Pain," AllHipHop.com, http://www.allhiphop.com/editorial/?ID=212; Katz, Mark, 2012, *Groove Music: The Art and Culture of the Hip-Hop DJ* (New York: Oxford University Press); Light, Alan, ed., 1999, *The Vibe History of Hip Hop* (New York: Three Rivers Press); Nelson, George, 1998, *Hip Hop America* (New York: Viking Press); Nuzum, Eric, s.v. "Censorship Incidents," "Parental Advisory: Censorship in America," http://

ericnuzum.com/banned/incidents/; Ogg, Alex, 2002, *The Men behind Def Jam: The Radical Rise of Russell Simmons and Rich Rubins* (New York: Omnibus); Parker, Chris, 2004, "The Trial of Sean Combs: An Illustrative Tale," *Rock N Roll Quarterly*, November 17, Web page http://indyweek.com/durham/2004-11-17/rrq4.html; Pough, Gwendolyn D., 2004, *Check It While I Wreck It: Black Womanhood, Hip Hop Culture, and the Public Sphere* (Boston: Northeastern University Press); Rose, Tricia, 1994, *Black Noise: Rap Music and Black Culture in Contemporary America* (Hanover, NH: Wesleyan University Press); 2Pac2K.de, s.v. "Tupac Rumors Alive and Well," http://www.2pac2k.de/cgi-bin/articles.pl?73.txt; Rabaka, Reiland, 2012, *Hip Hop's Amnesia: From Blues and the Black Women's Club Movement to Rap and the Hip Hop Movement* (Lanham, MD: Lexington Books); Schloss, Joseph Glenn, 2009, *Foundation: B-boys, B-girls, and Hip-Hop Culture in New York* (New York: Oxford University Press).

HO

This is a term derived from the African American English pronunciation of "whore." Ho (sometimes hoe) employs the African American grammar and pronunciation pattern of final and postvocalic "r," in which the "r" sound found at the end of a word or after a vowel is not heard. The word demonstrates the way African Americans creatively manipulate language to signify on white society. Although no longer as coded as it once was, an early humorous story concerns the way those outside the community might translate or misinterpret the meaning of the word as "hoe" the garden tool, as opposed to ho'. Geneva Smitherman argues that the word is as follows:

> A generic reference to any female, used by males and females, women use the term to refer to close friends and intimates, as well as to antagonists and rivals. . . . A reference to a male or female who engages in sex indiscriminately. A reference to a female who engages in sex for free (older meaning). In this sense, the ho is contrasted with the prostitute, ho is perceived as more principled because she works for a living, i.e. she engages in sex as a business. (Smitherman, 135)

In early traditions of **toasts** and the **dozens** of the late 1960s and 1970s, the term occurs specifically in regard to sexuality: "Back in forty-two when the poor man had nothing to do, / All the hoes had made plans / To f*ck each other like a natural man / So I went to this ho house" ("At the Whorehouse," Dance, 234). The recording of the tale conveys the particular variations and adjustments to the term made by the speaker of this particular toast. The spelling of ho alternates between keeping the "e" or dropping it altogether. Despite the difference in spelling, the speaker establishes that ho/hoe also could mean a prostitute/whore who does have sex for money, and it explains why one must always consider the context of the word, rather than assume fixed meaning.

Over the years, African Americans have also used the term in reference to African American males who have sex with numerous women, now commonly called "players" by **hip-hop** communities. In the same way that Otis and Carla Redding redefined "tramp" as a marker of black male sexual promiscuity in their classic

soul duet of the same title, African American **rap** artists of the 1980s and 1990s once employed the generic reference to both males and females who are sexually promiscuous. In Whodini's classic rap song, "I'm a Ho" (Jive/RCA/BMG, 1988), the three rappers proclaim, "I'm a ho / you know I'm a ho. / How do you know? / because I just told you so."

In other hip-hop lyrics, ho becomes a marker of expression used as a type of call-and-response while at a party or on the **dance** floor. For example, Naughty By Nature's "Hip Hop Hooray" (Tommy Boy Records, 1999) extended the rejoinder "Hey! Ho! Hey! Ho!" to make use of the variant meaning of "ho." This use of the term ho actually dates back farther, to the 1920s and 1930s, when Cab Calloway incorporated ho as a call-and-response party starter in his scatting tune "The Hi-De-Ho Miracle Man":

> Sister Green came to me for my love recipe,
> Said she'd heard about my miracle plan,
> Sister Green is now okay,
> Takes a treatment everyday,
> From the Hi-De-Ho Miracle Man!
> He's the Hi-De-Ho Miracle Man!
> Hi-de-hi-de-hi-de-hi!
> Ho-lo-lo-lo!

Time and again, African American culture (music, literature, folkore, and comedy) revises and changes the term for its own needs. Despite the various uses of the term, it remains controversial for its perceived ideology of demeaning women. Although the term, which was dominant during the 1980s and 1990s, is still used, it has gone the way of other black terms, to be replaced by fresher and less co-opted words such as "chickenhead," "skeeza," and "hoochie."

LaMonda Horton-Stallings

Further Reading

Adams, T.M., and D.B. Fuller, 2006, "The Words Have Changed but the Ideology Remains the Same: Misogynistic Lyrics in Rap Music," *Journal of Black Studies,* 36: 938–957; Dance, Daryl Cumber, 1978, *Shuckin and Jivin: Folklore from Contemporary Black Americans* (Bloomington: Indiana University Press); Majors, Clarence, 1994, *Juba to Jive: A Dictionary of African-American Slang* (New York: Viking); Monk-Turner, Elizabeth, and D'Ontae Sylvertooth, 2008, "Rap Music: Gender Difference in Derogatory Word Use," *American Communication Journal,* Vol. 10, No. 4: pp. 1–12; Reid-Brinkley, Shanara R., 2008, "The Essence of Respectability: Black Women's Negotiation of Black Femininity in Rap Music and Music Video," *Meridians: Feminism, Race, Transnationalism* 8 (1): 236; Rose, Tricia, 2008, *The Hip Hop Wars: What We Talk About When We Talk About Hip Hop—and Why It Matters* (New York: Basic Civitas); Rizoh, 2009, "11 Rap Songs to Disrespect Women To," www.http//therapup.net (Accessed November 1, 2015); Smitherman, Geneva, 2000 [1994], *Black Talk: Words and Phrases from the Hood to the Amen Corner* (Boston and New York: Houghton Mifflin); Stephens, Dionne P., and April L. Few, 2007, "Hip Hop Honey Or Video Ho: African American Preadolescents' Understanding of Female Sexual Scripts in Hip Hop Culture." *Sexuality & Culture* 11 (4): 48–69.

HOODOO

The word "Hoodoo" can be both a noun describing African American magical practices, particularly in the Mississippi Valley area of the **South**, and a verb meaning to cast a spell or hex on someone. Related words include "**conjure**," "tricking," "goopher dust," "**mojo**," and "rootwork." Some people also use the word "Vodou" as a synonym. Practitioners are known by many names, including Hoodoo doctors, two-headed doctors, Hoodooists, and Hoodoos.

The word "Hoodoo" did not appear in printed sources until the late 19th century, when white authors began to use it in reference to conjure practices in the New Orleans area. Its philological origins remain debatable. In 1893, Brander Matthews stated that the term was initially a word used in the theater world to mean anyone who brings ill fortune. During the early 1930s, Zora Neale Hurston argued in favor of an African origin. She believed that it developed from "juju," a West African word for magic. While either, perhaps both, might be true, "Hoodoo" is most likely a derivative of "Vodou." In common parlance, the two are frequently interchangeable. Moreover, a similar process of evolution occurred in Missouri, where "Voodoo" developed into the localized "noodoo."

During the 19th century, however, there was no distinction between the words "Hoodoo" and "Vodou." Today, most scholars use "Vodou" to designate an African American religion that is derived from the combination of Afro-Haitian Vodou with various European, **Native American**, and African religious systems. They use "Hoodoo" to describe the magical practices associated with but largely independent of the religion. This distinction is a 20th-century invention. According to at least one 19th-century authority, "Vodou" was the term used by whites for the entire spiritual complex of both magic and religion. African Americans reportedly preferred "Hoodoo" to describe the same thing. Thus, the only real distinction between the words was who tended to speak them.

Early Hoodoo was confined to the Mississippi Valley, though many of its customs resembled conjure, which was practiced elsewhere in the American South. One major distinction was that in the area around New Orleans, Hoodoo had its own set of gods and goddesses, most of whose pedigrees can be traced to the West African traditional faiths of the Fon, Ewe, Yoruba, and related peoples. There is also evidence that Kongolese beliefs had a significant impact in the area. Though we know little about these deities, several of their names have survived the passage of years. A few of the more prominent were Blanc Dani, the chief god; Lébat, spokesman of the spirit world; Monsieur d'Embarass, god of death; and Monsieur Agoussou, the deity of love. Gods were also known outside of Louisiana, though we know even less about them than those of New Orleans. In Missouri, for example, black people called on Samunga. About all that is known of this deity is that he was called on by people gathering mud, which was apparently to be used for magical purposes. Hoodoo doctors, in addition to working magic, frequently acted as priests and priestesses for the gods and periodically presided over major religious ceremonies, the most important of which was the annual St. John's Eve **dance** on the shores of Lake Pontchartrain.

In many respects, early Hoodoo differed little from other forms of conjure. Both Hoodooists and conjurers from outside of the Mississippi Valley told fortunes, located lost objects, performed spells, and cursed enemies for their paying clients. A few items, however, were more common along the Mississippi than elsewhere. "Frizzly chickens," which were chickens whose feathers curl upwards towards their heads, were used as a protection against malevolent conjure more often in Louisiana than along the Atlantic coast; the belief was that the chickens were immune to curses and conjure or that they could literally safely carry away cursed objects from potential victims. The same trend appeared in particular spell components, such as beef hearts and tongues, which figured prominently in New Orleans Hoodoo but were rare elsewhere.

Hoodoo and Vodou began to grow increasingly distinct in the late 19th century. Following emancipation, the non-Christian religious elements of African American belief began to disappear in the face of growing Catholic and Protestant orthodoxy. By the end of the century, most African Americans were abandoning the deities of Vodou in favor of the Christian God, a process accelerated by the advent of the Spiritual Church, which continued to recognize multiple spirits who operated within a nominally Christian framework. Nevertheless, the magical system of Hoodoo survived, continuing to develop even without its original religious underpinnings. In time, it would incorporate many elements of Christian belief, to the degree that Zora Neale Hurston was comfortable with calling the Bible the greatest conjure book in the world. Not until the 20th century was well advanced and the old faith forgotten did Hoodoo become a system distinct from historical Vodou. Today, most scholars treat the word "Hoodoo," shorn of its religious elements, as a synonym for "conjure."

As with other forms of conjure, Hoodoo has conferred power on its believers. Practitioners rose to positions of leadership in their communities. Marie Laveau, the "Voodoo Queen of New Orleans," inspired both fear and admiration in contemporaries and remains well known even today. Others, like King Alexander of St. Joseph, Missouri, and Dr. John of New Orleans, were important personages in their day, though succeeding generations have largely forgotten them.

Believers could also benefit from the power of Hoodoo. Its spells promised love, money, revenge, success, good luck, health, and virtually any other desire to those who had faith. In some cases, successful practitioners also offered practical advice, herbal medicine, and social influence that helped their clients attain what they sought. Most important, though, was the hope that it gave to a historically oppressed people.

At present, many African Americans are returning to Hoodoo as an expression of African American culture. This trend has found its most visible expression in Literary Hoodoo, a movement that seeks to make African American magic relevant to today's society by translating it into written works with transformative powers. For example, poet Ishmael Reed depicts Hoodooists as **tricksters** who undermine white power through magic. Such works are giving African American magic a new vitality and helping to revive its practice, making it more visible than it has ever been before to both white and black Americans.

Jeffrey E. Anderson

See also: John the Conqueror, High; Native American and African American Folklore

Further Reading

Anderson, Jeffrey Elton, 2007, *Conjure in African-American Society* (Baton Rouge: Louisiana State University Press); Anderson, Jeffrey E., 2008, *Hoodoo, Voodoo, and Conjure: A Handbook* (Greenwood); Covey, Herbert C., 2008, *African American Slave Medicine: Herbal and Non-herbal Treatments* (Lanham: Lexington Books); Hazzard-Donald, Katrina, 2013, *Mojo Workin': The Old African American Hoodoo System* (Urbana, IL: University of Illinois Press); Hurston, Zora Neale, 1931, "Hoodoo in America," *Journal of American Folklore* 44: 318–417; Hyatt, Harry Middleton, 1970–1978, *Hoodoo—Conjuration—Witchcraft—Rootwork*, 5 vols. (Hannibal, MO: Western Publishing Company); Long, Carolyn Morrow, 2001, *Spiritual Merchants: Religion, Magic, and Commerce* (Knoxville: University of Tennessee Press); Owen, Mary Alicia, 1892, "Among the Voodoos," in *The International Folk-lore Congress 1891: Papers and Transactions* (London: David Nutt), pp. 230–248; Young, Jason R., 2007, *Rituals of Resistance: African Atlantic Religion in Kongo and the Lowcountry South in the Era of Slavery*, 1st ed. (Baton Rouge: Louisiana State University Press).

HOUSE NEGRO

See Field Negro/House Negro

HUSH/BUSH HARBORS

Secretive, often religious, meetings held by slaves took place in remote locations known as hush harbors or bush harbors. Historian Lawrence Levine's seminal text on African American cultural history and practice, *Black Culture and Black Consciousness: Afro-American Folk Thought from Slavery to Freedom*, recognizes that a serious consideration of black thought, experience, and knowledge cannot be accomplished without revealing the existence of and the tactical import of hush harbors as sites where "slaves broke the prescription against unsupervised or unauthorized meetings by holding their services in secret, well hidden areas" (Levine, 41). In informal, unofficial meeting places, enslaved and free African Americans could share among themselves the minds they hid from their masters. Referred to as bush harbors, cane breaks, hush arbors, and, in some cases, **praise houses**, these places were hidden, secretive, or quasipublic sites that functioned under the radar of general public surveillance. Because of their secretive nature and function, histories of hush harbor practices and rhetorics are by definition difficult to come by. Fortunately, oral histories from the participants themselves provide insight into hush harbor practices.

For example, "The Clandestine Prayer Meeting," a section in *The Trouble I've Seen: The Big Book of Negro Spirituals*, provides an accessible, poignant, and paradigmatic introduction to hush harbors. Hush harbors were spaces of rhetorical education and knowledge in which everyday talk and discourse reflecting African and African American imaginations, aspirations, subjectivities, and worldviews were taken seriously. Folk and vernacular-grounded forms and artists such as Negro **spirituals** (e.g., "Steal Away"), the **blues** (e.g., **jook joint** themes), **jazz** (e.g., Charles Mingus's music), **hip-hop** culture (e.g., Nappy Roots), African American theater (e.g., August Wilson's plays), visual arts (e.g., Robert Peppers's mixed media exhibit "Hush Harbors, a commentary on church burnings), and African American literature (e.g., *The Portable Promised Land*) echo or make reference to African American hush harbors.

Hush harbor forms and rhetorics that enter the public sphere often legitimize the "authenticity" of African American performers. For example, the Fisk University Jubilee Singers did not become a national popular-culture phenomenon until they sang their material with vocal inflections and sensibilities culled from hush harbor culture. Chitlin circuit plays such as "Beauty Shop" and "A Good Man Is Hard to Find" continue to be more popular with African American audiences than the more mainstream fare in part because they participate in the cultural touchstones and commonplace circumstances of African American hush harbor places and cultures that for a period of time existed on the fertile lower frequencies of black communal life. Modern manifestations of hush harbors can be found in (some) jook joints and clubs, beauty shops, **barbershops**, churches, book clubs, black poetry slams, **hip-hop** freestyle competitions, and black Web sites.

Vorris Nunley

See also: Church, The Black; Hip-hop; Jook/Juke

Further Reading

Evans, Freddi Williams, and Erin Bennett Banks, 2008, *Hush Harbor: Praying in Secret* (Minneapolis: Carolrhoda Books); Levine, Lawrence W., 1977, *Black Culture and Black Consciousness: Afro-American Folk Thought from Slavery to Freedom* (London: Oxford University Press); Nunley, Vorris, 2011, *Keepin' It Hushed: The Barbershop and African American Hush Harbor Rhetoric* (Detroit: Wayne State University Press).

INSTRUMENTS, FOLK

Just as music has played a central role in all known cultures of African heritage, folk instruments have also been an essential and consistent element. These are defined as instruments made by those who actually play them. In most cases, African American folk instruments have reflected a connection with African traditional performance practices and instruments. In addition to singing in a strange land, slaves and later generations of African Americans made and played instruments as a part of their musical traditions. The study of musical instruments reveals innovation and ingenuity in the creation of a new material culture. Biographies of musicians, photographs, **slave narratives**, oral histories, journal articles on specific instruments, and general histories of diverse genres of African folk music offer information on the making of musical instruments, and the roles they played in their respective cultures.

Slave captains sometimes encouraged dancing aboard slave ships to preserve the slaves' health. Slaves on the ships had their first opportunity to improvise makeshift instruments for this purpose (Epstein). Therefore, prior to reaching the American shores, slaves were continuing their musical traditions, albeit on various makeshift instruments to accompany dancing. Some of these homemade instruments were eventually supplanted with manufactured instruments, and in many cases manufactured instruments were modified to achieve a certain aesthetic preference.

To continue their tradition of drumming in the United States, slaves employed certain adaptational strategies. African-style drums survived in the Caribbean and parts of South America but did not fare as well in the United States. Reasons for this include laws prohibiting the playing of drums and the performance of African dancing in many of the American colonies. As a result, slaves often used their bodies as instruments, in forms such as clapping and patting juba, both ways of keeping rhythm in the absence of actual drums. Bur drums were made in some parts of the United States. Drums were constructed by stretching a skin over a rice mortar in the Atlantic Coast's Sea Islands; also, slaves would invert an eel pot and stretch a skin over it, as was done during a **Pinkster** festival in New York prior to the Revolutionary War.

Slaves and freedmen made other types of improvised drums. In southern Mississippi early in the 20th century, Eli Owens's grandfather constructed a drum from a barrel with the use of tacks to fasten the head (Evans). Other drums were made from hollow logs to which slaves stretched a skin over one end. In addition, slaves made tambourine-like drums; some were made from gourds and barrels, and there were square-framed drums as well. Simulated drums without skins included the use of a metal bucket or a syrup can for a drum, holding the open end to the belly and tapping on the other end with the hand (Evans). Throughout the Caribbean and parts of South America much more elaborate drum-making traditions flourished.

Besides drums, a number of homemade stringed instruments appear in the literature. From several descriptions, gourd **banjos** seem to have been common in the United States by the mid-18th century. The banjo probably spread out from Virginia to neighboring states, including its use among free blacks along the Eastern shores of Virginia and Maryland as well as perhaps New Orleans. The making of a banjo was described in a novel set in Louisiana between Baton Rouge and New Orleans in the 1850s. "The bowl of a large gourd with a long straight neck was cut away and the seeds and contents removed; a coon-skin was stretched and covered over the hole and dried. Five strings of homemade materials passed from the apron over a small bridge and attached to the keys on the neck" (Epstein). In *The Old Plantation*, a watercolor painting dating from the late 18th century and housed at the Abby Aldrich Rockefeller Folk Arts Center in Williamsburg, Virginia, a four-string gourd banjo with three long strings and one short string is depicted. Several descriptions confirm that gourd banjos were popular instruments of slaves, although the number of strings varies. In all probability, slaves made banjos at different times and in different places with varying numbers of strings. Several sources confirm a very active black tradition of banjo playing. For example, Gus Cannon fashioned his first banjo from a bread pan and a broom handle.

The fiddle was the favorite companion instrument to the banjo. Slave fiddlers were highly valued and played for white and black recreational events. In the memoir *Twelve Years a Slave*, New York freedman Solomon Northup recounts his kidnapping and sale into slavery in Louisiana. His ability to play the fiddle helped improve his situation until he obtained freedom. While numerous slave fiddlers played the European violin, others constructed their instruments. A slave narrative from Georgia described making a fiddle out of a large-sized gourd with a long wooden handle as a neck; it featured catgut strings and was played with a bow made from a horse's tail (Epstein). Gourd fiddles were found in Georgia, Alabama, Mississippi, Louisiana, Tennessee, and Texas. In Texas, fiddles also were fashioned from cigar boxes, sardine cans, and tobacco tins in place of gourds. In terms of African instruments, the gourd fiddle resembled the *goge*, a single-string fiddle found in the Savannah belt of West Africa that was played with an arched bow (Minton 1996). Slave musicians also used sticks, bones, or knitting needles to beat on the strings of the fiddle, a custom they called "beating straws."

Slaves also made musical bows. Eli Owens made a bow for folklorist and writer David Evans in the early 1970s. According to Owens, the musical bow consisted of a flexible stick (chinaberry wood is favored) with a string about five feet long tied at each end of the stick. Owens used 100-pound-tested nylon fishing line for the string. His great grandfather's bows had a friction peg at the far end that allowed for the tuning of the string. A hole was bored into a small tin cup for a baking soda can that was then placed over the end of the stick with the string attached about two or three inches from the end. This provided amplification and also served as a rattle. The string was then plucked. Similar instruments were made by slaves in other countries, including the berimbau in Brazil.

The "diddley bow" was found mainly in the northwest section of Mississippi and adjacent parts of Arkansas and Tennessee. Players constructed diddley bows using three- or four-foot lengths of broom wire or baling wire attached to the wall of a house, a porch post, or a board. Two bottles, rocks, or other hard objects were inserted as bridges at each end, and a drinking glass or a bottle was slid along the wire to produce the sound (Evans).

Another common instrument was the one-string bass, which consisted of an inverted five- or ten-gallon bucket or an aluminum washtub with a length of rope attached to the tub's bottom and tied to the end of a four-foot stick. This instrument has a prototype known as the ground harp, which was found in Central Africa.

In the 1920s and 1930s, jug bands were popular in the **South**. Cannon's Jug Stompers and the Memphis Jug Band were the best known of these early bands. Gus Cannon attached his coal-oil jug to a neck harness (like a racked harmonica). He would blow across the mouth of the jug to produce a bass-like sound that was similar to that of a tuba.

Quills were also noted in the slave narratives. Owens demonstrated and made a model set of quills for Evans. They were made out of fishing-pole cane cut into several lengths, with one end of each closed by a node of the cane and the other end open. The open end was cut diagonally and then plugged with stoppers made of a dried hardwood, leaving a very narrow opening. Another opening was cut in the side of each quill to allow the sound to escape. This was essentially a set of tuned whistles. Another type of quill is the simpler panpipe, with the blowing end entirely open. Each set of quills played five or seven different notes. Quills were apparently very popular in parts of the South and accompanied some of the early **blues**. For instance, Henry Thomas used a neck harness to play quills as he sang and also played guitar, in much the same manner as later solo performers would use the harmonica. **Jazz** drummer Baby Dodds played quills as a youth. Quills or panpipes were also made by slaves and later generations in other parts of the world. For example, in South America a similar instrument was found among indigenous native populations. The intersection of the two traditions provided opportunities for innovative uses of the quills.

Other common instruments found throughout the diaspora include wooden blocks, pots and pans, bottles, and cowbells struck percussively; whistles; diverse kinds of flutes (such as the fife in the southern United States); stamping tubes (long, hollow wooden or bamboo tubes that make a deep, resonating sound when stamped straight down against the ground); thumb pianos, such as those used in mento bands (versions of the African mbira); shakers (gourds with beads woven around them or with small, hard objects such as pebbles or grain placed inside); rattlers (a wooden stick rubbed against the jagged edge of a bone, for instance); conch shells; homemade guitars; and kazoos.

The kazoo is an instrument reportedly invented by Alabama Vest, a black man in Macon, Georgia. Vest engaged a clockmaker named Thaddeus von Clegg to help him make a prototype kazoo to Vest's requirements and get it patented. The kazoo is similar to an African instrument called a mirliton, which also has a vibrating membrane.

Although in contemporary times, many instruments are store-bought and electrified, the making of traditional folk instruments still continues in many parts of the diaspora. This is especially true of folk instruments that have held central or even dominant positions in African musical traditions. The best example is probably the drum. Another good example is the steel pan drum. What has happened in many modern African communities is that local instrument makers have emerged as small businessmen and businesswomen, serving primarily the needs of local musicians. Such developments help to ensure the continued importance of instrument-making traditions.

Willie Collins

Further Reading

Andersen, Leslie, 2015, "African American Roots and Branches of the 5-String Banjo: A Selective Videography," *Notes* 72 (1): 203; Epstein, Dena J., 1977, *Sinful Tunes and Spirituals: Black Folk Music to the Civil War* (Urbana: University of Illinois Press); Evans, David, 1994, "The Music of Eli Owens: African Music in Transition in Southern Mississippi," in *For Gerhard Kubik: Festschrift on the Occasion of His 60th Birthday*, ed. August Schmidhofer and Dietrich Schuller (Frankfurt am Main, Germany: Vergleichende Musikwissenschaft); Katz-Hyman, Martha B., and Kym S. Rice, 2011, *World of a Slave: Encyclopedia of the Material Life of Slaves in the United States* (Santa Barbara, CA: Greenwood); Minton, John, 1996, "West African Fiddles in Deep East Texas," in *Juneteenth Texas: Essay in African-American Folklore*, Publications of the Texas Folklore Society, no. 54, ed. Francis E. Abernethy, Patrick B. Mullen, and Alan Govenar (Denton: University of North Texas Press).

IRONWORK
See Blacksmithing

J

JAZZ

Jazz is commonly considered to be the first "American" music, in the sense that it originated in and was disseminated throughout the United States as its own distinctive style; however, **blues** probably holds this distinction. Jazz developed primarily in southern African American communities around the turn of the 20th century and combines elements of brass band music, ragtime, and blues. However, jazz also borrows from a wide spectrum of older cultural and folk traditions that exposes the blending of American boundaries. For many African American musicians, this sense of hybridity became a way to invoke African polyrhythms and syncopated beats—all while developing the thoroughly organic concept that would become known as jazz. Jazz, then, emerged at a cultural moment when ethnic styles and diverse musical methodologies were reaching a point of critical dispersion. New Orleans, Louisiana, near the turn of the 20th century, became a vortex and point of assemblage where African Americans were able to flesh out these sounds.

A distinctive characteristic of jazz is its constant use of improvisation as well as call-and-response configurations between players. Jazz breaks from Western musical tradition, in which musicians compose and then try to play their music by following the written piece with utmost precision. Rather, jazz musicians use a musical piece only as a blank canvas of sorts; they use an old form only to add to, paint over, and modify it. A song might begin with an established beat or melody, then swerve into unknown territory. While the musicians usually return periodically (or finally) to a common theme, what makes jazz unique is its ability to move in indeterminate directions while maintaining a delicate balance of continuity and spontaneity. Jazz bands are often led by an arrangement of horns in the foreground, but a drummer, pianist, or bassist can prominently enter the scene when "called" in. It is also important to note that jazz was frequently coupled with a loose and rhythmic style of corresponding **dance**.

In terms of folklore, jazz is significant because of ties to and intersections with African American lived experience; one cannot detach the music from the material and economic conditions out of which the sounds emerge. The music is not only a reflection of material circumstances but also quite literally an enactment of social engagement dedicated to (and composed of) African American traditions and customs. Historical shifts from enslavement to emancipation and segregation all influenced and were intertwined with the musical conception of jazz. On a very basic level, the inherent improvisation of jazz is an embodiment of the African American experience of survival, rumination, and creative expression in relation to oppressive socioeconomic forces. It is impossible to trace the origins of jazz to any single time or place, since it was a collaborative endeavor spanning numerous geographical regions from the blurry moment of its conception. However, in terms of a general sense of historical and geographical roots, jazz can at least be traced to the antebellum period in and around New Orleans. This site was crucial for at least two main reasons: remnants of African culture were carried on there, and large brass bands in the area offered African Americans a wide array of instruments and older musical forms to experiment with and explore.

Early in the history of jazz, bands did not play to earn money but instead as a way of cultivating a collaboratively creative subculture; jazz was the nightly complement to the long days of menial jobs of many African Americans. Even as jazz began to be conceived of as an actual, coherent (if permanently capricious) style, there was no musical notation written down. Jazz musicians ubiquitously held that no form of musical notation could accurately relay the feel of an improvised performance. In this sense, then, jazz was more concerned with presentation than with recordable (or rehearsed) composition. For the jazz purist, composition only happens once; arrangement is a product of who is performing—and who is listening—in the moment. This attention to the unique energy in a specific venue on a given night is reminiscent of oral folk tradition, in which stories are modified or built depending on who is telling and who is listening.

Jazz soon became somewhat of a commodity, though, and was appropriated and adapted as a fresh form of entertainment in a range of social sectors that cut sharply across racial and class divides. In the urban red-light districts of New Orleans, for example, jazz became a way for African American musicians to be gainfully employed. Jazz—or at least the borrowed sound of jazz—was also becoming the choice music for upscale parties outside of the African American communities of its origin. By the 1920s, jazz was being performed in Chicago, and distinct regional styles were beginning to take shape elsewhere. At this point of the style's popularization and dispersal across the country, white jazz bands were being formed, as well; often, though, they hired African American musicians to arrange and compose the sets for upper class (predominantly white) dance parties and live performances. (While this went against the original grain of improvisational jazz, these new "swing" bands still relied on free, call-and-response sessions to supplement the prepared music.) Many African Americans were able to capitalize on this popularization, though; Count Basie and Duke Ellington became two of the more successful swing artists, and their bands were active across multiple decades.

Another movement in jazz departed from the trend of the larger, more methodical swing bands, as smaller groups began to rally around the original ideas of improvisation and creativity rather than working from the popularized melodies of swing. The style these bands played was called "bebop" and included the works of Dizzy Gillespie, Thelonious Monk, Charlie Parker, and Max Roach. This new/old jazz came out of a heavily localized African American consciousness in and around Harlem. A strain of bebop grew into "free jazz," which featured an even more committed return to spontaneous composition and simultaneous "harmolodics," a term coined by free jazz saxophonist Ornette Coleman. John Coltrane is another example of a free jazz artist. Toward the middle of the 20th century, musicians such as Miles Davis and Stan Getz developed the soft dynamics and ballad approach that became "**cool** jazz." Miles Davis went on to inspire yet another, later strain known as "fusion jazz"—a style that was eclectic, experimentally electronic, and yet drew from the roots of blues and gospel. Fusion continues to be the most recognizably appreciated form of jazz, although many contemporary artists (e.g., Wynton Marsalis) have worked toward a return to the traditional sounds of early jazz.

This brief history of jazz obviously glosses over the intricate stylistic shifts and specific nuances of particular artists and groups. From a folklorist perspective, though, what is perhaps most compelling about jazz

Trumpet virtuoso Dizzy Gillespie inspired the bop revolution along with Charlie Parker, and became a founding father of modern jazz. (Library of Congress)

are the inextricable ties—and continual returns—to the African American lived experience. Rather than functioning as a corollary expression of or metaphor for certain sociomaterial conditions, jazz is in constant interaction with its own context and ambience. As a rich, ever-expanding field of artistic possibilities, jazz delicately balances newness and heritage, spontaneity and tradition. While subgenres of jazz are constantly splitting and morphing, what remains is the intense commitment to something like a communicative arena in which what happens musically is immediate—it cannot really ever be repeated or effectively composed.

This sense of immediacy reflects both the tightly woven nature of the African American ethnic fabric as well as its porous quality; jazz works from a basis of commonality but always with an eye out for the unexpected or inspired twist. Additionally, the music can never be dissociated from its present community, and this allows for folk aspects such as evening entertainment, impromptu **storytelling**, and the values of family, love, friendship, and home in the midst of turbulent race and class politics. Artists of other media, including painters, writers, and filmmakers have also tapped the deep reservoir of jazz lore in order to explore significant folk aspects of African American culture as it comes through this distinctive music. In the 1990 **film** *Mo' Better Blues*, for example, writer and director Spike Lee explores the mythos around and implications within the African American culture of jazz at the turn of the 21st century.

The African American invention of jazz becomes a project involved with folklore because of its strong sense of lineage and descent. That is, musicians not only call and respond to other players in the present moment but also are in continual conversation with a longer tradition of ideas, sounds, and rhythms. While this collaborative spirit is not entirely unique to jazz, what stands out is the strong sense of ethnic identity associated with the music. Players are not only communicating aesthetic statements and provocations but also are grappling with shared material conditions of an entire ethnic culture as well. This communication takes place across at least several centuries of shared history of oppression, segregation, and denigration. Jazz functions as an expressive form of folklore, then, for its ability to convey and connect specific ethnic histories while also opening up space for creativity and innovation. In short, jazz becomes a projective gesture that yet maintains its ties to a rich tradition of African American cultural narratives.

Christopher S. Schaberg

Further Reading

Giddins, Gary, and Scott Knowles DeVeaux, 2009, *Jazz* (New York: W. W. Norton); Gioia, Ted, 2011, *The History of Jazz* (New York: Oxford University Press); Heble, Ajay, and Rob Wallace, 2013, *People Get Ready: The Future of Jazz is Now* (Durham, NC: Duke University Press); Levey, Josef, 1983, *The Jazz Experience: A Guide to Appreciation* (Englewood Cliffs, NJ: Prentice Hall); Milkowski, Bill, and Joe Lovano, 2011, *Legends of Jazz* (Verceli, Italy: White Star).

JEMIMA, AUNT

This advertising character based on the antebellum slave "mammy" figure was used to promote Aunt Jemima Pancake Flour, the first nationally distributed ready-mixed food and one of the earliest products to be marketed via personal appearances and advertisements featuring its namesake. The name "Aunt Jemima" was derived from an old slave song that was adapted to the stage by a popular minstrel show performer and brought to the world of advertising to marry advances in food production with popular nostalgia for the antebellum **South**. The concept of "Aunt Jemima" might be appropriately said to be a subject of white American folklore as well as African American folklore.

In 1889, a duo of speculators in St. Joseph, Missouri, named Chris Rutt and Charles Underwood created the self-rising pancake mix that would eventually bear Aunt Jemima's name. They had purchased a bankrupt mill and planned to make it successful by developing a new product that would create demand for flour in a depressed market. Thus, they settled on developing a foolproof and less labor-intensive pancake mix that would only require the addition of water. They experimented with a variety of recipes in the summer of 1889 before settling on a mixture of wheat flour, corn flour, lime phosphate, and salt. The product was originally named "self-rising pancake flour" and sold in bags. In the fall of 1889, Rutt was inspired to rename the mix after attending a minstrel show, during which a popular song titled "Old Aunt Jemima" was performed by men in blackface, one of whom was dressed as a slave mammy of the plantation South. The song, which was written by African American singer, dancer, and acrobat Billy Kersands in 1875, was a staple of the minstrel circuit and was based on a song sung by field-hand slaves. The words to the first verse are:

> I went to church the other day,
> Old Aunt Jemima, Oh! Oh! Oh!
> To hear them white folks sing and pray,
> Old Aunt Jemima, Oh! Oh! Oh!
> They prayed so long I could not stay,
> Old Aunt Jemima, Oh! Oh! Oh!
> I knew the Lord would come that way,
> Old Aunt Jemima, Oh! Oh! Oh!

(Manring, 61)

Rutt and Underwood contributed the name but failed to market their product successfully and sold their milling company to a larger corporation owned by R. G. Davis of Chicago. He transformed the local product into a national one by distributing it through a network of suppliers and by creating a persona for Aunt Jemima. Davis hired Nancy Green, a Kentucky slave in her childhood, to portray Aunt Jemima at the 1893 Chicago World's Fair. She served pancakes from a booth designed to look like a huge flour barrel and told stories of her "memories" as a cook on an "Old South" plantation. Her highly publicized appearance spurred thousands of orders for the product from distributors. Davis also commissioned a pamphlet detailing the "life" of Aunt Jemima. She was depicted as the historically real house slave of a Colonel Higbee of Louisiana, whose plantation was known across the South for its fine food and most notably its pancake breakfasts. The recipe for the pancakes was a secret known only to the slave woman. Sometime after the war, the pamphlet said, Aunt Jemima was remembered by a Confederate general who had once found himself stranded at her cabin. The general recalled her pancakes and put Aunt Jemima in contact with a "large northern milling company," which paid her to come North and supervise the construction of a modern factory to produce large quantities of the secret mix. This pamphlet formed the fundamental background for decades of future Aunt Jemima advertising.

The story was expanded upon and illustrated in an advertising campaign in American women's magazines during the 1920s and 1930s. The ads were the work of James Webb Young, a legendary account executive at the J. Water Thompson advertising agency in Chicago. He collaborated with the great American painter N. C. Wyeth, who was famous as the illustrator of books such as *Treasure Island* and *The Last of the Mohicans*. The ads were usually full page and full color, and they ran regularly in *Ladies' Home Journal*, *Good Housekeeping*, and *The Saturday Evening Post*. They were panoramas depicting the leisure and splendor of the plantation South as the Higbee plantation hosted grand gatherings of visitors from across the region. Aunt Jemima Pancake Flour was marketed as perhaps the ultimate labor-saving product by drawing an explicit parallel between the work of a house slave and the work the product saved a housewife. A line from a 1927 advertisement read, "Make them with Aunt Jemima Pancake Flour and your family will ask where you got your wonderful southern cook."

Nancy Green, the original Aunt Jemima, continued in the role until her death in an auto accident in 1923. She was replaced by Anna Robinson, a heavier woman with a darker complexion. The image on the box and in ads was adjusted to resemble her more closely. Later, actresses Aylene Lewis and Edith Wilson portrayed the mammy in some advertisements, and Lewis performed as Aunt Jemima at Aunt Jemima's Pancake House in Disneyland, which opened in 1957. However, the advertising character, which had often been the subject of criticism in the African American press, came under greater scrutiny in the 1950s and 1960s. Local chapters of the National Association for the Advancement of Colored People (NAACP) pressured schools and county fair organizers not to invite Aunt Jemima to appear. Wilson, in 1967, became the final woman to play Aunt Jemima in advertisements when Quaker Oats fired her and canceled its TV ads. Quaker Oats also took Aunt Jemima's name off the Disneyland restaurant in 1970; Lewis was the last woman to portray Aunt Jemima on the company's behalf.

Throughout the 1960s, Aunt Jemima's skin became lighter, and Quaker Oats made her look thinner in print images. In 1968, the company replaced her bandanna with a headband and made her look somewhat younger. Her image still appeared in print advertisements, but for the most part the character did not speak or appear to live on a slave plantation. In 1989, Quaker Oats made the most dramatic alteration to Aunt Jemima since her introduction 100 years earlier, removing her headband to reveal a head full of graying curls and adding earrings and a pearl necklace. The company said it was repositioning the brand icon as a "black working grandmother."

In 1993, Quaker Oats created a series of television ads for the pancake mix featuring the singer Gladys Knight as a spokeswoman and using Aunt Jemima's face only as a logo. The campaign ran very briefly. While Aunt Jemima now maintains a low profile in the advertising world, the former slave continues to rank as one of the most recognizable trade names in North America. Aunt Jemima pancake mix and syrup remain market leaders in the United States, and in the 1990s Quaker Oats even licensed the use of her name and image for a line of frozen breakfast products manufactured by another company.

For African Americans, Aunt Jemima represents the tenacity of American racism, embodying the long-standing need for white Americans to perpetrate the mammy stereotype that romanticizes slavery and plantation life. In her essay "'Now Then—Who Said Biscuits?' The Black Woman Cook as Fetish in American Advertising, 1905–1953," Alice Deck argues that Aunt Jemima symbolizes the white fixation on domestic, black, female bodies, a practice that invokes the magical qualities of blackness while reinforcing the subordinate position of African Americans. A close parallel would be the portrayal of Uncle Ben on rice boxes. Despite African American objections to her image dating from roughly the 1920s to current days and the wider controversy surrounding her image in the late 20th century,

Aunt Jemima remains one of the most successful advertising icons of modern times.

M. M. Manring

Further Reading

Behnken, Brian D., and Gregory D. Smithers, 2015, *Racism in American Popular Media: From Aunt Jemima to the Frito Bandito* (Santa Barbara, CA: Praeger); Davis, Judy Foster, 2007, "Aunt Jemima Is Alive and Cookin'? An Advertiser's Dilemma of Competing Collective Memories," *Journal of Macromarketing* 27 (1): 25–37; Deck, Alice, 2001, "'Now Then—Who Said Biscuits?' The Black Woman Cook as Fetish in American Advertising, 1905–1953," in *Kitchen Culture in America: Popular Representations of Food, Gender, and Race,* ed. Sherrie A. Inness (Philadelphia: University of Pennsylvania Press), pp. 69–94; Finley, Cheryl, 2014, "Visual Legacies of Slavery and Emancipation," *Callaloo* 37 (4): 1023–1032; Kern-Foxworth, Marilyn, 1994, *Aunt Jemima, Uncle Ben, and Rastus: Blacks in Advertising, Yesterday, Today, and Tomorrow* (Westport, CT: Praeger); Manring, Maurice M., 1998, *Slave in a Box: The Strange Career of Aunt Jemima* (Charlottesville: University Press of Virginia); McElya, Micki, 2007, *Clinging to Mammy: The Faithful Slave in Twentieth-century America* (Cambridge, MA: Harvard University Press); Wallace-Sanders, Kimberly, 2008, *Mammy: A Century of Race, Gender, and Southern Memory* (Ann Arbor: University of Michigan Press).

JIM CROW

Jim Crow was the name given to a caricature of African Americans common in the minstrel tradition as well as the name for a system of discrimination against black people in the American **South**. "Weel 'bout, and turn 'bout / And do ges so / Eb'ry time I weel 'bout / I jumps Jim Crow" were the song lyrics that white minstrel Thomas "Daddy" Rice popularized in the United States in the 1830s. He claimed he heard an elderly and crippled Louisville black stable man perform the song in 1828. Employing burnt cork to blacken his face, red lipstick to exaggerate his lips, too-short and tattered clothes, animated movements, and wild grimaces, Rice mockingly imitated the singing, dancing, and general deportment of enslaved Africans (or Negroes, as they were called then). The grotesque caricature of African American life and culture was enthusiastically embraced by a white public that constantly felt compelled to justify their enslavement and general disdain for blacks.

American historians have found it difficult to explain how a **dance** created by a black stable man and vulgarly recreated by a white man to assuage the consciences of white slaveholding audiences became synonymous with American apartheid. However, the historical reality is that the minstrel show reinforced the already prevalent racist notion that blacks were subhuman or, at the least, certainly inferior to whites. In essence, "Jump Jim Crow" was minstrelsy's theme song, and as a result it represented much more than entertainment; it became white America's medium to plant the seeds of superiority in whites and inferiority in blacks.

The Jim Crow system was apartheid plain and simple, with separate (and rarely equal) accommodations for blacks and whites. For example, a 1914 Louisiana statute required separate entrances at circuses for blacks and whites, a 1915

Oklahoma law sanctioned segregated telephone booths, and a 1920 Mississippi law made advocating social equality or intermarriage between whites and blacks a crime. In Kentucky, separate schools gave way to separate textbooks, and a law that stated that no textbooks issued to a black child would "ever be reissued or redistributed to a white school child" or vice versa. In like manner, Florida went so far as to stipulate that textbooks for black children be stored separately from those for white children.

The South was the citadel of Jim Crow even as World War II came to a close in 1945, with almost all social spaces imaginable segregated. Churches, hospitals, schools, colleges, prisons, cemeteries, restaurants, theaters, swimming pools, water fountains, and bathrooms were designated either for whites or blacks but not under any condition accessible to both. Even courtrooms bowed to the blazon of Jim Crow, with black witnesses swearing on one Bible and whites on another. In the South, babies were delivered in segregated hospitals, children were educated in segregated public schools, and upon death, Southerners were buried in segregated cemeteries.

White Southerners relied on the racist **mythology** they created around the Reconstruction era (1865–1877) to defend their deeds, claiming that uneducated and unsophisticated black voters had been bamboozled by northern "carpetbaggers" who opportunistically moved south after the Civil War (1861–1865). The proponents of Jim Crow also turned to the propaganda of the southern white press, which seemed to continuously publish sensational and distorted accounts of alleged crimes committed by black Americans. This gave rise to white terrorist violence against blacks, which was underwritten by the legally sanctioned system of racial segregation, the police, and the extralegal activities of several white terrorist groups. Among the most notorious of the white terrorist organizations, the Ku Klux Klan maimed and murdered thousands of African Americans for attempting to exercise their right to vote and for endeavoring to participate in American social life.

The Ku Klux Klan and its "Invisible Empire" can be said to have been the backbone of the Jim Crow system. Many erroneously believe that the Klan was simply a southern social phenomenon, but recent scholarly research has revealed that only 15 percent of its membership during the 1920s resided in the South. The Klan population of New Jersey was higher than that of Alabama; the Klan membership of the city of Indianapolis, Indiana, alone was nearly double that of the states of South Carolina and Mississippi taken together; and at its height in 1924, the Klan claimed some 7 million to 10 million members throughout the United States.

The Jim Crow system of American apartheid was also aided by white supremacist trends in scholarship at the beginning of the 20th century, when pseudosciences like eugenics were employed to bolster arguments that blacks were genetically inferior to whites. The civil rights movement of the 1950s and 1960s brought several legal and social changes, such as an end to de jure segregation and the beginning of black integration into white public schools and universities. However, the death of de jure segregation gave birth to de facto segregation, and though Jim Crow officially died in the 1960s, his children inherited his legacy and carried it into the 21st century.

Reiland Rabaka

Further Reading

Alexander, Michelle, 2010, *The New Jim Crow: Mass Incarceration in the Age of Colorblindness* (New York: New Press); Cell, John W., 1982, *The Highest Stage of White Supremacy: The Origins of Segregation in South America and the American South* (Cambridge: Cambridge University Press); Dailey, Jane, Glenda Elizabeth Gilmore, and Bryant Simon, eds., 2000, *Jumpin' Jim Crow: Southern Politics from Civil War to Civil Rights* (Princeton, NJ: Princeton University Press); Higginbotham, F. Michael, 2013, *Ghosts of Jim Crow: Ending Racism in Post-racial America* (New York: New York University Press); Lewis, Catherine M., and J. Richard Lewis, 2009, *Jim Crow America: A Documentary History* (Fayetteville: University of Arkansas Press); Lhamon, William T., Jr., 2003, *Jump Jim Crow: Lost Plays, Lyrics, and Street Prose of the First Atlantic Popular Culture* (Cambridge, MA: Harvard University Press); Litwack, Leon F., 1998, *Trouble in Mind: Black Southerners in the Age of Jim Crow* (New York: Alfred A. Knopf); Packard, Jerrold M., 2002, *American Nightmare: The History of Jim Crow* (New York: St. Martin's Press); Rabinowitz, Howard, 1978, *Race Relations in the Urban South, 1865–1890* (New York: Oxford University Press); Valk, Anne M., and Leslie Brown, 2010, *Living with Jim Crow: African American Women and Memories of the Segregated South*, 1st ed. (New York: Palgrave Macmillan); Williamson, Joel, 1984, *The Crucible of Race: Black-White Relations in the American South since Emancipation* (New York: Oxford University Press); Woodward, C. Vann, 1974, *The Strange Career of Jim Crow*, 3d rev. ed. (New York: Oxford University Press); Wormser, Richard, 2003, *The Rise and Fall of Jim Crow* (New York: St. Martin's Press).

JIVIN'

Jivin' is a strategy or a rhetorical style of speaking used to gain advantage over a person or a situation. Jivin' is also referred to as "whupping the game," and its meaning is sometimes linked with its relative, shuckin'. Shuckin' and jivin' are forms of misleading communication. According to Thomas Kochman, "'shucking,' 'shucking it,' 'shucking ad jiving,' 's-ing and j-ing,' or just 'jiving,' are terms that refer to one form of language behavior practiced by the black when interacting with The Man (the white man, the Establishment, or any authority figure), and to another form of language behavior practiced by blacks when interacting with each other on the peer-group level" (Kochman, 246). Generally, shuckin' is a defensive means of protecting oneself, and jivin' is an offensive method used to "obtain some benefit or advantage" (Kochman, 251). Motive is a distinguishing factor between jivin' and shuckin'. In some situations, the terms can be used simultaneously. For example, an individual can "shuck to whup the game" by "[assuming] a guise or posture or perform[ing] some action in a certain way that is designed to work on someone's mind to get him to give up something" (Kochman, 251). In other situations, both terms may refer to lying. As an example, "Don't jive me," is translated to mean, "Don't lie to me."

Kochman provides illustrations on how jivin' operates. In one example, a woman wears an older dress to work for white employees in the hope of obtaining a raise. She is considered to be jivin'. Kochman includes a quote from Malcolm X in another example of jivin': "Whites who came at night got a better reception; the several Harlem nightclubs they patronized were geared to entertain and jive [flatter, cajole] the night white crowd to get their money" (Malcolm X, 87). In this scenario, African Americans manipulate their performance for their personal benefit (Kochman, 251). In another example from Malcolm X's autobiography, an African American man instructs him "how to make the shine rag pop like a firecracker" while shining shoes (Malcolm X, 48). He describes this sound as a "jive noise." The "jive noise" is an exaggerated sound designed to give the appearance of flair, speed, and exerted effort. This tactic is employed to receive good tips. All of these examples illustrate how jivin' may be performed not only via speech but also through strategically constructed maneuvers.

The tactics above are much more likely to be effective posed against someone who is not aware of African American communication styles and their functions. In jivin', African Americans have developed a means to gain control of situations and over white people. On the other hand, jivin' is not so effective against other African Americans who are "able practitioners" in various communication strategies (Kochman, 253). When jivin' is practiced within the African American community, it "often has play overtones in which the person being put on is aware of the attempts being made and goes along with it for the enjoyment of it or in appreciation of the style involved" (Kochman, 253).

Gladys L. Knight

Further Reading

Burley, Dan, 1990 [1973], "The Technique of Jive," in Alan Dundes, ed., *Mother Wit From the Laughing Barrel: Readings in the Interpretation of Afro-American Folklore* (Jackson: University Press of Mississippi), pp. 206–221; Calt, Stephen, 2009, *Barrelhouse Words: A Blues Dialect Dictionary* (University of Illinois Press); Hamm, Theodore, 2008, "Dan Burley's Original Handbook of Harlem Jive," (*The Brooklyn Rail*, Dec. 12) www .brooklynrail.org accessed November 3, 2015; Jonnes, Jill, 1999, *Hep-cats, Narcs, and Pipe Dreams* (John Hopkins University Press); Kochman, Thomas, 1972, "Toward an Ethnography of Black American Speech," in *Rappin' and Stylin' Out*, ed. Thomas Kochman (Urbana: University of Illinois Press), pp. 241–264; Shelley, Lou, 1945, *Hepcats Jive Talk Dictionary* (Derby, CT: T.W.O. Charles Co.); X, Malcolm, 1965, *Autobiography of Malcolm X* (New York: Grove Press).

JOHN THE CONQUEROR, HIGH

The root known as High John the Conqueror is employed in African American **Hoodoo**. It is carried in the pocket and rubbed when needed, kept in the house as an amulet, "fed" or "dressed" with various substances, boiled to make baths and floor wash, soaked in whiskey, oils, and perfumes to make an anointing substance, or incorporated into the **charm** assemblages called **mojo** bags and lucky hands. One also hears of Little John, Low John, Running John, Southern John, and other members of the "John" family. These are used in the same manner as High John but are not considered to be as potent. Another root, Chewing John the Conqueror, is chewed, and the juice is spat in the vicinity of the person or situation that one wishes to influence. All of the John the Conqueror roots are used for protection from enemies and malevolent spirits; for luck in gambling, business, and money matters; to get a job; to obtain a favorable outcome in court cases; and for success with women. None of the John roots is ingested for medicinal purposes.

African American root charms like John the Conqueror probably have their origins in the religious and magical practices of the Kongo-related peoples of Central Africa, the largest ethnic group to be enslaved in the American mid-Atlantic states. Among the Kongo peoples, twisted, swollen, phallus-shaped roots, representing power and masculinity, were incorporated into the charm assemblages called *minkisi*. The roots of *munkwiza*, a member of the ginger family, were chewed and spat to ward off enemies and detect sorcerers.

The use of a protective root charm that may have been John the Conqueror is found in the narratives of former slaves Frederick Douglass of Maryland and Henry Bibb of Kentucky, both of whom recounted experiences of the 1830s. Reports submitted in 1878 by black students at Virginia's Hampton Institute also indicated that enslaved people carried John the Conqueror roots as amulets or chewed them and spat the juice.

The roots collectively known as John the Conqueror were native to the southeastern United States and were still harvested in the wild into the mid-20th century. It has been conjectured that jack-in-the pulpit (*Arisaema triphyllum*), Solomon's seal (*Polygonatum odoratum*), beth root (*Trillium* species), or some species of wild morning glory (*Ipomoea*), all of which have large, twisted, or swollen tubers, rhizomes, or taproots, might have served southern Hoodoo doctors as John the Conqueror root.

St. John's wort (*Hypericum perforatum*) has frequently been misidentified as John the Conqueror. Books on European **herbalism** and folk medicine state that the flowers, leaves, and stems were used to heal wounds, protect against lightning, and drive away evil spirits. The roots of St. John's wort are a branching, fibrous mass, not at all conducive to being carried as an amulet or chewed. There is no record of any part of the St. John's wort plant being employed by African Americans for magical or medicinal purposes.

Present-day spiritual supply stores offer Mexican jalap (*Ipomoea jalapa*) as High John the Conqueror, beth root as Southern John, and Asian galangal (*Alpinia galanga*) as Chewing John. These particular roots were probably chosen because they are easily obtained, cheap, and have an extended shelf life.

In traditional western Central African belief systems, every natural object is believed to have an indwelling spirit that can be summoned to the aid of human beings. In the language of the Kongo people, this spirit is called Mooyo, from which comes the African American word "mojo." The name High John the Conqueror suggests that a potent personality inhabits this magical root. This spirit may be equated with Funza, the Kongo spirit of power and masculinity, which is also embodied in a root that was incorporated into Kongo *minkisi*. High John may also have West African antecedents. In his role as a protector against human enemies, authority figures, and malevolent spirits, he resembles Gu, the Fon and Yoruba warrior spirit of iron and warfare. His function as a bringer of luck in gambling, business, and money matters relates him to Eshu, the **trickster** spirit who governs chance and the **crossroads**. In his role as a "conqueror" of women, he is related to

Shango, the handsome and virile spirit of thunder and lightning. Although High John the Conqueror has parallels among the deities of Haitian Vodou and Cuban Santería—Ogou/Ògún, Legba/Eleguá, and Changó—he plays no role in either of these religions and is unique to the American South.

Zora Neale Hurston associated the indwelling spirit of High John the Conqueror root with the African American slave trickster hero Old John, a man of great strength and cunning. Stories of Old John and his adversary Old Marster constitute a cycle of folk narratives that parallel the better-known tales of **Brer Rabbit**. Other folklore texts assert that the character of High John is synonymous with St. John the Baptist, the man who baptized Jesus, preached in the wilderness, was tempted, and conquered Satan.

The prototype for High John the Conqueror could also have been a historic person, possibly a powerful Hoodoo doctor who became associated in the minds of believers with this African spirit. The word "high" connotes authority, strength, and potency, and in coastal Maryland and Virginia a conjurer was called a "high man."

High John the Conqueror, the indwelling spirit of a magical root, would appear to be a mélange of African deities, a legendary slave trickster, and a Christian saint, possibly combined with one or more powerful conjurers. In all of these aspects, High John personifies a strong, dark, virile, masculine spirit who protects his devotees and brings them success, wealth, and luck. He represents the resiliency and empowerment of black people in surviving slavery and its aftermath of poverty and racism.

Carolyn Morrow Long

See also: Conjure; Magic Shops

Further Reading

Anderson, Jeffrey, 2007, *Conjure in African American Society* (Baton Rouge: Louisiana State University Press); Hazzard-Donald, Katrina, 2013, *Mojo Workin': The Old African American Hoodoo System* (Urbana, IL: University of Illinois Press); Hurston, Zora Neale, 1943, "High John de Conker," *American Mercury* 57: 450–458; Hyatt, Harry Middleton, 1970–1978, *Hoodoo—Conjuration—Witchcraft—Rootwork*, 5 vols. (Hannibal, MO: Western Publishing Company); Long, Carolyn Morrow, 2001, *Spiritual Merchants: Religion, Magic, and Commerce* (Knoxville: University of Tennessee Press); Thompson, Robert Farris, 1983, *Flash of the Spirit, African and Afro-American Art and Philosophy* (New York: Vintage Books).

JOKES

Jokes are narratives designed to evoke humor and lighten the mood, and often to evoke laughter. Jokes can take many different forms, including riddle jokes, joke cycles, and stories. The narratives may be as lengthy as a folktale or as short as a few sentences. The length of jokes can vary, from those that are as long as **folktales** to those that may be only a question and a simple answer. Jokes can occur in almost any context, from the sacred to the profane, and they can refer to a wide and diverse range of subjects.

Jokes are typically forms of indirect discourse, and are often strategies to communicate critical and unflattering messages about specific people or groups of people. They are generally recognized by scholars as disguised forms of aggression, but have the appearance of being innocent. As such, they are socially acceptable ways through which to mediate tensions, or to say things that it would be unacceptable to say in an open and direct fashion. To accomplish these functions, jokes use such devices as irony, double entendre, sarcasm, satire, innuendo, **signifying**, and ambivalence. Understandably, jokes have been an important form of folklore in African American culture. They have allowed for expressions of anger; catharsis and bonding through humor and laughter; attacks on whites and systems of power that have enslaved and oppressed black people; desires for freedom and equality; and the rhetorical reversal of social power, so that those who have been oppressed gain the upper hand.

Many African American jokes refer to the plight of blacks in racist American society. They often make fun of the inconsistencies in the unjust social and political system wherein black people are both physically and intellectually needed, but yet are treated as beasts of burden. Jokes are thus as much tools for survival as they are pastimes and entertainment. In the "John tales," for example, a slave named John consistently outwits the "butt" of the jokes, the slave owner. John is the human counterpart to **Brer Rabbit**, the trickster. Although **tricksters** such as John are often self-deprecating, they are respected for their ability to survive and for their joking, tongue-in-cheek disposition toward a master. John jokes represent him as harmless and unassuming, while African Americans watch as he manipulates the slave owner into doing what he wants them to do. In one story, John steals three of his master's pigs and is unexpectedly visited by the master, who looks in the pot and sees the pigs cooking. John says that it's the darnedest thing because he put three possums in the pot, and who ever heard of three possums turning into pigs?

Many other jokes also refer to racism and social oppression. In one of these, a cook dreams that she went to heaven. The next morning, when she tells her cohorts the dream, they ask her whether the blacks in heaven had to work in the kitchen. She responds indignantly that she never went into the kitchen. In another, a black man and a white man are walking along the road, and the white man reaches over and takes a tick off the black man's neck. The black man tells him, "It's mine. Give it back." The joke is that whites do not permit blacks to have anything in America; even the most undesirable things are appropriated.

Jokes can occur in any setting and have any number of functions. Sometimes **preachers** tell or allude to jokes from the pulpit. One preacher alluded to a joke with the question, "Who in the hell left the gate open?" The question is the punch line in a joke about a little dog that sits on the front porch and barks up a storm each day as the big dogs pass by the front gate. But the gate is always locked and thus keeps the little dog safe. One day, though, the little dog begins barking at passing dogs, and in a fit of excitement and boldness, rushes off the porch so that he can sit by the gate and taunt the other dogs. He is terrified to find that the gate is open and in horror, he asks, "Who in the hell left the gate open?" The preacher is signifying on someone in the congregation who has a habit of boasting, assuming that they are protected by some form of social etiquette or otherwise. He is warning the person, suggesting that they may not be as protected as they imagine they are. The congregation "gets" the joke, because they are familiar with the story, and quite possibly understand to whom the preacher's message is directed.

Jokes are, of course, the main form of folklore for black comedians, who use a combination of traditional material and jokes that they create themselves. The performance of humor found in comedy routines goes back to animated styles of **storytelling**, as early as the slavery period. The first professionalization of African American humor was in the early 19th century, in the form of medicine and minstrel shows, which gave way to vaudeville entertainment in the early 20th century, and to traveling road shows in which black comedians performed for all-black audiences. Watkins writes that "these comics, performing in tents and so called 'dark' houses, before dark audiences, were among the first black professional comedians subtly to alter the minstrel stage presentation of black humor. Just as self-deprecation was a salient element of black folk humor, it was also present in the works of early comedians" (Watkins). Many entertainers from vaudeville, Broadway comedies, and the road show tradition later went on to become the first generation of "black entertainment superstars" (Watkins). The routines of comedians have also consistently addressed racism and served some of the same functions as folk humor. From the jokes of Moms Mabley and Redd Foxx to Richard Pryor and Dave Chappelle, black comedians have used jokes as a tool to critique racism and to push back against the oppression of African Americans.

Laura C. Jarmon

Further Reading

Bailey, Constance, 2012, "Fight the Power: African American Humor as a Discourse of Resistance." *Western Journal of Black Studies* 36 (4): 253; Brewer, J. Mason, 1968, *American Negro Folklore* (Chicago: Quadrangle); Dorson, Richard M., 1967, *American Negro Folktales* (Greenwich, CT: Fawcett Publishers, Inc.); Haggins, Bambi, 2007, *Laughing Mad: The Black Comic Persona in Post-Soul America* (New Brunswick, NJ: Rutgers University Press); Jarmon, Laura C., 2003, *Wishbone: Reference and Interpretation in Black Folk Narrative* (Knoxville: University of Tennessee Press); Littleton, Darryl J., 2008, *Black Comedians on Black Comedy: How African-Americans Taught Us to Laugh* (New York: Applause Theatre and Cinema Books); Stanzak, Steve, 2012, "Manipulating Play Frames: The Yo Mamma Joke Cycle on YouTube," *Children's Folklore Review* 34: 7; Watkins, Mel, 2002, *African American Humor: The Best Black Comedy from Slavery to Today* (Chicago: Lawrence Hill Books); Watkins, Mel, 1999, *On the Real Side: A History of African American Comedy* (Chicago: Lawrence Hill Books).

JOOK/JUKE

Jook joints are rough-hewn, one-floor nightclubs, typically in the rural American **South**, where working-class African American patrons gather to **dance**, drink, eat, gamble, fight (when need be), and socialize to **blues** music, live or recorded. "Jook is the word for negro pleasure house," wrote folklorist and novelist Zora Neale

Hurston. "Musically speaking, the Jook is the most important place in America. For in its smelly shoddy confines has been born the secular music known as blues and on blues has been founded **jazz**. The singing and playing in the true Negro style is called 'jooking.'"

The cultural importance of the jooks, both for African Americans and the larger world, can hardly be overstated. The jukebox found in every bar and nightclub across America—which in our day spins CDs and in an earlier era spun 45 rpm "singles"—began as a way of modernizing the jooks by replacing the live guitar player or piano man with an electrically powered device. The riveting performance styles and iconic presences of African American blues men and blueswomen such as B. B. King, Howlin' Wolf, Muddy Waters, Koko Taylor, and Big Mama Thornton were honed in country jooks and their urban equivalents. Jook performers offered their working-class black audiences not merely good-time entertainment and Saturday-night release but also an image of heroic potency that sustained community morale in the face of economic exploitation and the deadly physical intimidation that characterized life in the **Jim Crow** South. "I'm the hoochie-coochie man," sang Muddy Waters in a blues hit that exemplified the jook attitude. "Everybody knows I'm here!" The jook was a crucial arena within which black expressive mastery was forged, black self-determination was insisted upon, and black collective survival was celebrated.

The distant origins of the jooks lie in West Africa, with the religiously grounded festive dances that were a pervasive part of community life. As African slaves were slowly transformed into African Americans on southern plantations, "a clear demarcation emerged between sacred, ceremonial dance and the secular dancing associated with festivities and parties" (Hazzard-Gordon, 15–16). It was the latter sort of dances, and the slave fiddlers and **banjo** players who played them, that became the core elements of the Saturday-night "frolics" that marked antebellum life and anticipated the jooks. In the post-Reconstruction period, as African American freedmen began to remake their social world within the confines of segregation, the jooks emerged along with a new and heavily rhythmic music that the younger generation began to call "blues." Alcohol became a part of black sociality in a way it had not previously been—antebellum slave culture had been essentially dry, except for **Christmas**—and a sensual new blues dance called the "slow drag" spread through the southern jooks.

Jook people, as the patrons of these rowdy establishments were called, were held in disrepute by some members of black southern communities, particularly those with religious objections to couples dancing together and the audible celebration of sexual desire. Violence was a more serious problem. Virtually every blues musician who has written or been interviewed about jook life mentions the knives and guns, the "cuttings and shootings," that frequently marred Saturday night festivities. Yet the violence, too, had a cultural importance. It was a marker of frontier vitality and a way of arbitrating interpersonal disputes when the white law refused to take black grievances seriously. It was also an aspect of black Southern life that both the bluesmen themselves and many African American writers found a compelling subject for their art.

Jitterbugging in a juke joint on a Saturday evening outside Clarksdale, Mississippi, November, 1939. (Library of Congress)

Zora Neale Hurston led the way in the use of jooks as a literary setting. A native Floridian, she made repeated trips in the late 1920s and early 1930s to the Polk County region of that state, investigating the blues culture of the local jooks. In both *Mules and Men* (J. P. Lippincott, 1935) and *Dust Tracks on a Road* (J. P. Lippincott, 1942), she celebrates larger-than-life jook women such as Big Sweet, Lucy, and Ella Wall—women who wielded switchblades with deadly proficiency and were as willing to use them on the white boss as they were on each other. An iconic cultural institution and trope of dirty-Southern authenticity, the jook plays an important role in novels by J. J. Phillips (*Mojo Hand*, New Directions, 1966), Albert Murray (*Train Whistle Guitar*, Northeastern University Press, 1989), Alice Walker (*The Color Purple*, Harcourt Brace Jovanovich, 1982), Walter Mosley (*RL's Dream*, Washington Square Press, 1995), and Clarence Major (*Dirty Bird Blues*, Berkley House, 1996). The jook has also been the subject of works by visual artists, such as Jacob Lawrence.

Contrary to reports of its demise, the down-home jook catering to an African American clientele is still very much alive and well in certain parts of the contemporary South, particularly Mississippi. Although Junior Kimbrough, who presided over a legendary jook in the hill-country hamlet of Chulahoma, died in 1998 and his establishment burned down the following year, bluesman Willie King still plays to a community crowd every Sunday night at Bettie's Place, a jook in Prairie Point; similar scenes can be found at Po' Monkey's Lounge in Merigold, Red's Lounge in

Clarksdale, and Wild Bill's in Memphis, Tennessee. Although the House of Blues chain tried mightily during the 1990s to recreate this down-home ambiance at nightclubs in Hollywood, Boston, and New Orleans (see "Million-Dollar Juke Joint: Commodifying Blues Culture" in the Further Reading section), the "shoddy confines" of the back-country jook celebrated by Hurston remain the original and still most vital home of the blues.

Adam Gussow

Further Reading

Cheseborough, Steve, 2008, *Blues Traveling: The Holy Sites of Delta Blues.* 3rd ed. (Jackson: University Press of Mississippi); Cook, Alex V., 2012, *Louisiana Saturday Night: Looking for a Good Time in South Louisiana's Juke Joints, Honky-Tonks, and Dance Halls*, 1st ed. (Baton Rouge: Louisiana State University Press); Gussow, Adam, 2002, *Seems Like Murder Here: Southern Violence and the Blues Tradition* (Chicago: University of Chicago Press); Hazzard-Gordon, Katrina, 1990, *Jookin': The Rise of Social Dance Formations in African American Culture* (Philadelphia: Temple University Press); Hurston, Zora Neale, 1995, "The Jook," in "Characteristics of Negro Expression," in *Zora Neale Hurston: Folklore, Memoirs, and Other Writings* (New York: Library of America); Lieberfeld, Daniel, 1995, "Million-Dollar Juke Joint: Commodifying Blues Culture," *African American Review* 29 (2): 217–221; Pearson, Barry Lee, 2003, "Jook Women," *Living Blues* 34 (5) (September–October): 103–113.

JORDAN (RIVER, LAND)

The Jordan River figures prominently throughout African American religious folklore in virtually all genres: narrative forms, spirituals, gospel music, sermon traditions, and various folk art. The Jordan River flows from Israel, north of the Sea of Galilee, and empties into the Dead Sea. It serves as the boundary between Israel and Jordan and, further south, between Jordan and the disputed West Bank territory. The Jordan River's place in African American folklore is based on its biblical significance, and it appears in both the Old and New Testaments. The river and the land surrounding Jordan are first described in the book of Genesis as being like "the garden of the Lord." To the Israelites traveling out of the desert wilderness after their enslavement in Egypt, the Jordan River Valley was the sign that they had reached "the land of milk and honey," that is, the "Promised Land" given them by God, where they would be free from oppression.

The Old Testament story of Elijah is one of the most significant in African American religious folklore. After parting the waters of the Jordan, Elijah crossed the river bed on dry land and was taken up to heaven in a chariot of fire. In part because of this story, the Jordan River became a symbol in African American folk belief of the crossing from this life to the next—the soul's release from its earthly body and passage into heaven. However, the river also was a symbol of moving from harsh circumstances such as slavery to a time and place where black people could be free and could experience the joy and celebration that came with making it to the Promised Land.

The symbolic significance of the Jordan River continued in the New Testament gospels, in which John the Baptist lowered Jesus into the Jordan's waters and then lifted him up—a ritual symbolic of new birth. This ritual, known as **baptism**, continues to be a central component of African American Protestant theology. Baptism encompasses the belief that, to be converted, one must be "born again." The old life of sin and separation from God must be left behind and the new life then devoted to the fulfillment of God's will. Thus, the Jordan as a symbol of passage to eternal life was extended, for it is only through baptism and repentance that salvation is attained.

For African American slaves in the antebellum South, the Ohio River became their Jordan. Flowing south and then west from Pittsburgh to Illinois, the Ohio River served as the boundary between slave and free territories, making it the final crossing into what was, for escaped slaves, the Promised Land. In this way, references to the Jordan River in African American religious folklore make both a spiritual and literal connection to the ultimate goal of freedom: the freedom from sin attained through baptism, freedom from earthly toil through God's promise of Paradise, and freedom from slavery through the crossing of its waters. While the River Jordan serves as a central theme in a variety of folk media, a survey of African American spirituals alone provides a sense of how frequently it occurs. Specific examples of spirituals and gospel songs that include the motif of the Jordan River include "Swing Low, Sweet Chariot," "Roll, Jordan, Roll," "Get Away Jordan," and "Down by the Riverside."

Nancy A. Clark

See also: Biblical Characters; Sermons

Further Reading

Lovell, John, 1972, *Black Song: The Forge and the Flame: The Story of How the Afro-American Spiritual Was Hammered Out* (New York: Macmillan); Pinn, Anthony, B., Stephen C. Finley, and Torin Alesander, 2009, *African American Religious Cultures* (Santa Barbara: CA: ABC-CLIO).

JUKE JOINTS
See Jook/Juke

JUMP ROPE RHYMES/GAMES
Children, adolescents, and even adults perform jump rope rhymes and games in African American cultures across a wide variety of regions. This involves skipping or jumping rope to the rhythm of a saying, song, riddle, story, or lyric. Many jump rope games and rhymes are performed and circulated in families, on playgrounds, at schools, and during religious events, and some forms can be traced back many centuries.

Jump rope rhymes exhibit a tremendous amount of variety, and the verses of a rhyme may include directions for how to jump, counts or descriptions for the frequency or speed of jumping, predictions about the jumper's failure or success in the game (and in life), and a tremendous range of themes, characters, plots, word play, rhyme patterns, and line lengths.

The content of a given jump rope rhyme may focus on family, authority figures, social institutions like school or church, the weather, animals, love, sin, and any number of topics. Furthermore, according to Roger D. Abrahams, many jump rope rhymes include an antitaboo and antiauthoritarian tone directed against teachers, parents, police, and church leaders, as well as different kinds of taunts, parodies, judgments, morals, sayings, and fantasies (Abrahams 1969, xxiv).

While there are documented cases of boys and men performing jump rope rhymes and games, it is a pastime primarily performed by girls and women. Furthermore, some scholars and collectors have argued that it is primarily an urban tradition, arising out of congested areas that offer few public arenas for group play. According to Abrahams, "Jumping Rope, especially jumping in groups to the accompaniment of the game-rhymes, is essentially an urban phenomenon," but many folklorists have collected jump rope rhymes in rural areas as well (Abrahams 1969, xvii).

Abrahams also says that it is important to recognize jump rope rhymes and games as performative (Abrahams 1969, xvi). That is, jump rope rhymes require and demonstrate verbal agility, creativity, and social interaction at a sophisticated level. There are multiple levels of meaning evident in most jump rope rhymes, starting with their functional use (they keep time for the jumper and the rope swingers) and including the literal and symbolic meanings of the rhymes. Jump

African American girls practice their double-dutch routine in New York City, 2003. Double-dutch competitions are held throughout the United States. (AP Photo/Kathy Willens)

rope rhymes and games may also be a way to compete and act out competitive scenarios, and they may also be a medium for subverting or upholding social norms or taboos.

Similarly, in her article "The Serious Side of Jump Rope: Conversational Practices and Social Organization in the Frame of Play," Marjorie Harness Goodwin discusses the functional aspect of this form of play. She argues that games of jump rope require players to make numerous decisions over the course of a single game and that the process also requires negotiating disputes among the jumpers, rope turners, and audiences (Goodwin, 324). For Goodwin, the game of jump rope frames the disputes and negotiations of daily life, allowing for the creation and recreation of a special kind of social order within the game (Goodwin, 327).

Also, Kyra D. Gaunt's analysis of the significance of the **double dutch** games played by younger African American girls focuses on the relationship between jump rope rhymes and games and other African American verbal and musical traditions. In "Translating Double-Dutch to Hip-Hop: The Musical Vernacular of Black Girls' Play," Gaunt explores the connections between urban forms of double dutch and their potential connections to "hyper-masculine" and highly sexualized **hip-hop** cultures.

Gaunt argues that black girls' performances in double-dutch games on the playground or in the street results in the enactment of a social and musical identity in the performance of those rhymes and games (Gaunt, 288). For Gaunt, these complex identities as represented in jump rope rhymes and games are central to "an enculturational process" through which "black social musicking and a gendered ethnicity are learned." Gaunt sees double-dutch rhyming and playing as a blending of public and private spheres as well as a merging of the cultural past and present (Gaunt, 274). She further suggests that double-dutch performances can be important for understanding black women's performances in other traditions (Gaunt, 288).

Many scholars have proposed classification systems for jump rope rhymes. For example, Brian Sutton-Smith in *Games of New Zealand Children* examines the history of children's play by documenting jump rope rhymes (Sutton-Smith). In another study, Sue Hall proposes the categories of "Fundamentals," "Combinations of Play Jumping," "Counting," "Hot," "Verses with Pantomime," and "Single Line Chants" (Hall, 713). Also, Bruce Buckley's study of jump rope rhymes proposes a classification system based on the style of jumping (Buckley, 99–111), and Ruth Hawthorne organizes her collection based on a list of variables in any given jump rope game (Hawthorne, 113–126).

Other brief collections of jump rope rhymes include Ed Cray's study, which is focused on the Los Angeles area (Cray, 119–127), and Teri John's short documentation of rhymes collected from Raleigh, North Carolina; Detroit, Michigan; Buffalo, New York; southern California; and northern Illinois (John, 15–17).

Jump rope rhymes and games persist as a vibrant form of African American verbal art. For example, African American schoolchildren compete at double dutch competitions throughout the United States, and the traditions have been documented by nationally syndicated columnist Anna Quindlen, whose column about the American double dutch champion team, The Dynamos, highlighted the dexterity and neighborhood tradition exhibited by African American girls on the grade-school playground. Quindlen wrote that the girls she observed one day shortly before the annual National Double Dutch Tournament recited, "Who's on the go? You know. The Dynamos," as their audience of classmates chorused, "The Dynamos, The Dynamos," and stared at the performers while "cheering, dreaming, about what it would be like to cartwheel . . . right into the whirling arcs of two opposing jump ropes, to do spread eagles and buck jumps while the ropes go round and round" (Quindlen, 27).

Jacqueline L. McGrath

See also: Games, Folk

Further Reading

Abrahams, Roger, 1980, *Counting-Out Rhymes: A Dictionary* (Austin, TX, and London: University of Texas Press); Abrahams, Roger, 1969, *Jump-Rope Rhymes: A Dictionary* (Austin, TX, and London: University of Texas Press); Buckley, Bruce R., 1966, "Jump Rope Rhymes: Suggestions for Classification and Study," Keystone Folklore Quarterly 11: 99–111; Cray, Ed, 1970, "Jump-Rope Rhymes from Los Angeles," *Western Folklore* 29: 119–127; Gaunt, Kyra D., 1998, "Dancin' in the Street to a Black Girl's Beat: Music, Gender, and the Ins and Outs of Double-Dutch," in *Generations of Youth: Youth Cultures and History in Twentieth-Century America*, ed. Joe Austin and Michael Nevin Willard (New York: New York University Press), pp. 272–292; Gaunt, Kyra Danielle, 2006, *The Games Black Girls Play: Learning the Ropes from Double-Dutch to Hip-Hop* (New York: New York University Press); Gaunt, Kyra Danielle, 1997, "Translating Double-Dutch to Hip-Hop: The Musical Vernacular of Black Girl's Play," in *Language, Rhythm & Sound: Black Popular Cultures into the Twenty-First Century,* eds. Joseph K. Adjaye, and Adrianne R. Andrews (Pittsburgh, PA: University of Pittsburgh Press), 146–163; Goodwin, Marjorie Harness, 1985, "The Serious Side of Jump Rope: Conversational Practices and Social Organization in the Frame of Play," *The Journal of American Folklore* 98 (389): 315–330; Hall, Sue, 1941, "That Spring Perennial—Rope Jumping!" Recreation (March): 713–716; Hawthorne, Ruth, 1966, "Classifying Jump Rope Games," *Keystone Folklore Quarterly* 11: 113–126; John, Teri, 1973, "A Collection of Jump Rope Rhymes," *North Carolina Folklore Journal* 21: 15–17; Quindlen, Anna, 1983, "Riding Two Ropes to the Double Dutch Top," *New York Times,* June 11, p. 27; Saloy, Mona Lisa, 2011, "Sidewalk Songs, Jump-rope Rhymes, Clap-hand Games of African American Children," *Children's Folklore Review:* 33: 35; Sutton-Smith, Brian, 1959, *Games of New Zealand Children* (Berkeley and Los Angeles: University of California Press).

JUMPING THE BROOM

Jumping the broom is a ritualized, ceremonial activity associated with weddings in which the betrothed jump over a broom to mark their formal union. The broom is held by two people, one at each end, horizontal to the ground. This rite of passage is most likely an Africanism that pays homage to the separation of village life from wilderness. In many parts of West **Africa**, the broom plant (*Sorghum bicolor L. Moench* or *Sorghum vulgare*), which is of African origin, represents the wild, untamed nature of the forest, as do other natural grasses (United States Department of Agriculture, Natural Resources Conservation Service [USDA-NRCS]). In Africa and the diaspora, brooms are cultural objects that are steeped in magical and spiritual folklore, as they are associated with feared orishas (gods) like Obaluaiye in the Ifa stories of the Yoruba people and the orixa Babalu Aye of Cuba. In the Afro-Bahian Candomblé religion of Brazil, the broom is a power object, called *shashara*, which is danced with the air of a royal scepter (Thompson, 61–68). With stories, material culture, songs, and **dances** employing brooms, it is clear that they symbolize wilderness as both a place and a concept (Vogel, 11).

The wild quality of the broom plant represents untamed nature, serving as a metaphor for the state of couples before marriage. When a couple jumps over the broom, they are enacting a physical and psychological shift from wild, undomesticated life to settled, civil, domesticated life (Bird, 43–57). Jumping the broom was a way of marking weddings that was used in the Americas by enslaved Africans whose legal rights, including the right to be legally married, were denied (Hope Franklin, 185–213).

Jumping the broom became a part of American wedding ceremonies during the slavery era and continues to the present day in the African American community as well as in other groups. The ritual has become in contemporary American culture an expression of Afrocentric pride and is such a widespread component of weddings that many small businesses specialize in manufacturing brooms designed for these occasions.

Stephanie Rose Bird

Further Reading

Bird, Stephanie, 2004, *Sticks, Stones, Roots and Bones: Hoodoo, Mojo and Conjuring with Herbs* (St. Paul, MN: Llewellyn Worldwide Publishers); Foster, Frances Smith, 2010, *Til Death or Distance Do Us Part: Love and Marriage in African America* (New York: Oxford University Press); Hope Franklin, John, 1969, *From Slavery to Freedom: A History of Negro Americans*, 3rd ed. (New York: Vintage Books); O'Neil, Patrick W., 2009, "Bosses and Broomsticks: Ritual and Authority in Antebellum Slave Weddings," *The Journal of Southern History* 75 (1): 29–48; Parry, Tyler D., 2015, "Married in Slavery Time: Jumping the Broom in Atlantic Perspective," *Journal of Southern History* 81 (2): 273–312; Thompson, Robert Farris, 1987, *Flash of the Spirit: African and Afro-American Art and Philosophy* (New York: Vintage Books); USDA-NRCS, 1995, "Sorghum: National Plant Data Center; FAO Food and Nutrition Series, No. 27" (Rome, Italy: Food and Agriculture Organization of the United Nations); Vogel, Susan, 1989, *Wild Spirits, Strong Medicine: African Art and the Wilderness*, ed. Enid Schildkrout (New York: The Center for African Art).

JUNETEENTH

An emancipation celebration, Juneteenth is recognized all over the United States. On June 19, 1865, Union Army officer Major General Gordon Granger arrived in Galveston, Texas, and made the following announcement:

The people of Texas are hereby informed that, in accordance with a proclamation from the Executive of the United States of America, all slaves are free. This involves an absolute equality of personal rights and rights of property between former masters and slaves, and the connection heretofore existing between them becomes that between employer and hired labor. The freedmen are advised to remain quietly at their present homes and work for wages.

Thus was established one of the most enduring Emancipation Day celebrations in the United States, popularly known as "Juneteenth," which marks the formal end of African enslavement. President Abraham Lincoln had signed the Emancipation Proclamation to go into effect on January 1, 1863, for those states that were in succession against the Union. However, that decree was not implemented in Texas for more than 17 months after the original emancipation order was to have taken effect. By the time of Granger's announcement, Lincoln had been assassinated, the Confederate forces had been defeated and had formally surrendered at Appomattox Court House, and most other southern states were reeling from the defeat and adjusting to a new social reality.

Juneteenth was one of several emancipation observations. There were others in Oklahoma, Kentucky, Tennessee, Alabama, North Carolina, and South Carolina, but by far the longest lasting has been the Texas observance, held annually on June 19. Initially, the day had a functional purpose. During the period when the state was occupied by federal troops, black leaders, white missionaries, and other good Samaritans of the Freedmen's Bureau used the date to instruct newly freed blacks about their rights and entitlements as free citizens. Gradually, the date took on a more festive atmosphere. This direction continued throughout the balance of the 19th century and into the 20th and 21st centuries.

Certain traditions came to be associated with the Juneteenth observance into the 20th century. Some of the practices date back to **festivals** set in African tradition during the colonial era. There was, for example, a parade in which a "Juneteenth king and queen" might be selected through balloting. Another feature of the early Juneteenth observation was to invite any formerly enslaved Africans in the area to be given a place of honor (such as in the parade) and given the opportunity to recount for a younger generation their experiences in bondage. Some formerly enslaved African Americans who had left Texas and escaped to Mexico via the Underground Railroad returned specifically for the Juneteenth observance.

As the holiday became more festive, public entertainment, **family reunions**, and other events became more prominent. In places such as Dallas, rodeos were the center of the celebration. Food was and is important in the celebrations, and an emphasis on **barbecues** is standard. All kinds of meats are cooked and shared. Some participants also make unique dishes, and in some locations, like Austin, there are cook-off contests. Wearing red and having red foods like watermelon, red soft drinks, and strawberry pie is also symbolic at the Juneteenth celebration. In some Texas localities, people donned plantation-style dress replete with red bandanas.

For reasons that are not very clear, the Juneteenth holiday lost its appeal throughout Texas during the 1950s and 1960s. The explanation frequently offered is that this period, encompassing the struggles of the civil rights movement, contrasted unfavorably with a holiday that harkened back to an era of black enslavement; Juneteenth was simply out of vogue and seen as an antiquated celebration. By the 1970s, however, there was renewed interest. In 1979, State Representative Al Edwards introduced a bill to the Texas legislature making June 19 an official state holiday. It was subsequently signed into law and has been recognized as such since 1980.

By the 1990s, as a result of Texans moving to other parts of the country and the general interest in reviving African American folkloric traditions, Juneteenth has been recognized and celebrated nationwide. There is even a Juneteenth international Web site that posts holiday events taking place around the world. From Dallas to Detroit, June 19 has captured the imagination and inspired African Americans to revisit their heritage in numerous ways.

Christopher Brooks

Further Reading

Conner, Robert C., 2013, *General Gordon Granger: The Savior of Chickamauga and the Man Behind "Juneteenth"* (Philadelphia: Casemate); Hume, Janice, and Noah Arceneaux, 2008, "Public Memory, Cultural Legacy, and Press Coverage of the Juneteenth Revival," *Journalism History* 34 (3): 155; Juneteenth Web site, http://www.juneteenth .com; Murray, Julie, 2012, *Juneteenth* (Edina, Minn: ABDO Pub. Co.); Nelson, Vaunda Micheaux, and Drew Nelson, 2006, *Juneteenth* (Millbrook Press); Peppas, Lynn, 2011, *Juneteenth* (New York: Crabtree Pub. Co.); Wiggins, William H., Jr., 1990, *Oh Freedom! Afro-American Emancipation Celebrations* (Knoxville: University of Tennessee Press).

K

KWANZAA

This annual, African American, **Christmas**-season holiday is celebrated December 26 through January 1. Philosopher, activist, and Us (a Los Angeles–based black community organization) leader, Maulana Karenga, established the political and cultural holiday in Los Angeles, California, in 1966 as a means of strengthening the African American community through seven basic principles, each assigned a Swahili name and a day of observance:

1. *umoja* (unity)
2. *kujichagulia* (self-determination)
3. *ujima* (collective work and responsibility)
4. *ujamaa* (cooperative economics)
5. *nia* (purpose)
6. *kuumba* (creativity)
7. *imani* (faith)

Adapting facets of a 1920 declaration by Jamaican-born black nationalist Marcus Garvey, Kwanzaa rituals use the colors black, red, and green to represent, respectively, African people, the continuing struggle for justice, and hope for youth and the future. Families celebrate Kwanzaa by lighting seven candles (*mishumaa saba*), each representing a Kwanzaa principle, in a candleholder (*kinara*). They drink from a unity cup (*kikombe cha umoja*) and place on a mat (*mkeka*): crops (*mazao*), which symbolize African agricultural traditions; ears of corn (*vibunzi*), one for each child in the family; and gifts (*zawadi*), which are awarded to children who have honored commitments during the year.

By the end of the 20th century, an estimated 13 million people had begun to celebrate Kwanzaa in the United States alone. However, amid a vague, popular-culture awareness of the holiday, mistaken beliefs arose about its origin and purpose. Some Americans have considered Kwanzaa a religious occasion, easily lumped with other nonmainstream winter holidays such as Hanukkah, Ramadan, Oshogatsu, and the winter solstice, and thus characterized it as an "alternative" to Christmas. The specific religious bent of the holiday is falsely believed to be mystical and, as Karenga put it, "spookistic," loosely related to traditional African religions employing idol worship and juju. In truth, Kwanzaa is a secular, cultural holiday to be celebrated by all African Americans, regardless of faith. Although Kwanzaa incorporates specific principles and rites aimed at the spiritual elevation of its practitioners, it does not preclude the observance of Christian, Jewish, Muslim, Shinto, pagan, or other religious holidays. The rituals associated with

Some of the important symbols of the Kwanzaa celebration. (Aleasa Word/Dreamstime.com)

Kwanzaa, which include lighting candles and, in the West African tradition, offering libations to the ancestors, are designed to reinforce African Americans' self-concept and enhance social unity.

Kwanzaa's placement during the already festive week between Christmas and New Year's Day, however, was deliberate. The length of the celebration allows for the dedication of one full day for reflection upon each of the seven principles. It also marks a period when most schools and offices are closed, Americans spend more time with their families, people are preparing emotionally and spiritually for the coming of a new year, and after-Christmas sales allow for the purchase of gifts to be less financially burdensome to low-income African American families. Unlike their Christmas counterparts, Kwanzaa gifts are neither mandatory nor given unconditionally; in this regard, Kwanzaa does offer an alternative to the rampant commercialism associated with Christmas and Hanukkah in the United States.

Closely tied to the belief that Kwanzaa is derived from an African religion is the even more widespread idea that it is an African holiday rather than an American holiday for people of African heritage. Many African nations do celebrate harvest, or "first fruits," thanksgiving **festivals** and mark each harvest as the beginning of a new year. This tradition helped inspire the establishment of Kwanzaa, and the name itself is derived from the Swahili word for "first fruits" (*kwanza*). However, no Africans celebrated a holiday called Kwanzaa before 1966, and no traditional African holiday employs all of the same symbols and practices as Kwanzaa. This mistaken belief arose from the prevalence of African symbols (harvest crops, mats, a Zulu-based candleholder), African rituals (such as the East African *harambee*, a call to unity), and an African language (Swahili) being used in Kwanzaa practices, as well as the close connection between Kwanzaa principles and the values of many African tribes.

At the time that the holiday was created, in the 1960s, African American culture was immersed in a wave of Afrocentrism, a trend manifested in the importing of African art, the popularization of African hairstyles and fashion, a surge in giving black children African or pseudo-African names, an increase in political black nationalism, and a desire among young people of the African diaspora to reconnect with their roots on the ancestral continent. Infusing Kwanzaa with African imagery, Karenga and Us hoped to reach a broad range of African Americans through the promotion of a shared cultural heritage—and to perhaps avoid resistance to Kwanzaa by leaders and members of African American organizations not aligned with Us. Karenga has suggested, however, that resistance surfaced nonetheless and that **rumors** that Kwanzaa is a continental African holiday arose from deliberate attempts to deny Us and Karenga proper credit for Kwanzaa's invention. He also has speculated that Americans' eagerness to believe Kwanzaa came directly from Africa is rooted in a racist suspicion that African Americans are incapable of the creativity required for making a wholly new celebration using original customs and traditions.

Still, the link to the continent and history of **Africa** is fortified through the holiday's storytelling. In modern celebrations of Kwanzaa, African Americans have drawn from traditional tales of the African diaspora and have created or adapted stories that reinforce the seven principles of Kwanzaa, the *nguzo saba*. The West African **folktale** in which a fish swallows Anancy the spider and his seven sons must rescue him, for example, serves as a reminder of the principle of *umoja* (unity). The tale of the three tests, in which small animals outsmart a tiger, speaks to *kujichagulia* (self-determination). The principle of *ujima* (collective work and responsibility) surfaces in the Igbo tales of Mbeku the **tortoise** and the animals that work together to evade his persistent trickery. Such folktales have gained popularity in modern American culture through their recorded performances by African American celebrities. New writers, in the spirit of *kuumba*, have penned original Kwanzaa **fables** that draw on the experiences of American children. Some children's Kwanzaa stories link Christmas traditions to Kwanzaa, thus pushing the holiday further into mainstream culture.

Karen Pojmann

Further Reading

Allen, Reniqua, 2013, "Legitimized Blackness? Kwanzaa, Citizenship, and Newark," *Western Journal of Black Studies* 37 (4): 272–284; Ayub, Mariam, s.v. "The Story behind Kwanzaa," Festivals.com, http://festivals.com/features/holidays/kwanzaa.aspx; Bumpus, Eshu, s.v. "Kwanzaa: The Seven Principles in Folktales," Folktales.net, http://www.folktales.net/Kwanza1.html; Chocolate, Deborah M. Newton, 1999, *My First Kwanzaa Book* (New York: Scholastic); Gay, Kathlyn, 2007, *African-American Holidays, Festivals, and Celebrations: The History, Customs, and Symbols Associated with Both Traditional and Contemporary Religious and Secular Events Observed by Americans of African Descent* (Detroit: Omnigraphics); Geller, Brian, 1996, "A Holiday of Cultural Expression with No Religious Ties," *Independent Florida Alligator*, December 4 (also available online, http://www.alligator.org/edit/issues/96-fall/961204/a01kwanz.htm); Karenga, Ron, 1977, *Kwanzaa: Origin, Concepts, Practice* (Inglewood, CA: Lawaida Publications); Mayes, Keith A., 2009, *Kwanzaa: Black Power and the Making of the African-American Holiday Tradition* (New York: Routledge); Medearis, Angela Shelf, 1997, *The Seven Days of Kwanzaa* (New York: Scholastic); Official Kwanzaa Web Site, http://www.officialkwanzaawebsite.org; St. James, Synthia, 1997, *The Gifts of Kwanzaa* (Morton Grove, IL: Albert Whitman & Company).

L

LAWMAN, THE

In black folklore, lawmen are usually white characters associated with the police force and judicial system. These characters are essentially the evolution of captains and crews of slave ships, patty-rollers, slave owners and overseers, **night riders**, and members of the Ku Klux Klan. They are the postbellum, modern, and post-modern portraits of those figures in American—and other New World African—societies who are assigned the tasks of policing and attempting to destabilize black communities: meting out inhumane punishments for alleged crimes and enacting ritualized violence against the individual and the social black body. The lawman motif appears in genres as diverse as song (**blues**, **jazz**, reggae, calypso, and **rap**), **folktales**, **jokes**, graffiti, **aerosol art**, and **toasts**, and carries with it a number of consistent and, in some cases, unique nuances.

In rural blues the lawman appears as a mythologized figure, customarily referred to as "the High Sheriff." Granted power somewhere between that of a slave owner and the grim reaper, the High Sheriff is invested with the license to come, take away, and kill or imprison members of the black community. Although there is sometimes an ambivalence expressed toward the accused, songs are never sympathetic toward the sheriff. Barefoot Bill's "Big Rock Jail" exemplifies the sheriff motif (Sackheim, 302). The song, which begins, "The high sheriff been here / Got my girl and gone," also suggests that, in spite of her shortcomings, the speaker's lover is innocent and has been unfairly imprisoned. Her innocence is reflected in lines such as, "Well listen mister / What have my baby done?" and "You took her gun and / Hit her razor hand / And you went wrong 'cause / She ain't never harmed a man." The continuities between representations of colonial authority and the sheriff are reflected in the last lines of the song, "I say my baby in jail and / I can't get no sleep / I don't get nothing but the / Mean old high sheriff" (Sackheim, 302).

While songs like "Big Rock Jail" register the helplessness of black people in the face of the "law," other songs point to the sheriff's weakness when contrasted with defiant or "**baad**" black folk (usually men). For instance, in Henry Thomas's "Bob McKinney," the bold masculinity of the **bad man** eclipses the authority of the sheriff:

> Bobby said to the high sheriff
> Maybe you think I'm going to run
> If I had another load
> Me and you have some fun
> Wasn't he bad
> Yes wasn't he bad

(Sackheim, 71)

Comparable dynamics pertain in other songs in which lawmen are pitted against bad men. In one example the sheriff cowardly orders the deputy to go after **Stagolee**, to which the deputy responds by resigning:

> The high sheriff said, "Go bring me dat bad man Staggerlee here."
> The deputy pulled off his pistols and he laid them on the shelf.
> And said, "If you want dat bad man you got to go 'rest him by yo'self."
>
> (Levine, 414)

Motifs intricately connected to lawmen are those of the judge, jail, and jailer. Judges are customarily depicted as sadistic enforcers of the gateway between the two societies, white and black, and quick to mete out the severest penalties—more for the sake of emphasizing the power of white society than for the sake of justice. So coming before the judge has a special significance in black folklore, serving as a modern site for the replication of the slave system. Black characters have dealt with this dilemma and its related psychological crises in a variety of manners. Texas blues artist and raconteur Lightnin' Hopkins tells the story of being taken "up 'for the judge" for having run his own car in the ditch. He confronts and undermines the power of the court through **signifying** and humor, under which lies a warrior's defiance and contempt for the system and its perpetrators. The judge asks Hopkins, "Is you ever been up before me, boy?" to which Hopkins responds, "I don't know suh. What time do you get up?"

Jail resonates throughout African American folklore as the designated social space in which black people can be physically enslaved, having been targeted and taken from their communities by lawmen, and sentenced to jail terms by the judge. For some, limited stays in jail seem comparable to the Middle Passage, in which slaves were held below decks on ships crossing the Atlantic. Although the reality of jails and prisons often involved groups of prisoners, song narratives often offer a singular perspective, with a focus on feelings of isolation. Bessie Smith's "Jailhouse Blues," which begins with a spoken allusion to the police ("Lord, this house is gonna get raided / Yes sir"), exemplifies the sense of isolation and pain of being away from, and perhaps losing, one's community of friends. Smith sings, "Thirty days in jail with my back turned to the wall / Look here Mr. Jail Keeper, put another gal in my stall," and later, "I don't mind being in jail, but I got to stay there so long / When every friend I had is done shook hands and gone" (Sackheim, 52). Perhaps no other song expresses these sentiments better than Blind Lemon Jefferson's "Prison Cell Blues." Jefferson sings:

> Getting tired of sleeping in this low down lonesome cell. . . .
> Got a red-eyed captain and a squabbling boss
> Got a mad-dog sergeant, honey, and he won't knock off. . . .
> I asked the gov'ment to knock some days off my time
> Well the way I'm treated I'm 'bout to lose my mind.
>
> (Sackheim, 74)

The prison becomes less like the Middle Passage and more like slavery in the songs of those who have been given lengthier sentences, for example, in songs by

Delta blues singers such as Robert Pete Williams and Bukka White, who sang of the notorious Parchman Farm penitentiary in Mississippi.

The parallels between slavery and prison continue in references to escape and death sentences, both of which are found in Victoria Spivey's "Blood Hound Blues." The speaker in the song has been imprisoned and sentenced to the electric chair for killing her partner, who was physically abusing her. She escapes and is being tracked by a posse and bloodhounds: "I broke out of my cell when the jailer turned his back / But now I'm so sorry blood hounds are on my track" (Sackheim, 56). The escape motif is common in rural blues, as are images of being tracked by dogs, as in Robert Johnson's "Hellhounds on My Trail." Lawmen such as sheriffs are assumed to be heading the posses.

As times change and songs and narratives reflect more the Northern, urban reality of African American life, the High Sheriff becomes the Police, and later, the FBI and CIA. The idea that black people have been automatically perceived by policemen as criminals was present in the folklore as early as the beginning of migration from rural to urban areas and from the South to the North. Accompanying this idea is the belief that black people have historically been viewed as objects for target practice by gun-happy policemen. Memphis Minnie sings, in "Nothing in Rambling":

> I walked through the alley
> With my hand in my coat.
> The police start to shoot me
> Thought it was something I stole.

> (Sackheim, 57)

These sentiments are an integral part of reggae, **rap**, and **hip-hop** music, all of which contain much more militant articulations of the continuities between "the law" and colonialism. In Bob Marley and the Wailers' reggae song "I Shot the Sheriff," for instance, the speaker snaps under the pain of years of oppression and harassment, shoots the sheriff, and becomes a fugitive. Similarly, in the film *The Harder They Come*, Ivan, the rude boy and central character, becomes legendary by shooting a policeman, becoming a fugitive, and managing to taunt the authorities and evade capture for a considerable period of time. Such figures are placed within the context of Rastafari-influenced ideology that sees no substantial break between past times of slavery and colonialism and contemporary oppressed and policed postslavery societies.

In the United States, controversy has centered on rap lyrics in which the cops are declared enemies of black people. The tables are turned in these songs, as rappers encourage those in the black community to take up arms against lawmen ("pigs") who have no regard for black life. Songs by artists such as Ice-T ("Cop Killer") and Kool G Rap and DJ Polo ("Live and Let Die") have been at the heart of this controversy. Many in mainstream America were appalled not only by the lyrics of "Cop Killer" but also by the marketing strategy for the CD (which was shipped in miniature body bags). However, those who reacted most strongly to the song failed to place it the larger context of relationships between lawmen and the black community. Armed resistance by black people dates back to slave uprisings and is illustrated more recently by groups like the Black Panther Party and Deacons for Defense and Justice. Incidents such as the televised beating of Rodney King, widely publicized shootings of African Americans by policemen, the prevalence of arrests for "driving while black," and statistics on the numbers and percentages of black men in American prisons have drawn more national attention to the inequities of "the law."

Abuses by lawmen have also been a recurring motif in urban **legends** and **rumors**. As Patricia Turner notes, many such stories have centered on violent murders or assaults on black people by lawmen, with some of these stories sparking riots. She writes, "With fire, water, and like weapons capable of complete bodily destruction, the powers that be seemed intent on eliminating blacks one by one from American streets, American cities, American factories—the entire American landscape" (Turner, 56). Not only do lawmen such as the police recur in African American rumors and legends, but so do more specialized lawmen such as FBI and CIA agents. Such officials are often part of rumors that assume the presence of conspiracies on the part of the U.S. government to wipe out African Americans. For example, the FBI and CIA are pictured in some rumors as the killers of political figures such as Malcolm X and Martin Luther King. They also have been implicated as killers in such race-specific crises as the Atlanta child murders, a wave of murders of black children in the 1980s.

The lawman in African American folklore has been one of the most consistently revised and socially relevant motifs. It continues to have tremendous social currency and to influence perceptions and relationships between those in black communities and officers of the legal system. This is unlikely to change any time soon, as assaults continue into the 21st century, garnering ongoing media attention and triggering national debates, conversations, and varied forms of protest, such as the Black Lives Matter movement.

Anand Prahlad

Further Reading

Levine, Lawrence W., 1977, *Black Culture and Black Consciousness* (New York: Oxford University Press); Sackheim, Eric, ed., 1975 [1969], *The Blues Line: A Collection of Blues Lyrics* (New York: Schirmer Books); Turner, Patricia, 1993, *I Heard It through the Grapevine: Rumors in African-American Culture* (Berkeley: University of California Press).

LAYING ON HANDS

The laying on of hands is a spiritual practice in which a religious functionary places one or both hands palms down on the top of another person's head while saying a **prayer** or blessing for healing or "receiving the Holy Spirit." After an individual has hands laid on her or him, she or he may be "slain in the Spirit"—a phenomenon in which the individual falls backward or falls down. There are usually one or two persons behind the person to catch her or him and then gently lay the person on the floor. While lying upon the floor, the person may appear unconscious and remain in this seemingly unconscious state for many minutes or may recover immediately. Most individuals who have experienced this phenomenon report feeling a warm sensation spreading throughout the entire body followed by a feeling of deep peace and contentment.

Another phenomenon an individual may experience after having hands laid on him or her is referred to as "catching the Spirit." While in this state, the person might start dancing, shout praises unto God, or run in place or around the sanctuary in an exuberant fashion. The person may remain in this state of ecstasy for many minutes or recover in a relatively short period of time. Once the person is no longer in a state of exuberance, he or she has then moved into a state referred to as "the Spirit was spent." It is believed that the Holy Spirit, having demonstrated his power in the individual, now leaves the person with a deep, relaxed feeling of peace. This practice, which has historically been found among varying groups in different parts of the world and in varying historical periods, has had connections with "faith healing."

For African Americans, this spiritual practice has sometimes been associated with the need to release the sadness and anguish from having to fight to be full participants in and enjoy the full rights of citizenry in American culture. It tends to be found in certain denominations but not in others, for example, among "African American Holiness-Pentacostal ("Sanctified") and Spiritual churches," in which "Black divine healers use a variety of techniques, including laying-on of hands, anointing with oil, using blessed water, and applying prayer cloths to the sick body" (Baer, and Singer, p. 242).

The function of this ritual is sometimes likened to the experience of slaves singing songs and **spirituals** about the "by-and-by." Slaves were not experiencing justice on the earth, but they trusted that their lives would be joyous in heaven, or the "by-and-by." Therefore, participation in spiritual experiences such as the laying on of hands created the solace needed to continue the struggle of living under oppressive circumstances.

African Americans are of diverse opinions about religious phenomena such as the laying on of hands. Many artists and political activists see the practice as just another shackle created by white society that produces stagnation within the African American community. Those who ascribe to this viewpoint feel that evangelical religions reinforce subordinate behavior instead of facilitating actions that might alter the plight of African Americans. Others feel that spiritual experiences such as the laying on of hands are empowering and demonstrate the reality and power of a divine being and reaffirm the imminent change in social status that will result from divine justice.

Shawnrece D. Miller

Further Reading

Alexander, Estrelda, 2011, *Black Fire: One Hundred Years of African American Pentacostalism* (Downers Grove, IL: IVP Academic); Baer, Hans A., and Merrill Singer, 2002, *African American Religion: Varieties of Protest and Accommodation* (Knoxville: University of Tennessee Press); Bremer, Thomas S., 2015, *Formed From the Soil: An Introduction to the*

Diverse History of Religion (Chishester, West Sussex: Wiley Blackwell); Brown, Candy Gunther, 2011, *Global Pentecostal and Charismatic Healing* (New York: Oxford University Press); *Encyclopedia Britannica*, accessed October 28, 2004, s.v. "Hands, Imposition of," Encyclopedia Britannica Premium Service, http:www.brittanica.com/eb/article?tocld=90313257; Pinn, Anthony B., 2005, *The African American Religious Experience in America* (ABC-CLIO); Thwing, Warren, 1978, *A Hand Book for New Charismatics* (Fort Worth, TX: McElhaney Printing & Publishing).

LEGENDS

Legends are a category of folk narrative. They tell a story of some kind. There are three major categories, or genres, of narrative folklore—legend, **myth**, and **folktale**. Like myths, legends are stories believed to be true by both teller and hearer. But they differ from myths in that they take place in "real time" or in a historical past that is identifiable, and they typically focus on the dramas of people rather than on divine characters.

The spread of legends—through word of mouth, in print, and increasingly, on the Internet—is similar to the spread of **rumors** (unverified accounts of supposed events). Indeed, rumors may become legendary in scope as they acquire narrative content and motif structures. Though legends may deal in magical, supernatural, or otherwise bizarre incidents, they are seen to be straightforward accounts of concrete events and for this reason are highly variable in structure and topic. Broadly speaking, legends frequently speak to current cultural fears: the threat of various real and imagined enemies, technology gone awry, the dissemination of disease, fast-food culture, and the realm of the supernatural are all favorite topics. These narratives are meant to account for the extraordinary experiences of everyday people. People who tell legends often give their narratives "validating formulas" such as "This happened in our neighborhood," "My aunt told me that this happened to her friend," and "I think I read this in Dear Abby" (Brunvand, 159). Like most folklore, legends are migratory—that is, they exist in many places with slight variations. However, a legend may take on the names, geographical features, or histories of specific places and thus become a "localized" version of a migratory legend. Conversely, even a highly local legend may eventually alter and diffuse outward, becoming a migratory legend.

There are many subcategories of legend, and several of these are commonly found in African American folk culture. The historical legend features fictionalized versions of key events in African American cultural history. Closely related to this subgenre is family folklore and the personal legend, or "memorate." Actual history undergoes the process of becoming narrative through repetition across generations and cross-pollination between families. In this way, legendary motifs become standardized. Several common topics for these types of legends are important. There are stories of miscegenation, where family features are attributed to a white father (often a plantation owner and often influential—a state senator, for example, or even occasionally a U.S. president). Narratives of unusually kind or wicked masters and mistresses are mingled with tales of ancestors defying the masters in inventive ways (e.g., by running away, learning to read and write in secret, or accepting various forms of aid from a sympathetic white person). Encounters with racist whites, including the Ku Klux Klan, are common, as are recorded recollections of the moment in which a former slave received news of his or her emancipation.

Supernatural legends are supposedly factual narratives, told in either the first or third person, of encounters with the "other world" in the form of monsters, spirits, ghosts, magical animals, and so forth. In African American culture, the most common characters in supernatural legends include witches (or **conjure** women and men), ghosts (or haunts), and bogeymen (or boogermen), who steal lazy or disrespectful children away from their elders.

The urban legend (and the related rumor) is perhaps the most common legend type of all across contemporary American cultures, regardless of ethnicity or heritage. Urban legends are narratives in a modern (but not necessarily urban) setting; they are characterized by a suspenseful story line, an insistence upon the veracity of the story, and a more or less overt warning or moral. A rumor often contains the skeletal structure of the legend, perhaps without the full narrative sequencing. Critics argue that the African American "rumor mill" stretches back to the beginning of American slavery. For example, a common slave-ship rumor among African prisoners (fostered by their captors) was that the whites were going to kill and eat the prisoners when they reached land. During Reconstruction, a number of rumors were spread by former slave owners to discourage blacks from migrating north. For instance, ex-slaves were told that Northerners were running a slave trade to Cuba. Another story that circulated among blacks and whites alike warned that "night doctors" kidnapped and murdered blacks on the city streets, thus creating cadavers for medical dissection. This legend was built upon prevalent suspicions of modern medicine and science. Some versions of this legend put the night doctors in clothes of bright white—the color not only of lab coats but also of Klan robes. Other versions insisted that the night doctors wore black; this allied them not only with the garb of southern patrollers but, more subtly and disturbingly, also with black skin itself. Indeed, in some versions, the night doctors were themselves black.

More contemporary rumors, many of which have become full-blown legends, accuse various corporations, restaurants, and government agencies of racist conspiracies against African Americans. Some contend that the Snapple iced tea label features a slave ship and that the Ku Klux Klan owns the company. Other rumors have accused clothing designer Tommy Hilfiger (or, alternatively, Liz Claiborne) of making openly racist remarks about their black clientele. Still other rumors have postulated that popular food chains routinely contaminate foods served in African American communities; Church's Chicken, for instance, has been accused of adding an agent that causes sterility in African American males, while Kentucky Fried Chicken restaurants in black neighborhoods are rumored to serve rat in place of chicken. Several AIDS conspiracy theories have gained legendary status among African Americans. Those who study legends and rumors have argued that this folkloric form gives people a figurative language in which to frame their cultural fears and longings, their sense of oppression and injustice, and their suspicions and mutual intolerances. Thus, urban legends serve to protect black communities from various forms of assault by ensuring their suspicion of outside entities that have historically exploited them.

Molly Clark Hillard

See also: Grapevine, The

Further Reading

Brunvand, Jan Harold, 1986, *The Study of American Folklore: An Introduction* (New York: W. W. Norton); Dance, Daryl Cumber, ed., 2002, *From My People: 400 Years of African American Folklore* (New York: W. W. Norton); Moody-Turner, Shirley, 2013, *Black Folklore and the Politics of Racial Representation* (Jackson: University Press of Mississippi); Roberts, John, 2009, "African American Belief Narratives and the African Cultural Tradition," *Research in African Literatures* 40 (1): 112–126; Turner, Patricia A., 1993, *I Heard It through the Grapevine: Rumor in African-American Culture* (Berkeley: University of California Press); Turner, Patricia A., and Gary Alan Fine, 2001, *Whispers on the Color Line: Rumor and Race in America* (Berkeley: University of California Press).

M

MAGIC SHOPS

By the late 20th century, various magical and occult belief systems had become increasingly popular. All of these belief systems have specific products necessary to their practice. To serve the practitioners of various belief systems, shopkeepers maintain stores that specialize in spiritually related merchandise for practitioners of black, folk religions and **herbalism**.

By far the most common sources of this revival in magical and occult beliefs were reworked ancient European, particularly Celtic, pagan religions. However, African American magical belief systems such as **Hoodoo**, Vodou, **conjure**, and root work, though they have been practiced continuously for centuries, also experienced a renaissance. In addition, because of changes in immigration trends, the Afro-Cuban religion, Santería, has become more common in the United States in recent years, as has traditional Haitian Vodou and Mexican *Curandererismo* and *Brujeria*.

Originally products for these religions were created, collected, and provided by local practitioners. At the turn of the century, however, American products began being mass-produced, including items used in African American folk religions and spiritual practices. The shops that sprang up to sell these products, however, have not been generally called "magic shops." (Although businesses for new age, Celtic-based religions might be called "magick shops," and scholars Arthur L. Hall and Peter G. Bourne called purveyors of spiritual merchandise "magic vendors" to distinguish them from actual practitioners.) Earlier in the 20th century, a spiritual store might have been called a "Hoodoo drugstore," or a "candle store." Hoodoo drugstores were pharmacies with African American clientele that not only provided standard, doctor-prescribed medicines but also magical products, for example, **High John the Conqueror** root and ingredients for **charms** or **mojos**. A candle store, as the name implies, sold candles as well as other magical products. Some stores were called "Hindu stores" because the clientele related knowledge of the occult to Indian "swamis." In addition to retail outlets, various wholesale companies began selling spiritual merchandise. Many of these were "novelty" or "curio" companies. More mainstream suppliers also sold various types of magical supplies. Botanical companies, not surprisingly, sold items for magical as well as medicinal purposes.

Even companies not connected to religion, magic, or medicine began to produce spiritual merchandise. For example, toiletry and cleaning supply companies transformed some of their existing products into magical charms. The rise of mail-order marketing in the early 20th century helped all of these types of companies sell spiritual products. In particular, small-scale, independent entrepreneurs were able to reach national audiences through ads in the backs of magazines. However, in the 1930s local, state, and federal agencies began cracking down on the spiritual merchandise mail-order industry. Mail-order companies run by African Americans were targeted in particular and charged with conducting fraud through the U.S. Postal Service.

In recent years, with the growing popularity of various magical and occult belief systems, the marketplace has again stepped in to provide the necessary products. With the rise of Afro-Caribbean and Latin American immigration, botanicas and *yerberias* have become increasingly common. Like the mail-order businesses at the turn of the 20th century, today the Internet provides spiritual merchandisers or magic vendors national, even international, access to prospective consumers. Papa Bones, for example, has its own Web site and advertises itself as "the largest Voodoo and Occult store in the United States." Another large Internet retailer is The Lucky Mojo Curio Company, run by author Catherine Yronwode, who also sells her various books on the site. Lucky Mojo sells supplies for a variety of beliefs including "African-American hoodoo, Pagan magick, and other Witchcraft traditions" and for "Hindu, Buddhist, Catholic, Protestant, Muslim, and Jewish religious and magical traditions."

A great many scholars have examined folk medicine and magical beliefs among African Americans, but Carolyn Morrow Long is the only scholar who has focused extensively on the business side of these beliefs. Her book, *Spiritual Merchants: Religion, Magic, and Commerce*, was published in 2001. Other scholars who have included the subject in their studies include Arthur L. Hall and Peter G. Bourne as well as Loudell F. Snow, who wrote "Sorcerers, Saints and Charlatans: Black Folk Healers in Urban America," and "Mail Order Magic: The Commercial Exploitation of Folk Belief," among many other articles.

Hilary Mac Austin

See also: Conjure; Herbalism; Mojo

Further Reading

Anderson, Jeffrey, 2007, *Conjure in African American Society* (Baton Rouge: Louisiana State University Press); Anderson, Jeffrey E., 2008, *Hoodoo, Voodoo, and Conjure: A Handbook* (Greenwood Press); Baer, Hans A., 1982, "Toward a Systematic Typology of Black Folk Healers," Phylon (1960–) 43 (4): 327–343; Hall, Arthur L., and Peter G. Bourne, 1973, "Indigenous Therapists in a Southern Black Urban Community," *Archives of General Psychiatry* 28 (January): 137–142; Long, Carolyn Morrow, 2001, *Spiritual Merchants: Religion, Magic, and Commerce* (Knoxville: University of Tennessee Press); Mitchem, Stephanie Y., 2007, *African American Folk Healing* (New York: New York University Press); Snow, Loudell F., 1978, "Sorcerers, Saints and Charlatans: Black Folk Healers in Urban America," *Culture, Medicine and Psychiatry* 2 (1): 69–106; Snow, Loudell F., 1979, "Mail Order Magic: The Commercial Exploitation of Folk Belief," *Journal of the Folklore Institute* 16: 44–74.

MARDI GRAS

Mardi Gras is French for "Fat Tuesday," the name referring to the final day of feasting that occurs before the fasting and abstinence of the Christian penitential season of Lent leading up to Easter. Mardi Gras is a single day, the day before Ash Wednesday, which itself marks the beginning of Lent. This pre-Lenten carnival celebration is ritually observed along the U.S. Gulf Coast, particularly in Louisiana. However, it is the culmination of a celebratory season that in New Orleans is held to begin on Twelfth Night, January 6. Although technically this season is referred to as Carnival, this entire time period is commonly called Mardi Gras or the Mardi Gras season. Because Easter is a moveable feast and Lent thus begins at a different time each year, Mardi Gras does not have a fixed date. The best-known Mardi Gras celebration is that which takes place in New Orleans, although the celebration in Mobile, Alabama, is large and has a long history, and Mardi Gras festivities in rural Louisiana have become better known in recent years.

In New Orleans, Carnival is a time of gaiety and good feeling, but it is also a complex **festival** season in which people participate in different ways and that has a variety of social and cultural functions. Although Mardi Gras comes out of Catholic tradition, some non-Catholics traditionally have participated.

It is a focus for private activities like parties and family gatherings, although a large number of elaborate parades provide the central public focus. Street costuming takes place, principally on Mardi Gras day itself, the festival thus providing a venue for assuming fantasy identities. The streets also provide a place for public revelry, especially at parades and mainly on Mardi Gras day in certain parts of the city. The city government provides an infrastructure of safety, sanitation, and permits, but Carnival celebrations primarily are put on by private organizations generally called krewes, which commonly have formal balls and organize parades (although not all krewes participate in parading). Historically these organizations were all-male groups, although today there are women's krewes. Krewe membership relates to social status, with some of these organizations conferring greater social prestige upon members than others, resulting in forms of social and racial inclusion and exclusion and in Mardi Gras being in part a forum for expressing class, racial, and other cultural identities. Carnival krewes also serve as important connectors for business and social contacts. For the members of the socially elite "old-line" krewes, Mardi Gras functions as an aspect of a debutante system through which eligible young women "come out" and are "presented" to society, notably at formal balls, and Mardi Gras is central to the elite's social season.

Black participation in and influence upon Mardi Gras in New Orleans is complicated. In many ways African Americans engage in the same behaviors as others, such as attending parades or enjoying public celebrations (although their doing so sometimes has been discouraged by public policy; at one time, for example, blacks were not permitted to wear the masks that whites commonly assumed as parts of their costumes, and segregation limited the places where blacks celebrated). Historically, however, black culture and society have had a distinctive role in shaping Mardi Gras, and Mardi Gras also has been a particular focus of black/white political and social relations.

Mardi Gras is a tradition introduced by the French into their colony of Louisiana. Nonetheless, African elements entered the tradition early through the plantation societies of the Caribbean and the American **South**, though this influence is not

A Mardi Gras Indian in full costume, New Orleans, 2011. (Tulane University Public Relations)

well understood. The "official" Twelfth Night beginning of the Mardi Gras season suggests a tie to plantation revels of the **Christmas** season and to the Junkanoo Festivals of the black Caribbean. Prior to the 1850s, Mardi Gras in New Orleans was characterized by small, unorganized groups of street maskers and some random parading, which probably stemmed from African and Afro-Caribbean as well as European traditions, although there is little information on the extent of black participation in these forms of celebration. Over the years important, distinctively African American, Mardi Gras traditions developed. The Mardi Gras Indians are one such traditional group, composed of African Americans who "mask Indian," that is, who dress in elaborate, self-made costumes modeled on Native American dress and who belong to "tribes" or "gangs" and march on Mardi Gras day. They have developed **dances** and a body of songs that are the only true folk music of urban Mardi Gras (other Mardi Gras songs and parade music coming out of the worlds of pop and marching band music). Another such traditional group is Zulu (formally the Zulu Social Aid and Pleasure Club), an organization of African Americans who today put on one of the most important parades and whose costumes and behaviors lampoon a particular image of "Africa."

The present-day form of Mardi Gras in New Orleans—exclusive balls and stately, well-organized parades with expensive, elaborately constructed floats—began to take shape in the 1850s. At that time many residents of the city were repelled by the boisterous, Carnival-like behavior of street maskers and revelers. Groups of upper-class citizens created organized parades to defuse what they saw as uncontrolled street violence. This development of Mardi Gras created, then, a type of social control, and some Mardi Gras organizations—cementing as they do a political and social establishment—have also played a role, albeit an indirect one, in the control of African Americans and other minorities. For example, members of elite krewes probably aided the organization of the White League, which opposed Reconstruction and black political ambitions of that era (the Comus parade of 1872 was bitterly satirical of Reconstruction government and blacks). Members of elite krews also played a role in the deadly lynchings of Sicilian Americans in 1891.

Since the 1850s Mardi Gras in New Orleans has been dominated by an Anglo-French social elite. Therefore blacks, as well as working-class whites and members of certain ethnic groups (notably Italians and Jews), have historically been excluded from some forms of participation in the festival, notably those associated with the rituals of high society. They have responded by broadening and enriching the festival by creating their own forms of celebration. Zulu, whose parade originally was a ragtag affair with no fixed route (and thus in the spirit of earlier street masking), not only gave blacks a parading organization of their own but also served to make fun of the elite krewes and of white stereotypes of African culture. Upper-class blacks formed their own socially elite organizations, such as the Original Illinois Club, which held their own exclusive balls for their own debutantes. The Indians, whose origins are murky and the subject of controversy, created their own unique social organization and performance contexts. Working-class people of many ethnic heritages also formed their own organizations and made their own occasions, such as the "truck parades" that follow the elite Rex Parade on Mardi Gras day. LGBTQ and affluent people snubbed by old-line krewes have formed their own krewes, often putting on parades that are far more lavish than those of the old-line krewes. Certainly, elements of class and ethnic division remain in New Orleans's Mardi Gras but in fact are ignored by most people, who traditionally simply have enjoyed the spirit of revelry. In 1992 the New Orleans city council enacted an ordinance that prohibited the granting of parade permits to organizations whose membership remained racially segregated. Although this ordinance provoked considerable controversy and led to the withdrawal of several groups from parading, it further democratized Mardi Gras.

Rural, French Louisiana celebrates a very different form of Mardi Gras, one that seems to have little historical connection to New Orleans' Carnival, at least in its later developments. The rural form consists of costumed and masked revelers (often called *les Mardi Gras*) who make a circuit of homes, farms, and businesses on horseback or in wagons or trucks. They may perform mischievous tricks, dance, sing (a band of musicians usually accompanies a group), and request or beg for donations of food or money. Officials called *capitaines* provide a degree of order and organization. The gift of a live chicken, which has to be chased, has become an iconic event within the larger action. The use of the donations to create a communal meal is indicative of rural Mardi Gras celebrations that stress solidarity and unity. Rural Mardi Gras is participated in by both white Cajun and African American Creole groups, though their respective performance styles differ in various ways. In recent years there has been some controversy over the use of racial stereotyping in costuming and over individual maskers playing racial "others." Rural Mardi Gras has been revived and has become increasingly popular after a moribund period in the mid-20th century. Historically, the revelers were male, with women providing support services, but today there are women revelers as well.

Some Louisiana small cities and towns have Mardi Gras parades that imitate those of New Orleans. A town may have two parades: one predominantly black, the other white. In Lafayette, the central city of rural, French Louisiana, a tradition of Mardi Gras street maskers in African American Creole neighborhoods has continued and is being revitalized. There were concerns about the future of Mardi Gras in the wake of Hurricane Katrina, in August of 2005. Besides the widespread flooding and devastation of properties, up to 600,000 households were displaced, and by 2015, only 78 percent of the population had returned to New Orleans. Poverty rates and crime continue to be major challenges, and significant rebuilding remains. However, the spirit of the city, with its "deep-rooted **jazz**, **blues** and carnival culture" continues to endure (Batist), and thus, Mardi Gras celebrations continue to be held and to function as one of the most significant cultural events for African Americans and other groups in New Orleans.

Frank de Caro

Further Reading

Batist, Danielle, 2015, "A Decade after Katrina, Mardi Gras Rolls On," http://www.contributoria .com, Accessed November 5, 2015); Becker, Cynthia, 2013, "New Orleans Mardi Gras Indians: Mediating Racial Politics from the Backstreets to Main Street," *African Arts* 46 (2): 36–49; Breunlin, Rachel, 2013, "Bridge Work: Repatriating Mardi Gras Indian Photography with the House of Dance and Feathers," *African Arts* 46 (2): 50–61; Cohen, Ariella, 2008, "Conflict in N.O. About Who Owns Cultural Image of Mardi Gras Indians," *New Orleans CityBusiness*; Gaudet, Marcia, and James McDonald, eds., 2003, *Mardi Gras, Gumbo, and Zydeco: Readings in Louisiana* Culture (Jackson: University Press of Mississippi); Gay, Kathlyn, 2007, *African-American Holidays, Festivals, and Celebrations: The History, Customs, and Symbols Associated with Both Traditional and Contemporary Religious and Secular Events Observed by Americans of African Descent* (Detroit, MI: Omnigraphics); Gill, James, 1997, *Lords of Misrule: Mardi Gras and the Politics of Race in New Orleans* (Jackson: University Press of Mississippi); Kinser, Samuel, 1990, *Carnival American Style: Mardi Gras at New Orleans and Mobile* (Chicago and London: University of Chicago Press); Mitchell, Reid, 1995, *All on a Mardi Gras Day: Episodes in the History of New Orleans Carnival* (Cambridge, MA: Harvard University Press); Skipper, Jodi, and David Wharton, 2015, "Diasporic Kings and Queens: Lafayette's Black Mardi Gras Performances in Historical and Hemispheric Contexts," *Southern Quarterly* 52 (4): 133; Turner, Richard Brent, 2009, *Jazz Religion, the Second Line, and Black New Orleans* (Bloomington: Indiana University Press); Vaz, Kim Marie, 2013, *The "Baby Dolls": Breaking the Race and Gender Barriers of the New Orleans Mardi Gras Tradition*, 1st ed. (Baton Rouge: Louisiana State University Press); Watts, Lewis, and Eric Porter, 2013, *New Orleans Suite: Music and Culture in Transition*, 1st ed. (Berkeley: University of California Press); Wehmeyer, Stephen C., 2010, "Marching Bones and Invisible Indians: African American Spiritualism in New Orleans, Past and Present," *Southern Quarterly* 47 (4): 43.

MOJO

"Mojo" can be a name for a **charm** made by a conjurer; it can also be a synonym for "**conjure**," "**Hoodoo**," "rootwork," "tricking," "goofer," and the various other terms for African American magic. Mojo charms are also known as hands, gris-gris, tobies, and jacks. Some common variants of "mojo" are "moojoo," "mojoe," "joomoo," "jomoo," and "Joe Moe."

Mojos were the chief goods produced by conjure men and women. Their function was to manipulate supernatural forces to bring about practical results. During the early 20th century, when the first printed references to mojos appeared, they might have been designed to work for either evil or good. For example, one African American man from Georgia described harmful mojos as bottles filled with graveyard dirt, nails, blood, and hair, with the blood and hair presumably belonging to an intended victim. Conjurers fashioned such charms for paying clients who wished to harm their enemies. Each mojo was then hidden by either client or practitioner in a place where the intended prey was likely to come into close proximity with it. Favorite hiding places were the interiors of mattresses or under a few inches of dirt in front yards.

As time progressed, mojos took on a primarily benevolent role. They have served most commonly to win love for their possessors and bring success in gambling. Others were said to grant wishes, allow their bearers to take on the form of various animals and/or inanimate objects, and protect their owners from harm. Mojos designed for good most commonly took the form of red flannel bags containing a variety of lucky materials, which might include graveyard dirt, **High John the Conqueror** root, lodestones, Adam and Eve root, vinegar, five finger grass, and any number of other powerful conjure agents.

Though the evidence is sparse, "mojo" and its variants appear to have first gained popularity as words designating charms in the states bordering the Mississippi River, particularly Louisiana and Mississippi. Scholars have yet to determine the exact origins of the term. Some argue that it is a corruption of the English word "magic." More likely, it has an African ancestry. One contender is a West African word, *mojuba*, a type of prayer. The *mojuba* **prayer** remains the central supplication in the Yoruba-derived Santería religion of Cuba, in which it is used as an invocation to the spirits. Another possibility is that "mojo" derives from a BaKongo word, *mooyo*. *Mooyos* were the spirits that dwelt within BaKongo *minkisi* charms and gave them their power. The last explanation is the most likely in that it roughly matches the known American usage of "mojo" to mean a charm. As was commonly the case, the fine points of the African spiritual systems that originally supported the conjure practice gradually faded from view or were replaced by Christian equivalents. In the case of mojos, the *mooyos* themselves were forgotten and their name given to the physical charms.

A major problem with all explanations of the term's origins is that there is little evidence to suggest that "mojo" was the original form of the word. In fact, during the early 20th century, "jomo" and similar variations were almost as popular as "mojo." The possibility exists that the word derived from an as yet uninvestigated African term.

One thing is certain, however. The use of "mojo" and its variants had spread throughout the **South** by the 1930s and 1940s. Harry Middleton Hyatt discovered that they were used in North Carolina. Interviewers working for the Works Progress Administration (WPA) found them in Georgia as well. The spread of blues music and the growth of the spiritual products industry during the early 20th century likely helped popularize the term "mojo." **Blues** songs, many of which emanated from Mississippi and Louisiana, frequently contained references to mojo, as did many of the manufactured products sold by mail-order spiritual supply companies. The Mystic Mojo Love Sachet, for example, was a top seller among Georgian blacks during the 1930s. With the term highly visible in the consumer products and music of the era, it would have been natural for African Americans to apply the term to their own brands of magic.

Jeffrey E. Anderson

Further Reading

Anderson, Jeffrey Elton, 2007, *Conjure in African-American Society* (Baton Rouge: Louisiana State University Press); Georgia Writers' Project, Savannah Unit, 1986, *Drums and Shadows: Survival Studies among the Coastal Negroes* (Athens and London: University of Georgia Press); Hazzard-Donald, Katrina, 2013, *Mojo Workin': The Old African American Hoodoo System* (Urbana, IL: University of Illinois Press); Hyatt, Harry Middleton, 1970–1978, *Hoodoo—Conjuration—Witchcraft—Rootwork*, 5 vols. (Hannibal, MO: Memoirs of the Alma Egan Hyatt Foundation, and Western Publishing Company); Thompson, Robert Farris, 1983, *Flash of the Spirit: African and Afro-American Art and Philosophy* (New York: Random House); Yronwode, Catherine, 1995–2000, "Blues Lyrics and Hoodoo," Lucky Mojo Curio Company Web Site, accessed March 2, 2004, http://www.luckymojo.com/blues.html.

MONKEY, THE SIGNIFYING

A popular **trickster** figure in African American narrative poetry, the Signifying Monkey is known for disempowering opponents through a technique of using clever rhyme and rhetorical word play known as "**signifying**." The Monkey is both defined by and representative of the act of signifying, which is a language game or style of innuendo, cajoling, insult, deceit, or indirect and figurative doublespeak. More than just a folk hero who has mastered the technique of satirical word play, the Monkey literally is the technique. It is the character that signifies upon something—that "wreaks havoc upon the Signified" (Gates, 52). This usually takes the form of a withering verbal assault meant to deflate, demystify, delionize, or otherwise render powerless someone through linguistic play. This trickster figure as a motif in black folklore and **mythology** is known to have originated in black cultures in **Africa**, the Caribbean, and South America, and to have been carried by slaves to the New World. According to Gates, the trope can be traced back to a larger, collectively unified trickster figure known as Esu-Elegbara, who appears in numerous black cultures across the diaspora.

In the African American oral tradition, signifying is commonly known as a way of dismantling an opponent or oppressor through satirical rhyme and/or rhetorical assault. This assault often takes the form of insult and needling but need not be restricted to them; deceiving the other, stultifying the other, talking around the other, or speaking through hand and eye gestures are also common modalities of signifying. The act tends to be figurative instead of literal; it has been described as "the language of trickery, that set of words or gestures which arrives at direction through indirection" (Abrahams, 74). As early as the 18th century, instances of signifying, while not yet named as such, have been recorded in black songs, tales, and poetry. In such instances, slaves commonly used rhymes and lyrics to signify upon their oppressors through a process of satirical jargon and clever word play. The act of "signifying" thus accomplishes two goals: (1) the empowerment of the signifier, who signifies upon someone or something, through (2) the disempowerment of the signified, upon whom the signification is directed. In the African American tradition, signifying is a technique of linguistic play in which the more clever and artful the technician, the more superior he or she becomes to the other.

As a rhetorical strategy, signifying as such can be historically traced directly to the Signifying Monkey tales. These tales, or **toasts** as they are customarily known, are narratives typically depicting three characters—the Monkey, the Lion, and the Elephant—with the Monkey being physically the weakest but rhetorically the most powerful of the three. In most versions of the tale, the guileful trickster Monkey relays to the Lion some form of insult allegedly coming from the Elephant. This insult is a figurative one, but the Lion takes it literally and demands that the Elephant apologize. The Elephant refuses and proceeds to bash the Lion, dethroning him of both his ego and his status as "king of the jungle." Realizing that he had been duped all along, the emasculated Lion confronts the Monkey in a rage. This prompts the Monkey to signify upon the lion through a barrage of ridicule and insult. In some versions of the tale, the Monkey then falls from his branch to be set upon by the Lion but escapes through more artful signifying that confuses the Lion into letting him go. In the end the Lion, the dupe, whose physical power over the weaker trickster Monkey is unquestioned, nevertheless cannot understand the true meaning of the Monkey's satirical play on words and is rendered powerless as a result. The Monkey's triumph therefore lies in his wit and reason.

While humor and linguistic gymnastics are ostensible facets of the Monkey tales, the stories' common themes of power struggle and role reversal speak to the oppressive history from which the tales originate—African American slavery. Many scholars thus interpret the tales as **slave narratives** celebrating self-empowerment over an oppressive Other; the Monkey, the physically weakest and most helpless character in the stories, nevertheless reverses the Lion's status as "king" through strength of mind. The Monkey's use of signifying is the means by which the Lion is insulted, stultified, deceived, led astray, and thereby rendered powerless. The fact that the Lion is disempowered by the Monkey, the latter being a classically racist image often ascribed to African Americans during the time of slavery, represents a final and ironic act of what scholar and literary critic Henry Louis Gates called "repeating and reversing." In this way, African Americans are taking the racist image of themselves as monkeys and both repeating and reversing it in the form of the Signifying Monkey, the rhetorical genius and playful artisan who beats the Lion, not with physical strength but with his mind. This repeating and reversing is in itself an act of signifying; it is as much the purpose of the tales as it is the trickster Monkey's own technique.

Gates gave this mythical trickster figure new life when, in his famous work *The Signifying Monkey: A Theory of African-American Literary Criticism*, he cited it as a metaphor for African American literary discourse. For Gates, the Monkey represented more than just the artful pugilist, the Iago deceiver, the bandying genius. Gates argued that what he called "Signifyin(g)," and the trickster Monkey who represents it, "constitutes all of the language games, the figurative substitutions, the free associations . . . which disturb the seemingly coherent linearity of the syntagmatic chain of signifiers" (Gates, 58). In other words, the poems exist as a "play of differences," where no fixed text exists and emphasis is placed rather on the continual repeating and reversing of the same text, not the creation of new ones. It is this principle of repetition and reversal which Gates cited as "crucial to the black vernacular forms of Signifyin(g)," and represented for Gates a "trope for black intertextuality in the Afro-American formal literary tradition" (Gates, 64).

While many theorists have argued that the tales of the Signifying Monkey posit a black/white binary opposition in American society, Gates took issue with this conclusion as too simplistic. For him the Monkey tales are a form of daydream of the "Black Other," in which the reversal of power relationships is fantasized. Gates emphasizes that the third party in the tales plays just as important a role as do the two primary characters, the Lion and the Monkey. The Monkey does not simply insult the Lion but also blames it on the Elephant, the third party in the story. "The third term both critiques the idea of the binary opposition and demonstrates that Signifyin(g) itself encompasses a larger domain than merely the political. It is a game of language, independent of reaction to white racism or even to collective black wish fulfillment vis-à-vis white racism" (Gates, 70). Thus, while signifying is a technique used in response to white racism, its existence is not determined by that racism. It is a technique of language play and word difference historically tied to black culture "which black people learn as adolescents, almost exactly like children learn traditional figures of signification in classically structured Western primary and secondary schools" (Gates, 75). Through signifying, Gates argues, a sense of blackness arises via the rhetorical process of repeating and reversing, and it is this very process that the tales of the Signifying Monkey symbolize.

Ultimately, the Signifying Monkey becomes for Gates a metaphor for the role of the literary critic. The critic as trickster in this case is a person who "lifts one concept from two discrete discursive realms, only to compare them" (Gates, 65). In other words, signifying can mean any form of rhetorical play in which an existent text is subverted not through the creation of a new text but through the repetition and revision of one that exists already. Here the Signifying Monkey becomes the inspiration for a new way of seeing the role of literary theory in African American discourse. "When one text Signifies upon another text, by tropological revision or repetition and difference, the double-voiced utterance allows us to chart discrete formal relationships in Afro-American literary history. Signfiyin(g), then, is a metaphor for textual revision" (Gates, 88).

For Gates, the Signifying Monkey is not just a **folktale** but also a powerful metaphor for black discourse. The character of the Monkey remains a symbol of wordplay and self-empowerment for many. The Monkey's status as a trickster whose mastery of language empowers it with the ability to both affirm itself and reverse oppressive power relationships has inspired generations, from slaves in the American **South** to black literary critics and musicians of present day.

The most common poetic form in which Signifying Monkey tales appear is the rhyming couplet pattern A-A-B-B. However, this form can also be modified to a variety of other patterns, including, for instance, A-A-B-B-C-C, A-A-BB-C, or A-A-B-C-C. Rhyming is an important way in which the humorous element of these poems is delivered. Their retelling over generations has spanned both oral and music traditions. In black music for example, influential **jazz** and **blues** artists such as Count Basie, Otis Redding, Wilson Pickett, Willie Dixon, and many others have recorded songs about signifying or about the Signifying Monkey itself. In the following lines, the Monkey is signifying to the Lion, inciting him to start a fight with the elephant:

> He said, "Mr. Lion, Mr. Lion, I got something to tell yo today."
> He said, "This way this motherf*cker been talking 'bout you I know you'll sashay."
>   (two times)
> He said, "Mr. Lion, the way he talking 'bout your mother, down your cousins,
> I know damn well you don't play the dozens.
> He talking your uncle and your aunt's a damn shame.
> Called your father and your mother a whole lot of names."
>
> (Abrahams, 115)

The motif of the Signifying Monkey, along with the poetic and rhetorical elements the tale embodies, continues to be an enduring component of African American culture.

Alysia E. Garrison

Further Reading

Abrahams, Roger D., 1963, *Deep Down in the Jungle: Negro Narrative Folklore from the Streets of Philadelphia* (Chicago: Aldine Publishing Co.); Gates, Henry Louis, Jr., 1988, *The Signifying Monkey: A Theory of African-American Literary Criticism* (New York: Oxford University Press, Inc.); Jackson, Bruce, ed., 1974, *Get Your Ass in the Water and Swim Like Me: Narrative Poetry from Black Oral Tradition* (Cambridge, MA: Harvard University Press); Joyce, Ann, 2008, "A Tinker's Damn: Henry Louis Gates, Jr., and the Signifying Monkey Twenty Years Later," *Callaloo: A Journal of African-American and African Arts and Letters* 31 (2): 370; Khan, Khatija, 2012, "Signifying the Monkey: Rhetorical Modes of Expressions in African American Music: The Case of KRS-one," *Muziki* 9 (1): 35; Wald, Elijah, 2014, *Talking 'Bout Your Mama: The Dozens, Snaps, and the Deep Roots of Rap* (New York; Oxford University Press).

MOTHER WIT

This popular term in the realm of African American folk traditions describes a combination of wisdom and common sense, especially knowledge acquired by mothers and grandmothers through life experience. According to folklorist Alan Dundes, in his preface to *Mother Wit from the Laughing Barrel*, mother wit is often expressed in folklore forms (such as stories, songs, **proverbs**, **jokes**, oral histories, rhymes, and parables) and passed down through generations (Dundes, xvi). As Jacqueline D. Carr-Hamilton wrote, it can also be defined as "the collective body of female wisdom—both formal and informal, oral and written, spiritual and social—passed on from generation to generation by African American females"

(Carr-Hamilton, 72). It is a tradition that encompasses the collective knowledge and strength of black women, enabling them to "survive their diaspora experience in the Western World" (Carr-Hamilton, 72).

However, mother wit can be circulated and known by men and women, and while its matrifocal roots lie in a wide variety of African cultures, ranging from Yoruba, Mende, and BaKongo, the tradition is maintained strongly in black communities today. For example, Ronnie W. Clayton explored the power and depths of mother wit as a form of education in his 1990 analysis of the wit and wisdom of former slaves, in *Mother Wit: The Ex-Slave Narratives of the Louisiana Writer's Project.*

Other instances of traditional mother wit may be found in examples of history and literature. Frederick Douglass recollected his mother's and grandmother's wisdom in *My Bondage and My Freedom*, and Zora Neale Hurston's *Their Eyes Were Watching God* represents the tradition of mother wit in the character Nanny, who scolds, instructs, and comforts her granddaughter Janie with common sense and plain talk about the workings of the world. In Toni Morrison's *Beloved*, Baby Suggs is a grandmother and **preacher** whose mother wit and life-learned lessons included the caveat that "freeing yourself was one thing; claiming ownership of that freed self was another."

Jacqueline L. McGrath

Further Reading

Carr-Hamilton, Jacqueline D., 1996, "Motherwit in Southern Religion: A Womanist Perspective," in *"Ain't Gonna Lay My 'Ligion Down": African American Religion in the South*, ed. Alonzo Johnson and Paul Jersild (Columbia: University of South Carolina Press); Clayton, Ronnie W., 1990, *Mother Wit: The Ex-Slave Narratives of the Louisiana Writer's Project* (New York: Peter Lang); Douglass, Frederick, 1855, *My Bondage and My Freedom* (New York: Miller, Orton, and Mulligan); Dundes, Alan, ed., 1990, *Mother Wit from the Laughing Barrel: Readings in the Interpretation of Afro-American Folklore* (Jackson: University of Mississippi Press); Hurston, Zora Neale, 1978, *Their Eyes Were Watching God* (Chicago: Lippincott); Morrison, Toni, 1987, *Beloved* (New York: Plume).

MYTHOLOGY

In the field of folklore, myth does not mean, as it does in popular speech, something that is false. Instead, mythology is a system of religious belief, and myths are the narratives that accompany and validate this system. Myths are sacred narratives that are different from **legends** and **folktales**. Unlike folktales, myths are believed to be true by the people within the cultural group where they are found. Folklorists are not concerned with the scientific or historical truth of myths, but simply with whether those who tell them consider these narratives sacred truths. Hence, the term in folklore does not imply that something is false or imagined.

Myths typically involve gods and divine forces, and offer rationales for the structure of the universe and the relationships between human beings, the cosmos, and the supernatural. So, all people have myths, insofar as all known groups of people have some religious system with stories about a god or gods, creation, and life after death.

Because there are multiple religious systems found among African Americans, there are just as many systems of mythology and narratives. For example, African American culture includes various forms of Christianity, Islam, Judaism, Vodou, Buddhism, and African-derived religions such as Santería that have migrated from the Caribbean or Latin America. Historically, however, Christianity has been the most pervasive religion among African Americans, and of Christian denominations, Baptists have had the most influence on black culture. The black Baptist faith is based on a cosmological system derived from the Old and New Testaments of the Holy Bible (in most cases, the King James Version) and includes stories of Jehovah, Jesus, Daniel, Moses, and the Holy Ghost.

Despite the differences in cosmological perspectives, the mythology of African people tends to have overlapping emphases and recurrent motifs. These motifs engage issues such as suffering and liberation from bondage, rebirth, faith and endurance, personal and intimate connections to God, prophecy, and heavenly rewards. Thus, black mythology going back to the slavery period has tended to see life as a sacred journey and to focus on its trials and triumphs. So, the narratives of Moses leading God's people out of bondage, the parting of the Red Sea, Daniel in the lion's den, Shadrach, Meshach, and Abednego in the fiery furnace, the trials of Job, the story of Jonah in the belly of the whale, and the visions of prophets in the desert, for example, figure prominently in the Christian-based mythologies of black people throughout the diaspora. Myths (sacred narratives) centering on rebirth have also been prominent; for example, the baptism of Jesus by John the Baptist, Ezekiel preaching to the valley of dry bones, the resurrection of Christ, and the ascension of the chosen ones to heaven at the end of Revelation.

In living mythological systems, there are recurrent rituals for enacting and retelling the core myths of the group and for invoking and reexperiencing the presences of the divinities. One can view, for example, the evangelical **sermon** in the black Baptist church tradition as an enactment of sacred myths being retold by the priests of that faith. In this context of worship, there are clearly defined aesthetic standards by which to evaluate the **preacher**'s performance. For it is not enough that the myths simply be retold, they must be conveyed in such a manner that enables the congregation to collectively reexperience them. Furthermore, the priest, whether it be a Baptist minister, a Vodou hougan, or a Lucumi priest, is responsible for invoking the presence of the deity, which may or may not "possess" someone but whose presence is clearly felt by all in attendance. Thus the figures in a lived mythological system are far more than ideas or symbols; they are lived experiences of the divine.

Mythological systems are ever-evolving phenomena in which divine figures are reinterpreted, added, and sometimes dropped. Such is the case with people of African descent in the Western world. In addition to myths that have historically been part of a Christian—or African-based—system, prominent historical figures sometimes seem to enter the realm of the mythological. Such figures often inhabit a space somewhere between legend and myth, where the boundaries of history and mythology fade and the two come together. For example, leaders of slave rebellions, insurrections, and maroon communities in the Caribbean (e.g., Sister Nanny,

Cudjoe) have sometimes become more than just human beings. They have become forces in the consciousness of black people. Figures such as Dr. Martin Luther King Jr., Malcolm X, and Fred Hampton in the United States, inhabit this space, as do Steve Biko, and Nelson Mandela (among others), in South Africa. A common, complimentary set of visual icons on the walls of many African American homes includes a picture of Jesus and Dr. Martin Luther King Jr. Similar arguments can be made about the roles of artists, such as John Coltrane, within certain black communities. Haile Selassie's deification by Rastas is a more obvious example, along with the special place given to Marcus Garvey by numerous religious movements.

The evolution of legendary figures to mythological ones, however, is a lengthy process that involves the erasure of historical facts about the person's life, due to memory loss or other factors. It would also involve the emergence of specific narratives or stories (myths) about the person that would essentially represent their role in the mythological system. The advent of modern technology, in which the facts about people's lives seem permanently archived and constantly revisited, makes the completion of this process more difficult and less likely.

Anand Prahlad

Further Reading

Courlander, Harold, 1976, *A Treasury of Afro-American Folklore* (New York: Crown Publishers); Erskine, Noel Leo, 2014, *Plantation Church: How African American Religion was Born in Caribbean Slavery* (New York: Oxford University Press); Hart, William, 2008, *Black Religion: Malcolm X, Julius Lester and Jan Willis* (Basingstoke: Palgrave Macmillan); Levine, Lawrence W., 1977, *Black Culture and Black Consciousness* (New York: Oxford University Press); Raboteau, Albert J., 1978, *Slave Religion: The "Invisible Institution" in the Antebellum South* (New York: Oxford University Press); Raboteau, Emily, 2013, *Searching for Zion: The Quest for Home in the African Diaspora* (New York: Atlantic Monthly Press); Sernett, Milton, C., ed., 1999, *African American Religious History: A Documentary Witness* (Durham: Duke University Press).

N

NATIVE AMERICAN AND AFRICAN AMERICAN FOLKLORE

Few other cross-cultural traditions offer as potentially rich a field of study as African–Native American folklore. The knowledge of cultural merging between African and Native Americans is commonly alluded to in African American folk culture, often with ambivalence.

Relying on speculative evidence for a cross-Atlantic current that might have facilitated early navigation between Africa and the Americas, some scholars have argued that cultural exchanges between Africans and Native American people began before the slave trade (Van Sertima). Nevertheless, the pervasive contact between and the cultural merging of African and Native peoples beginning with the slavery period are more easily documented.

History of African American and Native Contact

As more historical work is done on the colonial period in the Americas, many commonly held images about the ethnic makeup of slave societies are being challenged and revised. In particular, it is becoming evident that Native people played a more central role in the cultural development of black and white cultures than has previously been imagined. For example, large numbers of Native peoples shared the experience of enslavement, depending on the political climate of certain colonies and states, and many Native slaves were not freed until the end of the Civil War. Native American enslavement took several forms. Initially, thousands of Native Americans were enslaved and shipped to European cities. European nations such as Spain, France, and England enslaved millions of Native Americans throughout the Americas, in many cases shipping these slaves from one nation to another (e.g., from the United States to the Caribbean, from one Caribbean nation to another, and from the Caribbean to the United States). Native Americans were also often kidnapped, taken from colonial schools, or sentenced to slavery by criminal courts (Brennan, 2–5). Hence, from the earliest period Native Americans often worked alongside African slaves in Europe, Africa, and throughout the colonies, resulting in "the creation of culturally and racially mixed communities" (ibid., 7). Because this phenomenon has been conventionally overlooked in scholarship, it is unclear to what extent slave societies were, generally speaking, African–Native communities. Certainly the influence of Native American culture would have varied from one locale to another, but current suggestions are that it was generally quite significant.

Native American traditions blended with, and enriched, much of African American folklore. (Western History Collections, University of Oklahoma Library, Phillips 975)

In addition to the development of enslaved African–Native communities, other such culturally mixed groups emerged as the following phenomena occurred: (1) runaways from both groups formed maroon societies; (2) runaway African American slaves were accepted into Native American nations; (3) free African Americans and free Native Americans married and formed communities; and (4) autonomous Native American nations held African slaves, in a similar fashion to the European slave system. It was common throughout the United States for Native nations to accept fugitive African Americans. For example, fugitive African Americans found homes, married, had families, and participated in—or were absorbed into—nations such as the Senecas, Pequot, Montauk, Onodagas, and Ninisinks of the Northeast; the Seminoles, Lumbee, Mattaponi, Gingaskin, Choctaw, Chickasaw, Creek, Cherokee, Alabama, and Nanticoke of the Southeast; and the Chippewa, Comanche, Crow, and Plains Indians of the western United States. There are numerous historical, well-known African Americans who found homes among Native nations. These would include, for example, Pierre Bonga, who married into the Chippewa nation; Edward Rose, a Cherokee–African American; and James Pierson Beckwourth, who married and served for several years as a chief. However, the names of most such men and women are unknown.

The intermarriage of free African Americans and Native Americans and the evolution of African–Native American communities was especially common in "the mid-Atlantic, southern Atlantic and northeastern regions" (Brennan, 15). Lorenzo Green has postulated that one reason for the large numbers of intermarriages in states such as Connecticut, Rhode Island, and Massachusetts was because there were few legal barriers and a relative absence of African American women. In such states, colonial law tended to treat Native American and African Americans the same, creating similar social conditions for the two groups and encouraging a sense of shared experience. For example, both groups were prohibited from "selling goods, lighting bonfires, begging for money, drinking in public taverns, dancing, gambling, [. . .] or holding social gatherings" (Brennan, 14).

One of the better-known African–Native nations is the Garífuna (Black Caribs), who resulted from the merging of indigenous Carib people and escaped slaves from the Ibo, Yoruba, Fon, Fanti-Ashanti, and Kongo nations, all of whom joined in the 17th century on the island of Saint Vincent. The Garífuna were eventually removed and resettled on the island of Roatán, near Honduras, and remain a strong, independent cultural group, with many folkloric traditions, including song, **dance**, music, speech, foodways, and religion. The Garífuna are found today in parts of Honduras, Nicaragua, and the United States.

Maroon settlements of Native and African American people were also common during the slavery period. Historians have noted the prevalence of such communities and Maroon nations in the southeastern and northeastern United States (Aptheker; Brennan; Jones). These nations were especially feared by colonial powers, and were under frequent attack. Many of the names assumed by these nations reflected their determination to resist colonization and remain independent, for example, "Disturb Me If You Dare," "Come Try Me If You Be Men," and "I Shall Moulder before I Shall Be Taken." Two of the largest such nations included the Dismal Swamp maroon nation, located in Virginia and North Carolina, and the Seminole Nation of Florida (Brennan, 8).

Many Native American nations also held African and African American slaves. These included the Seminoles, Choctaw, Chickasaw, Cherokee, and Creek. The nature of the enslavement varied from one nation, locale, and historical period to another, and ranged from the kind of cruelty that characterized many white-owned plantations to African Americans being given relative freedom to build their own houses, cultivate their own crops, and intermarry freely with members of the enslaving nation.

No matter what the circumstances were that brought African American and Native American people together, there was a significant exchange and merging of cultural traditions and folklore. The prevalence of such names as "griffon," "half-blood," "half-breed," "mulatto," "mustee," "mamaluco," "mestizo," "branco," "Black Indian," and "Indian-Negro," which were commonly applied to the unions of the two groups, reflects the prominence of intercultural exchanges. Many examples of African–Native American groups exist today, but are often caught in a political limbo between the two groups. Many Native American nations, the United States government, and African Americans resist granting these groups the rights extended to members of the Native American nations, or to fully accept them into African American culture.

Folklore

Unfortunately, the influences of Native American culture on African American folklore have hardly been researched. For the most part, this remains an incidental topic rather than one to which folklorists devote their full attention. However, some general comments can be made about the intersections between Native and African American traditions.

Most of the critical work done in this area has focused on elements in folktales and myths, and in particular Rabbit tales. Generally speaking, the assumptions have been that cultural borrowing in regard to Rabbit tales was fundamentally a one-way phenomenon; that Native Americans adopted the African rabbit **trickster** figure and made him a part of their tradition. Until recently, the most emphatic argument regarding Rabbit tales had been made by Alan Dundes, who contended that tales with the rabbit motif found among Native Americans were of African origin. Dundes's argument is based largely on finding documented cases of these motifs from African or African American tales in indexes such as Stith Thompson's, and the absence of such cases for Native American tales. More recently, scholars have pointed to the flaws in Dundes's argument. The most obvious weakness is that motif and tale type indexes have thus far been very European-centered, containing relatively little documentation for Africa, and even less for Native America. Furthermore, most of the recorded materials that do exist for Native America were collected in the 20th century, and there are only scant records of the materials from the earlier periods (Gay, 102–103).

Recent scholarship has recognized that Native American folklore also had a central rabbit trickster figure. David Elton Gay, along with others, suggests that Rabbit tales represent a syncretic process through which African Americans and Native Americans merged elements of both their traditions. For example, Gay argues that the change from the African trickster name Anancy/Anansi to the African American name **Brer Rabbit** reflects Native American influence. He argues further that African American versions of African trickster tales are more similar to Native American versions than to African, another indication of Native American influence. In her discussion of southeastern Rabbit tales, Sandra Baringer notes that before the publication of **Uncle Remus** tales by Joel Chandler Harris, "ethnologists had noted the similarities between Brer Rabbit stories and Rabbit stories among the Creek and Cherokee— in particular, two almost identical tales: the well-known tar baby tale, and Rabbit's race with the turtle or terrapin" (Baringer, 116). She goes on to discuss specific motifs from African American Brer Rabbit tales that are absent from African sources, but that are prevalent in Native American tales, for example, the "raining fire" motif. She cites as one example the tale in which an animal, such as Alligator, asks Brer Rabbit what trouble is. Brer Rabbit responds by setting the field on fire, replying with "I'll show you trouble." According to Baringer, the "raining fire" motif in African American tales takes on some of the sacredness it has in Cherokee and Creek stories.

A number of other syncretic motifs have been suggested in Brer Rabbit tales. These include the portrayal of the rabbit trickster as a dancer, healer, and musician. In both African and Native American cultures, the rabbit represents an animal figure who "holds the power of music and dance that is the key to communicating with the spirit world" (Baringer, 128). These elements are reflected in such stories as "Bur Jonah's Goat," "The Dance of the Little Animals," "Why Mr. Dog Runs Brer Rabbit," and the "Red Hill Churchyard." Such syncretisms reflect in part the overlapping emphasis on dancing and drumming as means through which to communicate with the spirit realm, and the association of certain animals with spirits, which are core elements of both African and Native American traditional cultures.

The merging of spiritual beliefs and drumming and dance traditions was at times evident in the actual day-to-day lives and ritual events of Africans and Native Americans during the slavery period. For example, some scholars have suggested that Natchez slaves sent to Saint-Domingue (today's Haiti), as well as survivors of the Petro Indians, merged cultures with the West African groups enslaved there. This cultural merging included an exchange of knowledge about herbs and natural healing, beliefs in spirits, and perspectives on cosmology and mythology. Hence, the development of Vodou would have included not only elements of African and European culture and Christianity, but also of Native American culture (Berry, Foose, and Jones, 201–202). So, the influx of slaves, planters, and freedmen from Haiti into New Orleans, and the emerging religion of Vodou there, likely had Native American influences.

The Native American influence surfaced in New Orleans in a very public manner as a part of the **Mardi Gras** Carnival, in the emergence of the Mardi Gras Indians around 1880. The Indian had been a prominent element in the carnival traditions of the Caribbean since the mid-19th century. For example, in Trinidad, Carnival masks included the Red, Black, and Blue Indians. Sources indicate that the first Indian mask in New Orleans Carnival was worn by Becate Batiste, who was an African–Native American. However, the Mardi Gras Indians have historically used the Black Indian personas more symbolically than as an actual claim to dual African and Native American ancestry (Berry, Foose, and Jones, 206). The proud sentiments found in the chants and songs of the Mardi Gras Indians often reflect those found among maroon, African–Native communities of the slavery period. The costuming and social hierarchies of the groups (who refer to themselves as "tribes") acknowledge and affirm the cultural affinities between African and Native American nations led by chiefs, who enact their rituals through music, chanting, and dance. Thus, the Mardi Gras Indians seem to recognize a cultural history that is not often represented in textbooks, and that is not a central part of either the American or African American historical narrative. The unique musical traditions of these tribes have had a profound influence on many contemporary African American and other musical traditions, including **jazz**, for instance, and the Mardi Gras Indians have become almost cultural icons, sought out by photographers, journalists, and ethnographers.

Many other areas in which there have been cultural exchanges and syncretisms between African and Native Americans bear mention, although little has been written about them. Inasmuch as Native Americans and African Americans have been brought together by historical circumstances in so many diverse interactions, we can speculate that basic areas such as foodways, healing practices, agricultural practices, and spiritual beliefs were mutually influential. Undoubtedly, like European Americans, African Americans were influenced by Native knowledge in regard to hunting, trapping, tool making, boat building, and other fishing-related traditions. Hopefully, many additional studies will emerge in this area that will provide us with more insights into the syncretisms of specific areas of folklore.

Anand Prahlad

Further Reading

Aptheker, Herbert, 1969, *American Negro Slave Revolts* (New York: International Publishers); Baringer, Sandra K., 2003, "Brer Rabbit and His Cherokee Cousin: Moving beyond the Appropriation Paradigm," in *When Brer Rabbit Meets Coyote: African–Native American Literature*, ed. Jonathan Brennan (Urbana: University of Illinois Press), pp. 114–138; Berry, Jason, Jonathan Foose, and Tad Jones, 2003, "In Search of the Mardi Gras Indians," in *When Brer Rabbit Meets Coyote: African–Native American Literature*, ed. Jonathan Brennan (Urbana: University of Illinois Press), pp. 197–217; Brennan, Jonathan, ed., 2003, *When Brer Rabbit Meets Coyote: African–Native American Literature* (Urbana: University of Illinois Press); Coleman, Arica L., 2013, *Blacks in the Diaspora: That the Blood Stay Pure: African Americans, Native Americans, and the Predicament of Race and Identity in* Virginia (Indiana University Press); Dundes, Alan, 1965, "African Tales among the North American Indians," *Journal of American Folklore* 29 (3): 207–219; Forbes, Jack D., 1993, *Africans and Native Americans: The Language of Race and the Evolution of Red-Black Peoples* (Urbana: University of Illinois Press); Gay, David Elton, 2003, "On the Interaction of Traditions: Southeastern Rabbit Tales as African-Native American Folklore," in *When Brer Rabbit Meets Coyote: African–Native American Literature*, ed. Jonathan Brennan (Urbana: University of Illinois Press), pp. 101–113; Green, Lorenzo, 1968, *The Negro in Colonial New England* (New York: Atheneum); Jones, Rhett S., 1977, "Black and Native American Relations before 1800," *Western Journal of Black Studies* 1: 155; Katz, William Loren, 1986, *Black Indians: A Hidden Heritage* (New York: Atheneum); Littlefield, Daniel F., 1979, *Africans and Creeks: From the Colonial Period to the Civil War* (Westport, CT: Greenwood Press); Littlefield, Daniel F., 1977, *Africans and Seminoles: From Removal to Emancipation* (Westport, CT: Greenwood Press); Miles, Tiya, 2005, *Ties That Bind: The Story of an Afro-Cherokee Family in Slavery and Freedom. Vol. 14* (Berkeley: University of California Press); Murray, David, 2007, *Matter, Magic, and Spirit: Representing Indian and African American Belief* (Philadelphia: University of Pennsylvania Press); Van Sertima, Ivan, ed., 1992, *African Presence in Early America* (New Brunswick, NJ: Transaction Publishers); Van Sertima, Ivan, 1976, *They Came before Columbus* (New York: Random House).

NIGHT RIDERS

This is a folk term used by African Americans to refer to ghosts, "patter rollers," Ku Klux Klan members, and "night doctors." Night riders were generally white men who used various disguises, schemes, and tactics as a means of terrorizing blacks at night to manipulate, control, and suppress them. Night riders first appeared in slavery times and persisted through the early 1900s, affecting both Southern and Northern blacks. Whites exploited the African-based beliefs about the supernatural maintained by many African Americans; beliefs in ghosts, witches, witch doctors, and malevolent spirits. Whites then instigated fear by spreading **rumors** and making regular "night rider" appearances. Blacks also sustained their own fears through ghost stories and night rider tales.

The first night riders were white masters or overseers who, disguised as ghosts, haunted the fields and slave quarters. One slave stated that he was "so afraid of ghosts until you couldn't shove [him] off on the porch at night" (Fry, 61). Later, the police patrollers, also known as patterollers, were established to help prevent slave escapes and revolts. One ex-slave said the pattyrollers were "tall and most usually wore white robes [though not always], sometimes dar head would jes turn roun and roun and be looking at you fust from de front and den frum his back. Dey wuz something like de ghosts but dey sometimes had paddles an effen dey caught you den you had a paddlin" (ibid., 87). This illustrates how patrollers used tricks and violence to exacerbate the slaves' fear of the supernatural and keep them in their state of bondage.

The Ku Klux Klan, which started after the emancipation of the slaves in 1865, used similar guises and tactics, primarily for the purpose of regulating race relations and preventing black migrations to the North. The members were known to augment their white hoods and robes with horns, fierce-looking masks, and artificial red eyes. Klansmen also performed fear-inducing skits, and used props such as human or animal body parts, and noisemaking devices. One ex-slave said that these demonstrations, which often included mutilations, burnings, and lynching, would "[scare] the poor Negroes to death" (ibid., 142).

Closely associated with night riders, Night doctors were individuals who allegedly abducted living bodies for scientific or medical experiments. Whites created rumors about night doctors who preyed specifically on blacks in Northern cities. Whites hoped to further discourage blacks from leaving white farms to pursue opportunities in the North. When many blacks did move North, they carried the rumors with them, and they embellished on the old tales. Among these tales was Sam McKeever, a black man touted to be a night doctor. These stories could be used to explain the fear blacks had of walking the streets alone at night, as well as the disappearance of loved ones. In this way, the fear of night riders continued to control the way blacks conducted themselves and perceived the world in which they lived.

Fears expressed through rumors about night riders were reinforced by historical violence against black bodies, in southern and Northern states. Such violence included medical experimentation on living African Americans and body snatching of cadavers for dissection in medical schools. Such examples as the Tuskegee experiment, when hundreds of African American men unwittingly became lab rats in a syphilis study, validated these concerns. Recent research also indicates that African Americans were often used as test subjects for new surgical experiments and demonstrations at teaching hospitals (Leilani). Unfortunately, the legacy of night riders continues to resonate in actual instances of medical experimentation with black bodies (Skloot), and continues to influence perceptions that African Americans have toward the medical establishment.

Gladys L. Knight

Further Reading

Fry, Gladys-Marie, 1975, *Night Riders in Black Folk History* (Knoxville: University of Tennessee Press); Halperin, E. C., 2007, "The Poor, the Black, and Marginalized as the Source of Cadavers in the United States Anatomical Education," *Clinical Anatomy* 20, 489–495; Leilani, Doty, 2007, "Renewing Trust in Regular (Allopathic) Medicine and Research," *SELAM International Newsletter,* 9 (1); Skloot, Rebecca, 2010, *The Immortal Life of Henrietta Lacks* (New York: Crown Publishers).

NONVERBAL COMMUNICATION

Nonverbal communication includes forms of communication that rely on movement and visual cues rather than on speech. It may occur by itself or in concert with oral communication. It carries messages that cannot be expressed solely through words, such as feelings and attitudes; information; and messages for which words may be inadequate, inappropriate, or disadvantageous. As such, nonverbal communication is rooted in movements and expressions of the body and external objects.

During slavery and in subsequent periods, African Americans did not have the freedom to express their true thoughts and feelings around white people. Thus, much of their communication has been secretive and coded. As a result, forms of nonverbal communication have been especially important and have become, by necessity, highly developed. An emphasis on many forms of nonverbal communication was also a part of the African cultural heritage that slaves brought with them to the New World. As scholars such as Robert Farris Thompson have demonstrated, the high value placed on an ability to express oneself kinetically, through the body, has been one of the consistent cultural aesthetics across most regions of Africa. This aesthetic is rooted in the belief that the body is sacred and that expressions of the body are, in fact, expressions of the spirit. The high regard, and necessity for, nonverbal communication in African American cultures is reflected in many genres and folk forms.

There are two basic types of nonverbal communication. First are those that are inscribed on objects. Examples of these continue to exist over time in forms of material culture; for instance, aerosol art, a symbol painted on a barn, or coded messages in quilt patterns. Second are temporal performances that leave no record in material culture and exist only in the moment in which they are being performed. These would include a gesture, such as nodding one's head to mean "no," shrugging one's shoulders to mean "I don't know," movements in **dance**, or a secret handshake.

Temporal Performances

Among the most vibrant of African American nonverbal traditions are vernacular dance traditions, which, in combination with music, across time and space, have effectively communicated emotion, mood, and attitude in play, courtship, and disputes. African American dances combine movements and music derived from **Africa**, Europe, and the Americas to convey many different emotional realms, convey ideas, offer social critique, converse with human and supernatural forces, and occasionally to narrate stories. Dance forms have permeated black life in many secular and religious contexts since Africans were brought to the New World and continue to be a central activity throughout diverse regions and groups in the United States. The often-elaborate steps and gestures that accompany dance are examples of the artistic beauty of nonverbal communication. By way of example, Susan Phillips traces the "C-Walking," or "Crip Walking" dance common among gang members in Los Angeles back to dances among slaves, and argues that the dancers use their bodies to spell out the names of people and places (62).

Gestures are one of the most prevalent forms of nonverbal communication, occurring in diverse contexts and conveying a wide range of messages, emotions, and ideas. Many gestures have their roots in African cultures, and are widely dispersed throughout the diaspora—for example, the commonly known "suck teeth" or "cut eye." "Suck teeth" refers to sucking air inward through the teeth, making a sound almost like an inverted hiss. The gesture is used in a dismissive fashion, sometimes to signal disgust. "Cut eye" refers to a sideways type of glare directed at someone in defiance or anger. A child who has been disciplined might glare at the adult out of the corners of his or her eyes, to which the adult may reply, "Don't you be cutting your eyes at me!" Placing one's hands on one's hips, and either tilting to one side or allowing the hips to "slip" to one side is another African-derived gesture, which can communicate different meanings depending on the social context. A young girl enacting this gesture among her peers might be communicating a playful "sassiness," whereas a woman who uses the gesture with her partner might be indicating that she is "putting her foot down."

A plethora of gestures is associated with greeting rituals in African American culture. There are countless variations of handshakes, for instance. One type of handshake is associated with Baptist church services, and consists of two people gripping each other's hands and swinging them back and forth in time to the song that is being sung during the invocational segment of the church service. Many organizations have secret handshakes or other greetings that are known only to members of the group. One of the most common gestures is "giving skin," "giving five," or "high-fiving," which has many different variations and extends beyond greeting rituals to numerous other contexts. Giving skin might involve one person holding both hands out at waist level, palms up, while another person slaps the first person's hands with their palms down. In some cases, the action would then be reciprocated. Other variations include the same gesture, but with one hand; giving skin while holding the hands outward and at head level; turning the back of the hand to the other person's palm; sliding the palms slowly across each other; touching only the fingers; clasping fingers as the palms are slid away from each other; snapping the fingers as the palms are slid away from each other; or a combination of these variations in a particular sequence. As with other forms of folklore, creativity and spontaneity characterize nonverbal communications, and so variations on such gestures as giving skin are ongoing. Also, as with many other forms of African American folklore, this one has been thoroughly absorbed into the American mainstream. High-fiving, for instance, is by now a core element of bonding and celebratory rituals among American athletes.

Another large group of gestures are associated with styles of standing and walking. For instance, Benjamin Cooke describes, among other stances, the "**pimp** stance" (feet apart, hands behind the back, torso tilted to one side as if "checking someone out"), the rapping stance (shoulder lowered, one leg forward, head leaned toward the other person), and the player's stance. A variety of stances and facial expressions among women signal different responses to these predominantly male postures. A variety of walking styles are also discussed, including the "chicken walk" and the "pimp walk," a rhythmic, pronounced style of walking in which a person communicates his manliness and "**cool**."

Other gestures can carry nationalistic meanings. The best known of these is perhaps the gesture for black power that emerged in the 1960s: a fist raised high in the air. At the time the gesture originated it indicated political sympathy for the militant stance toward the U.S. government taken by the Black Panther Party, which included demands for the rights of first-class citizenship and a determination to gain equal rights even if it meant doing so through armed struggle. Since then, the gesture has come to signify one's political leanings toward black nationalism, even though it does not necessarily mean that one is in favor of taking up arms.

From these few examples, one can get a glimpse of how abundant the variety of gestures commonly used by people of the African diaspora are, and of how central a role they play in everyday culture. From a simple nod (meaning yes), to the crossing of arms (indicating "no way"), to the jerking of the head slightly upward to mean "what's happening," or raising the shoulders and holding them there (meaning "I have absolutely no idea what that boy was thinking!"), gestures are as important a part of communication as are spoken words.

Inscribed on Material Culture

Clothing, hairstyles, tatoos, and other forms of bodily adornment (or costuming) are also types of nonverbal communication. For instance, there have long been traditions of head adornments, such as hats, in African American culture. Examples that come readily to mind include hats worn by women in church and those worn by male "players." The importance of hats to personal identity is reflected in the ballad of **Stagolee**, in which Stagolee shoots Billy Lyons because Billy accidentally knocks his hat off. At the core of costuming traditions is an aesthetic that places an emphasis on personal style, on the way that one's style communicates critical information about one's values and inner spirit, and the idea that one's personal energy should be in a vibrant call-and-response relationship with the energies of others around one. At times messages conveyed through dress and adornment are social and political, and at other times they may be simply personal statements.

African American hairstyles are also a form of personal and social communication. The traditional craft of hair braiding illustrates a practice dating back to ancient African cultures, in which the designs and styles of the braids can inform viewers of the social status, age range, political orientation, and regional identity of the wearer. The rise of the Afro and cornrows in the 1960s signaled Afrocentric attitudes and a movement toward embracing African-derived elements of black culture. When dreadlocks were first worn by Rastafari in Jamaica, they embodied even more radical ideas. They symbolized not only an embrace of African culture and an attack on Europeanized aesthetics, but also a declaration of belief in a very specific set of religious and political ideas, including repatriation to Africa and the belief in Haile Selassie as the living God. Over time, such styles have taken on different meanings, but in most cases, they are still worn to make some specific statements about a person's social and/or political orientations. This is true of many different hair styles.

Costuming and bodily adornment have taken many forms in African American culture and continue to be among the primary means of communicating nonverbally. It is difficult to imagine contexts in which these areas of nonverbal communication are not apparent. They are obvious in religious and secular contexts in practically every part of the diaspora. Whether the contexts are ones in which there is an intense focus on costuming (such as **festivals** and Carnival), or everyday social spaces such as in homes or on the street, people find ways within their economic means to talk with their costuming and with their bodies. It may be gestures as simple as the tilt of a hat, the shine of a shoe, the color of an earring, a gold tooth, a multicolored fingernail, or the crease in a pair of pants.

Examples of nonverbal communication can be found as well in visual arts. **Aerosol art**, the painting of words, designs and other visual images on public spaces such as the sides of buildings, under bridges, or on the sides of subway trains, is one of the most prevalent folk forms of African American visual culture. The creations of "taggers," or "aerosol artists" are often messages to other artists, gang members, or members of the larger communities from which they come. Quilting is another form that has sometimes incorporated specific messages. According to some critics, quilts containing messages about escape routes were often hung on the clothesline during the slavery period to aid the journeys of slaves on the Underground Railroad, making their way out of the South to freedom in Northern states. Nonverbal communication is one of the primary modes of folklore in African American cultures.

Anand Prahlad and Phyllis M. May-Machunda

Further Reading

Byrd, Ayana D., and Lori L. Tharps, 2001, *Hair Story: Untangling the Roots of Black Hair in America* (New York: St. Martin's Press); Cooke, Benjamin G., 1972, "Nonverbal Communication: Time and Cool People," in *Rappin' and Stylin' Out: Communication in Urban Black America*, ed. Thomas Kochman (Urbana: University of Illinois Press), pp. 19–31; Fry, Gladys-Marie, 1990, *Stitched from the Soul* (New York: Dutton Studio Books); Greene, Deric M., and Felicia R. Stewart, 2011, "African American Students' Reactions to Benjamin Cooke's 'Nonverbal Communication Among Afro-Americans: An Initial Classification,'" *Journal of Black Studies* 42 (3): 389–401; Herskovits, Melville, 1941, *The Myth of the Negro Past* (New York: Harper & Brothers); James, Willis Laurence, 1972, "Romance of the Negro Folk Cry in America" in *Mother Wit from the Laughing Barrel: Readings in the Interpretation of Afro-American Folklore*, ed. Alan Dundes (Englewood Cliffs, NJ: Prentice-Hall); Leone, Mark P., and Gladys-Marie Fry, 1999, "Conjuring in the Big House Kitchen: An Interpretation of African American Belief Systems, Based on the Uses of Archaeology and Folklore Sources," *Journal of American Folklore* 445 (112): 372–403; Phillips, Susan A., 2008, "Physical Graffiti West: African American Gang Walks and Semiotic Practice," in *Migrations of Gesture,* eds. Carrie Noland, and Sally Ann Ness (Minneapolis: Jefferson, NC: McFarland), 31–69; Thompson, Robert Farris, 1974, Exhibit Catalog, *African Art in Motion: Icon and Act*, National Gallery of Art, Smithsonian Institution, Washington, DC (Los Angeles: University of California Press); Tobin, Jacqueline L., and Raymond G. Dobard, 1999, *Hidden in Plain View: The Secret Story of Quilts and the Underground Railroad* (New York: Doubleday); Wiggins, William H., Jr., 1987, *O, Freedom! African American Emancipation Celebrations* (Knoxville: University of Tennessee Press).

P

PAPER BAG TEST

The "paper bag test" is among the most archetypical "complexion legends" in the African American community. These legends reflect realities of colorism within the African American community that are an outgrowth of racism and white supremacy. Starting with the ideology that white was the sign of intelligence and civilization, slave traders and plantation owners tended to assign dark-skinned women and men to field labor. Lighter-skinned men and women were more often house servants and skilled laborers (also possibly because of their blood relationship with an owner or one of his male relatives). As a result of this white-defined hierarchy and because of kinship realities, in many African American communities in both the antebellum and post–Civil War eras, wealthier blacks were often mulatto and lighter skinned. To protect themselves from these light-skinned blacks, whites developed various tests to ensure that blacks weren't passing into white society. Some light-skinned blacks, adopting the racism of the world around them, then developed their own tests and denied dark-skinned blacks access to their organizations in order to "protect" themselves from the "stain."

The paper bag test, in particular, has a profound resonance within the African American community. The test was used to judge if a person was light-skinned enough to be admitted to a variety of African American institutions. If a person was "darker than a brown paper bag," they were too dark to be accepted. Audrey Elisa Kerr has studied these tales and interviewed African Americans all over the country. She found a large number of such stories in New Orleans, (particularly about the traditionally Creole sections such as the Seventh Ward). One woman, who had heard the tale from her mother, told Kerr "with absolute certainty" that the paper bag test started "in Appaloosa, Louisiana, at the turn of the [20th] century." Some places, in order to stop women who might "pass" as lighter skinned through the use of skin-lightening creams, tested the bags against women's arms. As Kerr points out, "It is quite revealing that the social faux pas was not holding a paper bag to a guest's arm, but attempting to enter the party 'wearing' dark skin."

Whether based in fact or not, paper bag test tales are told in every region of the United States and in about every type of bourgeois African American institution from churches, sororities, and social clubs to nightclubs, restaurants, and parties. They have been used in the plot lines of television shows such as "Frank's Place." Lawrence Otis Graham wrote of a test in his book *Our Kind of People*. Toni Morrison talked about the test in a New Yorker interview.

While today the stories are almost always relegated to a safe past, the fact that paper bag test tales (and other complexion lore) are still popular only verifies that there is still a point to the stories and a need for them to be told.

Hilary Mac Austin

Further Reading

Esmail, Ashraf, and Jas M. Sullivan, 2006, "African American College Males and Females: A Look at Color Mating Preferences," *Race, Gender & Class* 13 (1/2): 201–220; Kerr, Audrey Elisa, 2005, "The Paper Bag Principle: Of the Myth and the Motion of Colorism," *Journal of American Folklore* 118 (469): 271–289; Kerr, Audrey Elisa, 2006, *The Paper Bag Principle: Class, Colorism, and Rumor and the Case of Black Washington, D.C.*, 1st ed. (Knoxville: University of Tennessee Press); Monk, Ellis P., 2014, "Skin Tone Stratification Among Black Americans, 2001–2003," *Social Forces* 92 (4): 1313–1337; Wilder, JeffriAnne, 2010, "Revisiting 'Color Names and Color Notions': A Contemporary Examination of the Language and Attitudes of Skin Color Among Young Black Women," *Journal of Black Studies* 41 (1): 184–206.

PIMP, THE

Pimps are men who are usually thought of as petty criminals who make their living off the proceeds of illegal female prostitution. The figure of the pimp, however, takes on a much more complex role in African American folk tradition. Dismissed as a low-level nuisance to be locked up or ignored by mainstream culture, the pimp instead often stands as a figure of stature and a representation of masculine pride and dignity in the black community. It is the pimp's refusal to abide by societal convention that marks him as a figure of resistance, much like his close cousins the **trickster** and the **Bad Man**. His principle ambition is to "get over" without having to "slave" in the "square's world"—in other words, the pimp wants to support a rich lifestyle without having to work. To this end he relies on the labor of women, using only his wit and guile to control them. The pimp, then, is a "gentleman of leisure" and a consummate manipulator; he employs verbal dexterity and psychology to convince his women—often called his "**hoes**," "ladies," "**bitches**," "stable," or "family"—to use their bodies to make money for him. His powers of persuasion (or "game") must be so compelling that his women will do anything for him and endure everything he does to them—all so that they can forfeit every cent of the money they have earned after working each night on the "strip." The pimp's "game" is often so perfect that his women will not think of themselves as victims of exploitation; instead, they see themselves as having "chosen" to be part of a family. As members of this "family," their job is to take advantage of men, most of whom are white, often called "tricks," whose supposed deficient masculinity, sexual curiosity, or uncontrolled perversion makes them vulnerable prey.

In this way, the pimp disrupts the power structure of society, taking advantage of those who, under different circumstances, would seek to use him for their own profit. The pimp takes pride in having his ladies "trick" politicians, fathers, business owners, and other "squares," allowing these men to indulge in illicit activities that conflict with their daytime morality. In this way the pimp stands as a radical subversive, laying waste to the conventions of middle-class society, living fast, and dressing flamboyantly to announce his status as outsider to that boring world. Wild style and sartorial flair are high context markers of the pimp's success. A pimp must not only look good and ride in style; he must speak with a golden tongue and be fluent in the language of the street. These are the traits that have made the pimp a staple of black folk tradition. Traditional "**toasts**" such as "Pimping Sam" and "Hustlin' Dan" celebrate not only the resourcefulness of the pimp, they highlight him as a figure of unflinching confidence and robust sexuality. As a result, the pimp has become a representation of black masculinity in black cultural tradition, a figure of resistance to the emasculating oppression of white society.

It has been possible, then, for the black community to celebrate the triumphs of the pimp for generations in tales, toasts, **films**, and songs, even while his profession clearly exploits and often brutalizes women. The fact that he must resort to less than desirable methods to negotiate a world of ambivalent morality and constant injustice only reinforces his relevance to a group that must survive in the same world he inhabits. The pimp's willing disregard for the law takes on a special kind of utility and acts to model self-reliance and ambition. Ultimately, he is marked as "**cool**" because he rejects all that is conventional.

This veneration of the pimp in black folk culture has only seemed to intensify during the last 30 years. Influential critic and historian Robin D. G. Kelley argues that the pimp's status as a figure of respect for black males during the late 1960s and early 1970s reached unprecedented levels. He writes that "[t]he Pimp, not just any 'baaadman,' became an emblematic figure of the period, elevated to the status of hero and invoked by Hollywood as well as in the writings of black nationalist militants like H. Rap Brown, Eldridge Cleaver, Bobby Seale, and Huey P. Newton" (1996, 215). This influence can be seen most clearly manifested in black popular culture through the defiant heroes of the blaxploitation film era such as "Goldie" from *The Mack* (1973) and other rebellious pimp-like characters such as "Sweetback" (*Sweet Sweetback's Baadasssss Song*, 1972) and "Youngblood Priest" (*Super Fly*, 1972), who perform the principle characteristics of the pimp as trickster or revolutionary figure. The fascination the pimp held during that time has not waned in contemporary black folk culture; in fact, it has become even more evident. Pimp motifs continue to serve as an essential element of black vernacular street culture. For instance, the use of the word "pimp" as a verb connoting the ability to take advantage of a person or situation for personal gain has gained popularity to the extent that it has become a part of the lexicon of popular culture. Other slang words that originated with pimping and street life such as "hustle" or "hustler," "mack," "player," "pimped out," "trick," and "game" have become mainstays of **hip-hop** culture and hence popular culture as well.

This continued use of the pimp as icon has extended through the 1980s, showing up in the music of **rap** superstars such as Ice-T, Ice Cube, and Too Short. References to pimps in the 1990s and in the first part of the 21st century have become even more mainstream, as pimps have become the subjects of feature films like the Hughes Brothers' *American Pimp* (1999) and as hip-hop artists have gained a solid foothold in the world of popular music, releasing songs such as Jay-Z's "Big Pimpin'" and 50 Cent's 2003 hit, "P.I.M.P." These examples demonstrate the crossover of the pimp figure from black folk culture into American popular culture, a movement that reflects the growing influence that black vernacular culture continues to have as a determiner of "coolness" in youth culture.

David Todd Lawrence

See also: Baad

Further Reading

Dagbovie-Mullins, Sika A., 2013, "Pigtails, Ponytails, and Getting Tail: The Infantilization and Hyper-Sexualization of African American Females in Popular Culture," *The Journal of Popular Culture* 46 (4): 745–771; Hall, Susan, and Bob Adelman, 1972, *Gentleman of Leisure: A Year in the Life of a Pimp* (New York: New American Library); Kelley, Robin D. G., 1996, *Race Rebels* (New York: Free Press); Metcalf, Josephine, and Will Turner, eds., 2014, *Rapper, Writer, Pop-cultural Player: Ice-T and the Politics of Black Cultural Production* (Burlington: Ashgate Publishing Limited); Milner, Christina, and Richard Milner, 1972, *Black Players: The Secret World of Black Pimps* (New York: Bantam Books); Munby, Jonathan, 2011, *Under a Bad Sign: Criminal Self-Representation in African American Popular Culture* (Chicago: University of Chicago Press); Quinn, Eithne, 2001, "'Pimpin' Ain't Easy': Work, Play, and 'Lifestylization' of the Black Pimp Figure in Early 1970's America," in *Media, Culture, and the Modern African American Freedom Struggle*, ed. Brian Ward (Gainesville: University Press of Florida); Van Deberg, William, 1997, *Black Camelot: African-American Culture Heroes in Their Times 1960–1980* (Chicago: University of Chicago Press).

PINKSTER CELEBRATIONS

The Pinkster celebration is a **festival** celebrated by African Americans in major cities, particularly throughout New York, that has its original roots in the culture of the Dutch. "Pinkster" comes from the Dutch term for Whitsuntide or Pentecost, and the celebration of Pinkster began in the land that is now New York when Dutch settlers arrived in the 17th century. Men and women of African descent soon remade the ceremony into a ritual of their own, and by 1750 it was generally considered an African American celebration. Pinkster festivals lasted anywhere from three days to a week and drew, according to one observer, a "motley group of thousands" (White 1989, 68).

In 1867, Dr. James Eights recalled his childhood Pinkster experiences. "The younger members of the family—both white and colored" were "adorned in all their varied finery," provided with "numberless small coins," and sent out to attend the Pinkster festivities "[u]nder the careful guidance of a trusty slave." When they arrived at "the far-famed Pinkster hill," they found the premises already quite full of people. The ceremony that Eights witnessed was an early example of multicultural celebration in America, "consisting chiefly of individuals of almost every description of feature, form and color, from the sable sons of **Africa**, neatly attired and scrupulously clean in all their holiday habiliments, to the half clad and blanketed children of the forest, accompanied by their squaws . . . and boys and girls of every age and condition were everywhere seen gliding to and fro amid this motley group" (Eights, 42–43).

Eights clearly enjoyed the opening day of Pinkster, where he witnessed "wild animals, rope dancing, circus-riding, and the playing ground of all simple gaming sports." Yet his recollection skimmed quickly past this first day. The real celebration could not begin then, as it was "considered vastly ungenteel for the colored nobility to make their appearance on the commencing day." On the second day, King Charley, the "venerable, sovereign king," appeared. "Charles originally came from Africa," Eights related, "having, in his infant days, been brought from Angola, in the Guinea gulf." Charley was regal, and his right to govern lay upon a solid foundation. His African ancestry was a part of that foundation, as was the importance of his owner, "[o]ne of the most ancient and respectable merchant princes of the olden time, then residing on the opposite bank of the Hudson." Charley was, moreover, "tall, thin, and athletic" and had reached an age that would accord him the respect given to any elder in an African community, as "the frost of nearly seventy winters had settled on his brow" (Eights, 43–44).

Presiding over the group, King Charley reigned supreme. He appeared before his followers in a "broadcloth scarlet coat, with wide flaps almost reaching to his heels, and gayly [sic] ornamented everywhere with broad tracings of bright golden lace." Upon his feet he wore "yellow buckskin, fresh and new, with stockings blue, and burnished silver buckles to his well-blacked shoe"; upon his head rested a "tricornered cocked hat trimmed also with lack of gold" (Eights, 45). Such bright clothing emphasized the celebratory nature of the gathering. At the same time, the ceremony functioned as a reminder of the freedom that slaves experienced for just this short period of time. Charley's outfit, then, was a vibrant reminder of the flash of freedom that Pinkster provided.

About the practice of allowing slaves to have a few days off to celebrate **Christmas**, Frederick Douglass wrote, "These holidays serve as conductors, or safety-valves, to carry off the rebellious spirit of enslaved humanity" (Douglass, 300). Pinkster functioned similarly. Though Douglass decried the tendency of such safety valves because they released the tension that might otherwise have erupted in revolt, the opportunity to gather in large groups outside of the controlling influence of whites provided a valuable opportunity to perform African-inspired song and **dance**. In fact, though ceremonies like Pinkster may have lessened the tendency toward open revolt by making slavery somewhat endurable, it can be argued that they allowed, rather than prevented, resistance. Historian Sterling Stuckey has observed that "dance can be an extremely subtle means of perpetuating values before the very eyes of those looking on in contempt, or with fascination—or some combination of the two. When the oppressor had no handle on its meaning, as was the case in this country, opportunities for using it as a cultural weapon were enormously enhanced." As such, Stuckey concluded, African-influenced dance in the United States was "an act of resistance" (Stuckey, 53–54).

The values perpetuated "before the very eyes" of a mixed audience were indeed African and African American. The foreignness of African culture to a young white boy is belied by Eights' language. He described the music as "singular in the extreme." The instrument employed was unfamiliar to him: "a symmetrically formed wooden article usually denominated an eel-pot, with a cleanly dressed sheep skin drawn tightly over its wide and open extremity." The playing upon these instruments, though it was quite familiar to those of African descent, struck Eights as alien as well: he observed Jackey Quackenboss "beating lustily with his naked hands upon its loud sounding head, successively repeating the ever wild, though euphonic cry of Hi-a-bomba, bomba, bomba, in full harmony with the thumping sounds." Familiar with the African emphasis on communality, Quackenboss' audience joined in, as his "vocal sounds were readily taken up and as oft repeated by the female portion of the spectators not otherwise engaged in the exercises of the scene" (Eights, 45–46).

Moreover, African and African American dance accompanied African and African American instruments, music, and patterns of audience participation. Pinkster dance took place in a ring, with the king on occasions weaving his way among the dancers, who appeared to have paired off in couples. This dance provided an important opportunity to remember one's connections with Africa as well as to emphasize the black nationalist connections developing between all slaves and freed blacks in America. As Stuckey has observed, "African peoples shared too many dance characteristics across ethnic lines for there to have been one form of dance to the exclusion of all others, and very few, if any, dance formations would have been frozen in time, the impulse to improvisation alone opening the way to ethnic intermingling of dance movement." Thus the Pinkster festival played an important role by allowing persons of African descent to celebrate their heritage at the same time that they created a new identity that would be a necessary element in individual and group resistance.

Jennifer Hildebrand

See also: Congo Square; Election Day

Further Reading

Dewulf, Jeroen, 2013, "Pinkster: An Atlantic Creole Festival in a Dutch-American Context," *The Journal of American Folklore* 126 (501): 245–271; Douglass, Frederick, 1987, "Narrative of the Life of Frederick Douglass," in *The Classic Slave Narratives*, ed. Henry Louis Gates Jr. (New York: Penguin Group); Eights, James, 1971, "Pinkster Festivities in Albany," in *Readings in Black American Music*, ed. Eileen Southern (New York: W. W. Norton); Stuckey, Gay, Kathlyn, 2007, *African-American Holidays, Festivals, and Celebrations: The History, Customs, and Symbols Associated with Both Traditional and Contemporary Religious and Secular Events Observed by Americans of African Descent* (Detroit, MI: Omnigraphics); Sterling, 1994, "The Skies of Consciousness: African Dance at Pinkster in New York, 1750–1840," in *Going through the Storm* (New York: Oxford University Press); White, Shane, 1994, "'It Was a Proud Day': African Americans, Festivals, and Parades in the North, 1741–1834," *Journal of American History*, 81: 13–59; White, Shane, 1989, "Pinkster: Afro-Dutch Syncretization in New York City and the Hudson Valley," *Journal of American Folklore*, 102 (January/March): 68–75.

PORCH SITTERS

Front stoops, front windows, porches, verandas, and front yards have all had their place in the perpetuation of oral traditions. None, however, has been more effective than the front porches of the American **South**. Initially influenced by the warm weather and, after air conditioning, by the general love of lore, people in the southern United States have gravitated to the front porches of their homes as well as to the porches of various business establishments in the South.

In the days before air conditioning became widespread in black communities, front porches provided the pause between a long day's work, usually in agriculture, and the time needed to allow the house to cool down before retiring. African Americans in rural and semirural areas up until the sixth and seventh decades of the 20th century would congregate in chairs or in porch swings and while away the early evening hours. In the absence of funds to pay for fancy mosquito retardants, they would routinely light rags in a bucket, smother the flame, and allow the smoke to drive away the mosquitoes.

In the quiet of relaxation, they would share the day's adventures, carry on general conversation, and tell the stories that are the essence of the black oral tradition: how John escaped by running barefooted when Old Marster came in a sheet and pretended to be "the Lawd"; how haints haunted houses; how Railroad Bill managed to escape "every time." This was also the setting for stories about racial

Men sitting on the porch of a country store in Gordonton, North Carolina, July 1939. (Library of Congress)

injustices and how certain black persons escaped from the South under cover of darkness when sharecropping conditions became too much to bear.

Not only did porch sitters occupy the space in the early evening hours: porches were in use for most of the day. Children would play there; women could gather there to shell peas, shuck corn, or peel peaches; and **quilting** horses might be set up for a group of women to join in conversation and creativity.

Porches were designed to enable sitters to engage in conversation with passersby. Indeed, it could be argued that porch sitting was only fully legitimated when persons on the porch engaged with each other or with persons passing by. While a lone human being could sit on a porch—as many frequently did—that was not as dynamic and not as contributive to the perpetuation of folk traditions as interactive porch sitting could be.

No matter their conversation or engagement, porch sitters used the space to define an acceptable, liminal area for social interaction. Strangers could be received on the porch without inviting them inside the house. Nosey neighbors could be contained in this space without the host or hostess seeming inhospitable. And of course the community of tradition bearers, however that tradition might have been defined, could use the space to perpetuate whatever lies they wanted to tell.

Folk traditions in the African American South, therefore, are strongly identified with front porches that, by their very spatial locations, were separated from the usual demands of domestic or agricultural work. Porch sitters understood this time-out designation and carried on traditions that illustrate the integral ties between space and creativity in perpetuating many forms of folklore.

Trudier Harris

See also: Folktales; Jokes; Legends; Storytelling

Further Reading

Donion, Jocelyn Hazelwood, 2000, *Swinging in Place: Porch Life in Southern Culture* (University of North Carolina Press); Harris, Trudier, 2003, "Porch Sitting as a Creative Southern Tradition," in *Summer Snow: Reflections from a Black Daughter of the South* (Boston: Beacon), pp. 48–65; McGregory, Jerrilyn, 2010, *Downhome Gospel: African American Spiritual Activism in Wiregrass Country* (University Press of Mississippi).

POTTERY

Pottery is a clay-based folk craft to which African Americans contributed. Folk potters, by definition, learn group-shared designs and handcrafting methods through informal, face-to-face training. Such traditional learning could occur by apprenticeship, but in the **South**, where the black population was concentrated, one typically became a folk potter by being born or marrying into an Anglo-American "clay clan," the oldest of which had British pottery roots. This emphasis on kinship to maintain the craft had the effect of excluding African Americans; by comparison, there was greater African American involvement in the related clay craft of brick making. Asked in 1968 why there had been so few black folk potters, Guy Dorsey, whose white family made pottery for four generations in Georgia, put it this way:

"It seems that when it got into one family, nobody else ever got interested" (Burrison, 50). There were, however, some notable exceptions to this generalization.

Colonial and Antebellum Periods

The earliest ceramics possibly made by African Americans are what archaeologists have dubbed "Colonowares." Some of these hand-built, unglazed, low-fired vessels from 18th- and early 19th-century Virginia and the Carolinas echo the shapes of European wares. First thought to have been made by southeastern Indians for trade to settlers, a concentration of Colonowares on low-country South Carolina plantation sites suggests the alternative possibility that they were made by slaves for their own use. Since the clay-working technology of either Native America or West Africa could have produced Colonowares, they may also have been the creolized products of contact among Indians, African slaves, and Europeans. Whoever made them, there is little doubt that they were used extensively by South Carolina's slave population.

The antebellum black potters for whom records survive worked in white-owned shops and probably began with such tasks as digging and processing clay, then acquired, by apprenticeship, the skill that most defines a southern folk potter: "turning" or "throwing" (shaping on a potter's wheel). Known slave potters include David Jarbour, who worked at the Wilkes Street Pottery in Alexandria, Virginia, from 1826 to 1841, and Captain Cribbs of Lamar County, Alabama, whose master, potter Peter Cribbs, had migrated from Ohio in the late 1820s. (Captain and his son, Major Cribbs, later potted for Peter's widow after he died in 1854.) Abe Spencer, a free black potter, worked in Virginia's Shenandoah Valley before and after the Civil War: in 1860 he worked at Harrisonburg (probably for Thomas Logan) and later at Strasburg for Samuel Bell. For a brief time in the 1870s he evidently marketed his own wares.

There was a concentration of antebellum black potters in the old Edgefield District of west central South Carolina, where entrepreneurial workshop owners made substantial use of slave labor. It is estimated that before the Civil War, more than 50 slaves were involved in the craft there. Most go unnamed in records, but a few, such as Buster (listed as a "turner" in Amos Landrum's 1835 property transfer to pottery owners Reuben Drake and Jasper Gibbs), have been identified.

Dave, Edgefield Potter-Poet

The most famous African American folk potter, and the one about whom most is known, is David Drake of Edgefield District. For a slave artisan he was allowed the rare freedom of signing (as "Dave") and inscribing his own poetry on his work. His wares are also remarkable for their size, the largest of which—two jars dated May 13, 1859, and now in the Charleston Museum—stand almost three feet tall and would have each held about forty gallons. That they were intended for preserving plantation meat after the fall butchering is suggested by poems incised in flowing script in the damp clay: "Great & noble jar / Hold sheep goat or bear" and

"Made at Stoney Bluff / For making lard enuff." Produced when Dave was nearly sixty (and, according to oral history, missing a leg) and signed "Dave and Baddler," the two jars are thought to have been thrown in sections with a slave assistant cranking the wheel while Dave added clay coils to finish the top.

Of Dave's documented creations (more than a hundred), the majority are wide-mouthed food-storage jars that, with their British-derived shapes and brown or green alkaline (woodash- and lime-based) glazes, are in accord with the local stoneware tradition. A dozen or so narrow-necked jugs by him also are known, the larger ones meant for cane syrup. Dave's early wares are relatively small and evenly thrown, while those of the 1850s are lumpier. His jars, whose shapes vary from bulbous to straight-sided, have wide lug handles (four on some of the largest), a short neck, and rolled rim—details seen on jars by Harvey Drake, Dave's first master. Dave's jugs often have a dimple impressed in the lower terminal of the loop handle. With or without his own name, his later owner's initials, "Lm" (Lewis Miles), in Dave's characteristic hand, usually are present. Other production marks (perhaps not exclusive to Dave) include an incised U, X, and two parallel lines. Gallon capacity is indicated by punctated dots, an Edgefield marking system possibly meant to aid illiterate customers who may have included plantation cooks.

A few biographical facts can be pieced together from archival sources and the evidence of the pots themselves. Born in 1800, at the age of 18 Dave became the property of Harvey Drake—partner in the Pottersville Stoneware Manufactory established about 1815 by Dr. Abner Landrum—and likely learned the craft from Drake in the 1820s. In about 1830 Dave worked at Landrum's newspaper, the *Edgefield Hive*, where he probably learned to read and write (in 1837 South Carolina made it illegal to teach literacy to slaves); his cursive style echoes a typeface used by Landrum on an 1832 circular. The pride Dave must have taken in this empowering skill is indicated by his choice of embellishment and his poetic tribute on a jar dated April 14, 1859, just after Landrum died: "When Noble Dr. Landrum is dead / May guardian angels visit his bed." In a pot-poem dated four days later, Dave seems to be identifying himself with the periodical while marking his birthday: "Hive is eighteen hundred + fifty nine / Unto you all I feel inclined." He may have continued as a turner at Pottersville after Harvey Drake's death in 1832, when the shop was taken over by Harvey's brother, Reuben. The first identifiable Dave pot is dated 1834, unsigned but with a brief poem in his hand. Another unsigned pot from 1836 contains a sardonic report on a farm catastrophe in quatrain form: "Horses, mules and hogs / All our cows is in the bogs—/ There they shall ever stay / Till the buzzards take them away."

By 1840 Dave had passed to Abner Landrum's son-in-law, Lewis Miles, who ran a pottery shop on his Stoney Bluff plantation; a jar dated that year is inscribed, "Dave belongs to Mr. Miles / Where the oven bakes & the pot biles." It was at that time that Dave began to sign his work: his ceramic output evidently so benefited Miles financially that he was given the freedom to declare his identity and express himself in a manner denied to other slaves. Some 30 Dave pots are inscribed with poems, a couple of them repeats. All but the sardonic one quoted above are couplets (two-line stanzas), their brevity suited to the limited space available. No other

southern folk potters routinely versified their work, the nearest community of poetic potters being that of Montgomery County, Pennsylvania (and those rhymes
were in German). So what was Dave's source of poetic inspiration? Brief poems
appeared as fillers in the newspapers to which he would have had access, but their
formal diction was at odds with his more vernacular language. African American
oral poetry, in particular the stanzas of **spirituals** and **work songs**, comes closer to
the mark.

As with some Pennsylvania German and English pot-poetry, certain Dave
rhymes refer to the ware's function, as with "A very large jar which has 4 handles /
Pack it full of fresh meat—then light candles" on a 25-gallon jar with four lug handles probably meant for freshly butchered meat to be sealed in brine with melted
tallow. The nonpoetic inscription on another Dave jar seems to have been commissioned for a specific recipient: "Think of me when far away, Rosa D'La Never.
Mr. Milton Miles, Edgefield" (Milton was the eldest son of Lewis Miles, and Rosa
was a neighbor). This raises the question of whether Lewis encouraged the poetry,
perhaps even charging extra for a customer request. Other rhymes raise the possibility of Dave receiving some payment for his work: "I made this jar for cash /
Though its called lucre trash."

The subjects of Dave's poems range from the sacred to profane. Some exhort piety ("I made this jar all of cross / If you don't repent you will be lost," his last known
poem, dated 1862, on a pot with an ash glaze that melted in a crisscross pattern) or
point to familiarity with the Bible ("I saw a leppard & a lions face / Then I felt the
need of grace," likely inspired by Chapter 13 of the Book of Revelation). Others are
romantic ("Another trick is worst than this / Dearest Miss, spare me a kiss," and "A
pretty little girl on a virge / Volcanic mountain, how they burge"). The latter especially begs the question of meaning, which in some cases was clearly personal and
unlikely to be fully understood today. Certain Dave rhymes may even have been
subtly subversive and meant for other literate slaves. A 30-gallon, broad-shouldered
jar dated July 4, 1859, bears the inscription, "The fourth of July is surely come / To
blow the fife and beat the drum." Was this simply commemorative, or was it an
ironic comment on Dave having to work on the national holiday (reminiscent of
Frederick Douglass' 1841 speech on the slave's view of Independence Day)? Further, might the reference to drumming, banned in South Carolina's 1740 Slave Act
as a possible incitement to rebellion, have had a hidden meaning? Another Dave
pot-poem, "I wonder where is all my relations / Friendship to all—and every nation," appears to be a less ambiguous statement on the breakup of slave families.

In the 1840s, Dave was "farmed out" to the workshops of John Landrum (Abner's brother) and John's son, B. F., then returned by 1849 to Lewis Miles; his last
signed pieces are dated 1864. A contemporary description of the potter-poet in an
1863 Edgefield Advertiser editorial shows that he enjoyed some prominence in his
community:

> [W]e happened to meet DAVE POTTERY (whom many readers will remember as the
> grandiloquent old darkey once connected with . . . the Edgefield Hive) in the out-
> skirts of his beloved hamlet. Observing an intelligent twinkle in his eye, we accosted
> him in one of his own set speeches: "Well, uncle Dave, how does your corporosity

seem to sagatiate?"—"First rate, young master, from top to toe. I just had a magnani-mous bowl-ful of dat delicious old beverage, buttermilk." Who has not often felt his buttermilk as Dave did.

After the Civil War, Miles moved his shop to Miles Mill (later called Sunny-brook), on the railroad, which became a more industrialized operation following his death in 1868. The 1870 census for nearby Graniteville lists David Drake, age 70, as a black turner, indicating that Dave took his early master's surname and continued to work at Miles Mill after the emancipation of 1863. He probably died sometime in the 1870s. Archaeological excavation of the Stoney Bluff shop site and oral history interviews with Dave's descendants should reveal further details about this "**John Henry**" of the potter's trade.

Edgefield People Pots

African American potters in Edgefield District produced a substantial number of humanoid vessels referred to as face jugs, although a few represent full figures or are sculpted on non-jug forms (e.g., cups, jars, pitchers). Those made between 1863 and 1865 by slave workmen at Colonel Thomas Davies' Palmetto Firebrick Works at Bath, South Carolina, have bulging eyes and bared teeth of inset white clay. After corresponding with Davies, ceramics historian Edwin A. Barber de-scribed them (with no mention of the makers' motivations) in 1909: "These curi-ous objects . . . possess considerable interest as representing an art of the Southern negroes . . . the modeling reveals a trace of aboriginal art as formerly practiced by their ancestors in the Dark Continent." Sixty years later, Yale University art histo-rian Robert Farris Thompson advanced Barber's suggestion of African origins and argued that later, white face-jug makers such as north Georgian Cheever Meaders appropriated the "Afro-Carolinian" tradition. What has been learned since then complicates the picture.

Anthropomorphic clay vessels were indeed made in West Africa, perhaps early enough for the idea to be brought by slaves. The Yungur of Nigeria made portrait pots called *wiiso* to contain ancestral spirits at shrines, and the Mambila of Came-roon made similar figural vessels with white clay sometimes highlighting features. However, there were also European traditions of humanoid ceramics, such as the German *Bartmannkrüg* or bellarmine, a salt-glazed stoneware jug with a bearded face molded on the shoulder. John Remmey likely brought this tradition from the Rhineland to colonial New York, and face vessels made in the early 1800s by his descendants are the earliest known Euro-American examples. A white potter named Thomas Chandler may have met the Remmeys up North before moving to Edgefield District, where he made a smiling face jug in the late 1840s. Did Chan-dler bring the Northern tradition to South Carolina, resulting in the merging of European and African ideas? As for Cheever Meaders (whose son, Lanier, popular-ized face jugs in the 1970s), he inherited a white tradition of them from William Hewell, who probably acquired it from the Fergusons, who had migrated from Edgefield District. One is left to conclude that there were separate black and white face-jug traditions that may have influenced each other but had different meanings for each group.

The Postbellum Period

With emancipation and the end of the Civil War, African American potters continued to work in Edgefield District, especially at the Miles Mill pottery. A large, cylindrical umbrella stand with a toothy face is thought to have been made there about 1870 by Dave in collaboration with a former Thomas Davies worker. A figural bottle depicting a seated man in a military uniform, with dark iron highlights and melted-glass runs from the epaulets, is attributed to a black potter named Jim Lee at the Roundtree-Bodie Pottery, also about 1870. Alkaline-glazed tombstones with inlaid white-clay inscriptions, signed by black potter F. E. Justice and dated 1868, were discovered in a local African American cemetery. By 1880 a black potter named Josh Miles (a probable former slave of Lewis Miles) was operating his own "Jug Factory" on Shaw's Creek and employing six workers.

During the Civil War, two Edgefield potters, Marion Durham (white) and John Chandler (former slave of Thomas Chandler), migrated to Guadalupe County, Texas, where they formed a rare interracial pottery partnership near an existing shop operated with slave labor by Reverend John Wilson. When Wilson sold out to Durham in 1869, three of his free black workmen—Hyrum, James, and Wallace Wilson—left to open their own pottery shop, producing salt-glazed stoneware until 1884. In northern South Carolina, at the pottery center known as Jugtown in Greenville County, a black potter named Rich Williams operated his own shop in the early 1900s; he may have been related to Milage Williams, a freed black Edgefield District potter.

Of the 450 or so folk potters who have worked in Georgia, only three African Americans, active relatively late, have been identified. When white Washington County potter Lucius Jordan retired in about 1880, he sold his shop to Oscar Kitchens, an African American who had probably worked for Jordan earlier. Kitchens' ownership was short-lived, however, as his mortgage was foreclosed before he could pay it off. In the early 1900s, a black potter named Bob Cantrell worked for White County shop owner William Fowler ("Daddy Bill") Dorsey, learning the craft while assisting other hired potters there. Lanier Meaders remembered Cantrell as "a good jar turner; the only black man I ever knew who could" (Burrison, 50). And in the late 1930s, Demory Lipscomb made pottery for Hall County shop owners Barney Colbert and Ray Holcomb.

As a young black man, Elbert Rutledge learned to turn simple rabbit-feeding dishes and chimney-flue thimbles from white potters Norman and Hennin Miller in Perry County, Alabama, continuing to work for Norman and then his widow into the 1970s. Finally, in the mid-1970s, the last Mississippi folk potter, Gerald Stewart of Winston County, hired a black high school student named Wicks Edmonds to help in his shop. Edmonds graduated from preparing clay to throwing before leaving for better-paying work.

Conclusion

Black participation in American folk pottery, especially during the antebellum period, almost certainly has been underestimated; it is hard to imagine, for example, that Georgia potters who owned slaves didn't employ some in their workshops, despite the lack of evidence. And the extent to which utilitarian pieces surviving in collections and farm outbuildings, not visibly distinguishable from the work of white potters, were actually shaped by black hands may never be known. But this much is certain: Dave's poetic pots and Palmetto Firebrick Works face vessels are now among the most highly sought American ceramic antiques and are eloquent messages, not yet fully decoded, about the lives of enslaved African American artisans.

John A. Burrison

Further Reading

Baldwin, Cinda K., 1993, *Great and Noble Jar: Traditional Stoneware of South Carolina* (Athens: University of Georgia Press); Bishir, Catherine W., 2015, *Crafting Lives: African American Artisans in New Bern* (Chapel Hill: The University of North Carolina Press); Brown, Michael K., 2002, *The Wilson Potters: An African-American Enterprise in 19th-Century Texas* (Houston: Museum of Fine Arts, Bayou Bend Collection and Gardens); Burrison, John A., 1983, *Brothers in Clay: The Story of Georgia Folk Pottery* (Athens: University of Georgia Press); Ferguson, Leland, 1980, "Looking for the 'Afro' in Colono-Indian Pottery," in *Archaeological Perspectives on Ethnicity in America*, ed. Robert L. Schuyler (Farmingdale, NY: Baywood Publishing Co.), pp. 14–28; Koverman, Jill Beute, ed., 1998, *I Made This Jar . . . The Life and Works of the Enslaved African American Potter, Dave* (Columbia: McKissick Museum, University of South Carolina); Todd, Leonard, 2008, *Carolina Clay: The Life and Legend of the Slave Potter Dave* (New York: Norton); Vlach, John Michael, 1990, *The Afro-American Tradition in Decorative Arts* (Athens: University of Georgia Press).

PRAISE HOUSES

Praise houses were places for the celebration of the highly syncretic form of African American religion found throughout the low country of Georgia and South Carolina. According to Samuel Lawton's 1930s study, the more correct name is "pray's house." Lawton found that the worshippers in South Carolina had intended to name the place in accordance with its function in society: it was the house where one went to pray ("way oner go fur pray," as his informant on Saint Helena island explained). Most of his interviewees, Lawton observed, either used the term "pray houses" (leaving the "s" off of "prays") or "pray-ers house."

The pray's house was one of several places where Africa met the United States and the two blended to form a religion that reflected the spiritual traditions of both. The religion of the pray's house evolved during slavery as a space to house the "brush arbor" tradition of slaves who met in the brush, out of sight of the master, to come to a new understanding of the spiritual powers that had placed them in this new land and cruel situation. In these meetings, slaves and their descendants "sang, prayed, shouted, testified, preached, planned their escape, and otherwise did what they felt spiritually led to do" (Johnson, 10).

After the Civil War, the pray's houses remained an important institution among the former slaves. The leaders of the pray's houses were the leaders of the community, underscoring the lack of a separation between the secular and sacred worlds among people of African descent. A white missionary complained that such leaders inhibited their efforts to convert the freedmen and women: Father S., as one such leader was known, had such power that his followers "appeared spellbound, not to move or think without him" (quoted in Creel, 196).

Pray's houses allowed the preservation of musical traditions as well as religious ones. Guy and Candie Carawan visited a pray's house on St. John's Island, attending all-night ceremonies known as the **Christmas** Watch and the New Year's Watch. As the congregation took turns to preach, pray, sing, and **shout** (underscoring the communal nature of religion), the Carawans taped them, providing a primary source of first importance.

The blending of traditions—musical and religious, sacred and secular, American and African—appears in the following description provided by Charlotte Forten, a northern black who traveled south to teach the newly freed men and women. After the praise-meeting closed, she observed, the participants "all shake hands in the most solemn manner." Then "as a kind of appendix, they have a grand 'shout' during which they sing their own hymns." At the first shout that she saw, she observed "the wild whirling dance of the shouters." An "old blind man, whose excitement could hardly be controlled," particularly struck her. Other Northerners who traveled to the **South** to teach and convert the former slaves also highlighted the difference between pray's house religion and mainstream American worship, describing it as "pagan" and "savage." One noted the African connection when he described the shout that followed a religious ceremony as "a strange, barbaric Central-African dance and song" (quoted in Creel, 298–299).

Pray's houses remained prevalent in the low country until roughly the 1970s. A much smaller number of them remain today.

Jennifer Hildebrand

See also: Ring Shout; Spirituals

Further Reading

Creel, Margaret, 1988, *"A Peculiar People": Slave Religion and Community-Culture among the Gullahs* (New York: New York University Press); Johnson, Alonzo, 1996, "'Pray's House Spirit': The Institutional Structure and Spiritual Core of an African American Folk Tradition," in *Ain't Gonna Lay My 'Ligion Down*, ed. Alonzo Johnson and Paul Jersild (Columbia: University of South Carolina Press), pp. 8–38; Lawton, Samuel, 1939, *The Religious Life of Coastal and Sea Island Negroes* (Nashville, TN: George Peabody College for Teachers); Manigault-Bryant, LeRhonda S., 2014, *Talking to the Dead: Religion, Music, and Lived Memory Among Gullah-Geechee Women* (London, Durham: Duke University Press); Young, Jason R., 2007, *Rituals of Resistance: African Atlantic Religion in Kongo and the Lowcountry South in the Era of Slavery*, 1st ed. (Baton Rouge: Louisiana State University Press).

PRAYER

Prayer is the practice of communicating with gods, deities, and forces of nature, natural phenomena, or other forms of the supernatural. Channels of communication can include speaking, dancing, singing, music, or simply thinking. Modes of communication are also diverse, and can include, for instance, salutation, praise, thanksgiving, petition, confession, dedication, and testifying. Prayer is one of the most central practices and forms of oral narrative among people of African descent in the New World.

Prayer traditions in African American culture can be traced back to the slavery period, and include influences of both African and European religious practices. Some of the earliest examples of communal prayer were among slaves in brush arbors or **hush harbors** (some of these were actual structures made of wooden poles supporting a roof or green branches, and others were less formally constructed or were simply secret spaces where slaves gathered at night). The brush arbors were the first "invisible institution." Water-soaked quilts, blankets, and large black iron pots filled with water helped to mute the sounds of the worshippers. It was in the context of the brush arbor where slaves found their distinctive voices in prayer and in song influenced by their diverse African heritages, their knowledge of Christianity, and the horrific experiences of their enslavement. According to Sobel, "The fondest memories of many ex-slaves centered on these secret meetings. They were the highpoint of communal as well as individual emotional life: they were the scene of spirit travels" (p. 170).

The importance of prayer in African American tradition is suggested by the name given to hush harbors and the communal spaces that they later developed into—the "pray's house" (or **praise house**). Pray's houses, which have been found throughout the South Carolina and Georgia low country, were spaces where slaves gathered to pray, testify, sing, preach, and plan escapes. They were contexts in which African styles of worship blended with European and white American influences to produce unique musical and oral forms. In these early forerunners of modern New World African religious institutions, such as the black Baptist church, Vodou, Santería, and so on, contemporary traditions of black prayer were born.

Another common context for prayer dating back to the slavery period is the "prayer meeting," sometimes called "prayer services." Prayer meetings were popular in the context of camp meetings from around the 1780s to the 1830s. They were commonly held on plantations, and were autonomous and frequently unsupervised. Prayer meetings on plantations often consisted of a scripture reading, someone talking about a biblical event, and/or the singing of hymns, interspersed among prayers. Prayer meetings are still an important part of church communities in contemporary societies.

Prayer bands were another early development centering on the prayer tradition. Prayer bands consisted of itinerant or permanently settled groups who frequently prayed together. They were drawn from Methodist and Baptist congregations and traditionally focused their prayers on freedom and uplifting those who were sick or bereaved. Rev. Charles O. Boothe, the first minister of the Dexter Avenue Baptist

Church in Montgomery, Alabama, observed, "we organized a prayer band to pray for our freedom. We met outside of the little town, under a large oak tree, on every Friday night" (Boothe).

In the African American Baptist tradition, the structure of prayers tends to be highly formalized, and church members learn the form from frequent exposure as they grow from children to adults in the church community. However, church members emphasize that the essence of prayer is a feeling that comes from "the Holy Spirit." Novice prayer sayers begin by memorizing sentences and phrases heard from elder deacons, deaconesses, preachers, and other lay members who are experienced prayer sayers. Novices memorize sentences and phrases from traditional prayers, and the prayer sayers experiment by adding their own words and phrases, emphases, and performative qualities to their prayers.

Based on personal fieldwork and collection of prayer in Alabama, and the subsequent analysis of transcriptions, this author has noted two types of prayers: (1) standard and (2) improvisational, although there are probably more types than these. The standard prayer incorporates a number of memorized phrases that have been in circulation in oral and written tradition from the earliest through the contemporary time period. Portions of these texts are drawn from sermons, songs, and biblical passages, and these are combined traditional phrases that originated within black communities, and with individually created phrases and ideas. Examples of traditional and somewhat formulaic phrases from the different sections of prayer include:

Salutation:
"Eternal God, Father of Abraham, Isaac, and Jacob
Almighty! And all-wise God, our heavenly Father!
Tis once more and again,"

Body:
"Touched us with the fingertip of love. . ."
"The blood was still running warm in our veins. . ."
"Strengthen us where we are weak; and build us up where we are torn down"
"You are a heart fixer and a mind regulator"

Closure:
"Done been called everything but a child of God"
"When this old world can no longer afford me a home"

Such prayers will often make use of a recurring refrain, such as "Oh Lawd, Oh Lawd," or "Oh Lawd, Oh Lawd my Father," or "Oh Lord, Oh Jesus," which will recur throughout the prayer. The prayer sayer will often petition the Lord for their prayers to be sincere and from the heart, with such phrases as "Don't let me bow here for no form and either fashion; no outside shoe to your unfriendly world; let me bow with a pure and honest heart." In contrast to the standard prayer, the improvisational prayer is spontaneous and creative, drawing from an immediate event and the present state of the prayer sayer, and contains far less traditional and formulaic phrases.

The performances of prayers in the **black church** are dynamic events characterized by call-and-response interactions between the prayer sayer and the congregation. Prayer sayers often employ devices such as chanting, just as preachers do during their sermons. Since the earliest times prayer events have included moaning, groaning, verbal responses from the congregation, hand clapping, and sometimes crying and shouting. (Moans here refer to vocal utterances, phrases, or sentences that were repeated by members of the congregation, musically, almost as if being sung.) For example, someone might utter the phrase, "Come in the building, if you don't stay long," as a response to parts of a prayer. Or someone might utter chanted phrases, such as, "Yes Lord," or echo phrases from the prayer sayer. Frequently, music plays softly in the background as prayers are being spoken, and at times the instruments respond just as voices do, with a call-and-response emphasis on portions of the prayer.

But the church is not the only social context in which prayer occurs. Prayers can occur in smaller groups, such as within families (before meals, for instance), on occasions when church members visit the sick and shut-in to pray with them, or before meetings in secular environments. Prayer has also become prevalent in unexpected public spheres, such as among athletes and entertainers. And prayer can be an activity that people engage in at times when no one else is present. Furthermore, prayer is found among many different religious groups throughout the diaspora, and directed toward diverse deities and spiritual powers. For instance, traditional invocations of loas or orishas in religions such as Vodou or Santería can be considered forms of prayer. At times, prayer has apparently been a mode of communication through which worshippers appeal to priests within these more African-based religions. Zora Neale Hurston recorded a prayer spoken by a Vodou supplicant to the New Orleans Hoodoo priestess Marie Laveau. The structure of the prayer is not too different from that which characterizes prayers within the black Baptist church, though the content is quite a departure. In fact, the spirit of the following prayer to Laveau recalls prayers from books of the Old Testament, in which God is being asked to destroy the prayer sayer's enemies: "Oh, Good Mother. I come to you with my heart bowed down and my shoulders drooping, and my spirits broken; for an enemy has sorely tried me; has caused my loved ones to leave me [. . .] On my knees I pray to you, Good Mother, that you will cause confusion to reign in the house of my enemy and you will take their power from them and cause them to be unsuccessful" (*Mules and Men*, 204).

The efficacy of prayer among cultures of African descent in the New World cannot be overstated; it permeates religious and "secular" life. The most important aspects of prayer include (1) an emphasis on individuals developing a direct channel of communication with divine powers, and further, an intimate relationship with gods or deities, and (2) an emphasis on communicating with the deity in a communal setting, in which the community can witness and share moments of divine connection. Underlying both of these ideas are several related convictions. One is that prayer is a method through which to invoke the ultimate source of power, which is necessary for surviving and thriving within an oppressed context. A second is that one's life is defined by the integrity of one's communication with the divine. And the third is that one should never fail to testify to "what he has done for me." As the traditional gospel song says, "Jesus is on the main line, tell him what you want, call him up and tell him what you want." Prayer, then, is a genre of invocation, healing, and testimony, central to many New World African cultures and religious groups.

Willie Collins

Further Reading

Battle, Michael, 2006, *The Black Church in America: African American Christian Spirituality* (Malden, MA: Blackwell Publishers); Boothe, Charles O., 1895, *The Cyclopedia of the Colored Baptist of Alabama* (Birmingham: Alabama Publishing Co.), p. 107; Collins, Willie R., 2004, Interview with Deacon William T. Guice, Victory Baptist Church, Los Angeles, CA, November 27; Collins, Willie R., 1988, "Moaning-and-Prayer: A Musical and Contextual Analysis of Chants to Accompany Prayer in Two Afro-American Baptist Churches in Southeast Alabama," PhD diss., University of California, Los Angeles; Johnson, Alonzo, 1996, "'Pray's House Spirit': The Institution Structure and Spiritual Core of an African American Folk Tradition," in *Ain't Gonna Lay My 'Ligion Down: African American Religion in the South,* ed. Alonzo Johnson and Paul Jersild (Columbia: University of South Carolina Press); Maynard-Reid, Pedrito U., 2000, *Diverse Worship: African-American, Caribbean & Hispanic Perspectives* (Downers Grove, IL: InterVarsity Press); Pinn, Anthony B., Stephen C. Finley, and Torin Alexander, 2009, *African American Religious Cultures* (Santa Barbara, CA: ABC-CLIO); Sobel, Mechal, 1979, *Trabelin' On: The Slave Journey to an Afro-Baptist Faith* (Westport, CT: Greenwood Press); Spann, Thomas, 1994, "An Interpretation of an African-American Prayer," in *Journal of Religious Thought* 51 (2).

PREACHER, THE

In *The Souls of Black Folk* (1903), W. E. B. Du Bois wrote, "The Preacher is the most unique personality developed on American soil. A leader, a politician, an orator, a 'boss,' and idealist—all these he is, and ever, too, the center of a group of men." But the preacher is also the center from which many veins of folk narrative, performance styles, and aesthetics in black culture emanate, and about which many narratives are told. Clearly the history and fundamental function of the African American preacher is complicated and complex. However, there are several sometimes subtle themes that run through African American religious and secular discourse that provide useful aids in understanding the black preacher. The first theme revolves around the black preacher's relationship with both traditional African and western European theology and religious practices. A second theme entails the black preacher's dual role as both a sacred and secular leader. Finally, a third theme involves the black preacher's place in the **black church** and the church's influence on African American culture and civilization in general.

The evolution of the black preacher began during the slavery period, with antecedents for spiritual and political leaders in both African and European cultures. Observers from the slavery period commented frequently that preachers were often men with unusual leadership abilities, were illiterate but were still in charge of ritualized ceremonies, such as weddings, funerals, and baptisms. Because of laws making it illegal to teach slaves to read, it was difficult for slaves in general to become literate, and preachers were no exception. But illiteracy did not prevent preachers from accessing knowledge of biblical texts, as biblical stories circulated in oral tradition, stemming from sources such as Sunday school lessons and becoming widely disseminated among enslaved people. The oral nature of biblical texts, in fact, provided enslaved people with greater freedom to interpret and embellish the stories in ways that reflected their own experiences and beliefs. Elements such as the evangelical and poetic style of sermonizing; the belief in being "called" to preach; the tension between serving the spiritual and political interest of the black community, while at the same time being closely monitored by whites; and the often uneasy negotiation between African and European religious influences were all present for the slave preacher and have continued to characterize this figure in modern times.

Even during the slavery period, black preachers were regarded with esteem. Raboteau observes, "By comparison with other slaves, some preachers were privileged characters" (*Slave Religion*, p. 233). For example, preachers were often exempt from hard labor and were allowed to travel from one plantation to another to lead services. At the same time, preachers posed a threat to the institution of slavery and so were watched closely by whites. Hence, they had to temper their sermons and at least appear, when around whites, that they were not condemning slavery or inspiring slaves to seek their freedom. In many cases, they were forced by plantation owners to deliver messages of servitude. As Raboteau notes, preachers were viewed as both "a force for accommodation to the status quo" and as forces "for the exercise of slave autonomy" (p. 238). Historically speaking, black preachers were much more likely to be leaders in the struggle for freedom, and many were key figures in slave rebellions. Beginning in the slavery period and moving into the 21st century, preachers have been the dominant political spokesmen in black culture, a role consistent with that of the black church as the overwhelmingly dominant institution in the black community.

The black preacher has been further challenged by the complexities of merging cultural elements from African, European, and Native cultures. From the slavery period on, Christianity has been only one of numerous spiritual practices found in black communities. On plantations, for instance, **conjure**rs commanded as much power and respect as preachers. Other plantation practices included **herbalism** and other traditional forms of healing influenced by African and Native American sources. Then there were the slaves and later generations who chose what has historically been referred to as "secular" paths, including, for example, dancing and fiddling, activities sometimes called "the devil's work" by those of Christian persuasion. However, recent scholars such as Jon Michael Spencer have argued that "the devil's work" actually represents alternative forms of religiosity. In the context of slavery and since, the preacher has had to mediate between diverse ideologies and practices, synthesizing cultural elements in ways that would be undeniably Christian while at the same time being comfortable and empowering for communities whose experiences and worldviews are distinctively African American. In as much as African American religion evolved through the process of syncretism, preachers bore the responsibility of helping to craft belief systems and rituals that were syn-cretic, yet "Christian."

The black preacher's role as a political and social figurehead, at every historical moment since the slavery period, is widely recognized and discussed by historians, sociologists, and political scientists. Less emphasized, but of equal significance, is the preacher's role as the central figure in the development of black discourse and performance styles. The African priest-healer was called on not simply to save lost souls but to soothe mutilated psyches and invoke deities or angels that could in-spire the enslaved to do more than suffer through their misery. Drawing from the religiosity of their African past and coupling it with the coercive Christianity of their present, black preachers produced a staggeringly wide range of interpretive insights, narrative techniques, sound signals, and body language to express the often inexpressible pain and frustration of their enslaved sisters and brothers.

Blending the evangelical style of early American preaching with African oratori-cal elements and a uniquely African American sensibility, the black preacher devel-oped what is perhaps the most influential performative aesthetic in the Americas. Black evangelical preaching is typically characterized by the use of vivid imageries and innovative metaphors, **storytelling**, **signifying**, humor, and a kinetic style referred to as stylin' out, which involves innovative vocal techniques such as moan-ing, shouting, and uses of rhythmic repetitions that rouse congregations to ecstatic and frenzied emotional states. These elements extend back to the slavery period and were often noted by colonial writers. Hence, renowned preachers of the earli-est period, such as John Jasper, share a performative tradition with contemporary preachers, such as Rev. C. L. Franklin or Dr. Martin Luther King Jr. Aesthetic tributaries leading from the central figure of the preacher include performers of countless genres of music, narrative, visual art, dress, and **dance**. For example, **soul**, rhythm and **blues**, blues, **jazz**, **hip-hop**, funk, and so on can trace their per-formative modes to the black preacher. The same can be said of many comedians and dancers. Even the structures and aesthetics underlying works by many visual artists and writers have been influenced by those associated with the black preacher and sermonizing.

As one might expect, preachers have often entered the realm of **legend** and my-thology in black folklore. But, like clergymen in many societies, black preachers have also been the focus of **jokes** and **preacher tales** that portray them in an un-favorable light. The general character flaws highlighted in such lore include dis-honesty, pompousness, greed, insatiable appetites, hypersexuality, and infidelity. Preachers are thus portrayed, for example, as inviting themselves to Sunday dinner and eating up all of the fried chicken, or being sexually involved with countless women in the church congregation. It is certainly not unusual for cultures to target the most powerful members in narratives that lampoon them; in fact, such narra-tives are testimony to the wide-ranging influence of the preacher. As was the case during the slavery period, contemporary African Americans recognize the impor-tance of the preacher in addressing the spiritual and social needs of the black com-munity and admire and respect those who are strong and courageous enough to meet these challenges.

African American preachers continue to provide a unique brand of leadership, spiritual council, and core inspiration for the essence of the African American artistic spirit.

Reiland Rabaka

Further Reading

Best, Felton O., ed., 1998, *Black Religious Leadership from the Slave Community to the Million Man March: Flames of Fire* (Lewiston, NY: Edwin Mellen Press); Dallam, Marie W., 2007, *Daddy Grace: A Celebrity Preacher and His House of Prayer*, 1st ed. (New York: New York University Press); Dickerson, Dennis C., 2010, *African American Preachers and Politics: The Careys of Chicago* (Jackson: University Press of Mississippi); Hamilton, Charles V., 1972, *The Black Preacher in America* (New York: Morrow); Johnson, Joseph A., Jr., 1971, *The Soul of the Black Preacher* (Philadelphia: Pilgrim Press); Lanzano, Stanley F., 2013, *True Places: A Lowcountry Preacher, His Church, and His People* (Columbia: University of South Carolina Press); Mitchell, Henry H., 1990, *Black Preaching: The Recovery of a Powerful Art* (Nashville: Abingdon Press); Raboteau, Albert J., 1978, *Slave Religion: The "Invisible Institution" in the Antebelum South* (New York: Oxford University Press); Taylor, Clarence, 2002, *Black Religious Intellectuals: The Fight for Equality from Jim Crow to the Twenty-First Century* (New York: Routledge); Walker, Clarence Earl, and Gregory D. Smithers, 2009, *The Preacher and the Politician: Jeremiah Wright, Barack Obama, and Race in America* (Charlottesville: University of Virginia Press); West, Cornel, and Eddie S. Glaude, Jr., eds., 2003, *African American Religious Thought: An Anthology* (Louisville, KY: Westminister John Knox Press); Wilmore, Gayraud S., 1983, *Black Religion and Black Radicalism: An Interpretation of the Religious History of Afro-American People*, 2d ed. (Maryknoll, NY: Orbis); Young, Henry J., 1977, *Major Black Religious Leaders*, 1755–1940 (Nashville: Abingdon).

PREACHER TALES

The term "preacher tales" refers to humorous, often satirical, **folktales** told by or about preachers. Because the African American **preacher** has always occupied a place of honor and influence in the black community, it is not surprising that he would also become a central character in African American folklore. For as W. E. B. Du Bois asserts in *The Souls of Black Folk* (1903), the black preacher is "the most unique personality developed by the Negro on American soil." In his role as God's voice on earth, the black preacher enjoyed a special relationship with the people who depended upon him for spiritual guidance and leadership in the black community. Further evidence of the importance of the black preacher in the African American literary and folk traditions is confirmed in the prominence of preachers in works of such writers as Paul Laurence Dunbar, James Weldon Johnson, Zora Neale Hurston, James Baldwin, and Toni Morrison. Black storytellers have long been fascinated by the **black church** and the black preacher who also served as spiritual leader, counselor, and politician. Moreover, the black preacher who inspired the preacher tales interacted with the folk in three primary sites: the church, community at large, and as an honored guest in homes of his parishioners. Therefore, preacher tales generally are set in one of those spaces.

J. Mason Brewer and Zora Neale Hurston, the two most notable black folklorists of the 20th century, collected a rich body of preacher tales that reflect the religious, social, political, and cultural interests of the folk, preserving for future generations a sense of the language practices, especially the emphasis on oral performance, that developed among the folk in black communities at the turn of the century and well into the early 20th century. Brewer published *The Word on the Brazos: Negro Preacher Tales from the Brazos Bottoms of Texas* in 1953, and although Hurston collected the tales for *Every Tongue Got to Confess: Negro Folktales from the Gulf States* in the 1920s, the manuscript was not published until 2001. For Hurston and Brewer, the most significant attribute of black folk preachers was their mastery of the language; their ability to become a poet in the pulpit. Hurston and Brewer's preacher tales demonstrate their keen ear for the black vernacular, but they also highlight the moral failures of the black preacher.

Brewer compares his preacher tales to medieval exempla: illustrative stories intended to call attention to a moral, to teach a lesson, to direct listeners toward specific virtues such as honesty and piety and warn against vices such as greed and disrespect for God. One finds a similar focus in Hurston's preacher tales. While the African American preacher tales bear a striking similarity to the medieval exempla in terms of their didactic purpose, there are also significant differences. Whereas the exempla were used primarily within the context of a sermon, the black preacher tales were told most often as discrete narratives in informal settings such as cotton fields, social gatherings, on the porch of the country store, at dances, picnics, etc. Also, the preacher tales depend heavily on humor to convey their message, and as Hurston insists, there is no such thing as a folktale without a message. Frequently, preacher tales incorporate social and political commentary into the narratives, illuminating issues such as racial discrimination and prejudice.

Structurally, the typical preacher tale as recorded by Brewer and Hurston follows a three-part pattern. The tale usually begins with a narrative voice establishing a context or frame by commenting on a piece of folk wisdom that relates in some way to a preacher. The speaker then "calls to mind" or remembers a tale or comic anecdote to illustrate the moral articulated in the introductory comments. For example, in one of Brewer's tales entitled "The Preacher and His Farmer Brother," the narrative voice observes that in the Bottoms "in de same fam'ly, you kin fin' some of de bestes' preachuhs dat done evuh grace a pulpit, an' a brothuh or sistuh what ain't nevuh set foot in de chu'ch, ez long ez dey live." With that introductory comment, the narrator then "calls to min'" Revun Jeremiah Sol'mon. A brief tale involving "Revun Sol'mon and his brothauh Sid, What ain't nevuh set foot in a chu'ch house in his life" follows. The tales conclude with a "clincher" statement, a humorous observation that confirms the narrator's point.

Thematically, the preacher tales not only satirize the foibles—moral weaknesses of black preachers—but they also offer valuable insights into the social, cultural, and political conditions that affected black preachers and their congregations. For example, boss men treated the workers like slaves, restricting their freedom of movement and refusing to allow time off for burying the dead during the work week. To gain a measure of control over their environment, black preachers often assumed the role of **trickster**. For example, in "The Preacher Who Walked on Water," Elder Washington enlists the help of his deacon to build a "suppo't for a plank out in the river" to make it appear as though he can walk on water like Jesus and Peter. In another tale entitled "Reverend Black's Gifts from Heaven," the preacher hides his son in the attic of the church with a sack of groceries. When he gives the signal, the little boy throws down a particular food item. The preacher claimed that the food was sent from heaven at his request. However, the preachers' schemes are always exposed, making them a laughingstock while conveying a moral.

Both entertaining and instructive, the African American preacher tales embody the folk wisdom of the people at the lowest rung of the socioeconomic ladder. They provide a window through which we can glimpse the rich culture that sustained African Americans in the late 19th and early 20th centuries.

Elvin Holt

See also: Preacher, The; Sermons

Further Reading

Byrd, James W., 1967, *J. Mason Brewer: Negro Folklorist*, Southwestern Writers Series, no. 12 (Austin: Steck-Vaughn Company); Rucker, James 'Sparky', 2008, "The Preacher's in the Pulpit: Old-time African American Preacher Tales," *Appalachian Heritage* 36 (3): 87; Thomas, Lorenzo, 1996, "The African-American Folktale and J. Mason Brewer," in *Juneteenth Texas: Essays in African-American Folklore*, ed. Francis E. Abernethy et al. (Denton: University of North Texas Press); Turner, Darwin T., 1975, "J. Mason Brewer: Vignettes," *CLA Journal* 18 (June): 570–577.

PROVERBS

Proverbs are short, often witty statements having the ring of ancient wisdom. Besides seeming to embody the wisdom of the ages, proverbs often contain all the elements of formal poetry. For example, one finds alliteration, assonance, rhyme, parallelism, and metaphor in many proverbs. Proverbs are also often humorous. Structurally, proverbs can be divided into two halves: a topic, and a comment about that topic. For instance, in the proverb "Hard times will make a monkey eat cayenne and cry his eyes out," "Hard times" would be the topic, and the remainder of the proverb would be the comment about that topic.

Proverbs are one of the most widely used forms of spoken folklore in African American culture. Undoubtedly, the prevalence of proverbs among New World African people is a direct influence of African culture, in which proverbs are revered. Not only have proverbs been always relied upon in African societies to add spice to everyday conversation and gain points in arguments, but they have also played more specialized roles. For instance, the effective use of proverbs has been a major factor in the outcome of court cases, and proverbs have been a staple in educational lessons among many groups. Proverbs have also traditionally served as a rhetorical means through which to offer advice, make sarcastic remarks, make comments in a roundabout way so as not to evoke negative responses, to warn or shame, and to censure socially inappropriate behavior. The saying "Proverbs are the work horses of speech" captures the idea that this small form is perhaps the most important conversational genre throughout the African continent. The importance of proverbs has carried over into the cultures of the Americas.

The pervasiveness of the proverb tradition among African Americans reflects the continuity of African-speaking strategies and cultural aesthetics that endure in the new world. For instance, proverbial speech remains so important in part because the emphasis placed on metaphorical and colorful speaking that characterizes African cultures persists among groups with African heritages. Moreover, in African American culture, just as in **Africa**, those who can speak with thoughtfulness and wisdom tend to be held in great esteem.

A further reason for the significance given to proverbs in African American culture has to do with the quality of coded speech they embody. From the earliest moment of contact with Europeans, Africans had, by necessity, to develop coded dimensions of their language. The veiled meanings of proverbs have allowed African Americans to communicate secret messages to each other and secretly direct critical comments toward whites in power. Just as other forms of folklore (tales, for instance) have been historically coded to appear to communicate innocuous messages while actually conveying socially dangerous thoughts and ideas, proverbs have sometimes been used similarly. As an example, one enslaved man responded to accusations that he had been stealing from his master's garden with, "Well don't the Bible say that you reap what you sow?" During the slavery period, the proverbial expression, "Auntie's coming," was used to mean that freedom was imminent. "Let's turn the wash pot bottom down tonight" referred to secret, nocturnal celebrations that slaves held in the woods. Because of their coded natures, such phrases could be used around white people without arousing suspicion.

One of the most frequent occasions of proverb use is by adults to children. In many instances this usage helps to impart widely held values and norms, and in other cases, it communicates beliefs or expectations particular to a given community, family, or individual. The use of proverbs to children can also be a way of censoring their behaviors. Proverbs are effective tools in influencing children because of their aura of ancient wisdom, and also because they tend to cause those hearing them to stop and think. Often inherent in the proverb when used by an adult to a child is a particular lesson that can be applied not only to the situation at hand, but to similar situations that may arise in the future. A child who is overly concerned about their appearance might be told, for instance, "Beauty is only skin deep," to instill that the most important qualities are internal traits, not aspects of outward appearance. Or children pointing the finger at someone else while being equally guilty may be told, "The pot calling the kettle black." In communicating to children the importance of being selective about their friends, an adult might offer, "If you lie down with dogs, you get up with fleas," or "If you fool with trash, it'll get in your eyes."

In many cases proverbs said to children contain warnings about how their actions can lead to either punishment or other undesirable consequences. For example, they may be warned with, "If you make your bed hard, you have to lie in it," or "A hard head makes a soft behind." Many such African American proverbs stress the reciprocity of actions and consequences in life. Two of the most popular are "What goes around comes around" and "You reap what you sow."

The adult-to-child use of proverbs is not the only context in which traditional expressions are found. They are often used among adults to address adult issues, social topics, situations, or crises that may arise or recur. The plight of living in a society that promotes white standards of beauty over those of people of color is addressed by the proverb, "The blacker the berry, the sweeter the juice." This is used to convey that black women are sexier, more beautiful, etc. "Last hired, first fired" refers to the unfortunate but age-old treatment of African Americans in many parts of the American work force.

Proverbs are also often used in **signifying**, capping, or other forms of verbal dueling. "Don't let your mouth write a check that your ass can't cash," is used as a taunt or a dare by someone. "A dog that brings a bone will carry one," is sometimes used to directly criticize someone who is gossiping. Unfortunately, at times proverbial signifying contains elements of humiliation and occurs not just between peers, but also in cases where adults are speaking to children. In one case when a girl riding in the back of the car with her boyfriend started to whistle a tune, her mother responded with the proverb, "A whistling woman and a crowing hen will never come to any good." The proverb was used to mean that it is just as unnatural for a woman to whistle as it would be for a hen to crow. In other words, whistling is "unladylike." Examples such as this one reflect the use of proverbs to put down or shame others.

The African tradition of sung proverbs also survives in the New World, and there are many examples in song lyrics. While religious songs such as **spirituals** and **gospels** contain relatively few examples, secular song genres—for instance, **blues**, **soul**, rhythm and blues, and **rap**—frequently incorporate proverbs into their lyrics. In some cases proverbs in popular music are addressed to a lover. For example, a traditional blues stanza goes, "You never miss your water baby, till your well runs dry / you never miss your baby until she says goodbye." But other kinds of issues are addressed as well, as in this blues lyric: "Way a tree falls, that's the way it lie / The way a man live, that's the way he die." And in song lyrics, just as in conversation, proverbs are used to offer advice. For example, the blues lines, "Don't burn down the bridge, cause you might want to come back / cause the grass ain't no greener, on the other side of the track," are used to warn a lover to think twice about leaving. The list of proverbs in soul, and rhythm and blues lyrics is equally as long as the list for blues. Common examples of these include "Actions speak louder than words" from Otis Redding's "Hard to Handle," and the well-known "Different strokes for different folks," from Sly and the Family Stone's "Everyday People." Rap and **hip-hop** demonstrate their grounding in traditional folk culture with the use of proverbs, among other genres. Common expressions used by rap artists include "If the shoe fits, wear it," "A hard head makes a soft ass," and "Do unto others."

Proverb use in African American culture is an art form, and similar to other folk arts, it involves periods of apprenticeship, a conscious striving for mastery, and an appreciation of the art by those within African American communities. Individuals who master the art are referred to by folklorists as "proverb masters," and they collect and practice items just as storytellers or other folk artists do. Proverb masters are usually known for their wise sayings within the communities in which they reside.

Although the stock of proverbs within African American communities is largely traditional, new expressions are being created and circulated all the time. For instance, the expression "Different strokes for different folks" is likely of African American origin. We could witness the invention and popularizing of another proverb during the O. J. Simpson trial. The phrase invented and used by Johnny Cochran, O. J. Simpson's attorney, during the closing arguments of the trial gained instant, large-scale exposure and entered the American and African American vernacular almost immediately. The expression, "If the glove doesn't fit, you must acquit," has been transformed in many subsequent uses; however, it remains a recognizable proverb whose origins can be easily traced. Other such expressions, many of which are short-lived, arise frequently in African American communities. The expression "Keep it real," which is associated with the hip-hop community, is an example of a proverb created very contemporarily. As long as eloquent and metaphorical speech is prized in the African American community, proverbs should continue to be one of the most important conversational genres.

Anand Prahlad

Further Reading

Baker, Christopher, 2013, "A Trip with the Strange Woman: Amiri Baraka's Dutchman and the Book of Proverbs," *South Atlantic Review* 78 (3–4): 110; Daniel, Jack, Geneva Smitherman-Donaldson, and Milford A. Jeremiah, 1987, "Makin' a Way Outa No Way: The Proverb Tradition in the Black Experience," *Journal of Black Studies* 17: 482–508; Doyle, Charles Clay, 2014, "'A Way Out of No Way': A Note on the Background of the African American Proverbial Saying," *Proverbium: Yearbook of International Proverb Scholarship* 31: 193–198; Folly, Dennis [Sw. Anand Prahlad], 1982, "Getting the Butter from the Duck: Proverbs and Proverbial Expressions in an Afro-American Family," in *A Celebration of American Family Folklore*, ed. Steven J. Zeitlin, Amy J. Kotkin, and Holly Cutting Baker (New York: Pantheon Books), pp. 232–241; Ndulute, Clement, 2009, "African and African American Plantation Proverbs: Connections and Chasms," *Griot* 28 (2): 12; Prahlad, Sw. Anand, 1996, *African American Proverbs in Context* (Jackson: University Press of Mississippi); Prahlad, Sw. Anand, 2001, *Regae Wisdom: Proverbs in Jamaican Music* (Jackson: University Press of Mississippi); Roberts, John W., 1978, "Slave Proverbs: A Perspective," *Callaloo* 1: 129–140.

Q

QUILTING

The African American quilting tradition dates back to the slavery era. Since making textiles and clothing was central to plantation life, a slave with an aptitude for sewing, weaving, spinning, and/or quilting was likely to be valued. Although most slave quilters remain anonymous, books such as Gladys-Marie Fry's *Stitched from the Soul: Slave Quilts from the Antebellum South* (1990) document a handful of talented individuals—usually identified only by their first names—and their works. Both men and women made quilts, and it was common for slave women to work with their white mistresses on quilts for the household. The most famous African American quilter of the 19th century was a freed slave named Harriet Powers (1837–1911), who made two spectacular quilts now housed in the Smithsonian's National Museum of American History and the Museum of Fine Arts, Boston. Considered masterpieces of the black folk art tradition, these Story-Bible Quilts artistically depict Bible stories as well as historic events. Powers is a unique figure in that she was recognized as an artist at the time that she made her quilts. In fact, the wives of several Atlanta University professors commissioned Powers' second Story-Bible Quilt in 1895. African American quilt making is a multifaceted folk art form that includes items made out of necessity as well as objects intentionally created as art. As scholars have written, historically many utilitarian quilts have incorporated designs that can be linked to African textiles, Masonic symbols, and early Euro-American quilt designs. By contrast, quilts made in the latter decades of the 20th century are often created as art objects, although they also reference historical aspects of the African American experience and reflect styles that are similar to utilitarian quilts. Although artistic and utilitarian impulses need not be mutually exclusive, the definition of the art—its display and the attempt to preserve it—discourages its use in everyday life. The co-existence of these different types of quilts has often resulted in quilt art being judged by a different set of standards than other types of art, even other textile art. For example, in a public museum lecture by the story quilt artist Faith Ringgold, an audience member asked Ringgold whether she sometimes felt her quilts were misplaced on the gallery wall (Ringgold 1998). The audience member wondered if Ringgold wished that people would use her quilts. Faith Ringgold tartly replied that she had put enormous effort into her quilts, and that she would not look kindly on people sleeping beneath them. In this sense the intention of the creator is important. By the same token, quilts never meant to be displayed as art objects have increasingly found their way into museums. In that context, they have gained status due to the changing valuation of African American textile arts, the shifting perspectives on objects once classified as craft rather than art, and the desire to preserve examples of African American material culture for posterity.

In recent decades, African American quilts have entered the popular cultural vernacular in surprising ways. In the year 2000, the television miniseries *Sally Hemings: An American Scandal*, which recounted a highly romanticized version of the relationship between Thomas Jefferson and his slave Sally Hemings, included a very telling segment that featured a quilt. In the first scene, Thomas Jefferson shows a group of male slaves the architectural model for Monticello, his plantation in Virginia. Then, Jefferson walks toward a group of women and children, among them Sally and her mother, Elizabeth Hemings, who are gathered around a quilt hanging on a frame. When asked by Jefferson, "What have we here?" Sally's mother Elizabeth explains that the quilt portrays the Hemings family. As Elizabeth points to squares that depict figures, her description of each family member makes it clear that the white Jeffersons and the black Hemingses are related through intimate bonds between white southern men and enslaved black women. The familiar aspects of this sequence include the idea that quilting is a domestic, female activity. At the same time, the scene references the late 1990s revelations about the relationship between Jefferson and Hemings, which has long been a part of African American oral history but was consistently denied by prominent historians. In 1998, DNA research proved that male descendants of Hemings are genetically related to male descendants of Jefferson. The miniseries used this contemporary information to imagine historical circumstances in which African Americans used one of the forms of expression available to them—quilting—to write their own version of events into a historical record that denied their experience, in the context of a society that made it illegal for slaves to read and write.

The comparison between quilting and writing is just one analogy that is frequently used to interpret quilts. The discipline or field of specialization of the observer strongly influences the ways that a quilt is "read." For a writer, especially a historian, quilt details such as patterns, stitching, ties, and width of fabric are clues both to artistic intention and the historical circumstances that influenced the creation of the quilt. The historical study of African American quilts involves a significant amount of conjecture based on clues that are partial and incomplete. In Jacqueline Tobin and Raymond Dobard's *Hidden in Plain View: A Secret Story of Quilts and the Underground Railroad* (1999), the scholars investigate a "quilt code" revealed to them in the mid-1990s as an oral tradition by an African American woman from South Carolina. Based on her story, Tobin and Dobard assert that familiar patterns such as the Monkey Wrench, the Wagon Wheel, and the Log Cabin were deployed in black quilts of the antebellum period to instruct slaves about how to escape to the North and freedom. Tobin and Dobard build upon earlier research by scholars such as Maude Wahlman, which examines the relationship between patterns in African American quilts and West African textiles. For example, scholars assert that black Americans continued the symbolic use of color prevalent in West African textiles, which symbolized their belief in the curative and protective uses of color.

Quilt scholars have also linked the tendency to asymmetry in black quilt aesthetics to West African beliefs that evil travels in straight lines. Tobin and Dobard agree that evidence such as color and line indicates that quilts, like African textiles, were imbued with protective powers. *Hidden in Plain View* includes research on American and British Masonic symbols, arguing that an African American freemasonry group established in the late 18th century by free men of color was likely to have played an instrumental role in aiding fugitive slaves. For example, Tobin and Dobard point out that the Nine Patch pattern, which is strongly geometric, has references to African symbols, Masonic emblems, and early American quilt patterns. They also write that diamonds arranged in a specific pattern, known as **Crossroads**, was code for Cleveland, Ohio, one of the main destinations on the Underground Railroad. Tobin and Dobard claim that the quilt pattern called Wagon Wheel or sometimes Carpenter's Wheel wagon wheel symbolized a means of escape, as fugitive slaves were often hidden in the secret compartments of wagons. Another example builds on the fact that African American quilt tops are often tied rather than stitched down. The use of ties on quilts by Black Americans was often interpreted as a sign of poor workmanship. However, Tobin and Dobard suggest that the number of knots placed on quilt ties was encoded information that told slaves when to escape. An increasing number of knots on the ties of quilts aired out in the slave quarters signaled to those escaping that the date of departure was approaching.

Ultimately, *Hidden in Plain View* makes a convincing case for the continuity between West African symbols, American quilt patterns, and some Masonic emblems. However, despite the compelling nature of the argument, interpreting quilt patterns as encoded messages remains highly conjectural. This is due not only to the lack of material evidence—the rarity of African American quilts from the pre–Civil War period—but also to the highly protective nature of secret societies both in West **Africa** and the Americas, and to the necessary secrecy that shrouded how fugitive slaves managed to escape. By the same token, while it is difficult to verify how quilts reference historical events, contemporary African American quilts often tell fascinating stories of everyday life. For example, in a 1940 quilt called The Overhaul Quilt by a Texan woman named Beulah Smith, the use of old clothing contained a reference to a humorous tale. The quilt included a pair of pants worn by the father of the quilt's owner. One can see the dark impression left by a back pocket, as well as a patched area from a run-in with a bull that the owner of the pants had as a young boy. In another example, Texas quilter Anita Knox described inspiration for a quilt coming to her in a supermarket checkout line as she suddenly saw the façade of a restaurant across the street in a new way (*Flash of the Spirit*, 2003).

Quilting is a uniquely American art that has been subjected to the characteristically American practice of racial segregation. It is common to speak of "black" and "white" quilt styles. However, as many scholars have pointed out, the tendency to racially classify quilt styles has resulted in overgeneralizations. Generally speaking, European American quilts such as those in the Amish and Pennsylvania Dutch traditions are associated with precise geometric shapes, very detailed piecing or patchwork, and tiny, meticulous stitching. European Americans have also been associated with slower-paced quilt work and the creation of quilts for display. By contrast,

African Americans are associated with improvisational quilt styles and so-called "unusual" color combinations. Their tendency to use large, irregular stitching or ties in place of stitching is likened to a utilitarian as opposed to an aesthetic impulse, as well as quilts that are produced more quickly and less meticulously. It is not hard to note the ways that such seemingly objective descriptions are complicit with racial stereotypes. "White" quilts are orderly, intricate and muted, while "black" quilts are bold and sloppy. The reality, of course, is far less polarized. As Tobin and Dobard have written, "The African American quilt is a cultural hybrid" (35). The examples of geometric, abstract, and figurative quilts made by black Americans very capably demonstrate that they work in the full variety of quilt idioms.

Traditionally quilts have been classified even lower on the hierarchy of artistic value than vernacular or outsider art—labels that have been used to distinguish work by self-taught artists from work by those trained in the fine art tradition. Quilts are most often considered crafts—although occasionally they have been elevated to the status of folk art. In recent decades, such distinctions have become increasingly blurred, very often because it is now recognized that they may mask biases of gender, race, class, and region. A prominent example of this phenomenon was one of the most talked-about museum shows of the fall 2002 season, the exhibit "The Quilts of Gee's Bend." The exhibit originated at The Museum of Fine Arts in Houston and was eventually displayed at the prestigious Whitney Museum of American Art in New York. It contained 70 quilts from Gee's Bend, an isolated enclave in rural Alabama where several generations of African American women in

Quilters in Gee's Bend, Alabama, display one of their quilts, 1965. (Bob Adelman/Corbis)

a number of families have created quilts of exceptional beauty and originality. That an institution like the Whitney would devote an exhibit to objects made by unknown black women from Alabama is evidence of significant cultural shifts. On one hand, the prestige of the museum lends the quilts an undeniable aura of credibility and cements their value in the high art realm. At the same time, these quilts are irresistible to a jaded urban elite because they are marketed as authentic objects from a place that is economically impoverished yet ethnically "pure." In fact, the women of Gee's Bend have been "discovered" more than once during the 20th century. Photographers of the Works Progress Administration (WPA) extensively documented Gee's Bend in the 1930s because it was located in one of the poorest counties of the United States, and the African American tenant farmers there lived in deplorable conditions. The quilters were also celebrated by the New York art world in the 1970s, when for a brief period of time their quilts were actually sold in Bloomingdale's. While the 21st-century rediscovery of these quilts is wonderful for a contemporary audience, it is important to note the cyclical fashion in which folk art or craft can gain entry into the fine art world. Does this type of attention represent superficial trends or is it a sign of more significant change?

One of the most persistent problems in keeping track of African American material culture derives from the fact that objects are not kept and passed down the generations. Although historians such as Gladys-Marie Fry have done a laudable job of finding examples of antebellum quilts made by black Americans, the majority of these objects have not survived, and examples of 19th-century African American quilts are rare. As the prominent historian Bing Davis once remarked, "Slaves were not brought to America. Africans were brought to America, and there they were enslaved" (Tobin and Dobard, 2). Although the West African practice of oral tradition persisted among black Americans and accounts for the retention of much of what we know about that history, it is also the case that African American communities have been subject to continuous ruptures such as migration and economic hardship that cause cultural memory to become fragmented, and material culture to be undervalued. Thus, when it comes to quilts, patterns with origins in West African textile traditions may be used with no knowledge on the part of the quilter about the provenance of the pattern. Or, as is the case with many families where quilts were made as a matter of necessity, people may remember the women in their families making quilts and remember sleeping under them, but they were used until they wore out, or perhaps even destroyed once they were no longer needed. One of the women in the group of quilters from Gee's Bend Alabama recalls burning dozens of quilts because "they thought they were junk."

One of the striking things that many critics have noted about black quilt aesthetics is how much they have in common with work by some of the most revered examples of modern art. This aspect of "appreciation" of African American quilts is controversial in that the modernist aesthetic of 20th-century Europe and America has often been informed by African art traditions that have been ignored by art historians. Artists such as Faith Ringgold and Robert Colescott have explicitly critiqued this hypocritical aspect of traditional art history. Such scholarship celebrates Africanisms in European masters such as Matisse and Picasso yet fails to recognize the work of African artists. Moreover, for hundreds of years Africa was stereotyped as having no meaningful culture or art prior to being colonized.

An example of the way that quilts can be related to modern art is the pattern Nine Patch, which strongly resembles the Hausa (Nigerian) eight-knives design that dates from the 17th century. By the same token, the eight knives design also bears a striking resemblance to the minimalist grid of 20th-century abstract art. Many of the quilts from Gee's Bend have been compared to the grid aesthetic used by artists such as Josef Albers and Piet Mondrian. For example, in Lutisha Pettway's 1950 quilt entitled "Bars," the strips of denim from used pants creates just such a grid pattern. The contrasting shadings reflect different rates of fading and the darkened patches where pants pockets once were. Pettway's quilt illustrates how a utilitarian quilt created from old denim work clothes is at the same time a beautiful object that evokes historical detail as well as contemporary art aesthetics.

As Tobin and Dobard state, the African American quilt is a hybrid object. It incorporates many cultural and aesthetic influences, not all of which are intentional on the part of the individual quilter. Although oral histories in African American communities are rich sources of historical information, they are fragmented and incomplete. Therefore, the creative impulse among African American quilters may not be linked to an explicit source that can be easily identified. However, whether the initial impulse behind making a quilt is necessity or the leisure to make an art object, a unique creative aesthetic deeply informs African American quilts. They remain one of the most important folk art objects in the African American tradition.

Caroline A. Streeter

Further Reading

Arnett, William, ed., 2002, *The Quilts of Gee's Bend* (Atlanta: Tinwood Books); Fry, Gladys-Marie, 1990, *Stitched from the Soul: Slave Quilts from the Antebellum South* (New York: Museum of American Folk Art and Dutton Studio Books); Grace Museum, 2003, *Flash of the Spirit: African American Quilts*, Abilene, Texas; Klassen, Teri, 2009, "Representations of African American Quiltmaking: From Omission to High Art," *The Journal of American Folklore* 122 (485): 297–334; Lyons, Mary E., 1993, *Stitching Stars: The Story Quilts of Harriet Powers* (New York: Aladdin Paperbacks); Museum of African American Life and Culture, 1986, *Broken Star: Post–Civil War Quilts Made by Black Women*, Dallas; Ringgold, Faith, 1998, "A Conversation with Faith Ringgold," lecture in conjunction with the exhibit "Dancing at the Louvre: Faith Ringgold's French Collection and Other Story Quilts," May 9, University Art Museum, Berkeley, CA; Tobin, Jacqueline, and Raymond Dobard, 1999, *Hidden in Plain View: A Secret Story of Quilts and the Underground Railroad* (New York: Doubleday); Turner, Patricia A., 2009, *Crafted Lives: Stories and Studies of African American Quilters* (Jackson: University Press of Mississippi); Wahlman, Maude Southwell, and John Scully, 1983, "Aesthetic Principles in Afro-American Quilts," in *Afro-American Folk Arts and Crafts*, ed. William Ferris (Boston: G.K. Hall); Wahlman, Maude Southwell, and John Scully, 1983, *Black Quilters* (New Haven, CT: Yale Art Gallery); Webber-Bey, Deimosa, 2014, "Runaway Quilt Project: Digital Humanities Exploration of Quilting During the Era of Slavery," *Journal of Interactive Technology and Pedagogy* 6; Woolfork, Lisa, 2009, *Embodying American Slavery in Contemporary Culture* (Urbana: University of Illinois Press).

R

RABBIT, BRER

Brer Rabbit (Buh Rabbit, B'Rabby, Ber Rabbit, "Compére Rabbit") is one of the world's most famous **trickster** figures and one of the most popular **folktale** characters in black folklore of the African diaspora. Rabbit as trickster appears in Buddhist folktales, stories from India, European lore, Cherokee and other **Native American** tales, and most visibly in the diaspora of African folklore, flowing into and then out of the southeastern United States. Brer Rabbit came to the attention of white Americans through Joel Chandler Harris's Uncle Remus: *His Songs and His Sayings* (1880) and *Nights with Uncle Remus* (1883). Four more volumes of Brer Rabbit and related tales appeared before the end of Harris' career. Two-thirds of the 185 Brer Rabbit tales and related animal stories that Harris gathered show direct African lineages; the balance derive primarily from European and Native American lore. On one level, Brer Rabbit stories are pure entertainment, augmented by the body language, intonation, and audience-conscious performance styles of the narrators. But the sociology of these stories consistently imports themes about the struggle for food, shelter, land, sexual favors, and status from continental **Africa** into parts of the Caribbean, South America, and the United States. Brer Rabbit and his smaller friends, such as Brer Tarrypin, must resort to trickery and mind games to survive or, better, prevail in a jungle alive with dangerous, larger animals. **Brer Fox**, Brer Wolf, Brer Bear, and other larger creatures are not only adversarial animals on the prowl for food and power; they also symbolize the slave owners, overseers, and field bosses in the American **South**. Like the trickster, John, of the "John and Old Master" tale cycle, Brer Rabbit is continually putting one over on a larger, predatory foe. And beyond mere survival, Brer Rabbit reflects the desires on the part of the enslaved for advancement; that is, acquiring more wealth, status, and power.

As Lawrence Levine has argued, the Brer Rabbit tales were not simply entertaining examples of wish fulfillment for enslaved African Americans: they offered practical strategies for navigating the treacherous waters of the slavery system, staying alive, and gaining whatever small advantages might be available within that system. The tales are centered on struggles of power, most often as allegories about the abilities of the weak to defeat and take power away from the strong. Levine writes: "The many tales of which these are typical make it clear that what Rabbit craves is not possession but power, and this he acquires not simply by obtaining food but by obtaining it through the manipulation and deprivation of others" (p. 110). Perhaps reflecting the experience of enslaved Africans, the Brer Rabbit tales depict an irrational universe in which there is a constant state of conflict and

Illustration from Joel Chandler Harris's, *Uncle Remus and His Friends* (1892), shows Brer Rabbit seated on a rock, telling stories. (Library of Congress)

in which the behaviors of animals (people) are arbitrary and capricious. Thus, they mediate the sometimes gray area created by conflicting tensions within slave life. For example, survival often depended on actions that would be considered by the morals of slaveholders, and even of Africans and African Americans, as immoral.

As the nature of the **trickster** is to disrupt the social order and call into question issues of morality and boundaries, it is understandable that Brer Rabbit was so popular among the enslaved. In what is likely the world's most celebrated example of the stick-fast folk motif and of the effectiveness of reverse psychology, Brer Rabbit escapes Brer Fox's tar-baby trap after he discovers that punching out the "stuck-up" female figure who won't give him the time of day has suddenly backfired. Brer Fox then comes out of hiding and deliciously rehearses a whole litany of methods for killing Brer Rabbit—by hanging, drowning, or roasting him, or by tearing him limb from limb. Brer Rabbit quickly puts his brain to work and tells Brer Fox repeatedly that all of those actions will be fine, so long as the fox does not throw him into the dreaded **briar patch**. Of course, that's exactly where Brer Fox flings him; and when he lands there, Brer Rabbit jubilantly reminds the fox that he had been "Bred and bawn in a brier-patch!" Uncle Remus's litany of possible deaths for the rabbit by burning, hanging, drowning, or mutilation is simultaneously an inventory of tortures inflicted on slaves. The stories are barely disguised allegories of slavery, in all its violence and inhumanity.

Part of Brer Rabbit's legacy as an archetypal trickster is that he is also an amoral boundary-crosser. He is not above reneging on an agreement with other animals to share food, for example. In the sociology of these stories, across the African diaspora and other folk traditions, too, one can understand why slave-hero Rabbit would seize any opportunity to outmaneuver and take revenge on the more predatory animals who have been threatening his life—as he does, for example, when he arranges for Fox to be caught and killed by Mr. Man, or when he cooks Granny Wolf in a pot, in a ruse to cure her sickness, and then feeds her head to Wolf. But in a more disturbing story, which has variants in Native American folklore and elsewhere, Rabbit gets powerfully hungry in the middle of the night and devours the communal butter supply that he, Fox, and Possum have collected. Moreover, Rabbit smears butter on Possum's mouth to pin the blame on him. The next morning, Possum tries to defend himself and, unwisely, proposes that the animals agree to a fire-jump test, figuring that the critter who had eaten all that butter would not be able to clear the flames. But hapless and unathletic Possum himself falls into the flames and dies.

Brer Rabbit tales have continued among African Americans, although they have become less and less common. In later versions of the tales, however, attitudes toward Brer Rabbit have quite naturally changed from those of the slavery period. One kind of change has been the incorporation of elements reflecting the time periods in which the tales might appear. For example, tales told in the postbellum era might reflect the social dynamics of that period, which were different than those of the slavery era. In one tale, Rabbit is the sharecropper working for the Bear (the boss). The tale reflects the frustrations of black sharecroppers who were routinely cheated by the land owners and provides a mocking picture of the boss, and an instance in which Rabbit, the sharecropper, comes out ahead (Levine, 323). Of course, the language of the tales has changed, as it has in African American speech in general, and the dress of characters reflects that of whatever historical moment the tales appear in. Another change has been a reinterpretation of Brer Rabbit's antics, sometimes in negative ways. African American audiences in the 20th century have been often disturbed by Brer Rabbit's unprovoked attacks or trickery of other animals, and in some locales, Brer Rabbit's defeat is a recurrent motif in the tales (Levine, 377). Although Brer Rabbit is remembered and tales may be occasionally told, Rabbit has been largely replaced by trickster figures that reflect more accurately the social circumstances, aesthetics, and political sensibilities of contemporary African Americans.

As a folk hero, Brer Rabbit is a living example, quite literally, of the values of resourcefulness, courage, endurance, and native intelligence. Yet among his other influences, the trickster also stirs up the neighborhood, violates expected norms, keeps the power structures off-balance, and threatens the expected social or moral order of things—including the order of things among his own, smaller-sized classes of animals.

R. Bruce Bickley Jr.

See also: Fables; Folktales; Storytelling

Further Reading

Abrahams, Roger D., 1985, *Afro-American Folktales: Stories from Black Traditions in the New World* (New York: Pantheon Press); Carpio, Glenda, 2008, *Laughing Fit to Kill: Black Humor in the Fictions of Slavery* (New York: Oxford University Press); Chase, Richard, ed., 1955, *The Complete Tales of Uncle Remus* (Boston: Houghton Mifflin); Dorson, Richard M., ed., 1958, *American Negro Folktales* (Bloomington: Indiana University Press); Green, Thomas A., 2009, *African American Folktales* (Westport, CT: Greenwood Press); Levine, Lawrence W., 1977, *Black Culture and Black Consciousness:*

Afro-American Folk Thought from Slavery to Freedom (New York: Oxford University Press); Sperb, Jason, 2012, *Disney's Most Notorious Film: Race, Convergence, and the Hidden Histories of Song of the South* (Austin: University of Texas Press).

RAP

The term "rap" can describe both a stylized way of speaking and a popular musical form that developed in the 1970s in New York City. In the vernacular, the term "rap" has historically referred to a colorful, smooth, persuasive, and manipulative kind of speech that customarily reaches its most eloquent form in the repertoire of the **pimp**. As the ultimate wordsmith in the world of the street, the pimp is a secular parallel to the **preacher**, who is the most masterful speaker in the world of religion. The status accorded both of these figures in their respective social realms indicates the tremendous weight given to artful speaking in the African American community. Speaking goes far beyond the function of communicating information and becomes a means to claim cultural territory and status through the projection of one's public persona. Kochman suggests that there are two basic elements of rap: the personality-style component and the informational component. He suggests further that the personality-style component is the most important in affecting the listener. In a typical scenario, for instance, the pimp uses his raps to convince women to become prostitutes in his "stable" and keep them there once they join.

Both the poetry and the performance styles of rapping as a form of speech are highly elaborate, but the most important element is the personality-style of the speaker. Thus, rappers are admired not only for their verbal acuity, but also for their ability to persuade others to give them whatever it is that they are asking for. Rapping can also refer to a stylized way of narrating a story (e.g., "running something down" or "running a game" on someone—trying to trick or hustle someone out of their money).

Rap, the Musical Genre

The first phase of what would become rap music started around 1972, when New York City youth (primarily African American, though there were Puerto Ricans and whites as well) began to move away from the disco club scene, where there were increasing incidents of violence, to return to neighborhood parties in the Bronx. Early DJs like Kool Herc, Afrika Bambaataa, Pete Jones, Grandmaster Flowers, and Grandmaster Flash would set up mobile sound systems in parks and at block parties, where the crowds would evaluate them on their equipment (particularly the size and power of their amplifiers) and the music played. These developments in New York were directly influenced by the Jamaican traditions of "sound systems," DJ talk-overs, and other sound experiments that were brought by Jamaican musicians and artists who had settled in the Bronx and in other areas of New York with large black populations. This was prior to any "rapping," other than the occasional shout-out from the DJ to friends and audience members; essentially, these block parties were simply outdoor clubs, where people went to **dance**.

The second phase of rap music began in the mid-1970s, when DJs began to incorporate rappers, or emcees (MCs, short for Master of Ceremonies) into their performances. Kool Herc brought on emcees Coke La Rock, Clark Kent, and Jay Cee to form the Herculords, bringing a team dynamic to the parties in which the emcees would rap intermittently, throwing out stock phrases like "get up" or "jam to the beat," mostly in an effort to excite the audience to dance. There were a number of emcees that ran with DJ crews at this time, but it was still the DJ that was far and away the star of the show. Grandmaster Flash's group, the Furious Five (Melle Mel, Cowboy, Raheim, Kid Creole, and Mr. Ness), would later set the standard for rapping with a technique they called "trading phrases," in which the various emcees would go back and forth with rhyming couplets, synchronized with the DJ's music.

The early commercial successes of recorded rap music, most famously Sugarhill Gang's 1979 hit "Rapper's Delight," constitute the art form's third phase, from the late 1970s through the mid-1980s. During this time, rap artists were recorded primarily by independent record companies, and the emphasis shifted away from the DJ and more toward the rappers themselves, who, as the "mouthpiece" of the rap sound, presented more commercially viable commodities, as their sound could be localized in a body that could then be packaged for public consumption. This was the time period in which Afrika Bambaataa would begin experimenting with what he called "techno-pop" (most notably with his group Soulsonic Force on the 1982 album *Planet Rock*), using synthesizers and drum machines to complement the developing rap sound. This use of electronic sound would dovetail in the mid-1980s with the use of sampling, the digital reproduction of bits of recorded material, using equipment like the Akai MPC. Sampling would eventually be considered the fundamental unit of rap music production.

The fourth phase of rap music, the mid-1980s through the early 1990s, is considered by many to be "the golden age" of rap. It was during this period that the art form exploded commercially, moving wholly into the mainstream of American culture. Rap music simultaneously diversified its sound tremendously, with new subgenres emerging seemingly at every turn: there was the political rap of Boogie Down Productions and Public Enemy; "conscious" or "five-percenter" rap, as that of A Tribe Called Quest or the Jungle Brothers; the "hippy" rap of De La Soul; "gangster" or "gangsta" rap, exemplified by N.W.A, Schoolly-D, and Ice-T; as well as more and more entries into the already established world of "party" rap by performers like Run DMC, the Beastie Boys, and Biz Markie.

In 1994 rap came to a crossroads. Two hugely important albums were released: Nas's debut *Illmatic* and Common's sophomore LP *Resurrection*, both of which raised the bar for lyric writing in rap music, with intricate narrative pieces like "N.Y. State of Mind" by Nas, or Common's extended metaphor in "I Used to Love H.E.R." Both albums were hailed as classics, garnering both critical and commercial accolades. Nas's album took the by-now–familiar "gangsta" rap themes and refined and expanded on them; Common's album grew more out of the five-percenter tradition. The art form would have to take one path or the other, and ultimately it would head in the direction laid out by Nas, perhaps due to the added influence

Contemporary rapper Nas performs at "Carmelo Anthony Powers Through the Hudson," in New York, October 20, 2011. (Brian Ach/AP Images for Jordan Brand)

of Dr. Dre's album *The Chronic*, released the year before, as well as another 1994 debut masterpiece, the Notorious B.I.G.'s *Ready to Die*. By the middle of the decade, "gangsta" rap would be fully entrenched, becoming the ubiquitous version of "rap music" in the mainstream. Needing new points of differentiation in the creative void left by the singularity of this new, monolithic, popular form, feuds like the much-publicized East Coast–West Coast rivalry between Biggie Smalls (the Notorious B.I.G.) and 2Pac (Tupac Shakur) began, injecting intrigue into the cultural landscape.

The latter half of the 1990s saw rap music move from being one popular art form among many to being at the center of global popular culture. Today its influence extends across the range of cultural production, from television and movies to the visual and performing arts, and everything in between.

Folkloric Elements of Rap

The musical genre of rap is related to the vernacular use of the term in a number of ways. Rap music inherited the emphasis on stylized performance and self presentation that characterizes the conversational genre of rap. Similar to the conversational genre, rap music looks to the figure of the pimp as a role model for eloquent and inventive orality. Hence, rap artists draw upon multiple oral genres associated with the pimp, street culture, and with the black underworld (subcultures involved in illegal activities and whose behaviors are outside of what is acceptable within mainstream black communities). For example, **toasting** traditions and the **dozens** play a significant role in the lyrical structures (rhymed couplets, for example) and sensibilities of rap music, and both of these genres have close associations with street culture and with pimps. Figures such as Iceberg Slim, a reformed pimp turned novelist, is revered by many rappers, especially artists of gangsta rap. Key components of rap dialect are obvious borrowings from pimp subculture, for instance, "**ho**" and "**bitch**." Elements of black militancy are also incorporated into rap music, and one can see influences from cultural heroes such as Malcolm X and members of the Black Panthers. Such components are evident in the militant positions taken by many rappers toward the police or other authorities who have histories of abusing black people. These elements come together with the tradition of the **bad man** to create a new kind of tough persona suited for the contemporary social milieu.

Similarly to Jamaican DJ talk-over (one of rap's early influences), rap also incorporates a vast array of influences from oral tradition. One finds frequent uses of **proverbs**, for instance, in rap lyrics, occasional lines drawn from children game songs, and frequent allusions to other black song genres. One key characteristic of rap is its tendency to invite reinterpretation not only of elements of black oral tradition and culture, but of world culture. In this way, sampling is far from imitation; rather, it is a form of social critique. There are also abundant elements drawn from the gospel tradition and from worship in the **black church** in general—as there are in most black popular music forms. Although the deep-voiced monologues from 1970s "**soul**-rappers" like Isaac Hayes and Barry White may have been more immediate influences than church, these were themselves influenced by the poetics of black **prayer** and **testifying** traditions. One can see in the call-and-response interactions between rap performers and their audiences some of the same dynamics that one would witness in a black Baptist church service; the waving of the hands in the air, for instance, which is typically associated with "getting the spirit" in church. Perhaps the most prominent influence of the church is the **sermon**-like delivery of many rap performances, which are parallel in performance style and intensity to those of preachers.

Rap music and subculture are the latest in a historical chain of black musical traditions that incorporate and reinterpret diverse elements of African American folklore. And, like some of these other genres, rap music has also been responsible for creating new traditions; for instance, styles of dress, gestures, dialect, and dance forms.

Anand Prahlad and Dan Thomas-Glass

See also: Hip-hop; Toasts

Further Reading

Barnes, Sandra L., 2008, "Religion and Rap Music: An Analysis of Black Church Usage," *Review of Religious Research* 49 (3): 319–338; Bonnette, Lakeyta M., 2015, *Pulse of the People: Political Rap Music and Black Politics* (Philadelphia: University of Pennsylvania Press); Dyson, Michael Eric, 1993, *Reflecting Black: African-American Cultural Criticism* (Minneapolis: University of Minnesota Press); George, Nelson, 1999, *Hip Hop America* (New York: Penguin Books); Harkness, Geoffrey Victor, 2014, *Chicago Hustle and Flow: Gangs, Gangsta Rap, and Social Class* (Minneapolis: University of Minnesota Press); Kochman, Thomas, 1972, "Toward an Ethnography of Black American Speech Behavior," in *Rappin' and Stylin' Out: Communication in Urban Black America*, ed. Thomas Kochman (Urbana, University of Illinois Press), pp. 241–264; Oware, Matthew, 2011, "Decent Daddy, Imperfect Daddy: Black Male Rap Artists' Views of Fatherhood and the Family," *Journal of African American Studies* 15 (3): 327–351; Pavlic, Ed, 2006, "Rap, Soul, and the Vortex at 33.3 RPM: Hip-Hop's Implements and African American Modernisms," *Callaloo* 29 (3): 956–968; Perkins, William Eric, ed., 1996, *Droppin' Science: Critical Essays on Rap Music and Hip Hop Culture* (Philadelphia, PA: Temple University Press); Potter, Russell A., 1995, *Spectacular Vernaculars: Hip-Hop and the Politics of Postmodernism* (Albany: State University of New York Press); Rabaka, Reiland, 2012, *Hip Hop's Amnesia: From Blues and the Black Women's Club Movement to Rap and the Hip Hop Movement* (Lanham, MD: Lexington Books); Reeves, Marcus, 2008, *Somebody Scream: Rap Music's Rise to Prominence in the Aftershock of Back Power*, 1st ed. (New York: Faber and Faber); Rose, Tricia, 1994, *Black Noise: Rap Music and Black Culture in Contemporary America* (Middletown, CT: Wesleyan University Press); White, Miles, 2011, *From Jim Crow to Jay-Z: Race, Rap, and the Performance of Masculinity* (Urbana: University of Illinois Press).

REMUS, UNCLE

Uncle Remus was a "human syndicate" created by Joel Chandler Harris from several black storytellers he had met while working from 1862 to 1866 as a printer's devil on Joseph Addison Turner's Turnwold Plantation outside Eatonton in Putnam County, Middle Georgia. Ultimately taking his name from Rome's Romulus and Remus legend, the narrator's more immediate namesake was an elderly black gardener Harris met in Forsyth, Georgia. While serving as associate editor of the *Atlanta Constitution*, Harris wrote several newspaper dialect sketches that portrayed

Uncle Remus as a reluctant city dweller. When Harris began telling his newspaper readers **Brer Rabbit** rural black dialect tales, his stories proved to be so popular that in 1880 Harris published *Uncle Remus: His Songs and His Sayings*, which was a volume of these **folktales** together with songs and pithy sayings gathered from slaves on plantations and Atlanta street sketches. Harris would publish *Nights with Uncle Remus* in 1883 and four more volumes of Remus stories during his lifetime, including, in 1895, a revised, A. B. Frost–illustrated edition of his first book. Two more volumes would appear posthumously, followed in 1955 by *The Complete Tales of Uncle Remus,* a collection of all 185 tales edited by Richard Chase.

As Robert Hemenway notes, Uncle Remus has been one of the most enduring characters in American literature, popular culture, or folklore, much like **Aunt Jemima**. Harris was a conservative white male newspaperman writing for mostly white readers during Reconstruction and post-Reconstruction, and his creation, Uncle Remus, is extremely complex. Uncle Remus is actually only one of several narrators created by Harris, but he is the most well-developed one. In *Nights with Uncle Remus*, three other black narrators are created and also tell folktales: Aunt Tempy, the uppity and privileged cook in the big house; 'Tildy, the often-sassy house maid; and Daddy Jack, an elderly **Gullah** black shaman from the Sea Islands of Georgia who performs stories complexly counterpointed with musical themes. Remus's character gradually evolves in the later Uncle Remus collections, even as his young white listener grows up and marries, eventually sending his son to learn at the knee of the seemingly ageless old man, as he himself had done a generation earlier.

The Uncle Remus character was one of many depictions of black people created during the Reconstruction era that promoted the romantic, southern, white fantasy that slaves loved slavery, adored their masters, and preferred to remain in subservient roles on plantations rather than moving north, owning their own land, and/or developing their own communities and economic ventures. Hemenway writes in the Introduction to the 1982 edition:

> Uncle Remus was created by an author with a sentimental attachment to a plantation memory. Bald, bearded, bespectacled, Remus is a former slave who does odd jobs around the plantation after emancipation. He tells his stories night after night to a little white boy, son of a plantation owner, unfolding to him in grandfatherly fashion the "mysteries of plantation lore." Remus has, Harris tells, "nothing but pleasant memories of the discipline of slavery." This fictional creation of a white Southerner was welcomed by an audience that wanted to believe Remus was a representative of his race; Uncle Remus is a cousin of those nineteenth-century minstrels who blackened their faces to entertain with jokes and songs. He is, in a way, white. (Hemenway, 8)

Unfortunately, the fantasy of black characters and attitudes toward slavery did not disappear with the passing of Reconstruction, or even with the changes that occurred in American society as a result of the civil rights movement. The immense and continued popularity of Uncle Remus suggests that the narrative of the happy slave still competes with more realistic, historical evidence about the slavery experience. But Uncle Remus is more complex than even his role in the romantic portrayal of slavery would suggest. He served as a shadow side of Harris's personality, referred to by Harris as "the other fellow." In a letter to his daughter, Harris wrote:

> You know, all of us have two entities, or personalities. That is the reason you see and hear persons "talking to themselves." They are talking to the "other fellow." I have often asked my "other fellow" where he gets all his information and how he can remember, in the nick of time, things I have forgotten long ago; but he never satisfies my curiosity. Sometimes I laugh heartily at what he writes . . . it is not my writing at all; it is my "other fellow" doing the work and I am getting all the credit for it. He is a creature hard to understand, but, so far as I can understand him, he's a very sour, surly fellow until I give him an opportunity to guide my pen in subjects congenial to him; whereas, I am, as you know, jolly, good-natured, and entirely harmless.
>
> Now, my "other fellow," I am convinced, would do some damage if I didn't give him an opportunity to work off his energy in the way he delights. (Hemenway, 11)

We learn from further research on Harris's life that his other fellow is essentially Uncle Remus, and that Harris retreats to this shadow self in order to overcome his pathological shyness and to be able to converse with others. The "other fellow," though, speaks in black dialect and performs in black mannerisms. According to Hemenway, "Harris apparently had a deep need to imagine himself as Uncle Remus. When the 'other fellow' took over his writing in the voice of Uncle Remus, that fellow was a black man of Harris' childhood, a plantation figure who told stories that Harris' mind had long forgotten" (16). Harris often referred to himself as Uncle Remus, signed his letters as Uncle Remus, and was referred to by the U.S. president as Uncle Remus. Hemenway has suggested that Uncle Remus was, then, a kind of minstrel or blackface character created by Harris out of a set of complex psychological and social factors.

There has been consistent controversy over the character of Uncle Remus, and the response to the character often depends on the critic's point of view. Linguists, for instance, have been impressed with the accuracy of black dialect captured and reproduced by Harris. Other critics are extremely critical of the earlier Uncle Remus but feel that his character evolves in latter presentations that transcend mere stereotype. Undeniably, one of the appeals of Uncle Remus is that the stories, along with the romantic setting in which the elderly black man is telling tales to a little white boy, evoke a sense of "racial utopia in which black and white love one another and share a childhood" (Hemenway, 19). As such, however well-developed Uncle Remus may be, he remains a rhetorical symbol of black servility that has historically placated white fears about black anger and retribution and has been a salve for white guilt. In an important symbolic move, author and folklorist Julius Lester published four volumes of Brer Rabbit tales, dropping the Uncle Remus character and narrating the tales himself.

The Uncle Remus tales are Harris's rendering of African American **trickster** stories about the exploits of Brer Rabbit, **Brer Fox**, and other "creeturs." Florence Baer has confirmed that two-thirds of these celebrated trickster tales—which comprise the largest gathering of African American folktales published in the 19th century— derive their deep structures and primary motifs from African folktales that were brought to the New World and then retold and elaborated upon by African American slaves living in the southeastern United States. The remaining stories have their roots in European and **Native American** folklore, but stories about the rabbit and hare as tricksters appear widely in both Eastern and Western cultures.

The Brer Rabbit stories have been translated into at least 30 foreign languages and have had an impressively wide influence on writers and on popular culture, generally. Writers indebted to Harris include Mark Twain, Charles Chesnutt, Zora Neale Hurston, Flannery O'Connor, William Faulkner, Ralph Ellison, Toni Morrison, and Van Dyke Parks and Julius Lester (who have retold the Uncle Remus tales in richly illustrated, multivolume sets). Many writers and intellectuals during the Harlem Renaissance, however, were upset with Harris's presuming to speak for the African American folk experience. Eatonton's other famous literary personality, Alice Walker, argues that Harris effectively stole a major part of the black folk legacy from its authentic African American creators. Harris's stories have been critiqued for their racial humor, more appropriate, at times, for the minstrel stage than for serious folklore recreation. Robert Hemenway sees Uncle Remus, in some episodes, in the same tradition with Aunt Jemima; but he also advises readers not to dismiss the tales in protest of the racist context in which they are presented.

On one narrative level, Uncle Remus appears to be telling only entertaining animal tales, drawn nostalgically from the pre–Civil War, Old **South** plantation tradition, which typically highlight the stupidity of the physically stronger animals. In the introduction to his first volume of Uncle Remus tales, however, Harris acknowledges the allegorical significance of the stories he sought to retell. Clearly, Brer Rabbit is the black slave's alter ego and trickster hero, and the so-called stronger animals represent the white slave owners. On deeper rhetorical, symbolical, and archetypal levels, furthermore, Uncle Remus's role is to initiate his young white listener into the complex realities of adult life. Yet at the same time, Uncle Remus has been a rhetorical strategy for educating entire generations of readers about the destructive power plays and status struggles among members of the animal kingdom who clearly represent socially and ethnically different, jealous, contentious, and even openly warring members of the human race itself.

Readers and listeners are challenged to find the value in stories that contain important messages about human beings, while remaining aware of the complicated and often negative social elements reflected in the character Uncle Remus.

R. Bruce Bickley Jr.

See also: Briar Patch; Storytelling

Further Reading

Baer, Florence E., 1981, *Sources and Analogues of the Uncle Remus Tales* (Helsinki: Folklore Fellows Communications); Bickley, R. Bruce, Jr., 1981, *Critical Essays on Joel Chandler Harris* (Boston: G. K. Hall) [see especially Louis D. Rubin Jr., "Uncle Remus and the Ubiquitous Rabbit," Darwin T. Turner, "Daddy Joel Harris and His Old-Time Darkies," and Bernard Wolfe, "Uncle Remus and the Malevolent Rabbit": Take a Limber-toe Gemmun fer ter Jump Jim Crow"]; Bickley, R. Bruce, Jr., 2000, *Joel Chandler Harris: A Biography and Critical Study* (Lincoln, NE: iUniverse); Bickley, John T., and R. Bruce

Bickley Jr., 2003, "Folklore Performance and the Legacy of Joel Chandler Harris," in *Nights with Uncle Remus* (New York: Penguin Classics); Brasch, Walter M., 2000, *Brer Rabbit, Uncle Remus, and the "Cornfield Journalist": The Tale of Joel Chandler Harris* (Atlanta: Mercer University Press); Cartwright, Keith, 2001, *Reading Africa into American Literature: Epics, Fables, and Gothic Tales* (Lexington: University Press of Kentucky); Chase, Richard, ed., 1955, *The Complete Tales of Uncle Remus* (Boston: Houghton Mifflin); Harris, Julia Collier, 1918, *The Life and Letters of Joel Chandler Harris* (Boston: Houghton Mifflin); Hemenway, Robert, 1982, "Introduction, Author, Teller, and Hero," in *Uncle Remus: His Songs and His Sayings* (New York: Penguin Classics); Inge, Thomas M., 2012, "Walt Disney's Song of the South and the Politics of Animation," *The Journal of American Culture* 35 (3): 219–230; Keenan, Hugh T., 1993, *Dearest Chums and Partners: Joel Chandler Harris's Letters to His Children. A Domestic Biography* (Athens: University of Georgia Press); Okpewho, Isidore, 1994, "The Cousins of Uncle Remus," in *The Black Columbiad: Defining Moments in African American Literature and Culture*, ed. Werner Sollors and Maria Diedrich (Cambridge: Harvard University Press); Peterson, Christopher, 2011, "Slavery's Bestiary: Joel Chandler Harris's Uncle Remus Tales," *Paragraph* 34 (1): 30–47; Piqueras, Fraile, María del Rosario, 2007, "Harris's Short Animal Stories: A Socio-linguistic Point of View," *Rœ L: Revista Electrónica De Lingüística Aplicada* 6: 31–40; Sundquist, Eric, 1993, *To Wake the Nations: Race in the Making of American Literature* (Cambridge: Harvard University Press); Wagner, Bryan, 2009, *Disturbing the Peace: Black Culture and the Police Power After Slavery* (Cambridge, Mass: Harvard University Press); Walker, Alice, 1988, "The Dummy in the Window: Joel Chandler Harris and the Invention of Uncle Remus," in *Living by the Word: Selected Writings, 1973–1987* (New York: Harcourt Brace Jovanovich), pp. 25–32; Walker, Alice, 1981, "Uncle Remus: No Friend of Mine," *Southern Exposure* 9 (2): 29–31;

RING SHOUT

The North American ring shout can be defined as a religious service that includes singing, percussion, **dance**-like movement, and heightened emotional expression, and that takes place in a ring formation. The shouters steadily increase the intensity of their devotions until they begin to feel the presence of the Holy Spirit in their midst. Once the spirit has been invoked, the **shout** becomes an expression of communion.

When describing the ring shout, many commentators have observed a series of key factors that make this form of group religious song and bodily movement unmistakable. First, the song sung during the performance of the shout is always in a call-and-response form. Second, the singing is repetitious, rhythmic, and sung with escalating fervor often for an hour or more. Third, during the singing, worshippers often move single file around in a counterclockwise direction. Fourth, when moving around in the circle, participants worship with feet, arms, bellies, hips—in fact, with their whole bodies. Fifth, the ring shout was always observed to take place after a formal preaching service or **prayer** meeting had concluded. Finally, many of those who have observed ring shouts—including John and Alan Lomax, James Weldon Johnson, W. E. B. Du Bois, Lydia Parrish, and the authors of the influential 19th-century book titled *Slave Songs of the United States* (1951/1867)—have considered them to be of West African origin.

Traditional ring shout dance, Savannah, Georgia. (Courtesy of the Georgia Historical Society, 1349-179-3002-01)

In the past, ring shouts seem to have been mostly associated with the coastal areas of South Carolina and Georgia. Historians have made this association in part because during the Civil War something of a rehearsal for Reconstruction took place on offshore islands of South Carolina before the Confederacy had been defeated. During this period, educators who came to work with the freedmen on the Sea Islands wrote and published detailed descriptions of the phenomenon. Subsequent generations of folklorists followed the path these early observers blazed. Yet the ring shout also thrived in the mid-Atlantic area surrounding the Chesapeake and Delaware Bays, which was, along with the coastal Southeast, a hearth area for African American culture in general. Other observers, however, have noted ring shouts as far west as Texas and in the large cities of the North.

Today, many scholars consider the ring shout to have been the most important religious ritual of enslaved Africans and the first generation of freedmen. Based on research with contemporary ring shout groups in the Chesapeake Bay area of Maryland and Delaware, the present author has concluded that the centrality of the ring shout to early African American Christianity has its roots in the sociological patterns of the rural African American communities that nurtured it. From the 19th century on, the cohesion of rural African American communities of this area was maintained by traditions of economic and social reciprocity. When one family needed to harvest corn, for example, others in the area would come help them. In return the recipients of such aid would help the others who helped them. The social pattern of mutual aid extended into religious life. When one church held a camp meeting where ring shouts would be featured, for example, leading members of the prayer meeting groups that featured ring shouts (called singing and praying bands) from other churches came to help build the spirit, holding their own services on the campgrounds of the host church. In return, the singing and praying band of the host church would visit the camp meetings of those who visited and performed at its event.

The sociological aspect of this tradition of mutual aid also had an aesthetic and spiritual dimension. Aesthetically, mutual aid is articulated in the call-and-response nature of the ring shout songs that the singing and praying bands would sing. Spiritually, the traditions of mutual aid in society—in which each individual, each family, and each church is a recipient of the help of the others during the course of a year—can be represented by a ring of worshippers in motion, representing a harmonious community in action. Finally, singing and praying band members commonly maintain that the spirit "runs from heart to heart and breast to breast." This spiritual solidarity expressed by the ring shout is the culmination of the traditions of grassroots social solidarity.

All of these patterns of mutuality articulate African-derived attitudes about the ideal relationship of the individual to the group. While these cultural patterns may be of African origin, this kind of reciprocity proved adaptive during the oppressive periods of slavery and its aftermath in the American **South**. This is why the ring shout became a central religious service in slavery and afterward.

Finally, participants held the shout after the formal preaching service or prayer service for several reasons. First, the ring shout took shape at a time when those living in slavery on rural plantations or farms had little access to officials of the more institutional church. When the institutional church became established in these communities, it often frowned on the supposedly unorthodox ring shout. Thus, the shout was excluded from formal religious practice and held semisecretly after such a service had been completed. But the ring shout was also an expression of community and communion. As the culmination of a service and the highest expression of religious sensibility of its participants, it belonged at the end of formal religious service like an exclamation point belongs at the end of an emphatic sentence.

Jonathan C. David

See also: Spirituals

Further Reading

Allen, William Francis, Charles P. Ware, and Lucy McKim Garrison, eds., 1951 [1867], *Slave Songs of the United States* (New York: Peter Smith); Busia, Abena P. A., 2006, "Ring Shout for the Ancestors," *The Journal of African American History* 91 (4): 372–373; Courlander, Harold, 1963, *Negro Folk Music, U.S.A.* (New York: Columbia University Press); Du Bois, W. E. B. 1996 [1899], *The Philadelphia Negro* (Philadelphia: University of Pennsylvania Press); Floyd, Samuel A., Jr., 1991, "Ring Shout! Literary Studies, Historical Studies, and Black Music Inquiry," *Black Music Research Journal* 11: 265–287; Hazzard-Donald, Katrina, 2011, "Hoodoo Religion and American Dance Traditions:

Rethinking the Ring Shout," *Journal of Pan African Studies* 4 (6): 194–212; Johnson, James Weldon, and J. Rosamond Johnson, eds., 1977 [1925], *The Books of American Negro Spirituals* (New York: Da Capo Press); Lomax, John A., and Alan Lomax, 1947, *Folksong U.S.A.* (New York: Duell, Sloan & Pearce); Parrish, Lydia, 1942, *Slave Songs of the Georgia Sea Islands* (New York: Creative Age Press); Rose, Willie Lee, 1964, *Rehearsal for Reconstruction: The Port Royal Experiment* (New York: Bobbs-Merrill Co.); Thompson, Katrina Dyonne, 2014, *Ring Shout, Wheel About: The Racial Politics of Music and Dance in North American Slavery* (Urbana: University of Illinois Press); White, Bryson C. M., 2014, "Death of the Ring Shout," *Black Theology: An International Journal* 12 (1): 44–57.

RUMORS

Rumors are a folk genre of speculative talk. Daryl Cumber Dance also defines rumors as "beliefs that circulate widely with no discernable source and with at least a degree of believability, usually transmitted orally" (p. 616). Rumors are traditionally created and maintained by word of mouth, and scholars such as Patricia Turner have collected and analyzed them. Turner examines numerous rumors within African American culture and explores how they, like the related genres of **legend**, **mythology**, and tales, have affected the African American worldview.

In *I Heard It through the Grapevine: Rumor in African American Culture*, Turner describes how rumors are often created as a result of fear, trauma, or ambiguity. She also suggests that rumors serve important functions within the communities in which they are found and offer windows into the fears and tensions impacting particular groups. For instance, one of the earliest rumors among enslaved Africans was that the white slave traders were cannibals. At the same time, similar rumors circulated among Europeans about African people. Such rumors demonstrate key functions of this genre of folklore. First, they address fears, anxieties, and uncertainty. They also help to reinforce the boundaries between one group and another and to identify one's own group by ascribing unfavorable characteristics to others. In other words, "those people do that, but we don't." Finally, rumors help to justify social customs and political policies. For whites, these cannibal rumors helped to justify the slave trade and the inhumane treatment of the slaves. For Africans, the rumors were an effort to make sense out of a traumatic experience and served as an expression of their deepest fears about their uncertain fates.

During the slavery period, slave owners utilized elaborate methods to exploit beliefs and rumors of the slaves. For instance, whites took advantage of the slaves' belief in spirits, ghosts, and **conjuring** to make slaves fearful of rebellion and attempts at escape. An ex-slave stated how "[slaves] were very superstitious as our masters would tell us tales to scare us and make us do nothing but what he told us to do" (Fry, 63). Slave owners went so far as to dress up like ghosts or monsters to terrorize slaves.

Whites also spread rumors to create tensions among slaves. On the plantation, white masters claimed that certain slaves "were bad Negroes" (ibid., 53). This "kept slaves mad at one another" and "provoked suspicion," thus undermining plantation revolts and uprisings (ibid., 53). Slave owners sowed the seeds for rumors about

Native Americans to discourage slaves from fleeing and seeking refuge among Native groups. Because tribes often harbored runaway slaves, whites manufactured stories that described "bizarre, painful, and slow deaths suffered by victims of Indian capture" (ibid., 50).

Following the emancipation, rumors emerged among African Americans reflecting primarily their suspicion and distrust of the government and white authorities, as well as the deeply held belief that the white government actively sought their genocide. Rumors furthermore focused on the experiences of segregation and discrimination against African American people. Such sentiments are understandable given the historical experiences of African Americans, beginning with enslavement, the reneged promises for **40 acres and a mule** that occurred shortly after emancipation, and continuous terrorism at the hands the Ku Klux Klan, law enforcement agencies, and other white American citizenry since that time. Hence rumors took on additional functions as cautionary narratives and stories substantiating negative beliefs about the government and white America in general. For example, it was rumored that, because of his ethnicity, the famous African American boxer, Jack Johnson, was denied a seat aboard the Titanic. Such rumors illustrate the "degree of believability" and even truth that a historically inaccurate story can contain.

Contemporary rumors continue to implicate such groups as the Ku Klux Klan, the FBI, the CIA, and large corporations in a variety of assaults, abductions, murders, poisonings, and assassinations of and conspiracies against black people. Rumors emerged, for instance, linking the CIA and FBI to the Atlanta child murders of the late 1970s and early 1980s.

Turner notes that the unfortunate aspect of rumors is that they often lead to a perpetuation of cultural stereotypes and distrust rather than facilitating steps toward resolving these social ills. Hence social events are often read through the lens of rumors, which predispose African Americans to draw certain conclusions, sometimes erroneously. It seems likely, though, that rumors will continue to exist as long as racism continues to be a defining experience of African American life.

Gladys L. Knight

See also: Folktales; Legends

Further Reading

Dance, Daryl Cumber, ed., 2002, *From My People: 400 Years of African American Folklore* (New York: W. W. Norton); Fry, Gladys-Marie, 1975, *Night Riders in Black Folk History* (Knoxville: University of Tennessee Press); Kerr, Audrey Elisa, 2006, *The Paper Bag Principle: Class, Colorism, and Rumor and the Case of Black Washington, D.C.* (Knoxville: University of Tennessee Press); Turner, Patricia A., 1993, *I Heard It through the Grapevine: Rumor in African American Culture* (Berkeley: University of California Press).

S

SACRED STEEL GUITAR

Sacred steel is the popular term for a vibrant African American tradition of sacred music played on the electric steel guitar practiced in more than 300 small Holiness-Pentecostal churches found in nearly 30 states. The tradition has been passed down through four generations.

"The House of God, Which Is the Church of the Living God, Pillar and Ground of the Truth, Inc., Keith Dominion" and the "Church of the Living God, Which He Purchased with His Own Blood, Jewell Dominion" are two related churches. In the late 1930s, musicians who heard the electric steel guitar played by Hawaiian artists took up the instrument and began to play it in worship services. Brothers Troman and Willie Eason of Philadelphia, Pennsylvania, and Lorenzo Harrison of Ocala, Florida, were among the earliest church musicians. Influential second-generation steel guitarists include Henry Nelson of Florida and New York, and Maurice "Ted" Beard Jr. and Calvin Cooke, both of Detroit.

Because their belief system emphasizes individual conversion and avoids the world outside their church—even other Holiness-Pentecostal churches—the steel guitar traditions of the Keith and Jewell Dominion churches evolved for nearly 60 years with a minimum of external influences. The Keith and Jewell Dominions have similar but distinct styles. In the early 1970s, some Keith Dominion steel guitarists began to play the more complex pedal steel guitar, a configuration of the instrument which continues to gain favor in that church. The older eight string "lap," or "Hawaiian," nonpedal instrument remains predominant in the Jewell Dominion.

Over the years, the electric steel guitar became the dominant musical instrument in both churches, albeit it has slipped somewhat in the Jewell Dominion in recent years. The instrument might be seen occasionally in other African American churches, but only in the Keith and Jewell Dominion churches has it achieved the position of dominance. While both traditions are rooted in Hawaiian popular music and have been influenced by country music and **blues**, the sound is distinctly African American gospel. Characteristics of the music include close imitation of ornamented African American gospel vocal technique and rhythmic "frams" or stums. The Keith Dominion steel guitarists are especially noted for the use of elaborate melismas, often executed on one string. Melismas played on a treble string imitate the singing voice; those executed on a bass string result in a dramatic "moan."

The steel guitarist leads the church band to provide extended periods of intense, rhythmic "praise" or "**shout**" music to aid congregants in their efforts to become infused with the Holy Ghost. Congregants **dance** ecstatically without partners, and they clap and shout. The presence of the Holy Ghost may be manifested by involuntary body movements; glossolalia, or speaking in tongues; and sometimes fainting, or "falling out." A steel guitarist who can consistently work a congregation into wholesale spirit possession is valued as a great asset to worship services.

The steel guitarists also work closely with ministers and other speakers to provide dramatic emphasis to **sermons** and testimonies. In the Keith Dominion, the steel guitarist leads the band in a swinging medley of instrumental **spirituals** as ushers lead congregants in a jaunty procession past the offertory collection plates placed near the altar. The steel guitarist also leads the band to provide a musical backdrop for periods of meditation and to accompany vocalists and choirs.

Musicians learn informally by watching, listening, and imitating. A large percentage of steel guitarists begin their musical careers as drummers. Praise music is improvised over a few conventionalized core musical structures. New tunes or "licks," which are successful in moving congregations, pass quickly through the national network of musicians. Although female congregants generally greatly outnumber males and many females are in leadership positions within both dominions, there are very few female steel guitarists.

The Keith Dominion is the larger of the two organizations, with about 8,000 members who attend approximately 200 small churches in more than 20 states, primarily in the East. Members of the Keith and Jewell Dominion churches emphasize the importance of marrying within the church community. With such a small pool of membership to draw from, nearly everyone is related.

In the 1990s, recordings of several of the musicians were released by Arhoolie Records and distributed internationally. The recordings were heralded by many as an important American vernacular music "discovery." The term "Sacred Steel," taken from the title of the initial Arhoolie release, came into popular use in the public sector. Sacred Steel bands such as the Campbell Brothers of Rochester, New York, the Lee Boys of Florida, and, most notably, Robert Randolph of New Jersey, now tour internationally. In 2003 Randolph signed a rockstar–magnitude recording contract with Warner Brothers. He was nominated for two Grammys in 2004. The popularity of Sacred Steel music in the public sector has influenced many youngsters within the churches to play the instrument, and today the tradition is probably stronger than ever.

Robert L. Stone

Further Reading

Baer, Hans, and Singer, Merrill, 2002, *African American Religion: Varieties of Protest and Accommodation*, 2nd ed. (Knoxville: University of Tennessee Press); Bucuvalas, Tina, 2012, *The Florida Folklife Reader* (Jackson: University Press of Mississippi); DuPree, Sherry Sherrod, 1989, *Biographical Dictionary of African-American Holiness-Pentecostals, 1880–1990* (Washington, DC: Middle Atlantic Regional Press); Hays, Cedric J., and Robert Laughton, 1992, *Gospel Records, 1943–1969: A Black Music Discography* (Milford, NH: Big Nickel Publications); Lewis, Meharry H., 2002, Mary Lena Lewis Tate: *"A Street Called Straight"—The Ten Most Dynamic and Productive Black Female Holiness Preachers of the Twentieth Century* (Nashville, TN: The New and Living Way Publishing Co.); Payne, Wardell J., ed., 1995, *Directory of African American Religious Bodies,*

2nd ed. (Washington, DC: Howard University Press); Ruymar, Lorene, 1996, *The Hawaiian Steel Guitar and Its Great Hawaiian Musicians* (Anaheim Hills, CA: Centerstream Publishing); Stone, Robert L., 2010, *Music in American Life: Sacred Steel: Inside an African American Steel Guitar Tradition* (Champaign: University of Illinois Press).

SASS/SASSY

This term indicates a quality of bold assertiveness and defiance usually associated with African American girls and women. "Sass" functions as both a verb and a noun and is also used in adjective form as "sassy." For example, someone might say, "She sure is sassy," or "She is full of sass," or "Don't sass your teacher." Sass is akin to "spunk" and connotes someone who is bold, spirited, and refuses to submit to authority. When applied to children or young women, sass shares similarities with terms such as "mannish," which are applied to young men. Such terms suggest that young people are behaving or interacting with adults inappropriately, that they are being too grown up. In particular, sass refers to verbal transgressions of authority, such as "talking back" to adults. When applied to women, sass is a traditional strategy employed by black women when negotiating with authority figures or in their general attitudes and demeanors. In social interactions, sass can be a way of extemporaneously asserting self-worth and personal dignity through spontaneous verbal utterances intended to shift the balance of power away from another person who might dominate or marginalize the woman. In public performances, sass can be an attitude that communicates that the woman is proud, assertive, and not going to take any kind of abuse or domination.

In African American oral tradition, "sass" came to refer to a mode of discourse that black women employed when negotiating their roles within their own families, as well as within American society. Sometimes utilized as a means of self-defense and, when necessary, as a verbal weapon, sass served as a mechanism by which black women might overcome the constraints placed upon them by their gender- and race-defined societal roles. Within African American culture, sass provided black women with an effective means of "talking back" to authority figures (primarily slave owners but also fathers or husbands) in protest of unfair or inhumane treatment. For black women, sass represented an act of protest whose primary purpose was to foster action rather than reflection. During the era of slavery, black women utilized sass principally in their attempts to negotiate their own physical survival, whereas after emancipation, black women increasingly used sass to achieve social and spiritual fulfillment.

The idea of "talking back" can be applied not only to verbal interactions but also to public presentations of self as well as performance styles. For example, legendary blues artist Bessie Smith embodied the essence of sass in the lyrics of her songs, her vocal style and nuances, and mannerisms on stage. Other performers who have projected sassy attitudes include Mamie Smith, Nina Simone, and Tina Turner. Sass can be conveyed through nonverbal channels, such as gestures (e.g., hands placed on the hips, arms crossed, or a defiant glare) and costuming (a hat cocked to the side).

Sass has been transformed in African American fiction and poetry, as well as in autobiographical writings, by black female authors. According to scholar Joanne Braxton, sass infuses several important literary texts written by black women, including Harriet Jacobs's *Incidents in the Life of a Slave Girl*, Zora Neale Hurston's *Dust Tracks on a Road*, and Maya Angelou's *I Know Why the Caged Bird Sings*. Characters such as Janie (Hurston's *Their Eyes Were Watching God*) and the various women speakers in Ntozake Shange's *For Colored Girls Who Have Considered Suicide/ When the Rainbow Is Enuf* represent women whose growth involves learning to be sassier. Sass was also an important element of black women's poetry of the Black Arts Movement, illustrated by poets such as Nikki Giovanni and Sonia Sanchez, whose work reflected a militant anger and defiance. In their written efforts to empower themselves within a marginalizing society, black female writers adapted the mode of verbal persuasion inherent to sass (in which attitudes of righteousness and moral outrage were directly and emotionally communicated), yet their writings were directed toward a general audience, which signified a shift from the traditional usage of sass primarily within specific interpersonal contexts.

Specific origins of the term "sass" are difficult to determine. Theories have been suggested, but they may be in the realm of folklore. For example, one theory posits that the word "sass" was derived from the name of the West African "sassy tree," whose bark, according to African mythology, produced a poisonous liquid concoction that the wives of the male trickster god Exu were forced to drink after they were accused of being witches. *Merriam Webster's Collegiate Dictionary* suggests that the term is derived from "sauce" and the vernacular use of "saucy" to describe a spirited person. Such theories, though, remain just that, as thus far no scholars have focused on the etymology of the term. Whatever its origin, sass remains a key concept in African American folklore.

Ted Olson

Further Reading

Braxton, Joanne M., 1989, *Black Women Writing Autobiography: A Tradition within a Tradition* (Philadelphia: Temple University Press); Dunn, Stephane, 2008, *"Baad Bitches" and Sassy Supermamas: Black Power Action Films"* (Urbana: University of Illinois Press); Jarmon, Laura C., 2003, *Wishbone: Reference and Interpretation in Black Folk Narrative* (Knoxville: University of Tennessee Press); Stevens, Joyce West, 2009 [2002], *Smart and Sassy: The Strengths of Inner City Black Girls* (New York: Oxford University Press).

SEA ISLANDS

See Gullah

SERMONS

Sermons are a form of religious oration and are perhaps the most prominent narrative and performance genre in African American culture. The genre developed in the slavery period as a synthesis of white evangelical influences, elements of

African oral performance, and reservoirs of African American creativity, and has continued to thrive and evolve. Research on the African American sermon tradition has tended to focus on three major related aspects of the form: content, structure, and performance styles.

The content of African American sermons has historically centered on biblical stories and has been very applicable to the everyday lives of black people. Preachers have primarily "dealt with the problems and realities confronting [their] people, as they cope with the demands and stress of daily living" (Smitherman, 87). Most often, preachers have favored stories that contain dramatic events and that lend themselves to allegorical comparisons to the social circumstances confronting African Americans. Until around the early 20th century, stories were largely derived from books of the Old Testament, but moving into the 20th century, African American sermons focused more and more on the New Testament. Popular Old Testament stories or dramatic motifs upon which sermons have been traditionally based include Daniel in the lion's den; Ezekiel in the valley of dry bones; the various episodes of the enslavement and freedom of the Israelites; Shadrach, Meshach, and Abednego in the fiery furnace; Jonah in the belly of the whale; the tower of Babel; and various episodes from the book of Genesis. Popular New Testament motifs include the crucifixion and episodes from the book of Revelation. The themes of political and personal liberation have been most prominent in black sermons and reflect the insistence of black **preachers** on using texts that speak to issues that dominate black consciousness.

Structurally, sermons include an opening, a climactic middle, and a closing. Preachers often begin with a prayer, a spontaneous song, and/or a passage from the Bible. During the opening part of the sermon, the preacher is usually in a talking mode. After reading the biblical passage upon which the sermon is based, he or she spends some time talking about it, sometimes giving historical context for the passage. This part of the sermon, which uses a more intellectual, "teacherly" mode, gradually gives way to the next phase, in which the preacher becomes more animated and dramatic. The second part of the sermon is typically more emotional. It is performed through the use of dramatic gestures, shouts, and other devices intended to evoke emotional responses from the congregation. The call-and-response pattern so prevalent in many African American traditions characterize this section of the sermon, as members of the congregation respond to the rhythmic chants of the preacher with shouts and other formulaic phrases. In the closing section of the sermon, the preacher gradually "cools down" and enters a mode that is somewhere between the talking and dramatic modes. The "doors of the church are opened" during this phase, and those who are not members are invited to come to the front and declare their commitment to join. Typically this last part of the sermon is accompanied by music and sometimes by singing from the choir and congregation.

The performances of sermons typically contain a number of stylistic features and word play. For example, repetition begins early on, when the preacher announces the title of the sermon and then goes on to reiterate it at selected moments throughout the sermon. It is also apparent in portions of the second part of the sermon in which certain phrases are repeated as chanted lines. At other times, words, catchy phrases, and even sounds are repeated to emphasize certain messages and intensify the speech (Smitherman, 142–143). The preacher may even repeatedly ask his congregation, "Can I get a witness?" if the audience is too quiet. Word play encompasses a wide variety of devices, such as dialect or vernacular speech, **signifying**, metaphors, florid language, rhymes, chants, tone, and talk-singing. According to Smitherman, "The preacher [may or may not be] university-educated, but he must be able to 'talk that talk' (preach in Black English style and lingo)" (p. 90). Historically, "many black preachers swung easily between congregations of rough, dialect-speaking field hands and congregations of house slaves, urban slaves, free Negroes, and even whites. Most impressively, many were able to preach effectively to all at once" (Genovese, 268).

Another commonly employed device in sermons is signifying. Signifying is an indirect method of commenting on a topic or insulting someone. It is usually done to demonstrate one's verbal dexterity and to generate humor. For example, one preacher signified during a sermon when he said, "Y'all know, the Lord sees and watches everythang we do; whether we be in the church or out. And I just wanta let y'all know one thang: Everybody talkin bout Heaven ain goin there!" (Smitherman, 120). Such comments generate laughter and applause and succeed in conveying a subtle message to a specific person in the congregation without drawing attention to that individual.

Sermons are sometimes embellished with live instruments, spontaneous outcries, and religious shouts or dances. The preacher himself may embellish a sermon with facial gestures and expressive body movements. The following description suggests the dynamism of the sermon performance and how the words are only one of many levels of texts occurring throughout:

> The successful minister makes use not only of his powerful oratory and his captivating singing voice (he often breaks into song), or leads congregation into song, but all sorts of body movements: he claps his hands, prances, dances, rocks, jumps up and down and stomps, often waving his hands frenetically. He suddenly freezes, then he dramatically starts again (sometimes with a loud clap of the hands and a sudden shift in the direction in which he was moving). He may even leave the pulpit and move through the audience, comforting, cajoling, challenging, inviting, accusing. His hand gestures and facial expressions add impact and often humor to his delivery. (Dance, 252)

Sermon styles have been one of the foundations upon which many other forms of black oratory rest. For example, the performance styles of **blues** singers, such as B. B. King or Muddy Waters, or that of rhythm and blues artists, like James Brown, draw upon the aesthetics of the black sermon.

Gladys L. Knight

See also: Spirituals

Further Reading

Brewer, J. Mason, 1968, *American Negro Folklore* (Chicago: Quadrangle Books); Costen, Melva Wilson, 2007 [1993], *African American Christian Worship*, 2nd ed. (Nashville:

Abingdon Press); Courlander, Harold, 1976, *A Treasury of Afro-American Folklore* (New York: Crown Publishers); Dance, Daryl Cumber, ed., 2002, *From My People: 400 Years of African American Folklore* (New York: W. W. Norton); Genovese, Eugene D., 1972, *Roll, Jordan, Roll: The World the Slaves Made* (New York: Random House); Hobson, Christopher Z., 2012, *The Mount of Vision: African American Prophetic Tradition, 1800–1950* (New York: Oxford University Press); LaRue, Cleophus, J., 2011, *I Believe I'll Testify: The Art of African American Preaching* (Louisville, KY: Westminister John Knox Press); Pinn, Anthony B., Stephen C. Finley, and Torin Alexander, 2009, *African American Religious Cultures* (Santa Barbara, CA: ABC-CLIO); Rosenberg, Bruce, 1988, *Can These Bones Live? The Art of the American Folk Preacher* (Urbana: University of Illinois Press); Simmons, Martha, and Frank A. Thomas, eds., 2010, *Preaching with Sacred Fire: An Anthology of African American Sermons, 1750 to the Present* (New York: W. W. Norton); Smitherman, Geneva, 1977, *Talkin and Testifyin: The Language of Black America* (Detroit: Wayne State University Press); Turner, Henry McNeal, and Andre E. Johnson, 2010, *An African American Pastor Before and During the American Civil War* (Lewiston: Edwin Mellen Press); White, Shane, and Graham J. White, 2005, *The Sounds of Slavery: Discovering African American History through Songs, Sermons, and Speech* (Boston: Beacon Press).

SHOUT

African American shouts are both a reference to **dance** and movement related to religious worship and a verbal or musical utterance asserting an African/African American interpretative frame of meaning.

The "shout" has often been associated with the "**ring shout**," a religious dance performed by slaves and later generations of African Americans. Often performed in **praise houses**, the ring shout was a unique, ecstatic, rhythmic dance or movement where the feet would not cross to distinguish its primarily sacred orientation from more secular movement. Immersed in the African-derived social-rhetorical form of call-and-response, the ring shout asserted both individual and communal African American beliefs and experiences. The ring shout was a channel of movement and communication through which individuals and communities addressed a variety of issues from enslavement to African/African American spiritual and cultural uplift. A contemporary practitioner of this folk/vernacular form is the McIntosh County Shouters.

The term "shout" also refers to more spontaneous, excited responses to **sermons**, singing, or being "touched by the spirit" in African American churches. Shouting could take the form of simple utterances, such as "Amen!" as well as more elaborate expressions such as waving the hands in the air, jumping, dancing, or "getting happy."

The African American shout can be understood as a manifestation of a counter-interpretative lens. Black expressions that exceeded or resisted the interpretative frames of whites, or that were due to the presence of African elements or a content/style that were not acceptable to dominant culture performance expectations and values, were categorized as shouts beyond sense, or as black noise. However, these utterances often reflect the expression of African/African American subjectivity, interiority, and feeling and convey a spirit and understanding beyond the capacity of language to capture.

Geneva Smitherman (1977) discusses the secular use of the shout and its connection to **soul** music concerts. In brief, the shout, like other African American religious practices, migrated to what is considered by scholars as "secular" contexts, as black concert goers have tended to respond to singers in much the same rhetorical fashion that they respond to preachers. The shout has also been used by singers as a metaphor for sex, as noted in John Lee Hooker's, "We're doing the shout." The term has become a standard way of those in the **hip-hop** community of dedicating a song to someone: "I want to give a shout out to all the brothers from Compton." Hence, the shout is not only a religious symbol for a uniquely African-derived form of expression in religious settings, but it is also a way of infusing so-called "secular" contexts with sacred significance. It reflects an African-influenced insistence on a more holistic spirituality that is signified by a willingness to surrender to the spirits, and offers an implicit, negative critique of the more Western, compartmentalized view of religion and identity.

Vorris Nunley

See also: Church, The Black

Further Reading

Cruz, Jon, 1999, *Culture on the Margins: The Black Spiritual and the Rise of American Cultural Interpretation* (Princeton, NJ: Princeton University Press); Rosenbaum, Art, and Johann S. Buis, 1998, *Shout Because You're Free: The African American Ring Shout Tradition in Coastal Georgia* (Athens: University of Georgia Press); Smitherman, Geneva, 1977, *Talkin and Testifyin: The Language of Black America* (Detroit: Wayne State University Press); Thompson, Katrina Dyonne, 2014, *Ring Shout, Wheel About: The Racial Politics of Music and Dance in North American Slavery* (Urbana: University of Illinois Press); White, Bryson C. M., 2014, "Death of the Ring Shout," *Black Theology: An International Journal* 12 (1): 44–57; White, Shane, and Graham J. White, 2005, *The Sounds of Slavery: Discovering African American History through Songs, Sermons, and Speech* (Boston: Beacon Press).

SIGNIFYING

Signifying is a speech act involving indirection. Signifying is a cultural tradition within African American communities that can be expressed and defined in various ways. In "Signifying, Loud-Talking and Marking" (1972), Claudia Mitchell-Kernan addresses several ways in which signifying is used. She explains how Roger D. Abrahams describes signifying as a "**toast**, a carp, a cajole, a needle and lie," as well as a means "to circumvent, make fun, and to trick someone" (Mitchell-Kernan, 310). Mitchell-Kernan points out that these forms of signifying can also refer to shucking and marking, and she also discusses Thomas Kochman's assertion that signifying occurs when "the signifier reports or repeats what someone else has said about the listener" in order to "arouse feelings of anger and hostility," and also when the signifier taunts another person in order "to arouse feelings of embarrassment, shame, frustration, or futility, to diminish someone's status" (ibid., 311). Both Abrahams's and Kochman's notions of signifying are commonly found in the **Signifying Monkey** stories. According to other scholars, signifying also occurs within verbal insult games, such as the **dozens**, sounding, or woofing. Less studied is Mitchell-Kernan's definition, which states that signifying "refers to a way of encoding messages or meanings" (ibid., 309). This definition describes signifying at its essence as it is used in a wide array of communication events, from the preacher's sermon to everyday interactions.

According to Mitchell-Kernan, "signifying involves the recognition and attribution of some implicit content or function which is potentially obscured by the surface content or function" (p. 312). Signifying is also dependent upon the signifier's motive (which varies), how the signifier conveys meaning, and how the target of signifying interprets the message (ibid.). Moreover, signifying allows an individual to express his or her message without having to confront the target directly. The socially acceptable or easily digested message stands as a metaphor for the intended message. In this way, "the apparent meaning of [a] sentence 'signifies' its actual meaning" (ibid., 319). Mitchell-Kernan provides an example of this point in an exchange between a husband and a wife. The husband dresses up for work, which is not his normal routine. The wife asks the husband where he is going. He says that he is going to work. The wife then responds by signifying, "[You're wearing] a suit, tie and white shirt? You didn't tell me you got a promotion" (ibid., 316).

The apparent meaning of this remark is the wife's suggestion that her husband's job now requires him to wear a suit. This serves as an acceptable justification of her husband's suit and tie. Her intended message is "that he is not going to work; moreover, [she believes] he is lying about his destination" (ibid.). This exchange prevents a direct confrontation between the husband and wife. If the husband is savvy, he will know that his wife is suspicious of his behavior and has an opportunity to correct it, thus avoiding a full-blown encounter. In any given signifying act, the signifier must expertly and cautiously allude to his or her real meaning. In the same respect, the target of signifying must be able to identify the signifying remark and interpret the messages within it. The target may save face or receive recognition if he or she is able to signify back. Expert signifiers are adept at using the popular jargon and phrases of the day, and are knowledgeable of the values and shared knowledge within their community. Importantly, the initial signifiers have the advantage since they "[reserve] the right to subsequently insist on the harmless interpretation rather than the provocative one" (ibid., 316).

Signifying has distinct features. These features include the use of humor and the exchange of cultural knowledge and values. Other aspects include audience participation, negative commentary, verbal and nonverbal cues, and stylistic and artistic effect. Humor is often used to disguise the intended message. In another example provided by Mitchell-Kernan, an informant named Barbara jokingly asks, "Are you one of those Negroes who don't eat chitlins?" (ibid., 312). Humor acts as a buffer to Barbara's intended remark, which implies that her target is an assimilationist (ibid., 313). In order to correctly interpret the intended message, the participant must understand that chitlins (**chitterlings**) is a traditional African

American meal and that Mary is expressing her belief, shared by some African Americans, that chitlins are valued in the African American community. Also relevant to this speech act is the signifier's stylistic effect. Mary exemplifies this in the way she words her question rather than simply asking, "Do you like chitlins?"

Mary and Mitchell-Kernan are both present when Barbara poses her question. Mary, in her own defense, responds by signifying back at Barbara:

> That's all I hear lately—soul food, soul food. If you say you don't eat it you get accused of being saditty [affected, considering oneself superior]. (matter of factly) Well, I ate enough black-eyed peas and neckbones during the depression that I can't get too excited over it. I eat prime rib and T-bone because I like to, not because I'm trying to be white. (sincerely) Negroes are constantly trying to find some way to discriminate against each other. If they could once get it in their heads that we are all in this together maybe we could get somewhere in this battle against the man. (Ibid., 312)

Mary's response indirectly assesses what she believes is Barbara's intended message: African Americans who do not eat soul food are acting white. Moreover, "Negroes," in this context, signifies on Barbara. Mary believes Barbara is discriminating against African Americans because their dietary habits are not traditional. She also attempts to unify all African Americans by pitting them against who she believes is the common enemy—"the man." "The Man" is slang for the white power structure.

Mitchell-Kernan offers another example of individuals engaged in signifying. In this example, three young men approach Mitchell-Kernan in a park. One of the men initiates a conversation by saying "Mama, you sho is fine" (p. 318). Mitchell-Kernan jibes, "That ain't no way to talk to your mother" (ibid.). In this statement, "mother" indicates Mitchell-Kernan. Mitchell-Kernan's message implies that the young man is too young to come on to her. The dialog continues with both participants signifying in a casual and witty manner. This exchange is laced with multiple meanings including moments where the young man acknowledges Mitchell-Kernan's adeptness at signifying. Essential to this exchange is Mitchell-Kernan's understanding that the young man "does not expect to be taken seriously" and is "not attempting to engage the hearer in anything other than a conversation. He is merely demonstrating his ability to use persuasive language. He is playing a game, and he expects his addressee and audience to recognize it as such" (ibid., 319). For Mitchell-Kernan to dismiss the young man and walk away angrily would break the rules of the game. Also significant to this encounter is the role of the other men who intermittently interject with laughter and comments such as "Talk that talk" (ibid., 318). An audience, however, is not required. Signifying can occur between two individuals. Nevertheless, an audience's responsiveness and participation enhance the signifying performance. The audience is also expected to interpret the verbal and nonverbal cues and messages in order to respond appropriately.

Mitchell-Kernan points out how signifying often consists of messages that "carr[y] some negative import for the addressee" (p. 314). The example above is an exception as it illustrates how signifying can be executed as a form of flattery. **Preachers** also may engage in signifying during a sermon. Although the remarks may be negative, they serve to teach or "bring home" a pertinent message. Negative comments directed at an individual may include "What a lovely coat; they sure don't make coats like that anymore. (Glossed: Your coat is out of style)," and "You must be going to the Ritz this afternoon. (Glossed: You're looking tacky)" (ibid., 318).

Signifying is also "thought of as a kind of art—a clever way of conveying messages" (Mitchell-Kernan, 317). The art is an element of many different kinds of speech genres among African Americans, including **jokes**, the dozens, sounding, capping, songs, and **sermons**. Mitchell-Kernan asserts that it takes "skill to construct messages with multi-level meanings, and it sometimes takes equal expertise to unravel the puzzle presented in all of its many implications" (ibid.). Some messages can even be imparted and understood nonverbally. Generally, messages consist of nonverbal and verbal cues. **Nonverbal** cues include any body movements or facial expressions which lend understanding to the signifier's message, such as the "highly stylized leer" the young man wore while signifying to Mitchell-Kernan (ibid., 319). The nonverbal cues also augment the entire performance. Signifiers tend to utilize black speech and voice modulation while engaged in signifying. Often the word "n*gger" is used, as well as popular phrases (ibid., 322–323). Voice modulation can be used to direct an audience away from the obvious message to the underlying message. Moreover, "A speaker's artistic talent is judged upon the cleverness used in directing the attention of the hearer and the audience to this shared knowledge" (ibid., 321).

Gladys L. Knight

See also: Monkey, The Signifying

Further Reading

Khan, Khatija, 2012, "Signifying the Monkey: Rhetorical Modes of Expressions in African American Music: The Case of KRS-one," *Muziki* 9 (1): 35; Li, Stephanie, 2012, *Signifying Without Specifying: Racial Discourse in the Age of Obama* (New Brunswick, NJ: Rutgers University Press); Mitchell-Kernan, Claudia, 1972, "Signifying, Loud-Talking, and Marking," in *Rappin' & Stylin' Out*, ed. Thomas Kochman (Urbana: University of Illinois Press), pp. 315–335.

SIGNIFYING MONKEY
See Monkey, The Signifying

SINGING AND PRAYING BANDS

The Singing and Praying Bands of tidewater Maryland and Delaware, and formerly of southeastern Pennsylvania, are a regional variation of the larger **ring shout** tradition that many scholars consider to have been the most important religious service of enslaved Africans and their African American descendants in North America in the 19th century. The bands of the mid-Atlantic region grew out of Methodist prayer meeting groups that held weekday and Sunday evening services at many **black churches**. When African American churches began to hold outdoor camp meetings in the summer and fall, the leaders of the **prayer** meetings did the organizing. At these African American camp meetings, prayer meeting groups, referring to themselves as "Singing and Praying Bands," from many neighboring churches, came and sang and prayed, one band at a time, each band performing as a self-contained unit. As such, in the 19th and 20th centuries, the African American Methodist camp meetings of this area became showcases for the ring shout. Under the umbrella of Methodism, then, a regional African-derived folk religious tradition continued to thrive. In the late 20th century, however, the band tradition began to dwindle: all of the churches in a network of churches in the Chesapeake and Delaware Bay areas combined enough members to form only a single performing unit. While the same people participate in this group from week to week, the group itself travels each week to different church and camp meetings.

A Singing and Praying Band service begins after a preaching service has been completed. All the band members come forward to the cross aisle of the church; that is, to the area between the first row of pews and the altar rail. Placing a bench or a row of folding chairs in the center of the cross aisle, the men stand with their backs to the altar, facing the congregation remaining in the pews. The women of the group face the men, with the bench or chairs separating the two sexes. Beginning slowly and at a low pitch, a leader lines out—the bands say "gives out"—the first line of an old multiversed hymn in a tune that is traditional to the bands. The singing ensemble follows, singing the first line of the hymn through after the leader. The leader then gives out the next line, and the group sings after him or her. So it goes throughout the hymn. Gradually, the singing rises in pitch and tempo. At the conclusion of the hymn, the bands sing the final line over and over as a meditation to invoke the Holy Spirit.

After the first hymn, another band member prays an impassioned prayer that also focuses on a highly stressed invocation for the spirit to descend onto the congregation then and there. The bands follow by raising another traditional "give-out" hymn and offering another prayer. After two "give-out" hymns and two prayers, another member of the group is called upon to raise what the bands refer to as a "straight hymn." This type of hymn consists of a short, much-repeated chorus, to which rhymed narrative couplets are added. Outsiders might refer to straight hymns as "**spirituals**." While the initial give-out hymns might be penitential in mood, the straight hymns tend to be ebullient. The Holy Spirit having been invoked, and the spiritual well-being of the worshippers having been restored, the bands complete their service in joy. Gradually, the band members on the end of the lines turn to the side, pull themselves closer to the leaders, and the lines of singing men and women transform themselves into a singing and hand-clapping circle. Some members jump off the floor and land with a thud, adding a percussive, drum-like sound to the performance.

After singing the chorus of the straight hymn over and over with increasing enthusiasm, the band begins to march. In a maneuver common to ring shouts around the country, the bands first march counterclockwise around the bench between the women and the men. Then they march down the aisles of the church; weather permitting, they march out onto the churchyard, march around the campground, and eventually form a circle and continue to sing. New leaders move one at a time into the center of the hand-clapping ring to add new verses. Gradually the singing dies down. The service is over.

The first person to mention the Singing and Praying Bands by name was the famous 19th-century AME Bishop Daniel Alexander Payne. In his autobiography, Bishop Payne wrote that in 1851, he had vicious arguments with band members as he attempted to suppress the group at Bethel AME in Baltimore. If we examine even earlier reports of African American religious practice in the mid-Atlantic, however, we can trace the band service further into the past. In 1817, Quaker schoolboys outside of Westtown in southeastern Pennsylvania witnessed a black group marching around a campground singing a spiritual chorus in a way that clearly is an early version of today's band service. In 1819, a white minister named John Fanning Watson also witnessed a group of black worshippers singing a chorus in a circle on a camp meeting site outside of Philadelphia. In late antebellum times, another white minister, named John Dixon Long, observed an African American prayer meeting in Maryland in which members remained in their seats in the pews and sang and prayed until the conclusion of the meeting, at which time they came to the front of the church, formed a circle, and sang.

It would appear that the Singing and Praying Band service as performed today grew from such a tradition that began during the earliest days of Methodist evangelism among African Americans in the mid-Atlantic region. Later, the bands combined the relatively standard Methodist prayer meeting format and the ring shout that John Dixon Long described to form a seamless service. This service continues to be performed in the 21st century and is one of the earliest forms of African American expressive culture still surviving.

Jonathan C. David

Further Reading

David, Jonathan, 1994, "The Sermon and the Shout: A History of the Singing and Praying Bands of Maryland and Delaware," *Southern Folklore* 51: 241–263; David, Jonathan, 2007, *Together Let Us Sweetly Live: The Singing and Praying Bands* (Champaign: University of Illinois Press); Long, John Dixon, 1969 [1857], *Pictures of Slavery in Church and State* (New York: Negro Universities Press); Murphy, Clifford R., 2014, "The Singing and Praying Bands of Maryland and Delaware," *Smithsonian Folkways Magazine* Fall/ Winter; Payne, Rev. Daniel Alexander, 1969 [1886], *Recollections of Seventy Years* (New York: Arno Press); Richards, Chris, 2012, "Singing and Praying Bands Take Musical Ministry to the Masses," *Washington Post* June 14; Watson, John Fanning, 1819, *Methodist Error: Or Friendly, Christian Advise, to those Methodists, Who Indulge in Extravagant Religious Emotions and Bodily Exercises* (Trenton, NJ: D & E Fenton).

SLAVE NARRATIVES

"No more slavery chains for me, no more, no more. No more slavery chains for me, many thousand gone" (Spiritual).

Slave narratives are a unique genre of African American folklore and are also regarded as the earliest form of African American literature. They document and detail an epoch of black experience in this country's history. Numbering in the thousands, the narratives range from relatively brief accounts to full-length manuscripts. There are accounts from celebrated names, as well as those from obscure field hands. For the purpose of this discussion the narratives can be separated into two categories: (1) literary narratives from the antebellum period (i.e., the colonial period through the Civil War) and postbellum eras; and (2) the 1930s federally funded Works Progress Administration (WPA) project, which attempted to document the narratives and experiences of formerly enslaved Americans.

Ante- and Postbellum Narratives

Prior to the mid-19th century, the majority of slave narratives were detailing African enslavement outside the United States, mostly in Europe. In 19th-century United States, the narratives became vehicles for a nascent abolition movement. Their intent was to show the brutality of African enslavement and document the humanity of the enslaved individuals. There were many such narratives in the antebellum era. Several fit into what were known as captivity narratives (i.e., detailing dramatic escape attempts, recapture, or the horrible treatment endured in the event of recapture). Henry Bibb, for example, held in captivity in Kentucky, attempted to escape several times and provides a vivid example:

> Many tears were shed on that occasion by our friends and relatives, who saw us dragged off irons to be sold in the human flesh market. No tongue could express the deep anguish of my soul when I saw the silent tear drops streaming down the sable cheeks of an aged slave mother, at my departure; and that too, caused by a black hearted traitor who was himself a slave.

Other well-known narratives of the 1830s and 1840s were produced by Frederick Douglass, William W. Brown, and William and Ellen Craft, among others. These and many others deal with working and living during slavery, religion, superstition, and music.

Religion as a theme in slave narratives is pervasive, as an excerpt from *From Slave Cabin to the Pulpit* makes clear:

> Sometimes the slaves meet in an old log cabin, when they find it necessary to keep watch. If discovered, they escape if possible; but those who are caught often get whipped. Some are willing to be punished thus for Jesus' sake. . . . In some places, if the slaves are caught praying to God, they are whipped more than if they had committed a great crime. The slaveholders will allow the slaves to dance, but do not want them to pray to God. (Randolph)

Indirectly related to religion was a strong presence of superstition and other folk beliefs among the captives. Many narratives give a vivid picture of such practices, for instance not letting a red-headed woman into your house before 7:00 a.m. because she is clearly a witch, howling dogs as a sign of someone's impending death, or sweeping floors only in the morning because any other time of day could produce conflict such as fights among loved ones. In his narrative, Henry Bibb speaks of "conjuration":

There is much superstition among slaves. Many of them believe in what they call "conjuration," tricking, and witchcraft; and some of them pretend to understand the art, say that by it they can prevent their masters from exercising their will over their slaves. . . . I was led to believe that I could do almost as I pleased, without being flogged. So on the next Sabbath my conjuration was fully tested by my going, and staying away until Monday morning without permission. When I returned home, my master declared that he would punish me for going off; but I did not believe he could do it while I had this root and dust; and as he approached me, I commenced talking saucy to him. But he soon convinced me that there was no virtue in them. He became so enraged at me for saucing him that he grasped a handful of switches and punished me severely in spite of all my roots and powers.

Music was also an important aspect of slave life, as reported by the narratives. In *Twelve Years a Slave* (1857) Solomon Northup, a free man and itinerant violinist in New York, tells of his experience being lured to Washington, D.C., by the promise of a playing engagement, only to be drugged, kidnapped, and sold into enslavement in Louisiana. After being enslaved, he describes a **Christmas** gathering:

When the viands have disappeared, and the hungry maws of the children of toil are satisfied, then, next in the order of amusement, is the Christmas dance. My business on these gala days was always to play on the violin. The African race is a music-loving one. . . . My master often received letters, sometimes from a distance of ten miles, requesting him to send me to play at a ball or festival of the whites.

Funerary musical activities are described in the narrative account of Gus Feaster from Union, South Carolina:

On de way home from de funeral, de mules would perk up a little in dey walk and a faster hymn was sung on the way home. When we got home, we was in such a good mood from singing de faster hymns and de funeral soon be forgot. (South Carolina Narratives, p. 51)

And from James Deane in Baltimore, Maryland, an account of a routine music-making session:

After work was done, the slaves would smoke, sing, tell ghost stories and tales, dance [and make] music, [with] homemade fiddles. Saturday was work day like any other day. We had all legal holidays. Christmas morning we went to the big house and got presents and had a big time all day. (Slave Narratives, Vol. VIII, p. 8)

These "upbeat" excerpts do not minimize, however, the brutality and forced labor that these enslaved persons faced.

The WPA Narratives

The most comprehensive and systematic collection of narratives from enslaved Americans documenting their experiences took place in the 20th century. In the late 1930s, the federally sponsored Works Progress Administration (WPA) embarked on a massive project to preserve the stories of those African Americans who had been enslaved in the previous century. There were close to 100,000 former captives still alive around the country at that time. Many of the informants who participated in the project were enslaved just before, during, or near the end of the Civil War. At the time of the interviews most were in their eighties and nineties. The accounts from the WPA project attempted to capture the language and inflexions more faithfully than the somewhat "sanitized" narratives of the ante- and postbellum periods. Many of these accounts were recorded, as was the case with Fountain Hughes, who was born enslaved in Charlottesville, Virginia, in 1848. He narrates the experience of many after the war:

> An soon after we found out we was free, why then we was bound out to certain people to certain people. . . . An' we would run away, an' wouldn' stay with them. Why then we'd jus' go an' stay anywhere we could. Lay out at night in underwear. We had no home, you know. We was just turned out like cattle. You know like you turn out cattle in a pasture? Colored people did have nothin'.

Even though there were difficulties with the WPA project (e.g., using white interviewers instead of African American, which might have put the informants a little more at ease), it remains one of the most significant records of this brutal era. These narratives hold immense value in providing information about the folk beliefs and practices of African Americans during the slavery period. They have been influential in countless studies of African American history and culture; for example, Lawrence Levine's *Black Culture and Black Consciousness* (1977), Albert Raboteau's, *Slave Religion* (1978), and Anand Prahlad's *African American Proverbs in Context* (1996). In fact, one could go so far as to suggest that the narratives have been the single most important source in the modern revisions of African American culture found in departments of history, religion, and others that focus on understanding black culture. Besides being reservoirs of information, they document the humanity and the indomitable spirit of those who either escaped captivity or outlived it to tell their stories.

Christopher Brooks

Further Reading

Andrews, William L., ed., 1993, *African American Autobiography: A Collection of Critical Essays* (Englewood Cliffs, NJ: Prentice Hall); Andrews, William L., 2011, *Slave Narratives After Slavery* (New York: Oxford University Press); Andrews, William L., and Henry Louis Gates Jr., eds., 1999, *The Civitas Anthology of African American Slave Narratives* (Washington, DC: Civitas/Counterpoint); Ashton, Susanna, and Robyn E. Adams, 2010, *I Belong to South Carolina: South Carolina Slave Narratives* (Columbia: University of South Carolina Press); Crew, Spencer R., Lonnie G. Bunch, Clement Alexander Price, and Federal Writers' Project, 2014, *Slave Culture: A Documentary Collection of the Slave Narratives from the Federal Writers' Project* (Santa Barbara, CA: Greenwood); Federal Writers' Project, 1941, *Slave Narratives: Folk History of Slavery in the United States from Interviews with Former Slaves, Vol. VIII, Maryland* (Library of Congress); Federal Writers' Project, 1976 [1940] *Slave Narratives: A Folk History of Slavery in the United States from Interviews with Former Slaves South Carolina Narratives, Part I* (St. Clair

Shores, MI: Scholarly Press); Foster, Frances Smith, ed., 1994, *Witnessing Slavery: The Development of Ante-Bellum Slave Narratives* (Madison: University of Wisconsin Press); Fulton Minor, DoVeanna S., Reginald H. Pitts, Louisa Picquet, Mattie J. Jackson, and Cornelius Wilson Larison, 2010, *Speaking Lives, Authoring Texts: Three African American Women's Oral Slave Narratives* (Albany: State University of New York Press); Goodwin, Ronald E., 2013, *Remembering the Days of Sorrow: The WPA and the Texas Slave Narratives*, 1st ed. (Buffalo Gap, TX: State House Press); Randolph, Peter, 2000, *From Slave Cabin to Pulpit* (Chapel Hill: University of North Carolina Press); Rawick, George P., ed., 1972, *The American Slave: A Composite Autobiography* (Westport, CT: Greenwood); Southern, Eileen, ed., 1983, *Readings in Black American Music* (New York: W. W. Norton); Work Projects Administration, 2006, *Slave Narratives: A Folk History of Slavery in the United States Project* (Gutenberg Literary Archive Foundation).

SLIDE GUITAR

Slide guitar is a guitar technique, associated with **blues** and some types of **gospel** music, in which the performer slides a hard, smooth object over the steel strings of the instrument to produce a whining, crying, and percussive sound. The technique is first noted in African American folk music near the beginning of the 20th century in Georgia and Mississippi and elsewhere in the Deep **South**. The earliest players typically used the back of a knife blade or knife handle, a glass bottle or bottleneck, a metal tube, or a beef bone to slide on the strings. The technique has two sources, one African and the other Polynesian. The African source is a type of one-stringed instrument found in Central Africa and typically played by adolescent boys as a music learning device. It consists of a section of the central stalk of a raffia palm leaf, from which a sliver of fiber is raised but not detached. This length of fiber becomes the "string." The leaf stalk is usually placed over a bowl or a hole in the ground, which serves as a resonating chamber. One player strikes it in even rhythm with two sticks, while a second player slides a bowl or cup along its length, creating counter rhythms and pitch variations.

In the United States, this African instrument developed into a single-player instrument found mostly in an area from central Georgia to Louisiana, in which the player, usually also an adolescent boy, strikes a metal wire mounted on a board or wall and slides a glass bottle along it. This instrument is called by a variety of names, including one-stringed guitar, diddley bow, bo-diddley, and jitterbug. The technique was transferred by some players to the guitar, and its influence is apparent in the playing of such artists as Bukka White, Son House, and Fred McDowell. This style of slide guitar is highly percussive and features repeated riffs. The other style is derived from Hawaiian guitar and is more melodic and harmonic, featuring long musical lines, sometimes played within chords, picked out on the guitar with the sliding device. This style arose in Hawaii from unknown sources in the last two decades of the 19th century, but it did not make a major impact on the American mainland until 1915.

Black American players were influenced by both styles, and by the time they began to make recordings in the 1920s the two styles had often become blended. The results can be heard in the work of some guitarists of the 1920s and 1930s who specialized in the slide style, such as bluesmen Sylvester Weaver, Tampa Red, Casey Bill Weldon, Kokomo Arnold, and Oscar Woods, and gospel artist Blind Willie Johnson. The slide style was adapted to the electric guitar in the years following World War II and is especially prominent in the work of blues artists such as Muddy Waters and Elmore James, both based in Chicago but originally from Mississippi. The steel guitar, an electrified adaptation of Hawaiian guitar, also became popular in these years in the field of country and western music. It was adopted by black musicians in some Pentecostal Holiness sects and has remained popular there to the present day. Many white blues revival and blues-rock musicians have taken up slide guitar, whereas among black players it has lost much of its popularity in recent decades.

David H. Evans

See also: Blues; Sacred Steel Guitar

Further Reading

Evans, David, 1970, "Afro-American One-Stringed Instruments," *Western Folklore* 29: 229–245; Evans, David, 1995, "Bottleneck Blues," liner notes for recording (Testament TCD 5021); Stone, Robert, 1995, "Sacred Steel," liner notes for recording (Florida Department of State Audio Cassette FFP-107); Troutman, John W., 2013, "Steelin' the Slide: Hawai'i and the Birth of the Blues Guitar," *Southern Cultures* 19 (1): 26–52; Unterberger, Richie, 2003, "Blues Slide Guitar," in *All Music Guide to the Blues*, 3rd ed., ed. Vladimir Bogdanov, Chris Woodstra, and Stephen Thomas Erlewine (Ann Arbor, MI: All Media Guide), p. 696; Wald, Elijah, 2010, *The Blues: A Very Short Introduction* (New York: Oxford University Press).

SORORITY FOLKLORE

Sororities are groups of women in a social organization governed by a constitution.

African American sororities include Alpha Kappa Alpha (1908), Delta Sigma Theta (1913), Zeta Phi Beta (1920), and Sigma Gamma Rho (1922). Members of the sororities fondly refer to one another as "soror" (sister) and acknowledge each other with special handshakes and calls. The lore of black sororities is found in the initiation rituals, calls, probate shows, and step shows.

Interested women attend "rush," an information meeting where they learn the application process. Yet many women begin their preparation long before "rush" in a process commonly referred to as "pre-line." "Pre-line"—now illegal—occurs before formal acceptance to the sorority, and "on-line" (which is now termed membership intake process because of excessive hazing practices) is the time period after the candidate learns of her acceptance to the sorority. Women accepted for membership refer to their period of initiation as pledging or being "on-line."

Pledging is filled with sorority folklore. Pledges create tall tales to prove their pledge process is the most difficult. The idea of being "on-line" finds its roots in the African slave trade. Upon arriving in the New World, slaves were chained together in a single-file "line" and given one name for the "line." In the New World, the slaves were also given a new name. This tradition is reflected in the sorority initiation rituals. Each line member receives a name that reflects her character (e.g., Everready, Resistor, Poison, Dark and Lovely, and Quiet Storm). The initiates form a single file, back-to-belly-line according to height and are instructed not to allow anyone to break their "line." Each line is given a line name that characterizes the entire line. For example, "half and half" might refer to a line in which half of the girls did not "pledge." Lines with only one person are usually termed "solitaire," "most precious dove," "only the strong survive." Other line names are "envy," "N.S.Y.N.C.," "Divine Ivies," or "Thirteen Souls of Perfection."

This pledge period is marked by several other traditions and ends with "hell night"—members of the sororities that didn't participate in the pledge's process interrogate them through a variety of rituals and traditions. Sorority "lines" commonly bite an onion, pass an egg from each of their line sister's necks, learn greetings, memorize Greek-letter organizations' history, and recite the Greek alphabet. It is also common during pre-line and line for the girls to dress alike; not wear makeup, get their hair done, or speak to men; avoid eating foods of any sorority's colors; and not walk on grass. These traditions unify the members, establish a sisterhood, and symbolically purify them for their rebirth as sorority women.

Hand gestures and sorority calls define each sorority and are used to distinguish sororities and acknowledge their presence at large events (football games, step shows, etc.). AKAs have the "pinky" and "The Ivy." DST forms a pyramid. The Dove, the "Z," and the "kitty" (most common) represent ZFB. S-G-Rho extends three fingers while the ring finger and thumb meet.

The calls are: "Skee-Wee" (AKA), "Oo-oop" (DST), "Eee-i-Kee!!" or "Zkitty!" (ZFB), and "Ee-Yip" (S-G-Rho). Only members should make the calls, which are rooted in the West African call-and-response tradition. An AKA might say "1–9" and her sorors would respond "0–8." When a Zeta calls "Z-Phi," her sorors respond "Sooo Sweet!"

Other traditions mark each sorority as well. AKAs are known as "pretty girls." Their signature step, "Serious Matter," is a prissy step to a four beat. When this step is performed, the steppers do not smile while alternating the "serious matter" refrain with verses. An example is "Delta Sigma Theta in your red and white / You think you're the best / but you lost the fight / Eve was not a Delta / and this you should know / because Alpha Kappa Alpha started the show / This is a serious matter." Zeta's are renowned for their superior "stepping skills" and finer womanhood motto, and always during probate shows (pledges are presented to the community after their pledge period and initiation ritual) salute their **fraternity** brother, Phi Beta Sigma. Zetas are the only sorority constitutionally bound to a Greek-letter fraternity. Other sororities, such as AKA and DST, have unofficial brothers because members married men in those fraternities. A strong DST tradition is their elephant walk or duck walk. It is common for members to chant, "Boom, boom / quack, quack. I can't stand my sexy self." DST is also known for incorporating African dance steps in their step shows. S-G-Rho performs a poodle step, their sorority mascot. They also step with canes inherited from their "brother" fraternity, Kappa Alpha Psi.

All these traditions are usually demonstrated in step shows that are carnivalesque in nature. Sororities choreograph a show in which they often "crack on" or insult other sororities and imitate their steps to project their own sorority's greatness. A Delta chants, "There is no one who can step quite like us you see / that includes Aky, Gamma Rho, and ZFB" during the show. An S-G-Rho asserts her superiority in a history chant: "Seven women / in 1922 / got together at Butler U. / They set out on a mission / seven decades ago / to establish this sorority / Sigma Gamma Rho! / We come unique / not like the rest / the ladies of Sigma / are nothing but the best. / Besides gold, the color is blue, / we dedicate this step to Mary Lou." For example, Zetas chant "its a serious matter but not for me / this is a serious matter for DST / Delta Sigma Theta you think you're the best / but everybody knows you're an AKA reject / you're not successful in anything you do / if you're not copying Zeta, you're trying to be a Que!"

Other sorority lore such as information regarding initiation and **funeral** rituals, symbolism of the shield, the handshake or "grip," recognizing a soror, and the pledge song are sacred and privileged to membership.

Lisa C. Lakes

See also: Stepping

Further Reading

Brown, Tamara L., Gregory Parks, and Clarenda M. Phillips, 2005, *African American Fraternities and Sororities: The Legacy and the Vision* (Lexington: University Press of Kentucky); Chandler, Danver Ann, 2006, "A Celebration of an African American Sorority: Alpha Kappa Alpha Sorority, Inc.," *Black History Bulletin* 69 (1): 22; Fine, Elizabeth C., 2003, *Soulstepping: African American Step Shows* (Urbana: University of Illinois Press); Greyerbiehl, L., and D. Mitchell, 2014, "An Intersectional Social Capital Analysis of the Influence of Historically Black Sororities on African American Women's College Experiences at a Predominantly White Institution," *Journal of Diversity in Higher Education* 7 (4): 282–294; Henderson, Jarrad, 2013, *Beyond this Place: Documenting the Visual History of African American Fraternities and Sororities* (University of Missouri–Columbia); Ross, Lawrence C., Jr., 2002, *The Divine Nine: The History of African American Fraternities and Sororities* (New York: Dafina); Whaley, Deborah Elizabeth, 2010, *Disciplining Women: Alpha Kappa Alpha, Black Counterpublics, and the Cultural Politics of Black Sororities* (Albany: SUNY Press).

SORROW SONGS
See Spirituals

SOUL

Soul is a quality of African American music, **food**, writing, and so on. The term is not easy to define but involves deep feeling, black traditions, and pride in being African American. Although soul is by no means restricted to music, this almost ineffable quality is perhaps most easily delineated through the development of the musical genre. Soul appears in the names of **gospel** groups of the 1940s and 1950s, and there was a form of **jazz** in the late 1950s that was called soul jazz. However, it was rhythm and blues with the addition of certain gospel feelings and forms that finally came to be called soul music.

Rhythm and blues developed from classic and country blues when, essentially, jazz moved away from the regular rhythms required for dancing and into more abstract forms. Rhythm and blues that was geared to a young audience became rock and roll in the 1950s, while the more adult and often sexually explicit form continued to keep the original name and following. Then, in the early 1960s, singer Clyde McPhatter began to use the "surge singing" style of Mahalia Jackson and Clara Ward in songs with gospel harmonies and lyrics that were virtually gospel. He was followed by Jackie Wilson and Ray Charles, the latter of whom adapted some gospel songs with slight word changes. ("I've got a savior" becomes "I've got a woman.") He also adapted gospel techniques such as the call-and-response pattern between lead singer and backup group or audience. James Brown went even further, transforming the performance venue into a sanctified church where all that was missing was the religion. The result electrified the popular music world.

Former gospel singer Sam Cooke was far less raw but no less effective in soul ballads. He strongly influenced Otis Redding and Al Green. When Aretha Franklin emerged in the late 1960s, soul music enjoyed a surge of popularity. One of the first women to sing soul, Franklin had a tremendous, extremely well-trained voice and such intensity of feeling that not only did she become the "Queen of Soul," but for many she was the definition of soul. It has even been speculated that her perfect embodiment of soul led to the genre's decline in popularity. No one could surpass her, so people didn't try. While Aretha was considered the Queen, James Brown was called "The Godfather of Soul" and "Soul Brother Number One." More than any other artist, Brown transformed most genres of American popular music, as he also pioneered Funk and Rhythm and Blues, and continues to be an influence on more recent genres such as **Hip-hop**. "Sweet soul" developed after 1970, and both Franklin and Brown continued to perform.

In the late 20th and early 21st centuries, the word soul was frequently used to describe a cuisine that was based on African American cooking traditions, including fried chicken, greens cooked with ham, black-eyed peas and sweet potato pie. It also became a general term for positive qualities in any field of black endeavor. The term is a reference to some effable quality that defines the essence of blackness, emphasizing its distinctness from whiteness. In his essay "The Language of Soul," author Claude Brown refers to the nation of "Soulville" and "Soul people," who live within the Western world but are separated from it by the aesthetic norms that characterize black culture. Perhaps the longest running black television program was titled *Soul Train,* a music variety show that aired from 1971 through 2006. Soul connotes a deep, heartfelt, and spiritual way of being, in contrast to a more mechanical, logical, and "cold-hearted" attitude attributed to white America by black people. Also embodied in the term is the history of struggle, survival, and the ability to improvise and be creative that has enabled black people to rise above the historical circumstances of life in the Western world. "Soul" suggests the cultural process of taking foreign and sometimes meager materials and creatively transforming them into something unique, dynamic, and artful. Hence, soul has been applied to music, foodways, speech, dress, **dance**, and other elements of black culture.

Kathleen Thompson

See also: Soul Food; Speech, Folk

Further Reading

Brackett, David, 2004, s.v. "Soul Music," in *Grove Music Online* (New York: Oxford University Press), www.grovemusiconline.com; Brown, Claude, 1972, "The Language of Soul," in *Rappin' and Stylin' Out*, ed. Thomas Kochman (Urbana: University of Illinois Press), pp. 134–139; Gordon, Robert, 2013, *Respect Yourself: Stax Records and the Soul Explosion* (New York: Bloomsbury); Kopano, Baruti N., and Tamara Brown, 2014, *Soul Thieves: The Appropriation and Misrepresentation of African American Popular Culture* (New York: Palgrave Macmillan); Neal, Mark Anthony, 1999, *What the Music Said: Black Popular Music and Black Public Culture* (New York: Routledge); Ritz, David, 2014, *Respect: The Life of Aretha Franklin* (New York: Little, Brown and Company); Smith, R. J., 2014, *The One: The Life and Music of James Brown* (New York: Gotham Books); Talevski, Nick, 1998, *The Unofficial Encyclopedia of the Rock and Roll Hall of Fame* (Westport, CT: Greenwood Press); Vincent, Rickey, 2013, *Party Music: The Inside Story of the Black Panthers' Band and How Black Power Transformed Soul Music*, 1st ed. (Chicago: Lawrence Hill Books); Werner, Craig, 2004, *Higher Ground: Stevie Wonder, Aretha Franklin, Curtis Mayfield, and the Rise and Fall of American Soul* (New York: Crown).

SOUL FOOD

Soul food refers to African American foodways, particularly those culinary traditions thought to have derived from the black Atlantic slave trade and U.S. chattel slavery. Although soul food has reference to the "comfort foods" of diverse ethnic groups, during the late 1960s and early 1970s the term gained popular usage in the United States as a synonym for black southern—or "down home"—cooking. It is important to bear in mind, however, that the actual history of African American dietary practices should be distinguished from the emergence and evolution of soul food as a distinct ideological concept, one that has circulated since the 1960s through venues ranging from private conversations and community events to popular film, television, music, and cookbooks. In this sense soul food might be said to encompass not only the ongoing evolution of living culinary traditions but also the politicized creation of imagined culinary pasts.

The underpinnings of soul food encompass at least three overlapping developmental phases. First, European colonialism and the black Atlantic slave trade resulted in a synthesis of foods and cooking techniques indigenous to **Africa** with those indigenous to Europe and the New World. For example, whereas culinary historians have traced the origins of yams and watermelon to Africa, as well as techniques such as deep fat frying and one-pot stewing, other foods commonly associated with **soul**, such as collard greens and corn, are said to have originated in Europe and the Americas, respectively. Second, enslaved Africans learned how to use relatively expensive ingredients such as ham, chicken, eggs, butter, refined sugar, and white flour in cooking for slave owners while also creating healthful and palatable meals for themselves and their families: they supplemented rations consisting largely of inexpensive pork and corn products with wild game, seafood, fruits, vegetables, and herbs derived from hunting, fishing, foraging, and gardening. Third, successive waves of black migration from the rural **South** to the urban North, Midwest, and West in the decades between the Civil War and World War II not only dispersed southern black dietary practices across the United States but transformed them in the process by giving many African Americans little choice but to consume mass-produced foods and by disrupting the oral transmission of culinary knowledge from generation to generation.

Together these developments set the stage for the emergence of soul food in the mid-1960s, as the civil rights movement was beginning to give way to the more confrontational politics of black power. The former movement had its base primarily in black southern churches. Just as food had historically played an important role in the sustenance of African American communities during and in the years immediately following slavery, it also played a role in sustaining the civil rights protesters—primarily via the famed culinary expertise of the "church sisters." But, at the time, food itself was not widely understood as a site of political contestation. As the movement shifted from a southern battle over integration to a northern struggle spearheaded by a younger generation of urban activists fighting for black power, however, many black nationalists began using the term "soul" to valorize the cultural forms created through a history of black oppression. Though most commonly associated with music, soul was increasingly used by the late 1960s to refer to a wide array of black cultural practices, including cuisine. From 1969 through 1971, soul food cookbooks, newspaper and magazine columns, restaurants, and cafeteria menus proliferated.

Yet even as many African Americans began embracing soul food as a symbol of black resilience and solidarity in response to centuries of white oppression, others were much less sympathetic to what they considered an inauthentic fad. Whereas Black Panther Eldridge Cleaver ridiculed soul food as a form of middle-class black "slumming," comedian-turned-political-activist Dick Gregory and Nation of Islam leader Elijah Muhammad claimed that in its popular guises soul food was tantamount to racial genocide. Gregory insisted that slaves had eaten not high-fat, salty, and sugar-laden foods such as fried chicken, biscuits, and sweet potato pie, but instead "soil food"—a primarily vegetarian diet of whole grains, fresh fruits, and vegetables seasoned with lard. Chef Edna Lewis similarly argued that soul food emerged from northern urban poverty and that the then-popular fixation on **chitterlings**, grits, and greens bore no authentic relationship to the wide array of fresh fruits, grains, meats, and vegetables that have historically constituted the southern black diet. Working from a different perspective, cookbook author Vertamae Smart-Grosvenor also challenged the association between soul food and the U.S. South by critiquing popular understandings of soul food as consisting of "massa's leftovers," by working to identify the African roots of American dietary practices, and by redefining soul food to include the culinary history of peoples of the African diaspora around the world.

These debates over the origins, ingredients, healthfulness, authenticity, and meanings of soul food have continued up to the present. Their biggest impact is to be found in the continued growth of a subgenre of health-oriented soul food cookbooks that attempt to recreate traditional recipes using different ingredients (for example, canola oil instead of lard) in order to address widespread concerns about the high rates among African Americans of diet-related health problems such as obesity, diabetes, and heart disease. But by the late 1990s, the widespread success of a Hollywood film and spin-off television series titled "Soul Food" demonstrated that the term also continued to function—as indeed it had from its inception—as an acknowledgment of black spiritual as well as physical health needs. Soul food might thus be seen to refer not only to African American culinary traditions but also to a widely felt hope that communal wisdom derived from centuries of struggle against white domination not be forgotten.

Doris Witt

See also: Barbecue; Folk Foods; Soul

Further Reading

Bates, Kelsey Scouten, 2012, "Comfort in a Decidedly Uncomfortable Time: Hunger, Collective Memory, and the Meaning of Soul Food in Gee's Bend, Alabama," *Food and Foodways* 20 (1): 53–75; Harris, Jessica, 1995, *The Welcome Table: African-American Heritage Cooking* (New York: Simon & Schuster); Miller, Adrian, 2013, *Soul Food: The Surprising Story of an American Cuisine, One Plate at a Time* (Chapel Hill: University of North Carolina Press); Opie, Frederick Douglass, 2010, *Hog and Hominy: Soul Food from Africa to America* (New York: Columbia University Press); Poe, Tracy, 1999, "The Origins of Soul Food in Black Urban Identity: Chicago, 1915–1947," *American Studies International* 37 (1): 4–33; Root, Waverley, and Richard de Rochement, 1976, *Eating in America: A History* (New York: William Morrow); Toppin, Shirlyn, 2006, "'Soul Food' Theology: Pastoral Care and Practice Through the Sharing of Meals: A Womanist Reflection," *Black Theology: An International Journal* 4 (1): 44–69; Van DeBurg, William L., 1992, *New Day in Babylon: The Black Power Movement and American Culture, 1965–1975* (Chicago: University of Chicago Press); Witt, Doris, 2004, *Black Hunger: Soul Food and America* (Minneapolis: University of Minnesota Press).

SOUTH, THE

The South is a region of the United States characterized by specific folkways and historically by particular ethnic settlement patterns and by its allegiances to the confederacy. Mythologically, it often represents the home and birthplace of African Americans; a kind of hell out of which black American culture emerged and with which it has a love/hate relationship.

The U.S. Census Bureau defines the following 16 states as constituting the South: Alabama, Arkansas, Delaware, Florida, Georgia, Kentucky, Louisiana, Maryland, Mississippi, North Carolina, Oklahoma, South Carolina, Tennessee, Texas,

Virginia, and West Virginia. The South is often further divided into geographic areas consisting of the Deep South, which includes Mississippi, Alabama, Georgia, Florida, and South Carolina; the Up-South, which includes the border states of Delaware, Maryland, Virginia, and West Virginia; and the mid-South, which includes Tennessee, North Carolina, and Kentucky. Other regions of the South include ethnically distinct Louisiana with its Creole and Cajun folkways, the Appalachian folk culture and that of the Ozark Mountains, and the **Gullah** folk traditions of South Carolina and the Georgia Sea Islands. Aside from a geographic South, there exists a cultural South, which extends to include Missouri. On the other hand, many people do not consider Delaware southern, neither geographically nor culturally, and many parts of Texas as well as southern Florida have become less southern culturally due to shifting demographics.

The region always has been culturally diverse with folk traditions from Ireland, Scotland, England, Germany, and France, as well as Spain, Portugal, and various parts of **Africa**. All of these folkways as well as **Native American** influences contributed to the lore of the American South. However, the area south of the Mason-Dixon Line received more enslaved Africans than did any other region of what eventually became the United States of America. This large African presence in the South was a decisive factor in shaping southern folk culture, from **folktales** to cuisine.

Many African traditions once thought to have been lost during the Middle Passage remained intact in spite of the efforts of slaveholders to season or strip Africans of all cultural vestiges from their homeland. Through the oral tradition, body language, facial expressions, humor, and sentiment, cultural and racial memory survived. The massive numbers of black people in the South were not only able to retain African survivals in terms of words and language patterns (Gullah and Sea Island, for instance) and African lore, but they created new **myths**, tales, songs, **jokes**—a new world lore.

Chief among the African American folk traditions of the South is folk music. Black folk music consists of the **spirituals, blues, jazz, work songs**, and **field hollers**. The **banjo**, an instrument introduced by slaves, was based on the West African instrument called the *banjar*, constructed of a calabash gourd and gut strings. During slavery drums were outlawed (except in selected localities, such as New Orleans), as slaveholders were aware of the West African tradition of the talking drums. Used as a means of communication for slave rebellions, the drum was the heartbeat of African music. African American folk music substituted for the missing drum with homemade instruments like jugs, bottles, and washing boards to keep rhythm; also used was body percussion called hambone, a rhythm created by using the hands to hit or slap the thigh or chest. While Black folk music began in the South, it spread and influenced all of American music.

The **spirituals** or "Sorrow Songs," as W. E. B. Du Bois called them, were a culmination of African rhythms and Christian imagery. While many of the lyrics of the spirituals came directly from the Bible, often these biblical lyrics were encoded messages for the enslaved to escape their hell on earth and not an expression of their willingness to wait for freedom in the great hereafter as first thought by those who studied the traditions. The spiritual "Swing Low Sweet Chariot" was the signal that Harriet Tubman was coming to carry the enslaved to freedom. "Jacob's Ladder" was another song shrouded in Biblical imagery but intended for instructions to a better life on earth. "Follow the Drinking Gourd" was a secular song within the same tradition.

Storytelling, while not exclusive to the South, is a central part of southern culture and a mainstay in African American culture. Folktales, many of which have African origins, especially the animal tales, were a means for enslaved people to pass on ethnic mores and wisdom. They also provided an outlet for signifying or talking about the slave owners and/or white people in general. These animal tales, once thought of as quite simplistic, served as social criticism and were political attacks on the injustice of those in power. **Brer Rabbit** was a metaphor for the slave, whereas Brer Bear, large and powerful, symbolized the great white planter. Brer Rabbit lived by his wits, as did all of the enslaved people of the South. Many of the tales bear the mark of highly sophisticated metaphor, initially dismissed by whites as slave superstitions. **High John the Conqueror** is one example of the African understanding of Spirit and the absolute need for forgiveness within the human experience.

Southern cultural traditions all bear the mark of that peculiar institution of slavery. Southern cuisine often referred to as **soul food** was greatly influenced by black cooks. As with music and other aspects of African American folk culture, enslaved people used what was available to them. **Chitterlings**, fatback, neck bones, hog maws, pig feet, pig tail, and mountain oysters became "soul food" because these were the foods available to the slaves after the owners had taken for themselves the most nutritious parts of whatever was available. Given what was left, these Africans in America created delicacies. They did so by combining traditional African seasonings like salt, onion, garlic, and an abundance of peppers. Vegetables like okra, eggplant, and pumpkin were imported either with or by the enslaved men and women from Africa. Poke salad, pokeweed, mustard, kale, and collard greens were vegetables that were boiled and seasoned with fatback, called salt pork in some areas of the South, or with some other meat, such as hog maws, and eaten with cornbread or hoecake. The juice from the boiled greens, called pot likker, was eaten like broth, often with day-old cornbread crumbled in the bowl.

In the South, also known as the Sunbelt, heat and high humidity produced what is known as porch culture and southern drinks to accompany the **porch sitters**. Sweet tea, which is still popular throughout the South, the famed mint julep, wines made from southern grown fruits, blackberries (dewberries), Muscadine grapes, and peaches were typical southern drinks served ice cold. Folk made their own drinks, sang, and told stories (or lies, as the case might be), while sitting on front porches of shotgun houses (West African architectural style) or in clean-swept yards reminiscent of African compounds to pass the time and catch a cool breeze before the inventions and affordability of air conditioning and television.

The South figures prominently in African American oral traditions. Genres such as blues, jokes, **legends**, and folktales often reflect some of the ambivalence that African Americans have toward the region and its culture. It was in the periods following slavery when African Americans migrated north and west that this ambivalence emerged. In black southern mythology, the North had, during the slavery period, been a land of "milk and honey," of freedom and equality. When African Americans began migrating north only to be met with different forms of racism and with cultural and familial isolation, the South took on a new significance. On the one hand, many of those who had left the South began to view it in nostalgic terms, remembering the close bonds of black communities but also the slower pace of life. At the same time, the horrors of southern life were not forgotten. Hence, the South became a mythological land into which one might wander in hopes of becoming spiritually renewed through contact with loved ones, but in which one had to always be aware of ever-present dangers. Lawrence Levine describes comedian Moms Mabley's attitude toward the South as representative of the general attitude among African Americans in the North:

> She referred to the South as "down home," the place which harbored so many relatives and friends and which was still symbolic of much of Afro-American culture. Yet more often the South was spoken of as something exotic, aberrant, and dangerous which was better left behind. She referred to it as "down there," "behind the scorched curtain," and "no man's land number two." (p. 364)

Leaders in the New South have made great efforts to distinguish it from the stereotypical Old South defined as the "Bible Belt" Christian fundamentalist or fanatic, politically conservative or racist, place of vigilante justice and Ku Klux Klan violence. Following the success of the civil rights movement, many African Americans began to return to the so-called New South. At the beginning of the 20th century, 90 percent of African Americans lived in the South. By 1970 the numbers had dwindled to less than 50 percent. The great out-migration was reversed in the 1980s, though, as many African Americans began moving back to the South. Most, however, relocated to Southern urban centers, such as Atlanta, giving rise to a different image of the South in the minds of many black people. Still intact, however, are the icons of the Old South, including the rebel flag and other images of the Confederacy, although widespread resistance to many such icons have gained nationwide attention. Organizations such as the League of the South and the Southern Agrarians represent new efforts to resist the liberal democracy expressed by many citizens of the New South. Perhaps the newest aspect of African American southern lore is that it is now urban rather than rural. While blues, jazz, rhythm and blues, and **gospel** remain classic, urban lore with its **toasts**, jokes, and **signifying** is growing in popular culture. **Hip-hop** is a popular urban form of folklore in many southern cities. Atlanta, Miami, Houston, and New Orleans are cities with growing multicultural communities: Hispanic, Asian, and transplanted Northerners, black and white, who sometimes outnumber native Southerners.

Nagueyalti Warren

Further Reading

Baker, Bruce E., and Brian Kelly, 2013, *After Slavery: Race, Labor, and Citizenship in the Reconstruction South* (Gainesville: University Press of Florida); Harris, Trudier, 2009, *The*

Scary Mason-Dixon Line: African American Writers and the South, 1st ed. (Baton Rouge: Louisiana State University Press); Holloway, Joseph E., 1990, *Africanisms in American Culture* (Bloomington: Illinois University Press); Levine, Lawrence W., 1977, *Black Culture and Black Consciousness: Afro-American Folk Thought from Slavery to Freedom* (New York: Oxford University Press); Nettles, Saundra Murray, 2013, *Necessary Spaces: Exploring the Richness of African American Childhood in the South* (Charlotte, NC: Information Age Pub., Inc.); Sharpless, Rebecca, 2010, *Cooking in Other Women's Kitchens: Domestic Workers in the South, 1865–1960*, 1st ed. (Chapel Hill: University of North Carolina Press; Turner, Lorenzo D., 1973 [1949], *Africanisms in the Gullah Dialect* (Ann Arbor: University of Michigan Press); Walker, Sheila S., 2001, *African Roots/American Cultures: Africa in the Creation of the Americas* (Lanham, MD: Rowman & Littlefield).

SPEECH, FOLK

Folk speech is the linguistic expression of the masses of people of African descent in the United States. It is a Creole language that forms part of the family of Atlantic Creoles that emerged as a consequence of the trafficking of African peoples into the Western Hemisphere by European colonizers. The African American variety of Atlantic, Anglophone Creoles—like other varieties such as **Gullah** and Jamaican Creole, or patois—evolved from a pidgin language that combined the grammatical elements of West African Mande and Central African Niger-Congo languages with lexical items from the English language. African American folk speech is also referred to as black English, African American English, black communications, Ebonics or U.S. Ebonics, black dialect, black idiom, ghetto talk, street talk, Africanized English, black vernacular, and black talk, among other appellations. African American folk speech expresses the conditions of enslavement and resistance and the celebration of black life and black folkways in America. It speaks to the repression of African tongues under the system of slavery in the Americas and the coerced use of European languages. Even as African peoples were forced to acquire a new vocabulary, they retained lexical items from their original languages. Words such as "yam," "**gumbo**," "**banjo**," "gorilla," "**jive**," and "goober" represent a long list of terms that have been retained and that, through cross-culturation, have become part of the American English language. Diction, however, is described by modern linguists as the most superficial aspect of a language. The grammatical structure, specifically phonetic, morphological, syntactic, and semantic systems, is identified as the most significant aspect of a language. Grammatical structures reflect the cognition or mental system of human beings. This structure allows humans to formulate and interpret words and sentences and construct meaning. Examples of African American grammatical patterns that have been retained from African languages include the absence of consonant clusters and final consonants, zero-copula use, use of double subjects, minimal or simplified usage of inflections, and use of syntax to indicate possession.

In maintaining grammatical structures that are still comparable to West and Central African language systems, the African American folk, thereby, also retained a worldview that recalls their traditional African heritage. An integral aspect of that worldview is the primacy of the spoken word. In traditional African society, the spoken word has procreative force. It is the means through which African peoples ordered their world and determined their existence within it. Words actualize life and life events are actualized. Through naming rituals, for instance, newborns come into life. Things take on the quality of their designations, and incantations are as much a part of a creative process as the artifact created. All traditional rituals and ceremonies are accompanied by words. The spoken word, then, is potent and serves as a source of empowerment. The spoken word constitutes a fundamental aspect of the cultural legacy of African Americans and all diasporan Africans. And oral tradition is described by some scholars as "the fundamental vehicle for gittin' ovuh'" in black America.

African American folk speech represents the continuation of **Africa** in America, and it speaks to the adaptive power and resiliency of African peoples and African culture. The survival of Africans under conditions of bondage, economic exploitation, and social and political oppression in the Americas and the Caribbean is attributed to their retention of African oral traditions. Encoded in lyrics of songs, preached between the poetic prose of folk **sermons**, and narrated in the in-between lines of **fables** and **folktales** were the desires for freedom as well as the directions for escape. The release of tension and sublimated aggression can be detected in the refrains of **work songs** and **trickster** tales and in the laughter evoked from **jokes**, "lies," and the verbal game of **signifying**. The wisdom of social graciousness, and the skill and art of what to say and when, is expressed in parables, **proverbs**, and the general African American penchant for indirect communication. Through oral forms such as these and the rituals of verbal interplay, the African American folk embodied their worldview, life lessons, and strategies of survival, transmitting their precepts, principles, and philosophy of life from generation to generation.

Modes of discourse, which facilitate the communication process of the African American folk, include the rhetorical dynamics of call-and-response, signifying, and narrative sequencing. Call-and-response is considered a basic "organizing principle" of African American folk speech. For any speech act to have significance, it must be issued in the sociocultural context of community. A speaker or storyteller requires a listener or audience that will spontaneously interact with the speaker. The speaker's statement or story (the call) evokes an answer (the response) from the listener. This dynamic is apparent in **storytelling**, **field hollers**, folk sermons, and political speeches. It is apparent, as well, in African American folk music such as **blues** songs, instrumental **jazz** and jazz riffs, **rap**, and **hip-hop** music. The dynamic of call-and-response, as it integrates the voices of speaker and listener, functions as a means of establishing or reinforcing group identity and community. It also expresses an appreciation for interdependency and complementarity, and evidences the attempt of African American folk to achieve balance and harmony— fundamental aspects of the traditional African worldview.

Signifying is the verbal ritual of insult, the act of verbal dueling, and the art of verbal play in a general sense. As a **game** involving insult exchange, signifying is designed to verbally put down one's opponent. The opponent is expected to return in kind. Though potentially combative, the inspiration of the game is to entertain and evoke laughter, challenging the participants to draw upon their store of wit and clever repartee or to create it on the spot. The **dozens**, or mother-rhyming, broadcasting, specifyin', and checkin', are all forms of signifying as ritual insult. Sweet talkin' and talking around a subject are examples of signifying in the general sense of verbal play. Boasting, **toasting**, and **testifying**, which can be employed in signifying speech acts, are also examples of narrative sequencing. This dynamic demonstrates the ability of a speaker to tell a complex story that includes a multiplicity of digressions before returning to the main point of the story. Rhetorical devices that characterize African American folk speech and embellish oral performance are alliteration, repetition, rhyming, mimicry, and tonal semantics.

A communication system that is generated from an African grammar and uses English words imbued with an African sensibility, African American folk speech is arguably a language separate and distinct from American English. In spite of the social stigma associated with the usage of African American folk speech, it is spoken by a majority of African Americans. It constitutes the basis of African American written traditions and is a distinct and prominent feature in African American literary texts. Even as African Americans gained access to formal education—which was denied them—and developed skills in standard English usage, ranging from moderate facility to mastery, many, empowered with the ability to code-switch, choose to identify with and express themselves through the patterns of African American folk speech. And, as linguists and other scholars write, African American youth are consciously re-creolizing the language. These phenomena, on the one hand, attest to the problem of cultural illiteracy in the educational process and the continued need of African American language as a counter-cultural discourse. And on the other hand, they speak to the African American affirmation of their African heritage and their appreciation of the folk and the pattern and rhythm of African American folk speech.

Deborah G. Plant

See also: Dozens, The; Jim Crow; Monkey, The Signifying; Mother Wit; Signifying.

Further Reading

Abrahams, Roger D., ed., 1985, *Afro-American Folktales: Stories from Black Traditions in the New World* (New York: Pantheon); Delpit, Lisa, ed., 1998, *The Real Ebonics Debate: Power, Language, and the Education of African American Children* (Boston: Beacon); Dillard, J. L., 1972, *Black English: Its History and Usage in the United States* (New York: Random House); Gilyard, Keith, 1996, *Let's Flip the Script: An African American Discourse on Language, Literature and Learning* (Detroit, MI: Wayne State University); Holloway, Joseph and Winifred Vass, 1993, *The African Heritage of American English* (Bloomington: Indiana University Press); Hurston, Zora Neale, 1979 [1935], *Mules and Men* (Bloomington: Indiana University Press); Hurston, Zora Neale, 1983, *The Sanctified Church* (Berkeley: Turtle Island); Kearse, Randy, 2006, *Street Talk: Da Official Guide to Hip-Hop & Urban Slanguage* (Fort Lee, NJ: Barricade Books); Minnick, Lisa Cohen, 2009 [2004], *Dialect and Dichotomy: Literary Representations of African American Speech,* (Tuscaloosa: University of Alabama Press); Mitchell-Kernan, Claudia, 1973, "Signifying," in *Mother Wit from the Laughing Barrel: Readings in the Interpretations of*

Afro-American Folklore, ed. Alan Dundes (Englewood Cliffs, NJ: Prentice-Hall), pp. 310–328; Rickford, John R., and Russell John Rickford, 2000, *Spoken Soul: The Story of Black English* (New York: Wiley); Smitherman, Geneva, 2000, *Black Talk: Words and Phrases from the Hood to the Amen Corner* (Boston: Houghton Mifflin); Smitherman, Geneva, 1977, *Talkin and Testifyin: The Language of Black America* (Detroit, MI: Wayne State University); Vass, Winifred, 1979, *The Bantu Speaking Heritage of the United States* (Los Angeles: Center for Afro-American Studies, University of California).

SPIRITUALS

Sometimes referred to as "Sorrow Songs," spirituals are the 18th-century song crea-tions of enslaved African Americans who sought to express their religious beliefs in a way that was uniquely meaningful to them. It is a tradition born of the union of African traditional performance practices and American socioreligious elements. The slaves created spirituals, commonly known as "Negro spirituals," in contexts free of white control—fields and "**praise houses**." These songs commented on their love for God, the desire for freedom, the total disdain for the institution of slavery, and their plans for secret meetings or escape as expressed in the familiar lines, "Steal away to Jesus, I aint got long to stay here."

The origin of the spiritual is not known, and scholars who study the musical form have not come to any theoretical agreement. Some scholars consider the spir-itual to have started during the Second Great Awakening, also referred to as the Camp Meeting Revival Movement (1780–1830). The largest and most historical meeting was held in Logan County, Kentucky (1880). The interdenominational and interracial continuous religious services held over several days under tents in rural areas later became an American institution. Some scholars have credited the white spiritual, which emanated "Traditional Spiritual" from these meetings, with being the model for the black spiritual. On the other hand, scholars like Eileen Southern, author of *The Music of Black Americans: A History* (1997), support the premise that many of these folk songs might have been created first by northern African Ameri-can church congregations. These congregations used the Protestant hymn style and revised the texts to coincide with their experiences and needs while maintaining the original melody and harmony. Although the exact origin may not be known, there is overwhelming technical evidence and documented historical accounts (John Lovell Jr. and Dena Epstein) that have demonstrated that the spiritual far antedates the Second Great Awakening and is not an adaptation of white religious song. Cur-rently, scholars generally believe that several composition processes were used to create the spiritual: a) combining elements from old songs to create new ones; b) improvising on existing songs; and c) creating songs from new materials. How-ever, the main premise is that the African American spiritual is an African musical expression that combines song, body movements (**shout/dance**) and instruments (hand clapping and foot stomping), which are adapted to the American context. In recent decades, most scholars have not been interested in the original sources of text and melodic material because the process of "communal recreation" refashioned the songs into characteristic African American sacred folksongs.

Musical Performance Practices

The structural form and performance style associated with spirituals are derived from West African musical practices. In West Africa, the origin for most of the slave population, cultural mores govern group singing at musical events. These principles require the participation of group members who are present. Individuals become involved through singing, dancing, hand clapping, foot stomping, or some combination of these. These practices also provided the accompaniment.

The concept of group participation is further reinforced in the structural formula of the song itself. The songs, spontaneously created by an individual and/or group, were sung in an emotional antiphonal style of an unpredetermined length. Throughout West Africa, many songs subscribe to the antiphonal, call-and-response, or leader-chorus structure, in which the leader spontaneously improvises text, time, and melody, and the remaining group members respond with a short receptive phrase that can also be expressed by making slight changes in time, text, or melody.

The antebellum spiritual is based on this same call-and-response structural principle—one which allows for latitude and flexibility on the part of the leader (the call) and at the same time allows other group members to participate by singing short repetitive responses (the chorus). Although some songs are sung in harmony and some in unison, heterophony appears to have been more common. Heterophony is the resulting sound when deviation from the basic melody occurs, when tones are too high, or when there is a need for textual emphasis or more variety.

Spirituals were sung in many contexts during the slavery and postbellum periods, sometimes in groups, but also by individuals. The only musical accompaniment was hand clapping, foot stomping, or the sounds of a work tool, such as an axe, keeping the rhythm. They could be sung by enslaved people working in groups in the fields; by individuals doing domestic work in the slave owner's house; among groups of people at religious gatherings such as worship services in **hush harbors**; and by people engaged in any variety of activities in their own cabins or homes, e.g., cooking, cleaning, gardening, or as lullabies singing babies to sleep.

The spiritual is rooted in complex African rhythms. The basic pulse of the song is usually supplied by hand clapping and foot stomping, since drums were not allowed during slavery. The melody lines produce cross-rhythms that move within a different rhythmic pattern than the basic pulse. The resulting concept is polyrhythm, which is one of the most striking features of slave music. The melodic lines are usually original, with shouts, moans, groans, cries, and word interjections woven into the melody. Although other scales were used, the pentatonic, or five-tone, scale was more prevalent. Henry Edward Krehbiel, the music critic, confirmed this predilection for pentatonic scales after examining 527 spirituals. There is also a large frequency of lowered thirds and sevenths, known as "blue notes."

Song texts are direct, full of irony, and very symbolic. They are marked by vivid imagery, using the technique of personification with emphasis on metaphoric figures of speech. Although some spiritual verses rhyme, because spirituals were spontaneously created and improvised, rhyming was not essential to the creator. The songs are performed in black dialect, and texts are generally taken from the Bible, ministers' **sermons**, psalms, Protestant hymn motifs, and phrases and comments on everyday life experiences. There is a preponderance of biblical stories about Adam and Eve, Jonah and the whale, Mary and Martha, David and Goliath, and Paul and Silas. Some of the recurring scriptural heroes in the song texts are Jacob, Moses, Daniel, Gabriel, Job, and, of course, Jesus Christ. Other themes involving traveling, rivers, fighting, and escape are also prevalent. From the accounts of former slaves, we find that many spirituals had double meanings and were used as code songs for communication purposes on the Underground Railroad and to comment on slave owners, racism, and on the horrors of slavery. Scholars such as Lawrence Levine have suggested that the actual focus of spirituals was as much political as religious, or even more so. For example, slaves drew parallels between themselves and the Israelites in captivity, and between Pharoahs and slave owners. Hence, when they sang, "Go Down Moses, tell old Pharoah, set my people free" they were singing about their own plight. Such terms as "heaven" in spirituals, then, can be interpreted as freedom from slavery. These sacred songs are based on religious concepts, but they are invariably interpreted by the context of the slaves' everyday life experiences.

Dissemination

The unaccompanied spiritual served as the most important African American musical tradition up to the Civil War. After this period, this sacred music of sorrow, rebellion, and hope was transformed along with the slave populace. Thus, the spiritual spread beyond the African American community and began to be disseminated and popularized in other ways, including through publications, touring ensembles, individual performers, and classical arrangements and adoptions.

The classic 1867 anthology *Slave Songs of the United States* was the first published collection of spirituals. This landmark book represented the first systematic effort to collect and preserve the songs created by enslaved African Americans. To ensure authenticity, the editors—William Francis Allen, Charles Pickard Ware, and Lucy McKim Garrison—notated most of the melodies and words directly from the singers themselves. The final product was a rare musical treasure containing complete melody lines and lyrics for more than 130 songs, arranged by geographical region.

Publication of other anthologies and scholarly examinations of spirituals continued well into the next century. James Weldon Johnson's set of anthologies—*The Books of American Negro Spirituals: Including The Book of American Negro Spirituals and the Second Book of Negro Spirituals* (1977 [1925,1926])—is known not only for the collection of spirituals but also for the informative and frequently quoted preface. Natalie Curtis-Burlin (1918) and John W. Work (1940) published two other significant anthologies.

However, one of the most important scholarly examinations of African American spirituals was Henry Krehbiel's *Afro-American Folk Songs: A Study in Racial and*

National Music (1914). Other publications explicating the historical, cultural, musical, and aesthetic treatments of the spirituals proliferated during the early 20th century. W. E. B. Du Bois' essay "Of the Sorrow Songs" was one of the most salient essays on the folk spiritual. It was published in his book, *The Souls of Black Folk* (1903). Another important essay that followed was Alain Locke's "The Negro Spirituals" (1925). These works were most significant for the early 20th century and rendered a level of validity and credibility to this sacred folk music genre. Collectively, these publications exalted this art form and brought it to the forefront for concert treatment more than any other black idiom during the early 20th century.

Part of the challenge of Reconstruction after the Civil War was to help educate blacks to survive the overwhelming economic and social struggle they faced. Therefore, the Freedmen's Bureau and several missionary societies established educational institutions both in the North and the **South** for newly emancipated slaves. While struggling to survive, these institutions encountered financial problems.

Students at Fisk University in Nashville, Tennessee, made an effort to alleviate some of the financial strain by embarking on a singing tour for profit. The Fisk Jubilee Singers toured America and Europe from 1871 to 1878, performing choral and quartet arrangements of black spirituals in the classical style. They were the first to perform in concert such songs as "Go Down Moses," "Swing Low, Sweet Chariot," "No Auction Block for Me," "Steal Away to Jesus," and many more, which have been in circulation over a century and still persist in the repertoires of present-day gospel singers. The Jubilee Singers performed a mixed repertoire of sacred and secular songs, but as a rule the spirituals or jubilee songs were always rendered a cappella.

The success of the Fisk group influenced the formation of other black university choirs who also specialized in singing the sacred repertoire of black America. Groups from Hampton Institute in Virginia and Tuskegee Institute in Alabama joined the Fisk Jubilee Singers in being the first university choirs to introduce black spirituals to the American and European concert stage. These schools were also dedicated to the preservation and development of these sacred folk songs.

In the university context, the arranged or concert form of the folk spiritual was created. This version of the spiritual mirrored the emergence of a new environment and a new social class of African Americans. As they became more educated and more assimilated into Euro-American culture, spirituals were simultaneously transformed by the synthesis of West African musical practices and aesthetic principles with those of Western Europe.

As illustrated by the emergence of the classically arranged spiritual from the traditional folk spiritual, black sacred music is in constant evolution, and the next phenomenon to evolve was the community-based vocal group. These local quartets emerged from the tradition of the Fisk Jubilee Singers. This mixed ensemble from Fisk University also featured an all-male quartet, which sang four-part arrangements of the same repertoire, consisting mostly of spirituals. Known as jubilee quartets, these groups from various black colleges eventually toured independently and established the a capella singing tradition as a genre in its own right. By the late 1920s, this unaccompanied singing style had been preserved on record and was featured live on radio broadcasts as well.

Other examples of the synthesis of West African and Western European musical concepts are from the late 1800s, when several European and American composers used African American spirituals as a basis for major works. Antonín Dvořák from the Czech Republic served as director of the National Conservatory of Music in New York from 1892 to 1895. One of his African American students, Harry T. Burleigh, who happened to be a composer and vocalist, influenced Dvořák's use of themes, employing the idioms of spirit in major works. He composed a symphony, *From the New World* (No. 9 in E minor), and two chamber compositions, both for strings: the "American" quartet (Op. 96) and a quintet (Op. 97). Michael Tippett's composition, which is one of the most important and beloved oratorios of the 20th century, *A Child of Our Time* (1939–1941), integrates five African American spirituals into its structure.

In terms of the postslavery first generation of African American composers, we owe a tremendous amount of debt for their tenacity in the use and development of the folk spiritual. Referred to as African American "nationalist" composers by Eileen Southern, they either wrote classical arrangements of spirituals or composed other works inspired by spirituals. This nationalistic movement incorporated African-derived motifs into artistic works or based the entire work on African motifs. These composers of the late 19th and early 20th century were a part of a collective movement later known as the Harlem Renaissance. Among the most memorable and celebrated composers were Harry T. Burleigh, Samuel Coleridge-Taylor, Clarence Cameron White, William Levi Dawson, Robert Nathaniel Dett, Hall Johnson, John Rosamond Johnson, Florence Price, and William Grant Still.

Similarly, African American concert artists have done their share to help disseminate and preserve the African American spiritual. Those artists, who won wide acclaim at home and abroad, are Roland Hayes, Paul Robeson, Marian Anderson, H. T. Burleigh, Mahalia Jackson, Leontyne Price, Jessye Norman, and Kathleen Battle.

The African American spiritual, an expression created by the antebellum folk community for their total—sacred and secular—life experience, has a large populace appeal. It became useful and instructive to people in many different cultures and fields of study. Over the years, its influence has not diminished. This is evident by the non–African American groups and individuals that perform in the genre. This broad worldwide adoption of the folk spiritual attests to its uniqueness and universal appeal.

Joyce Marie Jackson

See also: Biblical Characters; Hush/Bush Harbors

Further Reading

Allen, William Francis, Charles Pickard Ware, and Lucy McKim Garrison, eds., 1995 [1867], *Slave Songs of the United States* (New York: Dover Publications); Backfish, Elizabeth, 2012, "'My God Is a Rock in a Weary Land': A Comparison of the Cries and Hopes of the Psalms and African American Slave Spirituals," *Christian Scholar's Review* 42 (1): 11; Caffery, Joshua Clegg, 2013, *Traditional Music in Coastal Louisiana: The 1934*

Lomax Recordings (Baton Rouge: Louisiana State University Press); Du Bois, W. E. B. 1982 [1903], "The Sorrow Songs," in *The Souls of Black Folk* (New York: New American Library); Hudson, Martyn, 2012, "Five African American Spirituals and Michael Tippett's a Child of our Time," *Race and Class* 54 (2): 75–81; Johnson, James Weldon, Lawrence Brown, and J. Rosamond Johnson, 1977 [1925, 1926]1973 [1925], *The Books of American Negro Spirituals: Including The Book of American Negro Spirituals and The Second Book of Negro Spirituals* (New York: Da Capo Press); Kelley, James B., 2008, "Song, Story, or History: Resisting Claims of a Coded Message in the African American Spiritual Follow the Drinking Gourd," *Journal of Popular Culture* 41 (2): 262; Krehbiel, Henry Edward, 1962 [1914], *Afro-American Folk Songs: A Study in Racial and National Music* (New York: Frederick Ungar Publishing Co.); Levine, Lawrence W., 1977, *Black Culture and Black Consciousness: Afro-American Folk Thought from Slavery to Freedom* (New York: Oxford University Press); Locke, Alain, ed., 1925, "The Negro Spirituals" in *The New Negro: An Interpretation* (New York: Albert and Charles Boni); Lovell, John, 1986 [1972], *Black Song: The Forge and the Flame* (New York: Paragon House Publishers); Maultsby, Portia, 1976, "Black Spirituals: An Analysis of Textual Forms and Structures," *The Black Perspective in Music* 4: 54–69; Nielson, Erik, 2011, "Go in de Wilderness: Evading the 'Eyes of Others' in the Slave Songs," *Western Journal of Black Studies* 35 (2): 106–117; Peretti, Burton W., 2009, *Lift Every Voice: The History of African American Music* (Lanham, MD: Rowman & Littlefield Publishers); Southern, Eileen, 1997 [1971], *The Music of Black Americans: A History* (New York: W. W. Norton).

SPORTS

African Americans have historically had a troubled and ambiguous relationship with American sports. On the one hand, the black body in motion has always held a special attraction for white Americans. On the other hand, these same spectators have been reluctant to grant black people as a whole full status as human beings and American citizens. Thus, from the beginning African Americans have been in a tenuous situation when participating in American sports. Sports have also historically been one of the few avenues through which African Americans could advance economically and socially. The first integrated sport, horse racing, provided opportunities for slaves to travel, accrue money, and sometimes gain their freedom. Similar opportunities have attracted many black athletes to their sports in later generations. But just as sports posed challenges during the slavery period, participation in modern athletics has meant walking a political tight rope. Within the context of racism and the ensuing tension for blacks who participated in sports, folklore has functioned in a variety of ways, both for and among the athletes and among the black communities from which they came.

The most obvious example of folklore related to African Americans in sports is the elevation of athletes to heroic and often legendary status. To some extent, the structure of sports, going back to Greco-Roman times, has fostered the idea of the athlete as cultural hero. However, this tendency becomes all the more magnified in the case of African Americans, relative to their communities. However strongly black athletes may have wanted to simply be accepted as American or as just another member of a team, they have invariably been forced into serving as representatives of their "race." Hence their triumphs and failures are those of the entire "race" of black people. From the earliest entrance of African Americans into sports in the early 17th century as jockeys, through the era of segregation, and up to the present, black communities have embraced athletes as cultural heroes and granted them legendary status. Athletes such as Joe Louis, Henry Aaron, or Muhammad Ali have held places in black American consciousness reserved for larger-than-life figures who embody almost mythical energy. Just as tricksters like **Brer Rabbit**, John, or Anancy often symbolize the triumph of the weak over the strong, successful athletes represent the potential for black people to compete with and win against overwhelming odds—often, against whites and white society.

A comparison between **tricksters** and athletes is not far-fetched and, in fact, suggests another use of folklore in sports. Black athletes have frequently employed the trope of the tricksters in negotiating the tensions of their careers, including the issue of how to present themselves in almost "no win" situations with the media. The famous (of his day) jockey, "Monkey" Simon, who was an African-born racer of the early 19th century, was known for his trickster-like mannerisms. According to reports, he was famous for his cutting, spontaneous sarcasm, which he directed toward any and all, regardless of their rank or social class. It has been conjectured that he was able to get away with it because of the combination of his extraordinary talent and his physical deformity and small size. His most famous exchanges were probably those he had with General Andrew Jackson (who would go on to become president). The two carried on competitive exchanges over a period of several years, which were intensified as Simon defeated Jackson's horses and then taunted Jackson, who grew more and more enraged. At one point, when Jackson was furious after losing, Simon remarked publicly to him, "Gineral, you were always ugly, but now you're a show. I could make a fortune by showing you as you now look, if I had put you in a cage where you could not hurt the people who came to look at you" (Hotaling, 54).

Mocking white privilege and cruelty has been a consistent motif in the employment of tricksterism by black athletes. The first black boxing heavyweight champion, Jack Johnson used similar strategies. He often presented himself as "devil-may-care," entertaining the press with jokes and playful antics. In the days before his famous fight with the "Great White Hope," James Jeffries, he staged a mock whipping, where he invited a white press member to kneel while he actually whipped him (playfully), as slave owners and overseers had whipped their slaves. One contemporary example of the **trickster** would be heavyweight champion Muhammed Ali, who not only donned the guise of a mischief maker with the press, but with his opponents as well. The "rope-a-dope" strategy used against Joe Frazier, for instance, was as cunning as tricks devised by Brer Rabbit. Another contemporary trickster is basketball player Dennis Rodman, now retired, who was known for his tattoos, tantrums on court, ever-changing hair colors, and public cross-dressing.

Black athletes, like those of any ethnic group, also use a variety of magical beliefs. For example, many players have their "lucky" jersey, "lucky" glove, or other articles of clothing, paraphernalia, etc. that they feel will bring them good luck in their competitive endeavors. Those who participate in team sports have quite naturally developed coded languages, gestures, and other in-group communications and symbols that strengthen the sense of cohesiveness of the group and enable players to "talk" to each other without their communications becoming public. Other gestures, such as "high-fiving," and elements of **folk speech**, such as "talking trash," have become public and are so widely emulated that they are now a general part of the sports world. Celebratory behaviors, such as the dancing of black football players, can also be best understood in the context of folk traditions. They are not simply spontaneous outpourings of emotion, but marked displays signifying blackness that can be seen as responses to the ongoing tensions faced especially by black athletes. Such trickster-like antics are often sharply criticized by the press, in part because of the assumption that, given their wealth and status relative to others in American society, black athletes should be grateful and have nothing to complain about.

African American participation in sports also gives rise to many festive events. Some of these are large-scale events such as homecomings, which include parades, scheduled dinners, parties, and other activities. But others are small-scale festive events that take place in homes or community centers. In most cases they involve some type of foods, beverages, and an atmosphere of lively partying.

A final use of folklore among African Americans in sports is the integration of religious motifs. This is most obvious in examples of group **prayer** and even **testifying**. But religious motifs occur in not-so-obvious ways as well. For example, the way in which basketball players think and talk about the game also incorporates elements of non-Christian worship. In descriptions of the Chicago Bulls' championship runs of the 1990s, for instance, the metaphor of "riding" was frequently used. Players spoke in terms of their "riding" on the back of Michael Jordan in ways reminiscent of how Vodou worshippers speak of the "loas" riding them. One got the impression that, besides being a great athlete, on the basketball court Jordan was the equivalent of a **conjurer**, or **preacher**, whose special talents extended to his ability to invoke a spiritual energy that could lift his fellow teammates to incredible heights of achievement. It is interesting that two of Jordan's predecessors had names that suggested similar things about their abilities: "Dr. J" (Julius Erving) and "Magic" Earvin Johnson. Others have noted this element, for example, poet Quincy Troupe in his well-known poem, "A Poem for 'Magic.'" Troupe's poem depicts Johnson as a juju-man, a conjurer, placing him and other black athletes in the cultural context of African-derived spiritual tropes. This reimagining of the African American in sports is important in that it draws upon the entire cultural history of blacks in the New World as a context for appreciating their performances within the confines of sports arenas. In fact, it repositions black athletes as practitioners in long-standing traditions of black, spiritually inscribed arts and as serving black communities, rather than as glitzy entertainers serving the historical needs of white America for black bodies in motion.

Anand Prahlad

See also: Festivals; Nonverbal Communication; Rabbit, Brer; Trickster

Further Reading

Ashe, Arthur R., Jr., 1988, *A Hard Road to Glory: A History of the African-American Athlete 1919–1945*, vol. 2 (New York: Amistad Press); Early, Gerald Lyn, 2011, *A Level Playing Field: African American Athletes and the Republic of Sports* (Cambridge, MA: Harvard University Press); Hawkins, Billy, 2010, *The New Plantation: Black Athletes, College Sports, and Predominantly White NCAA Institutions*, 1st ed. (New York: Palgrave Macmillan); Hotaling, Edward, 1999, *The Great Black Jockeys: The Lives and Times of the Men Who Dominated America's First National Sport* (Rocklin, CA: Forum Publishing); Troupe, Quincy, 1996, *Avalanche* (Minneapolis, MN: Coffee House Press); Wigginton, Russell Thomas, 2006, *The Strange Career of the Black Athlete: African Americans and Sports* (Westport, CT: Praeger); Williams, Shawn L., *I'm a Bad Man: African American Vernacular Culture and the Making of Muhammad Ali* (Morrisville, NC: Lulu Publishing).

STAGOLEE

Stagolee is a classic **Bad Man** figure who shoots someone for accidentally touching or knocking off his Stetson hat. Of all the bad men in the African American oral tradition, Stagolee (Stackerlee, Stackalee) is probably the most widely known, and his exploits are probably the most widely recounted. It has been retold in genres of the ballad, **toasts**, **jazz**, **rap**, rhythm and blues, and in contexts including prisons, vaudeville shows, **barbershops**, **juke** joints, pool halls, brothels, on levees, on Northern street corners, and in Southern fields. Hundreds of blues recordings about Stagolee have been made, and artists as diverse as Duke Ellington, James Brown, Mississippi John Hurt, and Wilson Pickett have also recorded versions. Stagolee has also become a part of the white American tradition and has been recorded by artists such as Peggy Lee, Jimmy Dorsey, Neil Diamond, Bob Dylan, and the Grateful Dead, as well as by foreign bands such as the Clash and the Australian singer Nick Cave. In addition to his popularity in the oral tradition, Stagolee has been the basis for literary productions from authors including Gwendolyn Brooks, Howard Odum, James Baldwin, and Richard Wright (Brown, 2).

The basic plot of the narrative is that Stagolee is gambling with another man called Billy, when Billy either touches, wins, or knocks Stagolee's Stetson hat off. Stagolee responds by pulling his gun, which incites Billy to start begging for his life: "Oh please don't take my life / I got two lovely children / and a very lovely wife."

Stagolee declares that he could care less about Billy's children or his wife, and that because of Billy's transgression against his hat, he has to kill him. Stagolee shoots Billy, and in some versions he lands in jail. In other versions he is executed and goes to hell, but he is so **baad** that the **devil** gives him relative license, asking only that he not bother his wife.

There have been many speculative accounts debating whether Stagolee was a real historical person or simply a figure invented in oral tradition. Discovering the truth of his existence has been complicated by the **rumor** and **legend** process, which led many African Americans to claim that a bad man in their community had been the real Stagolee. In his seminal study of Stagolee, Cecil Brown writes, "But there was indeed a real Stagolee, a well-known figure in St. Louis's red-light district during the 1890s, a **pimp** who, when he shot and killed William Lyons, was the president of a 'Colored Four Hundred Club,' a political and social organization" (p. 11). Brown goes on to offer documented evidence, such as court records, police reports, and newspaper articles, to support his contention that Stagolee was actually a pimp named Lee Shelton, also known as Stack Lee. He was apparently a member of a group of pimps known as the "macks," who were extraordinarily elaborate and flashy dressers.

According to records, Shelton walked in to the Bill Curtis Saloon in the heart of the black, underworld district of St. Louis, between Morgan and Christy Streets, and began drinking with a man named William (Billy) Lyons. Eventually they began exchanging blows, purportedly over a disagreement about politics. In the exchanges, Lyons grabbed Shelton's hat and refused to give it back. Shelton then drew his .44 revolver and threatened to kill Lyons if he didn't return the hat. Lyons still refused and pulled a knife. Shelton shot Lyons and then "walked over to the dying man, who was still holding on to the bar, and said, 'N.., I told you to give me my hat!'" (Brown, 24). Shelton reportedly snatched the hat from Lyons, put it on, calmly walked out, went home, and went to bed. Billy Lyons was taken to the hospital and died in the early hours of the morning. Shelton was arrested, tried, and sentenced to prison, where he spent around 13 years of a 25-year sentence before getting out on parole. He continued to have trouble with the law and was sent back to prison a few years later, and he died there in 1912.

Brown writes, "The Stagolee song was born in the whorehouses and saloons of St. Louis, in the 1890s world of ward politics, racism, prostitution, and pimping. It was published as sheet music at least as early as 1924, but by 1911, six months before Lee Shelton's death, Negroes were already singing it in Georgia and the Carolinas" (p. 99). Before long it would be sung throughout the **South** and North, and it would grow rather than diminish in popularity over time.

The core elements of Stagolee's popularity in the oral tradition are his absolute indifference to moral laws, defiance of authority, his "baad-ness," and his "**cool**." The oral tradition loses sight of historical facts; for example, that he was a pimp and that, rather than engaging in heroic actions, he murdered another black man. Thus, we have to separate the historical figure from the legendary motif. The essence of his heroism in the motif is that, like **tricksters,** he operates outside of moral boundaries and does so with style. There is a celebration of willingness and ability to operate outside of the law, mainly because the law represents white society and its insistence on keeping black people oppressed and socially confined. Although the history of the actual person may have been obscured as the legend grew, the Stagolee of the legend was still someone who bore the signs of prosperity, as symbolized by his Stetson hat. And at the heart of the motif is the idea that Stagolee killed Billy because his manhood, signified by his hat and his general "sporting" appearance, had been symbolically challenged. Just as the merciless exploits of **Brer Rabbit** were celebrated by slaves who recognized in Rabbit qualities that might enable them to confront some of the inhumane horrors of their lives, contemporary African Americans have celebrated the ruthless but stylish nature of Stagolee and his unhesitating defense of his manhood. Embodied in the attitude toward Stagolee is some of the same ambivalence held toward the pimp in black communities. And in both cases, the premium placed on the stylish presentation of manhood and the ability to prosper outside of the law outweigh the inevitable social damages and transgression against even the black community. The community's embrace of the Bad Man or Bad "N*gger" are best understood in social context. As Brown notes, "For blacks, such rebellious figures were essential to survival in an era when white southerners were exploiting, threatening, and murdering African Americans with little fear of punishment" (p. 120). Despite the damaging side of the Stagolee motif, it provided inspiration for black people battling constantly against the forces of white racism.

Since its beginnings in the 19th century, the Stagolee motif has been adopted by many African American men in a variety of contexts as a signifier of their own masculinity and as a symbol for the rebellious, young black man who is only a step away from becoming a political revolutionary. For instance, Black Panther co-organizer Bobby Seale "often recited a Stagolee toast at social gatherings" and wanted to name his son Stagolee (Brown, 212). Seale saw Stagolee as the archetypal Bad "N*gger" who held great revolutionary potential. Stagolee's influence can also be seen in the toasting tradition, which is associated with black gangs and pimps. Within these contexts, the cold heartedness and rebelliousness are emphasized moreso than political revolution. In performances of Stagolee toasts, performers typically insert themselves into the narrative in ways that are not found in the song tradition. Usually, the toasts are quite lengthy and include numerous episodes, such as Stagolee shooting the bartender, having sex with multiple women during an orgy in the bar, shooting not only Billy but also his brother, and scenes of his trial.

The most recent influence of Stagolee has been in rap and **hip-hop**, which draws upon toast traditions as well as the subculture of gangs and pimps.

Anand Prahlad

Further Reading

Abrahams, Roger D., 1970 [1963], *Deep Down in the Jungle* (Chicago: Aldine Publishing Company); Brown, Cecil, 2003, *Stagolee Shot Billy* (Cambridge, MA: Harvard University Press); Jackson, Bruce, 1974, *"Get Your Ass in the Water and Swim Like Me": Narrative Poetry from Black Oral Tradition* (Cambridge, MA: Harvard University Press); Jemie, Onwuchekwa, 2003, *"Yo' Mama!": New Raps, Toasts, Dozens, Jokes & Children's Rhymes from Urban Black America* (Philadelphia, PA: Temple University Press); Levine, Lawrence, 1980 [1977], *Black Culture and Black Consciousness: Afro-American Folk Thought from Slavery to Freedom* (New York: Oxford University Press); Munby, Jonathan, 2011, *Under a Bad Sign: Criminal Self-Representation in African American Popular Culture* (Chicago; London: University of Chicago Press); Roberts, John W., 1989, *From Trickster to Badman: The Black Folk Hero in Slavery and Freedom* (Philadelphia: University of Pennsylvania Press); Wepman, Dennis, Ronald B. Newman, and Murray B. Binderman, 1976, *The Life: The Lore and Folk Poetry of the Black Hustler* (Philadelphia: University of Pennsylvania Press).

STEPPING

Stepping is a complex performance involving synchronized percussive movement, singing, speaking, chanting, and drama that developed among African American college **fraternities** and **sororities** as a ritual of group identity. Members of the nine historically black Greek-letter societies that comprise the National Pan-Hellenic Council celebrate their organizations through performances known as step shows, which present new members to the public (probate or neophyte shows). Members perform in competitive shows to raise money for social causes. Popularized in **films** and television programs such as *School Daze* (1988) and *A Different World* (1987–1993), stepping is now performed by multicultural, Asian, Latino, and occasionally white fraternities and sororities, as well as by community groups and youth in many African American **churches**. Stepping has become a dynamic and vital performance for the expression and celebration of African American identity.

The founders of the first black college fraternity, Alpha Phi Alpha, were closely associated with black Masonic societies and held their first initiation in 1906 at a Masonic Hall, where they borrowed Masonic costumes for their ritual. Stepping may have grown out of the popular drill team traditions of black mutual aid and Masonic societies and reflects the same kind of emphasis on synchronized clapping and stomping. There is a militaristic element apparent at times in the stepping or marching tradition, which may be related to this early influence.

The earliest written reference to what may be stepping on the Howard University campus appears in 1925, when an article on "Hell Week" in the campus newspaper describes Alpha Phi Alpha and Omega Psi Phi pledges "marching as if to the Fairy Pipes of Pan." Stepping grew out of the black Greek ritual of "marching on line," in which pledges expressed their brotherhood or sisterhood by walking in a line across campus, displaying their group's colors and symbols. Over the years, groups added singing, chanting, and synchronized clapping and stomping. Early shows were often in counterclockwise circles, but as stage performances for audiences became more common in the 1960s, line formations became prevalent. Terms for stepping vary among campuses and change over time and include such terms as demonstrating, marching, stomping, bopping, hopping, and blocking.

Stepping routines are orally composed and transmitted. When the stepmaster or leader is an adult, leading younger steppers, he or she may teach the routine by "breaking it down" into smaller rhythmic units which are imitated until everyone masters them. In groups in which everyone is the same age, composition is often collaborative. Circulating videotapes of step shows aid in the transmission process. A number of regional and national competitions, along with a televised nationally syndicated stepping competition and regional and national meetings of the nine black Greek-letter societies, further help to disseminate steps.

"Trade" or "signature" steps of the nine black Greek-letter societies are performed by college chapters throughout the nation and convey the character and style of the organizations. These trade steps have names and members within the black Greek system that recognize them as belonging to particular organizations by

Members of the University of Houston Alpha Phi Alpha fraternity perform during the Sprite Step Off Service Challenge in Houston, Texas, January, 2010. (Dave Einsel/AP Images for Sprite)

their visual and oral patterns. Nevertheless, other groups might also perform the trade steps of another organization to pay tribute to that group (called "saluting"), or to mock them (called "cracking"), by performing the step in an inept or comic manner. Some well-known signature steps include Alpha Phi Alpha's "The Grand-Daddy" and "Ice, Ice"; Alpha Kappa Alpha's "It's a Serious Matter"; Zeta Phi Beta's

"Sweat" and "Precise"; Phi Beta Sigma's "Wood"; and Iota Phi Theta's "Centaur Walk."

Stepping styles incorporate recent influences such as **break dancing** and **hip-hop**, as well as earlier elements from slave **dances**, such as patting juba and **ring shouts**, and aesthetic features common in Western and Central African dances. When drums were outlawed by slaveholding states, slaves used their clapping hands and stomping feet to create the rhythm for their dances. The counterclock-wise circular movement of early step routines recalls both patting juba and ring shouts, as well as the common dance pattern in Kongo culture. One of the most striking stances of African American stepping, the "get-down" position, in which steppers bend deeply from the waist or step with knees deeply bent, is common in **Africa**. Other features of African dance, according to Robert Farris Thompson, include call-and-response, dances of derision, striking moralistic poses, correct entrance and exit, personal and representational balance, establishing clear bound-aries around dances, looking smart, the mask of the **cool**, and polyrhythm or multiple meter. African American steppers exhibit all of these features as well, demonstrating the continuity of stepping with African culture.

Elizabeth C. Fine

See also: Break Dancing; Hip-Hop

Further Reading

Brown, Tamara L., Gregory Parks, and Clarenda M. Phillips, 2005, *African American Fraternities and Sororities: The Legacy and the Vision* (Lexington, KY: University Press of Kentucky); Fine, Elizabeth C., 2003, *Soulstepping: African American Step Shows* (Urbana: University of Illinois Press); Glass, Barbara S., 2007, *African American Dance: An Illustrated History* (Jefferson, NC: McFarland & Co.); Hughey, Matthew W., and Gregory Parks, 2011, *Black Greek-Letter Organizations 2.0: New Directions in the Study of African American Fraternities and Sororities* (Jackson: University Press of Mississippi); Kimbrough, Walter M., 2004, *Black Greek 101: The Culture, Customs, and Challenges of Historically Black Fraternities and Sororities* (Madison, NJ: Fairleigh Dickinson University Press); Malone, Jacqui, 1996, *Steppin' on the Blues: The Visible Rhythms of African American Dance* (Urbana: University of Illinois Press); Nomani, Asra Q., 1989, "Steeped in Tradition, 'Step Dance' Unites Blacks on Campus," *Wall Street Journal*, July 10, pp. A1, A4; Thompson, Robert Farris, 1979, *African Art in Motion: Icon and Act* (Los Angeles: University of California Press).

STORYTELLING

Storytelling is the act of communicating a narrative, usually through oral channels. Although there are contexts in African American culture that are set aside specifi-cally for narrating stories, contemporary storytelling occurs most frequently in everyday situations and conversation, for example, as people talk to each other at work, during a meal, on the telephone, and so on. Hence, there are many different kinds of storytellers, some who are masterful performers who entertain large groups, others who are equally skilled but whose audiences consist of other family members or friends, and still others who may not distinguish the stories they tell from the rest of their conversation in which the stories occur. One of the most common contemporary contexts for storytelling is within families. Stories may be told by highly skilled family members who are known in their communities as exceptional storytellers, but in most cases they are simply told by someone who wishes to share an experience, tell a **joke**, or communicate a rumor or urban **legend**. Storytelling can also occur in many other contexts and even as a part of other narrative performances. For instance, preachers customarily tell stories as a part of their **sermons**. It is common for singers in the **gospel** and **blues** traditions to narrate a story as the introductory segment to a particular song. The routines of most comedians revolve around storytelling, and politicians are known for including stories in their speeches.

Not surprisingly, there is a connection between the context, the type of stories that are told, and the performance styles used to tell the stories. During the slavery period stories were customarily told in the evening, as groups of slaves gathered in the quarters or outside at the end of long days of excruciating labor. Throughout the diaspora, storytellers of various skills told diverse kinds of tales to others in the plantation community. Folklorists would consider some stories memorates, or personal experience narratives. For instance, slaves told stories about their memories of Africa, the Middle Passage, or other experiences of their enslavement, including being whipped or attempts at escape. Stories about those who successfully escaped figured prominently among slave narratives, whether about actual slaves who fled north or legendary **flying Africans**. Stories and jokes about whites were also common, as were moralizing tales reinforcing such values as the importance of family ties, obedience, and devotion to God (Levine). Narratives about the supernatural, such as ghosts, duppies, or **hoodoo**, comprise another major category of tales. Stories most written about from the slavery period are the longer, more formulaic animal tales that include the exploits of **tricksters**, such as **Brer Rabbit**, John, or Anancy, and other colorful characters such as Bouki and Ti Malice, Brer Wolf, **Brer Fox**, and the buzzard.

Until the spread of television and other electronic media, storytelling was still a highly developed art form practiced by specialists in many New World African communities. While some of the stories and motifs from the slavery period have been continued in modern times, many of the older stories have fallen out of fashion and have been replaced by urban legends and other narratives more suited to contemporary concerns and experiences. Daniel Crowley documents and discusses Bahamian storytellers and elements of their art in *I Could Talk Old Story Good: Creativity in Bahamian Folklore*, as does Richard Dorson in *American Negro Folktales*. In works such as these we get glimpses of a time when communities gathered to hear storytellers perform, as well as insights into elements of their art. We also gain knowledge about the narrating of longer tales in traditions that extend back beyond slavery to storytelling in African societies. Although one can still find such traditions, they are not as common as they once were. As is the case with many forms of folklore and folk artists in today's societies, there has been a demand for professional storytellers to perform at events outside of their homes or communities. Thus there are storytellers who perform at festivals and in schools and community centers, and who record and market themselves in much the same way that artists of other genres do. Although the functions of stories in these settings are very different from those that apply when storytellers are performing among family, friends, or other community members, these occasions offer an opportunity for many non–African Americans to gain at least a brief exposure to this ancient tradition.

Functions

The functions served by stories are as diverse as the contexts and types in which they are found; however, there are some general functions that can be discussed. These include offering social commentary, providing opportunities for laughter, reinforcing group values and identity, imparting morals and teaching lessons, providing psychological release, providing a forum for the symbolic defeat of an oppressive society and the victory of the oppressed, and making persuasive arguments and illustrating the points of those arguments. As most scholars of African American tales have noted, trickster tales were important (among other reasons) because they offered a narrative arena in which the weaker character (the slaves), could outwit and defeat the stronger characters (slave owners). Scholars have also emphasized the importance of humor in providing slaves and later generations of African Americans a psychological mechanism through which to process the overwhelming emotional crises wrought by living within a hostile and oppressive environment, and to continue persevering and maintaining a positive state of mind. Stories and, more specifically, the arts of storytelling have been one of the major avenues of humor in African American culture. The negative critique of whites has often been paired with humor in black storytelling. Humor has also arisen from the portrayals of characters in the black community, for example, the **preacher**, Rastafarians, Bouki, Big Boy, and so on, and hinges not only on the texts of the stories but on the drama of their performances. The performance of stories helped to enliven and energize listeners, whether in the slavery period or in later centuries.

Performative Elements

New World African storytelling has historically been characterized by a number of performative elements and narrative features. One of these is the rhyming opening and closing formulas employed by storytellers in most parts of the diaspora. These are stock sentences or phrases that storytellers use to alert the audience that a story is about to begin and that the story has just ended. An example of a closing formula found in the United States is, "I stepped on some tin and it bent / And I skated on away from there" (Dorson 1967, 91). Another element of black storytelling is the formulaic insertion of a word into the story to elicit a response from the audience. The best known of these formulas is "Cric/Crack," which is found among French-speaking populations of the diaspora. At points during the story, the storyteller yells out "Cric!" and the audience yells back, "Crack!"

Call-and-response interaction between the narrator and the audience is a prominent feature of traditional storytelling events in black communities. In contrast to performances in which the audiences might sit quietly and listen to a tale being told, traditional storytelling included the background noises of people engaged in conversation, people coming and going, the noises of children playing, and the ongoing interactions between the narrator and members of the audience. Within this context, such conventions as "Cric/Crick" are more easily understood. Just as one of the primary tasks of the preacher is to perform in such a way that the congregation remains emotionally involved in the sermon, a primary challenge facing the storyteller is to employ devices that keep the audience not just engaged but actively involved in the performance. Hence, the audience helps to shape the performance and influences the length of stories, the motifs that are included or left out, and the dramatic devices that are employed and when they are used.

Scholars have commented on numerous other features found commonly in black storytelling traditions (Wolfson; Labov; Dorson 1967; Smitherman). These include direct speech, asides, repetition, expressive sounds, sound effects, motions, and gestures. The animation and dramatization of stories cannot be overemphasized. Collectors and scholars working with black storytellers invariably point out the extent to which every opportunity for the dramatic is seized. For instance, the voices of animals are exaggerated and tonal methods are used to distinguish one character's voice from another. Some voices are sung, and others humorously mimicked. Dorson writes that black storytellers

> not only fully utilize their oral resources but also gesticulate and even act out parts in exciting narratives. . . . To indicate continuous running, rather than a sudden sharp spurt, he drops his hands to his sides, spreads the fingers, and wiggles his wrists in a sideways motion, thus suggesting steady movement. Sometimes the reciter gets to his feet and weaves, writhes, gestures, and groans. . . . These histrionics build up to a small performance, the tale verging onto a drama or farce, and the audience rolling with laughter, exclaiming, commenting, and otherwise appreciating the efforts of the star. (1967, 53)

The dramatic devices employed by storytellers have sometimes been drawn from influences of popular entertainment, including in earlier times the minstrel show and vaudeville and, later, other forms such as black poetry readings and theater.

Black storytelling traditions have continued to evolve, reflecting the profound changes in Western societies from the slavery period until today. However, storytelling remains a core component of black folklore and continues to maintain some of the same characteristics and to serve many of the same functions that it did in earlier times.

Akua Duku Anokye

See also: Fables; Folktales; Nonverbal Communication

Further Reading

Ainsworth-Vaughn, Nancy, 1987, "The Lord Used, a Bottle of Mil, to Prove a Point: Cohesion and Coherence in Oral and Written Narratives," paper presented at the annual meeting of the Midwestern Modern Language Association, Columbus, OH; Champion, Tempii Bridgene, 2003, *Understanding Storytelling Among African American Children: A Journey from Africa to America* (Mahwah, NJ: Lawrence Erlbaum Associates); Collins, Brennan, 2012, "Raymond Andrews as Griot: Privileging Southern Black Communities through Oral Storytelling and Cultural History," *American Studies Journal* 56; Collins, James, and Sarah Michaels, 1986, "Speaking and Writing: Discourse Strategies and the Acquisition of Literacy," in *The Social Construction of Literacy*, ed. Jenny Cook-Gumperz (Cambridge, MA: Cambridge University Press); Dorson, Richard M., ed., 1967, *American Negro Folktales* (Greenwich, CT: Fawcett Publications, Inc.); Dorson, Richard M., ed., 1983, *Handbook of American Folklore* (Bloomington: Indiana University Press); Dorson, Richard M., 1960, "Oral Styles of American Folk Narrators," in *Style in Language*, ed. Thomas A. Sebeok (Cambridge, MA: MIT); Finnegan, Ruth, 1970, *Oral Literature in Africa* (London: Oxford University Press); Ford, Sarah Gilbreath, 2014, *Tracing Southern Storytelling in Black and White* (Tuscaloosa: The University of Alabama Press); Hua, Anh, 2013, "Black Diaspora Feminism and Writing: Memories, Storytelling, and the Narrative World as Sites of Resistance," *African and Black Diaspora* 6 (1): 30–42; Kochman, Thomas, 1981, *Black and White Styles in Conflict* (Chicago: Chicago University Press); Kochman, Thomas, comp., 1972, *Rappin' and Stylin' Out: Communication in Urban Black America* (Urbana: University of Illinois Press); Labov, W., 1972, "The Transformation of Experience in Narrative Syntax," in *Language in the Inner City* (Philadelphia: University of Pennsylvania Press); Levine, Lawrence W., 1977, *Black Culture and Black Consciousness: Afro-American Folk Thought from Slavery to Freedom* (Oxford: Oxford University Press); Ong, Walter J., 1982, "Oral Remembering and Narrative Structures," in *Analyzing Discourse: Text and Talk*, ed. D. Tannen (Washington, DC: Georgetown University Press); Smitherman, Geneva, 1977, *Talkin' and Testifyin': The Language of Black America* (Boston: Houghton Mifflin); Vaughn-Cooke, Anna Fay, 1972, "The Black Preaching Style: Historical Development & Characteristics," in *Language and Linguistics Working Papers, No. 5: Sociolinguistics*, ed. William K. Riley and David M. Smith (Washington, DC: Georgetown University Press); Wolfson, Nessa, 1982, *CHP: the Conversational Historical Present in American English Narrative* (Dordrecht, Holland: Foris Publications).

T

TAR BABY

See Rabbit, Brer; Remus, Uncle

TESTIFYING

Testifying is typically viewed and received as both a religious act as well as a communal act. It derived from the oral tradition of bearing witness and call-and-response. According to *Webster's American Dictionary* and the *King James Version Biblical Dictionary*, to testify is "to make a solemn declaration, verbal or written, to establish some fact; to give testimony for the purpose of communicating to others a knowledge of something not known to them; to declare a charge against one; to affirm or declare solemnly for the purpose of establishing a fact; to bear witness to; to support the truth of by testimony." To testify simply means to tell or to speak the experience into existence. In African American culture, a religious testimonial typically takes place within a church worship service in which the person testifying relates to the congregation an experience in which they were spiritually transcended. They bear witness to events that seem unclear or even unbelievable to others. Testifying means to tell stories of divine intervention and the guidance of the Holy Spirit in one's life. Historically, "to testify is to commit oneself and to commit the narrative to others: to take responsibility—in speech—for history or for the truth of an occurrence, for something which, by definition, goes beyond the personal" (Felman and Laub, 204). For worshippers, the act of testifying is spiritual and it serves as a significant part of **the black church**. They can only testify if there are witnesses present to receive their testimony and to acknowledge their transcendence. Testifying, in the spiritual sense, can have two dimensions: telling the truth to God about our lives and bearing witness to others about God's redemptive powers ("Practicing Our Faith").

"It is commonplace to note that religion is a vital part of both Black American history and today's Black community. Partly because Blacks were denied access to most institutions, the church became, after the family, the Blacks' most important institution, providing solace and solidarity, a positive self-image, emotional, and spiritual release, and an experimental model for leadership." Testifying, like shouting and preaching, is the common practice of spiritual relief. According to Rita Dove, "there is a tradition in the black church: we call it Testifying. It is the brave and humbling act of standing up among one's family, friends, and neighbors to bare one's soul, and to bear witness by acknowledging those who have sustained and nurtured the testifier along the way" ("testifying"). For example, African

American **preachers** often relate the stories of the enslavement of the Israelites and their deliverance to that of American slavery. The preacher would testify that if God delivered the Israelites from bondage in Egypt, Assyria, and Babylon, then he would also deliver them from slavery in the New World. If the congregation relates to and accepts the preacher's testimony, then they, in the nature of true call-and-response, will respond either verbally or physically in acceptance of his words. The testimony of a preacher evokes witnesses throughout the congregation, and they, in turn, will be able to testify to their own experiences.

"In testimony, people speak truthfully about what they have experienced and seen, offering it to the community for the edification of all. The practice of testimony [testifying] requires that there be witnesses to testify and others to receive and evaluate their testimony. It is a deeply shared practice—one that is possible only in a community that recognizes that falsehood is strong, but that yearns nonetheless to know what is true and good" ("Practicing Our Faith"). Testifying is a basic communal practice within worship services. Accordingly, it is a significant part of the King James Version of the Holy Bible. Followers of Jesus Christ were promised that they, too, would eventually be required to testify as he had to do when he faced a trial before councils and kings: "The Holy Spirit will give you words when you need them" (Mark 13:9–13). Those who choose to testify to the community often feel at a loss for words in the beginning of their witnessing process, but because of their faith and belief that they have been spiritually transcended, they await the Holy Spirit to give them the words to share with others about their experiences.

The practice of testifying has a history that moves it beyond just church services. Communal testifying can take the form of preaching, singing, or activism. For example, storytellers have told the history of African slaves as they survived in the New World. Songs have also given testifiers a way, other than through the spoken word, to make sense of their lives. The spiritual "Amazing Grace" evokes the compassion of the singer as well as the listeners. Martyrs, such as Sojourner Truth and Martin Luther King Jr., testified through their actions. They gave their bodies and lives to inspire others to bear witness to their experiences ("Practicing Our Faith"). Testifying has also become a significant part of the African American literary tradition. Its kinship with the **blues** aesthetic, which "is an ethos of blues people that manifests itself in everything done, not just in the music" (ya Salaam, 2), has made it a popular literary art form. Singing the blues creates an outlet for anguish and grief, and like testifying, it helps the person make sense of their life. According to Houston Baker, "the notion of resolution of earthly problems through motion is implied in the sound of the blues" (quoted in Moses). Toni Morrison, in *The Bluest Eye* (Washington Square Press, 1972 [1970]), has one of the main characters sing the blues of community through the oral tradition of bearing witness. The character testifies to the "community's lack of love and its transference of this lack" onto an innocent girl (Moses). Testifying signifies the manner in which a person may "shame the devil" and attest to the goodness, grace, and mercy of their god or the mere presence of hope in their lives.

Sharon D. Raynor

See also: Church, The Black; Prayer; Ring Shout

Further Reading

Atkinson, Yonne, 1996, "Creating Community: Call/Response and Witness/Testify in Toni Morrison's Beloved, Jazz, and Song of Solomon," unpublished paper, Twentieth Century Literature Conference, University of Louisville, Louisville, KY, February 24; Baker, Houston A., Jr., 1984, *Blues, Ideology, and Afro-American Literature: A Vernacular Theory* (Chicago, IL: University of Chicago Press); Campbell, Charles L. 2012, "I Believe I'll Testify: The Art of African American Preaching by Cleophus J. LaRue," *Theology Today* 69 (3): 349–351; Circle Association, "Testifying: A Tribute [to Gwendolyn Brooks] by Rita Dove, Poet Laureate of the United States," http://www.math.buffalo.edu/~sww/brooks/brookbiobib.html; Felman, Shoshana, and Dori Laub, 1992, *Testimony: Crisis of Witnessing in Literature, Psychoanalysis, and History* (New York: Routledge); Moses, Cat, 1999, "The Blues Aesthetic in Toni Morrison's The Bluest Eye," African American Review (Winter); "Practicing Our Faith: The Practices: Testimony," http://www.practicingourfaith.org/prct_testimony.html; Pinn, Anthony B., Stephen C. Finley, and Torin Alexander, 2009, *African American Religious Cultures* (Santa Barbara, CA: ABC-CLIO); Smitherman, Geneva, 1985, *Talkin' and Testifyin': The Language of Black America* (Detroit, MI: Wayne State University Press); ya Salaam, Kalamu, 1994, *What Is Life?: Reclaiming the Black Blues Self* (Chicago: Third World Press).

TITANIC, THE

The *Titanic* is a motif representing white hubris, growing out of the tragic sinking of the ship, the *Titanic*. The *Titanic* was a British luxury passenger liner that sank on April 14 and 15, 1912, en route from Southampton, England, to New York City. It was celebrated as the greatest ship that had ever been built, and was, in fact, the largest and most lavish ship that had been manufactured up to that time. Its design included a double-bottomed hull separated into numerous, supposedly watertight compartments. The *Titanic* was touted as not only the most luxurious ship ever made, but as unsinkable. The maiden voyage of the *Titanic* was a tremendous media phenomenon, in part because most of the passengers were from very prominent American and European families. The *Titanic* crashed into an iceberg about 400 miles south of Newfoundland and sank, killing 1,500 of its 4,000 passengers.

The sinking of the *Titanic* gave rise to **legends** and other kinds of folklore among varying groups of people in the United States and Europe. Ballads and broadsides commenting on the disaster were plentiful. As is often the case, the folklore reflects the attitudes, perspectives, and concerns of the particular groups from which it comes toward the multiple elements of the phenomenon. For many white Americans, there was a very positive attitude toward the *Titanic* and a pride in the technological achievement that it represented. There was, furthermore, a celebration and idolization of the wealthy families who were able to afford a ticket for the first voyage of this highly publicized ship. On the other hand, African Americans tended to view the *Titanic* in a very different light. For many in the black community, the *Titanic* symbolized the white man's belief in his own infallibility and was an ostentatious display of racism. It was rumored that the famous boxing champion, Jack Johnson, was denied a ticket on the ship. Hence, this is the perspective generally reflected when the motif appears in black folklore.

Although the motif is commonly associated with the **toasting** tradition, there is evidence that it circulated in black rural folklore in other genres as well. For example, **blues** singer Hi' Henry Brown recorded a song entitled "Titanic Blues," which relates some of the basic *Titanic* legend motifs (e.g., the ship's band was playing "Nearer, My God to Thee," as the ship was sinking). Another song version is also found in *Gumbo Ya-Ya* (1945), a collection of **folktales** from Louisiana. This version contains some motifs associated with the **toasts** and is believed to date back to the 1930s. Fragments of the modern-day toast can also be found in a 1920s minstrel tune called "The Traveling Coon" and in other early collections of folksongs. Blues singer Leadbelly also recorded a song about the *Titanic*, which focuses on the idea that Jack Johnson was ironically spared because he was not allowed on board.

The earliest complete, recorded version of the *Titanic* as a toast was collected in Harlem and published by Langston Hughes in the *Book of Negro Folklore* (1945), although it is likely that Hughes edited out all of the sexual and profane content. The basic plot of the toast is that only one black person, Shine, is allowed on the *Titanic*, and he has the job of shoveling coal to keep the engine running. When the ship hits the iceberg, Shine repeatedly goes up on deck to tell the captain that water is pouring in, and each time the captain patronizingly directs him to go back down to the boiler room and not to worry, because the ship is unsinkable. Finally, Shine jumps overboard. He is then offered money by the captain and offered sex by the captain's wife and the captain's daughter if he will come back and save them. Shine rejects their offers and outswims whales and sharks to make it back to Harlem, where, by the time that the news of the *Titanic* reaches Washington, he is already half drunk. In the narrative, he is the only survivor. Shine becomes an African American hero, symbolizing the black man who has sense enough to ignore the captain's orders and abandon a sinking ship. He also has pride enough in his heritage to not be tempted by white status symbols, and he has superhuman abilities, demonstrated by his outswimming the most formidable creatures of the sea.

Anand Prahlad

Further Reading

Abrahams, Roger D., 1970 [1963], *Deep Down in the Jungle: Negro Narrative Folklore from the Streets of Philadelphia* (Chicago, IL: Aldine Publishing); Free, Marvin D., and Mitch Ruesink, 2012, *Race and Justice: Wrongful Convictions of African Men* (Boulder, CO: Lynne Rienner Publishers); Hughes, Langston, and Arna Bontemps, 1958, *The Book of Negro Folklore* (New York: Dodd, Mead); Jackson, Bruce, 1974, *Get Your Ass in the Water and Swim Like Me: Narrative Poetry from Black Oral Tradition* (Cambridge, MA: Harvard University Press); Munby, Jonathan, 2011, *Under a Bad Sign: Criminal Self-Representation in African American Popular Culture* (Chicago: University of Chicago Press); Saxon, Lyle, Edward Dreyer, and Rober Tallant, 1945, *Gumbo Ya-Ya* (New York: Houghton Mifflin).

TOASTS

Toasts are prose narratives that are one of the most highly developed forms of black oral traditions. They incorporate other traditional forms, such as **signifying**, boasts, threats, **dozens**, epitaphs, etc. These entertaining narratives ridicule stupidity, gullibility, selfishness, weakness, braggadocio, audacity, and arrogance of victims while regaling the wit, guile, strength, and virility of protagonists. The most well-known toasts in black oral tradition are "**The Signifying Monkey**," "**The *Titanic***," and "Stackerlee" (**Stagolee**), and they all speak to these qualities in varying degrees. Clearly, these are not the kinds of toasts that one performs with drink in hand while celebrating a birthday, wishing newlyweds success, or drinking to a comrade's good health. These are distinctly African American, not European, and represent the best of black orature, black **sermons** notwithstanding.

Onwuchekwa Jemie calls the African American toast "a jazzy riff" on the conventional European drinking toast (2003, 52). This is not to say that its origins excluded drink. A natural conversational setting among black males might include the telling of toasts as a bottle of liquor is drained, as Anthony M. Reynolds attests in his collection (1974, 299). Similarly, Roger Abrahams discusses the manner in which African Americans may have coined the term in his 1970 collection *Deep Down in the Jungle: Negro Narrative Folklore from the Streets of Philadelphia* (1970 [1963], 109–111), suggesting that even though early minstrel shows influenced the tradition's emergence, toasts may have also derived from performing verse with drink in hand (ibid., 109). Yet, prohibition must have had an effect on such a function, and it therefore does not account for its popularity among male prisoners and others unable to purchase liquor. He and others distinguish between "society toasts" and **bad man** toasts (e.g., "Stackolee") and other toasts, such as "The Signifying Monkey," both of which have appeared in several collections. "Society toasts," unlike the other types, lack obscenities, are appropriate for mixed company, have a greater frequency of internal rhyme, have a moralistic tone, and obtain close identification between the storyteller and the main characters (Reynolds, 273–274).

In their performance, toasts showcase the speaker's skill in expressing the characteristics of the story's protagonist, often pitting a bad man/**trickster** against everybody else. A skillful raconteur combines rhymed couplets while displaying his voice inflections and body movement to mimic the hero and his foes. Jemie calls such a performance "the apex of the modern tradition of African-American oral poetry" in the introduction to *"Yo' Mama!" New Raps, Toasts, Dozens, Jokes & Children's Rhymes from Urban Black America* (2003).

Perhaps the most widely known toast appearing in African American folklore collections is "The Signifying Monkey." The main character, Monkey, is a symbolic construct, a trickster, and an antagonist who invites trouble. His words are dangerous because they are ridiculous, exaggerated, and outrageous; however, they succeed in stirring up trouble. In most versions of the toast, the Monkey incites the Lion to pick a fight with the elephant, who invariably badly beats the Lion almost to death. Other black toasts include familiar figures such as Stagolee, Railroad Bill, Dolemite, Piss-Pot Pete, and Shine.

Despite the exaggerations, the characters in toasts such as "The Signifying Monkey" are ones with which listeners and narrators identify to some extent. The monkey is the quintessential trickster who pits two individuals against each other by telling lies and insults, but the monkey sometimes survives by guile and wit. Lion is a bully and lacks the intelligence to know he is being signified on by the monkey, whereas the elephant is really the king of the jungle, given his sheer size, but he is also someone the insecure lion feels he must overcome to prove who is king of the jungle. Of course, it is the monkey who upsets the status quo and creates chaos.

"The *Titanic*" also incorporates many of these same features, but this time the protagonist is Shine, a character who shares qualities of the bad man as well as the hardman, and even the trickster. "The *Titanic*" is based on the sinking of the super luxury liner that, ironically, refused passage to blacks (including the famous prizefighter Jack Johnson) unless the passenger occupied a lowly position such as a servant, or, as in Shine's case, a stoker in the boiler room below. Because of the institutionalized racism practiced during this time (1912) of the ship's sinking, it is no wonder that such a toast would find considerable appeal among black audiences. Jackson included "The *Titanic*" in his 1974 collection *"Get Your Ass in the Water and Swim Like Me": Narrative Poetry from Black Oral Tradition*; a line in the toast is his book's title.

In black oral tradition, the *Titanic* toast proclaims the futility of earthly grandeur and riches while taunting whites for excluding blacks from the doomed vessel (including the black heavyweight champion of the world, Jack Johnson). This toast's relevance to racial tensions endures, even though the meaning such toasts have to those who perform and enjoy them will always be culturally specific. But the toast is more than a response to racial indignities. Shine is the only one intelligent enough to know the ship is sinking. Moreover, he is not only outrageous in his language as he thwarts the ultimate authority, the white ship's captain, but he has also impregnated the captain's daughter while refusing to acquiesce to her and others' pleas to save them, returning to land where he continues his life of drinking and debauchery as the super ocean liner goes down.

Bruce Jackson has offered some psychosocial functions of toasts as they occur in "certain kinds of parties, among youths hanging around street corners, [and] among inmates in jails and prisons" (Jackson, 123), while Wepman, Newman, and Binderman have compared and discussed culture heroes within toasts that black prisoners performed during the 1950s and 1960s (1976, 1–15), identifying themes and "culture hero" types characteristic of the genre, giving special attention to the bad man and the trickster. Other scholars, such as Labov, Cohen, Robins, and Lewis concur that toasts employ the trickster and bad man as protagonists (329–347), but Onwuchekwa Jemie argues that these basic categories are fragments of African American sensibility and may be seen as "existential nay-sayers . . . saying no to domination and exploitation [and] yes to freedom and self-mastery," rather than seen as childlike and amoral, as some scholars have argued (60). Nevertheless, these and other researchers have made available not only representations of folklore performances but also the typical contexts in which they emerge.

The recitations of "The *Titanic*" and "The Signifying Monkey" always bring laughter to an audience that understands the social milieu that has shaped such oral traditions, the challenge against an oppressive system, and the tremendous effort to survive in a racist society. The artistic forms of expression (boasts, signifying, invectives) contained in these narratives further illustrate the level of complexity and black aesthetic that such prose evinces in the hands of an experienced raconteur.

Richard Allen Burns

See also: Dozens, The; Stagolee

Further Reading

Abrahams, Roger, 1970 [1963], *Deep Down in the Jungle: Negro Narrative Folklore from the Streets of Philadelphia* (Chicago, IL: Aldine Publishing Company); Evans, David, 1977, "The Toast in Context," *Journal of American Folklore* 90 (356):129–148; Jackson, Bruce, 1975, "A Response to 'Toasts: The Black Urban Poetry,'" *Journal of American Folklore* 88 (348):178–182; Jackson, Bruce, 1972, "Circus and Street: Psychosocial Aspects of the Black Toast," *Journal of American Folklore* 85 (336): 123–139; Jackson, Bruce, 1974, *"Get Your Ass in the Water and Swim Like Me": Narrative Poetry from Black Oral Tradition* (Cambridge, MA: Harvard University Press); Jemie, Onwuchekwa, ed., 2003, *"Yo' Mama!": New Raps, Toasts, Dozens, Jokes & Children's Rhymes from Urban Black America* (Philadelphia, PA: Temple University Press); Johnson, James D., 1981, "An Instance of Toasts among Southern Whites," *Western Folklore* 40 (4): 329–337; Kearse, Randy, 2006, *Street Talk: Da Official Guide to Hip-Hop & Urban Slanguage* (Fort Lee, NJ: Barricade Books); Labov, William, Paul Cohen, Clarence Robins, and John Lewis, 1994 [1968], "Toasts," in *Mother Wit from the Laughing Barrel: Readings in the Interpretation of Afro-American Folklore*, ed. Alan Dundes (Jackson: University Press of Mississippi), pp. 329–347; Reynolds, Anthony M., 1974, "Urban Toasts: A Hustler's Point of View from L. A.," *Western Folklore* 33 (4): 267–300; Smitherman, Geneva, 2000, *Black Talk: Words and Phrases from the Hood to the Amen Corner* (Boston: Houghton Mifflin); Wepman, Dennis, Ronald B. Newman, and Murray B. Binderman, 1975, "A Rejoinder to Jackson," *Journal of American Folklore* 88 (348): 182–185; Wepman, Dennis, Ronald B. Newman, and Murray B. Binderman, 1976, *The Life: The Lore and Folk Poetry of the Black Hustler* (Philadelphia: University of Pennsylvania Press); Wepman, Dennis, Ronald B. Newman, and Murray B. Binderman, 1974, "Toasts: The Black Urban Folk Poetry," *Journal of American Folklore* 87 (345): 208–224.

TOM, UNCLE

The term "Uncle Tom" describes a black man who is loyal, submissive, and servile to white people. It is also used as a verb meaning to act in a manner characteristic of an Uncle Tom. Other variations on the term include the nouns "Uncle Tommery," "Uncle Tomming," and "Uncle Tommism," and the adjective "Uncle Tommish." Uncle Tom is the name of the hero of the famous abolitionist novel *Uncle Tom's Cabin, or, Life among the Lowly* by Harriet Beecher Stowe. Published in 1852, *Uncle Tom's Cabin* was a best-seller, America's first social protest novel, and the first novel to criticize slavery. The Fugitive Slave Law, passed in 1850, provided a catalyst for Stowe's antislavery writing, though abolitionism was a family affair. The Beecher family produced a number of religious leaders, reformers, and educators who embraced the cause. Stowe uses sentimentality to win her audience—who, at the time, were mostly white, educated, and middle class—over to her cause. Rather than arguing that slavery is wrong for moral or religious reasons, the novel instead emphasizes the ways that slavery tragically breaks apart families. This approach was enormously successful in the mid-19th century, but contemporary readers may find it unsatisfactory. Attitudes toward the novel, its argument, and its characters have changed, which explains why the term *Uncle Tom* has the meaning it does today. In a letter printed in *Frederick Douglass' Paper* on May 20, 1852, William G. Allen wrote, "Uncle Tom was a good soul, thoroughly and perfectly pious. Indeed, if any man had too much piety, Uncle Tom was that man." Allen's comment seems to anticipate 20th-century reactions to the character, for while Stowe sought to portray Uncle Tom as selfless, trustworthy, and devoutly Christian, many contemporary readers instead see him as a pushover, passive, obsequious, and even cowardly. For example, Uncle Tom remains loyal to Mr. Shelby, the white man he has served since childhood, even after Shelby sells him to the slave trader, Mr. Hadley. Hadley plans to bring Tom to the auction block in New Orleans, where he will be sold to a Southern plantation with far worse conditions than his former home in Kentucky. Shelby's maid Eliza runs away to prevent her master from selling her young son Harry and urges Uncle Tom to do the same, but he refuses, accepting his fate and turning to the Bible for comfort. Stowe intended to characterize Uncle Tom's actions as saintly or even Christ-like. But today, Uncle Tom may seem too fond of or devoted to his white owners and too content in slavery.

M. J. Strong

Further Reading

Allen, W. B., 2009, *Rethinking Uncle Tom: The Political Philosophy of Harriet Beecher Stowe,* (Lanham: Lexington Books); Del Guercio, Gerardo, 2012, *The Fugitive Slave Law in the Life of Frederick Douglass, an American Slave and Harriet Beecher Stowe's Uncle Tom's Cabin: An American Society Transforms its Culture* (Lewiston: The Edwin Mellen Press); Douglas, Ann, 1978, *The Feminization of American Culture* (New York: Avon Books); Garcia, Claire Oberon, Vershawn Ashanti Young, and Charise Pimentel, 2014, *From Uncle Tom's Cabin to the Help: Critical Perspectives on White-Authored Narratives of Black Life* (New York: Palgrave Macmillan); Mitchell, Margaret, 1996, *Gone with the Wind, with a New Preface by Pat Conroy and an Introduction by James A. Michener* (New York: Scribner); Richardson, Riché, 2007, *Black Masculinity and the U.S. South: From Uncle Tom to Gangsta* (Athens: University of Georgia Press); Spingarn, A., 2012, "When Uncle Tom Didn't Die: The Antislavery Politics of H.J. Conway's Uncle Tom's Cabin," *Theatre Survey* 53 (2): 203–218; *Uncle Tom's Cabin and American Culture: A Multi-Media Archive,* http://www.iath.virginia.edu/utc/; Stowe, Harriet Beecher, 2002, *Uncle Tom's Cabin, or, Life among the Lowly, with a New Introduction by Charles Johnson* (New York: Oxford University Press); Visser, Irene, 2008, "(In) Famous Spirituality: Harriet Beecher Stowe's Uncle Tom," *Spiritus: A Journal of Christian Spirituality* 8 (1): 1–22.

TORTOISE

Tortoise has been an integral character/figure of black oral tales dating back to Africa. It prominently turns up in stories of the Yoruba, Igbo, and Edo people of Nigeria; the myths of Central Africa; epics and fables of the Masai of Eastern Africa; and trickster tales from the slaves of the Southern United States and Caribbean. In some fables, tortoise is referred to as Ijapa/Ajapa. In spiritual mythologies, turtle emblematically represents the connection between heaven and earth. Ison (Eka Obasi, Obasi Nsi, Ibibio) is the West African goddess, "The Tortoise-shelled" who symbolizes the earth. Tortoise also evokes sexuality in West African myths. In Nigeria, the tortoise serves as a sign of the female sex organs and sexuality. Among the Azande of Africa, the tortoise can also be symbolically linked to the phallus and/or homoeroticism. In addition to being linked to gods/goddesses, the tortoise's shell links it to immortality and is considered a temporary dwelling place for souls making their way to nirvana. For this reason, tortoise is seen as the perfect representation of healing, and many African cultures associate the animal with shamanism. In Dahomean culture, tortoises in mythical narratives are fundamentally essential to understanding the importance of divination traditions. In these tales, tortoise is an outcast amongst other animals and unlike anything they have ever known or seen. In one story, tortoise is told, "You will always be a diviner because you have suffered much" (Herskovits, 193).

In African diaspora culture, tortoise transitions into turtle or terrapin, and it serves as a figure of tricksterism in African American folklore and literature. The earliest print acknowledgment of turtle occurs in Joel Chandler Harris's **Uncle Remus** tales, in which turtle is mentioned in competition with **Brer Rabbit**. Lawrence Levine's *Black Culture and Black Consciousness* (1977) explains that the turtle and terrapin occupy trickster spaces in African American folklore: "In the popular tales featuring a race between a slow animal and a swifter opponent the former triumphs not through persistence, as does his counterpart in Aseopian **fable** of the Tortoise and the Hare, but by outwitting and capitalizing on his weakness and shortsightedness. Terrapin defeats Deer by placing relatives along the route with Terrapin himself stationed by the finish line" (p. 115). Levine's reading explores the tortoise as a trickster of deception that relies on wit and intelligence as opposed to physical attributes.

LaMonda Horton-Stallings

Further Reading

Conner, Randy P., David Sparks, and Mariya Sparks, 1997, *Cassell's Encyclopedia of Queer Myths, Symbol and Spirit* (London and New York: Cassell); Herskovits, Melville, 1958, *Dahomean Narrative: A Cross-Cultural Analysis* (Evanston, IL: Northwestern University Press); Levine, Lawrence, 1977, *Black Culture and Black Consciousness: Afro-American Folk Thought from Slavery to Freedom* (New York: Oxford University Press); M'Baye, Babacar, 2009, *The Trickster Comes West: Pan-African Influence in Early Black Diasporan Narratives* (Jackson: University Press of Mississippi); Njoku, J. Akuma-Kalu, 2009, "'There's Got to be a Tortoise in It': Lore as the Conceptual Focus of Igbo Folklore," *Southern Quarterly* 46 (4): 159.

TRAINS

The train is a recurrent motif and one of the most ubiquitous motifs in African American folklore. It is found in many genres over the period from slavery through the early 21st century, not only in the United States, but also in parts of the Caribbean. Some have suggested a connection between the train and African divinity, Ògún, the deity of iron, progress, and civilization. Whether such a connection was made by slaves or not, the train is certainly imbued with mythic features, with living presence.

The train first appears in African American folklore in slave **spirituals**, in which it functions as a symbol of the journey toward freedom. Not only was the train a symbol of the network that secretly transported slaves out of slavery and into freedom in the North (the Underground Railroad), but it figured prominently in the lyrics of spirituals, where it sometimes replaced the image of the chariot bound for heaven (freedom). The train image appears in the following stanza, from "King David," for example:

Just as soon as you cease
Good Lord,
Children, from your sins,
Good Lord,
This-a train will start
Good Lord,
To take you in.

(Courlander, 305)

No other symbol, or for that matter, no other technological reality has been more central to **blues** culture. Trains represented transportation and mobility, and train yards were a common gathering place for itinerant black men, including musicians. But before that, slaves had been the primary labor for laying and maintaining the tracks. The same rhythmic, call-and-response of singing that has been widely documented among black work gangs in the postbellum and modern eras characterized the laying of track during the slavery period. Railroads were also one of the (if not the largest) employer of African Americans in the latter part of the 19th century. As much as the train captured the general imagination of Americans, it became for African Americans a mythical presence, and was woven throughout the lyrics and musical approaches of blues artists. Harmonica players and guitarists mimicked or celebrated the sounds of the train, which seemed to echo some of their own inner angst. Reportedly, boogie woogie piano style, which had a profound impact on blues music, emerged as an attempt to capture the rhythms and sounds of the train. In blues lyrics trains are sometimes avenues for freedom, and at other times vehicles that take one's lover away. The train is also reflected in ballads that found their way into the blues tradition, for example, "John Henry," who dies hammering a train tunnel through a mountain, and "Casey Jones." The train image recurs as well in urban blues, **gospels**, rhythm and blues, **soul**, **jazz**, reggae, and **hip-hop** music, as indicated by such titles as "Take the 'A' Train" (jazz), "This Train" (reggae), and "Nighttrain" (hip-hop). It is no accident, then, that the title of the most enduring black television show is *Soul Train* (1971–2006), and that the symbol for the show is a puffing engine.

Moving from the passenger and freight trains that captivated African Americans in the late 19th and early 20th century to the subway trains of cities such as New York has inspired new meanings that have merged with traditional ones. Like the trains of blues lore, subway trains also represented mobility and power, and the train yards have been spaces for communities of young men to gather and to create. For instance, in the 1970s **aerosol artists** gathered in subway train yards to paint and to socialize. They even referred at times to the subways as the "underground railroad." Trains, which they painted on, became for them the main medium for spreading their art, political messages, and reflections of their lives and communities.

Recognizing the importance of the train motif in African American folk culture, literary artists have often utilized it. For example, Albert Murray's *Train Whistle Guitar* (1974) revolves around the life of blues musician Luzana Cholly, whose music replicates sounds of a train. The train recurs in works by many other authors, including Amiri Baraka, James Baldwin, Langston Hughes, Zora Neale Hurston, Jean Toomer, and Sterling Brown.

Anand Prahlad

Further Reading

Courlander, Harold, ed., 1976, *A Treasury of Afro-American Folklore* (New York: Crown Publishers); Kornweibel, Theodore, 2010, *Railroads in the African American Experience: A Photographic Journey* (Baltimore, MD: Johns Hopkins University Press); McCombe, John, 2012, "The Stephen Dedalus Blues: Travel, Trains, and a Blues Sensibility in A Portrait of the Artist as a Young Man," *James Joyce Quarterly* 48 (3): 477–494; Miller, Ivor L., 2002, *Aerosol Kingdom: Subway Painters of New York City* (Jackson: University Press of Mississippi Press).

TRICKSTER

A trickster is an irreverent figure whose behaviors consistently disrupt the morals of a given society or group. Tricksters operate in the liminal space between the well-established social structures of a group and the chaos beyond. Typically, they delight in exposing the seams along which social mores are stitched together by violating them. Through his/her transgressions, group members experience a sense of psychic relief and a vicarious pleasure in listening to exploits that reflect some of their own desires. Paradoxically, the outrageous antics ascribed to tricksters also provide ongoing opportunities for groups to reaffirm the values that are most important to them. In many ways tricksters are the embodiment of creativity, of ingenuity, as they routinely reinvent the tools of social discourse, applying them in imaginative ways that suit their own purposes. Hence, while often serving as cultural heroes, they also define behaviors that are extremely outside of what is socially appropriate within the group.

Tricksters are found in cultures around the globe, and have historically been extremely popular in **Africa**. Common African tricksters include Anansi the spider, Hare or Rabbit, the **Tortoise**, and a number of divine figures such as Legba, Eshu, and Orunmila. Most of these were transplanted to parts of the Americas and served vital functions in slave and postbellum societies. The most important African-derived trickster figure in the United States was **Brer Rabbit**. Like animal trickster tales found in Africa, those in the United States revolve around the assault on a weak animal by a stronger one, and the ingenious ability of the weaker animal to defeat his foe, thereby upsetting or even reversing structures of power (Levine, 106).

Within African American slave culture, though, Brer Rabbit evolved beyond simply "slipping the yoke" and escaping the traps of larger animals. His development is understandable considering the complexities of black life under slavery. Operating within slavery meant mastering and coping with multiple sets of social morals and values, as well as systems of power. For example, slaveholders espoused a belief in God and Christianity but at the same time practiced the most horrendous greed, brutality, and inhumane treatment of other human beings imaginable. Besides coping with these two contradictory systems, the slaves had their own sets of social mores by which they lived. Their lives were troubled by a clash of inconsistent systems; a chaos, a jungle in which multiple forces worked against their survival and social values were enacted in the most arbitrary of fashions. Brer Rabbit evolved within this social reality. As Lawrence Levine points out, Brer Rabbit's driving impulse was advancement, not survival, and he "emerged not only as an incomparable defender but also as a supreme manipulator" (1977, 108). He wanted to better himself, to attain possessions, wealth, and most importantly, power. Although the exploits of Brer Rabbit may seem extreme to the sensibilities of later generations, it is understandable how he could have provided not only a sense of psychic relief for slaves but also a necessary symbolic conquest of their enemies. His behavior also mapped psychological and behavioral strategies for enduring, challenging, and undermining the structures of power inherent in the plantation reality.

Besides the African-derived tricksters, human figures also emerged in the folklore of the slavery and postbellum periods. One such figure was John, who is usually paired with Old Master. Operating within the human realm, John's adventures are more restrained than are Brer Rabbit's. Nor does John display the same extent of assault on established social morals as is characteristic of animal tales. The John tales are more overt depictions of a black man employing the strategies of the trickster in order to negotiate the tensions of his life as a slave. The structure of the tales revolves around competition between the two, John and Old Master. As such, the white slave owner and those he represents are portrayed as being motivated by their greed, but moreso by their psychological need to feel superior to black men. The tales suggest that John becomes a trickster because of the nature of his circumstances, and that one of his most effective weapons is his insight into the psychology of the white mind. It is this insight that not only enables him to win, but to win in ways that are most psychologically damaging to Old Master. There have also been a number of female tricksters in the African American tradition (e.g., Aunt Nancy, Ol' Molly Hare, and **Aunt Dicy**), but relatively few compared to the male figures.

In the time since slavery, the trickster has continued to evolve in African American culture and a host of social changes have had a profound impact on his development, for example, northern and western migration, segregation, integration, the civil rights and black power movements, etc. Because of these changes, figures associated with the plantation and rural life gave way to new personalities associated more with urban realities. An example of a modern trickster figure who emerged out of the urban environment is the **Signifying Monkey** of the **toast** tradition. Henry Louis Gates suggests the evolution of the Signifying Monkey in a lineage going back to African divine tricksters, such as Legba and Eshu. The Monkey is certainly a different kind of trickster than either Brer Rabbit or John. Whereas the latter two operate within the context of oppression and are usually motivated by systematic or direct assaults against them, the Signifying Monkey embodies the character of "he-who-exists-to-trick-and-create-mischief." His mission in life is to **signify**, to stir up trouble. He is best known for playing on the egos of larger animals, such as the Lion and the Elephant, and for manipulating them into fighting with each other.

John Roberts has discussed the further evolution of the trickster figure into the "**Bad Man**" in African American folklore. The Bad Man's character and motivations are distinct from either those of the plantation trickster or figures like the Signifying Monkey. If Brer Rabbit reflected the need for slaves to ritually reaffirm the potential of the weak to outwit and defeat the strong, then the Bad Man reflects the contemporary African American who "will not take any mess from anybody." His spirit is a combination of the mischievousness of tricksters found in folktales and the militancy demonstrated by groups such as the Black Panthers. As such, the Bad Man can be fierce and dangerously explosive; for example, **Stagolee** shoots Billy for simply knocking his hat off. But there can also be a playful side to Bad Men, for example, many of the interactions that Stagolee has with other characters in extended versions of toasts; or interactions that Railroad Bill has with the posses that are chasing him.

Modern examples of the trickster range from characters in folklore, black films, literature, and popular culture, and many times there is a conscious emulation of trickster behavior found in earlier examples of folklore. **Sports** figures, such as boxer Muhammad Ali or basketball player Dennis Rodman have crafted public personas that are clearly trickster figures. Comedians like Richard Pryor, Rudy Ray Moore, or Dave Chappelle integrated many elements of tricksterism into their public personas and comedic routines. Henry Louis Gates's exploration of signifying in black speech and literature suggests the presence of trickster motifs in much of African American literature. Elements of tricksterism permeate lyrics and performances of hip-hop and other popular music, for example, the costumes and stage props for many concerts. Although trickster tales are rarely told in contemporary African American culture, the spirit and rhetorical motifs of tricksterism remain essential strategies for negotiating race, and as such, continue to be important elements of black discourse in the 21st century.

Anand Prahlad

Further Reading

Borgatti, Jean, 2009, "Willie Cole's Africa Remix: Trickster and 'Tribe,'" *African Arts* 42 (2): 12–23; Courlander, Harold, ed., 1976, *A Treasury of Afro-American Folklore* (New York: Crown Publishers); Gates, Henry Louis, Jr., 1988, *The Signifying Monkey: A Theory of African-American Literary Criticism* (New York: Oxford University Press); Landry, H. Jordan, 2013, "Bringing Down the House: The Trickster's Signifying on Victimization in Harriet E. Wilson's Our Nig," *Callaloo* 36 (2): 440–460; Lavender, Isiah, 2009, "Lebert Joseph to the Rescue: A Positive Trickster in Paule Marshall's 'Praisesong for the Widow,'" *Journal of Caribbean Literatures* 6 (1): 109–124; Levine, Lawrence W., 1977, *Black Culture and Black Consciousness* (New York: Oxford University Press); M'Baye, Babacar, 2009, *The Trickster Comes West: Pan-African Influence in Early Black Diasporan Narratives* (Jackson: University Press of Mississippi); Nyawalo, Mich Yonah, 2012, "From Trickster to Badman to 'Gangsta': Globalizing the Badman Mythoform in Hip-Hop Music," (ProQuest Dissertations Publishing).

V

VISIONARY ARTISTS

Art that is based on an extremely personal vision and often inspired by direct supernatural encounters, dreams, and revelatory experiences is called visionary art. During the 1990s, there had been an increasing fascination among scholars, art collectors, and the general public in "visionary and outsider art," generally defined as "the art of obsessive visionaries or the patients of mental institutions"—people with no formal artistic training who are inspired to fulfill some extraordinary, personal creative vision (Hall and Metcalf, xii–xiv; Beardsley, 7–11). The art of such individuals often is said to be idiosyncratic or without precedent or tradition and isolated from the dominant culture and the mainstream art world (Rhodes, 7–22). Such art tends not to be based so much on community traditions and collective aesthetics, like folk art, but instead gives tangible form to a uniquely personal vision. This vision usually preoccupies the individual, who works fervently to create things, compelled by some supernatural power that is experienced through profound mystical experiences, encounters with divine beings or forces, dreams, altered states of consciousness, mental illness, or traumatic events (Beardsley, Hall, Manley). Formalistically, the art often is said to have a compulsive and obsessive quality, and the artist usually takes an uninhibited, nonconformist approach to creation, initially producing things without regard to mainstream recognition or the marketplace (Nasisse).

The concept of visionary art is related to the term "outsider art," which was coined by Roger Cardinal in 1972 as an equivalent for the French term *art brut*, which was proposed by the modernist painter Jean Dubuffet in 1949. For Dubuffet, *art brut* ("raw art") was made by people who were free of artistic training, "untouched" by culture, and existed outside of or against cultural norms (Dubuffet). The assumptions underlying the concept of outsider art are problematic from a folkloric perspective. The concept is inaccurate and dehumanizing; it emphasizes romantic and stereotypical notions of the eccentric or insane "artist as rebel," disconnected from society and free from societal influences, obsessively creating *art brut*. The term stigmatizes the artist as "Other," as primitive or pathological in relation to so-called normal people and culture. When applied to African Americans and other people of color, this label takes on even more disturbing, racist connotations.

The term "visionary art" has been proposed as a corrective to the denigrating connotations of "outsider art," with the new term designating those creations that are based on some sort of transformative spiritual experience and recognizing the important but often neglected influence of the religious origins and function of such art. The art of African Americans previously labeled as "outsiders" now is being considered in terms of African American religion, vernacular traditions, and even surviving African influences and aesthetic traditions that have been perpetuated and transformed (Wahlman, 1987; Wahlman, 2001). Furthermore, the art of such individuals must be viewed in terms of life history, social interactions, and personal motivations as well as within the larger context of racism, segregation, oppression, economic hardship, limited educational opportunities, and other struggles that many African Americans have faced.

There have been hundreds of African American visionary artists, and this limited discussion mentions only a few of the significant individuals who represent certain common themes or tendencies among such artists. Perhaps the most famous of these are James Hampton (1909–1964), Minnie Evans (1992–1983), and Sister Gertrude Morgan (1900–1980), each of whom has been referred to as among the great visionary artists of all time. Hampton based his shimmering, massive throne sculpture on divinely inspired private visions, prophecies from the book of Revelation, and broader African American vernacular traditions. Evans's luminous, symmetrically patterned drawings were inspired by her dreams and visions of other worlds. Morgan, who became a street **preacher** after visionary experiences, created vivid, colorful paintings as well as painted objects and music to express her religious devotion and mission.

Whether preachers, mediums, mystics, or clairvoyants, a large number of visionary artists assert that during a dream or trance state a voice or spirit

Jesus is my air Plane, by Sister Gertrude Morgan, one of the greatest visionary artists of all time, ca. 1970. (Smithsonian American Art Museum, Washington, DC/Art Resource, NY)

commanded them to create art. For Christian visionaries, this direct experience of the supernatural may be an accepted occurrence, regarded simply as "feeling the spirit," which is a part of one's faith. However, such art often expresses distinctive aspects of African American spirituality and possibly older African beliefs about spirit beings mingling freely with the living as guardian spirits guiding artists or as an animistic, spiritual power infusing all things. Such beliefs reflect a creolization of Christian and perhaps **Native American** traditions. (Adele, 16; Lawal, 40–41; Wahlman 1987, 28–29).

An example of an individual inspired by visionary experiences and African influences is Bessie Harvey (1929–1994), from Alcoa, Tennessee. She began creating things after a sickness and various life traumas, which lead to her spiritual calling. She had visions for most of her life and started seeing faces, souls, and figures in the natural world, which she believed was alive with God, spirits, and presences. She then began forming haunting, anthropomorphic sculptures from branches, roots, shells, and other found objects to bring out the inherent spirit and form within. This sort of art might seem idiosyncratic, but objects made from roots and natural materials have an extensive history in African art, and gnarled and twisted roots traditionally have been used as **charms** in African American folk practice (Adele, 78). For instance, a twisted root, or a "black snake root," is known as **High John the Conqueror** (Wahlman, 1987, 380). Harvey called her work "**hoodoo**," and clearly considered her art to be based in African American traditions and beliefs. The use of roots and branches with protective powers occurs among various other self-taught African American artists, including Willard "The Texas Kid" Watson, Sam Doyle, and Steve Ashby.

Jesse Aaron (1887–1979) also worked with roots and saw faces and figures in wood. He believed that they were put there by God and that he would "bring to life" the figures and faces through his carving. Like Harvey, Aaron suddenly began creating after a period of hardship (his wife lost her sight and he had tremendous debts and feelings of helplessness). In the middle of the night in July 1968, "the Spirit" woke him up and commanded him to carve wood, and he spent the next decade creating expressive faces and figures. In a similar manner, Tyrome H. Jordan (1967–), a prisoner in Texas, says he was filled with a spiritual power and began drawing colorful, obsessively detailed images of humans, animals, and creatures.

This kind of direct, numinous encounter is common among visionary artists, whether associated with evangelical Christianity, spiritualist churches, Hoodoo, other faiths, or uniquely individualistic mystical experiences. For example, trance states and visions are an accepted part of the African-based religion of Vodou, and numerous Vodou practitioners have created divinely inspired work. Hector Hyppolite (1894–1949), a Haitian painter and Vodou priest, was motivated by dreams and visions, and his art depicts Vodou **mythology** and the loas (deities). Pierrot Barra (1942–), another Vodou priest, creates elaborate, postmodern "Vodou things"—sacred sculptures, assemblages, and ritual objects that are communicated by the loas in dreams (Cosentino).

In the United States, communication with "the Spirit" informed the art of John "J. B." Murry (1908–1988), who lived in Sandersville, Georgia. In the 1970s, after he became disabled, he had a vision telling him to spread the word of God. He began creating divinely communicated script while in a trance, often drawing it on market receipts, bank calendars, and other scraps of paper. Murry made an estimated 1,500 drawings and writings that he called "spirit works." These elongated and wavy drawings have a ghost-like character and concern good and evil, heaven and hell, **conjure** men, and other religious and vernacular ideas. A session of **prayer** preceded Murry's deciphering of the sacred script, which only he could interpret by viewing the mysterious calligraphy through a glass of pure water drawn from his well (a practice based in African American folk traditions). He believed that God created the script by moving his hand, a vernacularized, visual form of "speaking in tongues" that is perhaps related to African script traditions (Nasisse, Wahlman, and Mhire, 56; Wahlman, 1987, 32–33).

The spirit of God also is believed to be the guiding force in the work of Simon Sparrow (1925–), who creates bas-relief collages and sculptures. His art is constructed from glitter, beads, costume jewelry, and found objects that are transformed into mystical assemblages that depict Christian iconography and mysterious imagery. Sparrow, a street evangelist living in Madison, Wisconsin, says that he is a channel for God's power and that his images of faces are actually visions of the spirits of deceased people.

Other well-known visionary artists inspired by spiritual forces include Elijah Pierce (1892–1984), who believed that God directed him to preach the word through **wood carving**; Joseph Yoakum (1886–1972), who created mysterious, dreamlike landscapes after God appeared to him in a dream and instructed him to draw; and Mary Tillman Smith (1904–1995), who constructed an elaborate **yard art** environment as a tribute to God. After a vision of an angel that predicted the end of the world, Zebedee "Z. B." Armstrong (1911–1993) began creating detailed apocalyptic calendars from an assortment of objects. William Edmondson (1870–1951), the first African American to have a one-man show at the Museum of Modern Art in New York in 1937, said that he was commanded by God in a vision to carve religious imagery on limestone gravestones and sculptures. Others motivated to create art because of religious experiences or magical forces include Clementine Hunter, Johnny Banks, David Butler, Juanita Rogers, Felix "Fox" Harris, the Reverend Johnnie S. Swearingen, and Joe Minter.

Lonnie Holley (1950–), who lives east of Birmingham, Alabama, is considered by some to exemplify the concept of a contemporary visionary artist. He spent much of his youth in foster homes and reform schools, and after a house fire killed two of his nieces, he attempted suicide. He prayed to God to help him with his grief, and was inspired to carve tombstones out of sandstone to mark his nieces' graves. He continued to carve sandstone, then wood, and ultimately created thousands of artworks and an entire yard art environment consisting of pieces of cast-off metal and other found materials. His art draws upon a wide range of African and African American traditions, such as spirit writing and ancestral shrines, and addresses poverty, oppression, suffering, and various other social problems.

Drawing upon his heritage and religious beliefs, Holley's work emphasizes ancestors, family, the life cycle, and his own role as a seer with a mission to help humanity progress spiritually. Although his environment may look like a bricolage of random junk to some people, his sculptures have symbolic and religious meanings and associated narratives that comment on aspects of contemporary culture or African American experience, such as racism, the importance of family, the dangers of drugs, and the need for spirituality. Like the work of various other African American visionary artists, Holley's environment may be seen as an elaboration of regional traditions of yard art and "yard shows" in the **South** as well as the importance of recycling and resourcefulness.

Holley's environment also seems influenced by African traditions of graveyard art. In this tradition, the grave itself is regarded as a sort of charm and decorated with white objects, clocks, mirrors, jars, glass, and other things that look watery—practices traced back to Kongo beliefs about the watery world of the ancestors and ancestral power (Wahlman, 2001, 159–161). His yard, filled with objects hanging from trees, is clearly related to traditions of the **bottle tree**. This practice, still found in the South, and originally a type of charm, can be traced back to Kongo graveyard tree charms (*minkisi*), involving protective ideas about glass, the connection between the living and the ancestors, and the function of the bottle tree to keep evil spirits away or lure them into the bottles (Wahlman 1987, 34–39; Wahlman 2001, 159–163). Various other African American artists, such as Dilmus Hall and David Butler, also hung protective objects in trees, influenced by these bottle tree and charm traditions.

Similarly, the art of Frank "Preacher" Boyle (1933–2001) focused on the powerful and multivalent meaning of bottles. Boyle had a successful life as a waiter in high-class establishments but later became an alcoholic and drug addict. After years of misery and despair, he had a life-changing religious vision, and he then wandered the streets of Memphis, collecting empty, discarded alcohol bottles, which he painted with expressive, eerie faces. In salvaging and artistically transforming these bottles into beautiful and symbolically protective objects, Boyle expressed his own transfiguration and used his art as a means to help other substance abusers.

Another individual whose art was inspired by visions but was also rooted in vernacular traditions was Nellie Mae Rowe (1900–1982). She believed her art was a gift from God, and she created paintings, found-object sculptures, and an entire yard art environment with glass and other objects hanging from trees (Wahlman 1987, 39–40). Although reflecting her deep Christian faith, her art also contains images of ancestral spirits, protective "**mojo**" amulets and charms, and objects based on "memory jugs," which are decorated vessels associated with funerary rites.

In a comparable manner, Mary Le Ravin (1905–1992), a healer and preacher, was guided by the Holy Spirit and her dreams to create fantastic sculptures from bones. Throughout her life she participated in various spiritual traditions, a number of which emphasized ecstatic religious experiences. She endured much adversity in her life and later started a storefront church in Los Angeles, cooking and ministering to the poor and homeless. Her divinely inspired art was rooted in her personal interpretation of the biblical meaning of bones as symbols of resurrection and life and death and perhaps in African-based beliefs about bones and their spiritual power. She considered her preparation and use of bones to be a sacred process, and like other artists mentioned, she saw faces, figures, and life forms within the bones. In addition to religious themes, her art pays tribute to African and African American cultures, leaders, and celebrities and draws attention to social issues, including racism, homelessness, violence, rape, the struggles of women, and other forms of social injustice.

Royal Robertson (1930–1997) was motivated to create art by visions of a different type, related to the trauma of his wife, Adelle, leaving him after 19 years of marriage. Tormented by his lost love and mocked by his neighbors, Robertson filled his yard with signs that contained attacks on Adelle and art that was influenced by comics, Christianity, and African motifs. He also began drawing scenes of futuristic cities, spacecraft, space people, and life on utopian planets, which he said were records of trance visions and dreams that had transported him to other worlds. Although his yard contained an ever-changing array of signs that condemned Adelle and unfaithful spouses in general, inside his house Robertson constructed shrines to Adelle, and his depictions of lost love and visionary cities in outer space covered nearly every inch of the interior walls. Although often categorized as a kook, Robertson, like many individuals, created art in an attempt to deal with emotional pain and feelings of loss. Rather than dismissing such individuals as abnormal, a folkloristic approach helps contextualize personal suffering and the ways that people try to cope with anguish and trauma through creativity.

An individual who was transformed by tragedy is Mr. Imagination (Gregory Warmack, 1949–), whose artistic career was launched after a nearly fatal shooting in 1978. After going into a coma and having a life-changing near-death experience, Mr. Imagination has devoted his life to creating things from found objects such as bottle caps, paintbrushes, and furniture. His work, inspired by visions and vague memories of soul travel to ancient civilizations, expresses his pride in his African American heritage, sense of royal African ancestry, and fascination with Egyptian themes. Mr. Imagination says he was spiritually chosen to create this art, and recycling has become a metaphor for his own rebirth and survival, as he gathers the refuse of everyday life and transforms junk into mythic and majestic jewel-like thrones, walking staffs, faces of black kings, and totems (Metcalf, 52–53). His art has helped him deal with additional hardship and suffering, such as the sudden death of his brother and the loss of his art in a fire. He sees himself as a minister of recycled art and a healer who is teaching the world about the value and beauty of castaway things, which represent the personal and spiritual renewal of one's life and community.

The relationship between misfortune, trauma, and creativity also is evident in the life and art of Frank Jones (1900–1969). Jones was born "special," with a **caul** (part of the fetal membrane) over his left eye, which his mother said would allow him to see spirits. Belief in the gift of visions and supernatural abilities for people born with the "spirit veil" is widely known in African American folk belief and in various other cultures. Jones took this prediction of supernatural vision seriously, and it later became the basis of his mysterious illustrations of supernatural beings.

Jones' life was beset by tragedies. His father left the family, his mother abandoned him on a street corner when he was three years old, and he was raised by various relatives and a woman he called Aunt Della. As a young man, he was unhappily married to several women who seemed to exploit his passive personality and faithful devotion. Later, he adopted an abandoned three-year-old girl but he was then accused of raping her by the wayward mother when he refused to give up the child and was sentenced to five years in prison. Things only got worse: Aunt Della was murdered in 1949, and Jones was convicted of being an accomplice in the crime, even though he did not seem to be involved. Then he was charged with rape again, another apparently phony charge. In retrospect, Jones is now believed to be innocent of his alleged crimes. However, in 1960, he did violate his parole, and as a result spent the remainder of his life in the prison in Huntsville, Texas. An illiterate man who was often regarded as mentally disabled, Jones was the victim of the injustices and racism of the judicial and prison system in Texas.

While in prison Jones began drawing "Devil houses" and "haints" (haunts) that he had been seeing for years as the result of his ability to peer into the spirit world with his left eye. He was familiar with Hoodoo beliefs, creating his own mojos, juju bags, and other fetish objects as means of protection (Steen, 13–14, 24–25). His art seems related to these Hoodoo traditions and often consists of elaborate structures with devils captured inside, drawn mostly in the protective colors of blue and red. His work may have been created in an attempt to protect himself from evil forces, both the real dangers of prison life and the ever-present demons that taunted him and that only he could see. Jones's drawings also resemble African magical designs that invoke spirits or gods, giving supernatural forces material form and capturing them in ornate, cell-like structures. His precisely patterned drawings clearly were a way to construct order and gain a sense of personal control, providing a temporary escape from his difficult life and reflecting his beliefs and widely held African American folk traditions.

In studying the lives of people described as "visionaries," one notices that many of them began creating art during or after a period of adversity or personal crisis. In these instances, the creative process often has enabled individuals to address stressful or painful experiences. Emotional trauma persists when individuals feel powerless and unable to take action against danger and suffering, and the act of creating is one way to regain the feeling of control over one's life and uncontrollable events and overwhelming emotions (Wojcik). Traumatic experiences may be so painful that they cannot be put into words, but creating material objects makes manifest and externalizes these unspeakable emotions and conflicts. The sense of increased self-esteem and the local acclaim that creating things may bring can help to offset feelings of loss, despair, and oppression as well.

The creation of visionary environments also is a way for solitary individuals to engage with their communities and express social commentary or protest. For example, Tyree Guyton (1955–) created the Heidelberg Project in a rundown part of Detroit's East Side as a form of demonstration and community renewal. In 1986, he began building sculptures in vacant lots using toys, bicycles, appliances, shoes, dolls, signs, crosses, stuffed animals, and other found objects. He also painted abandoned buildings, covering them with polka dots. He painted buildings and created these assemblages as a way to draw attention to the decaying neighborhood and the dilapidated buildings that were being used as crack houses. As a result of the attention Guyton's art environments received, the drug dealers left the neighborhood.

Although Guyton has some formal art training, he says his inspiration comes from dreams, the grandfather who encouraged him during times of despair, and his sense of a spiritual mission to renew his neighborhood. He sees his project on Heidelberg Street (where he grew up and one of the first African American neighborhoods in Detroit) as a way to transform urban blight and the dangers of the inner city into an artwork that will rejuvenate the community. A number of his creations involve social commentary, with piles and assemblages of hundreds of shoes symbolizing homelessness and his "OJ House" constructed as a blatant critique of media exploitation and the American obsession with celebrities. Although Guyton's creations have generated hostility from some city council and community members and a number of his structures were subsequently disassembled or destroyed by bulldozers, in recent years his art environments have received some recognition and support for the positive ways they have physically and spiritually transformed an impoverished part of the city.

Although visionary art frequently has been dismissed as eccentric and fanciful, it expresses deeply felt emotional, religious, and social concerns. African American visionary art often is created by people who are marginalized by race and disempowered economically and politically. Through their art, these individuals attempt to assert their voices, communicate significant ideas and values to others, and recreate and perhaps change their world according to their own visions. Such art also may challenge oppressive societal norms and the official order of things, whether racism, consumerism, sexism, and injustice or dominant concepts of "art," public space, freedom, and diversity of expression.

African American visionary art is a powerful and dynamic phenomenon that expresses the unique experiences of individuals as well as universal concerns, struggles, and hopes. Although expressing personal visions, the creativity and imagination of these artists often reflect the "flash of the spirit" and improvisational aesthetics associated with African-based traditions (Nasisse, 15; Wahlman 1987, 42–43; Beardsley, 178). Frequently this form of creativity has clear therapeutic functions and is an attempt to share personal experiences and traumas with others. Many of these self-taught individuals did not consider themselves artists or create things for fame or profit. They worked instead in an effort to convey a message, confront adversity and suffering, or heal themselves or others, emotionally, psychologically, physically, or spiritually. Their creations attest to the artistic mastery of solitary individuals—largely untrained, often impoverished, and usually unknown—and what they were able to accomplish in a lifetime. The lives and art of these women and men provide important insights into African American experience and culture and the power of human creativity.

Daniel Wojcik

Further Reading

Adele, Lynne, 1989, *Black History/Black Vision: The Visionary Image in Texas* (Austin: Archer M. Huntington Art Gallery, College of Fine Arts, University of Texas at Austin); Arnett, Paul, and William Arnett, eds., 2000, *Souls Grown Deep: African American Vernacular Art of the South,* vol. 1 (Atlanta, GA: Tinwood Books); Beardsley, John, 1995, *Gardens of Revelation: Environments by Visionary Artists* (New York: Abbeville Press); Bernier, Celeste-Marie, 2009, *African American Visual Arts: From Slavery to the Present* (GB: Edinburgh University Press); Cardinal, Roger, 1972, *Outsider Art* (London: Studio Vista); Cosentino, Donald J., 1998, *Vodou Things: The Art of Pierrot Barra and Marie Cassaise* (Jackson: University Press of Mississippi); Cubbs, Joanne, and Eugene W. Metcalf Jr., 1996, "Sci-Fi Machines and Bottle-Caps Kings: The Recycling Strategies of Self-Taught Artists and the Imaginary Practice of Contemporary Consumption," in *Recycled, Re-Seen: Folk Art from the Global Scrap Heap*, ed. Charlene Cerny and Suzanne Seriff (New York: Harry N. Abrams in association with the Museum of International Folk Art), pp. 46–59; Dial, Thornton, E. W. Metcalf, Joanne Cubbs, David C. Driskell, Greg Tate, and Indianapolis Museum of Art, 2011, *Hard Truths: The Art of Thornton Dial* (Indianapolis, IN: Indianapolis Museum of Art); Dubuffet, Jean, 1988, *Asphyxiating Culture and Other Writings* (New York: Four Walls Eight Windows); Hall, Michael D., and Eugene Metcalf Jr., eds., 1994, *The Artist Outsider: Creativity and the Boundaries of Culture* (Washington, DC: Smithsonian Institution Press); Lawal, Babatunde, 2000, "African Roots, American Branches: Tradition and Transformation in African American Self-Taught Art," in *Souls Grown Deep: African American Vernacular Art of the South*, vol. 1, ed. Paul Arnett and William Arnett (Atlanta: GA: Tinwood Books), pp. 30–49; Manley, Roger, 1989, *Signs and Wonders: Outsider Art inside North Carolina* (Raleigh: North Carolina Museum of Art); Nasisse, Andy, 1987, "Aspects of Visionary Art," in *Baking in the Sun: Visionary Images from the South*, ed. Andy Nasisse, Maude Southwell Wahlman, and Herman Mhire (Lafayette: University Art Museum, University of Southwestern Louisiana), pp. 8–27; Nasisse, Andy, Maude Southwell Wahlman, and Herman Mhire, eds., 1987, *Baking in the Sun: Visionary Images from the South* (Lafayette: University Art Museum, University of Southwestern Louisiana); Rhodes, Colin, 2000, *Outsider Art: Spontaneous Alternatives* (London: Thames and Hudson); Russell, Charles, 2001, *Self-Taught Art: The Culture and Aesthetics of American Vernacular Art* (Jackson: University Press of Mississippi); Steen, William, 1992, "Frank Jones: Devil Houses," in *Devil Houses: Frank Jones Drawings*, exhibit catalog (Philadelphia: Janet Fleisher Gallery); Wahlman, Maude Southwell, 2001, "African Charm Traditions Remembered in the Arts of the Americas," in *Self-Taught Art: The Culture and Aesthetics of American Vernacular Art*, ed. Charles Russell (Jackson: University Press of Mississippi), pp. 146–165; Wahlman, Maude Southwell, 1987, "Africanisms in Afro-American Visionary Art," in *Baking in the Sun: Visionary Images from the South*, ed. Andy Nasisse, Maude Southwell Wahlman, and Herman Mhire (Lafayette: University Art Museum, University of Southwestern Louisiana), pp. 28–43; Wojcik, Daniel, 2005, *Mysterious Technology: Flying Saucers and the Visionary Art of Ionel Talpazan* (Jackson: University Press of Mississippi).

W

WAKES

A wake is a vigil held for a deceased person prior to burial at which friends and family keep watch over the body. Wakes provide a time for family and friends to commemorate the departed and adjust to life without him or her. Festivities including laments, **prayers**, eating, and drinking occur throughout the night or nights prior to burial. Within African American wake traditions, **storytelling**, **dancing**, and gambling also play important roles. Wakes are not simply celebrations or commemorations, however. They are serious events required to ensure passage of the spirit of the deceased to a final resting place. While specific beliefs may vary, wakes are an important part of the **funeral** traditions among African American communities in the United States and the Caribbean.

Beliefs about spiritual life after death give shape to the wake event. Zora Neale Hurston notes that the spirit of the deceased may be most destructive during the time after death and before burial. This makes the wake a necessary ritual in many African American communities to ensure that the spirit of the deceased does not bother the living. In Alan Dundes's *Mother Wit from the Laughing Barrel*, Ruth Bass relates the events immediately following a death in Mississippi during the 1930s. Clocks remain stopped from the moment of death until after burial. All mirrors and glass-covered pictures are covered to avoid seeing one's reflection in the room with a dead body, or worse, the reflection of the deceased. The deceased might see his or her reflection, become enamored, and remain in the glass. Family and friends "set up" with the body until burial. Throughout this time, women continually wail, mourning the departed in improvised songs reciting the good qualities of the deceased.

In *Folk Beliefs of the Southern Negro*, Newbell N. Puckett also discusses "setting-up" with the deceased during this same period. He records the belief that the deceased is not really dead until burial, when the soul departs. During the time between death and burial, the body must never be left alone. Food is served for those coming to "set-up" with the body, and mourning songs are sung. Puckett also records comments from an elder complaining of the changing wake traditions. In the early 20th century, the elder said, traditions of praying and spiritual singing began to give way to storytelling or "annidotes all nite."

Wakes have a transforming effect on friends and family, not only helping them adjust to life without the departed but also re-creating their bonds as a family. In an interview with the creator of the American Audio Prose Library Kay Bonetti, writer John Edgar Wideman recounted his memories of his grandmother's funeral. Storytelling played a crucial role in renewing connections among family and friends. Wideman described the narrative performance: "Aunt May was drinking a lot of Wild Turkey. She is a little old lady and she sits in a chair and her feet don't touch the floor—and she began to tell stories. Everybody was telling stories but sooner or later she just took center stage and told the story of Sybela Owens and how my family came to Pittsburgh—I listened. I'd heard these stories before but it was the first time I had heard them in a way that made them special" (Wideman and Bonetti, 86). Perhaps more important, Wideman described his own reactions as he listened to these stories about his grandmother: "I was hearing her life. That was what was done at these wakes. You talk about the person who died, you talk about their friends, you talk about the time you saw them with ice cream on their chin and the crazy situations that person had been in; it's almost like a voodoo ritual where you talk down a departed spirit. A communal, a collective will forces the spirit of the departed person to return, and you draw strength and direction from that spirit" (Bonetti, 86). Storytelling in this context becomes a ritual event, reminding family and friends that the memory of the departed remains. By doing so, oral histories come alive, reminding family to keep alive their family histories and the memories of their ancestors.

Common threads weave throughout these traditions over time and space. Wakes continue to play important roles in the 21st century. Wake traditions, though, are changing. The growing use of funeral parlors in the 20th century, for example, allows the body of the deceased to be removed from the home. Practices of preparing the body no longer play an important part in the event. Beliefs encouraged by the presence of the body are mitigated. Burial times can be extended to allow all family members to arrive, a necessity because of the increase in migration today. This transforms wakes into not just a commemoration and celebration to ensure the departure of the deceased but also a reunion of the living. As in Wideman's account, wakes since the mid-20th century have provided social contexts to reconstitute family ties and retell family histories. In many parts of the Americas, immigration of different cultural groups into local neighborhoods has changed the participation in wakes and nine-night rituals. This results in a changing of the wake event itself. In all cases, however, wakes allow the living to come to terms with the loss of family and friends and to perform traditions that reestablish their basic beliefs about life and death.

Michele A. Goldwasser

Further Reading

Dundes, Alan, ed., 1973, *Mother Wit from the Laughing Barrel: Readings in the Interpretation of Afro-American Folklore* (Englewood Cliffs, NJ: Prentice-Hall); Puckett, Newbell N., 1926, *Folk Beliefs of the Southern Negro* (Chapel Hill: University of North Carolina Press); Wideman, John Edgar, and Kay Bonetti, 1986, "An Interview with John Edgar Wideman," *The Missouri Review 9*, 75–103. *Project MUSE, 2013*, https://muse.jhu.edu/; Williams, Regennia N., 2011, *Homegoings, Crossings, and Passings: Life and Death in the African Diaspora* (Porter Ranch, CA: New World African Press).

WOOD CARVING

The art of wood carving in the black Americas dates back to the earliest arrival of Africans from their homelands as slaves. Most West African nations had strong traditions of wood carving. Artists and craftspeople carved tools, utensils, bowls, stools, combs, staffs and walking sticks, masks, headrests, **game** boards, and weapons. Quite naturally, Africans transplanted from their homelands would continue to make functional and decorative wood carvings. Connections between African and African American wood carving traditions have been made by numerous scholars, beginning in the 1970s. Research before the 1960s in this area was summed up by Robert Farris Thompson when he stated that "few are likely to study a field believed not to exist." In his pioneering work on relationships between African and African American expressive cultures and, in particular, art, David Evans listed seven characteristics of African American sculpture that suggest African influence:

1. Monochromy or bichromy: One or two colors are used, usually black and/or red.
2. Smooth, luminous surfaces.
3. Equilibrated gestures: The sculpture is symmetrical and has a mood of repose.
4. Frozen faces: The face is calm and dignified.
5. Beaded, shell, or metal eyes.
6. Synoptic vision: Two or more vantage points are used simultaneously within the same frame of visual reference.
7. The repertory of motifs: Reptiles (frogs, lizards, **tortoises**, alligators, serpents) and human figures are the pervasive themes. (Evans, 144)

Scholars have identified the Georgia coastal region as one of the areas in the United States that has historically had the strongest tradition of wood carving. Reasons for this include the relative isolation of slaves and postslavery generations from the mainland and the larger ratio of African Americans relative to whites. Thus not only wood carving but also other African folk traditions have been retained by black people in this area more than in areas of the mainland. There exist oral accounts of African American men of the 19th century making various kinds of wood sculptures along the Georgia coastal area, including walking sticks, human or animal figures, utensils such as forks and spoons, and "whimsical objects—such as chains or balls-in-cages—from a single block of wood" (Vlach, 27).

The most commonly carved and highly developed sculptural form in the Georgia tradition, and perhaps in general, has been walking sticks, or canes. Numerous carvers have been discovered and interviewed by folklorists, who have examined the particulars of their aesthetics. One such carver is James Cooper of Yamacraw, also known as "Stick Daddy." Cooper's walking sticks displayed the same basic aesthetic features that characterize the work of most African American carvers. For example, his favorite visual motifs were reptiles such as lizards, snakes, turtles, and alligators. Folklorist John Michael Vlach described one of Cooper's canes:

Despite the thinness of the sticks, he incised deeply so that the snakes and alligators appear to stand out from the surface of the cane, even though they are carved in low relief. This effect is further enhanced by a contrast in finishes; figures are stained and polished, while the background of natural wood is left unfinished. In two instances, Cooper's walking sticks included other media: a black and white dye was used as a handle for one cane; another was topped by a flashlight handle with a small photo inserted in the end. (Vlach, 27)

Another Georgia coast sculptor was William Rogers, of Darien. Rogers's canes are thick and heavy compared to Cooper's, but he makes use of the same basic visual motifs. For instance, his canes also have alligator carvings and employ mixed media. Two other carvers from this region, William Brown and Crawford Smith, were known for their predominant use of the snake motif on their canes. One of Smith's canes has flashing rhinestones as the snake's eyes.

In addition to animal motifs on walking sticks, Georgia carvers also made sculptures of animals. Some of the artists mentioned above also carved animal figures. Artists known for their carvings of animals include Allen Parker, of Tatemville, and Jerome Carter, of Frogtown. Between them, they carved snakes, lizards, frogs, dogs, alligators, and rabbits as well as human figures. The Georgia coast artists also made forks and spoons with animals or human figures as a part of the design as well as trays, buckets, and mortar and pestles.

There was also a historical tradition of wood carving in areas other than the Georgia coast, some of which resulted from the inland migration of African Americans in the 19th century. The inland tradition has the same characteristics as carving along the coast. Canes are the most commonly found objects, and they contain the same motifs as walking sticks in the coastal tradition; for example, alligators and other reptiles dominate, and human figures are also found. Howard Miller, of Dixie, Georgia, is an inland artist whose work has been discussed by folklorists. Canes found in the 20th century in Mississippi lead scholars to believe that wood carving traditions also existed there in earlier centuries. The carvings bear close similarities to those found in Georgia.

One Mississippi carver whose work has been documented is Leon Rucker, who was raised by his grandfather, Lewis Rucker, an ex-slave who was knowledgeable about herbal medicine. Leon Rucker learned carving and herbal medicine from his grandfather. Rucker included not only the common motifs of reptiles on some of his canes but also mask-like human faces. Another Mississippi carver is Lester Willis, who was better known for his painting. Willis became prolific and skillful enough to make a relative living from his canes. Like Rucker's, Willis's walking sticks also included elaborate human figures.

There is some evidence of wood carving traditions in Missouri, although details remain sketchy. Evidence for a Missouri tradition hinges on the work of one carver, Henry Gudgell, who is credited with what is perhaps the greatest example of cane sculpture by an Afro-American. Gudgell was a slave who was born in Kentucky. Links between his carvings and other traditions of the **South** are unclear.

A handful of other examples of early wood carving have been found in New York and New Jersey. They deviate greatly from the traditions of the South. One is a figure of a female Native American, carved by a slave named Job around 1825 in New York. The second is the figure of a seated black man holding a bucket on his knees, which is dated around 1860, also from New York. A third example is a wooden "church chandelier" that was carved around 1890 by a black woodworker from Maryland, Luther Goins. The chandelier is an intricate assemblage of sticks that involves a complexity not usually associated with wood carving.

In addition to the strong traditions of carving in regions such as Georgia and Mississippi, many carvers have been documented in other regions, although the possible traditions out of which they may have come have not been extensively examined. Many known carvers across the country also incorporate influences from white American and other traditions more obviously than those from the strong, African-derived traditions of the Georgia coasts. Also characteristic of many carvers is an improvisational approach to their carving, which often leads to innovations in concept and design that are not easily ascribed to specific sources. Especially in the 20th century, carvers, like folk artists of any genre, are often exposed to many aesthetics and styles that might influence their work. Even in the work of these carvers, though, African aesthetic elements are usually present.

One example of a carver whose work reflects more diverse influences is George "Baby" Scott, who was born a slave in 1865 in Virginia. Scott employed a variety of materials for his carvings, including wood, soapstone, slate, and limestone. He had a special affinity for animals, and those who knew him suggested that his house was a small zoo. He kept three wildcats, two black bear cubs, two foxes, opossums, raccoons, snakes, and an alligator. Like many other African American carvers, Scott frequently employed animal motifs such as snakes, lizards, alligators, monkeys, and spiders. Also like other carvers, he made canes with animals such as snakes on them. However, his favorite animal subjects were birds, about which he had extensive knowledge, and most of these were carved in soapstone. The use of soapstone was influenced by the practice of schoolboys collecting this material to carve pipes. However, Scott was the first adult carver of the area to use soapstone. Of the African elements in his work, Adler writes:

> When dealing with a black American, the issue of possible African retentions is unavoidable. Many of Scott's pieces have what might be considered an "African" quality about them. The snake cane is more than the ordinary cane; spiders and reptiles make frequent appearances; the accretion of extra materials to the surface of the basic form occurs; there is a shiny, smooth surface on some of the carvings; there is a general lack of polychromed figures: all might be mentioned as "African" traits present in Scott's work. However, Scott's work as a whole is probably more the result of individualism rather than a knowledge of African roots. (Adler, 157)

Thus, Scott exemplifies African American carvers whose work employs African-derived elements and motifs but is also marked by other influences. Still, there continue to be many carvers in various parts of the country whose work is directly linked to traditions of black wood carving through family members or other relatives and who have made conscious choices to draw more upon African influences than upon others. One such artist is Claude Lockhart Clark, who lives in the San Francisco Bay Area. Clark is a trained artist with a master's degree in sculpture. His father was also a painter and printmaker as well as a professor of African and

African American art history at Merritt College in Oakland, California. Thus, Clark was exposed to the vast world of art. He became interested in African wood carving after meeting a Nigerian artist, Lamidi Olanada Fakeye, whose ancestors were Yoruba wood carvers. Clark went on to become his family's historian and a wood carver. Like many African American wood carvers, Clark has developed the art of carved walking sticks. His repertoire also includes trays, decorative boxes, masks, and stools.

Although, Clark emphasizes the element of individual innovation in his carvings, the most striking features are the similarities to traditional African wood carving. For instance, animals such as the tortoise recur in his work. The specific functions of his objects are quite different from those of comparable items in African societies. However, there are some connections. For instance, his stools symbolize for him connections to his family ancestry. In **Africa**, stools often housed the spirits of ancestors. Clark's stools house braided locks of hair from his female ancestors. Like Clark, many contemporary African American carvers carry on wood sculpting traditions that are marked by innovation in form and function but that continue to draw upon African influences.

Wood carving traditions have been continued not only in the United States but also in most parts of the diaspora. In many countries, including Haiti and Jamaica, links to African traditions are much stronger and more prevalent than in the United States. Some of the objects commonly carved in the Caribbean include walking sticks, masks, utensils, tools, animal and human figures, and furniture. In addition to reptile motifs, a popular motif in Caribbean walking sticks is the phallus, which is usually the top part of the cane. On many Caribbean islands, wood carving is one of the most prevalent forms of folk art marketed to tourists and is sometimes reflective of specific religious ideologies. For example, in Jamaica, Rastafari-inspired wood carvings proliferate. While one finds all of the items mentioned above on display at a myriad of vending sites, some of the most skilled craftsmanship goes into Rastafari mask carvings. Beyond the marketplace, wood carvings are also found in the contexts of traditional religions, often used in ceremonies or rituals. For instance, a carved wooden staff is sometimes a sacred object in Vodou ceremonies.

Although research in this area is not nearly as extensive as in many other areas of black folklore, wood carving represents one of the most vibrant and enduring traditions throughout the diaspora. In carved pieces of wood are inscribed historical and personal narratives, essences of **myths** and tales, spirits, and memories, sometimes so deeply that they seem to call to viewers with an uncanny magic.

Anand Prahlad

See also: Gullah

Further Reading

Adler, Elizabeth Mosby, 1983 [1975], "George 'Baby' Scott (1865–1945): A Carver and His Repertoire," in *Afro-American Folk Art and Crafts*, ed. William Ferris (Boston: G. K. Hall & Co.), pp. 149–159; Arnett, Paul, and William Arnett, 2000, *Souls Grown Deep:*

African-American Vernacular Art of the South (Atlanta, GA: Tinwood Books); Bishir, Catherine W., 2015, *Crafting Lives: African American Artisans in New Bern, North Carolina, 1770–1900* (University of North Carolina Press); Burchard, Hank, s.v. "Islands of Art," accessed February 2005, http://www.webster.edu/~corbetre/haiti/art/islands.htm; Evans, David, 1983 [1972], "Afro-American Folk Sculpture from Parchman Penitentiary," in *Afro-American Folk Art and Crafts*, ed. William Ferris (Boston: G. K. Hall & Co.), pp. 140–148; Sickler-Voigt, Debrah C. 2006, "Carving for the Soul: Life Lessons from Self-taught Artist O.L. Samuels." *Art Education* [H.W. Wilson - EDUC] 59 (3): 25; Vlach, John Michael, 1990, *The Afro-American Tradition in Decorative Arts* (Athens: The University of Georgia Press); Vlach, John Michael, 1991, *By the Work of Their Hands: Studies in Afro-American Folklife* (Ann Arbor, MI: U.M.I. Research Press).

WORK SONGS

Over the years, many different types of songs have provided accompaniment for many different kinds of work, including songs with lyrics as well as those that might have been hummed, clapped, or otherwise performed. The practice of accompanying work with music is an age-old element of African cultures that was transplanted to the Western world when Africans were taken into captivity and shipped across the ocean as slaves. The first written text of an African song was recorded by colonial explorer Mungo Park in 1880; since then, a plethora of popular and academic descriptions have followed. Park's account is interesting because it happens to have been a work song. Park had apparently been sitting beneath a tree all day and had no food to eat and no place to sleep. A woman pitied him and offered him food and shelter. The host and a group of other women were spinning cotton and sang as they worked. One of the women even composed extemporaneous verses about Park:

> The winds roared, and the rains fell;
> The poor white man, faint and weary,
> Came and sat under our tree.
> He has no mother to bring him milk,
> No wife to grind his corn.
>
> Chorus:
> Let us pity the white man.
> No mother has he to bring him milk,
> No wife to grind his corn.

(Southern, 17)

A similar kind of creativity and use of song to accompany work characterized the daily lives of slaves throughout the African diaspora. Observing the slaves sing as they worked, especially when they were working under brutal conditions, tended to mystify whites and in part contributed to their characterization of slaves as innocent, happy, and contented. The functions of work songs in slave and post-slavery life were complex, however, and reflected anything but contentment.

African American work songs can be grouped into two categories. First there are songs that may have accompanied work but were not specific to particular work situations. For example, a common image of slave life is one of groups of people singing **spirituals** as they labored in fields, picking cotton, cutting sugarcane, harvesting tobacco, plowing the earth, or chopping down trees. However, the spirituals sung by slaves in the fields were sung as well in other contexts such as religious meetings, for example. A second group of songs would be those that were specific to certain kinds of work, for instance, songs that accompanied the rhythm of chopping wood or rowing a boat. Research suggests not only that such songs were often specific to the work but also that many songs were specific to certain regions and even that "each plantation had its own repertory of worksongs" (Southern, 179). One can see why, for instance, this popular roustabout song might only have been sung in the context of boating:

> Molly was a good gal and a bad gal, too,
> Oh, Molly, row, gal;
> Molly was a good gal and a bad girl, too,
> Oh, Molly, row, gal.
> I'll row this boat and I'll row no more,
> Row, Molly, row, gal;
> I'll row this boat and I'll row no more,
> Row, Molly, row, gal.
>
> (Southern, 179)

Another group of songs related to specific tasks were "corn songs," which were sung at corn-shucking events. The following stanza comes from "Roun' de Corn, Sally," a corn-shucking song from Hungerford, Virginia, recorded in 1832.

> Hooray, hooray, ho!
> Roun' de corn, Sally!
> Hooray, for all de lub-ly la-dies!
> Roun' de corn, Sally!
>
> (Southern, 180)

Work songs during the slavery period functioned to establish a sense of community and to lighten the burden of forced and harsh labor. They dulled the tedious nature of the work, helped to energize slaves, and provided a means through which slaves could reaffirm their own humanity. Work songs also functioned to create an Africanized space and time within very hostile and foreign circumstances and facilitated the process of cultural affirmation that colonial slave owners sought to dismantle. Through shared rituals of song making, slaves could rise above their enslavement in spirit, if not physically.

Underneath the song rituals was an awareness of the immense healing properties of music, and within the institution of slavery such a balm was desperately needed. The spiritual and cultural function of work songs is reflected not only in particular lyrics but also in the freedom of bodily movement. In descriptions of slave work songs, writers invariably focus on the rhythmic beauty of the singers' bodies, as the music of their singing created for them a channel through which they could maintain the integrity of their corporeal identities.

Close analysis of work song rituals reveals that some of the same behavioral and ideological modalities that characterized religious services were present. For instance, when working in large groups, there was often a designated song leader whose leadership influenced the amount of work done, the tempo, and the mood. Singing in a call-and-response, or antiphonal, style, the leader often sang lines of the song, which were then answered or repeated by the rest of the group. One can draw parallels between song leaders and preachers or other leaders in contexts of religious services. Southern notes that slave owners were very attuned to the leader's function: "The importance of the song leader in affecting the amount of work to be obtained from a gang was well recognized by plantation owners. Frequently these leaders were excused from labor so that they could devote their entire energies to leading the singing, or they were given extra rewards as incentives" (Southern, 153). Southern notes an observer who captures some of these points in his description of grain harvesters.

> Fifteen or twenty "cradlers" swinging their brawny arms in unison as they cut the ripened grain, and moving with the regulated cadence of the leader's song. The scene repeated the poet's picture of ancient oarsmen and the chanter seated high above the rowers, keeping time with staff and voice, blending into one impulse the banks of the trireme.

> For such a song strong emphasis of rhythm was, of course, more important than words. Each mower kept his stroke and measured his stride by musical intervals. A favorite song for these harvesting occasions commenced: "Rise up in due time, due time, due time; / Rise up in due time, Ba-a! / Bleat like the old ewe, Ba-a! / Bleat like the old ewe, Ba-a." (Southern, 182)

Other genres of work songs that emerged out of the slavery period—some of which were characteristically sung in groups and others by men or women working alone—included lullabies and **field hollers**.

Traditions of work songs continued in the postbellum era, although, as time went on, there were fewer occasions of large groups working together and more and more instances in which workers found themselves working alone or in much smaller groups. In situations of sharecropping or small, black-owned farming, for instance, workers labored at many of the same tasks that the slaves did, but in smaller numbers. In these settings, however, work songs continued to be sung.

Traditions of work songs faced even greater challenges as African Americans moved north and settled in urban centers. "Hollers" and "cries" from street vendors were one of the few work-related song types that survived in the North. In general, the degree of technological advancement at any given time has been an important influence on work songs, as it has steadily altered the kind of labor that has been available. For instance, factory work did not offer the same opportunities for singing as did working in the fields. To this extent, the prevalence or decline of work song traditions has been different in various parts of the African diaspora.

One context in which strong work song traditions of large groups emerged in postbellum America was hauntingly similar to and, in fact, could be considered a variation on slavery—the context of prison work gangs. It would be difficult to witness groups of black men chained together with leg irons around their ankles, dressed in prison stripes and swinging hammers while white guards with pistols and shotguns stood watch over them and not think of slavery. The prison work gang system, like that of slavery, capitalized on the free labor of people who existed outside of the purview or consciousness of their fellow Americans. Even when, for some reason, those in the main society had been aware of these men, for the most part they remained impervious to their plights as human beings. They were, after all, criminals and prisoners of the American justice system, a group that Americans have typically looked upon with attitudes similar to the way that plantation owners and others in colonial times looked upon slaves.

Those who have written about the work song traditions of black prisoners lining tracks, busting rocks, digging trenches, or performing other tasks of manual labor have reflected some of the elements found in writings about slave workers. For example, it has been common practice for such groups to have a song leader, and songs have generally taken the form of call-and-response. Just as in songs of slaves, the song leader moderates the tempo of the work and sets the tone for the rest of the laborers. Also, like the slaves before them, prison labor crews have characteristically worked in rhythmic unison, the unified "Ha!" or the sound of the hammer on metal stakes, rails, or rocks having become almost legendary. The lyrics of prison work crews have touched on numerous topics, including the emotional longing to see loved ones, reflections on the circumstances that led to imprisonment, the particular labor at hand, and the cruelty of prison guards, or "drivers." Musically, and in terms of performance, there is a striking resemblance between spirituals, **hollers**, prison crew work songs, and the **blues**, which drew upon all of these other forms. For example, the prison camp song "Lost John" begins with four lines taken from a spiritual before turning into a song about an escaped prisoner rather than about an encounter with angels.

> One day, one day,
> I were walking along,
> And I heard a little voice,
> Didn't see no one.
> It was old Lost John,
> He said he was long gone,
> Like a turkey through the corn,
> With his long clothes on.

> (Courlander, 407)

Further lines from the same song comment on the harshness of prison camp labor.

> Oughta come on the river,
> Long time ago,
> You could find a dead man,
> Right on your row.
> Well the dog man killed him,
> Well the dog man killed him,

'Cause the boy couldn't go.
Wake up dead man,
Help me carry my row,
"Cause the row's so heavy,
Can't hardly make it.

(Courlander, 408)

On the one hand, prison crew work songs sometimes incorporated elements of other song genres, such as spirituals. On the other hand, they also had a tremendous impact on the evolution of blues music. Not only were lines from these songs occasionally borrowed by blues artists but the disposition of the singers toward the society that enslaved and imprisoned them also informed the blues conceptualization of what it meant to be black in America.

The evolution of the blues raises an interesting point insofar as work song traditions go. Typically, blues songs have been considered in the context of entertainment rather than work. However, one can make a strong argument for considering them as extensions of work song traditions in a modernized age. The chief motivations of the itinerant blues singer who sang on street corners, in **juke** joints, or in other venues, for instance, was the same as that of any other worker—economic gain and social status. The job of being a blues musician gained appeal for some of the same reasons that **sports** opportunities have appealed to many young African Americans in today's society—it offered economic reward and social status in a system in which there may have been few other opportunities that would have been as lucrative. In part, the reluctance to think of blues singing as an occupation results from the general American reluctance to view those in the creative arts as really "working." Theorizing "work" in the context of African American culture might help to clarify this issue.

Historically, black people have been simultaneously engaged in three different kinds of work, or at least have held three kinds of jobs. The first kind of work has been the forced labor that laid the foundation for the wealth of Western empires. The second kind of work has included the labor it took to survive and take care of one's family. The third kind of job has been culture building, work designed to strengthen and maintain community and culture, to gain freedom, and to advance as much as possible socially, politically, and economically. During the slavery period, slaves were forced to spend most of their time engaged in the first kind of work. However, they also had to find time for the second type of work, which included such activities as raising small gardens for themselves and also making sure they had time for the third type of work. Although this model of work has to be modified when applied to modern societies, the idea of multiple kinds of work is still applicable. The genre of "work songs" has typically been applied to the first kind of work, but perhaps it would be appropriate to extend the concept to these other kinds as well.

Work songs sung by groups of people or even individuals as they labor at agricultural, mechanical, or other kinds of tasks are less frequent as more societies become modernized and increasing amounts of work falls into the technological realm. However, instances of such work songs can still be found, and work song traditions are echoed in professionalized music making, reflecting basic changes in the forms of labor in contemporary societies.

Anand Prahlad

Further Reading

Conforth, Bruce M., 2013, *African American Folksong and American Cultural Politics: The Lawrence Gellert Story*, Vol. No. 19 (Lanham, MD: Scarecrow Press); Courlander, Harold, 1976, *A Treasury of Afro-American Folklore* (New York: Crown Publishers); Dargan, William T., and Isaac Watts, 2006, *Lining out the Word: Dr. Watts Hymn Singing in the Music of Black Americans*, Vol. 8 (Berkeley: University of California Press); Gioia, Ted, 2006, *Work Songs* (Durham: Duke University Press); Park, Mungo, 2000 [1799], *Travels into the Interior Districts of Africa*, ed. Kate Furguson (Durham, NC: Duke University Press); Ramey, Lauri, 2008, *Slave Songs and the Birth of African American Poetry*, 1st ed. (New York: Palgrave Macmillan); Southern, Eileen, 1971, *The Music of Black Americans: A History* (New York: W. W. Norton & Company); White, Shane, and Graham J. White, 2005, *The Sounds of Slavery: Discovering African American History Through Songs, Sermons, and Speech* (Boston: Beacon Press).

Y

YARD ART

This term refers to artistic material expressions found in outdoor spaces: yards and gardens. Studies of African American gardening and yard art traditions have been scarce until recently. Most extant works trace the distinctiveness and "flexible visual vocabulary" of these vernacular spaces to a process of creolization of African, European, and American traditions, a process that is continually evolving today due to such factors as increased urbanization, acculturation, and changes in American material culture in general.

Although the historical documentation of domestic outdoor spaces in Africa and among early African American slaves is scarce, available photographs and descriptions make clear that the yard adjacent to the house or cabin became an extension of the kitchen itself, filled with objects such as a washtub, a cutting table, a rain barrel, and a fireplace, as well as animals (e.g., hogs and chickens). Some African practices were not retained in the New World, but other African influences are readily observable, giving shape to elements of the New World landscape for the slaves, their descendents, and even Southern whites. According to Robert Farris Thompson, African retentions evident in the yards and gardens of contemporary African Americans reveal principles and iconography derived from the Central African kingdom of Kongo, where many of the captured slaves brought to the United States originated. Such Africanisms include mirrors, jars or vessels, emblems of motion (e.g., wheels, tires, hubcaps,

A bottle tree in a yard in Burnet, Texas. (Q-Images/Alamy Stock Photo)

hoops, pinwheels, directional orientation), cosmograms (i.e., representing four moments of the sun or the four stages of the soul, sometimes appearing in the form of diamonds or circles), herbs or flowers encircled protectively (i.e., with a tire or a rock border), trees hung with shiny objects (e.g., bottles, light bulbs, tinfoil, metal pieces), swept-earth yards, graveyard-type decorations (e.g., shells, pipes, rock piles), and an assortment of other objects (e.g., dolls, found images, stuffed or sculptured animals, seats, or "thrones") (Thompson, 1989, 124). Most practitioners (whose descriptions vary depending on age, class, and region) refer to their own ever-evolving activities as "yard work," "working in the yard," or "gardening," language that downplays the artistic significance in their work. Outside observers of these same yards prefer to speak of "dressing the yard" and "yard art," focusing on how the meaning and function of everyday objects, for example, are transformed to express essential values, aesthetics, and spiritual beliefs. In this schema, African American yards display continuities and consistencies in terms of organizing principles (e.g., motion, containment, figuration, and medicine) (ibid., 104).

Decorative ornaments, recycled materials, and the arrangement of yards are taken to be rich in meaning and associations for the owners. Mirrors on the porch, for instance, are said by scholars "to keep certain forces at a distance," jars or vessels placed near doors are said "to send back evil to its sources," bottle trees "ward off evil," tying and wrapping are "traditional ways of enclosing charms and . . . sealing intentions," and swept-earth yards are kept clear of plants and evil spirits (e.g., snakes) that could otherwise hide in vegetation. Moreover, natural features of the landscape (e.g., trees and rocks) become "invested with spiritual significance . . . interwoven with the life courses of individuals" (Gundaker, 61). It is important to note, however, in light of these theories that, when questioned about these meanings, practitioners rarely articulate such explicit views or philosophies. Many gardeners, in fact, deny African ancestry in their behavior; African influences apparently are "seen to be contrary to their [Christian] religious beliefs" (Westmacott, 103). Certainly there are some decorative impulses that are not as clearly linked to the spiritual or supernatural—for instance, artificial grass, painted or sculptured mailboxes, painted brick steps, pink flamingoes, chimes, and decorative arrangements of flowering plants. In either case, it remains clear that African American yard art is a material manifestation of unique personal experiences and cultural values that contains identifiable evidence of African, European, and New World influences and, most significantly, is always evolving to fit the aesthetic predilection of the gardeners.

LuAnne Roth

See also: Bottle Trees; Grave Decorations

Further Reading

Arnett, Paul, and William Arnett, eds., 2000, *Souls Grown Deep: African American Vernacular Art of the South*, vol. 1 (Atlanta: Tinwood Books); Gundaker, Grey, 1993, "Tradition and Innovation in African-American Yards," *African Arts* 26 (April): 58–71, 94–96; Gundaker, Grey, and Tynes Cowan, eds., 1998, *Keep Your Head to the Sky: Interpreting*

African American Home Ground (Charlottesville: University Press of Virginia); LeFalle-Collins, Lizzetta, 1987, *Home and Yard: Black Folk Life Expressions in Los Angeles* (Los Angeles: California Afro-American Museum); Mintz, Sidney W., 1974, "Houses and Yards among Caribbean Peasantries," in *Caribbean Transformations* (New York: Columbia University Press), pp. 225–250; Thompson, Robert Farris, 1983, *Flash of the Spirit: African and Afro-American Art and Philosophy* (New York: Random House); Thompson, Robert Farris, 1989, "The Song That Named the Land: The Visionary Presence of African-American Art," in *Black Art: Ancestral Legacy* (Dallas: Dallas Museum of Art); Westmacott, Richard, 1992, *African-American Gardens and Yards in the Rural South* (Knoxville: University of Tennessee Press).

Z

ZYDECO

Zydeco is a modern hybrid of various **dances** and folk music performed by the African American and African francophone descendants who historically inhabited the prairie lands of southeastern Texas and south central and southwestern Louisiana. In its earlier forms, zydeco had a variety of spellings, including the following: zarico, zotticoe, zodico, zordico, and zologo. Today the term is used to describe Louisiana's Creole music and is derived from what native Louisiana Creoles call *les haricots*, (pronounced "lay zarico") a French term which means "green beans" or "snap beans." The expression *les haricots sont pas salé*, (translated to "the snap beans are not salty") was later shortened to just *les haricots* and was meant to echo difficult times when people could not afford the desired salt pork for their beans. *Les haricots* became "le zydeco," which gave this new genre of music its name. In its initial conception, zydeco artists redefined the classic folk music that had existed in southwestern Louisiana but was unheard of outside of that area. Zydeco gradually became accepted as a major cornerstone of the African American folk tradition.

A more in-depth investigation into the etymology of zydeco suggests that the term is used in multifaceted ways. In southern Louisiana, the word zydeco has become synonymous with having a party. The meaning of the term has gradually grown to describe not just the music but is inclusive of the complete social scene. For example, participants go to a zydeco (the party) to do the zydeco (the dance—a syncopated two-step or jitterbug) to zydeco songs performed by zydeco artists. Modern analysis of zydeco music suggests more complex cultural and linguistic origins than had previously been identified. A debate regarding the spelling of the term among folklorists, ethnomusicologists, and other scholars suggests that due to earlier French and Spanish colonialism, the term is often cited as "Zarico," and that the present spelling represents its English phonetics. The term also has West African roots; several West African languages that were affected by the slave trade and colonialism have pointed folklorists to other places to look for its origins. Cajun folklorist Barry Jean Ancelet has suggested that the phonemes "za," "ré," and "go" are oftentimes linked with dancing or playing music in several West African cultures. For example, *a zaré* translates to "I dance" in the Yula culture. These cultural practices were transplanted with African slaves to the Americas and are a significant part to the legacy of zydeco.

Although a great deal of inconsistent information exists about its beginnings, zydeco, as many may think, is not Cajun in origin. As a result of British colonization of Nova Scotia during the 1750s, the French-speaking Acadians who inhabited the land were exiled. Thousands of those expatriates, along with the Spanish colonizers of the Mississippi River Delta region, were relocated to the Louisiana territory alongside other French and Spanish, African, and Afro-Caribbean refugees as well as Native American peoples who inhabited the land along Bayous Teche (Lafourche Parish), and the area of the Mississippi River between New Orleans and Baton Rouge. Dubbed as "Cajuns," a result of slurring "Acadians" by the natives, their culture was soon influenced by the surrounding cultures that existed in that region. One of the most notable influences was in the music. The Acadians brought with them their cultural affinity for performing songs and dance music, called "la-la" (an ancestor to zydeco), at evening house parties and other social events.

The heaviest influence on zydeco music comes from the Africans who were uprooted to southwestern Louisiana. Although the majority of Africans came to Louisiana as slaves from francophone West Africa, some also arrived as free people from the Caribbean following the Haitian Revolution. They brought with them—both free and enslaved—their unique aestheticism and other cultural values, including their musical skills. Creating a synthesis with the cultures of Louisiana's European colonizers and other local ethnic groups, their music was gradually absorbed into both of the developing Creole and Cajun cultures. Early forms of this manifestation began to be influenced further by additional tensions involving the African diaspora and the transatlantic slave trade. Over a period of time, a notable byproduct of this cultural convergence emerged in southwestern Louisiana; zydeco began to take its initial form. The musical expression's early stages and widespread socioeconomic and sociopolitical conditions were mirrored by the musicians in the titles and lyrics of most of the songs. In the early to mid–19th century, other immigrants began to make their mark on the art form. The most notable of the influences is the introduction of the Spanish guitar and the German piano accordion to the lineup of instruments. In the 1920s, the influence of the accordion/fiddle duo became a popular element of Cajun and Creole folk music. Some of the great early duets playing this musical type include black Creole accordionist Amédé Ardoin recording with white Cajun fiddler Dennis McGee. By the mid-1950s, zydeco was gradually developing into a fusion of traditional Cajun music with Creole rhythm and blues, and was beginning to take on a more concrete form, creating a confluence of folk tradition that is still in full bloom today.

Comprising a blend of modern rhythm and **blues**, folk, **jazz**, Cajun melodies (with French lyrics), country and western music, and more recently **rap** and **hip-hop**, zydeco artists borrowed much of the initial form for the music from Cajun musicians. Despite this influence, zydeco differs greatly from its Cajun ancestry. The most distinctive variation between the two forms of music is zydeco's substitution of an African-based rhythm, the *frottoir* (rub board), for the conventional triangle used in Cajun music. A rub board, an accordion, a guitar, a bass guitar, and drums now comprise the instruments of a traditional zydeco band. Dominated by the accordion, some modern zydeco bands expand this list by adding a saxophone, horns, and a keyboard. With some exceptions, the fiddle, which is a common instrument in Creole and Cajun music, lost its place in zydeco bands and was replaced with the rub board. Another distinguishable difference is that zydeco bands seldom play the waltzes that are common in Creole and Cajun music. Instead, zydeco incorporates a syncopated two-step or jitterbug, an upbeat-type sound.

Today zydeco music continues to evolve and can be heard all over the world as its distinctive sound resonates from clubs and bars alike. Much of the music tends to give acknowledgment to the early zydeco artists. In the 1990s, some bands began adding an additional element to the syncopated rhythm called "double clutching," which is a method of arranging the entire sound around the bass drum to emphasize the beat. To further enhance the musical form's crossover appeal, some newer bands, sometimes called "Zydekids," perform primarily in English and incorporate rap and other hip-hop forms, disco, **soul**, and reggae, attracting younger audiences. Some influential zydeco artists include Clifton Chenier, Buckwheat Zydeco, Queen Ida Lewis, and Alton "Rockin' Dopsie" Rubin.

Willie J. Harrell Jr.

Further Reading

Ancelet, Barry Jean, 2001, *Cajun Music and Zydeco: A (Very) Brief Overview* (Lafayette: Center for Cultural and Eco-Tourism, University of Louisiana at Lafayette); Ancelet, Barry Jean, 1988, "Zydeco/Zarico: Beans, Blues and Beyond," *Black Music Research Journal* 8 (1): 33–49; Dempsey, Tom, 1996, *Origins of Zydeco and Cajun Music* (Seattle: History—NW Zydeco Music and Dance Association); DeWitt, Mark F., 2008, *Cajun and Zydeco Dance Music in Northern California: Modern Pleasures in a Postmodern World* (Jackson: University Press of Mississippi); Fuller, R. Reese, 2011, *Angola to Zydeco: Louisiana Lives* (Jackson: University Press of Mississippi); Kuhlken, Robert, 1999, *Zydeco Music: A Brief Historical Geography w/ Web Links* (Ellensburg: Central Washington University); McNulty, Ian, 2011, *Louisiana Rambles: Exploring America's Cajun and Creole Heartland* (Jackson: University Press of Mississippi); Simonett, Helena, 2012, *The Accordion in the Americas: Klezmer, Polka, Tango, Zydeco, and More!* (University of Illinois Press); Tisserand, Michael, 1998, *The Kingdom of Zydeco* (New York: Arcade Publishing).

Selected Bibliography

Collections, Folklife, and Oral History

Abrahams, Roger D. 1992. *Singing the Master: The Emergence of African American Culture in the Plantation South.* New York: Pantheon Books.

Abrahams, Roger D., and John Szwed. 1978. *Afro-American Folk Culture: An Annotated Bibliography of Materials from North, Central, and South America and the West Indies.* Philadelphia: Institute for the Study of Human Issues.

Ancelet, Barry Jean, and Marcia Gaudet, eds. 2013. *Second Line Rescue: Improvised Responses to Katrina and Rita.* Jackson: University Press of Mississippi.

Baron, Robert, and Ana C. Cara. 2013. *Creolization as Cultural Creativity.* Jackson: University Press of Mississippi.

Brewer, J. Mason, ed. 1968. *American Negro Folklore.* Chicago: Quadrangle Books.

Brown, Frank C., ed. 1964. *North Carolina Folklore.* Vols. 1–7. Durham: Duke University Press.

Bucuvalas, Tina. 2012. *The Florida Folklife Reader.* Jackson: University Press of Mississippi.

Caponi, Gena Dagel, ed. 1999. *Signifyin(g), Sanctifyin', & Slam Dunking.* Amherst: University of Massachusetts Press.

Carawan, C., and G. Carawan. 1966. *Aint You Got a Right to the Tree of Life: The People of Johns Island, South Carolina, Their Faces, Their Words and Their Songs.* New York: Simon and Schuster.

Courlander, Harold, ed. 1976. *A Treasury of Afro-American Folklore.* New York: Crown Publishers.

Dance, Daryl Cumber, ed. 2002. *From My People: 400 Years of African American Folklore.* New York: W. W. Norton.

Dance, Daryl Cumber. 1987. *Long Gone: The Mecklenburg Six & The Theme of Escape in Black Folklore.* University of Tennessee Press.

Dance, Daryl Cumber, ed. 1978. *Shuckin' and Jivin': Folklore from Contemporary Black Americans.* Bloomington: Indiana University Press.

Dundes, Alan, ed. 1990 [1973]. *Mother Wit from the Laughing Barrel: Readings in the Interpretation of Afro-American Folklore.* Jackson: University of Mississippi Press.

Fauset, Arthur H. 1931. *Folklore from Nova Scotia.* New York: Memoirs of the American Folklore Society, vol. 24.

Fry, Gladys-Marie. 1975. *Nightriders in Black Folk History.* Knoxville: University of Tennessee Press.

Gwaltney, John Langston. 1980. *Drylongso: A Self-Portrait of Black America.* New York: Random House.

Harris, Joel Chandler. 1981 [1895]. *Uncle Remus: His Songs and His Sayings.* New York: D. Appleton.

Higginson, Thomas Wentworth. 1962 [1869]. *Army Life in a Black Regiment.* Boston: Beacon Press.

Hinson, Glenn, and William Ferris. 2009. *The New Encyclopedia of Southern Culture.* Vol. 14. Chapel Hill: University of North Carolina Press.

Hughes, Langston, and Arna Bontemps, eds. 1958. *The Book of Negro Folklore*. New York: Dodd, Mead & Co.

Hurston, Zora Neale. 1935. *Mules and Men*. Philadelphia: J. P. Lippincott.

Jackson, Bruce, ed. 1967. *The Negro and His Folklore in Nineteenth-Century Periodicals*. American Folklore Society, Bibliographical and Special Series, vol. 18.

Johnson, Guy B. 1968 [1930]. *Folk Culture of St. Helena Island, South Carolina*. Hatboro, PA: Folklore Associates.

Jones-Jackson, Patricia. 1987. *When Roots Die: Endangered Traditions of the Sea Islands*. Athens: University of Georgia Press.

Katz-Hyman, Martha B., and Kym S. Rice. 2011. *World of a Slave: Encyclopedia of the Material Life of Slaves in the United States*. Santa Barbara, CA: Greenwood.

Kerr, Audrey Elisa. 2006. *The Paper Bag Principle: Class, Colorism, and Rumor and the Case of Black Washington, D.C.* Knoxville: University of Tennessee Press.

Kimbrough, Walter M. 2003. *Black Greek 101: The Culture, Customs, and Challenges of Black Fraternities and Sororities*. Madison and Teaneck, NJ, and London: Fairleigh Dickinson University Press, and Associated University Presses.

LaRue, Cleophus, J. 2011. *I Believe I'll Testify: The Art of African American Preaching*. Louisville, KY: Westminister John Knox Press.

Levine, Lawrence W. 1977. *Black Culture and Black Consciousness: Afro-American Folk Thought from Slavery to Freedom*. Oxford: Oxford University Press.

Littlefield, Daniel F., Jr. 2001. *Africans and Seminoles: From Removal to Emancipation*. Jackson: University Press of Mississippi.

Miles, Tiya. 2005. *Ties That Bind: The Story of an Afro-Cherokee Family in Slavery and Freedom*. Vol. 14. Berkeley: University of California Press.

Mills, Quincy T. 2013. *Cutting Along the Color Line: Black Barbers and Barber Shops in America*. Philadelphia: University of Pennsylvania Press.

Montell, William Lynwood. 1970. *The Saga of Coe Ridge: A Study in Oral History*. Knoxville: University of Tennessee Press.

Moody-Turner, Shirley. 2014. *Black Folklore and the Politics of Racial Representation*. Jackson: University Press of Mississippi.

Morgan, Kathryn L. 1980. *Children of Strangers: The Stories of a Black Family*. Philadelphia: Temple University Press.

Parsons, Elsie Clews. 1943. *Folk-Lore of the Antilles, French and English*. New York: Memoirs of the American Folklore Society, vol. 26, Pt. 3: 457–487.

Parsons, Elsie Clews. 1969 [1923]. *Folk-lore of the Sea Islands, South Carolina*. Chicago: Afro-American Press.

Parsons, Elsie Clews. 1923. *Folk-Tales of the Sea Islands, South Carolina*. Memoirs of the American Folklore Society, vol. 16.

Powdermaker, Hortense. 1939. *After Freedom*. New York: Viking Press.

Pyatt, Sherman E., and Alan Johns. 1998. *A Dictionary and Catalog of African American Folklife of the South*. Westport, CT: Greenwood Press.

Rawick, George P., ed. 1972. *The American Slave: A Composite Autobiography*. 19 vols. Westport, CT: Greenwood Press.

Savannah Unit, Georgia Writers' Project (Works Progress Administration). 1940. *Drums and Shadows: Survival Studies among the Georgia Coastal Negroes*. Athens: University of Georgia Press.

Schoener, Allon, ed. 1968. *Harlem on My Mind: Cultural Capital of Black America 1900–1968*. New York: Random House.

Simmons, Martha, and Frank A. Thomas, eds. 2010. *Preaching with Sacred Fire: An Anthology of African American Sermons, 1750 to the Present.* New York: W. W. Norton.

Spalding, Henry D. 1972. *Encyclopedia of Black Folklore and Humor.* New York: Jonathan David Publishers, Inc.

Whitten, Norman E., Jr., and John F. Szwed, eds. 1970. *Afro-American Anthropology: Contemporary Perspectives.* New York: Free Press.

Woofter, T. J. 1930. *Black Yeomanry: Life on St. Helena Island.* New York: Henry Holt and Co.

Yount, Lisa. 1977. *Frontier of Freedom: African Americans in the West.* New York: Facts on File, Inc.

Zeitlin, Steven J., Amy J. Kotkin, and Holly Cutting Baker, eds. 1982. *A Celebration of Family Folklore: Tales and Traditions from the Smithsonian Collection.* Cambridge, MA: Yellow Moon Press.

Narrative: Tales, Legends, Myths, Film

Abrahams, Roger D., ed. 1985. *Afro-American Folktales: Stories from Black Traditions in the New World.* New York: Pantheon.

Abrahams, Roger D. 1970 [1963]. *Deep Down in the Jungle: Negro Narrative Folklore from the Streets of Philadelphia.* Chicago: Aldine Publishing.

Adams, Edward C. L. 1927. *Congaree Sketches, Scenes from Negro Life in the Swamps of the Congaree and Tales by Tad and Scip of Heaven and Hell with Other Miscellany.* Chapel Hill: University of North Carolina Press.

Bascom, William R. 1981. "African Folktales in America: 1. The Talking Skull Refuses to Talk." In *Contributions to Folkloristics*, ed. William R. Bascom, pp. 185–211. Meerut, India: Archana Publications.

Brewer, James Mason. 1976 [1958]. *Dog Ghosts and Other Texas Negro Folk Tales.* Austin: University of Texas Press.

Brewer, James Mason. 1976 [1953]. *The Word on the Brazos: Negro Preacher Tales from the Brazos Bottoms of Texas.* Austin: University of Texas Press.

Bristol, Douglas Walter. 2009. *Knights of the Razor: Black Barbers in Slavery and Freedom.* Baltimore: Johns Hopkins University Press.

Brown, Cecil. 2003. *Stagolee Shot Billy.* Cambridge: Harvard University Press.

Bryant, Jerry H. 2003. *Born in a Mighty Bad Land: The Violent Man in African American Folklore and Fiction.* Bloomington: Indiana University Press.

Dorson, Richard M., ed. 1967. *American Negro Folktales.* Greenwich, CT: Fawcett Publications, Inc.

Dunn, Stephane. 2008. *"Baad Bitches" and Sassy Supermamas: Black Power Action Films.* Urbana: University of Illinois Press.

Fine, Gary Alan, and Patricia A. Turner. 2001. *Whispers on the Color Line: Rumor and Race in America.* Berkeley: University of California Press.

Gonzalez, Ambrose E. 1964 [1922]. *The Black Border: Gullah Stories of the Carolina Coast.* Columbia, SC: The State Company.

Gonzalez, Ambrose E. 1974 [1924]. *The Captain: Stories of the Black Border.* New York: Books for Library Press.

Green, Thomas. 2009. *African American Folktales.* Westport, CT: Greenwood Press.

Horton-Stallings, LaMonda. 2007. *Mutha' is Half a Word: Intersections of Folklore, Vernacular, Myth, and Queerness in Black Female Culture.* Columbus: Ohio State University Press.

Hurston, Zora Neale. 1990 [1935]. *Mules and Men*. New York: Perennial Library.

Jackson, Bruce. 1974. *"Get Your Ass in the Water and Swim Like Me": Narrative Poetry from Black Oral Tradition*. Cambridge: Harvard University Press.

Jarmon, Laura C. 2003. *Wishbone: Reference and Interpretation in Black Folk Narrative*. Knoxville: University of Tennessee Press.

Jemie, Onwuchekwa, ed. 2003. *"Yo' Mama!": New Raps, Toasts, Dozens, Jokes & Children's Rhymes from Urban Black America*. Philadelphia: Temple University Press.

Lester, Julius. 1969. *Black Folktales*. New York: Grove Press.

Liebow, Elliot. 1967. *Tally's Corner: A Study of Negro Streetcorner Men*. Boston: Little, Brown and Company.

M'Baye, Babacar. 2009. *The Trickster Comes West: Pan-African Influence in Early Black Diasporan Narratives*. Jackson: University Press of Mississippi.

Munby, Jonathan. 2011. *Under a Bad Sign: Criminal Self-Representation in African American Popular Culture*. Chicago: University of Chicago Press.

Oster, Harry. 1968. "Negro Humor: John and Old Marster," *Journal of the Folklore Institute* 5: 42–57.

Roberts, John W. 1989. *From Trickster to Badman: The Black Folk Hero in Slavery and Freedom*. Philadelphia: University of Pennsylvania Press.

Rolston, Simon. 2013. "Prison Life Writing, African American Narrative Strategies, and Bad: The Autobiography of James Carr." *Multi-Ethnic Literature of the United States* 38 (4): 191–215.

Saxon, Lyle, Edward Dryer, and Robert Tallant. 1945. *Gumbo Ya-Ya: A Collection of Louisiana Folk Tales*. Boston: Houghton Mifflin.

South Carolina WPA Project. 1941. *South Carolina Folk Tales: Stories of Animals and Supernatural Beings*. Compiled by workers of the WPA in South Carolina. *Bulletin of the University of South Carolina* (October).

Turner, Patricia A. 1993. *I Heard It through the Grapevine: Rumor in African-American Culture*. Berkeley: University of California Press.

Wald, Elijah. 2012. *The Dozens: A History of Rap's Mama*. New York: Oxford University Press.

Wald, Elijah. 2014. *Talking 'bout Your Mama: The Dozens, Snaps, and the Deep Roots of Rap*. New York: Oxford University Press.

Wepman, Dennis, Ronald B. Newman, and Murray B. Binderman. 1976. *The Life: The Lore and Folk Poetry of the Black Hustler*. Philadelphia: University of Pennsylvania Press.

Williams, Shawn. 2007. *I'm a Bad Man: African American Vernacular Culture and the Making of Muhammad Ali*. Lulu.

Conversational Genres: Proverbs, Jokes, Riddles, Speech

Abrahams, Roger D. 1980. *Between the Living and the Dead*. Helsinki: Suomalainen Tiedeakatemia.

Abrahams, Roger D. 1990 [1973]. "Playing the Dozens." In *Mother Wit from the Laughing Barrel: Readings in the Interpretation of Afro-American Folklore*, ed. Alan Dundes, pp. 295–309. Jackson: University Press of Mississippi.

Abrahams, Roger D. 1976. *Talking Black*. Rowley: Newbury House Publishers.

Brown, H. Rap. 1990 [1973]. "Street Smarts." In *Mother Wit from the Laughing Barrel: Readings in the Interpretation of Afro-American Folklore*, ed. Alan Dundes, pp. 353–356. Jackson: University Press of Mississippi.

Burley, Dan. 1944. *Dan Burley's Original Handbook of Harlem Jive.* New York: D. Burley.

Daniels, Jack. 1979. *The Wisdom of Sixth Mount Zion from Members of Sixth Mount Zion and Those Who Begot Them.* Pittsburgh: Self Published.

Daniels, Jack, Geneva Smitherman-Donaldson, and Milford A. Jeremiah. 1987. "Makin' a Way Outa No Way: The Proverb Tradition in the Black Experience." *Journal of Black Studies* 17: 482–508.

Dillard, J. L. 1972. *Black English.* New York: Random House.

Harris-Lacwell, Melissa Victoria. 2004. *Barbershops, Bibles, and Bet: Everyday Talk and Black Political Thought.* Princeton, NJ: Princeton University Press.

Harrison, Deborah Sears, and Tom Trabasso, eds. 1976. *Black English: A Seminar.* New York: Lawrence Erlbaum Associates.

Holloway, Joseph E. 2005. *Africanisms in American Culture.* 2nd ed. Bloomington: Indiana University Press, 2005.

Kearse, Randy. 2006. *Street Talk: Da Official Guide to Hip-Hop & Urban Slanguage.* Fort Lee, NJ: Barricade Books.

Kochman, Thomas, ed. 1972. *Rappin' and Stylin' Out: Communication in Urban Black America.* Urbana: University of Illinois Press.

Majors, Clarence. 1994. *Juba to Jive: A Dictionary of African-American Slang.* New York: Viking Press.

Page, Mary H., and Nancy D. Washington. 1981. "Family Proverbs and Value Transmission of Single Black Mothers." *Journal of Social Psychology* 127: 49–58.

Prahlad, Anand (Dennis W. Folly). 1996. *African American Proverbs in Context.* Jackson: University Press of Mississippi.

Prahlad, Anand. 1982. "Gettin' the Butter from the Duck: Proverbs and Proverbial Expressions in an Afro-American Family." In *A Celebration of American Family Folklore*, ed. Steven J. Zeitlin, Amy J. Kotkin, and Holly Cutting Baker, pp. 232–241. New York: Pantheon Books.

Prange, Arthur J., Jr., and M. M. Vitols. 1990 [1973]. "Jokes among Southern Negroes: The Revelation of Conflict." In *Mother Wit from the Laughing Barrel: Readings in the Interpretation of Afro-American Folklore*, ed. Alan Dundes, pp. 628–635. Jackson: University Press of Mississippi.

Roberts, John W. 1978. "Slave Proverbs: A Perspective." *Callaloo* 1: 129–140.

Smitherman, Geneva. 1994. *Black Talk: Words and Phrases from the Hood to the Amen Corner.* Boston: Houghton Mifflin.

Smitherman, Geneva. 1986 [1977]. *Talkin' and Testifyin': The Language of Black America.* Detroit: Wayne State University.

Talley, T. W. 1922. *Negro Folk Rhymes.* New York: The Macmillan Co.

Watkins, Mel. 2002. *African American Humor.* Chicago: Lawrence Hill Books.

Music

Abrahams, Roger D. 1974. *Deep the Water, Shallow the Shore: Three Essays on Shantying in the West Indies.* Austin: University of Texas Press.

Allen, William F., C. P. Ware, and L. M. Garrison. 1951 [1867]. *Slave Songs of the United States.* New York: Peter Smith.

Armstrong, Louis. 1954. *Satchmo: My Life in New Orleans.* New York: Prentice-Hall.

Armstrong, Louis, and Thomas Brothers. 2001. *Louis Armstrong, in His Own Words: Selected Writings.* New York: Oxford University Press.

Ballanta-Taylor, Nicholas G. J. 1925. *Saint Helena Island Spirituals*. New York: G. Shirmer.

Baraka, Amiri (LeRoi Jones). 1963. *Blues People: Negro Music in White America*. New York: William Morrow and Company.

Bastin, Bruce. 1995. *Red River Blues: The Blues Tradition in the Southeast*. Urbana: University of Chicago Press.

Boyer, Horace Clarence. 1995. *How Sweet the Sound: The Golden Age of Gospel Music*. Washington, DC: Elliot and Clark Publishers.

Bryant, Jerry H. 2003. *Born in a Mighty Bad Land*. Bloomington: Indiana University Press.

Burrison, John A. 2007. *Roots of a Region: Southern Folk Culture*. University of Mississippi Press.

Caravan, Guy, and Candie Carawan, eds. 1963. *We Shall Overcome: Songs of the Southern Freedom Movement*. New York: Oak Publications.

Charters, Samuel B. 1967. *The Bluesmen*. New York: Oak Publications.

Conway, Cecelia. 1995. *African Banjo Echoes in Appalachia*. Knoxville, University of Tennessee Press.

Cooper, Carolyn. 1993. *Noises in the Blood: Orality, Gender, and the "Vulgar" Body of Jamaican Popular Culture*. Durham, NC: Duke University Press.

Cooper, Peter. 1997. *Hub City Music Makers: One Southern Town's Popular Music Legacy*. Spartanburg, SC: Holocene.

Courlander, Harold, ed. 1963. *Negro Folk Music. U.S.A.*, New York: Columbia University Press.

Dyson, Michael Eric. 1993. *Reflecting Black: African American Cultural Criticism*. Minneapolis: University of Minnesota Press.

Edwards, Paul. 2015. *The Concise Guide to Hip-Hop Music: a Fresh Look at the Art of Hip-Hop, from Old School Beats to Freestyle Rap*. New York: St. Martin's Griffin.

Epstein, Dena J. 1977. *Sinful Tunes and Spirituals*. Urbana: University of Illinois Press.

Evans, David. 1982. *Big Road Blues: Tradition and Creativity in the Blues*. New York: Da Capo Press.

Ferris, William R. 2009. *Give My Poor Heart Ease: Voices of the Mississippi Blues*. Chapel Hill, NC: University of North Carolina Press.

Fisher, Mark Miles. 1969 [1953]. *Negro Slave Songs in the United States*. New York: The Citadel Press.

Garland, Phyl. 1969. *The Sound of Soul*. New York: Pocket Books.

Gellert, Lawrence. 1930. "Me and My Captain (Chain Gangs)." *Negro Songs of Protest*. New York: Hours Press.

Gellert, Lawrence. 1934. "Negro Songs of Protest: North and South Carolina and Georgia." In *Negro Anthology*, ed. Nancy Cunard, pp. 366–377. London: Wishart & Co.

Gillespie, Dizzy, with Al Fraser. 2009 [1979]. *To Be or Not to Bop: Memoirs of Dizzy Gillespie*. Minneapolis: University of Minnesota Press.

Gioia, Ted. 2008. *Delta Blues: The Life and Times of the Mississippi Masters who Revolutionized American Music*. Jackson: University of Mississippi Press.

Gioia, Ted. 2011. *The History of Jazz*. New York: Oxford University Press.

Gordon, Robert. 2002. *Can't Be Satisfied: The Life and Times of Muddy Waters*. Boston: Little, Brown and Company.

Gregory, Hugh. 1998. *The Real Rhythm and Blues*. London: Blandford.

Guralnick, Peter. 1986. *Sweet Soul Music: Rhythm and Blues and the Southern Dream of Freedom*. New York: Harper & Row.

Halibut, Tony. 1971. *The Gospel Sound: Good News and Bad Times*. New York: Simon and Schuster.

Handy, W. C. 1926. *Blues: An Anthology*. New York: A. C. Boni.

Handy, W. C. 1970. *Father of the Blues: An Autobiography*. New York: Collier Books.

Harris, Sheldon. 1979. *Blues Who's Who: A Biographical Dictionary of Blues Singers*. New Rochelle, NY: Arlington House.

Haydon, Geoffrey, and Dennis Marks, eds. 1985. *Repercussions: A Celebration of African-American Music*. London: Century.

Johnson, James Weldon. 1925. *The Book of American Negro Spirituals*. New York: Viking Press.

Johnson, James Weldon. 1926. *The Second Book of Negro Spirituals*. New York: Viking Press.

Katrina Dyonne. 2014. *Ring Shout, Wheel About: The Racial Politics of Music and Dance in North American Slavery*. Urbana: University of Illinois Press.

Katz, Mark. 2012. *Groove Music: The Art and Culture of the Hip-Hop DJ*. New York: Oxford University Press.

Keil, Charles. 1966. *Urban Blues*. Chicago: University of Chicago Press.

Kemble, Frances A. 1863. *Journal of a Residence on a Georgian Plantation in 1838–39*. New York: Harper & Brothers.

King, B. B., with David Ritz. 2011 [1996]. *Blues All Around Me: The Autobiography of B. B. King*. New York: HarperCollins.

Krehbiel, H. I. 1962. *Afro-American Folksongs*. New York: F. Ungar Publishing Co.

Kubik, Gerhard. 2008. *Africa and the Blues*. Bloomington: Indiana University Press.

Levey, Josef. 1983. *The Jazz Experience: A Guide to Appreciation*. Englewood Cliffs, NJ: Prentice Hall.

Lewin, Olive, ed. 2000. *Rock It Come Over: The Folk Music of Jamaica*. Kingston, Jamaica: University of the West Indies Press.

Locke, Alain. 1968. *The Negro and His Music*. Port Washington, NY: Kennikat Press.

Lovell, John, Jr. 1972. *Black Song: The Forge and the Flame*. New York: Macmillan Co.

McKee, Margaret, and Fred Chisenhall. 1981. *Beale Black & Blue: Life and Music on Black America's Main Street*. Baton Rouge: Louisiana State University Press.

Mitchell, George. 1971. *Blow My Blues Away*. Baton Rouge: Louisiana State University Press.

Nelson, George. 1999. *Hip Hop America*. New York: Penguin Books.

Odum, Howard W., and Guy B. Johnson. 1964. *The Negro and His Songs*. Hatboro, PA: Folklore Associates, Inc.

Oliver, Paul. 1963 [1960]. *The Meaning of the Blues*. New York: Collier Books.

Oliver, Paul. 1970. *Savannah Syncopators: African Retentions in the Blues*. New York: Stein and Day, Publishers.

Olsson, Bengt. 1970. *Memphis Blues*. London: Studio Vista Limited.

Oster, Harry. 1969. *Living Country Blues*. Detroit: Folklore Associates.

Palmer, Robert. 1981. *Deep Blues*. New York: Penguin Books.

Parrish, Lydia. 1942. *Slave Songs of the Georgia Sea Islands*. New York: Creative Age Press.

Pecknold, Diane. 2013. *Hidden in the Mix: The African American Presence in Country Music*. Durham, NC: Duke University Press.

Pollard, Deborah Smith. 2008. *When the Church Becomes Your Party: Contemporary Gospel Music*. Detroit: Wayne State University Press.

Prahlad, Anand, Sw. 2001. *Reggae Wisdom: Proverbs in Jamaican Music*. Jackson: University Press of Mississippi.

Reagon, Bernice Johnson, ed. 1992. *We'll Understand It Better By and By: Pioneering African American Gospel Composers*. Washington, DC: Smithsonian Institution Press.

Roberts, John Storm. 1998. *Black Music of Two Worlds: African, Caribbean, Latin, and African-American Traditions*. 2nd ed. New York: Schirmer Books.

Rose, Tricia. 1994. *Black Noise: Rap Music and Black Culture in Contemporary America*. Middletown, CT: Wesleyan University Press.

Rowe, Mike. 1975. *Chicago Blues: The City and the Music*. New York: Da Capo Press.

Sackheim, Eric, ed. 1969. *The Blues Line: A Collection of Blues Lyrics from Leadbelly to Muddy Waters*. New York: Schirmer Books.

Shaw, Arnold. 1970. *The World of Soul*. New York: Paperback Library Edition.

Silvester, Peter. 1989. *A Left Hand Like God: A History of Boogie-Woogie Piano*. New York: Da Capo Press.

Southern, Eileen. 1971. *The Music of Black Americans: A History*. New York: W.W. Norton & Co., Inc.

Stewart-Baxter, Derrick. 1970. *Ma Rainey and the Classic Blues Singers*. New York: Stein and Day, Publishers.

Stone, Robert L. 2010. *Music in American Life: Sacred Steel: Inside an African American Steel Guitar Tradition*. University of Illinois Press.

Tisserand, Michael. 1998. *The Kingdom of Zydeco*. New York: Arcade Publishing.

Toop, David. 2000. *Rap Attack #3: African Rap to Global Hip Hop*. London: Serpent's Tail.

Vincent, Rickey. 1996. *Funk: The Music, the People and the Rhythm of the One*. New York: St. Martin's Griffin.

Wald, Elijah. 2010. *The Blues: A Very Short Introduction*. New York: Oxford University Press.

White, Newman I. 1965. *American Negro Folk-Songs*. Hatboro, PA: Folklore Associates, Inc.

Work, John W. 1940. *American Negro Songs and Spirituals*. New York: Crown Publishers.

Religion, Ritual, Folk Belief, Folk Healing

Alexander, Estrelda. 2011. *Black Fire: One Hundred Years of African American Pentacostalism*. Downers Grove, IL: IVP Academic.

Anderson, Jeffrey Elton. 2007. *Conjure in African-American Society*. Baton Rouge: Louisiana State University Press.

Archer, Jermaine O. 2009. *Antebellum Slave Narratives: Cultural and Political Expressions of Africa*. New York: Routledge.

Barnes, Sandra T., ed. 1997 [1989]. *Africa's Ogun: Old World and New*. Bloomington: Indiana University Press.

Battle, Michael. 2006. *The Black Church in America: African American Christian Spirituality*. Malden; MA: Blackwell Publishers.

Bird, Stephanie. 2004. *Sticks, Stones, Roots and Bones: Hoodoo, Mojo and Conjuring with Herbs*. St. Paul, MN: Llewellyn Worldwide Publishers.

Bird, Stephanie. 2009. *A Healing Grove: African Tree Remedies and Rituals for Body and Spirit*. Chicago, IL: Lawrence Hill Books.

Carter, Harold A. 1976. *The Prayer Tradition of Black America*. Valley Forge: Judson Press.

Cartwright, Keith. 2013. *Sacral Grooves, Limbo Gateways: Travels in Deep Southern Time, Circum-Caribbean Space, Afro-creole Authority*. Athens: University of Georgia Press.

Chireau, Yvonne P. 2003. *Black Magic: Religion and the African American Conjuring Tradition*. Berkeley: University of California Press.

Covey, Herbert C. 2007. *African American Slave Medicine: Herbal and Non-Herbal Treatments*. Lanham: Lexington Books.

Davis, Gerald L. 1985. *I Got the Word in Me and I Can Sing It, You Know: A Study of the Performed African-American Sermon*. Philadelphia: University of Pennsylvania Press.

Evans, Freddi Williams. 2014. *Congo Square: African Roots in New Orleans*. Lafayette, LA: University of Louisiana Press.

Fauset, Arthur Huff. 1971. *Black Gods of the Metropolis: Negro Religious Cults of the Urban North*. Philadelphia: University of Pennsylvania Press.

Fett, Sharla. 2002. *Working Cures: Healing, Health and Power on Southern Slave Plantations*. Chapel Hill: The University of North Carolina Press.

Franklin, Rev. C. L. 1989. *Give Me This Mountain: Life History and Selected Sermons*, ed. Jeff Todd Titon. Urbana: University of Illinois Press.

Frazier, E. Franklin. 1964. *The Negro Church in America*. New York: Schocken Books.

Harvey, Paul. 2011. *Through the Storm, Through the Night: A History of African American Christianity*. Lanham, MD: Rowman & Littlefield Publishers.

Hazzard-Donald, Katrina. 2013. *Mojo Workin': The Old African American Hoodoo System*. Chicago: University of Illinois Press.

Hurston, Zora Neale. 1934. "Characteristics of Negro Expression," "Conversions and Visions," "Shouting," "The Sermon," "Mother Catherine," and "Uncle Monday." In *Negro Anthology*, ed. Nancy Cunard, pp. 39–61. London: Wishart & Co.

Hurston, Zora Neale. 1938. *Tell My Horse*. Philadelphia: J. B. Lippincott.

Hyatt, Harry Middleton. 1970–1978. *Hoodoo-Conjuration-Witchcraft-Rootwork*. 5 vols. Memoirs of the Alma Egan Hyatt Foundation. Hannibal, MO: Western Publishing Company.

Johnson, Clifton H., ed. 1969. *God Struck Me Dead: Religious Conversion Experiences and Autobiographies of Ex-Slaves*. Philadelphia: Pilgrim Press.

Long, Carolyn Marrow. 2001. *Spiritual Merchants: Religion, Magic, and Commerce*. Knoxville: University of Tennessee Press.

Manigault-Bryant, LeRhonda S. 2014. *Talking to the Dead: Religion, Music, and Lived Memory among Gullah-Geechee Women*. Durham: Duke University Press.

Mays, Benjamin E. 1969. *The Negro's Church*. New York: Negro Universities Press.

Mays, Benjamin E. 1968. *The Negro's God as Reflected in His Literature*. New York: Russell & Russell.

Mitchell, Faith. 1999. *Hoodoo Medicine: Gullah Herbal Remedies*. Columbia, SC: Summerhouse Press.

Mitchell, Henry H. 1970. *Black Preaching*. Philadelphia: Lippincott.

Mitchem, Stephanie Y. 2007. *African American Folk Healing*. Berkeley: University of California Press.

Murray, David. 2007. *Matter, Magic, and Spirit: Representing Indian and African American Belief*. Philadelphia: University of Pennsylvania Press.

Nunley, Vorris. 2011. *Keepin' It Hushed: The Barbershop and African American Hush Harbor Rhetoric*. Detroit: Wayne State University Press.

Pinn, Anthony B. 2009. *Black Religion and Aesthetics: Religious Thought and Life in Africa and the African Diaspora*. New York, NY: Palgrave Macmillan.

Pipes, William H. 1951. *Say Amen Brothers: Old-Time Negro Preaching*. New York: William-Frederick Press.

Pitts, Walter F., Jr. 1993. *Old Ship of Zion: The Afro-Baptist Ritual in the African Diaspora*. New York: Oxford University Press.

Puckett, Newbell Niles. 1968. *Folk Beliefs of the Southern Negro*. Patterson Smith Reprint Series in Criminology, Law Enforcement, and Social Problems, no. 22. Montclair, NJ: Patterson Smith.

Raboteau, Albert J. 1978. *Slave Religion: The "Invisible Institution" in the Antebellum South*. New York: Oxford University Press.

Rosenberg, Bruce A. 1988. *Can These Bones Live: The Art of the American Folk Preacher*. Urbana: University of Illinois Press.

Tallant, Robert. 1962. *Voodoo in New Orleans*. New York: Collier Books.

Thomas, Kenneth, and Hugh Tulloch. 2008. *The Religious Dancing of American Slaves, 1820–1865: Spiritual Ecstasy at Baptisms, Funerals, and Sunday Meetings*. Lewiston, NY: Edwin Mellen Press.

Washington, Joseph R., Jr. 1964. *Black Religion: The Negro and Christianity in the United States*. Boston: Beacon Press.

Williams, Regennia N., ed. 2011. *Homegoings, Crossings, and Passings: Life and Death in the African Diaspora*. Porter Ranch, CA: New World African Press.

Material Culture: Art, Dance, Foodways, Crafts, Festivals

Abrahams, Roger. 1969. *Jump-Rope Rhymes: A Dictionary*. Austin and London: University of Texas Press.

Adler, Elizabeth Mosby. 1983. "George 'Baby' Scott (1865–1945): A Carver and His Repertoire." In *Afro-American Folk Art and Crafts*, ed. William Ferris, pp. 149–159. Boston: G. K. Hall & Co.

Angelou, Maya, and Jessica B. Harris. 2011. *High on the Hog: A Culinary Journey from Africa to America*. New York: Bloomsbury Press.

Arnett, Paul, and William Arnett, eds. 2000. *Souls Grown Deep: African American Vernacular Art of the South*. Vol. 1. Atlanta: Tinwood Books.

Banks, Ingrid. 2000. *Hair Matters: Beauty, Power, and Black Women's Consciousness*. New York: New York University Press.

Bishir, Catherine W. 2013. *Crafting Lives: African American Artisans in New Bern, North Carolina, 1770–1900*. Chapel Hill: University of North Carolina Press.

Bower, Anne L, ed. 2007. *African American Foodways: Explorations of History and Culture*. Urbana: University of Illinois Press.

Brown, Michael K. 2002. *The Wilson Potters: An African-American Enterprise in 19th- Century Texas*. Houston: Museum of Fine Arts, Bayou Bend Collection and Gardens.

Chalfant, Henry, and James Prigoff. 1987. *Spraycan Art*. London: Thames and Hudson, Ltd.

Chase, Judith Wragg. 1971. *Afro-American Art and Craft*. New York: Van Nostrand, Reinhold Co.

Christian, Marcus. 1972. *Negro Ironworkers of Louisiana, 1718–1900*. Gretna, LA: Pelican.

Coakley, Joyce V. 2006. *Sweetgrass Baskets and the Gullah Tradition*. Charleston, SC: Arcadia Publishing.

Congdon, Kristin G., and Tina Bucavalas. 2006. *Just Above the Water: Florida Folk Art*. Jackson: University Press of Mississippi.

Crown, Carol, and Charles Russell. 2007. *Sacred and Profane: Voice and Vision in Southern Self-Taught Art*. Jackson: University Press of Mississippi.

Daniels, J. Y. 2000. "Black Bodies, Black Space: A-Waiting Spectacle." In *White Papers Black Marks: Architecture, Race, and Culture*, ed. Lesley Naa Norle Lokko, pp. 194–217. Minneapolis: University of Minnesota Press.

Dark, Philip J. C. 1973. *Bush Negro Art*. New York: St. Martin's Press.

Davis, Gerald L. 1976. "Afro-American Coil Basketry in Charleston County, South Carolina." In *American Folklife*, ed. Don Yoder. Austin: University of Texas.

DeFrantz, Thomas F., ed. 2002. *Dancing Many Drums: Excavations in African American Dance*. Madison: University of Wisconsin Press.

Emery, Lynne Fauley. 1988. *Black Dance from 1619 to Today*. Princeton, NJ: Princeton Books.

Ferris, William. 1983. "James 'Son Ford' Thomas, Sculptor." In *Afro-American Folk Art and Crafts*, ed. William Ferris, pp. 129–139. Boston: G. K. Hall & Co.

Ferris, William. "Louis Dotson, One-String Guitar Maker." In *Afro-American Folk Art and Crafts*, ed. William Ferris, pp. 199–206. Boston: G. K. Hall & Co.

Ferris, William. 1983. "Othar Turner, Cane Fife Maker." In *Afro-American Folk Art and Crafts*, ed. William Ferris, pp. 173–180. Boston: G. K. Hall & Co.

Ferris, William. 1983. "Pecolia Warner, Quilt Maker." In *Afro-American Folk Art and Crafts*, ed. William Ferris, pp. 99–108. Boston: G. K. Hall & Co.

Freeman, Roland. 1996. *A Communion of the Spirits: African-American Quilters, Preservers, and Their Stories*. Nashville, TN: Rutledge Hill Press.

Fry, Gladys-Marie. 1986. *Broken Star: Post-Civil War Quilts Made by Black Women*. Dallas: Museum of African American Life and Culture.

Fry, Gladys-Marie. 1990. *Stitched from the Soul: Slave Quilts from the Antebellum South*. New York: Museum of American Folk Art and Dutton Studio Books.

Gaunt, Kyra Danielle. 2006. *The Games Black Girls Play: Learning the Ropes from Double-Dutch to Hip-hop*. New York: New York University Press.

Gay, Kathlyn. 2007. *African-American Holidays, Festivals, and Celebrations: The History, Customs, and Symbols Associated with Both Traditional and Contemporary Religious and Secular Events Observed by Americans of African Descent*. Detroit, MI: Omnigraphics.

Gottschild, Brenda Dixon. 2003. *The Black Dancing Body: A Geography from Coon to Cool*. New York: Palgrave Macmillan.

Gundaker, Grey. 1993. "Tradition and Innovation in African-American Yards." *African Arts* 26 (April): 58–71, 94–96.

Gundaker, Grey, and Tynes Cowan, eds. 1998. *Keep Your Head to the Sky: Interpreting African American Home Ground*. Charlottesville: University Press of Virginia.

Harris, Jessica. 1995. *The Welcome Table: African-American Heritage Cooking*. New York: Simon & Schuster.

Hazzard-Gordon, Katrina. 1990. *Jookin': The Rise of Social Dance Formations among African-Americans*. Philadelphia: Temple University Press.

Heywood, Duncan Clinch. 1937. *Seed from Madagascar*. Chapel Hill: University of North Carolina Press.

Hicks, Kyra E. 2003. *Black Threads: An African American Quilting Sourcebook*. Jefferson, NC: McFarland & Co.

Hood, Yolanda. 2000. "African American Quilt Culture: An Afrocentric Feminist Analysis of African American Art Quilts in the Midwest." PhD Dissertation. Columbia, MO: University of Missouri.

Klassen, Teri. 2009. "Representations of African American Quiltmaking: From Omission to High Art." *The Journal of American Folklore* 122 (485): 297–334.

Kriger, Colleen. 1999. *Pride of Men: Ironworking in 19th Century West Central Africa*. Portsmouth, NH: Heinemann.

Krug, Don, and Ann Parker. 2005. *Miracles of the Spirit: Folk, Art, and Stories from Wisconsin*. Jackson: University Press of Mississippi.

LeFalle-Collins, Lizzetta. 1987. *Home and Yard: Black Folk Life Expressions in Los Angeles*. Los Angeles: California Afro-American Museum.

Lepecki, Andre, ed. 2004. *Of the Presence of the Body: Essays on Dance and Performance Theory*. Middletown, CT: Wesleyan University Press.

Lyons, Mary E. 1993. *Stitching Stars: The Story Quilts of Harriet Powers*. New York: Aladdin Paperbacks.

Malone, Jaqui. 1996. *Steppin' on the Blues: The Visible Rhythms of African American Dance*. Urbana: University of Illinois Press.

Mazloomi, Carolyn. 1998. *Spirits of the Cloth: Contemporary African American Quilts*. New York: Clarkson Potter.

Miller, Adrian, 2014, *Soul Food: The Surprising Story of an American Cuisine One Plate at a Time*. Chapel Hill: University of North Carolina Press.

Miller, Ivor L. 2012 [2002]. *Aerosol Kingdom: Subway Painters of New York City*. Jackson: University Press of Mississippi.

Mitchell, Melvin L. 2001. *The Crisis of the African-American Architect: Conflicting Cultures of Architecture and (Black) Power*. New York: Writers Club Press.

Opie, Frederick Douglass. 2010. *Hog and Hominy: Soul Food from Africa to America*. New York: Columbia University Press.

Rabine, Leslie W. 2014. "These Walls Belong to Everybody: The Graffiti Art Movement in Dakar." *African Studies Quarterly: The Online Journal of African Studies* 14 (3): 89–112.

Rajakumar, Mohanalakshmi. 2012. *Hip Hop Dance*. Santa Barbara, CA: Greenwood.

Roach, Susan. 1998. *On My Way: The Arts of Sarah Albritton*. Jackson: University Press of Mississippi.

Rooks, Noliwe M. 1998 [1996]. *Hair Raising: Beauty, Culture, and African American Women*. New Brunswick, NJ: Rutgers University Press.

Rosengarten, Dale, Theodore Rosengarten, and Enid Schildkrout, eds. 2008. *Grass Roots: African Origins of an American Art*. New York: Museum for African Art.

Shawhan, Dorothy Sample, and Patti Carr Black, eds. 2005. *Spirit of the Delta: The Art of Carolyn Norris*. Jackson: University Press of Mississippi.

Stearns, Marshall, and Jean Stearns. 1968. *Jazz Dance: The Story of American Vernacular Dance*. New York: Macmillan.

Thompson, Katrina Dyonne. 2014. *Ring Shout, Wheel About: The Racial Politics of Music and Dance in North American Slavery*. Urbana: University of Illinois Press.

Thompson, Robert. 1993. *Face of the Gods: Art and Altars of Africa and the African Americas*. New York: Museum for African Art; Munich: Prestel.

Tobin, Jacqueline, and Raymond Dobard. 1999. *Hidden in Plain View: A Secret Story of Quilts and the Underground Railroad*. New York: Doubleday.

Turner, Patricia A. 2009. *Crafted Lives: Stories and Studies of African American Quilters*. Jackson: University Press of Mississippi.

Vlach, John Michael. 1990. *The Afro-American Tradition in Decorative Arts*. Athens: The University of Georgia Press.

Vlach, John Michael. 1999 [1991]. *By the Work of Their Hands*. Charlottesville: University Press of Virginia.

Vlach, John Michael. 1981. *Charleston Blacksmith: The Work of Philip Simmons*. Columbia: University of South Carolina Press.

Wahlman, Maude Southwell, and John Scully. 1983. "Aesthetic Principles in Afro-American Quilts." In *Afro-American Folk Art and Crafts*, ed. William Ferris, pp. 79–97. Boston: G. K. Hall & Co.

Warnes, Andrew. 2010. *Savage Barbecue: Race, Culture, and the Invention of America's First Food*. Athens: University of Georgia Press.

Westmacott, Richard. 1998 [1992]. *African-American Gardens and Yards in the Rural South*. Knoxville: University of Tennessee Press.

Witt, Doris. 1999. *Black Hunger: Food and the Politics of US Identity*. New York and London: Oxford University Press.

Index

Page numbers in **bold** indicate main entries in the text.

About the Editor, Advisors, and Contributors

Editor

Anand Prahlad is a professor of English at the University of Missouri, Columbia, where he teaches courses in creative writing, disability studies, folklore, and film. He has a doctorate in folklore and mythology from the University of California, Los Angeles, and has published extensively in folklore and literary journals. He is the author of two books of poems, *Hear My Story and Other Poems*, and *As Good as Mango*, and two academic works, *African American Proverbs in Context* and *Reggae Wisdom: Proverbs in Jamaican Music*. He is editor of *The Greenwood Encyclopedia of African American Folklore*, and has a third book of poems (*Hijra*) and a memoir (*The Secret Life of a Black Aspie*) forthcoming.

Advisory Board

Roger D. Abrahams is professor emeritus at the University of Pennsylvania in Philadelphia, where he was the Rosen Professor of Folklore and Folklife from 1985 until his retirement in 2002. He is also the founder of the Center for Folklore and Ethnography at the University of Pennsylvania. He is probably the most widely published folklorist in the field of African American folklore and one of the most influential contemporary scholars in the field of folklore in general, having over a hundred books and articles to his credit. His works include *Deep Down in the Jungle: Negro Narrative Folklore from the Streets of Philadelphia*; *Talking Black*; *African American Folktales: Stories from Black Traditions in the New World*; *Singing the Master: The Emergence of African-American Culture in the Plantation South*; and *The Man-of-Words in the West Indies: Performance and the Emergence of Creole Culture*.

Daryl Cumber Dance is a professor of English at the University of Richmond in Virginia. She has published extensively on African American and Caribbean literature and folklore. Her folklore studies include *Shuckin' and Jivin': Folklore from Contemporary Black Americans*; *Folklore from Contemporary Jamaicans*; *Long Gone: The Mecklenburg Six and the Theme of Escape in Black Folklore*; *Honey, Hush! An Anthology of African American Women's Humor*; and *From My People: 400 Years of African American Folklore*.

Trudier Harris is J. Carlyle Sitterson Professor of English at the University of North Carolina, where she teaches courses in African American literature and folklore. She is the author and editor of over 20 books, including *Exorcising Blackness: Historical and Literary Lynching and Burning Rituals* (1984), *Fiction and Folklore: The Novels of Toni Morrison* (1991); and *Saints, Sinners, Saviors: Strong Black Women in African American Literature* (2001). Her memoir, *Summer Snow: Reflections from a Black Daughter of the South,* was published in 2003. It was selected to inaugurate the One-Book, One-Community Reading Program in

Orange County, North Carolina, in 2003. Harris is currently working on a project on African American writers and the South.

Contributors

Aliyyah I. Abdur-Rahman is an associate professor of English, African and Afro-American studies, and women's, gender and sexuality studies at Brandeis University. She received a doctorate in English and American literature from New York University. Her teaching and research interests include 19th- and 20th-century African American literature, the history of women and gender, and 20th-century visual and media culture. She is a recipient of the Alice Richardson and Shortell-Holzer fellowships from New York University as well as a Ford Foundation fellowship. Her publications include *Against the Closet: Black Political Longings and the Erotics of Race* (2012). She is currently working on a second book, *Millennial Style: The Politics of Experiment in Contemporary African Diasporic Culture.*

Jeffrey E. Anderson is an assistant professor of history at Middle Georgia College. He has done extensive research in the area of African American folk magic. His first book, *Conjure in African American Society*, appeared in 2005.

Adrianne R. Andrews currently serves in the administrative position of ombudsperson for Smith College and Mount Holyoke College. She is also an adjunct lecturer in the Anthropology Department at Smith College. She is coeditor of *Language, Rhythm, and Sound: Black Popular Cultures into the 21st Century* (1997), has lectured extensively on the life and work of Zora Neale Hurston, and continues to conduct research and teaching related to African American folklore and folk culture.

Akua Duku Anokye is an associate professor of Africana language, literature, and culture at Arizona State University. Her research focuses on issues of orality and literacy in the African diaspora; a Ghanaian ancestress/deity as archetype in Africana women's literature; Ghanaian folktales, song, and dance; and oral histories. Among her publications are "Oral Connections to Literacy" in *Journal of Basic Writing* and "Private Thoughts, Public Voices: Letters from Zora Neale Hurston" in *Women: A Cultural Review.*

Hilary Mac Austin is an independent scholar and photo researcher. She served as a writer and photo editor for *Black Women in America: An Historical Encyclopedia, Second Edition* (2005). She was coeditor with Kathleen Thompson of three books: *America's Children: Images of Childhood from Early America to the Present* (2003), *Children of the Depression* (2001), and *The Face of Our Past: Images of Black Women from Colonial America to the Present* (2000).

Michael E. Bell has a doctorate in folklore from Indiana University, Bloomington; a master's degree in folklore and mythology from the University of California, Los Angeles; and a bachelor's degree in anthropology and archaeology from the University of Arizona, Tucson. Since 1980, Bell has been an independent public-sector scholar and a consulting folklorist at the Rhode Island Historical Preservation and Heritage Commission in Providence, Rhode Island. His book *Food for the Dead: On the Trail of New England's Vampires* (2001) was a BookSense 76 pick and winner of the Lord Ruthven Assembly Award for Best Nonfiction Book on Vampires.

R. Bruce Bickley Jr. is Griffith T. Pugh Professor of English at Florida State University, specializing in 19th-century American literature. He has published *The Method of Melville's Short Fiction* (1975) and seven books on Joel Chandler Harris and his legacies. He coedited with John T. Bickley the Penguin Classics edition of *Nights with Uncle Remus* (2003).

Stephanie Rose Bird was an assistant professor of painting and drawing at the Art Institute of Chicago from 1987 to 2003. She is currently an independent scholar, curator, and lecturer. Her artwork concerning West African traditional beliefs was included in the U.S. Department of State's Arts-in-the Embassy Program in Cotonou (Benin, Africa). Her book *Sticks, Stones, Roots and Bones: Hoodoo, Mojo and Conjuring with Herbs* (2004) explores African ethnobotany, African American folklore, ritual, and the magical and spiritual uses of plants. Subsequent publications include *Motherland Herbal: The Story of African Holistic Health* (2005), a practical guide that combines African and African American folklore, ethnobotany, health, and ritual; as well as *Four Seasons of Mojo: An Herbal Guide to Natural Living* (2006) and *Light, Bright, Damn Near White: Biracial and Triracial Culture in America* (2009).

Adam Bradley is an assistant professor in the English Department at the University of Colorado, Boulder. He received his doctorate in English from Harvard University, where he submitted a dissertation under the direction of Henry Louis Gates Jr. titled "The Liberation of Perception: Evil's Emergence in 20th Century African American Fiction." In addition, he is currently serving as collaborating editor of the scholarly edition of Ralph Ellison's second novel along with senior editor and Ellison's literary executor, John F. Callahan. His publications include *Book of Rhymes: The Poetics of Hip Hop*, *Ralph Ellison in Progress*, and *One Day It'll All Make Sense*.

Christopher Brooks is a professor of African American studies and anthropology in the School of World Studies at Virginia Commonwealth University. He is also a professional biographer. His most recent work in that genre, *"I Never Walked Alone": The Autobiography of an American Singer,* with African American opera singer Shirley Verrett, was published in 2003.

Richard Allen Burns earned his doctorate in anthropology/folklore at the University of Texas in 1990 and is currently an associate professor of English and folklore at Arkansas State University. While pursuing research on folklife in the Arkansas delta, he continues his research on military and prison folklore. He is revising and expanding his dissertation, "Texas Prison Folklore," to include an examination of southern prison folklore in general. Burns also helps organize Arkansas State University's Delta Blues Symposium, which is held at the Jonesboro main campus each spring.

John A. Burrison is Regents Professor of English and director of the folklore curriculum at Georgia State University. He is the author of *Brothers in Clay: The Story of Georgia Folk Pottery* (1983), editor of the "Folklife" section *of The New Georgia Encyclopedia* (online, 2004), and curator of the Folklife Gallery at the Atlanta History Museum and of the new Folk Pottery Museum of Northeast Georgia. He received his doctorate in folklore and folklife from the University of Pennsylvania.

Nancy A. Clark received her BA in English from the University of Missouri in 2003. She is interested in the fields of education and political advocacy.

Willie Collins is the principal of the Consortium for California Cultural Conservation, a cultural-resource consulting firm based in Oakland, California. Collins earned a doctorate in ethnomusicology specializing in African American music from the University of California, Los Angeles, and has worked in academic as well as in public-sector folklore in the cities of Los Angeles and Oakland. Collins has published numerous articles on African American folklore and music.

Cecelia Conway is a professor of English at Appalachian State University. *Atlantic Monthly* called her book *African Banjo Echoes in Appalachia* (1995) a "landmark study" and her 1998 coproduced Smithsonian Folkways CD *Black Banjo Songsters* a "rare collection" of music. She is also a comaker of award-winning films and videos, including *Sprout Wings and Fly: A Portrait of Fiddler Tommy Jarrell* and *African American Fiddler Joe Thompson and Friends*.

Jack T. Cooper is an associate professor of music at the University of Memphis's Rudi E. Scheidt School of Music. He has more than 70 pieces of music in print with Warner Brothers Publications, University of North Carolina Jazz Press, and several other music publishers. He is the recipient of grants from the National Endowment for the Arts, the Aaron Copland Foundation, the New York Conservatory for the Arts, the Southern Arts Foundation, and numerous other groups. He earned his doctorate in music composition from the University of Texas.

Stephen Criswell is a professor of English at Benedict College. He is the coeditor of *South Carolina Welcomes Y'all: Contemporary Folklife in South Carolina* (2005) and has conducted extensive research into African American family reunion traditions.

Jonathan C. David is a folklorist and writer living in Philadelphia. He is the author of *Together Let Us Sweetly Live: The Singing and Praying Bands*, a book about African American ring shouts.

Frank de Caro is a professor emeritus of English at Louisiana State University. He is the author or editor of several books, including *Re-Situating Folklore: Folk Contexts and Twentieth Century Literature and Art* (with Rosan Augusta Jordan, 2004) and *Louisiana Sojourns: Travelers' Tales and Literary Journeys* (1999).

Thomas F. DeFrantz is a professor and chair of the Women's Studies department at Duke University. He has published extensively on African American performance and is the author of *Dancing Revelations: Alvin Ailey's Embodiment of African American Culture* (2004) and *Hip Hop in Hollywood: Encounter, Community, Resistance* (2014). He is currently at work on a study of "beauty" in dance performance.

James I. Deutsch is a program curator at the Smithsonian Center for Folklife and Cultural Heritage, where he has helped develop festival programs on the Silk Road, building arts, World War II, and forestry. He currently serves as an adjunct professor in the American Studies Department at George Washington University (where he received his doctorate in 1991). Deutsch has also taught American studies classes at universities in Armenia, Belarus, Bulgaria, Germany, Kyrgyzstan, Norway, Poland, and Turkey. He has published a variety of articles and encyclopedia entries in the fields of film and folklore.

Samba Diop teaches Francophone literature and African cinema at Harvard University. He has published extensively on African and Francophone literature and film as well as on the African Wolof epic and oral traditions and literature. His most recent publication is *Epopées Africaines: Ndiadiane Ndiaye et El Hadj Omar Tall* (2003).

David H. Evans is a professor of music at the University of Memphis. He received his doctorate in folklore and mythology from the University of California, Los Angeles, in 1976. He is the author of *Tommy Johnson* (1971), *Big Road Blues: Tradition and Creativity in the Folk Blues* (1982), and *The NPR Curious Listener's Guide to Blues* (2005), and coauthor (with John Minton) of *"The Coon in the Box": A Global Folktale in African-American Tradition* (2001). He has also written many journal articles, book chapters, and record album notes, and produced many LPs and CDs of field and studio recordings. Evans is editor of the American Made Music book series for the University Press of Mississippi.

Elizabeth C. Fine is a professor and the chair of the Department of Interdisciplinary Studies at Virginia Polytechnic Institute. She is the author of *Soulstepping: African American Step Shows* (2003) and *The Folklore Text: From Performance to Print* (1994 [1984]). She is coeditor of *Performance, Culture and Identity* (Praeger, 1992).

Alysia E. Garrison is an assistant professor of English, African, and African American Studies, and Women's, Gender, and Sexuality Studies at Dartmouth College. She received her doctorate in English from the University of California, Davis.

Michele A. Goldwasser teaches at the University of California, San Diego. She has conducted field research in Trinidad, Venezuela, Belize, and Honduras. In her book *The Rainbow Madonna of Trinidad*, she analyzes the emergence of a miraculous, dark Madonna in the cultural franca of colonial Trinidad and examines its significance in contemporary society.

Adam Gussow is an associate professor of English and southern studies at the University of Mississippi. For 12 years he was the harmonica-playing half of Satan and Adam, a Harlem-based blues duo that toured internationally and recorded three albums on the Flying Fish label. He is the author of two books: *Mister Satan's Apprentice: A Blues Memoir* (1998) and *Seems Like Murder Here: Southern Violence and the Blues Tradition* (2002), the latter of which received the C. Hugh Holman Award from the Society for the Study of Southern Literature. His essays, reviews, and interviews have appeared in *Callaloo, African American Review, Southern Cultures, American Literature, Living Blues, Blues Access,* and many other publications.

Willie J. Harrell Jr. is an associate professor of English at Kent State University, where he teaches courses in African American literature and cultural studies and other ethnic literatures. His research interests include 19th-century American literature and cultural studies with an emphasis on African American literature and cultural studies, African American Jeremiadic rhetoric, slave narratives, Charles Chesnutt, Martin Delany, oral history, and historicizing text. He is editor of *We Wear the Mask: Paul Laurence Dunbar and the Politics of Representative Reality*, a collection of essays, and *Origins of the African American Jeremiad: The Rhetorical Strategies of Social Protest and Activism, 1760–1861*.

Jennifer Hildebrand is an associate professor in the History department at the State University of New York at Fredonia. She received her doctorate in 2003 and completed her dissertation, "'Another Life They Don't Show': African Cultural Practices in America," under Sterling Stuckey at the University of California, Riverside. She has also taught at the University of Nebraska, Lincoln.

Molly Clark Hillard holds a master's degree in folklore from the University of California, Berkeley, and a doctorate in English from the University of California, Davis. She is an assistant professor in the English department at Seattle University. She is the author of "Dangerous Exchange: Fairy Footsteps, Goblin Economies, and The Old Curiosity Shop" (*Dickens Studies Annual*, vol. 35). Her book, *Spellbound: The Fairy Tale and the Victorians*, was published in 2014.

Elvin Holt is a professor of English at Texas State University–San Marcos, where he specializes in American and African American literature. He has published essays on Zora Neale Hurston, Kristin Hunter, Wallace Thurman, Jarena Lee, Sherley Anne Williams, Alex LaGuma, and others. His most recent publication (with William Jackson) is "Reconstructing Black Manhood: Message and Meaning in Spike Lee's *Get on the Bus*."

LaMonda Horton-Stallings is an assistant professor of English at the University of Florida in Gainesville. Her areas of research and teaching are African American literature and culture and gender and sexuality studies. She is author of *Mutha Is Half a Word: Intersections of Folklore, Vernacular, Myth, and Queerness in Black Female Culture*.

Joyce Marie Jackson is an associate professor in the Department of Geography and Anthropology at Louisiana State University. Both a folklorist and an ethnomusicologist, she is currently completing a book on African American gospel quartets, is associate editor of the forthcoming *Encyclopedia of American Gospel Music*, and is the author of *Life in the Village: A Cultural Memory of the Fazendeville Community*. Her other research includes performance-centered studies on rituals in Africa and the African diaspora and the rural roots of jazz in southern Louisiana.

Laura C. Jarmon received a bachelor's degree at Howard University, a master's degree at Fisk University, and a doctorate at the Catholic University of America. She began teaching in 1972 and is currently a professor of English at the University of Tennessee, Martin. In 1993 she coedited *The Negro Traditions*, a collection of black folktales; in 1994, she authored *Arbors to Bricks*, a public research project; and she wrote *Wishbone: Reference and Interpretation in Black Folk Narrative*, published in 2003 and winner of a 2004 Choice Outstanding Book Award.

Gladys L. Knight is a former manager of the African American Museum in Tacoma, Washington. She is now preparing short stories, novels, and a screenplay, all based primarily on African American life and culture. She has made contributions to the *Encyclopedia of African American Literature*, published by Greenwood Press, and lectured on traditional African communities, African storytelling and dance, and slave life on plantations in the American South.

Lisa C. Lakes is a doctoral student in English at Florida State University. Her research interests are African American and diasporic literature. She serves as the program assistant for the university's First-Year Writing Program.

David Todd Lawrence is an associate professor of English at the University of St. Thomas in Saint Paul, Minnesota. He specializes in African American literature and culture as well as folkloristics, Afro-Futurism, and ethnographic writing. His current research explores the role of the pimp figure in black expressive culture, and a project with folklorist Elaine Lawless on a film and book about the African American community of Pinhook, Missouri.

Valerie Lee is a professor of English and women's studies at Ohio State University. The author of *Granny Midwives and Black Women Writers: Double-Dutched Readings* and editor of *The Prentice Hall Anthology of African American Women's Literature*, she publishes in the areas of critical race feminism, feminist theory, black women's literary studies, multicultural pedagogy, and folklore.

Carolyn Morrow Long is a research associate at the Smithsonian Institution's National Museum of American History. She has published several articles on African American folklore and is the author of *Spiritual Merchants: Religion, Magic, and Commerce* (2001). Her biography of Marie Laveau, *A New Orleans Voudou Priestess: The Legend and Reality of Marie Laveau*, was published in 2006.

M. M. Manring is the author of *Slave in a Box: The Strange Career of Aunt Jemima* (1998). He lives in Columbia, Missouri.

Phyllis M. May-Machunda is a professor and the chair of American Multicultural Studies at Minnesota State University, Moorhead. Trained as a folklorist and ethnomusicologist specializing in African American cultural traditions, her other research interests include multicultural studies, disability studies, and social justice. For several years prior to joining the faculty at Minnesota State University, Moorhead, she was employed as a folklorist at the Smithsonian Institution and conducted fieldwork on cultural traditions of African Americans throughout the South and Midwest. A native Iowan, she is a graduate of the University of Iowa and Indiana University.

Jacqueline L. McGrath is a professor of English at the College of DuPage, where she teaches writing, literature, and folklore studies. Her work has appeared in *Southern Folklore*, the *Journal of American Folklore*, and *Pif Magazine*. Her current project is a folklore studies textbook.

Bernard McKenna is an associate professor at the University of Delaware, where he teaches courses in Caribbean, Irish, and British literature. He has served on the editorial board of *The Caribbean Writer* and has published two books and numerous articles on Irish, Caribbean, and British literature and culture.

Shawnrece D. Miller is an assistant professor of English and the director of African studies at Stetson University. She is currently working on a manuscript titled "Eating and Drinking Culture: 'Soul Food' and Its Role in the Living Cultural Memory of Americans of African, Hispanic and Asian Descent."

Vorris Nunley is an associate professor in the Department of English at Pennsylvania State University, where he is focusing on the rhetoric of African American hush harbors. Nunley is coeditor with Keith Gilyard of *Rhetoric and Ethnicity* (2004), and author of *Keepin' It Hushed: The Barbershop and African American Hush Harbor Rhetoric* (2011).

Margaret M. Olsen is a professor of Hispanic & Latin American Studies at Macalester College. Her book publications include *Slavery and Salvation in Colonial Cartagena de Indias* and *La ceiba de la memoria: aproximaciones críticas*. She has published numerous articles and books about runaway slaves in colonial Spanish America and performances of urban space in New Orleans. She has also published essays on contemporary Caribbean literature.

Ted Olson teaches Appalachian studies and English courses at East Tennessee State University. He is the author of *Blue Ridge Folklife* and the editor of *Cross Roads: A Southern Culture Annual*, *The Bristol Sessions: Writings about the Big Bang of Country Music*, and the music section of the *Encyclopedia of Appalachia*.

Lucia Pawlowski earned her MA degree in English with an emphasis in folklore from the University of Missouri, Columbia, and PhD from The University of St. Thomas, where she is now an assistant professor. She continues to research and teach women's folklore, African American folklore, and critical theory.

Deborah G. Plant is an associate professor and Chair of the Department of Africana Studies at the University of South Florida. Her research, teaching, and professional publications focus on African, African American, and Afro-Caribbean writers. She has extensively researched the writings of Zora Neale Hurston and has published *Every Tub Sit on Its Own Bottom: The Philosophy and Politics of Zora Neale Hurston* (1995), and *Zora Neale Hurston: A Biography of the Spirit* (2007).

Karen Pojmann is a writer and editor in Columbia, Missouri. She manages magazine, website, social media, and podcast content—and content producers—in Mizzou Creative, the central communications department of the University of Missouri. She is a widely published freelance writer who has studied Igbo culture and folk traditions in Nigeria. Her current projects include a collection of poetry.

Reiland Rabaka is a professor in the Department of Ethnic Studies at the University of Colorado, Boulder. He earned his doctorate from Temple University and is a former visiting scholar in African American studies at the University of Houston. His teaching and research interests include African philosophy, Afro-Caribbean philosophy, African American philosophy, radical politics, critical social theory, and Africana women's studies. His work has been published in *Journal of African American Studies*, *Journal of Black Studies*, *Western Journal of Black Studies*, and *Jouvert: A Journal of Postcolonial Studies*, among others. His books include, *Hip-Hop's Inheritance: From the Harlem Renaissance to the Hip Hop Feminist Movement* and *Hip-Hop's Amnesia: From Blues and the Black Women's Club Movement to Rap and the Hip Hop Movement*.

Sharon D. Raynor is an associate professor in the Department of English and Foreign Languages at Johnson C. Smith University. She completed her doctorate in literature and criticism from Indiana University of Pennsylvania. She received both her bachelor's degree in English and her master's degree in multicultural literature at East Carolina University. Her most recent publications include "The World of Female Knowing According to Georgia

Douglass Johnson," which appeared in *College Language Association Journal*, and "Breaking the Silence: The Unspoken Brotherhood of Vietnam Veterans," which appeared in *North Carolina Crossroads*. She has also contributed to *The Encyclopedia of African American Literature*, *Dos Passos Review*, and *From around the Globe: Secular Authors and Biblical Perspectives*.

LuAnne Roth is an assistant teaching professor in the English department at the University of Missouri. Roth's research and teaching focus on folklore, film/media, and food studies. Roth is particularly interested in how food is used to negotiate the nexus of belief, class, ethnicity, gender, and race. Her foodways research appears as articles in the journals *Food, Culture and Society*, *Digest*, and *Western Folklore*, and as chapters in the volumes *Unsettling Assumptions: Tradition, Gender, Drag* (2014) and *Folklore/Cinema: Popular Film as Vernacular Culture* (2007). In addition to maintaining digital archives of scenes related to food/culture and legend, Roth is currently working on a book manuscript, "Talking Turkey," which examines media representations of the American Thanksgiving meal.

Walter Rucker, a native of Atlanta, Georgia, is an associate professor in the Department of History at Rutgers University. His research interests include Atlantic world/African diasporic history, pan-Africanism, slave culture and resistance, and social protest movements. He has delivered more than 20 professional talks and authored a number of journal articles, including works appearing in the *Journal of Black Studies*, *The Griot*, the *Journal of Negro History*, and *The Black Scholar*. His books include *The River Flows On: Black Resistance, Culture, and Identity Formation in Early America*, and *Gold Coast Diasporas: Identity, Culture, and Power*.

Christopher S. Schaberg is an associate professor in the English department at Loyola University. He has worked on projects ranging from advertisements for sports utility vehicles and their textual overlaps with American nature writing to airports and commercial airliners as ontologically liminal spaces in literature and film. His publications include *The Textual Life of Airports: Reading the Culture of Flight*.

Joko M. Sengova is currently an assistant in research and a GEAR UP faculty liaison in the Department of Child and Family Studies, Louis de la Parte Florida Mental Health Institute, University of South Florida–Tampa. He has taught, presented, and published extensively on the Gullah/Geechee language and culture, especially its potential links to his native Sierra Leone in West Africa. In his forthcoming essay, titled "'My Mother Dem Nyus to Plan' Reis': On Gullah/Geechee Creole, African Language Communication and Construction of African-American Identity," to be published in *Afro-Atlantic Dialogues: Anthropology in the Diaspora*, Sengova engages in a linguistic anthropological dialog focused specifically on Gullah/Geechee linkages to Africa and implications for Gullah/Geechee identity constructions and growing African-influenced consciousness in the United States and the African diaspora.

Robert L. Stone is an independent folklorist who serves as outreach coordinator for the Florida Folklife Program. He has been documenting the steel guitar traditions of the House of God, Keith Dominion, and the Church of the Living God, Jewell Dominion, since 1992. He has produced seven CD albums in the Arhoolie label's Sacred Steel Guitar series, served as director of the Arhoolie Foundation's Sacred Steel documentary video, and is writing a book on the subject. He is author of *Sacred Steel: Inside an African American Steel Guitar Tradition.*

Caroline A. Streeter is an associate professor of English and African American studies at the University of California, Los Angeles. Her most recent work appears in the journal *Callaloo* and the anthology *Black Cultural Traffic.* Her research interests and teaching areas include African American literary studies, critical mixed race studies, gender and sexuality, and African American film and visual art. Her publications include *Tragic No More: Mixed Race Women and the Nexus of Sex and Celebrity* (2012).

M. J. Strong is a doctoral candidate at the University of California, Davis. She studies 19th-century American literature and has completed a designated emphasis in feminist theory and research. Strong's work emphasizes issues of race, class, gender, and sexuality in the American fin de siècle period. Her other research interests include nostalgia, domestic labor, feminist science fiction, and popular culture. She presented a paper titled "Father of the Year: The Sanctification of Eminem in Popular Culture" at the Mid-Atlantic Popular/ American Culture Association's 2003 meeting. Strong teaches in the departments of English and Women and Gender Studies at the University of California, Davis.

Dan Thomas-Glass is earning his doctorate in English at the University of California, Davis. His areas of interest include the poetics of revolution, music and performance theory, and experiments in mass self-consciousness. He is author of *The Great American Beatjack Volume I* and *Daughters of Your Century.*

Kathleen Thompson is coauthor, with Darlene Clark Hine, of *A Shining Thread of Hope: The History of Black Women in America.* She was editor-in-chief of *Encyclopedia of Black Women in America* and recently served on the board of senior editors for Oxford University Press's revision of the landmark reference *Black Women in America: An Historical Encyclopedia.* She is president of OneHistory, an organization dedicated to making all voices of American history heard.

Nagueyalti Warren is associate dean for undergraduate education at Emory University and adjunct professor in the Department of African American Studies. She coedited *Southern Mothers: Fact and Fictions* and edited the forthcoming anthology *Temba Tupu! (Walking Naked) Africana Women's Poetic Self-Portrait.* Warren is a poet and Cave Canem fellow. She earned her bachelor's degree in English from Fisk University, master of arts degrees in English and Afro-American studies from Simmons College and Boston University, and a doctorate from the University of Mississippi. She is currently pursuing a master of fine arts degree in creative writing at Goddard College.

Yolanda Y. Williams is a performer, recording artist, actress, and educator holding faculty positions at the University of Minnesota in African/African American studies and Minneapolis Community and Technical College in the Music Department. Her courses cover black American music genres (e.g., jazz, rock and roll, blues, rhythm and blues) and world music. At Minneapolis Community and Technical College, she also directs two instrumental ensembles.

Doris Witt is an associate professor of English at the University of Iowa and also a student at the University of Iowa College of Law. She is the author of *Black Hunger: Soul Food and*

America (2004) and is currently developing a new research project in the area of food, race, and law.

Daniel Wojcik is professor of English and folklore studies at the University of Oregon. He is the author of *The End of the World as We Know It: Faith, Fatalism, and Apocalypse in America* (1997), *Punk and Neo-Tribal Body Art* (1995), and numerous articles on millenarianism, vernacular religion, and self-taught visionary artists.

www.ingramcontent.com/pod-product-compliance
Lightning Source LLC
Chambersburg PA
CBHW081426270326
41932CB00019B/3111